CHRISTIANITY IN

North Africa and West Asia

Editorial Team

CHRISTIANITY IN

North Africa and West Asia

Edited by Kenneth R. Ross,
Mariz Tadros, and Todd M. Johnson

CENTER FOR THE STUDY OF GLOBAL CHRISTIANITY

HENDRICKSON PUBLISHERS

Christianity in North Africa and West Asia

Hendrickson Publishers Marketing, LLC
P. O. Box 3473
Peabody, Massachusetts 01961-3473
www.hendrickson.com

Originally published in 2018 in Edinburgh, UK [under the title Christianity in North Africa and West Asia], by Edinburgh University Press Ltd
The Tun – Holyrood Road
12 (2f) Jackson's Entry
Edinburgh EH8 8PJ

Printed in the United States of America

First Printing — January 2020

Contents

Key Themes

Conclusion

Appendices

Series Preface

While a number of compendia have recently been produced on the study of worldwide Christianity, the distinctive quality of this series arises from its examination of global Christianity through a combination of reliable demographic information and original interpretative essays by indigenous scholars and practitioners. This approach was successfully pioneered by the *Atlas of Global Christianity 1910–2010*, published by Edinburgh University Press on the occasion of the centenary of the epoch-making Edinburgh 1910 World Missionary Conference.

Using the same methodology, the Edinburgh Companions to Global Christianity take the analysis to a deeper level of detail and explore the context of the twenty-first century. The series considers the presence of Christianity on a continent-by-continent basis worldwide. Covering every country in the world, it maps patterns of growth and/or decline and examines current trends. The aim of the series is to comprehensively map worldwide Christianity and to describe it in its entirety. Country-specific studies are offered, all the major Christian traditions are analysed and current regional and continental trends are examined.

Each volume is devoted to a continent or sub-continent, following the United Nations classifications. Through a combination of maps, tables, charts and graphs, each of the successive volumes presents a comprehensive demographic analysis of Christianity in the relevant area. Commentary and interpretation are provided by essays on key topics, each written by an expert in the field, normally an indigenous scholar. By the use of these various tools each volume provides an accurate, objective and incisive analysis of the presence of Christian faith in the relevant area.

The projected volumes in the series are:

1. Christianity in Sub-Saharan Africa
2. Christianity in North Africa and West Asia
3. Christianity in South and Central Asia
4. Christianity in East and Southeast Asia
5. Christianity in the Pacific
6. Christianity in Latin America
7. Christianity in North America
8. Christianity in Western and Northern Europe

9. Christianity in Eastern and Southern Europe
10. Compact Atlas of Global Christianity

As series editors, we rely heavily on the regional expertise of the dedicated third editor who joins us for each volume. Furthermore, each volume has its own editorial advisory board, made up of senior scholars with authoritative knowledge of the field in question. We work together to define the essay topics for the volume, arrange for compilation of the required demographic data, recruit the authors of the essays and edit their work. Statistical and demographic information is drawn from the highly regarded *World Christian Database* maintained by the Center for the Study of Global Christianity at Gordon-Conwell Theological Seminary (South Hamilton, MA, USA) and published by Brill. For each volume, a team of 35–40 authors will be recruited to write the essays, and it is ultimately upon their scholarship and commitment that we depend in order to create an original and authoritative work of reference.

Each volume in the series will be, we hope, a significant book in its own right and a contribution to the study of Christianity in the region in question. At the same time, each is a constituent part of a greater whole – the 10-volume series, which aims to provide a comprehensive analysis of global Christianity that will be groundbreaking in its demographic quality and analytical range. Our hope is that the Companions will be of service to anyone seeking a fuller understanding of the worldwide presence of the Christian faith.

Kenneth R. Ross and Todd M. Johnson
Series Editors

Volume Preface

This region, North Africa and West Asia, is where Christianity began, nearly 2,000 years ago. Many Christian communities today trace their histories back over the entire period. At the same time, there is no region in the world where Christians are more at risk of extinction, as civil wars, persecution and economic distress have resulted in a massive exodus of the Christian population. This volume documents that exodus while it is underway. The future of Christianity in the region is highly uncertain. At the same time, there is evidence of vitality and renewal. The picture is complex and multifaceted, defying generalisation and simplification. What is clear is that there is much at stake for Christians in this region, and much at stake for the region as the future of Christianity hangs in the balance.

In pursuit of understanding, this volume offers four angles of analysis. The first is demographic, using the methodology of the highly successful *Atlas of Global Christianity* (Edinburgh University Press, 2009) to present accurate statistical information in an attractive, user-friendly format. Maps and charts depict the status of Christianity regionally and in terms of the principal church traditions. As stated above, this profile is one of exodus and decline, although, since the 1970s, the Gulf states have welcomed large numbers of guest workers, many from largely Christian countries.

The second angle of analysis is at the country level. Account is taken of the presence and influence of Christianity in each of 25 settings in North Africa and West Asia. Scholars who are either indigenous or have long experience of the region have contributed interpretative essays that offer a 'critical insider' perspective on the way in which Christianity is finding expression in their context. Most countries are the subject of a dedicated essay, while, in a few cases, an essay covers neighbouring countries with significant affinity.

Thirdly, Christianity in North Africa and West Asia is considered in terms of its principal ecclesial forms or traditions. Five types of church are considered: Orthodox (both 'Eastern' and 'Oriental'), Catholic, Protestant, Anglican and Independent. In addition, the Evangelical and Pentecostal/ Charismatic movements, which cut across ecclesial affiliation, are examined.

Fourthly, selected themes are considered. Eight of these run right through the entire Edinburgh Companions series: faith and culture, worship and spirituality, theology, social and political context, mission and evangelism, gender, religious freedom and inter-religious relations. A further four have been selected specifically for this volume on account of their salience in the context of North Africa and West Asia: monastic movements and spirituality, ecclesiology, Christian media and displaced populations. Each of these themes is examined on a region-wide basis, deepening our understanding of features that are definitive for Christianity in this part of the world.

As is evident from the short bibliography offered at the end of each essay, this book rests on the body of scholarship that has illuminated our understanding of North African and West Asian Christianity, particularly the burgeoning literature of the past 25 years. Besides many detailed local studies, much insight has been derived from such attempts at overall analysis as Habib Badr et al.'s *Christianity: A History in the Middle East* (World Council of Churches, 2005), Betty Jane Bailey's *Who Are the Christians in the Middle East?* (Eerdmans, 2010), Andrea Pacini's *Christian Communities in the Arab Middle East: The Challenge of the Future* (Clarendon Press, 1998), Anthony O'Mahony and Emma Loosley's *Eastern Christianity in the Modern Middle East* (Routledge, 2010), Otto Meinardus's *Two Thousand Years of Coptic Christianity* (American University in Cairo Press, 1999) and Paul S. Rowe et al.'s *Christians and the Middle East Conflict* (Routledge, 2014). While resting on the preceding scholarship, this volume breaks new ground through its reliable demographic analysis, its contemporary focus, the indigenous authorship of its essays and the originality of the analyses. The essay authors employ a variety of disciplinary approaches – historical, theological, sociological, missiological, anthropological – as appropriate to their topics. Taken together, the volume offers a deeply textured and highly authoritative account of Christianity in North Africa and West Asia, one that will reward the attention of any who wish to deepen their knowledge of this subject.

Kenneth R. Ross
Mariz Tadros
Todd M. Johnson

August 2017

Contributors

Sara Afshari is a PhD student at the University of Edinburgh in the field of media, religion and culture. She is also co-founder and former Executive Director of SAT-7 PARS, a Christian television station for the Persian/Farsi-speaking world.
Christian Media

Ed Alden has served in Central Asia for the last 17 years, conducting research on Christianity in the region. He is a graduate of the University of Oklahoma and Southwestern Baptist Theological Seminary, USA.
Turkey

Najib George Awad is a theologian and poet originally from Syria. He is Associate Professor of Christian Theology and Director of the International PhD Program at Hartford Seminary, Connecticut, USA.
Inter-religious Relations

Katia Boissevain is a researcher in anthropology at the Centre National de la Recherche Scientifique (CNRS) in Aix-en-Provence, France. Her field of competence is religious anthropology of the Maghreb. She is the author of *Sainte parmi les saints: Sayyda Mannubiya* (Institut de recherche sur le Maghreb contemporain, 2007) and is currently co-editor of the journal *L'Année du Maghreb.*
Algeria and Tunisia

Charles Chartouni is Professor of Sociology and Politics at Lebanese University and St Joseph University and has taught at universities in Europe and America as well as in his native Lebanon. He was active as a politician and negotiator during the Lebanese civil war (1975–90) and has published extensively on the politics of difference and conflict resolution.
Lebanon

John Eibner is a managing director of Christian Solidarity International (CSI), with special responsibility for the Middle East and North Africa. He

has undertaken many human rights fact-finding missions to Sudan since 1992.
Sudan

Mark Farha is Assistant Professor of Politics and International Relations at Doha Institute for Graduate Studies, where he teaches in Arabic. He has written extensively on Lebanon and the Middle East, including *The Resisted Rise and Fall of the Secular State in Lebanon* (Cambridge University Press, 2018).
Social and Political Context

Kristian Girling is a postdoctoral research fellow at the School of Theology and Ministry, Boston College, USA. He completed his doctoral studies on the Chaldean Catholic community at the Centre for Eastern Christianity, Heythrop College, University of London, UK, in 2016.
Displaced Populations

Akram Habib is a veteran development manager and researcher with 20 years' work experience in the Middle East and is active in Christian media.
Libya

Gabriel Hachem is a professor at the Holy Spirit University of Kaslik (USEK) in Lebanon as well as editor-in-chief of the journal *Proche Orient Chrétien*. He has been a member of the International Theological Commission for the Roman Catholic Church since 2014 and has authored many books and articles on Eastern Christianity, ecumenism, ecclesiology and theological liturgy.
Ecclesiology

Hrayr Jebejian is General Secretary of the Bible Society in the Gulf. He is the author of *The Armenian's Path for Struggle and Existence* (in Armenian). A recipient of the Ambassador of the Motherland Medal from the Ministry of Diaspora of the Republic of Armenia, Dr Jebejian lives in Nicosia, Cyprus, with his wife and two children.
The Gulf: Bahrain, Kuwait, Oman, Qatar, Saudi Arabia, United Arab Emirates (UAE), Yemen

Todd M. Johnson is Associate Professor of Global Christianity and Director of the Center for the Study of Global Christianity at Gordon-Conwell Theological Seminary in South Hamilton, Massachusetts, USA.

He is also Visiting Research Fellow at Boston University's Institute for Culture, Religion and World Affairs, leading a research project on international religious demography.
Methodology and Sources of Christian and Religious Affiliation

Paolo Maggiolini is Research Fellow in Political and Social Transformations in the Arab World (Arab-Trans) for the Mediterranean and Middle East Programme and Research Assistant in History and Institutions of Asia at the Catholic University of Milan, Italy. He is the author of *Arabi Cristiani di Transgiordania. Spazi politici e cultura tribale (1841–1922)* [Arab Christians of Transjordan: Political Spaces and Tribal Culture (1841–1922)] (Franco Angeli, 2011).
Jordan

Duane Alexander Miller is Lecturer in Theology and Church History at Nazareth Evangelical Theological Seminary and adjunct faculty at Saint Mary's University in San Antonio, Texas, USA. He is the author of *Living Among the Breakage: Contextual Theology-making and ex-Muslim Christians* (Pickwick, 2016) as well as numerous articles on religious conversion to Christianity in the Middle East.
Independents

Elizabeth Monier is a Leverhulme Fellow in Middle Eastern Studies at the University of Cambridge, UK. She works on the contemporary history of the Arab world, focusing on minorities, sectarianism and identity.
Faith and Culture

Rima Nasrallah is Assistant Professor of Practical Theology at the Near East School of Theology, Beirut, Lebanon. Her specialty is in liturgical-ritual studies, with a focus on everyday practices in the East.
Worship and Spirituality

David Neuhaus SJ is a Roman Catholic priest and serves as Latin Patriarchal Vicar, responsible for Hebrew-speaking and migrant Catholics in Israel. He teaches biblical studies at various institutions in the Holy Land and is the author of numerous books and articles.
Israel

Eric N. Newberg is Professor of Theological and Historical Studies at Oral Roberts University in Tulsa, Oklahoma, USA. An ordained pastor of the

Evangelical Covenant Church, he is the author of *The Pentecostal Mission in Palestine: The Legacy of Pentecostal Zionism* (Wipf and Stock, 2012).
Pentecostals/Charismatics

Ewelina Ochab is a PhD candidate in international law and human rights and a legal researcher for ADF International. She is the author of *Never Again: Legal Responses to a Broken Promise in the Middle East* (Kairos, 2016).
Religious Freedom

Anthony O'Mahony is Reader in the History of Christianity at Heythrop College at the University of London, UK. He was founding director of Heythrop's Centre for Christianity and Interreligious Dialogue and now serves as director of Heythrop's Centre for Eastern Christianity. His numerous publications include *Christianity in the Middle East: Studies in Modern History, Politics and Theology* (Melisende, 2007).
Catholics

Anna Poujeau is a social anthropologist and researcher at the National Centre for Scientific Research (CNRS) in France. She is conducting research on Christian community and monasticism in Syria.
Monastic Movements and Spirituality

Mitri Raheb is President of Dar al-Kalima University College of Arts and Culture in Bethlehem, Palestine. A senior pastor of the Evangelical Lutheran Christmas Church in Bethlehem, he is the most widely published Palestinian theologian to date. His latest book is entitled *Faith in the Face of Empire: The Bible through Palestinian Eyes* (Orbis, 2014).
Protestants

Donna Rizk holds two master's degrees in theological studies, from Holy Cross Orthodox School of Theology and the University of Oxford, and is a PhD candidate in early patristics at King's College London, UK. Her research interests include gender in the Orthodox Church, Armenian and Coptic studies and the history of Christianity.
Gender

Bernard Sabella is a native of Jerusalem and is Associate Professor of Sociology at al-Quds University in the master's degree programme at the Centre for Jerusalem Studies. His academic interests are focused on Palestinian Christians and questions of identity and other challenges,

including emigration. In 2006 he was elected to the Jerusalem Christian quota seat in the Palestinian Legislative Council (Parliament).
Palestine

George F. Sabra is President and Professor of Systematic Theology at the Near East School of Theology in Beirut, Lebanon. He is the author of *Thomas Aquinas' Vision of the Church: Fundamentals of an Ecumenical Ecclesiology* (Matthias-Grünewald-Verlag, 1987) as well as other books in Arabic, and also editor of the *Near East School of Theology Theological Review.*
Theology

Yazid Said is a Palestinian-born Israeli citizen and an Anglican priest. He is Lecturer in Islam at Liverpool Hope University, UK, where his research is focused on Muslim–Christian relations and medieval Muslim political and legal thought. He is the author of *Ghazali's Politics in Context* (Routledge, 2017).
Anglicans

Silvia Serrano is Associate Professor in Political Science at the Université d'Auvergne and researcher at the Centre d'études des mondes russe, caucasien et centre européen (Cercec) at the Ecole des Hautes Etudes en Sciences Sociales, Paris, France. Her research focuses on the political sociology of the post-Soviet Caucasus. She is the author of *Géorgie: Sortie d'empire* (CNRS Editions, 2007) as well as numerous articles on the Caucasus.
Georgia and Azerbaijan

Heather J. Sharkey is an associate professor in the Department of Near Eastern Languages and Civilizations at the University of Pennsylvania, USA. Her books include *American Evangelicals in Egypt: Missionary Encounters in an Age of Empire* (Princeton University Press, 2015) and *A History of Muslims, Christians, and Jews in the Middle East* (Cambridge University Press, 2017).
Mission and Evangelism

Aho Shemunkasho is a Professor for Syriac Theology and director of the MA in Syriac Theology at the University of Salzburg, Austria. He comes originally from Turabdin in south-east Turkey and is a sub-deacon in the Syriac Orthodox Church.
Oriental Orthodox

Razek Siriani is a lay deacon in the Syriac Orthodox Church of Antioch, a researcher in Christianity of the East, a former director of education and international ecumenical relations at the Middle East Council of Churches and a former director of Relief Humanitarian Program for Refugees. He is originally from Syria and has translated *Towards the One Faith* into Arabic.
Syria

Mariz Tadros is Professor of Politics and Development at the Institute of Development Studies, University of Sussex, UK, where she co-leads the Power and Popular Politics Cluster. She is the author of *Copts at the Crossroads: The Challenges of Building Inclusive Democracy in Egypt* (American University in Cairo Press, 2013). Her research interests include religion in development, gender and development, political Islam, democratisation, unruly politics and security.
Introduction; Conclusion

Samuel Tadros is a senior fellow at the Hudson Institute, a visiting fellow at the Hoover Institution and a professorial lecturer at the School of Advanced International Studies, Johns Hopkins University, USA. He is the author of *Motherland Lost: The Egyptian and Coptic Quest for Modernity* (Hoover Institution Press, 2013).
Egypt

Georges Tamer is Professor of Oriental and Islamic Studies, Leader of the Centre for Euro-Oriental Studies and Director of the project Key Concepts in Interreligious Dialogue: Judaism, Christianity and Islam (KCID) at the Friedrich-Alexander University Erlangen-Nuremberg, Germany. He represents the Greek Orthodox Patriarchate of Antioch and All the East in the Central Committee of the World Council of Churches and has published widely in the fields of Arabic, Islamic and inter-religious studies.
Eastern Orthodox

Hratch Tchilingirian is an associate faculty member of the Oriental Institute, University of Oxford, UK. A sociologist by training, he has published many studies and articles on Armenian Christianity and religion over the last two decades.
Turkey; Armenia and Karabakh

Herman G. B. Teule is professor emeritus at Radboud University Nijmegen, The Netherlands, and University of Louvain, Belgium. Formerly he was

Head of the Institute of Eastern Christian Studies and has published extensively on the history and present-day situation of Middle Eastern Christianity, especially in Iraq, Syria, Lebanon and eastern Turkey.
Iraq

Iyad Twal is a Jordanian Catholic priest in the Latin Patriarchate of Jerusalem; Chairperson of the Department of Religious Studies at Bethlehem University; Professor of Philosophy, Dean of the Faculty of Theology and Philosophy at the Latin Seminary, Beit Jala; and pastor of Our Lady of Fatima Catholic Church in the Bethlehem area.
Jordan

Wafik Wahba is Associate Professor of Global Christianity at Tyndale University and Seminary in Toronto, Canada. He has taught theology and topics on global Christianity in the USA, the Middle East, Africa, Asia and South America and is author of several books and articles as well as a speaker at numerous international Christian conferences.
Evangelicals

Jack Wald has been pastor of Rabat International Church for 17 years. He received his DMin from Gordon-Conwell Theological Seminary in 2015 and has published a book derived from his thesis, *A Guide to International Church Ministry: Pastoring a Parade* (Barton-Veerman, 2016).
Morocco and Western Sahara

Anastasia Yiangou received her PhD from the University of London and is a historian of modern Cyprus. She is the author of *Cyprus in World War II: Politics and Conflict in the Eastern Mediterranean* (I. B. Tauris, 2010) and the co-editor of *The Greeks and the British in the Levant, 1800–1960s: Between Empires and Nations* (Routledge, 2016).
Cyprus

Gina A. Zurlo received her PhD from Boston University and is Assistant Director of the Center for the Study of Global Christianity at Gordon-Conwell Theological Seminary (South Hamilton, Massachusetts, USA). She is co-editor of the *World Christian Database* (Brill) and associate editor of the *World Religion Database* (Brill).
A Demographic Profile of Christianity in North Africa and West Asia; Methodology and Sources of Christian and Religious Affiliation

Introduction

A Demographic Profile of Christianity in North Africa and West Asia

Gina A. Zurlo

Majority Religion by Province, 2015

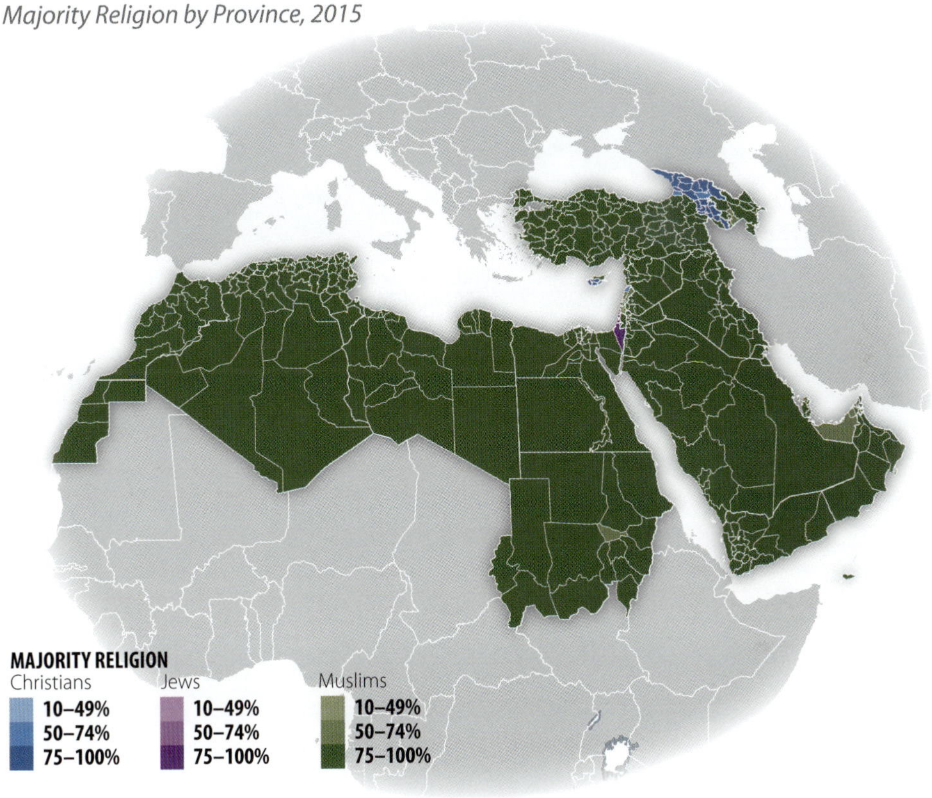

Although Christianity has been extant in the North Africa and West Asia regions for 2000 years, the region is predominantly Muslim today. From 1970 to 2015, Muslims have risen from 87% to 92% of the population. Historic Christian and Jewish communities have been declining proportionally due to political and social conflict.

Religions in North Africa and West Asia, 1970 and 2015

	1970		2015	
Religion	Adherents	%	Adherents	%
Muslims	147,487,000	87.3	440,182,000	91.5
Christians	11,550,000	6.8	24,913,000	5.2
Jews	2,568,000	1.5	6,409,000	1.3
Agnostics	4,123,000	2.4	4,590,000	1.0
Others	3,192,000	1.9	5,029,000	1.0
Total	**168,920,000**	**100.0**	**481,123,000**	**100.0**

Source: Todd M. Johnson and Gina A. Zurlo (eds), *World Christian Database* (Leiden/Boston: Brill), accessed April 2017. Figures do not add to 100% due to rounding.

Christianity in North Africa and West Asia, 1970–2015

Christians by Country, 2015

24.9 Million Christians, 5.2% of Population

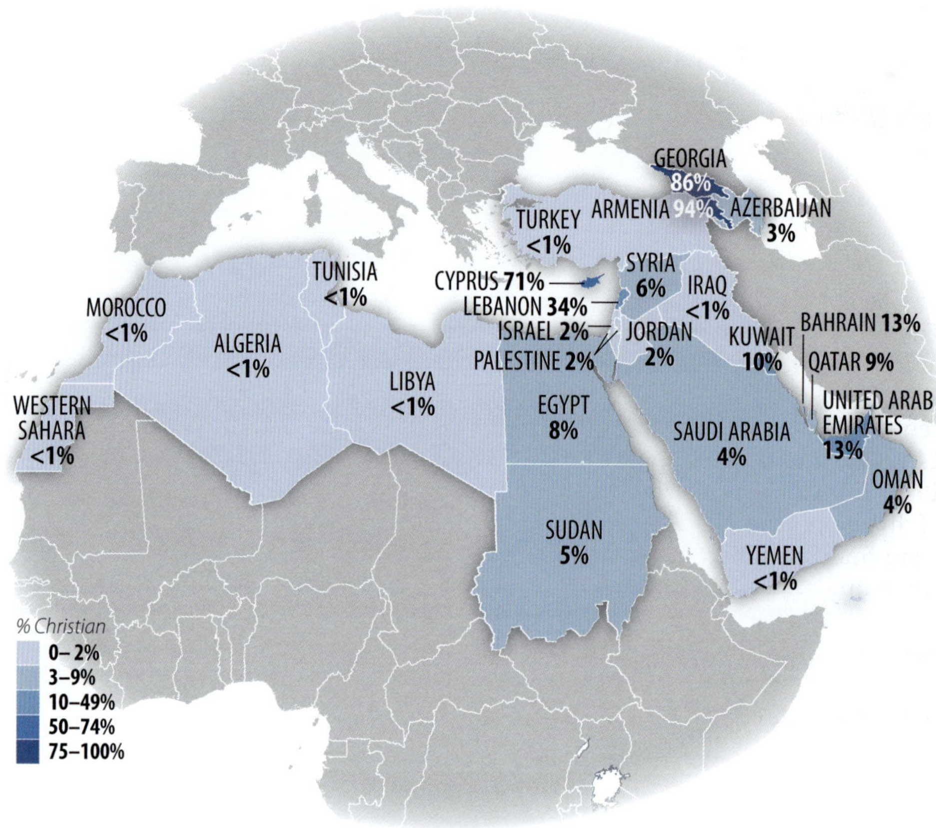

Christianity has a long history in North Africa and West Asia. The region is the birthplace of Jesus and as a result was the first region to receive the Christian message. St Paul visited numerous cities and planted churches in modern-day Turkey. Christianity began in Africa in the first century and by the second century it had reached Carthage (Tunisia).

Christians were in the majority in this region from the fourth century, but are the minority today except for in Armenia (94% Christian), Cyprus (71%) and Georgia (86%). Many countries in the region experienced decline in their Christian population between 1970 and 2015, such as Morocco, Iraq, Tunisia and Turkey. Most of these declines were due to death and emigration. However, some countries saw their Christian population increase, such as Saudi Arabia and the United Arab Emirates, because they receive a significant number of Christian migrant workers from South and Southeast Asia.

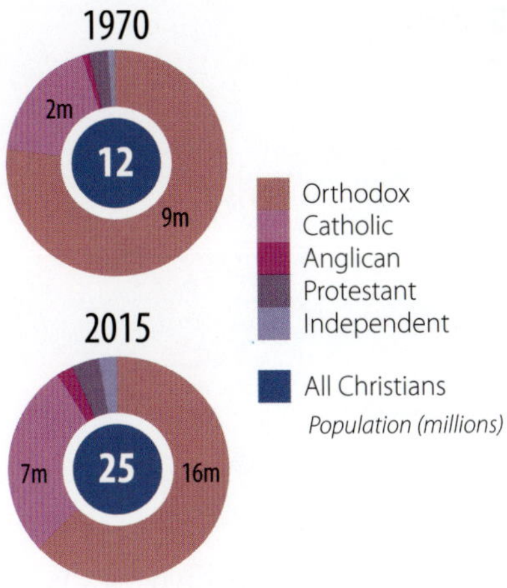

Major Christian Traditions, 1970 and 2015

Christianity in North Africa – West Asia has always been, and remains, majority Orthodox. There has been an increase in the proportion of Catholics (from about 1 in 6 Christians to about 1 in 3.5) and a corresponding decrease in the proportion of Orthodox. The slight increase in Protestants is due to missionary activity in the region.

Christians, 1970–2015

The proportional decline of Christians in the region has occurred since at least the beginning of the twentieth century, when Christians represented 14% (7 million) of the population. By 1970, Christians were 7% (12 million) of the population, and by 2015 they were 5% (25 million). Many Christian communities face severe persecution, resulting in emigration or death. Further, Christian birthrates below replacement level contribute to the religion's decline.

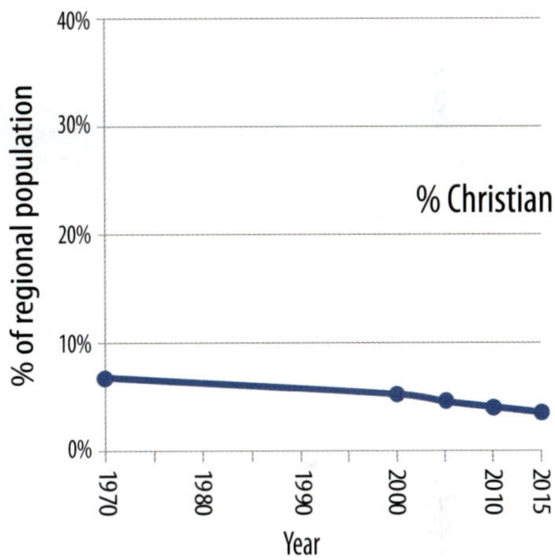

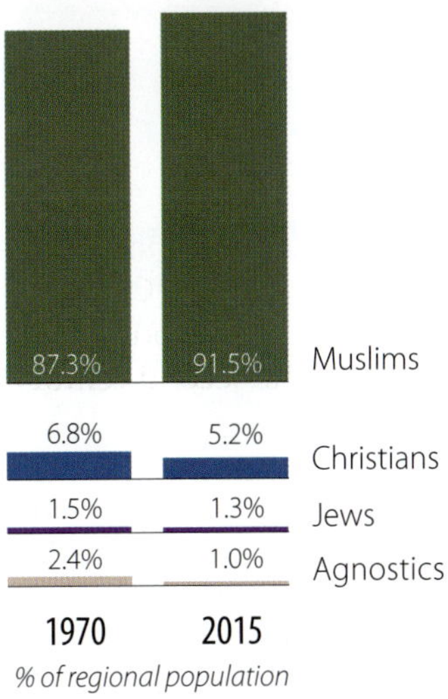

Religious Affiliation, 1970 and 2015

North Africa – West Asia is predominantly Muslim. Muslims have increased with the proportional decline of Christian and Jewish populations. Jews were 1.5% of the region in 1970 and decreased to 1.3% in 2015. Agnosticism has declined due to the collapse of communism in the region's three former Soviet states (Georgia, Armenia and Azerbaijan).

Note: Throughout this profile, traditions will not add up to total Christians in each region because of double-affiliation and the unaffiliated. Only the four largest religions are depicted.

Major Christian Traditions, 1970 and 2015

Christians

1970

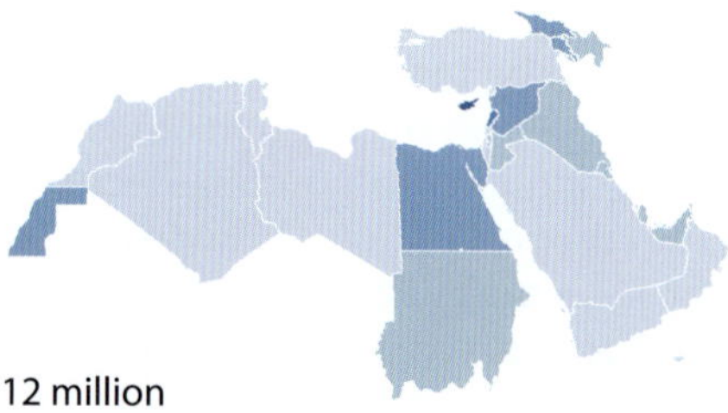

12 million

2015

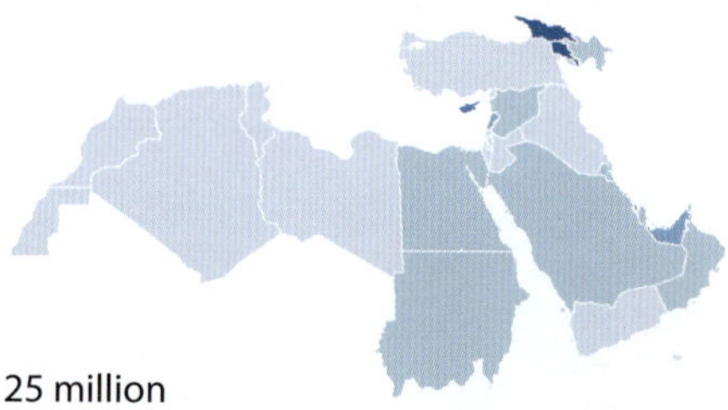

25 million

% of country population
- 0–2%
- 3–9%
- 10–49%
- 50–74%
- 75–100%

The largest Christian populations in North Africa – West Asia are found in Egypt (8 million), Georgia (3.5 million), Armenia (3 million), Sudan (2 million), Lebanon (2 million) and Saudi Arabia (1.4 million). Between 1970 and 2015, Christianity declined more quickly in North Africa (4.4% Christian in 2015) than in West Asia (6% Christian).

Anglicans

1970

0.1 million

2015

0.6 million

% of Christian population
- 0–2%
- 3–9%
- 10–49%
- 50–74%
- 75–100%

Anglicans have increased slightly in the region, though it still has a relatively small presence. Anglicans have a long history in Sudan, with the arrival of missionaries at the turn of the twentieth century. Decline of Anglicans in the Arabian Peninsula over the 45-year period was due largely to British decolonisation in the region. Anglicans are the third-largest Christian tradition in Turkey, after Orthodox and Catholics.

Catholics

Overall, Catholics have grown in the region from 1.2% of the population (2 million) to 1.5% (7.1 million). The portion of Catholics among Christians in some countries grew substantially between 1970 and 2015, such as Bahrain (42% to 83%), Kuwait (46% to 76%) and Lebanon (69% to 81%). Other Catholic populations dropped proportionally, such as in Algeria (76% to 8%). In other countries, the Catholic percentage of all Christians has remained high, such as in Iraq (55% in 2015), Israel (58%) and Tunisia (83%).

Independents

The largest Independent networks, where extant, are Muslim-background believers, or believers in Christ, who, for safety or other reasons, choose to remain publicly affiliated to Islam. Algeria has the largest population, where 70% of all Christians are Independents. There are also large clandestine communities of Christians in Tunisia, Morocco and Western Sahara.

Major Christian Traditions, 1970 and 2015

Orthodox

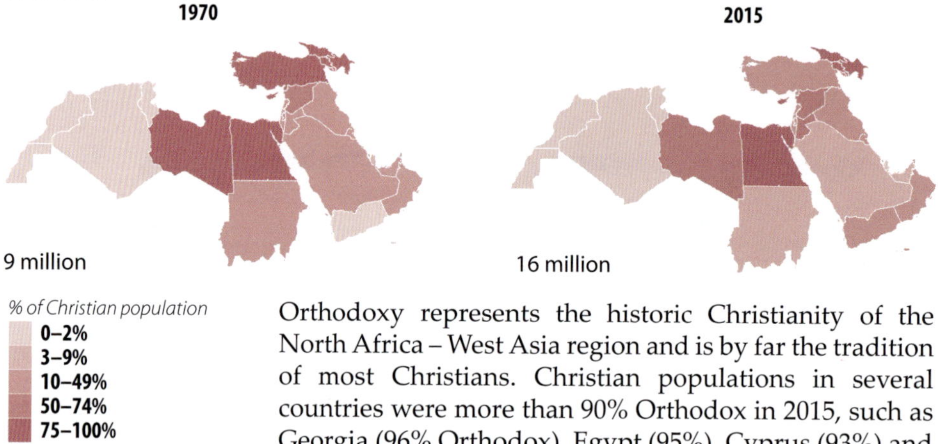

Orthodoxy represents the historic Christianity of the North Africa – West Asia region and is by far the tradition of most Christians. Christian populations in several countries were more than 90% Orthodox in 2015, such as Georgia (96% Orthodox), Egypt (95%), Cyprus (93%) and Azerbaijan (93%). The Orthodox declined proportionally between 1970 and 2015 in some countries with the introduction of other Christian traditions, such as in the United Arab Emirates.

Protestants

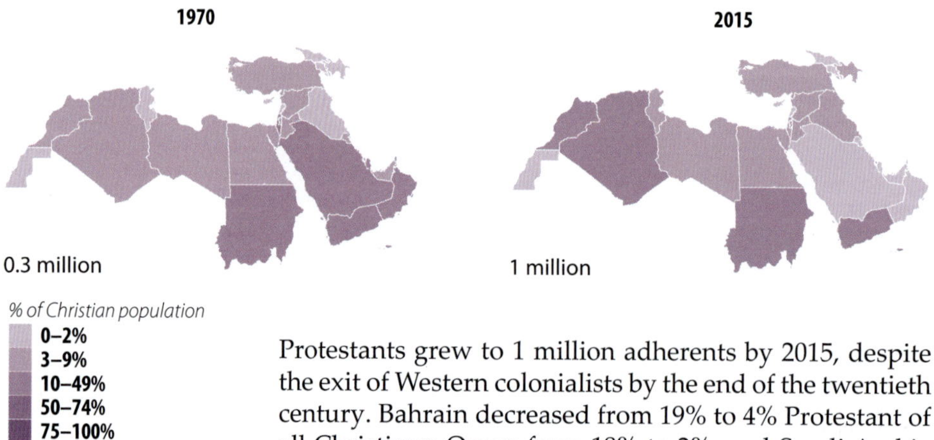

Protestants grew to 1 million adherents by 2015, despite the exit of Western colonialists by the end of the twentieth century. Bahrain decreased from 19% to 4% Protestant of all Christians; Oman from 18% to 2%; and Saudi Arabia from 38% to 1%. Christianity in Morocco declined at 2% per year between 1970 and 2015, though the proportion of Protestants increased from 5% to 11% of all Christians.

Movements Within Christianity, 1970 and 2015

Evangelicals

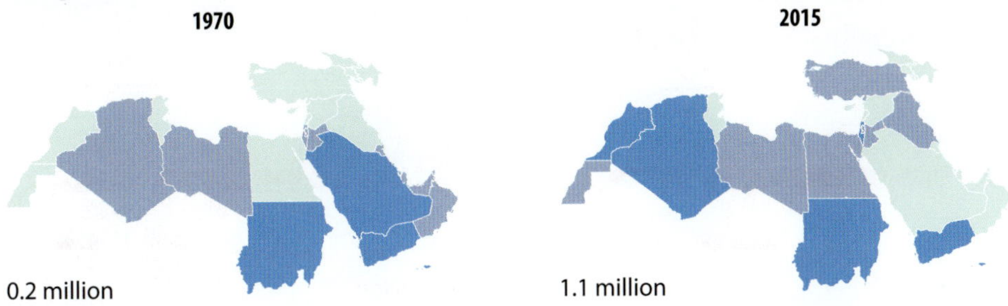

% of Christian population
- **0–2%**
- **3–9%**
- **10–49%**
- **50–74%**
- **75–100%**

Evangelicals are a minority movement in North Africa – West Asia, though there has been modest growth since 1970, from 2% to 4% of the region's Christian population. Algeria is home to the largest Evangelical community (39% of all Christians), largely due to its comparatively large community of secret Christians. Likewise, Morocco – where Christians are 12% Evangelical – is also home to a sizeable hidden Christian community that is also Evangelical in belief and practice.

Pentecostals/Charismatics

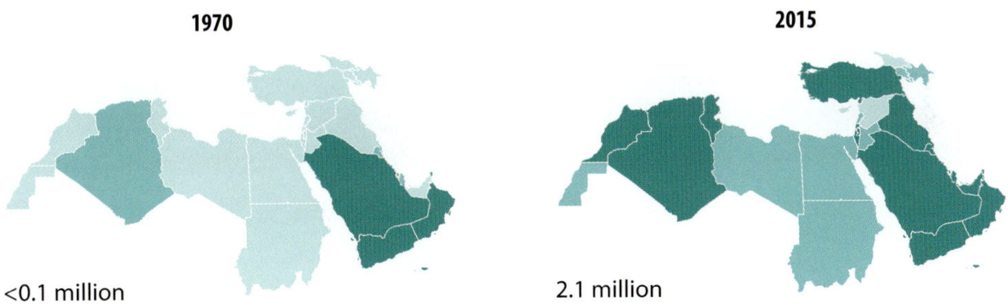

% of Christian population
- **0–2%**
- **3–9%**
- **10–49%**
- **50–74%**
- **75–100%**

Pentecostal and Charismatic Christianity grew faster than Evangelicalism in North Africa – West Asia from 1970 to 2015, and now represents 8% of the region's Christian population. However, in several countries Christians are more than 20% Pentecostals/Charismatics: Algeria (31%), Bahrain (24%), Iraq (21%), Israel (23%), Kuwait (21%), Qatar (26%), Saudi Arabia (26%) and the United Arab Emirates (25%).

Christianity In North Africa, 1970–2015

Christians by Country, 2015

9.9 Million Christians, 4.4% of Population

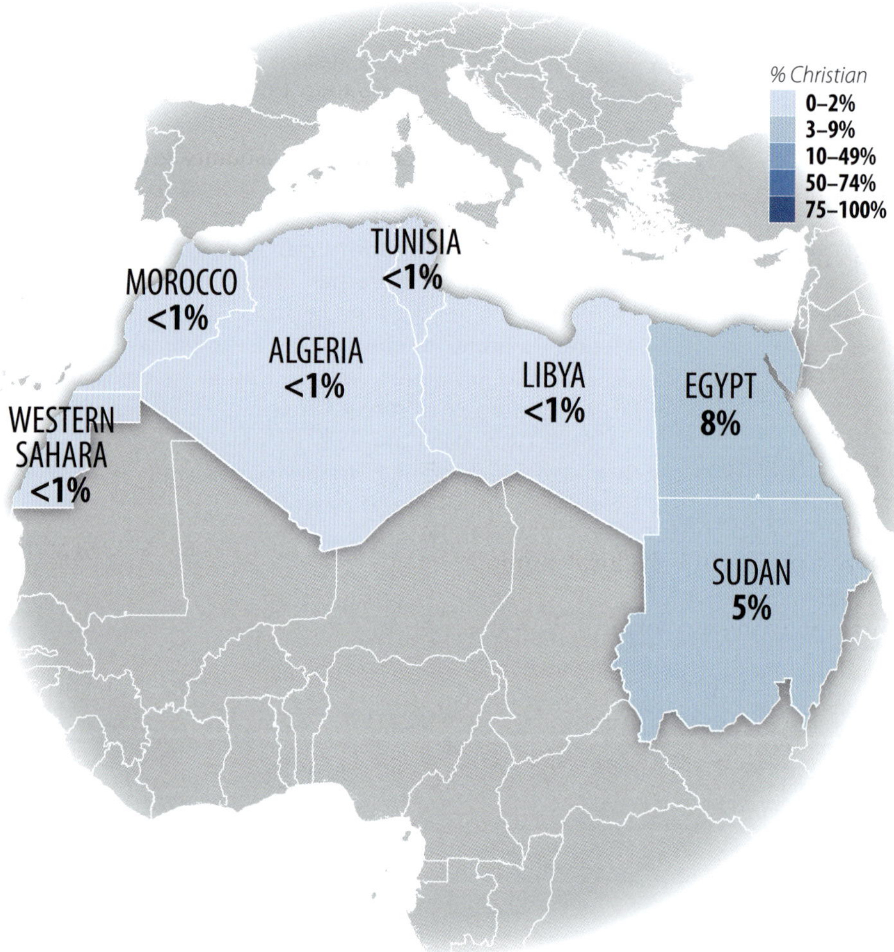

Christianity in North Africa declined from 6.3% of the population in 1970 to 4.4% in 2015, despite an increase in the overall number of Christians (5 million to 10 million). Christianity declined as a percentage in six of the seven countries in the region. The only exception to region-wide decline was Sudan, where Christianity rose from 3% of the population in 1970 to 5% in 2015.

Many Christians in North Africa have faced extreme persecution in the last several decades, resulting in an exodus, mainly to Europe. Religious minorities of all kinds were negatively affected by power struggles after the 'Arab Spring' of 2010–11 in countries such as Tunisia, Egypt, Libya and Morocco. Christianity in Western Sahara experienced the most drastic decline, dropping from 41% Christian to 0.2% in the 45-year period, largely due to the end of Spanish colonial rule in 1975. The remaining small Christian population there is composed almost entirely of Catholic foreigners.

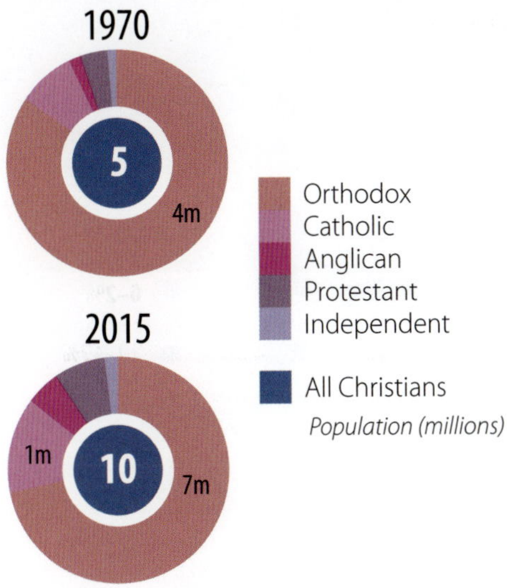

Major Christian Traditions, 1970 and 2015

In 2015, Christianity in North Africa was largely Orthodox (75% of all Christians) and Catholic (14% of all Christians). These traditions declined proportionally over the 45-year period, with gains in Protestant and, to a lesser extent, Independent Christians. Protestant Christianity grew as a result of missionary efforts in the region.

Christians, 1970–2015

Christianity in North Africa has declined from 6.3% of the population in 1970 to 4.4% in 2015. Political turmoil negatively impacted Christians, as did the end of Spanish colonial rule in the disputed Western Sahara territory. Decline was more precipitous after the Arab Spring in several countries.

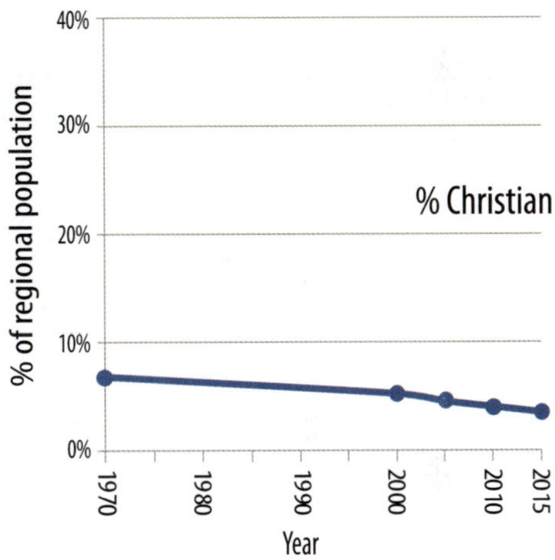

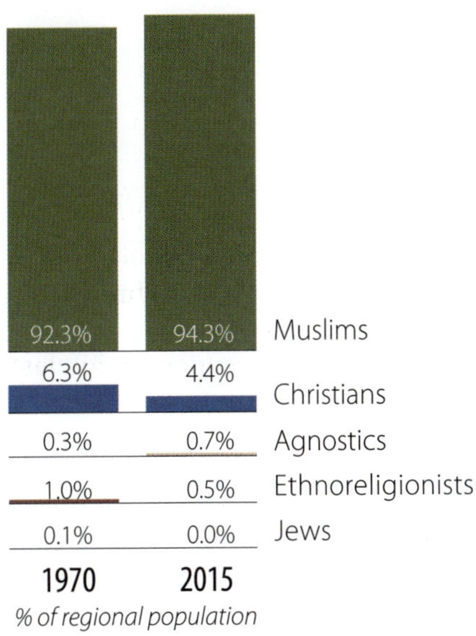

Religious Affiliation, 1970 and 2015

Many of the issues plaguing Christians in North Africa have also affected other religious minorities, such as Jews. In the last 45 years, Jews have transformed from a sizeable minority to near depletion in the region. The decline of Christians as a proportion of the region's population has occurred alongside continual increase of its Muslim population. Muslims grew from 92% of the population in 1970 to 94% in 2015.

Christianity in West Asia, 1970–2015

Christians by Country, 2015

15 Million Christians, 5.9% of Population

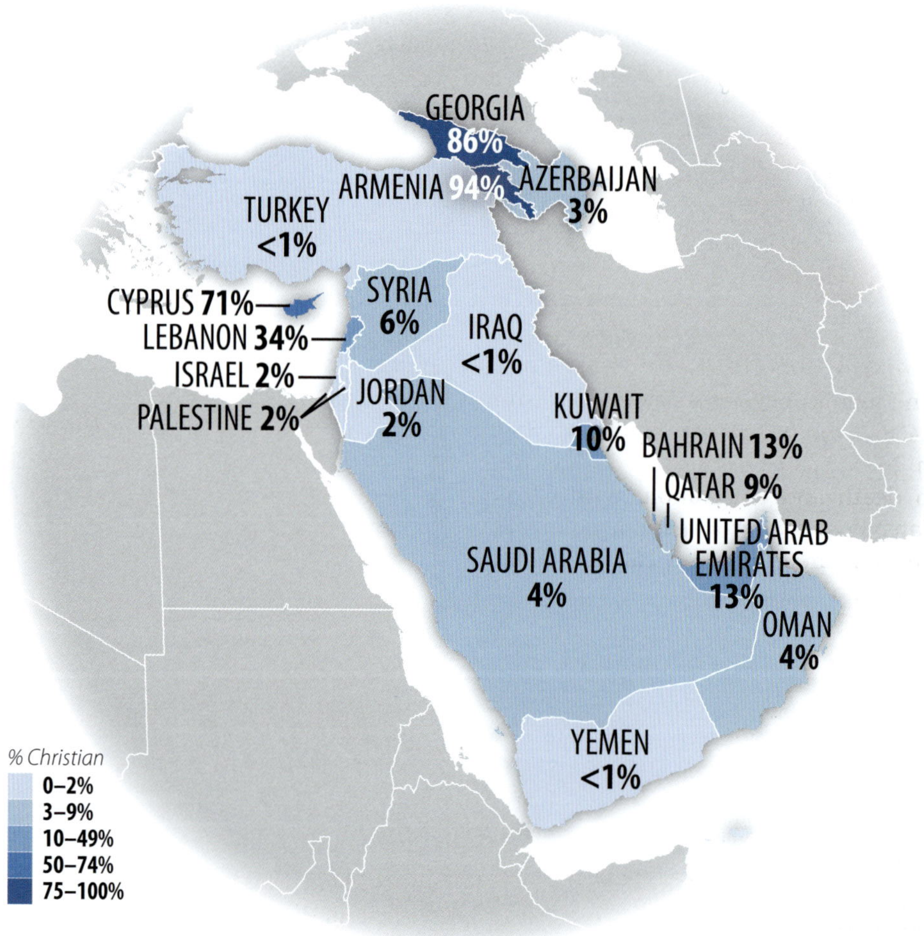

West Asia is culturally, politically and religiously very diverse. The region is home to historic Orthodox churches planted by direct spiritual descendants of Jesus's 12 Apostles in the first few centuries of Christianity. These Eastern churches thrived in the region until the Arab conquest of the seventh century. In the wake of Muslim rule, these churches entered 'survival mode', a state in which they essentially remain today.

Christians in Syria and Iraq have experienced acute suffering in the recent times, caught in the middle of civil wars and political struggles. Many Christians fled Iraq for Syria in the early 2000s only to be caught in the middle of the Syrian civil war, which began in 2011. Tens of thousands of Christians fled Syria for Jordan, Turkey and Lebanon.

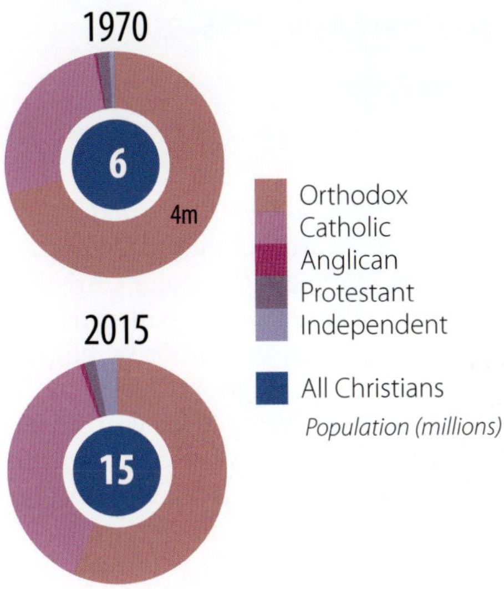

Major Christian Traditions, 1970 and 2015

Most Christians in West Asia are Orthodox (57% of all Christians in 2015) and Catholic (38% of all Christians in 2015). Some Protestant and Independent denominations have made modest increases in the region, such as small, new Pentecostal/Charismatic churches.

Christians, 1970–2015

Christianity in West Asia declined from 7.4% of the population in 1970 to 5.9% in 2015. Most of that decline was due to death and emigration, with Christians fleeing war-torn and politically unstable areas. It is unclear how many Christians have been martyred in the region, but they likely number in the thousands.

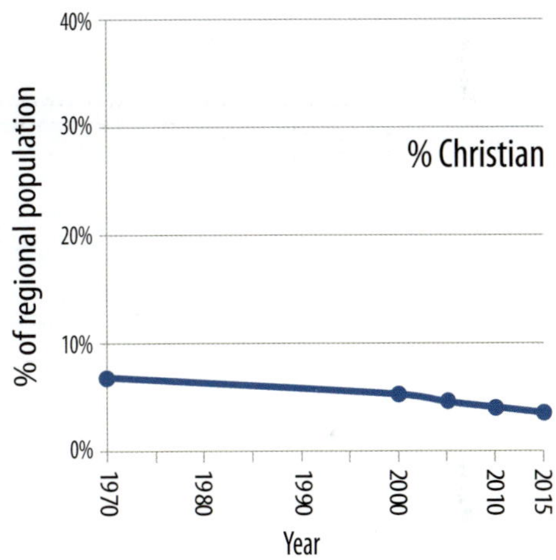

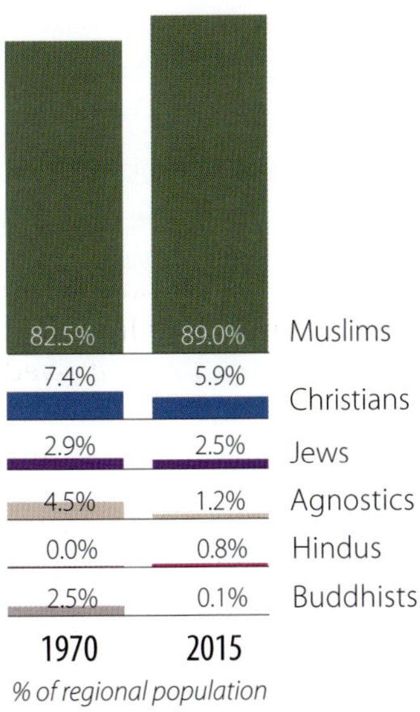

Religious Affiliation, 1970 and 2015

Muslims in West Asia remain the majority, rising from 83% of the population in 1970 to 89% in 2015. While Christians made numerical increases over the 45-year period (from 6 million to 15 million), they are in decline proportionally. Religious minorities of all kinds face challenges in this region: Christians, Jews, Buddhists and agnostics.

Future of Christianity in North Africa and West Asia, 2015–2050

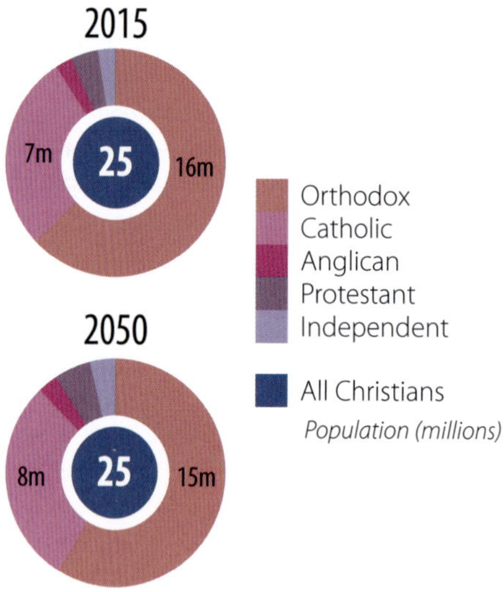

Major Christian Traditions, 2015 and 2050

Looking forward, Orthodox churches are likely to remain the major Christian tradition, although they will continue to face challenges as a minority religion in the region. Orthodox Christians in North Africa–West Asia will likely decline slightly in total and percentage terms from 2015 to 2050 while other traditions experience modest increases by percentage.

Christians, 2015–2050

By 2050, Christians will likely number 25 million in the region, 3% of the population. This is a substantial decrease from 5% in 2015. Without resolutions to conflict and strategies for refugees to return home, it is unlikely that the Christian situation in the region will improve.

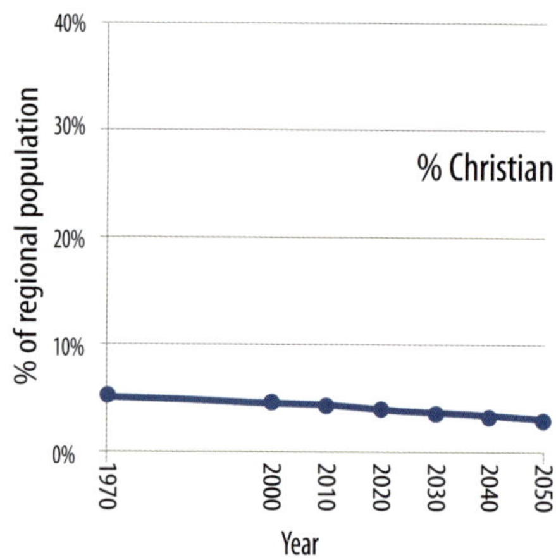

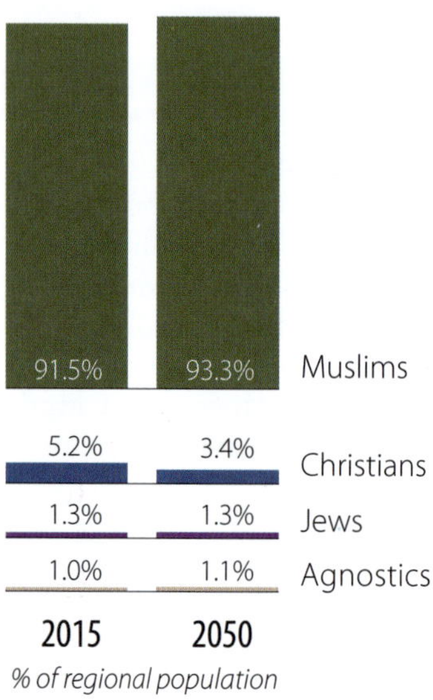

Religious Affiliation, 2015 and 2050

Between 2015 and 2050, the Muslim population in North Africa–West Asia will continue to grow both in size and as a percentage, at the cost of decreasing religious minorities in terms of percentage. Christians are likely to decline from 5% of the population in 2015 to 3%. Judaism is growing in Israel due to the high birth rates of Ultra-Orthodox Jews and therefore will likely keep its share of the region's population consistent into the future.

Christianity in North Africa and West Asia

Mariz Tadros

It is impossible to miss the poignancy of the timing of the release of this volume on Christianity in North Africa and West Asia (NAWA). The region witnessed the first genocide in the twenty-first century – that of the Christians and Yazidis at the hands of ISIS in Iraq. This juncture also marks 100 years since the genocide of the Armenian, Assyrian, Syriac and Chaldean Christians in the beginning of the twentieth century. Both genocides occurred at times of tumultuous reconfiguration of global and regional power and both have had devastating impacts on the demographics and coping trajectory of local Christian communities.

This volume tells the stories of the many faces and expressions of Christianity in 25 settings in the NAWA region in the twenty-first century, through a multi-vocal, multi-themed, multidisciplinary approach that is both historicised and contextualised. It recognises Christianity as a spirituality, as a religion and as a faith, as well as its interface with all aspects of material life (politics, culture and economics). In addition to presenting the most up-to-date statistical and demographic information, each country profile provides a brief local history of Christianity, with a particular focus on the twenty-first century, exploring the changing role and status of Christians and identifying critical historical junctures. Each essay seeks to capture the different religious traditions, denominations and expressions of spirituality, as well as the relationships between people, church and the broader community. Different authors give more weight to different features of lived Christianity, reflecting both their own positioning and their perspectives on the issues that they see as most influential for Christianity in their settings. Moreover, the volume comprises a number of thematic essays that address theological, social, cultural and political issues that converge and diverge within and across countries of the NAWA region.

This volume has a number of defining features. First, the region is home to the most ancient expressions and formations of Christianity. Second, Islam plays a very powerful role in the narratives of Christians across most of the countries in the region. Third, this is the region where Christians are facing the greatest existential risk. And fourth, there is an extraordinary plurality and diversity in Christian expression across denominational, ethnic, cultural and historical identifiers. This introduction is organised around these defining features. The chapter first highlights the historical, political and epistemological conundrums around engaging with the question of the Christians in the region, particularly with respect to the Middle East. It then briefly highlights the historical and contemporary interface between different sources of Islamic authority and the position of Christians in Muslim-majority contexts. This is further elaborated in the section that follows, where the influence of twenty-first-century political dynamics on Christian communities is discussed. Finally, the chapter provides a panoramic view on the mosaic of Christian denominations, their distinctive characteristics and the nature of relations across and within communities.

Whose Voice, Whose Standpoint?

With the exception of Cyprus, Georgia and Armenia (see the essays by Anastasia Yiangou, Silvia Serrano and Hratch Tchilingirian in this volume), Christians comprise a numerical minority in the countries presented. The United Nations (UN) defines a minority as:

> A group numerically inferior to the rest of the population of a State, in a non-dominant position, whose members – being nationals of the State – possess ethnic, religious or linguistic characteristics differing from those of the rest of the population and show, if only implicitly, a sense of solidarity, directed towards preserving their culture, traditions, religion or language. (United Nations High Commission for Human Rights, Office of the High Commissioner, *Minority Rights: International Standards and Guidelines for Implementation*, New York: United Nations, 2010)

As far as this definition is concerned, Christians in the NAWA region comprise religious minorities. The Christian communities as minorities in NAWA are in non-dominant positions, exercising varying degrees of power within their communities, from high levels of participation in countries such as Lebanon (see the essay by Charles Chartouni) to marginal levels in countries such as Iraq and Sudan (see the essays by Herman Teule and John Eibner). They also possess distinctive characteristics on account of their Christian faith, sometimes overlapping with an ethnic and linguistic identity (the Greeks, Armenians and Syriacs), sometimes expressing their Christian identity in secret, with no visible public manifestation. In all of these cases the distinct faith element has elicited a sense of solidarity, intent on preserving the religio-cultural heritage of the community.

However, to speak of Christian minorities, in particular with respect to the Middle Eastern countries, within the area covered is not without its problems. In some contexts, you are maligned if you describe Christians as a minority; in other contexts, you are undermined if you do not define them as such. In many cases, it depends on with whom Christians are engaging, whether locals or foreigners, the national context and what is happening in terms of geopolitics. In other words, the labelling of Christians in the NAWA region is both complex and contentious.

The legacy of colonialists' use of the term 'minority' has also inflected the term with highly contentious connotations. For example, Seteny Shami argues that the first time the word 'minority' entered the lexicon of terms used to describe Christians in the region was in the early 1920s in Egypt, when political elites were debating whether the new Egyptian constitution should include specific language concerning the protection of religious minorities (S. Shami, 'Aqaliliyya/Minority', in C. Gluck and A. Lowenhaupt Tsing (eds), *Words in Motion: Toward a Global Lexicon,* Durham: Duke University Press, 2009, 151–73). The labelling of non-Muslim communities as minorities was a political project, according to Shami, intended to justify colonialist control over matters of internal governance. When in 1922 Egypt gained its independence from Britain, areas remained in which Britain retained absolute control, including the defence of the interests of foreigners and non-indigenous minorities. Hence, for the pan-nationalist and pan-Arab resistance movements that reached their apex in the twentieth century, the use of the word 'minority' to refer to non-Muslim communities living in Muslim-majority contexts was anathema. Many champions of national liberation emphasised that their countries were not divided along religious lines and that to adopt such a rhetoric would be to allow colonialists to use divide-and-rule strategies. While a rhetoric emphasising unity and solidarity across the people might have encouraged patriotism, it also led to a policy intent on being blind to the prejudice and discrimination that populations suffered on account of their faith. In other words, it perpetuated a politics of denial as opposed to a policy of recognising and responding to religious pluralism.

Concurrently, within academic work on the Middle East, scholarship critiquing orientalism became popular, a trend that continues to this day with significant impact on the framing of Christians in the region. Its genesis lies in Edward Said's seminal work on orientalism, in which he critiques Western discourse on Islam as underpinned by an objectification of the religion and its followers and one that is inherently racist and colonialist. It followed that Western literature critiquing Christians as victims of persecution in Muslim-majority contexts came to be seen in the same light, as orientalist political projects intended to defame Islam. Closely intertwined with anti-orientalism was the emergence of the political project and scholarship of countering Islamophobia. The Council on American–Islamic Relations (CAIR) defines Islamophobia as:

> a closed-minded hatred, fear or prejudice toward Islam and Muslims that results in discrimination, marginalization and oppression. It creates a distorted understanding of Islam and Muslims and transforms diversity in name, language, culture, ethnicity, and race into a set of stereotyped characteristics. As such, Islamophobia is a system of both religious and racial animosity. (CAIR, 'Islamophobia 101', http://www.islamophobia.org/research/islamophobia-101.html, accessed 21 November 2017)

However, the line between rejecting narratives that are biased in the name of fighting Islamophobia and blocking any critique of individuals and movements whose words and actions have undermined the rights of Christians in the NAWA region is a very fine one. Sometimes, in a bid to avoid Islamophobia, there has been a purposeful negation or avoidance of the fact that Christians are a minority in the power-hierarchy sense of the word. As Mark Farha reflects in his essay 'Social and Political Context':

> Partly out of fear of being branded bigots, a number of scholars have also done their utmost to avoid attributing ideological origins to the crisis in Islamic political discourse in general, and to the discrimination and terrorist acts perpetrated by jihadists against Christian and other communities in particular. Yet in point of fact it must be understood that the Arab media sphere and the Internet are brim full not just with anti-Christian rhetoric but also with accusations of treason.

In some contexts, in contradistinction to the discourse that deems the labelling of Christian communities as minorities to be a colonialist political project, being recognised as a minority is the only pathway to secure a modicum of citizenship rights. For example, the Turkish government does not officially recognise the Syriac Orthodox Church, the Assyrian Christians, the Church of the East or the Chaldean Catholic Church, either as non-Muslim minorities or as legal entities. This is because when the Treaty of Lausanne was signed, extending protection to non-Muslim minorities to 'enjoy the same civil and political rights as Moslems' (Article 39), the Syriac Orthodox Church was not listed as one of the minorities in Turkey's compilation of religious groups residing on its territory. This means that even the recognition (very unequal) afforded to other Christian minorities in Turkey, such as the Greek and Armenian churches, is denied to the Assyrian Christians (see the essay on Turkey by Hratch Tchilingirian and Ed Alden).

Ironically, Christians are also called a minority by a political camp that would conventionally be seen as being at odds with the Western political 'colonialist' project identified by Shami. Some Islamist scholars in NAWA countries have described Christians as a minority in their countries, echoing the *dhimmi* discourse. For example, the late Sheikh Mohamed El Ghazali, a leading scholar of Sunni Islam, as well as several Salafi leaders have referred to Copts as the 'happiest minority in the world'. The aim of labelling the Copts as a minority in such a narrative is to emphasise that though a numerical minority, Christians enjoy privileges as a consequence of living under the protection of Islam (see the section 'Situating Christians in Islamic Paradigms', below). The use of 'minority' distinguishes them from a religious majority and highlights their 'religious otherness' while ignoring their unequal position. In a different context – that of contemporary Iraq, where sectarian affiliation trumps a more inclusive national political identity – Christians (and other groups) are identifying themselves as minorities in need of special protection against religious-based targeting. Without the legal guarantees of basic security, they fear that they will be particularly vulnerable.

It cannot be emphasised enough that political actors and their projects determine the outcomes of a particular labelling of Christians. For example, in the Arab region of NAWA, Christians once had no qualms about referring to themselves as Nazarenes (Nasarah). However, when the term began to be used by Islamists in the twentieth century to refer to Christians in a derogatory manner, this changed. (In the present essay as well as the concluding essay to this volume, the terms Islamist and Islamism do not refer to the Muslim population at large but to forces and movements who aspire to assume political power for the installation of a state run in accordance with their interpretation of Islamic Shariah.) In Syria and Iraq, radical Islamists, particularly ISIS, began to mark the homes of Christians with an 'n' (ن) for 'Nasarah', to single them out from non-Christian households so as to target them for payment of the Islamic *jizya* (see below) and for assault. As the assaults on Christians intensified, concerned Christians globally and fellow Iraqi Muslims began to use the sign 'n' to raise awareness of the plight of Iraqi Christians. This included a global social media campaign whereby Christians and others changed their profile pictures on Facebook and Twitter to a picture of the letter ن, thus demonstrating their support for their imperilled co-religionists. Iraqi Christians, while rejecting their labelling as 'Nasarah' by the Islamists, undoubtedly welcomed its appropriation by the international community to give recognition to the religious basis for their subjugation at the hands of ISIS. The implication is that the political nuances of words change as they are appropriated by different political actors to advance political agendas that enhance or circumscribe the rights of Christians in the region.

Similarly, Christians use multiple narratives to tell the story of their heritage. How they frame their identity (be it minority, community, citizens, nationals, Arabs) will vary dramatically according to the audience of their narrative. This volume actively sought contributions from scholars from the region, recognising that much of mainstream Western scholarship has reflected Western academic viewpoints and analysis. This is not to suggest that an 'indigenous viewpoint' is represented here; rather, there is a diversity of lenses representing differences as significant within communities as across them. The volume has sought to present a plurality of perspectives (rather than account for all forms of diversity) across a number of nexuses. These include religious affiliation (Orthodox, Catholic and Protestant scholars), disciplines (religion and philosophy, politics, sociology and history, among many) and background (academics, faith leaders, theologians and activists). The editors are conscious of the invisibility of many women scholars' contributions to mainstream academia in (and on) the region and have sought to redress this gap in this volume while acknowledging there is plenty of room for improvement.

This plurality also manifests itself in terms of intersecting identities – that is, how having a distinct religious but also ethnic or linguistic affiliation influences an individual's or a group's positioning. For example, what does it mean to be an Armenian or Assyrian living in Turkey or a Chaldean Catholic living in Iraq? What does it mean to be a Pentecostal pastor leading an underground ministry in English in Saudi Arabia? These intersecting identities have implications for the positioning of individuals and groups within a society where sometimes the stigma not only is one of being the 'religious other' but also is accentuated on account of being a minority within a minority. This subjects a group to prejudice both from the majority and from other Christian communities, who tend to see the group as not equally patriotic as them, or not as ancient, or as carrying a Western/foreign form of Christianity. This ultimately complicates the image of a mosaic of harmoniously aligned Christian communities, as relations of co-existence and mutual recognition are in negotiation at both the leadership and the grassroots levels.

While recognising the tensions and convergences across a plurality of identities, and without seeking to essentialise or minimise their significance, this volume is underpinned by a common standpoint, that of individuals who have a critical analytical lens on a subject that they consider to be of far-reaching significance for communities in the region and beyond.

Situating Christians in Islamic Paradigms

It is impossible to understand the context of contemporary Christianity in the twenty-first century independently of the multifaceted roles of Islam as a faith and way of life, ideology, system of governance and political project. One of the distinctive features of this volume is that almost every essay makes implicit or explicit reference to the interface between Christianity and Islam in terms of the latter's influence on political, economic and social system(s) more broadly. Who speaks in the name of Islam, the power they wield and the ideological underpinning of the political project that they champion all have enormous implications for the positioning, and indeed the very survival, of Christian and other non-Muslim minorities.

Islam was founded by Muhammad in the seventh century and emerged from Medina, which lies in modern-day Saudi Arabia. Islam began to spread in the region through conquests that began with Muhammad himself. The conquest by Arab forces of Syria (which was under Byzantine rule) in 634–41 then spread to Palestine and surrounding regions. Egypt, which was also under Byzantine rule, was conquered in 639–42 by the Muslim leader 'Amr ibn al-'As. Prior to the spread of Islam, these territories were mostly following the Christian faith, though encompassing different political leaderships, church hierarchies and traditions and other faiths as well. By the fourteenth century, in most of these conquered territories the demographic presence of Christianity had shrunk to one of minority as large segments of the population had converted to Islam.

The position of Islamic jurisprudence is critically important for understanding the influence of Islamic Sharia, both as a source of governance in many modern-day states and as a political project espoused by various Islamic movements competing to achieve political power. Islam is a religion that allows for multiple interpretations, meanings and inferences, which is reflected in the varied positions of Muslim–Christian relations within Islamic jurisprudence. Among the four schools of Islamic jurisprudence, there is agreement that the position of non-Muslims is first determined by whether they live in Dar al Islam (territory ruled by Muslims) or whether they are in Dar al Harb ('Domain of War'), territories ruled by non-Muslims, that is, Dar al Kufr ('unbelief'). The second qualifier is whether they would qualify for 'dhimmitude'.

Christians who reside in Dar al Islam and are People of the Book (as the majority of Christians in North Africa and West Asia came to be) would come under the covenant of dhimmitude. The basis of this covenant is that the Muslim majority will afford non-Muslims the right of abode and protection in return for the payment of a *jizya* (poll tax). Much of Islamic jurisprudence on the status of Christians in Muslim lands takes as a reference point the first covenant widely believed to be signed between Christians and the Islamic conquerors, what became commonly known as the Pact or Covenant of Umar. The Covenant of Umar was a treaty allegedly signed by the second Caliph, Umar Ubn al-Khattab, with the Christians of Syria after they were conquered by the Islamic army. The treaty contained a number of articles that set out the conditions upon which the Christians were to be granted the right to live and be protected from assault. Such conditions included restrictions on freedom of worship, such as 'We shall not build … new monasteries, churches, convents, or monks' cells, nor shall we repair … such of them as fall in ruins or are situated in the quarters of the Muslims'. It also included articles prohibiting public displays of religion and making freedom of conversion one way only, from Christianity to Islam: 'We shall not manifest our religion publicly nor convert anyone to it. We shall not prevent any of our kin from entering Islam if they wish it'. In addition, the treaty had a number of articles pertaining to distinct physical appearance and attire to differentiate non-Muslims from their Muslim counterparts: 'We shall show respect toward the Muslims, and we shall rise from our seats when they wish to sit'. Finally, discretion in religious practices so as not to offend Muslim sensibilities was mandated:

> We shall not display our crosses or our books in the roads or markets of the Muslims. We shall use only clappers in our churches very softly. We shall not raise our voices when following our dead. We shall not show lights on any of the roads of the Muslims or in their markets. We shall not bury our dead near the Muslims. (See https://sourcebooks.fordham.edu/source/pact-umar.asp)

From the seventh century and up to the instatement of modern-day citizenship in the nineteenth century, the terms of the Pact of Umar influenced the terms of engagement of Muslim rulers with Christian populations in their territories.

After the conquest of Constantinople, from 1453 and up to the nineteenth century, a large section of the Christian population in the NAWA region came under the rule of the Ottomans. Ottoman rulers used the millet system to organise religious groups within their territories. Though the benefits granted to each group varied, by and large the millet system offered a certain level of self-rule, in particular in the areas of family law, social and cultural autonomy, and election of group leadership. One of the key features was that religious leaders would be the representatives of their communities vis-à-vis the authorities. To a very large degree, the terms of engagement in many NAWA contexts today are such that Christian minorities are represented by their religious leaders, who mediate between them and the ruler, making requests from the community but also passing the authority-holder's wishes to the people. Such practices therefore have their historical genesis, although authority on both sides (within governments and within Christian communities) tends to be much more fragmented today, undermining a singular flow of command.

Relative to other parts of the globe at that time, the non-Muslim 'others' enjoyed a certain level of self-rule that allowed for their survival under the Ottoman Empire. In the twenty-first century, when so many religious minorities are facing existential threats, the idea that the solution might be in the revival of the millet system has been put forward. For example Nicholas Pelham proposes this as a solution pre-dating both the modern genocides witnessed in the region and the emergence of the modern nation-state (*Holy Lands: Reviving Religious Pluralism in the Middle East*, New York: Columbia Global Reports, 2016). However, it is important to note that as much as the millet system ensured the coexistence of minorities of different faiths alongside Muslim majorities, it was discriminatory at both state and society levels, and also instituted forms of discrimination and prejudice within Muslim populations themselves.

As Heather Sharkey notes in her essay 'Mission and Evangelism', some of the legacies of the past 'remain visible today in Middle Eastern and North African countries where laws limit or prohibit conversion from Islam while restricting marriage, inheritance and child custody in ways that favour Muslims – and above all, Muslim men'. Perhaps if the establishment of contemporary citizenship in modern-day states had been accompanied by religious pluralism, it also would have accorded all citizens freedoms irrespective of their religious identity. However, citizenship premised on full equality of status and rights was deeply circumscribed across most countries of NAWA. On the one hand, under the citizenship model instated in the Levant and Egypt, Christians were freed from the payment of *jizya* as they were allowed to assume responsibility with Muslims for the protection of the sovereignty of the state by joining national armies. In lieu of *jizya*, they paid taxes equal with the rest of the population and were supposed to enjoy equal access and opportunity to the services available to all citizens, irrespective of religious affiliation. On the other hand, where Islamic law continued to be one of the sources of legislation, formally or informally, some of the precepts of the Pact of Umar, such as restrictions on the construction and repair of churches, continued to inform policy, as in Egypt, Sudan, Turkey and Yemen.

The contemporary situation of Christians in NAWA is informed not only by Islamic doctrine. Political economy, leadership, numerical strength, nature of alliances and coalition politics, and regional reconfigurations all dramatically inform the status of Christians. However, one cannot ignore the interface between Islamic scholars' engagement with doctrine and ideology and the positioning and status of Christians. Contemporary Islamic jurisprudence has produced a broad spectrum of positions on Muslim–Christian relations. At one end of the spectrum are reformists who have resorted to *ijtihad* (reinterpretation of the text in the spirit of Islam). For example, the Islamist writer Fahmy Howeidy argued in his seminal book *Citizens, Not Dhimmis: The Position of Non-Muslims in Muslim Societies* (Cairo: Dar el Shorouk, 1985) that the citizenship contract abolished the *dhimmi* contract. Where non-Muslims (irrespective of whether they belong to the People of the Book or not) in modern nation-states participate fully in armies, pay taxes and contribute to all aspects of life in a Muslim community, there should no longer be a hierarchy of rights premised on religious affiliation, argues Howeidy, and all should be equal. Howeidy engages in *ijtihad* to show that the texts restricting the rights of non-Muslims should be read in a new light that recognises full equality of all citizens. His exegesis, however, has remained on the margins.

In the middle of the spectrum are scholars who recognise that religious affiliation is still an organising principle of rights in an Islamic *ummah* (nation). They represent mainstream contemporary Islamic thought on the position of Christians in Muslim-majority countries. Such scholars include a leading authority on Sunni Islam, Sheikh Yusuf el Qaradawy. He proposes that although Christians abiding in Dar al Islam might have the nationality of members of the Islamic *ummah*, their rights are tied to a number of qualifiers. The most important of these qualifiers is that Christians should show reverence and compliance to Sharia and should not challenge Islamic authority (though that it is not defined). The late Sheikh Mohammed Al Ghazali, a leading Sunni theologian, considered, for example, the objection by Copts in Egypt to the implementation of Sharia as a manifestation of disrespectful behaviour of non-Muslims to Islam. What will be considered offensive to the sensibilities of Muslims is very much open for contestation and debate, and very much based on the normative values that are espoused by those who rule and the prevailing societal ideas.

The question then becomes, what if Christians, from an Islamic jurisprudential point of view, are considered by the Muslim rulers to show disrespect to Islamic authority? It is important to note that the Pact of Umar came with a caveat in which the conquered Christians of Syria pronounced that 'If we in any way violate these undertakings for which we ourselves stand surety, we forfeit our covenant [*dhimma*], and we become liable to the penalties for contumacy and sedition'. One practical way in which respect for Islam is institutionalised through modern-day state legislative policy is the application of blasphemy laws. While such laws were intended to punish defamation against any religion, for the most part they have been applied in contexts such as Egypt, Tunisia and Sudan to punish anyone who shows disrespect to Islam. In many cases, blasphemy laws were applied predominantly to punish non-Muslims accused of defaming Islam (see Ewelina Ochab's essay 'Religious Freedom'), though they have also been applied to Muslims perceived to be non-conforming.

However, at the far end of the spectrum, some radical Islamist thinkers and movements would consider any sign of the non-subjugation of Christians to Islamic authority or their resistance to the imposition of Islamic Sharia as a sign of disrespect. Such disrespect would render the Covenant of Umar non-binding. In other words, the Muslim ruler's obligation to preserve their lives and afford them protection would be null and void. In such a case, Christians living in Islamic-ruled lands would be considered as of the same status as Christians living in Dar al Harb or Dar al Kufr. Jihad would apply to these Christians whose lives and property need not be spared and whose women can be taken as war booty. This is not outdated historical Islamic jurisprudence; rather, it informs the modern-day practice of some Islamists who consider the interpretations of Islamic jurisprudence presented by their leaders as authoritative. ISIS, for example, considered the People of the Book living under its territories as disqualified from the protection that the Covenant of Umar offered them on account of their transgression of the principle of showing allegiance and respect to Islam. They cited the insults waged by Christians against Islam as the basis for rejecting their protection. In one of their declarations, the leaders of ISIS stated:

> We believe that the factions of the People of the Book [i.e. Christians and Jews], and those of their ilk such as the Sabeans and others, are today in the Islamic State a people of war not enjoying a status of protection. They have violated what they agreed upon [with the Muslims] in numerous, countless regards. Therefore if they desire security and safety, they must create a new pact with the Islamic State in accordance with the conditions of the Pact of Umar that they violated. (Cited in Cole Bunzel, *From Paper State to Caliphate: The Ideology of the Islamic State*, Washington, DC: Brookings Institution, 2015, 40)

The significance of this is twofold. First, it interrogates the argument that Christians are guaranteed a privileged position across history as People of the Book, so long as they pay the *jizya*. Ultimately, if an Islamic authority (such as ISIS) considers that Christians show irreverence to Muslims, even the payment of *jizya* is not sufficient to secure them protection. Secondly, the line between what is Dar al Islam and Dar al Harb/al Kufr is a fine one. In the case of Egypt, ISIS declared that though the country is majority Muslim and being ruled by a Muslim leader, it is still categorised as Dar al Harb as they consider, first, the ruler (Al Sissi) as violating Sharia and, secondly, the Copts as showing a defiance and opposition to Islam, making them enemies who therefore must be killed. Hence, it should be noted that the position of Christians in the NAWA region is tied to the nature of the Islamic movement that is engaging with Islamic jurisprudence and the legitimacy and authority that movement wields within the populace.

Contemporary Juncture and Context

While political change is a feature of all contexts at all times, the publication of this volume comes at a critical juncture in the history of the Middle

East (though not necessarily all West Asian contexts). The confluence of a number of regional phenomena created this historic juncture: the series of popular uprisings in the region commonly referred to as the Arab Spring; the collapse of states (Libya, Yemen, Syria and Iraq); the emergence of ISIS; and the intensification of proxy wars involving global rivalry between the USA and Russia but also Shia and Sunni rivalry (among many). While all such phenomena have been brewing for a long time, they seemed to have converged to produce a major regional reconfiguration of powers, on a scale unparalleled since the collapse of the Ottoman Empire and the formation of the nation-states a century earlier. For Christians in the Middle East, the Arab Spring, which began in Tunisia in 2010 and spread to Egypt, Libya, Syria, Yemen and beyond, affected not only communities within these countries' borders but also neighbouring countries, such as Lebanon, Jordan, the Occupied Palestinian Territories and Gaza.

Since the uprising in Tunisia, the Arab region has witnessed the intense expression of people power in the form of mass mobilisation of citizens demanding bread, freedom and dignity, unprecedented in scale and intensity in modern times. However, the region has also witnessed the worst humanitarian disasters, with three states degenerating into civil war and chaos (Syria, Yemen and Libya), widespread statelessness and displacement and the threat of an outbreak of famine in Yemen in 2016. The notion of citizenship as a set of rights and duties underpinned by a national social contract between the individual and the state has been deemed redundant more than ever before in contexts where countries have fallen into civil war or suffered occupation (such as Iraq, first by the US-led coalition, then by ISIS).

All the peoples of the entire region have suffered directly or indirectly from growing insecurity, instability, loss of livelihood and wide-scale displacement, but the religious targeting of Christians in many of these settings at this critical juncture has had severe implications for religious diversity (see Kristian Girling's essay 'Displaced Populations'). In Libya, where Christians were already a small proportion of the population, predominantly of a migrant worker background, it is likely that, after the mass exodus that occurred between 2012 and 2014, the country is now virtually devoid of any Christian presence (see Akram Habib's essay on Libya). In Iraq, the percentage of Christians has dropped from 4% in 1970 to less than 1% today and similarly in Syria Christians were more than 10% of the population in 1970 but are now likely to be below 5% (see Herman Teule's and Razek Siriani's essays). In the land where Christ was born, the percentage of Christians in Israel is about 2% (see David Neuhaus's essay), 1.5% in Palestine and 3,000 persons in Gaza (see Bernard Sabella's essay). At the beginning of the twentieth century, Christians comprised more than

16% of the population of NAWA. Today, they likely comprise less than 5% and continue to decline significantly each year.

A century earlier, Christians in many parts of the Middle East also faced an existential threat, similarly against a background of major upheaval. Like a century earlier, today the existential threat to the Christian presence is exacerbated by global movements of arms, people and ideology across porous and volatile state boundaries where there are multiple sites of governance beyond that of the conventional state. Today, Christians are also victims of the proxy wars involving a wide array of regional and international actors, as eloquently mapped by Mark Farha in this volume.

Joshua Landis argues that:

> we are witnessing the rearrangement of populations in the region to better fit the nation states that were fixed after WWI. Some new borders are being drawn, such as those around the Kurdish regions of Iraq and perhaps Syria, but mostly, what we are seeing is the ethnic cleansing of much of the region to fit the borders. ('The Great Sorting Out: Ethnicity and the Future of the Levant', 18 December 2013 <https://qifanabki.com/2013/12/18/landis-ethnicity>, accessed 3 June 2017)

However, this suggests that the presence of ethnic/religious groups across artificially imposed state borders accounts for the cleansing of Christians in times of volatility in both the past and present centuries. Yet history is not necessarily tautological; neither is ethnic and religious annihilation in times of major political reconfiguration inevitable. In eastern Europe, for example, at the time of the breakdown of communist systems and the re-emergence of new states and political systems, the Hungarians negotiated a political settlement that ensured that religious and ethnic minorities are not 'sorted out' and are included in the new power configurations. Such a political settlement was dynamic and by no means easy to negotiate; however, it shows that it is possible to choose inclusivity and pluralism. A constellation of factors makes this possible: the nature of prevailing ideologies and the strength of pro-inclusion coalitions, as well as the collective strength of minorities themselves. It is also a matter not only of national choice but of foreign policy. As Mark Farha notes in his essay, 'amidst the greater tectonic forces pitting Saudi Arabia and Israel against Iran, and Sunni versus Shia, Christians usually find themselves as collateral damage, caught in the crosshairs at worst and suffering benign neglect at best'.

In this grim picture, there are exceptions. In the Levant, Jordan represents a case of 'positive deviance' where Christians thrive and, despite some challenges, enjoy citizenship rights with other Jordanians (see the essay by Paolo Maggiolini and Iyad Twal). Moreover, Christians in the Gulf, who are mostly workers and professionals from across the globe, have also seen a flourishing in their communities. Eric Newberg, Mark Farha and Hrayr Jebejian in this volume all note that Christians are constructing churches (sometimes even with governments donating the land) and worship freely in private and public spaces in a context where there is tolerance not only for old denominations (Catholicism and Orthodoxy) but also for newer churches (Pentecostals and Charismatics). The ripple effect has been particularly important for Arab Christians from other parts of the region who have found it difficult to stay in their own countries but for whom migration to the West is not feasible. These religious freedoms, however, are not shared across the entire Gulf region. As pointed by Hrayr Jebejian, in Saudi Arabia and Yemen, Christians operate via underground churches in a highly restrictive and intolerant environment. Moreover, in the North African contexts of Morocco, Algeria and Tunisia, Christian converts from Islam have organised into underground Christian movements of a very particular character (see the essays by Jack Wald and Katia Boissevain).

In parts of the NAWA region outside the Middle East, such as Cyprus, Armenia and Georgia (see the essays by Anastasia Yiangou, Hratch Tchilingirian and Silvia Serrano), Christians represent a majority and have witnessed revivals in the late twentieth and early twenty-first centuries. The most influential tradition in these contexts is the Orthodox, represented in the national churches where the intertwining of ethnic and religious identity is very strong. The nationalistic aspect of these churches has meant that in some cases (for example Georgia), pluralism within the Christian faith is sometimes circumscribed, in particular where a dominant church tradition is inimical to ecumenism and considers other churches as outsiders, as part of Western hegemonic projects.

Ecclesial Diversity Within the Christian Community

As noted above, whether in the Middle East, the Mediterranean or former Soviet countries in West Asia, the region is characterised by high levels of pluralism within the Christian faith. Representations of the Christian churches in the NAWA region have sometimes been fraught with a number of misconceptions that have contributed to their mis- or non-recognition. Sometimes churches were represented as extensions of Western imperialist ventures into the region in the nineteenth century, thereby denying roots that date back to the first century (see Heather Sharkey's essay). In many parts of the region in the nineteenth and twentieth centuries, local people referred to indigenous Christians as *khawagas* or foreigners, associating them with the churches established by the foreign communities. Gabriel Hachem, in his essay 'Ecclesiology', notes that this left the unfortunate legacy in which Christians were seen as corollaries of colonialism.

In these contexts, the churches arduously strove to represent themselves as indigenous churches with patriotic affinities to the nation-state, distinct from the churches established by missionaries. In some contexts such as Egypt, the church played an important role in the anti-British colonialist movement, while in Palestine the churches challenged Israeli encroachment on Palestinian land and defended the rights of the Palestinian people for sovereignty. With decolonisation and the growth in nationalist and pan-Arab movements in the twentieth century, Evangelical churches and the Catholic Church also sought to establish their local identities and national characters.

The emphasis on the patriotic and 'national' identity of the church remains one of the enduring characters of most of the churches across religious denominations in the NAWA region. Even churches that were established by Western missionaries have sought to emphasise their indigenous nature. This is critical for understanding church identity in the region, where the intersection of national and religious identity is strong whether Christians are a minority (as in Syria or Azerbaijan) or a majority (as in Cyprus or Armenia). In most of the Middle East, where Christians are a minority and struggles against Western foreign policy continue, the pressure to 'prove' the patriotic credentials of the churches is particularly high. Those that cling to an identity that is both religiously and ethnically different (such as the Greek and Armenian churches in Turkey) tend to suffer extreme stigma.

The accounts of the churches in the NAWA region presented by the authors in this volume show the plurality of religious traditions, leaderships and geographical spread. Within the NAWA region, the largest Christian tradition is the Orthodox faith. As Georges Tamer highlights in his essay 'Eastern Orthodoxy', the four patriarchates – Constantinople, Jerusalem, Antioch and Alexandria – together with Rome are the oldest churches of Christendom. They see themselves as a continuation of the first church, begun in Jerusalem, as described in the Book of Acts. They follow the Nicene Creed and lay emphasis on authenticity and intergenerational transfer of teachings and tradition, in particular with reference to a history anchored in stories of church fathers and mothers, martyrs and ascetics. However, the diversity within the Orthodox tradition is also striking. In addition to the diversity within Eastern Orthodoxy there is a great array of distinct expressions of Oriental Orthodoxy, particularly the Coptic, Armenian and Syriac churches, as described by Aho Shemunkasho in this volume.

Moreover, the intersection of ethnic affiliation (Armenian, Assyrian, Coptic, Greek and Syriac) with Orthodoxy renders some distinct cultural and linguistic expressions of the faith. Each church has its own leadership, headed by a patriarch, and its own holy synod. While many have their centres in the countries in which they originated, they have a universal outreach (the Armenian Orthodox Church extended over many countries in the NAWA region and in the diaspora in Europe and Northern and Latin America). The Coptic Orthodox Church has a large diasporic following in Europe and Northern America as well as in parts of Africa.

The second-largest church is the Catholic Church, which is estimated to have more than 7 million followers in the region. Again, there is no single expression of Catholicism. Catholicism in the NAWA regions exists in at least seven different expressions, each with distinct rites: Chaldean, Coptic, Syriac, Armenian, Melkite, Maronite and Latin (see Anthony O'Mahony's essay on Catholics). Each rite is headed by a (usually locally based) patriarch, who is appointed by the council of bishops (synod) but is confirmed by the pope in Rome. The largest Catholic Church in the NAWA region is the Maronite Catholic Church, which has more than 3.5 million followers. Anthony O'Mahony notes that what is particularly compelling about the Catholic Church in the NAWA region is how the demographic population shifts have affected religious expression. In the Gulf, guest workers from Asia and other parts of the world brought new expressions of Catholicism that thrived side by side with Eastern Catholic ones rooted in the region. Conversely, Eastern Catholics migrated to North and South America, Australia and Europe. For example, the Maronites number 700,000 in São Paolo, Brazil, though their origins lie in Lebanon. The disconnect between demographic origin and current citizenship poses a challenge for our understanding of Christian communities of the NAWA region but no longer situated there. How much of the 'Eastern' and 'Catholic' dimensions are maintained across generations who have left the NAWA region?

Within the Protestant churches there is also diversity in origin, expression, organisational structure and practice. Mitri Raheb's and Wafik Wahba's essays show that the earliest Protestant missions were the Presbyterians in Lebanon, Syria, Iraq and Egypt, and the Lutherans in Palestine. Yazid Said traces the history of the Anglican Church in the Middle East to the nineteenth century, which he argues cannot be disentangled with the 'history of British imperial interests'. However, all the 'mother' Protestant churches, whether of Presbyterian, Anglican or Lutheran origin, metamorphosed across the decades to embed new expressions of faith as they adapted to their contexts. Like their Catholic counterparts, the establishment of Protestant churches also meant the creation of regional and national forms of leadership. For example, as Said notes for the Anglican Church, metropolitan authority was handed from the Archbishop of Canterbury in 1976 to the provincial central synod, which elects two archbishops.

Not only did these churches influence the contexts in which they came to be established, but the context influenced them as well. In highly patriarchal Western societies of the nineteenth century, women were inhibited, by and large, from assuming leadership positions within church hierarchies. However, in missionary contexts in the NAWA region, women assumed leadership positions as preachers, teachers and co-founders of new churches. As Heather Sharkey notes in her essay on missionary work, previously all-male medical schools were challenged to open their doors to women under the rubric that their medical services were needed for overseas missionary work with women and girls.

What is particularly fascinating is the way, described in Eric Newberg's essay, in which the Pentecostal groups that were established in the NAWA region reversed the general direction of missionary activity from West to East to embark on their own mission activities, planting churches in other parts of the world. In contrast to the general picture of churches under threat in a context of persecution, the independent – usually underground – churches comprising 'believers from a Muslim background' (BMB) are experiencing rapid growth from Algeria to Iran and from Saudi Arabia to Syria, as described in Duane Miller's essay 'Independents'. While estimating their numbers is notoriously difficult, they are estimated to be in the hundreds of thousands, with the greatest concentrations being in Algeria (380,000) and Iran (100,000). Miller notes that since in most countries in the Middle East conversion from Islam is legally prohibited (and in some contexts considered a punishable crime), converts to Christianity remain secret believers. This has implications for the institutional form that BMB can assume. As Miller notes, 'while BMBs might teach or preach in a local church, they can never function as legal representatives of that church in terms of business transactions or issuing official documents like baptismal certificates. In other words, the "independence" is legally enforced'.

Historically, a point of agreement across the various churches is the Nicene Creed, a declaration of doctrine that lays a common foundation of understanding. However, attempts to sustain an ecumenical movement have been fraught with challenges. History, power dynamics and coping choices have all contributed to points of divergence and schisms. How these are narrated will point to different interpretations of where the responsibility for the schisms lie. As Gabriel Hachem indicates in his essay on ecclesiology, 'Theological debates of the fourth and fifth centuries led to painful separations that last to this day'. Perhaps the greatest schism in relations between the churches goes back to the Council of Chalcedon in 451, in which there was division over the divine and human natures of Jesus Christ. Even as historically different terminologies were used to articulate the orthodox faith, today it is generally recognised by the ancient churches that their Christological positions are similar.

As churches have moved into the twenty-first century, the labelling that bore a pejorative inference was abandoned, such as references to churches as 'Monophysites' or 'Anti-Chalcedonian' or 'Nestorians' or 'Jacobites'. The twenty-first century is witnessing an increase in bilateral and ecumenical dialogues that in the future might cumulate into a strong movement. The challenge is twofold at this stage: first, making ecumenical declarations of unity and solidarity a reality on the ground at a local level; and secondly, pluralising the voices and perspectives in ecumenical dialogues, to include those of youths, women and lay people, for example.

Diversity in Lived Spirituality

It is critically important to note that across the NAWA region, the realm of the spiritual is not clearly demarcated from that of the material, whether for Muslims, Christians or other religious groups. This is in no way to suggest that every topic, every struggle, every area is necessarily informed by a person's or community's 'religious lens'. Certainly, sometimes people's professions, classes, genders, political orientations or other identity markers have the overriding influence in informing how individuals and communities engage with their realities. However, sometimes there is an intersectionality of people's multiple identities that involves a spillover between the spiritual and material in both directions.

Among Christians in the NAWA region, faith, culture, history and ecclesiology are often enmeshed, constantly changing to adapt to volatile realities while simultaneously shaping and configuring their contexts in sometimes conspicuous and sometimes subtle ways. The authors in this volume tell powerful stories of the plurality of ways in which such dynamic agency of the interface between faith and context has manifested itself among Christians. The role of the church in the lives of Christians in NAWA is central even if it has sometimes witnessed a waxing and waning. While there is still great variety across individuals, groups and communities, many of the authors in this volume nonetheless highlight the permeation of the role of the church in the lives of its followers. This includes the performance of worship, in particular through the central role of the liturgy in the lives of the Orthodox and Catholic, which, as Rima Nasrallah notes in an essay on worship and spirituality, in the East is highly communal, participatory and multisensory. It also includes the role of the church in its celebration of ancient and modern saints and martyrs, which constitutes a core element of Christian consciousness in the NAWA region. Another expression is the Charismatic movements that have travelled across all denominations, old and new, in the region. Another still is the spread of Bible studies across denominations, brought about through Evangelical movements.

In contexts of extreme exclusion and marginalisation where Christians are a minority, the church has assumed a role beyond that of worship, offering to varying degrees educational and health services (see for instance the essay on Palestine, by Bernard Sabella) as well as space for building leadership and community.

While this has sometimes seemed like a story of 'cocoonisation', this is not to suggest that all churches cope through ghettoisation. Churches and Christian communities more broadly have made major contributions to culture, the economy and politics. Elizabeth Monier, in her essay on faith and culture, highlights some potent features of this in the area of art, music and even ideology (such as the role of Christians in building the pan-Arab movement in the nineteenth century).

One powerful story is of how Christians understand their history and how this informs their reading of the present situation and their future trajectory. For example, Elizabeth Monier shows how many communities have drawn on their ancient heritage, a pre-Islamic, pre-Arab one, which is simultaneously rooted in the local. This is critical for cultural expression and preservation on a number of levels. First, it provides a narrative that challenges the mainstream accounts of history that amplify the Arab and Islamic heritage, from one in which Christians are on the margins to one in which they can find pride and recognition. Secondly, it provides an 'anchor for their shared communal life within a Muslim-majority region' (Monier, this volume). This anchoring is critically important for intergenerational transfer of an affinity between faith and land of origin. Among the most powerful examples, notes Monier, are the Palestinian Christians, who speak of their faith as the 'living stones' to underscore the idea that their culture is rooted in the Holy Land, inherited from the very first Christians who established the very first church in Jerusalem. In Egypt, where the largest Christian population lies in the Middle East (though as a percentage of the population it is Lebanon), Copts conceive of their heritage as having pharaonic roots and take pride in the church of Alexandria as the lighthouse of Christian theology in the first centuries, as well as in the early formation of the monastic tradition. Similarly, in Syria and Iraq, Christians trace their Christian heritage back to the establishment of the early apostolic church, preceding the advent of the existing civilisations.

Moreover, communities have also sought to preserve their religious and cultural heritages by retaining the language used at the time of their adoption of the Christian faith. Rima Nasrallah in this volume notes that the use of ancient languages in worship is also one performative dimension of ecclesiology. The Assyrians' use of a form of Aramaic that was used by communities at the time of Jesus is a practice that reminds communities of the deeply spiritual roots of their faith. The use of Coptic in liturgy and as a language of communication in all Coptic villages again has its genealogy in the language used at the time when St Mark the evangelist brought Christianity to Egypt (see Samuel Tadros's essay on Egypt). The use of Armenian across NAWA and in the diaspora also bears witness to the enmeshment of cultural heritage and spirituality, as with the use of Byzantine Greek among the Greek Orthodox in NAWA and beyond. This is not always an easy process. Rima Nasrallah takes the example of Jerusalem, where Christians hold dear their Palestinian Arab identity: the use of Greek instead of Arabic and the appointment of Greek rather than Palestinian clergy have created tensions which have necessitated the adoption of innovative adaptation strategies.

Christians have negotiated their identity(ies) in highly diverse ways, some boasting of holding multiple identities simultaneously (Christian and Arab) while others conceive of their identities as distinctly non-Arab. The variations within groups are sometimes as significant as those across communities.

The flourishing of Christian communities in the NAWA region has required not only preservation of the old but also an energising through the new, or – in the words of Rima Nasrallah – making worship relevant to people's everyday lives so that it does not become 'museology'. The twentieth century witnessed 'revivals' that spilled over into the twenty-first century, such as a revival of the monastic tradition and religious pilgrimages. Many of the essays in this volume highlight the role of monasticism and religious pilgrimages as core elements of a dynamic Christian faith, culture and ecclesiology. It was in the deserts of Egypt that the first monastic communities emerged in the fourth century, as Anna Poujeau notes in her chapter, although as they spread to other regions and parts of the world they took on new modalities, expressions and organisational forms. Poujeau's essay on monasticism highlights that the same monastic revival movement swept across Syria, where, although 'in the 1950s only three Greek Orthodox monasteries were still active in the country, at the end of the year 2000 there were several dozen, as well as some Greek Catholic, Syriac Orthodox and Syriac Catholic monasteries'. Rima Nasrallah notes that the revival of monasticism became a centripetal force for serving the Christian communities through hosting retreats, meetings, conferences and youth activities. Najib George Awad notes in his essay 'Inter-religious Relations' yet another important role of monasteries, that of preserving heritage through conservation of manuscripts and artefacts across decades and centuries.

The region has also witnessed a number of powerful spiritual revivals. Rima Nasrallah in this volume cites two of these as being significant to this day: the emergence of the youth movement from within the Antiochian Greek Orthodox Church in the twentieth century and the Sunday School Movement within the Coptic Orthodox Church. Both these movements led to 'a spiritual revival, monastic renewal, evangelical engagement and liturgical awakening'. Other churches also continuously reconfigured from within; the Maronite Church in Lebanon reformed its liturgical practices, making it more Lebanese. Eric Newberg in his essay notes that in the past 50 years Charismatic renewal movements have emerged in the NAWA region, often influenced by free church movements, though also often couched in familiar Orthodox or Catholic terminology. These have had influential roles in strengthening belief, spirituality and communality.

There also was a proliferation of Christian broadcasting in the late twentieth century, a trend that shows no sign of waning in the twenty-first century. This is part of a broader surge of the role of technology in enhanced communication and outreach. Radio is still an important medium for communication, being cheap and widely accessible. Social media and its usage among young people has created platforms for consciousness-raising and at times mobilisation. Christian broadcasting, as Sara Asfari notes in her essay 'Christian Media', became an important medium for outreach to Christians from NAWA in their own languages, whether they lived in the region or in the diasporas. Asfari notes that as Islamic broadcasting increased its hate speech towards Christians, the sense of responsibility towards building people's repertoires of confidence and affirmation in their spirituality, culture and history also increased.

As with the plurality of churches and denominations, so too were the Christian broadcasting services plural, notes Asfari, in terms of their audiences. The reality was that the cultural background of Christians in the NAWA region has been becoming increasingly varied, on account of the vast Christian migrant population that works in the Gulf. Some of the migrants have brought to the NAWA traditions and ways of worship from their countries of origin in other parts of Africa or East Asia. Others have blended ancient rites with new forms of worship. For others still, there has been a cross-fertilisation of spirituality and culture across and within church communities.

While the theme has been the richness of pluralism and diversity, it is not only unity among Christians that is a challenge. Christian communities are not always multi-vocal internally. This is partly because in many contexts, civil society space for organising and mobilising is deeply circumscribed by authoritarian states. Hence the prospects of lay Christians organising to hold the church leadership accountable, whether from within the ecclesiastical structure or from outside, are very limited.

As Rima Nasrallah emphasises, most of the churches in the NAWA region have a patriarchal polity. This has meant that while women and young people often have space to participate in worship, they face major restrictions with respect to representation and leadership (of and within the community). The patriarchal nature of the church is to a large degree reflective of the nature of the societies and histories of the NAWA contexts more widely. In the NAWA region, both society in general and the institutional culture of the church revolve around the elders in the community. Nonetheless, the challenges facing youth in their assumption of leadership positions in the church are perhaps less daunting than those with respect to gender hierarchy. In some churches, the understanding of the biblical principle of eldership is associated not only with spiritual maturity but also age, which tends to exclude young people. However, across the NAWA region there are young clergy, including those assuming positions of high-ranking leadership and representation of their religious communities internally and externally. The same is not true for women. This is partly on account of the highly patriarchal gender hierarchies characterising most Arab and West Asian societies. In vernacular Arabic, the word for 'clergy' used by both Muslims and Christians translates as 'men of religion', even though in original languages used by many of these Christian communities, such as Greek/Coptic, the word is *ikliros*. The default mode is the exclusion of women from priesthood and leadership roles (except for secondary roles such as deaconesses, which are sometimes allowed in some churches). This, as Donna Rizk highlights in her essay on gender, is due to theological arguments, often deeply steeped in the culture. In February 2017, however, the Eastern Orthodox Patriarch of Alexandria ordained five African women in Congo to the order of the diaconate. Protestant, Evangelical and Pentecostal churches have also limited the assumption of leadership positions by women in the NAWA region, though, both historically and in contemporary times, there have been important breakthroughs. Historically, missionary women assumed leadership positions of significant influence (see Eric Newberg's essay). In contemporary times, on 26 February 2017, Reverend Raola Sleiman became the first-ever woman to be ordained as a pastor in the Middle East. The synod of the Presbyterian Church in Syria and Lebanon voted 23 to 1 in favour of her ordination, rendering her able to lead a congregation and perform the sacramental roles without the presence of a male pastor. While the Presbyterian Church is very small in the NAWA region, setting a precedent might inspire dialogues on this topic across the other churches, and possibly between them (though this has been a thorny topic).

Threat and Decline, Innovation and Adaptation

This introduction began on a sombre note, reflecting on a past and a present genocide, one at the beginning of the twentieth century and the other in the twenty-first. The existential threat facing Christians has reached its precipice in some parts of the NAWA region, most notably in Libya (where there has been an exodus of Christian migrants), in Palestine (where Christianity began) and in Iraq (where the population has shrunk to a fraction of what it was). While the political turbulence in the region has affected all settings directly or through ripple effects from neighbouring countries, a configuration of geostrategic and local factors has contributed to Christians and other religious minorities being made particularly vulnerable to a loss of presence. The essays in this volume suggest that the struggle for survival is far from over.

However, the story of Christianity in the NAWA region is not only about communities under encroachment, but also about communities' sense of enduring repertoires of power that extend back many generations. It is about communities' survival across hundreds of years, adapting to changing times, giving new meanings and expressions of faith and spirituality. In short, the story of the Christian communities in NAWA is also about the intergenerational transfer of knowledge and changing identity, with its strong interface with ancient languages (Aramaic, Greek and Coptic) as well as its own narratives of their history, their present and their future.

Moreover, it is also a story of the proliferation and flourishing of new expressions of Christianity in a context of high mobility across borders and spheres. Christians who have moved to the Gulf for professional and work purposes have established thriving multi-ethnic, multi-denominational churches. While they do not enjoy the full rights of citizenship (as migrant workers), the ability to worship freely has enabled Christians to contribute to the societies in which they are embedded economically, professionally and socially without having to negate their identity. Moreover, the establishment and growth of diaspora communities globally has extended these networks through communities united by their faith.

The story of Christians in NAWA is also one about adaptation and innovation. The contemporary use of media by Christian churches, leaders and organisations in the region enables outreach where it is not possible via face-to-face engagement. This resonates with the introduction of broad-based education for the people 200 years earlier, which paved the way for reformist movements to emerge within and across churches and for Christians to make a tangible contribution to popular culture, arts, politics and music. In the midst of uncertainty and opaqueness, what appears definitive is that there is a deep and nuanced enmeshment of the spiritual, political, social and cultural expressions of faith as lived by the Christians of the NAWA region, as the essays in this volume demonstrate.

Bibliography

Friedmann, Yohanen, *Tolerance and Coercion in Islam: Interfaith Relations in the Muslim Tradition* (Cambridge: Cambridge University Press, 2003).

Gaunt, David, Naures Atto and Soner O. Barthoma, *Let Them Not Return: Sayfo – The Genocide of the Assyrian, Syriac, and Chaldean_Christians in the Ottoman Empire* (New York: Berghahn Books, 2017).

Kalaitzidis, Pantelis, Thomas Fitzgerald, Cyri Hovorum, Aikaterini Pekridou, Nikolaos Asproulis, Guy Liagre, Dietrich Werner (eds), *Orthodox Handbook on Ecumenism* (Oxford: Regnum Books International, 2014).

Meral, Ziya, 'The Politics of Religious Minorities in Muslim-Majority States: Old Challenges and New Trends', *Review of Faith and International Affairs*, 9:2 (2011), 25–30.

Tadros, Mariz, *Copts at the Crossroads* (Cairo: American University in Cairo Press, 2013).

Countries

Morocco and Western Sahara

Jack Wald

During the French occupation, in the years before Moroccan independence in 1956, many French and Spanish Christians were living in the country. In these years Catholic and Protestant churches were built in all the major cities of Morocco, which still provide for the greatly reduced expatriate population. During the colonial period many missionaries were actively working in Morocco and many older people still remember men and women who cared for abandoned children, helped with education and provided medical care.

In Tangier there was even a Christian radio station broadcasting to Sweden (operated by Charismatic Christians), because Swedish stations were not permitted to broadcast messages about healing ministries.

In the years after independence, the Moroccan government began to assert its authority over the churches of Morocco. Church bells were removed and ministries to Moroccans had to relocate outside the country. In the late 1960s, an indigenous Moroccan church began to emerge. House church meetings were held in the homes of missionaries, often with more missionaries than Moroccans attending. In 1984 King Hassan II suspected a coup by Moroccan Christians and rounded them up to be interrogated in Casablanca. Those who did not recant were imprisoned and released after a few weeks. Most Moroccan Christians recanted; there was moral failure on the part of some leaders, and most of those meeting in house churches dropped away. From 1984 to 1995 house churches met in the homes of missionaries, but when these missionaries left, the house churches stopped meeting. In 1995, Moroccan Christians made the strategic decision to have churches meet in their own homes rather than those of the missionaries. By 1999 this transition, with a few exceptions, had been completed.

When Hassan II died in July 1999, there was much enthusiasm for the new king, Mohammed VI. He set a new tone from the beginning. For the first time in Moroccan history the king released photos of his wife to the public. With these photos he seemed to be sending a message to Islamic fundamentalists. In 2013, a photograph of the queen at a royal wedding in the Netherlands, wearing a modern dress and holding a glass of wine, was released to the public. There was a new transparency in Morocco and, from 2000 to 2010, there was a steady liberalisation. The press was given new freedoms, legislation was passed that gave women more rights and Christians fully expected legislation that would give them more rights. The number of house churches increased during these 10 years. One house church, for example, expanded to become a network of 23 house churches. It is estimated that during this time more than 4,000 Moroccans were meeting weekly in house churches throughout Morocco. There were church planting efforts and training programmes, all led by Moroccans.

During the years when George W. Bush was president of the USA, he was known as 'Mr Evangelical' and because the Polisario Front, which sought to oust Morocco from the disputed 'Western Sahara' (discussed below), was receiving a lot of support from US Evangelicals, the Moroccan ambassador was given instructions to court the Evangelicals. In 2004 and 2005 several US Evangelicals made high-profile visits to Morocco. The *wali* (mayor) of Marrakesh invited them to have a Christian music concert in 2005 at which Newsboys, Delirious, Phil Keaggy and others performed. In an Islamic backlash against this intrusion of Christians in such a high-profile way, the pastor of the international church in Marrakesh was deported. Over the years there were occasional periods when Moroccan Christian leaders were interviewed by the police, usually focused on whether or not the Christians were a threat to the monarchy. The conclusion was that Christians were not a direct threat. They were found to be patriotic Moroccans who loved their king. But they were viewed as an indirect threat to the monarchy because if their numbers grew, the Islamic fundamentalists would be inflamed – and they are a direct threat to the monarchy.

In general, however, the mood among Moroccan Christians was that things were going to get better. Then, in March 2010, it became clear that there was a 180-degree turn in Morocco. On the weekend of 5–7 March 2010, foreign Christians across the country were arrested. Ignoring due process and in violation of Moroccan law, people were taken to be questioned,

Christianity in Morocco, 1970 and 2015

	1970		2015		Average annual growth rate (%), 1970–2015
Tradition	Population	%	Population	%	
Christians	109,000	0.7%	34,800	0.1%	−2.5%
Anglicans	600	0.0%	1,600	0.0%	2.2%
Independents	1,400	0.0%	4,700	0.0%	2.8%
Orthodox	900	0.0%	570	0.0%	−1.0%
Protestants	5,000	0.0%	3,800	0.0%	−0.6%
Catholics	100,000	0.6%	22,500	0.1%	−3.3%
Evangelicals	1,300	0.0%	4,100	0.0%	2.6%
Pentecostals	800	0.0%	4,200	0.0%	3.7%
Total population	**16,040,000**	**100.0%**	**34,378,000**	**100.0%**	**1.7%**

Source: Todd M. Johnson and Gina A. Zurlo (eds), *World Christian Database* (Leiden/Boston: Brill), accessed March 2017.

allowed to pack a few things and then taken to the borders of Morocco to be deported. A total of 150 foreign Christians were deported, including the staff of a home for abandoned children in Ain Leuh. This was a family-based home and the 'parents' of these children, who were the only parents the children had ever known, were given just seven hours to say goodbye to their children and pack a few things. They were taken under police custody to a hotel at Casablanca airport, kept under guard for the night and then escorted by the police to the planes that flew them out of Morocco. Those deported came from all the cities of Morocco and from almost all the different Christian organisations represented in the country. Why this happened is not certain, but it is clear that a message was sent that Christians in Morocco needed to restrict their activities. During this period of deportations, the police interrogated Moroccans who were attending house churches and made it known they had inside informers. In Moroccan culture, people are not trusted until they earn the right to be trusted, so this caused those attending house churches to pull away from each other and, for the most part, house churches stopped meeting.

Since 2010 there has been a new movement among the youth of the church to restart house churches, but there is little or no national coordination. Mistrust causes each leader of a house church or a group of house churches to hide what is happening from others. Many who formerly attended house churches are now meeting by themselves, not wanting contact with other followers of Jesus.

The Internet has had a significant impact in this context. Each year more and larger groups form on Facebook to protest against the enforced fast during Ramadan. The Bible is readily available in Darija, the Moroccan Arabic dialect, and it is available in audio for the many who are illiterate. Brother Rachid, living in the USA but born and raised in Casablanca, broadcasts into Morocco, speaking in Darija. Some Moroccan Christians have begun putting their testimonies on YouTube, again speaking in Darija. During the deportations of 2010 the press made it clear for the first time that there are Moroccans who are Christians. This allows people who are drawn to faith in Jesus through radio, TV or the Internet to know that they are not alone.

Western Sahara

'Western Sahara' is regarded by Moroccans as an insulting description of what they think and feel is the 'Moroccan Sahara'. This is the key political issue for Morocco and affects business relationships, diplomatic relationships and all aspects of life. Moroccan Christians once rejected a version of an Arabic Bible that was smuggled into Morocco because it came with a map that labelled the Moroccan Sahara 'Western Sahara'.

Christianity in Western Sahara, 1970 and 2015

Tradition	1970 Population	1970 %	2015 Population	2015 %	Average annual growth rate (%), 1970–2015
Christians	31,600	41.1%	880	0.2%	–7.6%
Independents	0	0.0%	100	0.0%	5.3%
Catholics	30,000	39.0%	780	0.1%	–7.8%
Evangelicals	0	0.0%	30	0.0%	7.9%
Pentecostals	0	0.0%	70	0.0%	4.5%
Total population	**76,900**	**100.0%**	**573,000**	**100.0%**	**4.6%**

Source: Todd M. Johnson and Gina A. Zurlo (eds), *World Christian Database* (Leiden/Boston: Brill), accessed March 2017.

Living as refugees since 1975 has had a strong impact on Saharawi society. Two generations have known nothing else but living in the desert and waiting for a solution that would allow them to go back home. Hopelessness among the youth can make them receptive to extremists. The Sahara is home to a small number of Christian believers who can be readily identified, but no known house churches. Four known Christian ministries are active in the camps. Also, many Saharawi have been exposed to Christian influence elsewhere. Each summer children are brought to Spain, where many are hosted by Christian families. Many have studied in Cuba, where Christianity has been undergoing revival. There could be many who have privately embraced Christian faith but who are not visible and not connected because fear keeps them isolated from one another.

Conclusion

In the disputed Sahara, as well as in the rest of Morocco, the strongest pressure faced by Christians is cultural. The Moroccan government allows house churches to meet, as long as they do not become public. At the end of 2015, a Moroccan Christian wrote a letter to the king asking for permission to celebrate Christian faith openly during the Christmas season. As a result, the police conducted a series of interviews with leaders of house churches. In one of these interviews, the policeman asked if the Christians had enough people to fill a basketball arena. When the Christian said, 'no', the policeman replied, 'Then just keep quiet and don't bother us with this kind of public request'.

Bibliography

Garrison, David, *A Wind in the House of Islam: How God Is Drawing Muslims Around the World to Faith in Jesus Christ* (Monument, CO: WIGTake Resources, 2014).

Harris, Walter, *Morocco That Was* (London: Eland Books, 1921).

Algeria and Tunisia

Katia Boissevain

Christianity has had a long presence in this part of the Mediterranean, dating back to the Roman Empire. Its activities were later re-enacted during the French colonial period with the arrival of men and women of French, Spanish, Italian or Maltese origin. In the late nineteenth century, the Roman Catholic Church embarked on a vast mission of church building, to help and assist the colonial endeavour. This took effect in different ways, according to the political arrangement that France imposed on the country: colony for Algeria (1830–1962) and protectorate for Tunisia (1881–1956). Alongside the establishment of Catholic churches, the Reformed Protestants also ensured that places of worship were available. During this period of the French conquest, Cardinal Charles Lavigerie, Archbishop of Algiers, aimed to convert Muslim subjects.

Nowadays, aside from minor Christian groups (Europeans who stayed on after independence, American or African expatriates working there), small communities of local converts are emerging in Algeria and Tunisia. Over the last 20 years, conversion to Christianity has been developing, mainly in Algeria and to a lesser extent in Tunisia, in the form of Evangelical Protestantism or neo-Evangelical churches. More recently, since 2003, sub-Saharan African workers or students have also contributed to the revitalisation of the church, both Catholic and Protestant.

States and 'New' Religious Minorities

In Algeria, a discreet conversion movement has been at work since the early 1990s but received significant press coverage for the first time in 2004. The press campaign (by national media) highlighted the effectiveness of proselytism in Kabylia, the Berber region in the north of Algeria. The numbers were inflated (30% of the population in the region of Tizi-Ouzou) in order to inflame public concern and force the state to take measures. The main step was the passing in 2006 of a law concerning 'non-Muslim religions', which forbids religious celebrations outside defined religious buildings (and only with administrative authorisation) and proselytism. With no official numbers, conversions are difficult to estimate, but the Église Protestante d'Algérie (EPA, founded in 1972) is a federation of around 25 churches, comprising Reformed, Methodists, Lutherans and Evangelicals.

The Anglicans and Adventist converts are outside this federation. It is thought that membership of the federation numbers between 10,000 and 15,000, and those outside around the same. Despite the legal framework (since 2011 the EPA has been officially recognised by the state), regular attacks on Christian places of worship are reported and Christians are frequently taken to court on charges of proselytism.

In Tunisia, the numbers seem to be fewer still. Here again, official numbers are unavailable and the number of local Christian converts is estimated to be between 2,000 and 10,000. In contrast to Algeria, they are mainly to be found in urban settings, where they openly congregate in churches. Administrative intimidation also occurs and a subtle balance is at work between 'freedom of conscience, of belief and free expression of religion' (Article 6 of the 2014 constitution) and the prohibition of proselytism. Catholics, on the other hand, all of whom are foreigners, number around 20,000.

Leaving Islam and Becoming Christian

In both countries, when conversion to Christianity is discussed with Muslims, the question raised is that of apostasy (the negative side of the process), which is considered an act of religious treason. Indeed, it is common knowledge that were Sharia law to be followed, religious conversion would be punished by death. The fact that this sanction is a subject of debate and that no consensus emerges among Muslim scholars does not nuance opinion at the popular level. It is considered that the apostate (*murtad*) has turned his or her back on Islam and thus on the *ummah* (Muslim religious community) as a whole. The accusations of religious treason are debated in the press, in both Algeria and Tunisia, through vast campaigns that portray converts as a menace to the stability of the country. How do the men and women who have chosen to change religion counter the accusations of treason on the political and social levels?

Christianity in Algeria, 1970 and 2015

Tradition	1970 Population	1970 %	2015 Population	2015 %	Average annual growth rate (%), 1970–2015
Christians	100,000	1.0%	69,100	0.2%	−0.8%
Anglicans	800	0.0%	90	0.0%	−4.7%
Independents	16,100	0.1%	48,400	0.1%	2.5%
Orthodox	2,700	0.0%	1,400	0.0%	−1.5%
Protestants	4,400	0.0%	13,500	0.0%	2.5%
Catholics	76,500	0.5%	5,700	0.0%	−5.6%
Evangelicals	3,600	0.0%	27,000	0.1%	4.6%
Pentecostals	3,500	0.0%	21,400	0.1%	4.1%
Total population	**14,550,000**	**100.0%**	**39,667,000**	**100.0%**	**2.3%**

Source: Todd M. Johnson and Gina A. Zurlo (eds), *World Christian Database* (Leiden/Boston: Brill), accessed March 2017.

Since independence both Algeria and Tunisia have based their national construction on the idea of the strict equation between one country, one language and one religion, putting aside any social reality that contradicted this ideology, such as the Berber linguistic specificity. In Algeria, this ideology of unity has been shaken by the Berberist movement, but in Tunisia, nothing apart from the acknowledgement of its small Jewish community has come to contradict the equation 'Tunisian = Muslim'. Today, Protestantism, especially in its Evangelical form, is perceived as a religion imported from the USA. As such, it is not welcomed, since the USA is perceived to be a friend and supporter of Israel. This perception and Israel's centrality in Evangelical theology are no doubt the main reasons for the strong reactions Protestantism provokes.

Apostates/converts (depending on the point of view) are most often considered traitors: in an evolutionary understanding of religion, Islam is the last and most complete of the three revelations (Judaism and Christianity being the previous two). Converting to Christianity is therefore perceived as a pointless regression. When a conversion is announced, or discovered, families feel they have been cheated and abandoned and are often stunned by a secretly matured decision. Becoming Christian is interpreted by the others as a choice formulated against everything for which they have been raised. If it is a mistake to think that most Algerians or Tunisians conscientiously practise their ritual obligations, still it remains the case that a Muslim rhythm marks the day, the yearly calendar and the life rituals. Stepping aside and choosing the Christian religion is not only a break with the social body, but also a break with the social rhythm. When families interpret this change as an allegiance to the 'God of the French' or, worse still, of the USA, new converts often find themselves excluded, sometimes willingly, from family gatherings with religious connotations, such as circumcision ceremonies, weddings, birth or death rituals, Eid al-Fitr, Eid al-Adha and Mouled (birth of the Prophet Muhammad).

Christianity in Tunisia, 1970 and 2015

	1970		2015		Average annual growth rate (%), 1970–2015
Tradition	Population	%	Population	%	
Christians	27,300	0.5%	24,000	0.2%	−0.3%
Anglicans	150	0.0%	80	0.0%	−1.4%
Independents	1,200	0.0%	2,400	0.0%	1.5%
Orthodox	250	0.0%	230	0.0%	−0.2%
Protestants	630	0.0%	890	0.0%	0.8%
Catholics	25,000	0.5%	20,000	0.2%	−0.5%
Evangelicals	480	0.0%	660	0.0%	0.7%
Pentecostals	570	0.0%	2,400	0.0%	3.3%
Total population	**5,060,000**	**100.0%**	**11,254,000**	**100.0%**	**1.8%**

Source: Todd M. Johnson and Gina A. Zurlo (eds), *World Christian Database* (Leiden/Boston: Brill), accessed March 2017.

The other reproach formulated against converts is that they maintain an ambiguous relation with 'abroad' and are not loyal to their homeland. Critics might allege that many converts secretly hope that conversion will help them acquire a visa or a marriage to a foreigner (preferably a Westerner). As a result of such accusations, Algerian and Tunisian converts are constantly reaffirming their love for their nation and for their culture – which they dissociate from their religion. Whether on the 'Christians in Tunisia' website, where it is stated that we 'are Tunisian, we were born in Tunisia and we live in Tunisia', or in interviews collected by Karima Dirèche in Algeria, where converts among the Kabyle people in the north of the country give assurances that they would never leave the beauty of their land, the important issue is to demonstrate that one's religious identity was chosen spontaneously and not because of that actions of transnational Evangelical networks, which are, in any case, most of the time unknown to the converts themselves.

Intertwined Histories of Christianity

Contemporary Evangelical movements in Algeria and Tunisia reactivate discourses and representations of the ancient Christianity of North Africa as a means of legitimisation. In the fourth and fifth centuries, this form of Christianity was linked to Rome and allowed for the development of the Church of Africa, directed by the Bishop of Carthage. Today, during their worship, pastors often make reference to the ancient Christian martyrs in a compression of historical time, thus bridging the gap between the tortures endured by the first Christians and the vexations faced by converts. The figures of Cyprian, Tertullian and Saint Augustine are regularly called upon, and the theme of persecution and courage becomes a powerful ferment for converts' identity.

The Church of Algeria was founded by the creation of the Bishopric of Algiers in 1838. It was then mainly a Catholic Christianity linked to the Algerian colonial project, which it was hoped would expand throughout the country. The Berber regions attracted the greatest attention as they were considered to be less fully Islamised. This idea guided the action of the Archbishop of Algiers, Cardinal Charles de Lavigerie, who in 1868 founded the Missionaries of Africa, commonly known as the White Fathers and Sisters, devoted to the conversion of the Arabs and the peoples of Central Africa. As early as 1840, a Reformed mission followed, to serve soldiers and farmers who were settling.

Today, the Catholic churches in Algeria and Tunisia are not much solicited for religious conversions. Muslims turn more willingly to the Evangelicals. There can be several reasons for this. In 1957, the year of Tunisian independence, the Catholic Church still possessed around 100 church buildings and a lot of land. In 1964, the Vatican and the new Bourguiba government signed an agreement called the Modus Vivendi, in which the Tunisian government allowed the Catholic Church to remain in the country in exchange for much of the land and many of its religious buildings in its possession. Seven churches were left open for worship. Additionally, the church was required to officially renounce proselytism and solely direct its religious activities towards the existing Catholic community. The church was also allowed to maintain educational and health-oriented activities (hospitals) aimed at serving the Tunisian population.

Contrasting with this is the situation of the Protestant churches. Even though the Reformed Church was present in the region from the late nineteenth century (the first Protestant military chaplain, Georges Durmeyer, founded the Reformed Church of Tunis in 1882), no such agreement was passed, maybe for lack of a single interlocutor. As a consequence, the Protestants did not find themselves tied to this formal prohibition. In the 1990s, when Evangelical missionary networks came into play alongside the mainstream Protestants, they did not feel constrained in their desire to spread the Christian message, as their theology requires of them.

In both Algeria and Tunisia, Catholics are identified with the colonial period, whereas Evangelicals are perceived to be participating in a modern call to Jesus, both worldwide and local: worldwide because rhetoric insists on its supposed 'tidal wave' effect (in Latin America, Africa or Asia); and local because it taps into the ancient history of North Africa, particularly the pre-Arab, pre-Muslim, 'original' Berber identity. This Berber discourse is particularly effective in Algeria.

Furthermore, it has to be stressed that aside from the pastors and the formal religious hierarchy, local converts rarely make an issue of their denominational identity. Whether they are Methodists, Pentecostals or some other denomination, most of them define themselves simply as 'Christians', at best 'Evangelicals', embraced by the love of Jesus. They build their new religious identity in opposition to Islam and generally remain aloof from the theological differences between Christian denominations.

In Algiers, Monsignor Henri Teissier was the Catholic Archbishop until 2008, when he was succeeded by Ghaleb Bader. The leader of the Église Protestante d'Algérie was the American Hugh Johnson from 1972 to 2008; he was succeeded by Mustapha Krireche, who served until 2016, when he in turn was succeeded by Noureddine Benzid. In the Catholic Church in Tunisia, Illarion Antoniazi succeeded the Palestinian Maroun Lahham, who had been Bishop of Tunis from 2005 and then Archbishop from 2010 to 2012. The main Protestant churches in Tunis are the Reformed Church (led by eight pastors) and St George's Anglican Church. Their main mission is to provide for Western or African believers. Alongside this worship, during separate services, Tunisian pastors offer worship in the Tunisian dialect for the local converts. In order to be able to remain in the country without trouble, the foreign pastors must not undertake any proselytism towards the Tunisian community and are best advised to have very little contact.

Who Are the Christians?

Converts come from diverse sociological categories: young or old, men or women, highly educated, middle-class or socially fragile. People in their late teens or early 20s in Tunisia turn to Christianity with deep mystical passion and find in their new-found love of Jesus a way to affirm their own choices and differences with the social environment. In Algeria and more specifically in Kabylia, Karima Dirèche has shown how the religious choice is also a political one, set in the debate about Berber specificity, distinct from the Arab identity and therefore from the Muslim one. Their claim to a specific Algerian identity is consequently strengthened.

Moreover, the arrival of Christian sub-Saharan African migrants, be they students, workers or refugees, has had a great effect on the make-up of Christianity in the region. Having been quiet churches up to the 1990s, today they are loud and joyous places, with singing and passionate praising. Churches have had to adapt and call upon African priests and pastors to help lead this movement. Alongside these changes there has been an increase in intentional evangelistic outreach. As a consequence, African Pentecostal pastors (mainly from Nigeria and Côte d'Ivoire) convinced some locals to join their churches of different denominations.

Conclusion

Converts usually claim to have been attracted to Christianity either 'spontaneously', through a discussion with a friend, or thanks to radio, television or the Internet. The myth of endogenous calling is very strong and is deployed with the aim of counteracting accusations of being the toy of outside interests. For example, a Korean missionary is identified as an Arabic language student, a touching Christian song on the radio is heard as a personal call from God, and the mobile recording studio used for encouraging local Christian artists to write Christian songs is interpreted as 'really nice people here to help'. Local discourse makes every effort to minimise the implication that transnational Christian organisations (such as MENA – Ministère Evangélique parmi les Nations Arabophones) are behind the conversion of local people who have supposedly been caught unawares. However, Christian programmes are broadcast in the region and are listened to on the radio, watched on television and followed on the Internet. The existence of small communities of local converts to Christianity, despite their relatively small numbers, has a clear impact on public debates concerning freedom of thought or the way to deal legally with religious diversity.

Bibliography

Boissevain, Katia, 'Devenir chrétien évangélique en Tunisie. Quelques aspects d'une conversion en pays musulman à la veille de la révolution (2009–2010)', in Christophe Pons (ed.), *Jésus, moi et les autres. La construction collective d'une relation personnelle à Jésus dans les Eglises évangéliques: Europe, Océanie, Maghreb* (Paris: CNRS Editions, 2013), 147–87.

Ceillier, Jean-Claude, *Histoire des Missionnaires d'Afrique (Pères Blancs). De la fondation par Mgr Lavigerie à la mort du fondateur (1868–1892)* (Paris: Karthala, 2008).

Dirèche-Slimani, Karima, *Chrétiens de Kabylie, 1873–1964. Une action missionnaire dans l'Algérie coloniale* (Paris: Bouchène, 2004).

Kazdaghli, Habib, 'Les églises chrétiennes non catholiques et l'Etat tunisien depuis 1956', in Philippe Delisle and Marc Spindler (eds), *Les relations Eglises-Etats en situation post-coloniale: Amérique, Afrique, Asie, Océanie* (Paris: Karthala, 2003).

Soumille, Pierre, 'Eglise catholique et protestantisme français en Tunisie aux 19ème et 20ème siècles (années 1860–années 1960)', *Revue d'Histoire maghrebine*, 28 (2001–3), 117–40.

Libya

Akram Habib

Libya has a long but episodic Christian history. The Coptic Church believes that it was St Mark the Apostle, originally from the Libyan city of Cyrene, who first introduced Christianity to the country. By the end of the third century, the majority of the population of Libya was Christian and the presence of the church was extensive. Doctrinal divisions weakened the church, however, and made it easier for Islam to supplant Christianity from the seventh century onwards. The Islamic conquest was initiated by Uqba Ibn Nafi between 681 and 683 and, despite resistance and periodic rebellions, the result was the almost complete disappearance of Christianity. Only the remains of ancient churches bear witness to the early flourishing of Christian faith in this land. Even these remains have been jeopardised in recent times as ISIL militants have sought to eradicate evidence of the earlier Christian presence.

The Spanish occupation of Libya in the early sixteenth century re-introduced a Christian presence, particularly through the Knights of St John from Malta, who maintained a base in Tripoli for 21 years. The Knights of St John, together with all Christians who had settled in Libya during the period of Spanish rule, were expelled in 1551, when the country was occupied by the forces of the Ottoman Empire. Much later, in 1911, Libya was occupied by Italy, which encouraged its citizens to settle in the new colony. During the next 30 years some 200,000 Italians settled in Libya at a time when the total population was no more than 1 million. With the Italians came the Catholic Church, which established a considerable presence, particularly in the cities on the Mediterranean coast. Even after the end of Italian rule, in 1943, many Italians remained in Libya. It was only after Muammar Gaddafi came to power in 1969 that all Italians were expelled from the country in an event known as the 'Day of Revenge', 7 October 1970. Subsequently, the cathedrals and churches built during Italian rule were closed and the buildings used for other purposes.

Migrant Christians in Modern Times

The late twentieth century witnessed the rise of a new form of Christian presence in Libya as migrant Christians arrived in the country in large numbers. This development was prompted by the discovery of oil, the emergence of industry and the growth of the economy. Libya's small low population and its lack of skilled labour meant that there was an urgent need for foreign labour. Thousands of expatriate workers poured into the country, from Egypt, Sudan, various other African countries, Europe and North America. Many were Christians and so churches began to reappear to provide pastoral care for their members.

The Egyptian Coptic Orthodox Church became active once more in Libya as it sought to provide for the thousands of Coptic people who came to work as migrant labourers. Pope Shenouda III aimed to revive evangelism in 'the five western cities', as the territory of Libya is described in the Coptic tradition. On 12 December 1971 he consecrated Bishop Pachomius as bishop of the Beheira and Matrouh regions in Egypt and 'the five western cities'. On 27 March 1972, Pope Shenouda visited Libya at the invitation of President Muammar Gaddafi to participate in the General National Conference.

After the visit of Pope Shenouda and his meeting with Gaddafi, a number of Coptic Orthodox churches were established and opened. Among the most important were St Anthony's in Benghazi, St Mary's in Misurata and St Mark's in Tripoli. Additionally, Christian service centres were established in a number of cities, notably Bayda and Cyrene. All these churches and pastoral centres were under the authority of Bishop Pachomius, as Bishop of Beheira and the five western cities, who made his first pastoral visit on 17 January 1972. By 1996 it was estimated that there were 300 Coptic Christian families in Libya as well as some 15,000 Coptic migrant workers. By the time of the Libyan revolution, which began on 17 February 2011, there were three active Coptic churches in the country: St Mark the Apostle in the capital, Tripoli, under Pastor Timothy Bishara Adly; St Anthony, in Benghazi, under Pastor Paula Isaac Nashed; and St George, in Misurata, under Pastor Mark Zaghloul Paul.

Christianity in Libya, 1970 and 2015

	1970		2015		Average annual growth rate (%), 1970–2015
Tradition	Population	%	Population	%	
Christians	58,800	2.8%	46,600	0.7%	−0.5%
Anglicans	380	0.0%	60	0.0%	−4.0%
Independents	2,700	0.1%	1,700	0.0%	−1.1%
Orthodox	47,000	2.2%	27,800	0.4%	−1.2%
Protestants	3,900	0.2%	3,500	0.1%	−0.2%
Catholics	3,700	0.2%	11,200	0.2%	2.5%
Evangelicals	1,800	0.1%	1,500	0.0%	−0.4%
Pentecostals	390	0.0%	2,600	0.0%	4.3%
Total population	**2,114,000**	**100.0%**	**6,278,000**	**100.0%**	**2.4%**

Source: Todd M. Johnson and Gina A. Zurlo (eds), *World Christian Database* (Leiden/Boston: Brill), accessed March 2017.

The Catholic Church also built up a considerable organisation in Libya in modern times, with dioceses in Tripoli and Benghazi. From 1985 to 2017 Monsignor Giovanni Martinily served as Vicar Apostolic of Tripoli and Titular Bishop of Tabuda, leading the ministry of St Francis Church in Tripoli. The Bishop of Benghazi was Bishop Sylvester Carmel Magro, who had particular responsibility for Catholics of Maltese origin and who led the ministry of the Church of the Immaculate Conception, which closed after he left Libya on 13 February 2013. Numerous monastic foundations also have had to close their work and leave Libya after the revolution of 2011. These include the Monastery of the Holy Family in Darna, east of Benghazi, which had been serving in Libya for around 100 years, and the convent of the Franciscan Sisters of the Child Jesus in the town of Marj, between Benghazi and Darna.

Because of the thousands of Catholic migrant workers, staff and experts from all over the world, the Catholic Church built up a considerable network of pastoral service in modern Libya, but the unstable situation that developed in the aftermath of the revolution has imposed severe pressure on it. St Francis Church in Tripoli had to be closed after the pastor was shot by a gunman at the church door. The Church of Mary Immaculate in Benghazi, founded by Franciscan missionaries in 1858, was attacked by unknown individuals during Benghazi's troubles in February 2006. Then, on 17 May 2013, the church was bombed and seriously damaged.

The Anglican Church also established a presence in Libya, particularly through the work of the Church of Christ the King in the old city district of Tripoli. This church was providing pastoral care for Christians of many nationalities, including European workers in Libya as well as groups of Africans, Asians and Egyptian Protestants. The priest in charge was Vasihar Eben Baskaran, while Gus Ketola, a Canadian priest, led the English services, Ayobami Ayorinda led the work with the Africans and Samuel Iskander, an Egyptian priest, led the Arabic services. Before the revolution, this church was very active, with weekly Bible studies in addition to formal services. There are also Pentecostal churches in Tripoli and Misurata.

After the Revolution

Christian presence and activity has been severely inhibited in Libya since the revolution of 2011. The collapse of the national security apparatus and withdrawal of the police force introduced a situation of anarchy, exposing all citizens to the violence of criminal groups and placing Christian migrant workers in a particularly vulnerable position. Militant Islamist groups, such as Ansar al-Sharia, Nusra, ISIL and the Muslim Brotherhood, targeted Christians, who were forced to adopt a fugitive way of life. Kidnappings of men, women and children in return for ransoms, and sexual assault on women, assumed epidemic proportions, severely affecting whole communities. Despite such pressures, Christian migrant workers were initially reluctant to leave the country. Many had been working in Libya for years and were well integrated in Libyan society. They were also gainfully employed and the prospect of returning to unemployment in home contexts such as Upper Egypt was not attractive. Even when the churches closed their doors and evacuated their clergy, through community solidarity migrant Christians sought to sustain their presence.

This situation changed markedly in February 2015, when ISIL carried out a highly publicised beheading of a group of 21 Coptic Christians on the Mediterranean coast near Sirte. These were migrant workers, 13 of them from the village of Al-Our in Minya Governate in Upper Egypt, who, according to video footage, died with prayers to Jesus on their lips. Soon afterwards Coptic Pope Tawadros II announced that the 21 murdered Copts would be commemorated as martyr saints. Their fate illustrated all too vividly the vulnerability of Christians in Libya in the unstable situation prevailing in the aftermath of the revolution. It prompted a large-scale exodus of Christian migrant workers, most of whom returned to their homeland of Egypt. Reluctantly, many came to the conclusion that it was simply too dangerous to remain. The institutional presence of Christianity has been heavily depleted, and for the decreasing numbers of Christians who are still in Libya it is difficult to predict what the future might hold.

Bibliography

Ihsan, Abbas, *History of Libya Since the Arab Conquest Until the Beginning of the Ninth Century* (Benghazi: Libya House, 1967).

Oden, Thomas C., *Early Libyan Christianity: Uncovering a North African Tradition* (Downers Grove, IL: InterVarsity Press, 2011).

St John, Ronald Bruce, *Libya: From Colony to Revolution* (Oxford: Oneworld, 2011).

Sudan

John Eibner

Sudan has long been the scene of a 'War of Visions', to use an image employed by the Sudanese scholar and statesman Francis Deng. It is a conflict in which Muslim rulers have endeavoured to achieve unity of the multi-religious, multicultural country by means of state-enforced Arabisation and Islamisation. When Sudan achieved independence from Britain in 1956, the declared goal of the new Muslim-dominated government was to spread 'Islam and Arab culture in non-Arab and non-Islamic parts of the Sudan' and to achieve 'Islamic cultural unity'. For Sudan's new ruling elite, the restoration of Muslim and Arab supremacy after half a century of British (Christian) rule was perceived as a return to a natural Islamic order. Within this order, Christians were expected to accept politically and socially disadvantageous conditions of dhimmitude in accordance with the spirit, if not the letter, of Sharia norms. This state-sponsored process of social engineering has consistently encountered stiff resistance from the predominantly black African, Christian and tribal regions: South Sudan and the so-called 'Two Areas' – the Nuba Mountains and the southern Blue Nile region. Most of the resistors have dreamt of secession, while others, especially those with tribal roots in the Two Areas, sought the establishment of a religiously neutral, united Sudan, based on equal citizenship.

The term 'War of Visions' is not used altogether figuratively. Waves of violence have been a recurring feature of Sudan's history. Armed conflict erupted on the eve of independence as a Christian-led, southern-based resistance movement fought to prevent Arab Muslim hegemony. The Addis Ababa Peace Agreement of 1972 suspended combat and accommodated the country's religious diversity. But warfare erupted again in 1983 in response to the imposition of Sharia law. This war pitted the southern-based Sudan People's Liberation Army (SPLA) against the Khartoum government. Following the seizure of power in 1989 by Sudan's Muslim Brotherhood, Khartoum openly prosecuted the war as a jihad. The principal combat zones were areas with black African majorities, made up of Christians and tribalists. The Comprehensive Peace Agreement of 2005 suspended the war and permitted the adoption of an interim constitution that was 'mindful of religious, racial, ethnic and cultural diversity in the Sudan'. It also granted South Sudan the right of self-determination. In

January 2011 southerners voted for independence, thereby paving the way for the establishment of the Republic of South Sudan (RoSS) six months later. The Two Areas remained in the Republic of the Sudan (RoS).

The two great civil wars were catastrophic for those living in combat zones. Over 3 million black Africans perished, while more than 5 million were displaced. Despite the use of extreme violence – or perhaps because of it – efforts to Islamise proved to be counterproductive. In fact, one of the unintended consequences of the jihad was mass evangelism in rebel-controlled areas, conducted largely by Sudanese Christians, without much input from foreign missionaries. The result was a Christian majority in South Sudan and a significantly increased Christian population in the Two Areas. Another consequence was the mass migration of displaced black Africans to northern Sudan, starting with the great war-related famine of 1987–8. Their arrival and long-term residency swelled the ranks of Christians there, especially in the Khartoum area. Many of the new arrivals were mission-minded and helped strengthen the northern church.

The Sudanese government's decision to end hostilities in 2005 reflected the failure of forced Islamisation and Arabisation. Christianity had emerged from the civil wars stronger than ever. Revulsion at the brutal methods used as instruments of jihad was an important, perhaps decisive, factor in South Sudan's vote for independent statehood. Southern independence has at least suspended, if not ended, the War of Visions there, but it continues in the rump RoS in both its violent and non-violent guises. Already on the eve of southern secession, President Omer al-Bashir of the RoS announced that this development would result in an intensification of Islamisation. He said there would then be 'no time to speak of diversity of culture and ethnicity' and promised that 'Sharia and Islam will be the main source for the constitution'. The jihad then resumed in the Two Areas, pitting the armed forces

Christianity in Sudan, 1970 and 2015

	1970		2015		Average annual growth rate (%), 1970–2015
Tradition	Population	%	Population	%	
Christians	318,000	3.1%	2,016,000	5.0%	4.2%
Anglicans	90,000	0.9%	530,000	1.3%	4.0%
Independents	500	0.0%	19,900	0.1%	8.5%
Orthodox	107,000	1.1%	102,000	0.3%	−0.1%
Protestants	53,200	0.5%	256,000	0.6%	3.5%
Catholics	62,900	0.6%	1,099,000	2.7%	6.6%
Evangelicals	76,900	0.8%	407,000	1.0%	3.8%
Pentecostals	100	0.0%	141,000	0.4%	17.5%
Total population	**10,233,000**	**100.0%**	**40,235,000**	**100.0%**	**3.1%**

Source: Todd M. Johnson and Gina A. Zurlo (eds), *World Christian Database* (Leiden/Boston: Brill), accessed March 2017.

of the Islamist government against anti-Islamist Muslim, Christian and tribalist rebels of the Sudan People's Liberation Army–North (SPLA-N), a northern offshoot of the southern-based SPLA. The fighting has caused massive displacement. Some of the displaced have sought refuge in the neighbouring RoSS, while others have fled to tranquil parts of the RoS, especially the Khartoum area. The destruction of Christian homes, churches, schools and hospitals has been extensive.

The Sudanese government also continues to pursue its Islamist agenda outside the Two Areas war zones, using mainly threats and acts of low-level violence. The Christian community is impacted mainly by the harassment and occasional arrest of clergy, the confiscation or bulldozing of church buildings, and strict enforcement of Sharia's prohibition of conversion from Islam to any other faith. The government complements its repressive measures by promoting the conversion of non-Muslims to Islam in collaboration with Gulf-funded transnational Islamist *dawa* (proselytising; literally 'inviting') organisations. The War of Visions continues unabated.

The Christian Population

Just how many of the RoS's 39 million citizens are Christians cannot be defined with precision. Estimates vary widely. Past censuses have been few and far between and have never been a reliable guide to the size of the population, let alone its religious composition. For what it is worth, Sudanese authorities continue to say that Christians make up 3% of the population, or about 700,000 people. Despite the uncertainties surrounding official figures, it would be reasonable to assume that the RoS hosts well over 1 million Christians. Yet even if reliable statistics were available, we would still have to face the fact that there is no universally accepted definition of a Christian. The broadest definition, based on self-identification with the Christian community, will be used here.

Whatever their true number, the RoS's Christians are not characterised by homogeneity. Lifestyles and habits of worship are powerfully influenced by tribe, language, social and economic status, level of education, church affiliation, geographical location and degree of Christian commitment and zeal. The overwhelming majority of the RoS's Christians are culturally black African. Most have family roots in South Sudan or the Two Areas. Roman Catholics predominate, but many others identify with the Episcopal, Presbyterian, Pentecostal and other Protestant denominations. Worship and other aspects of church life reflect black African cultural traditions, even when Arabic is used as a lingua franca, as it often is, on account of the country's phenomenal linguistic diversity. Doctrinal dogmatism does not dominate the religious sensibilities of the mass of black African Christians, be they clergy or laity. In each of the denominations the level of commitment varies from occasional passive worshippers to those whose lives are overflowing with prayer, Bible reading, social service and evangelism.

While a distinct community of black African Christians is visible, neither southern-ness nor Christianity tends to be the strongest source of social identity. They often live in neighbourhoods and worship in congregations that are structurally tribal. Rites of passage, such as weddings and funerals, even when they encompass Christian worship, are usually strongly impacted by tribal customs. Religious syncretism is widespread, especially but not exclusively among the poor and illiterate, notwithstanding strong discouragement from the clergy. For example, the rituals of the tribal spearman still attract the respect and devotion of many Christians from the Dinka tribe. Similarly, the predictions of Nuer tribal prophets carry weight with many Nuer Christians. Polygamy is gradually declining, especially among the younger generation, but it is still widespread among southern Christians.

Well over half of black African Christians live below the national poverty line and are functionally illiterate, although there are literate black African Christians, with some education, who have achieved success in a trade, profession or commerce. Many of the poor live in slums and shantytowns, surviving on charity or through menial jobs. They worship more often in flimsy, makeshift structures made of rough-cut timber and roofed with tin or plastic sheeting than in the cathedrals of the historic churches. The gospel tends to be proclaimed by word of mouth, often in tribal languages, with pictures frequently used as tools for conveying Bible stories. Some still live as slaves of Arab Muslim masters in cattle camps, on farms and in households. Christians among them are normally forbidden to practise their faith. The low social status of black African Christians is reinforced by a prevailing Arab Muslim supremacist culture, within which black Africans are still often thought of by Arab Muslims as *abid* (slaves).

The black African Christian population in northern Sudan exploded during the last north–south civil war. Hundreds of thousands of southern Christians fled northward from the war zone. But with the end of the war in 2005 and the subsequent establishment of the RoSS, reverse migration took place. Nevertheless, according to the United Nations, about 0.5 million southerners reside in the Khartoum area today. The true figure is likely to be much higher.

The secession of southern Sudan has had an unsettling effect on the RoS's black African Christian population. The southern community is now significantly smaller than it was during the war years, and the issue of nationality has not yet been resolved. Many southern Sudanese have lost public sector jobs and have been subjected to social discrimination because they are no longer regarded as citizens. Some RoS officials have heightened tensions by threatening the deportation of southerners, with the state-controlled media sometimes whipping up anti-southern sentiment. The BBC reported, for example, that one major Khartoum newspaper with close ties to the government declared that southern Sudanese 'should go back to their country', claiming that some of them have a 'plan to destroy Sudan, and to occupy Sudan'. Such messaging, which the authorities amplify or tone down depending on immediate political interests, reinforces public perceptions of southern Sudanese Christians and tribalists as dangerous aliens and thereby exacerbates their sense of insecurity.

Similarly, war and extreme poverty have driven many Two Areas Christians from their war-torn native areas to Khartoum and other parts of the country. Roughly 3 million Sudanese are native to the Two Areas. The majority are Muslim, while Christians and tribalists constitute substantial minorities; Christians represent perhaps 20–25% of the population. Christianity is much stronger in the Nuba Mountains than in the Blue Nile region. Christians in the Two Areas tend to be poor and functionally illiterate. Most live in areas controlled by the government of Sudan, while the rest live under the rule of the SPLA-N.

Broad freedom of religion is promoted by the SPLA-N. Its mainly Muslim leadership is ideologically opposed to religious government. Christians in the Two Areas benefit greatly from this attitude. According to the retired Catholic Bishop of El Obeid, the Rt Revd Macram Max Gassis, 'Many of the Muslim commanders in the liberation movement of north Sudan respect the church and are helping the church to help the people. So there is a mutual respect.' This religious toleration, however, is offset by extreme physical hardship and trauma. Amnesty International reports that the inhabitants of these regions are 'living in desperate conditions, fleeing from relentless bombardment and seeking refuge inside foxholes and caves, with limited access to food, water and medical care'. Benjamin Barnaba of the New Sudan Council of Churches (NSCC) maintains that the Sudanese authorities aim to achieve either the submission of the resistant communities or their destruction by means of long-term, low-level warfare.

Christians in the Two Areas living in government-controlled regions, like their southern counterparts, can generally go to church, celebrate Christian festivals and participate in Christian education without direct obstruction, but not without complications. They experience all the commonplace racial and religious discrimination to which southern Christians are routinely subjected. Because of skin colour and Christian names, some Two Areas Christians are mistakenly thought to be 'alien' southerners, without full rights of citizenship in the RoS. Moreover, the state security apparatus and the Muslim population at large tend to suspect them, especially educated males, of acting as a fifth column for the SPLA-N. Arrest, imprisonment and torture for allegedly collaborating with rebels are very real dangers.

While most of the RoS's Christians belong to black African tribes, the RoS is also home to a significant and well established community of Copts of Egyptian ancestry. In 1993, it was estimated that Sudan's Coptic community numbered between 150,000 and 200,000. Substantial emigration has taken place since then. As a community, Copts are much more prosperous than most black African Christians. Sudan's Copts are more culturally bound to Egypt than to sub-Saharan Africa. Their churches, together with Khartoum's Coptic Club, are important social institutions for the community. Sudanese Copts are not victims of their government's Arabisation policies. Their ancestors were Arabised in Egypt many centuries ago. Christianity alone separates them from the mass of Muslims. It is on religious grounds that they are caught up in the War of Visions.

The decline of Sudan's Coptic community began in 1983 with the imposition of Sharia law. This act engendered doubts within the Coptic community about their long-term security. Human Rights Watch believed such anxiety to be justified and stated that 'The Copts had reason to feel unsafe and victimized'. Coptic fears were heightened when the Islamist media portrayed them as a subversive element in Islamic society. Emigration accelerated in the 1990s when Copts were conscripted as *mujahadeen* (jihadist) fighters, and systematic discrimination against them in public employment began. The authorities calibrate the anti-Copt campaigns according to immediate political interest. Waves of intimidation can be followed by broad troughs of calm.

Since the 1960s, Ethiopian and Eritrean Orthodox Christians have been added to Sudan's religious mix. Most have sought refuge in the north-east of Sudan, with many migrating to Khartoum. Today more than 100,000 displaced Eritreans live in Sudan, a good percentage of whom are Christians. While some stay long term as refugees, others use the RoS as a transit route for emigration to Europe.

Though small in number, Muslim converts to Christianity do exist. They come from both Arab and black African communities. These Christians tend to be invisible to outsiders on account of the security threats. Throughout the Muslim-dominated world, departure from Islam is seen as a grave, severely punishable offence. Violence against converts, including murder, is more often carried out by relatives and acquaintances than by the state, although apostasy is a capital offence according to Article 126 of Sudan's Penal Code of 1991. The outside world caught a glimpse of this grim reality in May 2014, when the media reported the conviction of an alleged Muslim convert to Christianity. Twenty-seven-year-old Meriam Yahya, the pregnant wife of a Christian and mother of a 20-month-old son, was sentenced to death by hanging. As a result of international protests, the Sudanese government eventually released Meriam from prison and allowed her and her family to leave the country. At the time of her trial, some of Meriam's Muslim relatives clamoured for her to be put to death to preserve the honour of the family.

All of the RoS's Christians, whatever their background, find the odds in life heavily stacked against them. Few can avoid a fate of discrimination, marginalisation, harassment or violent persecution because of their faith or cultural identity.

The Churches

The Sudanese churches are historically young. Perhaps because of their youthfulness, they take special pride in links between Sudan and the Bible. They identify closely with Old Testament references to the land of Kush. Isaiah 18, which speaks prophetically of the apocalyptic suffering and ultimate salvation of a people dwelling 'beyond the rivers of Ethiopia', is central to their self-perception. They also embrace the story in the Book of Acts of the conversion of the Ethiopian eunuch, an official at the court of a queen named Candace, whose capital many believe to have been located in northern Sudan. The Sudanese churches use these passages to anchor the faithful in a pre-Islamic biblical narrative.

There is no hard evidence of a Sudanese church emerging in Apostolic times. By the sixth century, however, the church had extended to Sudan from Egypt. Allied with powerful Nubian kingdoms, the church undergirded a vibrant Christian civilisation. The Sudanese church first came into contact with Islam in the mid-seventh century, when jihad warriors skirmished with Nubian troops in the Egyptian borderlands. The Christian kingdoms initially held their own, but they were ultimately unable to withstand the jihad dynamic emanating from Muslim neighbours. The last of the Christian kingdoms was overrun by the Muslim Funj Kingdom in the early sixteenth century. Soon thereafter, Christianity disappeared from Sudan. It had lost the first phase of the War of Visions.

Opportunity for Christian mission returned in the early nineteenth century. The largely independent Ottoman Khedive (Viceroy) of Egypt, Muhammad Ali, conquered Sudan in the 1820s. Muhammad Ali and his successors were modernising Muslims who opened the door of their domains to European Christian influence. By the 1870s, European Christians occupied powerful positions, while Egyptian Copts found business opportunities and employment in the state administration. Additionally, European Catholic missionaries appeared. But these developments proved to be false starts. The devastating Mahdist jihad (1881–98), in part a reaction against the reappearance of Christianity, put an end to the presence of church institutions for nearly two decades. The Mahdist episode of the War of Visions ended when a British-led army crushed the jihad, occupied Sudan and enabled London, through the Anglo-Egyptian Condominium, to rule the country in colonial style.

The new British authorities guaranteed that Christian missionary efforts were not directed at the country's Muslim majority in the north. They did allow missionaries freedom in the southern, largely un-Islamised black African parts of the country. The Closed Districts Ordinances Act of the 1920s diminished Arab Muslim influence in southern Sudan and the Two Areas. The provision of education was left largely to missionaries. The Catholic, Anglican and Presbyterian churches were able to gain an early foothold.

The Egyptian-migrant-based Coptic Orthodox Church also benefited immediately from the religious tolerance of the Anglo-Egyptian Condominium. Khartoum's Coptic Cathedral of St Mary the Virgin dates from the years of post-Mahdist reconstruction. In the early twentieth century, the Coptic Orthodox Church played a pioneering role in the provision of education and social services. Today, its showcase social programme is Khartoum's St Mark's Hospital. The Coptic Orthodox Church does not have a strong tradition of proselytising missionary outreach. Evangelism normally takes place within the community. While the Coptic Church does not actively seek Muslim converts, there are Muslims who come to faith in Christ through the witness of its members. The danger of evangelistic engagement with Muslims, no matter how low key, was highlighted in December 2012 when security agents arrested two Coptic priests for having allegedly converted a Muslim woman to Christianity. The convert fled abroad before she could be arrested.

The Catholic Church is the largest and most influential church in the RoS. It claims to have more than 1 million members and supports an extensive network of educational and medical facilities. The Catholic Church enjoys the prestige of having a long tradition in the Sudan. It also has the greatest financial and human resources. It benefits from the diplomatic presence of a papal nuncio in Khartoum. Following southern independence, the RoS's Catholic Church has been left with only two out of 10 dioceses: the Archdiocese of Khartoum and the Diocese of El Obeid. Ninety per cent of the Catholics in the RoS live in the Archdiocese of Khartoum.

The leading architect of Catholic mission was an Italian, Bishop Daniel Comboni. He energetically promoted the vision of an 'Africanised' church. The twin pillars of his programme for evangelism were quality education and liberation of black African slaves from their Arab Muslim masters. The goal of the former was to produce an indigenous, educated Christian leadership for an Africanised church. Comboni's success on this front can be seen in the network of Catholic schools that continue to bear his name. These schools, together with other social outreach, are often associated with the orders known as the Comboni Fathers and the Comboni Sisters. The goal of slave liberation was to identify the church with freedom of conscious for the black African tribes, a precondition for a truly Africanised church. Comboni's ideas continue today to animate Sudan's Catholic leadership. In recognition of his productive life and lasting vision, Comboni was canonised in 2003.

Three years before Comboni's sainthood was officially recognised, Pope John Paul II canonised Sudan's first native saint, Sister Josephine Bakhita, a liberated black African slave from Darfur, who died in 1947. Her canonisation expressed the church's solidarity with the lowest and most brutally abused strata of Sudanese society. Both Bakhita and Comboni are modern icons. Their pictures are often as visible in Catholic churches as those of Jesus Christ and the Virgin Mary. It is difficult to overstate the importance of these two icons for a largely illiterate and oppressed church as it is caught up in the ongoing War of Visions.

The Episcopal Church is the second largest in the RoS. It traces its origins to the activity of the Church Missionary Society at the beginning of the twentieth century. In the past, when British influence was strong, the Episcopalian leadership had considerable political and social influence. With the decline of Britain's global political and religious power, the Episcopal Church lost much of its weight. Increasingly it has had to fend for itself in an ever more challenging environment. Since the secession of South Sudan, it has been renamed the Episcopal Church of South Sudan and Sudan (ECSSS). The order of countries in the new name illustrates the fact that its centre of the gravity has shifted to the south. Of the ECSSS's 41 dioceses, only five are in the RoS. The northern province of the ECSSS is poor and fragile, resembling other Protestant churches rather than the Catholic Church. For example, in the Diocese of Wad Medani, the bishop reports that he has no salary or home of his own, and that every priest and administrator is a part-time volunteer.

Reformed churches make up the third-largest grouping of Sudanese Christians. The initial Reformed missionaries were American Presbyterians. The Sudanese Presbyterians soon became denominationally fragmented, with the southern-based, mainly Nuer Presbyterians forming the Presbyterian Church of Sudan (PCOS), and the Khartoum-based, mainly Coptic Presbyterians forming the Sudan Presbyterian Evangelical Church (SPEC). In the first decade of the twenty-first century, the SPEC stated that it had 8,000 members, 22 ordained clergymen serving 24 parishes, and 66 house groups that formed the nucleus of potential parishes. Like the Episcopalians, the PCOS changed its name to the Presbyterian Church of South Sudan and Sudan (PCSSS) and established headquarters in the RoSS rather than in Khartoum. It is difficult to gauge the current size of its presence in the RoS.

The Pentecostal Church of Sudan (PCS) grew out of the work of Scandinavian and East African missionaries in the second half of the twentieth century. Its main field of mission was in southern Sudan and in Khartoum. The PCS is reputed to be the fastest-growing church in the RoSS and has a visible presence in the Khartoum area. In 2003, there were 10 PCS congregations in the Sudanese capital, while today there are 20, according to a well informed traveller. Most of the new Pentecostal worshippers are black African tribalists or Christians from other denominations.

Many more small Protestant denominations are working in the RoS. Some have been present for decades, like the African Inland Church, the Sudanese Church of Christ and the Seventh Day Adventists. Others are the result of recent mission activity or denominational splits.

The churches that are anchored most deeply in Sudan's history are represented in the remarkably diverse Sudan Council of Churches (SCC), founded in 1965. They are the Africa Inland Church, the Catholic Church, the Coptic Orthodox Church, the Episcopal Church, the Ethiopian Orthodox Church, the Greek Catholic Church, the Greek Orthodox Church (Alexandria Patriarchate), the Presbyterian Church of Sudan, the Sudan Evangelical Presbyterian Church, the Sudan Interior Church, the Sudan Pentecostal Church and the Sudanese Church of Christ. The SCC describes its role as the coordination of education, advocacy, peace and reconciliation, and relief and development services. It is evident from this mission statement that while all member churches view the SCC as a manifestation of Christian unity, they place practical cooperation above theological dialogue. The SCC also participates in customarily sterile Christian-Muslim dialogue enterprises, the inspiration and funding for which normally originate in the West. Since 2014, the SCC has developed an offshoot known as the New Sudan Council of Churches (NSCC). The purpose of this RoSS-based entity is to serve the churches in the 'liberated parts' of the Two Areas – that is, the territory controlled by SPLA-N – without interference from the Sudanese government. Like the SCC, the NSCC aims to enable member churches to cooperate in service to the community and to act as a joint point of contact for ecumenical and humanitarian partners abroad.

Foreign partners continue to be important for all the Sudanese churches. While the churches have been thoroughly 'Africanised' in terms of personnel and operating culture, they are still largely dependent on non-Sudanese sources of income. It is not unusual for Protestant pastors and lay evangelists to be dependent for survival on non-church sources of income. The poverty of church personnel is especially acute in the SPLA-controlled parts of the Two Areas. Large-scale social-service programmes are usually funded almost exclusively from Western sources. While Sudan's churches are grateful for the significant humanitarian funding, the Secretary-General of the NSCC has noted that Western church partners provide very little support for what the Sudanese regard as their top priority: evangelism.

Churches in the RoS, as institutions, are subject to state-sponsored intimidation. One of the most headline-grabbing forms of harassment is the destruction, confiscation or closure of churches. A pattern has developed since the secession of southern Sudan whereby the authorities order such measures on the pretext of violations of zoning regulations or irregularities regarding land ownership records. Protestant churches that are less well connected internationally are more frequently targeted than the Catholic, Episcopal and Coptic communions. A prohibition on the building of new church premises complements this policy. In April 2013, the Sudanese Minister for Religious Guidance and Endowments announced that no new church licences would be issued. He justified the prohibition on the grounds that the post-independence migration of southerners to the RoSS had led to a lack of worshippers in the RoS – an assertion that is vehemently denied by church leaders.

Often unnoticed by the Western media are the extensive and systematic surveillance and hostile questioning of clergy, especially black African Protestants, with pastors of Nuba origins disproportionately subjected to such harassment. Usually detained pastors are eventually released without charge, but some cases go to court. For example, the Revds Yat Michael and Peter Yein Reith of SPEC were put on trial in 2015 and charged with espionage and inciting religious hatred. After having spent over half a year in prison, they were acquitted of these grave charges and released from prison, though convicted of minor offences.

As one Christian activist told *Morning Star News* in March 2016, 'Things are very difficult here in Sudan, as time after time we hear that a church leader is arrested'. The pattern of arrests, closures and demolitions demonstrates that today's War of Visions is being fought as one of attrition. This is painful for the RoS's churches, but they show no sign of succumbing.

Conclusion

On 24 June 2012, the customarily soft-spoken World Council of Churches, together with the All Africa Conference of Churches, condemned the Sudanese authorities' prosecution of the War of Visions. These ecumenical bodies declared:

> We once again regret that despite repeated rhetoric about freedom of religion and the protection of the minorities in the Republic of Sudan, the government

> policy seems to be bent on threatening and discriminating against Christians in Khartoum. By protecting religious fundamentalists who wreck mayhem and havoc on innocent civilians with impunity, the Republic of Sudan undermines the tenets on which a multi-religious society is based.

This sharp rebuke did not lead to change. Christianity in the RoS is more vulnerable than ever. The church now finds itself numerically and materially weaker than it was during the late north–south civil wars. As the secularisation of Europe and North America proceeds apace, less support is forthcoming from churches in the West. Moreover, there is a strong tendency on the part of Western partners to direct more resources instead towards churches in the religiously freer RoSS. The impoverished and struggling Christian community in the RoS must rely increasingly on its own meagre material resources. This 'simple weed', as the Episcopal Archbishop of Khartoum Ezekiel Kondo speaks of Christianity in the RoS, is in danger of being eradicated again, as it was in the early sixteenth century. But the Archbishop does not foresee defeat for the church in the War of Visions. 'We strongly reject the notion', he declared, 'that … there is only one religion, there is only one language [and] there is only one culture'. He furthermore prophesied that 'our children and grandchildren will be here for the next 100 years to come and beyond'. Few Sudanese Christians, despite their many trials and tribulations, think otherwise.

Bibliography

Copnal, James, *A Poisonous Thorn in our Hearts: Sudan and South Sudan's Bitter and Incomplete Divorce* (London: Hurst, 2014).

Deng, Francis M., *War of Visions: Conflict of Identities in the Sudan* (Washington, DC: Brookings Institution Press, 1995).

Guarak, Mawut Achiecque Mach, *Integration and Fragmentation of the Sudan: An African Renaissance* (Bloomington, IN: Author House, 2011).

Sanderson, L. P. and N. Sanderson, *Education, Religion and Politics in Southern Sudan 1899–1964* (London: Ithaca Press, 1981).

Wheeler, Andrew, 'Christianity in Sudan', in Zablon Nthamburi (ed.), *From Mission to Church: A Handbook of Christianity in East Africa* (Nairobi: Uzima Press, 1991), 37–80.

Egypt

Samuel Tadros

Egyptian Christians are called Copts. The word is derived from the Greek word for Egypt, *Aigyptios*. The number of Copts in Egypt is a highly politicised and contested issue, with no reliable figures available, though 8–10% of the population is the most likely, making Copts the largest Christian community in the Middle East.

Christianity was introduced in the country at the hands of Saint Mark the Evangelist, who, according to tradition, established the Church of Alexandria and was martyred in the city in AD 68. Christianity quickly spread from Alexandria to the countryside, with Christians constituting a majority of the population by the end of the third century. Successive waves of Roman persecution left their mark on the community, with the Church of Alexandria acquiring a reputation as the Church of the Martyrs. Recognising martyrdom as the cornerstone of its identity, the Church of Alexandria chose the beginning of the reign of the Emperor Diocletian, the worst oppressor of the church, in 284 as the starting point of the Coptic calendar known as the Calendar of the Martyrs.

By late antiquity, the Church of Alexandria emerged as one of the pillars of Christianity. The Catechetical School of Alexandria became one of the most important centres of theology under the leadership of Clement of Alexandria and Origen. In Egypt, numerous Christian traditions and sects were born, from Gnosticism to Arianism, and successive Coptic popes played an instrumental role in the theological disputes that ravaged the early church, with Saints Athanasius and Cyril I emerging as the key defenders of Christianity against heresies in the Councils of Nicaea and Ephesus. During the same period, the deserts of Egypt gave birth to Christian monasticism at the hands of Saint Anthony the Great and took a collective organised form in monasteries at the hands of Saint Pachomius. Attracting visitors from across the Roman world, the stories of Egypt's Desert Fathers would give birth to adoptions across the Christian world.

In 451 the dispute in the Council of Chalcedon over the natures of Christ led to a split in the universal church that proved irreparable. As a result, two competing patriarchs emerged in Alexandria, with the majority of Egyptians following their pope, Dioscorus I, and his successors forming what later became known as the Coptic Orthodox Church of Alexandria. A minority, referred to as Melkites, followed the competing Greek Orthodox Patriarch of Alexandria. The struggles between the two churches led to waves of persecution and deep bitterness and mistrust between both halves of the Christian world that continued until the modern era and that have limited attempts at rapprochement and unity.

The Arab/Muslim invasion of Egypt in 641 created a wall of separation between the country's Christians and the rest of the Christian world, allowing the Coptic Church to solidify its position as the national and dominant church of Egypt as its Greek Orthodox competitor continued to decline. Under the rule of Islam, Egypt's Christians were governed by the rules of dhimmitude, which tolerated their existence as a protected, yet second-class, community. Christians and other non-Muslims were forced to pay a yearly tax called *jizya*, restrictions were put on the building of churches and Christians were often required to wear specifically coloured clothes as a form of differentiation, as well as being barred from carrying arms or riding horses. Attempts to rid the civil service of Christians were launched throughout the centuries as the majority of the population became Muslim, often leading to persecution. The Muslim rulers often attempted to control the clergy as a means of controlling the community and influencing the behaviour of Ethiopia's rulers, given their control over the Nile's source. As a result, the lives of Copts under the rule of Islam witnessed successive waves of persecution followed by years of tranquillity.

Egypt likely became a Muslim-majority country by the tenth century, while Mamluk persecutions in the fourteenth century led to the steep decline of the Coptic community to its modern size. Conversion to Islam was a slow process, driven by a variety of causes, including conviction, persecution, the heavy tax burden of the *jizya* and advancement opportunities, as well as slow assimilation among the majority Muslim population. Besides losing a majority of its followers throughout the centuries, the

Christianity in Egypt, 1970 and 2015

	1970		2015		Average annual growth rate (%), 1970–2015
Tradition	Population	%	Population	%	
Christians	4,574,000	13.1%	7,673,000	8.4%	1.2%
Anglicans	1,000	0.0%	2,000	0.0%	1.6%
Independents	45,600	0.1%	118,000	0.1%	2.1%
Orthodox	4,252,000	12.2%	7,305,000	8.0%	1.2%
Protestants	137,000	0.4%	487,000	0.5%	2.9%
Catholics	139,000	0.4%	260,000	0.3%	1.4%
Evangelicals	102,000	0.3%	394,000	0.4%	3.1%
Pentecostals	43,000	0.1%	571,000	0.6%	5.9%
Total population	**34,809,000**	**100.0%**	**91,508,000**	**100.0%**	**2.2%**

Source: Todd M. Johnson and Gina A. Zurlo (eds), *World Christian Database* (Leiden/Boston: Brill), accessed March 2017.

Coptic Church had to adapt to changing circumstances by moving the papacy to Cairo in the middle of the eleventh century and adopting Arabic instead of Coptic as the language of liturgical readings in the middle of the twelfth century.

The encounter with modernity in the form of a French invasion in 1798 slowly led to changes in the conditions of the Coptic community. With restrictions on their advancement removed, many Copts rose to important positions in Egypt during the nineteenth and twentieth centuries, though their rise was often met with resentment by the majority. Modernity, however, posed significant challenges to the Coptic Church, as Catholic and Protestant missionaries began their work in the country, leading to the birth of the current denominational division in Egypt.

The Coptic Orthodox Church

As an apostolic church, the Coptic Orthodox Church traces its lineage to Saint Mark, who is considered its first pope. The current pope, Tawadros II, is the 118th in that sequence. The church's highest authority is the Holy Synod, currently composed of 125 bishops and the pope, who in traditional Coptic understanding is merely the first among equals. Until the 1970s that understanding prevailed, with the synod composed of only 20 bishops, making each a powerful figure within the church. Pope Shenouda III's (pope 1971–2012) practice of dividing dioceses following the death of their bishops and consecrating general bishops as assistants to the pope significantly diminished the synod's powers, making the pope the undisputed leader.

The Coptic clergy is divided into married clergy serving in the world and monks in the monasteries, with the latter being the pool from which bishops and a pope are chosen. The rationale behind having married priests has been to make them closer to normal life and problems as they take confessions. In the last few decades, however, monks have been increasingly sent out as priests, especially serving diaspora churches that cannot afford the costs of a priest and his family. The decline in Coptic monasticism throughout the centuries began to be reversed from 1948, when the first two university graduates were consecrated as monks, leading to the revival of abandoned monasteries and the establishment of new ones. There are around 30 Coptic monasteries today and more than 1,600 monks. Today's Coptic monastery is a flourishing small city in the middle of the desert, with monks working in land reclamation, cattle raising and carpentry. The modern monastery has become not merely a religious pilgrimage site for Copts, but also a centre of their identity as a unique people.

The church is in full communion with other Oriental Orthodox Churches in Armenia, India, Eritrea, Ethiopia and Syria, forming the

Oriental Orthodox family of churches. This full communion has resulted in numerous conferences at the top leadership levels, though grassroots cooperation between the churches remains weak outside of the lands of immigration. Dialogues have been launched with the Catholic Church, Eastern Orthodox Churches and the Anglican Church in order to bridge the gaps between the various denominations. A joint declaration between Pope Shenouda III and Catholic Pope Paul VI in 1973 solved the original dispute over the nature of Christ, though other differences that emerged over the course of centuries remain. Attempts at union with Eastern Orthodox Churches have moved further, although they continue to stumble over the question of past excommunications of Coptic saints such as Dioscorus I. In 2001 an agreement was signed with the Greek Orthodox Patriarchate of Alexandria to mutually recognise baptisms and marriages. The push for closer ties with other churches has acquired a new urgency under Pope Tawadros II, who visited the Vatican at the beginning of his papacy and is actively pushing for unifying Christmas and Easter dates.

As a traditionalist apostolic church, the Coptic Orthodox Church believes and practises the seven sacraments. Baptism and Confirmation are given at an early age, 40 days for boys and 80 days for girls, and baptised children partake in the Eucharist. Confession is also encouraged at a young age and is practised very frequently. Coptic boys are often consecrated at the lowest diaconal rank, Epsaltos, at a very early age. The lack of female deaconesses has been a source of controversy in recent years as women in the Coptic diaspora challenge their ecclesial exclusion. In Egypt, prayers are conducted in Arabic and Coptic, with the latter used more frequently in hymns. In the diaspora, the language of the local country is used in prayers and Coptic in hymns. The Coptic Orthodox Church venerates saints, with the Coptic Book of Saints, Synexarium, recognising all pre-schism saints and including some later ones. The process of canonisation is at the discretion of the Holy Synod. The last two saints canonised were Pope Kyrillos VI (1902–71) and Deacon Habib Girgis (1876–1951). Copts are deeply attached to their saints, with their icons found not only in churches but also in homes and carried in wallets. The most popular saints are the Virgin Mary, St George, St Mercurius, St Mina and St Demiana. Local celebrations of these and other saints are important dates in the Coptic calendar and their shrines attract hundreds of thousands of visitors.

By the time of the French invasion of Egypt, the Coptic Church had been in a state of decline for centuries. This was reversed at the hands of Pope Kyrillos IV (pope 1854–61), known as the Father of Reform, who opened modern schools to educate his flock (including young girls), imported a printing press and started training priests. His efforts were continued by Saint Habib Girgis, who laid the foundations of Sunday schools and rebuilt the theological school as an institution to educate future leaders of the church. Both efforts were carried on in the 1940s and 1950s by a generation of educated men and women within the Sunday School Movement, many of whom were later consecrated as priests and monks and in time bishops and pope. Under Pope Kyrillos VI, the young teachers of the Sunday schools finally began to take control of the church and revive it. The result has been a deep spiritual flourishing that continues to the present. Today, Copts are heavily involved in their churches, with hundreds of thousands of Copts serving in various capacities. A similar revival has taken place culturally, with traditional Coptic iconography revived by Isaac Fanous (1919–2007), who pioneered Neo-Coptic Art. Historical artefacts are housed in the Coptic Museum in Cairo. Attempts at reviving the Coptic language have been less successful. While for centuries the study of Copts and their language, manuscripts and traditions has been undertaken solely by Westerners, today a new generation of Copts are actively participating in scholarly studies of their heritage inside the church and through independent organisations such as the Orthodox Patristic Centre and the Saint Cyril Society. There has also been a growth of non-church civil society organisations that work in various charity and development fields, such as Coptic Orphans, as well as Coptic television channels.

Non-Coptic Denominations

While the Melkite community never entirely disappeared from Egypt, it remained small and weak throughout the centuries of Muslim rule. Beginning in the sixteenth century, the Roman Catholic Church attempted to bring the Coptic Church under its control. While early attempts focused on uniting both churches through a formal agreement signed by the Coptic pope acknowledging Rome's supremacy, the failure of such efforts led the Catholic Church by the eighteenth century to focus instead on converting Copts. This was aided by the important work that Catholic missionaries began performing in the country by the mid-seventeenth century, leading the Catholic community to slowly grow in number. The Catholic presence increased significantly following Napoleon's invasion of Egypt, as the country's modernisation efforts attracted Westerners and Levant Christians. By 1895, the head of the local Catholic community in Egypt was elevated to the patriarchate.

Today's Coptic Catholic Church is one of 23 Eastern Rite Catholic Churches in full communion with Rome. The size of the community remains small, with fewer than 200,000 followers, but its impact on the country is significant. Catholic schools run by various male and female monastic orders remain among the best in the country, and Catholic charity organisations play an important role in helping the country's impoverished.

Besides the Coptic Catholic Church, several other Eastern Rite Catholic churches are present in Egypt, such as the Maronite, Syrian Catholic, Greek Catholic, Chaldean Catholic and Armenian Catholic churches, as well as a Latin Catholic community. The 1952 military coup initiated a strong anti-foreigner campaign that severely impacted these churches, as many of their members left the country. Today, none of these churches maintains more than a few thousand members in Egypt, although some of their members continue to play an important role in the country's economy.

Historically, relations between the Coptic Orthodox Church and the Catholic Church in Egypt have been confrontational and bitter, with the Coptic Orthodox Church viewing Catholic conversion efforts as attempts to steal its followers, and both sides often engaged in theological disputes. Today, the relationship between the two communities has significantly improved, as they find themselves closer together in confronting both the Protestant and the Muslim challenges. In a historical first, Pope Tawadros II attended the enthronement of the Coptic Catholic Patriarch in 2013 as an indication of how close the two churches had become.

The Protestant presence in Egypt dates to the mid-nineteenth century, when missionaries from the American United Presbyterian Mission began arriving. Viewing the Coptic Church with its ancient rituals and theological positions as beyond redemption, they focused on converting Copts to Protestantism. Their work was aided by the first widely printed translation of the Bible into Arabic, completed in Beirut by Protestant missionaries in 1865. Initially the community grew much more slowly than its Catholic counterpart, as members often went back and forth between it and the Orthodox Church. The Protestant missionaries posed nonetheless a colossal challenge to the Coptic Orthodox Church, with their message of personal salvation, attack on church hierarchy and focus on Scripture, a message the Orthodox Church found alien and thus was unprepared to counter. Less successful were Protestant efforts in the field of education, which were never able to compete with their Catholic counterparts.

Today's Protestant community in Egypt is composed of 16 groups, the most prominent of which is the Evangelical Presbyterian Church – Synod of the Nile, followed by the Christian Brethren and the Assemblies of God, with smaller Pentecostal and Methodist communities. There is also an Anglican community numbering several thousand. There is continuous tension between the Anglican Church and the Synod of the Nile, which aims to bring the former under its jurisdiction. The exact number of Protestants in Egypt is impossible to determine given the diversity of the denominations they follow and the fluidity of many of these followers' relationships with the various churches. It is not uncommon to find people attending Protestant churches but having baptisms and marriages conducted in the

Orthodox Church. The Coptic Evangelical Organisation for Social Services plays an important role in development work among Egypt's poor, while the Bible Society of Egypt continues to be the main distributor of the Bible in the country. Several Arabic Protestant television channels are accessible in Egypt via satellite, and Protestant praise teams such as the Better Life Team are highly popular among Christians across denominations.

Relations between the Protestant and Orthodox churches in Egypt continue to be tense. The Coptic Orthodox Church resents continued Protestant attempts to convert Copts and is often fighting what it perceives to be the infiltration of Protestant ideas within its own ranks, which has led to high-profile excommunications of several Orthodox priests and monks in recent years. Especially worrying for the Orthodox Church are Protestant efforts to target youth through a more easily accessible church culture that incorporates Western music in its services. Yearly Protestant youth conferences are often the occasion of sermons by Coptic Orthodox bishops and priests warning their flock against attending such events.

The Greek Orthodox Patriarchate of Alexandria was born out of the split in the Egyptian church following the Council of Chalcedon in 451, with its patriarch ranking second after that of Constantinople in the Eastern Orthodox family of churches. Comprising a small community throughout the centuries, with many of its patriarchs residing in Constantinople, the church began to grow due to Greek migration to Egypt in the nineteenth century. Today, the church maintains a small following in the country, mainly composed of people of Greek or Levantine origin. The famous Saint Catherine Monastery of Sinai is Greek Orthodox but independent of the Patriarchate of Alexandria, being run by the autocephalous Church of Sinai.

Among the Muslims

Apart from a cross tattooed on the wrist of a Christian, or a Muslim woman's veil, in physical appearances it is impossible to distinguish Christians from Muslims in Egypt. Egypt's Muslims are simply the descendants of Copts who converted to Islam throughout the centuries, with a small addition of Arab and Turkish blood. Copts and Muslims have also lived side by side for centuries, with Egypt hardly witnessing the kind of geographical divisions or ghettoes associated with minorities in the rest of the Middle East. Copts historically have been more concentrated in the south of the country, given both its distance from the centre of authority – and hence persecution – and the destruction of the Coptic presence in the Nile Delta following the defeat of the successive Bashmurian revolts by the mid-ninth century. This is no longer the case, however, as urbanisation and the Islamist insurgency in the south during the 1980s and 1990s forced many

Copts to seek protection in Cairo. Having lived side by side for centuries, the relationship between Christians and Muslims was often fraught with persecution and discrimination, but there were also periods of coexistence and assimilation.

The arrival of European powers and the attempts at modernisation by Egypt's rulers in the nineteenth century liberated Copts from the shackles of dhimmitude, with the dress codes last imposed in 1817 and the *jizya* abolished in 1855, and opened for them the doors to jobs from which they had been barred, modern education and advancement in society. In 1908 a Copt, Boutros Ghali Pasha, was named Egypt's prime minister, though his appointment led to Muslim anger and his assassination. Coptic demands for equality in education, government funding and jobs took shape in a Coptic conference in 1911 but were rejected by their fellow countrymen in a counter-conference. The high point in the two communities' relationship came in 1919, when they joined together in demanding an end to British occupation. A flag with the crescent and the cross became the symbol of that national unity.

The relationship between Copts and the presidents who have ruled Egypt since the 1952 military coup has been mixed. Gamal Abdel Nasser had little interest in the community, as his gaze was fixed on a role in the wider Arab world. His economic policies negatively impacted a community that had excelled in the private sector as a result of being denied equality in public service. Copts had little appetite for an Arab identity in Egypt, which, unlike Levantine Christians, they never embraced. Yet the relationship between church and state remained cordial throughout his rule. Under President Anwar el-Sadat the relationship between church and state and the two men heading them came to a dramatic showdown. Sadat's conservative nature, his attempt to counter leftist opposition by aiding the Islamists, and the Islamist awakening in the universities that had started in the late 1960s were all sources of conflict. An attempt by Sadat to introduce Sharia law in Egypt was met with defiance by Pope Shenouda III, who had always believed the church had a role in defending the political rights of its followers. The inevitable showdown resulted in Sadat removing the state's recognition of Shenouda III as pope and banishing him to a monastery.

Under President Hosni Mubarak, the church and state worked to mend their relationship. Out of fear of the Islamist alternative and with Sadat gone, Pope Shenouda III emerged from the monastery in 1985 a changed man and maintained good relations with the state. His endorsement of Mubarak's rule continued until the very end, despite numerous disagreements over discrimination against Copts and especially problems related to the building of churches. Some Cairo-based Coptic youths supported the revolution of 2011, as did the Protestant community; however, the larger community remained anxious that it would give way to Islamist ascendancy. Their worst fears became reality as the security collapse that followed the revolution and the rise of Islamists on the national and local levels threatened the Coptic community's existence. The symbol of that threat became the attack on the centre of Coptic Christianity, Saint Mark Cathedral, where the bones of the church's founder are buried and where its current pope resides. Copts and their religious hierarchies enthusiastically endorsed President Mohamed Morsi's removal by the military in July 2013 and have supported President Abdel Fatah al-Sisi since, despite enduring the largest attack on their churches since the fourteenth century in August 2013 and despite the regime's failure to address their grievances.

Coptic grievances can be divided into four categories: legal restrictions, state discrimination, societal discrimination and violent attacks. Legal restrictions include limitations on building churches, with new churches requiring a presidential decree and the renovation of old ones approval by the governor, which is frequently not granted. A new church building law was passed in 2016 and endorsed by all of Egypt's denominations, though many Coptic activists raised concerns regarding its restrictive language. Legal restrictions also include the imposition of Sharia-based rules on civil issues such as inheritance laws.

State discrimination is manifested in the near-complete exclusion of Copts from positions of authority in the government, with Coptic representation in the military and police forces capped at an unofficial 1% and completely denied in the intelligence service. This is also true in other sectors of the state bureaucracy, including the complete exclusion of Copts from university leadership positions such as presidents and deans. State discriminatory policies are also evident in the near-complete exclusion of Coptic history from the educational system and the absence of Copts and their interests from the state-controlled media.

While Copts and Muslims continue to live together, societal discrimination against Copts has increased in the last few decades, with Copts increasingly denied access to things as diverse as sports clubs and jobs. The result of their increasing exclusion from the public sphere has been an exodus of Copts from the church and the church's attempt to provide for them. For the Copts, the church is not only for spiritual worship, but also for cultural, social and sports activities and leisure.

Attacks on Copts have increased dramatically in the past few decades, and especially since the 2011 revolution. Attacks usually take place following a rumour of Christians building a church, a Christian having an affair with a Muslim woman or a Christian insulting Islam. In all three cases Coptic homes and shops in the particular village are looted and burned.

Police absence and failure to prevent the attacks are followed by the state's unwillingness to punish the perpetrators, instead resorting to reconciliation sessions that often impose the demands of the angry mob on the Copts. This lack of legal punishment has created a culture of impunity that has become a culture of encouragement.

The Coptic Diaspora

Beginning in the fourth century, Ethiopia was part of the jurisdiction of the Church of Alexandria, with the Coptic Orthodox pope consecrating an Egyptian monk as bishop of the country. This relationship continued until the twentieth century, when the two churches separated. Today, only the Eritrean Orthodox Church follows the Orthodox Church of Alexandria, though recent political developments have put the relationship in jeopardy. Besides this historical relationship, the Coptic Orthodox Church was confined within the borders of Egypt, maintaining only a small presence in Jerusalem. Isolated from the rest of Christendom for centuries, the Coptic Orthodox Church developed its identity as the national church of Egypt, which profoundly affected its theology. The Egyptian invasion of Sudan at the beginning of the nineteenth century opened the gates for the growth of the Coptic presence there but left little impact on the church's identity.

This would dramatically change in the 1950s with the beginning of substantial Coptic emigration, driven by dwindling economic and career opportunities in Egypt as well as persecution and the growth of the Islamist threat. Initial migration in the 1950s and 1960s to Europe was soon overtaken by migration to the USA, Canada and Australia. Another destination for non-permanent emigration was oil-producing Arab countries in the Gulf as well as Libya. Determined to keep its followers, the Coptic Orthodox Church consecrated its first priest to serve in the West in 1964. Today, the Coptic Orthodox Church maintains more than 550 churches in the West, served by 30 bishops and hundreds of priests, with Coptic communities growing in places as far away as Latin America, Japan and Fiji. This growth in numbers and churches has been mirrored in the establishment of monasteries and theological seminaries to serve the diaspora community's needs.

The growth of a huge diaspora community has led to significant developments within the Orthodox Church. Assistance from other Christian churches to the Coptic Church in the initial phase of the establishment of its diaspora presence led to more cordial relations, cooperation through the World Council of Churches and the growth of communal interest in Christian unity, in terms of both doctrines and religious holidays. The Coptic Orthodox Church's minority position in the West and the lack of theological and spiritual literature in foreign languages forced Copts to depend on Eastern Orthodox literature, leading to the growth of a pan-Orthodox spirit in the diaspora; for instance, pan-Orthodox student groups have sprung up in American universities.

In the West, the Coptic Church is confronted with societal challenges from which its condition in Egypt had sheltered it, such as drugs, gay marriage, abortion and open-market competition among Christian denominations, new-age religions and atheism. Liberated from restrictions on missionary work and conversion within Egypt, the Orthodox Church abroad developed a strong missionary spirit, reaching out to local non-Egyptian communities. Consequently, the Coptic Orthodox Church has been increasingly forced to attempt to reframe its theology and appeal in universal terms, with varying degrees of success around the globe. The challenge of transformation from the national church of Egypt into a universal church continues to be one of the most important issues facing the church in the twenty-first century, as the balance inside the church continues to shift in favour of the diaspora church. The process of adoption is still ongoing and has witnessed conflict between traditionalists insisting on maintaining Coptic identity, traditions and rituals, and modernisers fearful of losing the next generation in the diaspora.

Egyptian Catholic and Evangelical migration to the West has had a lesser impact on both communities' internal development. Egyptian Catholics migrating to the West were absorbed within the wider Latin Rite network in the West or, to a lesser extent, within existing Eastern Rite Catholic Churches in the West, while Evangelicals either joined local Evangelical denominations or created Arab-Evangelical churches in the West, mixing with Palestinian and Levantine migrants.

Another significant development for the Coptic Orthodox Church has been the initiation of its missionary work in sub-Saharan Africa. Beginning in 1976 the Orthodox Church, with the consecration of Bishop Antonius Markos as Bishop for African Affairs, began establishing churches across the continent, where its appeal as a local African church and its lack of association with the heritage of colonialism led to significant success in attracting Africans. Today, the Coptic Orthodox Church has around 0.5 million followers in sub-Saharan Africa served by around 100 churches. The Greek Orthodox Patriarchate of Alexandria has enjoyed a similar expansion in Africa, though the number of converts has been smaller.

The Future of Christianity in Egypt

The decline of Christianity in the Middle East has continued with alarming pace in the past few decades, and Egypt is no exception. Yet despite huge waves of emigration and the persecution of Copts in Egypt, it is unlikely, barring complete state collapse, that the Christian presence in the country will be eradicated in the near future, as the community numbers over 7 million. More likely is the slow decline of the community as its better-off members continue to emigrate, leaving their less fortunate friends behind. The continued emigration will eventually lead to a shift in power within the Coptic Orthodox Church as the Coptic diaspora grows in number and power, impacting the ancient church's theology and worldview.

Bibliography

Guirguis, Magdi and Nelly Van Doorn-Harder, *The Emergence of the Modern Coptic Papacy* (Cairo: American University in Cairo Press, 2011).

Hassan, S. S., *Christians Versus Muslims in Modern Egypt: The Century-Long Struggle for Coptic Equality* (Oxford: Oxford University Press, 2003).

Meinardus, Otto F. A., *Two Thousand Years of Coptic Christianity* (Cairo: American University in Cairo Press, 2013).

Tadros, Mariz, *Copts at the Crossroads* (Cairo: American University in Cairo Press, 2013).

Tadros, Samuel, *Motherland Lost: The Egyptians and Coptic Quest for Modernity* (Stanford, CA: Hoover Institution Press, 2013).

Cyprus

Anastasia Yiangou

Cyprus, situated in the eastern Mediterranean, was one of the first lands to receive the Christian message, in the first century, and has since maintained a firm Christian presence. The vast majority of the population comprises Orthodox Christians. Other Christian denominations, most of which have a longstanding historical presence on the island, include the Armenians, Roman Catholics, Maronites and Anglicans.

Cyprus has come under Roman, Byzantine, Frankish, Venetian and Ottoman rule. In 1878 the British arrived on the island and, following an armed struggle for union with Greece (1955–9), the island eventually became independent in 1960; Archbishop Makarios III served as the Republic's first president. The constitution of the Republic of Cyprus recognised two communities on the island: the Greek and the Turkish. Armenians, Maronites and Latins, who were recognised by the constitution as religious groups, were given the option to decide which of the two communities they would join; all opted to join the Greek Cypriots. In 1974, following a coup d'état against Archbishop Makarios, Turkey invaded the island and occupied its northern part; thousands of people were killed, went missing or were expelled and displaced from their homes. The Republic of Cyprus – a member of the European Union since 2004 – remains the only entity on the island recognised by the United Nations and internationally, while a Republic of Northern Cyprus, illegally proclaimed in 1983, is recognised by Turkey alone. Religious freedom is protected in the Republic of Cyprus: all religious groups have the freedom to teach, practise, worship and observe according to the United Nations Universal Declaration of Human Rights.

According to the 2011 census, Cyprus has a population of 856,960, the great majority of whom belong to the Orthodox Church. Between 2001 and 2011 the percentage of the population bearing a foreign (non-Cypriot) nationality rose from 9.4% to 20.3%. Unavoidably this has influenced the demographics of Christianity, increasing the general influence of non-Orthodox people on the island.

Orthodox Christians

The Church of Cyprus has its origins in the apostolic era, as the island was evangelised by Saints Paul and Barnabas in the first century. Christianity secured a firm hold in Cyprus at an early date, as exemplified by the many Cypriot saints attested during the early Christian and Byzantine periods. Due to its close proximity to Antioch, Cyprus was initially administered from its patriarchate until the mid-fourth century, when the Cypriot ecclesiastical hierarchy sought to disengage itself from the Arian leadership in Antioch. In 431, the Council of Ephesus recognised the autocephalous status of the Cypriot Church, making it one of the oldest such churches. Orthodoxy flourished in subsequent centuries, but beginning in the seventh century the island suffered from several Arab raids, which did not leave church life unaffected. During the tenth century the Byzantines liberated the island and Orthodoxy was reinforced in the following years, while this period also witnessed the foundation of many churches and great monasteries on the island. In 1191 Richard the Lionheart took over the island en route to the Holy Land and bequeathed control of the island to the Knights Templar. Following the brief period of Templar occupation of Cyprus, Richard sold the island to the deposed King of Jerusalem, Guy de Lusignan. This signalled the onset of Frankish rule, during which the Latin Church was also founded. The authority of the Orthodox Church was undermined during Frankish (1191–1489) and Venetian rule (1489–1571). In 1571 the Ottomans took over, abolished the Latin Church and recognised the Orthodox Church as sole representative of the Christian population. The archbishop's role as the Ethnarch (protector and leader of the nation) had been shaped by the various occupations the island suffered over many centuries. In 1821, following the onset of the Greek War of Independence, the Ottomans hanged Archbishop Kyprianos along with many other members of the island's Greek Christian intelligentsia and clergy, alleging that they intended to join the revolution. Following these events the church in general and the office of the archbishop in particular

Christianity in Cyprus, 1970 and 2015

Tradition	1970 Population	1970 %	2015 Population	2015 %	Average annual growth rate (%), 1970–2015
Christians	469,000	76.5%	822,000	70.5%	1.3%
Anglicans	6,000	1.0%	10,000	0.9%	1.1%
Independents	2,200	0.4%	8,500	0.7%	3.0%
Orthodox	450,000	73.4%	765,000	65.7%	1.2%
Protestants	3,100	0.5%	5,900	0.5%	1.4%
Catholics	6,400	1.0%	11,300	1.0%	1.3%
Evangelicals	2,800	0.5%	6,300	0.5%	1.9%
Pentecostals	540	0.1%	13,900	1.2%	7.5%
Total population	**614,000**	**100.0%**	**1,165,000**	**100.0%**	**1.4%**

Source: Todd M. Johnson and Gina A. Zurlo (eds), *World Christian Database* (Leiden/Boston: Brill), accessed March 2017.

accrued an iconic significance in the collective Greek Cypriot consciousness. The arrival of the British in 1878 signalled the onset of a more liberal era, although church–state relations eventually became strained, particularly after the 1920s, because of the Greek Cypriot demand for union of the island with Greece (*enosis*). Following a national anticolonial struggle against the British during 1955–9, with the church at its forefront, Cyprus was declared an independent republic in 1960. Archbishop Makarios III, a seminal figure of the twentieth-century history of Cyprus, served as president of the Republic until his death in 1977. The Archbishop of the Nova Justiniana and all Cyprus (the formal title of the Archbishop of the Orthodox Church) is an influential figure in Cypriot society and politics.

For many years church administration was divided between four metropolitan seats: the archbishopric in Nicosia and the bishoprics of Kyrenia, Kition and Paphos. In 1973 two new seats were founded, for Limassol and Morphou. In 2007 the number of the Holy Synod members was further increased: the current archbishop, Chrysostomos II, who was elevated to the throne in 2006, increased the number of metropolitan regions as well as the episcopates so as to facilitate the convention of a Holy Synod, which, according to the Charter of the Church of Cyprus, governs the church. The inability to convene a Holy Synod brought the church more than once to an impasse during the twentieth and twenty-first centuries. The latest example was the inability to convene a congress between 2003 and 2006 when, owing to illness, the former Archbishop Chrysostomos I was unable to fulfil his religious duties. Having been elected to succeed Makarios III in 1977 and serving the Church of Cyprus during critical times, Chrysostomos I was dedicated, among other aims, to the safeguarding of the Orthodox faith and the promotion of inter-Orthodox and inter-Christian relations and succeeded in inspiring his people, especially those who had suffered as a result of the 1974 Turkish invasion.

Monasteries continue to play an important part in the daily life of Orthodox Christians as places of pilgrimage and in inspiring devotion. The nine active monasteries for men (including Kykkos, Stavrovouni, Machairas, St Neophytos, Chrysoroyiatissa and Trooditissa) and 16 for women (including St Nicholas Patron of Cats, St Kendeas, St George Alamanos and St Heraklidios) all form popular places of pilgrimage. Numerous churches and monasteries are also situated in the occupied areas. These are, however, in a dilapidated condition.

Sacramental mysteries include baptism, chrismation, communion, confession, unction, matrimony and ordination. For the spiritual needs of the faithful, oral and written sermons are regularly delivered. Orthodox Christians venerate icons of Christ, the Theotokos (Virgin Mary, the 'Birth-giver of God') and the saints as a means of expressing their honour. The

Eucharistic service, called the divine liturgy, has a central role in church life and activities and marks the high point of sacramental life. It is conducted by clergy and laity in a celebratory manner, as are baptisms and weddings. There is significant attendance in churches on Sundays as well as on feast days and midweek services, although nowadays many – especially in the urban areas – attend church services only on feast days. Fasting and prayer continue to play an important role in Orthodox spiritual life in Cyprus. Although traditional fasting is probably not practised to the extent it was in previous decades, certain periods, such as Advent – the liturgical period preceding Christmas – and Lent and the Holy Week – which prepare the faithful for Easter (Pascha), the resurrection of Christ – are considered highly important. In general, Orthodoxy plays a dominant role in the life of Cypriot Christians and until perhaps 1974, when the island was a predominantly agricultural society, it was inextricably related to the everyday life of the faithful. Even though the rapid transformation of the economy and society has led to a reduction in the number of the faithful who practise their religious duties on a daily basis, the bonds of Cypriot Christians with the Orthodox Church remain very strong.

The Church of Cyprus makes a major contribution to most aspects of Cypriot society. The various charitable institutions that function under church supervision form one aspect of this contribution. Such institutions include charitable fraternities, hostels for the elderly, children's campsites and orphanages. Furthermore, the church has contributed, and continues to contribute, significantly to the foundation of schools and libraries, both in the main towns of the island as well as in the rural areas. Moreover, it provides financial assistance to poor students, supporting through a scheme of scholarships their studies at a graduate level and offering accommodation to students studying abroad. This is the case in Athens, where a boarding house operates for Cypriot female university students who face financial constraint. Moreover, since 2013 – when Cyprus, like other parts of the world, has been experiencing an economic crisis – the church has been at the forefront of helping families who have suffered as a result of the profound financial difficulties. Similar actions for the relief of the faithful are undertaken in each archdiocese and metropolitan region.

The Orthodox Church is the founder of the Archbishop Makarios III Foundation, which has a deep impact on the cultural life of Cypriots as it houses the Byzantine Museum, a gallery and a library that hosts an important collection of rare books and journals relating to theology as well as a rich collection of books on Cypriot studies. The Foundation also includes an important nursing centre. The archbishopric is home to a conservation centre of ancient and rare icons, books and manuscripts. The Phaneromeni Library in Nicosia, one of the most important libraries on the island, was founded by and is maintained by the church. The church is also responsible for the publication of a monthly journal, *Apostolos Barnabas*. Sermons and religious programmes are broadcast via the radio and television channels. Finally, regular catechesis schools, schools of Byzantine music as well as ecclesiastical museums are in operation in the archdiocese and metropolitan regions.

The church assumes responsibility for the spiritual as well as material welfare of its clergy. This holds true in the case of the Apostle Barnabas Seminary, which provides full training for the priesthood. Furthermore, the Theological School of the Church of Cyprus was established in 2015 with the purpose of offering theological education at university level. The School began its operation with a four-year undergraduate programme, its mission being 'to educate people who will be able to serve the ecclesiastic, spiritual, social, cultural, educational and scientific mission of the church in the modern world and to serve the ministry of the church in general both locally and at the inter-Orthodox, inter-Christian and inter-religious level'.

The Orthodox Church is also renowned for sending many priests to serve in missionary capacities in other Orthodox communities abroad. During and since the era of Archbishop Makarios III, the Orthodox Church has been active in the mission to Africa. Cypriot donations built the seminary for East Africa at Nairobi, and the current Bishop of Kenya, Makarios Tyllirides, is himself a Cypriot.

The Orthodox Church retains good relations with all of its sister Orthodox Churches as well as with all other Christian denominations on the island. Since the mid-twentieth century it has been represented at most conferences of the World Council of Churches. It has been a member of the Council of European Churches since 1959 and is a founding member of the Council of Churches of the Middle East. The Church of Cyprus, led by Archbishop Chrysostomos II, participated at the Pan-Orthodox Council (Holy and Great Synod of the Orthodox Church) held in Crete in June 2016, the first to have been held since the schism of 1054.

Roman Catholics

Traditionally, the Roman Catholics of Cyprus were members mainly of the Latin religious group (Cypriot Roman Catholics of European or Levantine descent). Despite the fact that in recent decades the number of members of the Latin group has declined, the Roman Catholic presence on the island has been significantly reinforced. This is due to the arrival in Cyprus of many people of Catholic faith from Europe, Asia and Latin America. The Latin group has a longstanding historical presence on Cyprus. The founding of the Latin Church in the island dates back to the twelfth century with the arrival of the Franks following Guy de Lusignan's purchase of the island. The Latin Church was established on Cyprus in 1196. From that time the Latin archbishopric was based in Nicosia and there were three bishoprics, in Famagusta, Limassol and Paphos. The Roman Catholics exercised strong influence on the island during Frankish and Venetian rule. The conquest of the island by the Ottomans in 1571, however, resulted in the dissolution of the Latin Church, since it was the Orthodox Church that the Porte recognised as the only representative Christian Church on the island. During the British period (1878–1960), assisted by the general liberal administration and religious tolerance, the small but prosperous Latin community was strengthened. Today, the Latins (as with Maronites and Armenians) have an elected representative in the House of Representatives who acts as their link with the government.

Since the mid-nineteenth century, a resident Franciscan Vicar General has been serving in Cyprus, and the vicariate is housed in its own monastery in Nicosia. The Latin Catholic Church in Cyprus has four parishes (Nicosia, Larnaca, Limassol, Paphos) and comes under the Latin Patriarchate of Jerusalem. The Vicar General, since 2013 Fr Jerzy Kraj, further serves as the ex-officio representative in Cyprus of the pro-nuncio of the Holy See in Jerusalem. The major churches and chapels in operation include the Holy Cross Cathedral in Nicosia, the Catholic Church of St Mary of Graces in Larnaca and St Catherine's Church in Limassol. Following permission granted by the Orthodox Church, mass is also held at Orthodox churches in various places at Paphos, Limassol and Famagusta districts. Furthermore, as with all other Christian denominations' places of worship, Latin churches are also located in the occupied areas of Cyprus, such as Kyrenia and Famagusta. In Kyrenia the Church of St Elizabeth of Hungary stands out; mass is regularly celebrated there by the Latin priests of Nicosia. Other churches in the occupied areas remain either in a pitiful state or have been demolished by the Turks.

The first papal visit to Cyprus, in June 2010, was an event of major significance for the Catholic community and indeed for the island. During his visit Pope Benedict XVI prayed at the Pillar of St Paul in Paphos and was received by the president of the Republic and the archbishop of the Orthodox Church. He was further received at the Latin Church of the Holy Cross and the Maronite Church, where he met Latins and Maronites.

Over the years, the Roman Catholics of the Latin community were fully integrated into Cypriot society and contributed to all aspects of life. One notable example is in education, since the oldest school on the island, Terra Santa, was established as a boys' school by Franciscan monks in 1646. In 2013 Terra Santa (which now offers comprehensive education) and the University of Cyprus signed an agreement that recognised the Terra Santa School as a prototype and experimental model school of the latter. Other examples include the St Mary School in Limassol, which was founded in 1922 by Franciscan nuns. St Mary remains a popular school, well known for placing emphasis on the learning of foreign languages. The Catholic Church also supports the operation of a kindergarten at Mesa Chorio village in Paphos District, attended by children of various nationalities.

The contribution and impact of the Catholic Church in Cyprus stretches beyond education. The church is renowned for supporting centres for the protection of foreign workers as well as those in need. A notable example is St Joseph's Shelter of Foreign Workers, which operates in Nicosia. In the same city one can also find the oldest humanitarian association, St Anthony's Benevolent Society (founded in 1926). Another example can be found in Limassol, where the Catholic Church of St Catherine established the Shelter of St Francis, aiming to protect foreign workers, as well as the charity organisation of St Catherine. In Larnaca, the Association of St Joseph, Protector of the Needy was established in 2011 serving similar goals. Most of these associations and shelters are financially supported by the government. The community also participates in the Caritas Benevolent Organisation – Society of Cyprus. Similarly, the Latin Youth Community was also established in 2002.

Although the community does not have its own mass media, the local parish monthly church newsletters and the bimonthly letter from the representative of the community in the House of Representatives promote closer contact between members. Many prominent figures in Cypriot society are members of the Latin community, such as Sylvain Béraud, a distinguished researcher and historian; Andreas Karayan, an internationally distinguished painter; and members of the Pietroni, Cirilli and the Mantovani families, who have served in various posts, including as Latin representatives to the House of Representatives.

The Latin Catholic community therefore, although small, has a significant role in Cypriot society and contributes to its development. In recent years the demographics of the Roman Catholics have been influenced firstly by an increase in marriages with Greek Cypriots and secondly by the arrival of thousands of Roman Catholic believers from various parts of the globe. Following the accession of Cyprus to the European Union in 2004, thousands of people of Roman Catholic faith from Europe (mainly eastern Europe but also the central and western parts) have arrived on the island. In addition, past decades have witnessed the arrival of people from Southeast Asia and Latin America. These people are mostly women who work for Cypriot families, foreign students and people who work in embassies or for the United Nations. Many of these have settled permanently on the island. Although it cannot quite be said that these have been fully integrated into Cypriot society, their presence has nevertheless helped bolster the existence of a multicultural environment of acceptance and tolerance on the island.

Maronites

Maronites are members of the Eastern Catholic Church. The beginnings of their religious movement can be traced to St Maron, a Syriac Christian monk of the fourth century. Their presence on Cyprus dates back to the seventh century, when, seeking safety from Arab raids, they fled to the island from Syria and Lebanon. Successive waves of Maronites followed in subsequent centuries, particularly during Frankish rule, when their settlement was encouraged so as to bolster the Catholic presence. As a result, the Maronite Archbishopric of Cyprus was established in 1316 with Nicosia as its seat. However, the hardships experienced during the Ottoman period forced many either to convert to Islam or to join the Orthodox Church. The Maronite archbishop himself was forced to flee the island for Lebanon, where the archbishopric was relocated in 1673. From 1768 the Vicar General represented the archbishop in Cyprus, and this remained so until 1988, when the Maronite archbishopric returned to Nicosia. The Maronite diocese belongs to the Maronite Patriarchate in Lebanon and is subject to the Holy See. The archbishop, therefore, is elected by the Holy Synod of the Maronite Church in Lebanon and is confirmed by the pope. The present archbishop, Joseph Soueif, was elected in 2008, having succeeded Archbishop Boutros Gemayel. The Maronite diocese is divided into 11 parishes served by the clergy. These are located in the occupied areas as well as in the major cities in the non-occupied part of the Republic of Cyprus.

The Maronite Cathedral of the Virgin Mary of Graces is situated in Nicosia; other places of worship can be found in Limassol (such as St Marina and St Charbel, the latter constructed in 2003). The Maronites have organised themselves so as to protect their existing churches but have also founded new ones, especially since the church constitutes a meeting point for the members scattered all over the island. Indeed, new monasteries have been constructed in the Nicosia District – the monasteries of Prophet Elias in Kotsiatis (2006) and St Rebecca in Nicosia (2007). In Larnaca the faithful attend mass at St Joseph's Latin Nunnery. In Paphos, following permission from the Orthodox bishopric, they have been using Orthodox churches, testimony to the cordial relations between Christian denominations on the island.

The Maronite liturgy has traditionally been celebrated in Aramaic, although nowadays there are also parts translated into Greek. The liturgy in the Maronite Church is the result of its historical evolution and development and its interaction with multiple cultural, intellectual and social trends. The liturgy belongs to the Antiochene tradition and is a West

Syro-Antiochene Rite. Great emphasis is placed on the catechesis of the faithful: the Maronite Church runs nine catechesis centres on the island. Furthermore, in 2009 the Theological Centre St Efraim was founded under the auspices of the Maronite Archbishopric of Cyprus.

The Maronites have a strong attachment to their land and have formed a quiet rural community. Before the 1974 Turkish invasion they were mainly based in the four Maronite villages of Kormakitis, Asomatos, Karpasha and Ayia Marina, all now part of occupied Cyprus. While most Maronites were forced to flee into the non-occupied areas, others opted to stay. Their number, however, has decreased from around 2,000 to 130. Although they form an integral part of Cypriot society, the Maronites continue to consider themselves a distinct community. Determined to preserve their cultural identity, they place special importance on the role of social organisations and cultural clubs, as well as on mass media, in order to facilitate their consolidation and retain their distinct characteristics. In 2010 an ecclesiastical museum was established with the help of the A. G. Leventis Foundation at St George Cathedral in Kormakitis, while in the same village a folkloric museum was founded with financial help from the United Nations Development Programme and the Republic of Cyprus. While Maronites are educated in Greek schools and speak Greek fluently they also have their own Arabic/Aramaic language (Cypriot Maronite Arabic, CMA), recognised in 2008 by the Republic of Cyprus as a minority language. The Ministry of Education and Culture has undertaken an effort to implement a structured policy for the revival and preservation of CMA.

Armenians

Tradition has it that the Apostles Thaddeus and Bartholomew founded the Armenian Church – hence the title 'Apostolic'. In general, the theology and dogma of the Armenian Apostolic Church are based on the Bible and the canons and the teachings of the great Church Fathers of the fourth and fifth centuries. It also shares the doctrines of the ancient Eastern churches as adopted by the Councils of Nicea (325) and Constantinople (381). The liturgy, conducted in classical Armenian, is based on the missals of St Gregory the Theologian, St Basil of Caesarea and St John Chrysostom, with the addition of Armenian hymns. The overwhelming majority of the Armenians in Cyprus belong to the Armenian Apostolic Orthodox Church. There are also a small number of Armenian Protestants and a smaller number of Armenian Catholics.

Although Armenian Cypriots today are mainly descendants of the Armenian genocide survivors, their presence on the island is witnessed as early as 578, during the Byzantine period. Armenians have made an important contribution to the island's growth and development, first as soldiers and later as merchants and landowners and finally as craftsmen, entrepreneurs and people of the arts, letters and sciences.

The Armenian Prelature of Cyprus was established in 973 and has since maintained a continuous and firm presence on the island. The Prelature, currently led by Archbishop Nareg Alemezian (2014), is under the jurisdiction of the Catholicosate of Cilicia. Administration is exercised by the Armenian Ethnarchy (Azkayin Ishkhanoutiun) through the Diocesan Council (Temagan Joghov) and the Administrative Council (Varchagan Joghov). There are local parish committees in Nicosia, Larnaca and Limassol, including the committee for Christian instruction and the ladies' committee. The Prelature's charter consists of 102 articles and in its present form applies as of 2010.

For many years the Armenian Prelature building was situated in the Armenian quarter of Nicosia, within the medieval walls of the city. Like many other Cypriots, Armenians were dislocated during the intercommunal clashes of 1963–4. A new Prelature building was established in the non-occupied area of Nicosia. By initiative of the former Archbishop Varoujan Hergelian (1997–2014) its basement was renovated so as to host a variety of communal, cultural and charity events. The most important places of worship are the Cathedral of the Virgin Mary (Sourp Asdvadzadzin) in Nicosia, the Church of St Stephen in Larnaca and the Church of St George in Limassol. Since 2008, following permission granted by the Orthodox Bishop, the Armenians of Paphos use the Chapel of St George at the village of Chloraka for their services. There are also several important religious monuments in occupied Cyprus. A notable example is the Gothic Cathedral of the Virgin Mary within the walled city of Nicosia, which formed the centre of Armenian religious life until 1963–4. The Cathedral was restored between 2009 and 2013 with the help of the Armenian Ethnarchy, the Office of the Armenian Representative and funding by the UNDP-ACT and USAID. Two other significant monuments in occupied Cyprus are the Church of the Virgin Mary of Ganchvor (the Caller or Summoner) (Sourp Asdvadzadzin Ganchvor) within the walls of Famagusta and St Makarios Monastery (Sourp Magar Magaravank). The latter – a renowned place of pilgrimage originally built by Copts around 1000 – is located on the Pentadaktylos mountain range. As with other Christian places of worship in the areas occupied by the Turks, the monastery is in a pitiful condition. Since 2007, at the initiative of the Armenian Ethnarchy, annual pilgrimages to the monastery take place.

Armenians have made a significant contribution to Cypriot society and culture and have placed great emphasis on education; the first Armenian school was founded in Nicosia as early as the 1870s. In Cyprus the Armenian elementary schools are named 'Nareg' in memory of the monk, theologian and philosopher Krikor Naregatsi. In 2005 the Nareg Gymnasium was founded in Nicosia. The education provided is trilingual (Armenian, Greek and English) and the curriculum is equivalent to that of Greek Cypriot public schools, with an additional focus on Armenian language, history and religion. Special mention must be made of the Melkonian Educational Institute, built in the 1920s, initially to house orphans of the Armenian genocide. For decades the Melkonian remained a renowned secondary school (1934–2005) with an unparalleled impact on the Armenian Cypriot community. The school was administered by the New York-based Armenian General Benevolent Union (AGBU), which unilaterally closed it down in 2005, despite local opposition to the decision.

The Armenian Cypriot community has some very active cultural and social clubs, while charity, cultural and educational events are often organised, such as fund-raisers and bazaars, book fairs and exhibitions, theatre performances as well as academic lectures on Armenian history and culture. Armenians in Cyprus also have a long history of publishing their own journals and newspapers and run their own online media.

As with other religious communities, the demographics and dynamics of the Armenian Cypriot community has changed in recent times due to the increased number of marriages with Greek Cypriots and the arrival of Armenian political and economic immigrants due to the dissolution of the Soviet Union (1991), as well as to strife in the Middle East. Armenian was recognised as a minority language of Cyprus in 2002.

Anglicans, Protestants and Other Denominations

The Anglican Church of Cyprus was formed in 1878 as the island passed under colonial rule. St Paul's Cathedral in Nicosia and St George in the Forest are two beautiful examples of surviving colonial ecclesiastical architecture. In recent years, as is the case with Roman Catholics, the number of Anglicans has increased: most members are British expatriate retirees, although there are also Americans, Canadians and South Africans. The Anglican Church is led by an archdeacon and falls under the Diocese of Cyprus and the Gulf, which is part of the episcopal province of Jerusalem and the Middle East. The cathedral aside, Anglicans congregate in Larnaca (St Helena), Limassol (St Barnabas), Polis (St Luke) and Tala (St Stephen).

Furthermore, there are also smaller Protestant and Pentecostal churches in Cyprus, including the Church of God of Prophecy (established in 1935), the Church of God Pentecostal (1947), the Greek Evangelical Church (active since the late 1880s), the Nicosia Community Church (1953), the Seventh-day Adventist Church (1932) and the Reformed Presbyterian Church (1887). Most of these smaller communities have their congregations in the larger cities of the island.

Finally, the Jehovah's Witnesses began missions on Cyprus in 1925, where they were initially active at the village of Xylofagou in Larnaca District. Since then the number of Jehovah's Witnesses has increased; nowadays there are around 40 congregations both in urban and in rural areas of Cyprus. At least twice a year the Jehovah's Witnesses hold a general meeting.

Prospects

Christianity has been a distinctive trait of Cyprus since the first century. Today, religion and faith continue to play a significant part in the life of Cypriot Christians of all denominations and in society at large. In the next few decades, although it will likely continue to remain strong, Christianity will probably have to face the gradual increase of the non-religious population on the island.

Bibliography

Englezakis, Benedict, *Studies in the History of the Church of Cyprus, 4th–20th Centuries* (Aldershot: Variorum, 1995).

Hackett, John, *The Orthodox Church of Cyprus* (New York: Burt Franklin, 1972).

Hadjilyra, Alexander-Michael, *The Armenians of Cyprus* (Larnaca: Kalaydjian Foundation, 2009).

Mitsides, Andreas, 'The Church of Cyprus during the Twentieth Century', in Christine Chaillot (ed.), *The Orthodox Church in Eastern Europe in the Twentieth Century* (Frankfurt: Peter Lang, 2011).

Varnavas, Andrekos, Nicholas Coureas and Marina Elia (eds), *The Minorities of Cyprus: Development Patterns and the Identity of the Internal-Exclusion* (Newcastle upon Tyne: Cambridge Scholars Publishing, 2009).

Turkey

Hratch Tchilingirian and Ed Alden

Turkey's Christian history goes back to New Testament times. Paul and Barnabas were commissioned by the church in Antioch (modern-day Antakya) as the first missionaries to Asia Minor, now Turkey. Much of the Book of Acts is set in this region, where Paul made three missionary journeys to preach the Christian message, establish churches and strengthen the believers. His personal sacrifices were rewarded; once established, the churches in Asia Minor flourished. The Seven Churches in the Book of Revelation are all located in today's Turkey. It has been estimated that by the fourth century nearly half of Asia Minor had become Christian and it was established as one of the main centres of Christian faith. The Ecumenical Councils that defined the doctrines of the Christian faith were all held in what today is Turkey: Nicea (today Iznik), Constantinople (Istanbul), Ephesus (Efes) and Chalcedon (Kadıköy). However, the Christians of Asia Minor were sharply divided by language, loyalty and doctrine. Weakened by division, Christianity was unable to withstand the advance of Islam, which rapidly won the allegiance of a population whose faith was not deeply grounded and who resented heavy taxes and church control.

The Turkic tribes who came to the region embraced Islam around the year 1000. During the thirteenth century, new waves of Turkish tribes from central Asia entered Anatolia, with Osman, 'Sultan of the Gazis', setting up a rival state to the Byzantines, at Bursa. He and his successors, as initiators of the Ottoman Empire, pressed across the Dardanelles and into Europe. In 1453, Constantinople, chief city of the Byzantine Empire, fell to Mehmet II and his armies. Considered the beginning of the 'golden age' of the Ottoman Empire, it established a firm Muslim hold over what is now Turkey that continues to this day, with some 99% of Turkey's population professing Islam.

By the beginning of the twentieth century, the Ottoman Empire had been greatly weakened, and large parts of Turkey were occupied by the Allies in the aftermath of the First World War. This provoked the Turkish War of Independence, in which forces led by Mustafa Kemal (later known by the honorific title Atatürk – 'father of the Turks') were ultimately successful in gaining control of the country and proclaiming the Republic.

On 1 November 1922, the National Assembly in Ankara stripped the last Ottoman sultan of his power and proclaimed itself the sovereign authority. The Treaty of Lausanne, signed in July 1923, recognised the new state as the successor to the Ottoman Empire. By then the vast majority of Turkey's Christian population, namely Armenians, Greeks and Assyrians, had become victims of state-planned genocide. The Assyrians call it *Sayfo*, the 'year of the sword'.

The Treaty of Lausanne stated that non-Muslim minorities should 'enjoy the same civil and political rights as Moslems' (Article 39). They were supposed to 'have an equal right to establish, manage and control at their own expense, any charitable, religious and social institutions, any schools and other establishments for instruction and education, with the right to use their own language and to exercise their own religion freely therein' (Article 40). However, starting from the early days of the Turkish Republic, these basic rights enshrined in the Treaty were never fully granted to the Christian communities. Indeed, until today, the Greek and Armenian patriarchates do not have legal status in Turkey, which means they are unable to purchase or hold title to property or to press claims in court.

Starting in the 1920s, minority citizens were illegally profiled by state agencies, whereby a secret 'race code' was assigned to a person's ethnic identity – citizens with Greek origin were coded 1, Armenians 2, Jews 3, Syriacs 4 and other non-Muslims 5. In 1936, a government decree (*Beyanname*) put Christian and Jewish religious and community institutions under strict control of the state, freezing their wealth and philanthropic and cultural institutions. A major blow to Christians in Turkey was the 1942–4 'Wealth Tax' imposed by the state, which targeted non-Muslim minorities, especially the Armenians and the Jews. Its purpose was to reduce the influence of minorities in the economy, replacing the non-Muslim bourgeoisie with its Turkish Muslim counterpart. In 1955 tensions in Cyprus led to

Christianity in Turkey, 1970 and 2015

	1970		2015		Average annual growth rate (%), 1970–2015
Tradition	Population	%	Population	%	
Christians	290,000	0.8%	181,000	0.2%	−1.0%
Anglicans	2,000	0.0%	12,000	0.0%	4.1%
Independents	2,100	0.0%	19,700	0.0%	5.1%
Orthodox	226,000	0.7%	78,800	0.1%	−2.3%
Protestants	24,300	0.1%	15,000	0.0%	−1.1%
Catholics	26,500	0.1%	42,700	0.1%	1.1%
Evangelicals	5,100	0.0%	7,000	0.0%	0.7%
Pentecostals	490	0.0%	18,300	0.0%	8.4%
Total population	**34,772,000**	**100.0%**	**78,666,000**	**100.0%**	**1.8%**

Source: Todd M. Johnson and Gina A. Zurlo (eds), *World Christian Database* (Leiden/Boston: Brill), accessed March 2017.

orchestrated riots in Istanbul that targeted minorities, largely Greek but also Armenian businesses and homes. It caused an exodus of Greeks from Istanbul. Throughout the 1970s and 1980s Christian community properties and assets were confiscated, repossessed or redistributed by state agencies without compensation.

Modern Turkey: Implications for Christianity

Notwithstanding the advance of Islam, until the early twentieth century Turkey had a considerable Christian population, being a significant centre of both the Greek Orthodox and Armenian Orthodox traditions. Although Turkey has never accepted the validity of applying the term 'genocide' to the large-scale massacres of Armenian Christians that took place in 1915, the killings were on a scale that reduced the Armenian presence in Turkey to a small fraction of what it had been before the First World War. The genocide left the Armenians who survived traumatised and fearful. Their sense of vulnerability has been further compounded by the discrimination they have experienced since.

Atatürk, the founder and protector of the Turkish Republic, was determined to lead Turkey into modernity and fruitful relations with the Western world. He reshaped Turkish society by banning the veil and fez, requiring Turkish to be written in Latin script (devised by an Armenian Christian, Agop Dilâçar [Martayan], at Atatürk's request) and introducing a Swiss code of law. He insisted that Turkey must become a secular state and sought to distance the organs of the state from the country's Islamic heritage. The greatly reduced Christian population might have expected to enjoy equal rights in the secular state being created by Mustafa Kemal. In practice, they faced increased harassment, for example being hit more heavily than other communities by the tax regime. Periodically, they were also subject to violent attack, such as the attacks in 1955 on Christians in Istanbul. Despite its secular credentials, it became clear that the state would remain fundamentally Turkish and Muslim, with at best a precarious existence for those with other ethnic or religious identities. After the death of Kemal in 1938, the state allowed itself to be increasingly influenced by the Islamic faith of the great majority of its population, to the point where there is a conflation of Turkish and Muslim identity.

This trend is currently being consolidated under the government of Islamist Recep Tayyip Erdoğan. Nonetheless, after decades of legal restrictions and discrimination, the emergence of Erdoğan's Justice and Development Party (Adalet ve Kalkınma Partisi) as a leading political force in the early 2000s brought some much-needed relief to the Christian communities in Turkey. Armenian Patriarch Mesrob Mutafyan has enthusiastically said that 'the Erdoğan government has an open ear' for the

Christians. Unlike other parties, the Justice and Development Party was able to garner support and voters from the widest segments of society. Within a short time, the party shifted from its original dogmatic Islamist politics to conservative democracy. Since the 2000s, the government has restored the legal ownership of dozens of properties that had belonged to Christian communities, which were confiscated by the state over the decades. The Erdoğan government has been more respectful towards Christian religious heads and churches. Nevertheless, it remains to be seen whether full return of properties and complete restoration of minority rights will be fully implemented. Such concerns include, for instance, the reopening of church seminaries where future clergy could be trained, the legal status and independence of community schools, and freedom for church and community organisations to hold elections.

Greek Orthodox

The Greek Orthodox presence was dramatically diminished through the events that brought modern Turkey into being. Turkey and Greece had been at war, and under the terms of the 1923 Treaty of Lausanne 1.5 million Greeks living in Anatolia and Thrace were to be exchanged for the 500,000 Turks leaving Greek territory. This measure removed from Turkey the large majority of its Greek Orthodox population. Though Istanbul remains the seat of the Ecumenical Patriarch, the number of Greek Orthodox in Turkey today is very small. This is in contrast to the significant role and majestic history of the Greek Orthodox Church in the Byzantine Empire, when Constantinople was one of the most important patriarchal sees in all of Christianity. Today, even as the Ecumenical Patriarch is viewed as 'first among equals' among the Orthodox autocephalous churches and is considered the leader of 300 million Orthodox Christians around the world, the Turkish government does not recognise his 'Ecumenical' title. The Turkish state considers him the spiritual leader of the Greeks living in Turkey and refers to him as the local 'Orthodox Patriarch of Fener'. Fener is the neighbourhood in which the patriarchate's headquarters are located.

From 1924 the Turkish government constantly made life difficult for the Ecumenical Patriarchate, including attempts to promote the emergence of a Turkish Orthodox Church. Systematic efforts to encourage outward migration of Greeks, especially from the 1940s to the 1970s, were largely successful, and only a few thousand Greeks, generally of older age, remain in Turkey today. Most live in Istanbul, with some also on the Aegean islands of Gokceada and Bozcaada. The Greek community has been subject to constant harassment and their leaders and properties have been targets for acts of violence, including desecration, assassination and bomb attacks (including against the patriarchate's headquarters).

Armenian Orthodox

The Treaty of Lausanne provided for state recognition of the rights of the Greek, Armenian and Jewish communities as non-Muslim minorities but not for the institutional churches as such. Notwithstanding the catastrophic losses suffered during the First World War, the Armenian Orthodox remain by far the largest Christian tradition in Turkey, with around 70,000 adherents today, mainly living in Istanbul. Their ethnic and religious identities are inextricably intertwined. They form a strong community, running schools, newspapers and charitable activities. The Armenian Patriarchate operates under constant pressure as it lacks a clear legal status and has to engage in many disputes over confiscated properties and restrictions on church elections.

Their profile and numbers expose them to systematic discrimination. This has taken different forms at different times, including appropriation of their property; removal of cultural memory through destruction and renaming; social humiliation; and physical violence. The Armenians tend to be portrayed very negatively in official publications and in educational materials in Turkey. Despite being for centuries an integral part of Turkish society, Armenians are constantly made to feel like second-class citizens. The state apparatus is continuously mobilised to restrict and constrain the Armenian community.

As it comes to terms with living under such constant pressure, the Armenian community is pulled in opposite directions – between 'isolation' and 'integration'. The Armenian Orthodox Patriarchate and other leading institutions tend to favour isolation as the best strategy to secure the future of the Armenian community. They set great store by the preservation of the Armenian language, literature and religion as well as the maintenance of ethnic identity, resisting the growing trend towards mixed marriages. A contrasting vision of integration into mainstream Turkish society has been advocated by progressive Armenian intellectuals such as Hrant Dink, the writer and editor who was assassinated in 2007. They argue on the basis of democratic norms and equal citizenship rights. It appears that the growing trend in the Armenian community favours ending the isolation and moving further towards integration, openness and full participation in society, while seeking to preserve their Armenian identity.

One consequence of the genocide is the reality of Islamised Armenians in Turkey. Particularly women and children who survived were taken into Muslim families as wives, workers or slaves or were kidnapped and raised as Muslims. An estimated 2 million Turks and Kurds today have some Armenian ancestry. It has been estimated that one family in four in the eastern provinces of Diyarbakir, Hakkari, Bitlis and Van had a great-grandmother who was Armenian. In recent years a considerable number of

Islamised Armenians had sought baptism in the Armenian Church as a way of recovering the original religious and cultural identity of their ancestors. Armenian Patriarch Mesrob II estimated that between 80 and 120 have been baptised each year, while others recover their Christian identity by joining other churches. However, with the growing Islamisation of social and political discourse and public space in Turkey, such Armenians seem to have gone back into hiding.

Churches and schools, the institutional core of the Armenian community, operate amidst manifold administrative obstacles and financial challenges as well as occasionally being directly targeted by hostile forces. Restoration of churches has been a major concern of the Armenians but their efforts have been beset by many difficulties, notably legal obstacles. The reconstruction of churches in cities such as Diyarbakir, Kayseri and Antakya where there were large Armenian communities prior to the genocide represents an effort to restore the last remnants of the once rich Armenian Christian presence in these historic places.

Assyrians and Syriac Orthodox

There are an estimated 10,000–15,000 Syriac Orthodox in Turkey today, with deep historical religious roots in the south-east of the country, especially in the Tur Abdin region, which is dotted with churches and a dozen monasteries, such as Mor Gabriel, Mor Yacoub, Mor Malke and Zafaran. Throughout history these centres of religious learning have played a role in the theological, spiritual and cultural life of Syriac Christianity. Like other Christian communities, after years of subjection to what an archbishop called 'oppression and horror', more than half the Syriac population in Turkey lost their lives in the genocide during the First World War.

In 1924 Patriarch Ignatius Elias III Shakir (1917–32) was exiled and the official patriarchal see of the Syriac Orthodox Church was moved from the Zafaran monastery in Mardin to Homs in 1932 and then to Damascus in 1959. An eyewitness, Archbishop Gabriel Aydin, says, 'one day the governor of Mardin came to the Monastery to deliver a telegram from Atatürk [which read] "the clerical leader in the black cassock should leave Turkey immediately and should never ever return".' Despite his state-ordered exile, in 1931 the Turkish government issued a decree depriving Patriarch Elias of his Turkish citizenship. In 1937 another decree by the Turkish government banned the import of publications authored by Elias's successor, Patriarch Aphrem Barsoum, who was an advocate for the rights of the Syriac community. These measures were consistent with Atatürk's policy of secularisation. He had declared that the 'Orthodox and Armenian churches and Jewish synagogues which are based in Turkey should have been abolished together with the Caliphate'.

The Turkish state does not officially recognise the Syriac Orthodox Church or the Assyrian Christians, either as a non-Muslim minority or as a legal entity. The Syrian Orthodox community in Turkey is declining as a result of the military operations in the south-east and consequent outward migration. Like other Christian communities, the Syriac Orthodox also face perennial legal and administrative hurdles imposed by the state and society. One critical example is the case of the fourth-century monastery of Mor Gabriel. In 2008 the villagers in the vicinity of Mor Gabriel submitted a legal complaint to the courts that the monastery was occupying land illegally, including areas within the walls of the monastic complex. Turkish courts decided against the Syriac community and ordered the transfer of about 28 hectares of land owned by the monastery to the Turkish Ministry of Forestry and Water Affairs. Successive appeals have not reversed the decision. In 2017 the Turkish government seized more than 50 Syriac Orthodox properties in Mardin province, including monasteries, churches and cemeteries.

Catholics

There is a small but significant presence of the Catholic Church in Turkey. It is fragmented according to ethnic and ritual identity, including Armenian Catholic (Armenian rite), Roman Catholic (Roman rite), Greek-Byzantine Catholic (Greek rite), Syrian and Chaldean Catholic Churches. The largest expression of Catholicism is the community observing the Roman rite, found mainly in Istanbul, Trabzon and Adana districts. Its origins go back to the 1930s when Catholics of Italian and French origin moved to Turkey from the Levant. By the 1950s many of them had returned to Europe, but the Roman Catholic Church had by then attracted Assyrians, Maronites, Greeks and Armenians who lacked opportunity to worship with their own communities. Today around 20,000 people belong to the Roman Catholic Church. Fluctuating in numbers but never more than a few thousand strong is the Chaldean Church, drawing its adherents from among the Assyrians, including refugees from Iraq, and Christian Arabs from Syria and found mainly in Diyarbakir, Mersin and Istanbul. The Armenian Catholic community has greatly declined in numbers. Having been more than 100,000 strong before the genocide, it is now reduced to a few thousand. The Greek-Byzantine Catholic community is even weaker, with only a few dozen adherents today.

All the Catholic Churches have had to operate in a hostile environment, under constant suspicion from the authorities and facing direct persecution at times, with both the infrastructure and personnel of the church being targeted. In April 2005, an attempt was made to burn the St Paul Cultural Centre in Antalya. In February 2006, Fr Andrea Santoro was killed in

Trabzon, soon followed by the stabbing of Fr Pierre Brunissen in Samsun and Fr Adriano Francini in Izmir. In 2010, the Bishop of Iskenderun Luigi Padovese was repeatedly stabbed and then decapitated by his driver. The lack of religious tolerance and the attendant culture of violence in Turkey have taken a heavy toll on the leadership of the Catholic Churches.

Protestant Churches

The beginnings of Protestantism in Turkey can be traced back to the nineteenth-century work of the Anglican Church Missionary Society, the Basel Mission and the American Board of Commissioners for Foreign Missions. The latter was particularly influential among the Armenian community, leading to the emergence of the Armenian Evangelical Church. This flourishing movement came abruptly to an end with the genocide of 1915. The Armenian Evangelical Church had some 60,000 members before the genocide but has no more than a few hundred today. Other historic Protestant churches are also very small, including the Seventh-day Adventists, who have been present in Turkey since 1958.

It was not until 1961 that Protestant missionary work resumed in Turkey, with the arrival of workers from the American-based mission agency Operation Mobilization. Their work in literature distribution and church planting resulted in some Turks adopting the Christian faith, including Kenan Araz, who became a key figure in church leadership and relations with Muslims. This small movement was frequently subjected to police harassment and deportations but proved to be resilient. It was strengthened by the return to Turkey of individuals who had become Christians while living in Europe and who brought leadership qualities. A major achievement was the translation of the Bible into modern Turkish, with the New Testament being completed in 1987 and the entire Bible in 2001.

The risk of a violent reaction to Protestant missionary work was always present and was underlined when David Goodman, an Operation Mobilization worker, was shot and killed on his doorstep in 1979. Nonetheless, the Protestant movement has been growing – from a few dozen in the 1960s to an estimated 6,000 today, organised under the Association of Turkish Protestant Churches, commonly known as TEK. In terms of securing freedom of worship, a significant event was the visit in 1989 of Sir Fred Catherwood, Vice President of the European Parliament, at a time when Turkey was seeking closer relations with the European Union. He asked the Turkish government to allow Protestants to worship, in the same way that Catholics and Orthodox Christians were allowed. As a result, the government gave verbal assurance that fellowships needed only to inform the local *Vali*, or governor, of the meetings to avoid them being illegal. There are now fellowships meeting in 32 cities across Turkey.

Whereas initially most members came from an Orthodox background, today the majority are from a Muslim background. The vulnerability of such groups was underlined on 18 April 2007, when Necati Aydin, Ugur Yüksel and Tilmann Geske were brutally murdered in Malatya. They were working with a Christian publishing house and serving as leaders in the local Protestant church. Five young men, pretending an interest in Christianity, came to meet them. They then tied them up, videoed them with their cell phones and, with the police on their way, murdered all three. The case, including the public expression of forgiveness for the murderers by widows of two of the victims, attracted media attention. While there was an initial decline in participation at fellowship meetings throughout Turkey, the case appeared to prompt fresh interest in the Protestant movement, leading to a slight increase in attendance. Though still a marginal presence, the Protestant movement is growing in maturity and grappling with the question of what it means to be both Turkish and Christian in a context where the Islamic identity of the nation is being accentuated.

Although churches and believers experience more freedom today overall, the Protestant churches still have little in the way of official rights. There is no easy route for them to establish themselves officially as churches, to own property or to receive donations legally. Churches have engaged the government in dialogue about these issues through the work of TEK, but progress has been limited. The twenty-first century has seen bridges being built between many Protestant Church leaders and officials in the leadership of the Orthodox Churches. This cooperation has resulted in the development of resources that serve both. Significant areas of cooperation have been the SAT-7 Turk television station, which hosts programmes for both communities, and a growing openness to the use by Protestant congregations of vacant historical church buildings.

Conclusion

Despite the legacy of Atatürk and the secular state he created, it is clear that Islamic identity runs deep in Turkey and that 'Christophobia' is prevalent. Christianity is widely viewed as a dangerous alien ideology and as a threat to the unity and identity of the Turkish people. When Christianity is considered in public discourse it is often with reference to the Crusades or to Turkish–Greek conflict, thus framing Christianity in terms of enmity towards Turkey. Turkish perceptions are often cast in terms of perennial antagonism between Islam and Christianity. The press fans such hostility by consistently portraying Armenians as a sinister threat and exaggerating the extent of Protestant evangelism in order to arouse fear of a supposed danger to Turkish identity. The Turkish phrase *misyonerlik faaliyetleri*, used both in official reports and in nationalistic press coverage, can be translated simply as 'propagating activity', but it carries shades of propaganda, treachery and intrigue. Such language cultivates a sense that Christians are enemies, with malign intentions towards the people of Turkey. The resultant atmosphere is one in which it becomes possible to plan and carry out such assassinations as those of Hrant Dink, Bishop Luigi Padovese, and Necati Aydin, Ugur Yüksel and Tilmann Geske. Their violent deaths represent a grisly reminder of the vulnerability of the Christian community in a hostile environment. The difficulties facing Christian churches in Turkey cannot be underestimated. Nonetheless, both in historic Christian communities and in new movements there are resilience and vigour, born of the experience of keeping the faith in face of adversity.

Bibliography

Baum, Wilhilm, *The Christian Minorities in Turkey* (Vienna-Klagenfurt: Kitab Verlag, 2006).

Eibner, John, 'Turkey's Christians Under Siege', *Middle East Quarterly* (spring 2011), 41–52.

Ekmekçioğlu, Lerna, *Recovering Armenia: The Limits of Belonging in Post-genocide Turkey* (Stanford, CA: Stanford University Press, 2016).

Gaunt, David, Naures Atto and Soner O. Barthoma, *Let Them Not Return: Sayfo – The Genocide of the Assyrian, Syriac, and Chaldean_Christians in the Ottoman Empire* (New York: Berghahn Books, 2017).

Tchilingirian, Hratch, 'The "Other" Citizens: Armenians in Turkey Between Isolation and (Dis)integration', *Journal of the Society for Armenian Studies*, 25 (2016), 123–55.

Syria

Razek Siriani

It would be a mistake for any reader to confine the presence of Christians in Syria to the modern history of the country. We learn from the Book of Acts (11: 26) that it was in Antioch, which was the capital of Greater Syria in the first century, that the Apostles were first called 'Christians'. From that geographical and historical location Christianity spread east and west, to Asia Minor, Greece and Rome. The archaeology, shrines, remnants and literature of hundreds of churches and monasteries in northern Syria and southern Turkey present remarkable evidence of the early presence of Christianity. St Paul the Apostle was converted on the road to Damascus, lived in it and had his eyesight restored in the old city before launching his missionary work further north, to Rome. Ma'alula, a small carved village in the rocky mountains of southern Syria, is one of the very few places in the world where Aramaic, the language that Jesus spoke, is still spoken. Some Syrian Christians have an ethnic identity related to such ancient civilisations as the Aramean and Assyrian. Others – namely Armenians, Syriacs and Chaldeans – are survivors of the genocide committed by the Ottomans in the early twentieth century.

Syrian Christianity is marked by ecclesial division that has its roots in the fourth century. Originating in the Christological debates of the fourth and fifth centuries, the differing theological interpretations of that time have combined with cultural, ethnic and political identities to create deep divisions within Christianity in Syria. In particular, a division runs deep between the Byzantine and Greek on the one hand and the Syriac on the other, shaped by theological and political divergences in the fourth century.

The divided nature of Syrian Christianity has been compounded by further schisms, to the point where Syria has 11 different Christian traditions, each following its own theology, rites, identity, hierarchy, authority, administration, costume and language: Greek Orthodox of Antioch, Greek Melkite Catholic, Syriac Orthodox of Antioch, Armenian Orthodox, Maronite, Armenian Catholic, Syrian Catholic, Latin Catholic, Chaldean Catholic, Arab Evangelical (Presbyterian) and Union of Armenian Evangelical. Some of these church denominations were established by missionary work, either Catholic or Protestant. Others split from their original church to establish new churches, such as the Melkite and Syriac Catholic. The distinct identities of the Christian churches have meant that they have often been preoccupied with internal divisions while facing continuous conflicts, occupations, atrocities and persecutions in the region. Since the early 1960s, however, with the rise of the ecumenical movement, churches in Syria have transcended their theological differences and disputes and taken a path towards greater dialogue and unity, at least in relation to matters held in common. They have lifted many of the anathemas they had pronounced against one another. Nonetheless, each church has maintained its independence, hierarchy, rites, theology and doctrines, contributing to the richness of Christian heritage and identity.

Majority, Minority or Component?

On the eve of the Muslim Arab conquest of Syria (637–833) the majority of the inhabitants were Christians. It is believed that the Muslim Arabs did not conquer Syria by force but, rather, met with little resistance from the Christian inhabitants, especially the Syriac non-Chalcedonians (those who rejected the decisions of the Council of Chalcedon of 451 and did not conform to the rule of the Byzantines). The Syriac Christians, along with the Assyrians (Nestorians), looked on the Arabs as saviours from the Greek Byzantine Empire. By contrast, the Greek-speaking Christians regarded the newcomers as a threat to their religion and existence. Nevertheless, the presence of the new rulers imposed challenges on all Christian inhabitants of Syria – the new religion of Islam, a new language (Arabic), the formation of new common grounds for living together, and later on adherence to the new rules and laws of Islamic religious belief.

A few decades after the conquest, Christians found themselves under a regime that derived its laws from God (*Allah*) and denied other established laws. The Arab Muslims did not need to integrate into the society they had conquered but, rather, as conquerors imposed their laws and established

Christianity in Syria, 1970 and 2015

	1970		2015		Average annual growth rate (%), 1970–2015
Tradition	Population	%	Population	%	
Christians	667,000	10.5%	1,136,000	6.1%	1.2%
Anglicans	50	0.0%	4,600	0.0%	10.6%
Independents	2,600	0.0%	4,600	0.0%	1.3%
Orthodox	464,000	7.3%	714,000	3.9%	1.0%
Protestants	20,900	0.3%	33,500	0.2%	1.1%
Catholics	179,000	2.8%	386,000	2.1%	1.7%
Evangelicals	8,500	0.1%	11,400	0.1%	0.6%
Pentecostals	390	0.0%	22,800	0.1%	9.5%
Total population	**6,379,000**	**100.0%**	**18,502,000**	**100.0%**	**2.4%**

Source: Todd M. Johnson and Gina A. Zurlo (eds), *World Christian Database* (Leiden/Boston: Brill), accessed March 2017.

states (*Khilafa*). Christians found themselves obliged to conform to the new rulers, laws, culture and religion. Muslims used to consider Christians as the 'People of the Book' (*Ahl al-Kitab* – that is, those who held monotheistic beliefs). Christians were granted autonomy, allowed to remain in their faith and be protected as long as they paid the poll tax (*al-jizya*) to the Caliphate (the ruler in succession to the Prophet Muhammad).

The Arab Muslim conquests did not pass without some atrocities being committed against the non-Muslim inhabitants. The Christians did not resist the Arabs because they could not and had no will and capacity to do so. Instead, they accommodated to the Arabs while remaining faithful to their Christian religious identity. In fact, Christians in the first century after the Arab Muslim conquests helped the Muslims to establish their rule and state. Several well known Christians who lived in the ninth and tenth centuries were actively involved in the administration of Arab rule, while others contributed by translating books and manuscripts from the Greek and Syriac languages into Arabic.

Arabisation started to be enforced during the Caliphate of Al-Walid ibn Abd al-Malik (705–15), when all inhabitants of Syria as well as Egypt were forced to use Arabic as their primary language. This movement of Arabisation marked the beginning of the integration of Christians into Arab Muslim society. In order to protect themselves from any atrocities that might occur or accusations of infidelity, some Christians had no choice but to adopt and identify with Arabisation. Thus, the mother tongue of all Christians became Arabic, and many churches adopted it as the language of their liturgies and prayers.

Islam and Arabisation not only have affected the Christians' cultural identity but also have shaped their legislative perspectives, their behavioural affiliation to their religion, their ethnic belonging and, above all, their status as an autonomous entity. Christians realised that they could not remain an independent, united component of society. Neither could they fully preserve their social, cultural, ethical, religious and ecclesial behaviour. Nor could they freely express their political views in face of a ruling state that derived its law from the Qur'an and Sharia and could not separate Arabisation from Islam as a religion. Above all, Christians could not remain as a majority who could influence the other. Now they became a minority, likely to be influenced by the other.

The language of minority has long been a vexed issue for Christians. Many Christians in contemporary Syria, including church leaders, feel uncomfortable with the term 'minority', although it is a quantitative fact. To Christians, the term 'minority' signifies a non-authentic group of people protected by a dominant Muslim community. Prior to and during the current turmoil in Syria, many influential church leaders have preferred the term 'component' when referring to Christians in Syrian society and have utterly rejected the term 'minority'. They do this for three reasons: first, to emphasise the authentic presence of Christians in the region prior to Islam; secondly, to contest the claim of extremist Muslims that Christians are affiliated with the Western world; and thirdly, to maintain the situation of state protection of their presence and identity as citizens of Syria.

During the Ottoman Empire's rule over the Middle East and parts of Asia Minor for more than six centuries (1299–1923), Christians were treated as *Ahl al-Kitab* and were given state protection as *ahl al-dhimaa* ('people of protection'). This indicates that Christians were not treated as an authentic component of society but rather as a religious minority, along with other minorities, such as the Jews or Kurds. Furthermore, the Ottomans committed genocide against Armenian, Syriac, Chaldean and Greek Christians in 1915–16, which led many of them to escape to Syria.

After the First World War, Britain and France took over and mandated the Arab nations. The French took control of Syria and Lebanon. From 1920 to 1946 the French used a policy of 'divide and rule' and some Christians received preferential treatment. Christian missionaries from Europe flowed into Syria and established churches, schools and hospitals. Nevertheless, Syrian nationalists struggled against the French Mandate to keep the Syrian population undivided. Their ideas of equality for all the 'components' of society proved attractive to the people of Syria, at least to the educated elite, until independence was finally achieved in 1946. Some Christian leaders worked with their Muslim compatriots to overthrow the French Mandate.

Christianity in Modern Syria

Unlike the Lebanese Christians, after independence the Syrian Christians did not establish autonomous political parties or movements. They opted instead to play their part in creating and operating such political parties as the Ba'ath, the Communists and the Social Nationalists. Prior to 2011, Syrian Christians made up 6–8% of the population, some 1.5 million of the total 23 million population of Syria. Rather than foregrounding their ethno-sectarian identity, they stressed their loyalty to their country, its social framework and the existing political parties and recurring governments, which they expected to provide protection for them as full citizens. The Armenian Syrians, a distinct ethnic/linguistic group among Christians, did not exempt themselves from this loyalty to the nation. This stance explains Christians' involvement in military service, government jobs, civic society, education and health systems, and all other civic sectors in modern Syria, including the private sector. It is important to underline that Christians in modern Syria were not treated as *Ahl al-Dhimaa* as was the case under the

Islamic Caliphates and Ottoman Empire. Rather, they enjoyed the status of citizens with the full rights and obligations provided by the constitution, which was first passed during the French Mandate. In fact, since coming to power in 1971 the Ba'ath ruling political party has discouraged any emphasis on differences based on religion or ethnicity, viewing these as potentially divisive. While Christians regard their faith as a constituent part of their identity, their national loyalty has ensured that this does not set them at odds with their Muslim compatriots. They have consistently maintained open and tolerant relationships with Muslim fellow citizens, based on an ethic of coexistence.

Christians in Syria were influential in various sectors of society and contributed to the development of the country, yet they remained a numerical minority due to ongoing emigration and the higher birth rate among Muslims. The harsh effects of the internal and regional troubles in Syria's recurring wars from 1946 to 1973 prompted Christians, as well as other minorities, to look for a future outside their own country. Due to economic, social and internal turmoil with the Muslim Brotherhoods in the early 1980s, the emigration of Christians witnessed another increase. The rise of Islamist movements in opposition to the ruling party during this period signalled that the period ahead would not necessarily be a tolerant one for Christians.

Whether or not they are considered a minority, Christians maintain their identity and take their due part in national life. For example, in the national parliament Christians make up nearly 3% of the total membership. Christian MPs are elected through a national election process, but their names are either forwarded by their churches or selected by the ruling political party. In the cabinet, Christians represent 1% of the ministers. In other sectors, Christians can be employed like any other citizen, and they can occupy senior positions such as dean of a university or chief director of an institution.

Christians have also been at the forefront of cultural, economic and educational developments. Non-racist Christian thinkers and writers of the epoch after independence advocated liberal political, national and social reforms. In 1944, at the time of the French Mandate, Syria appointed a Christian Protestant prime minister, Fares Al-Khoury, an eminent politician who had opposed the French Mandate and participated in the struggle for independence, attained in 1946. He was also elected as a member of the United Nations Security Council to represent Syria from 1947 to 1948. Another prominent Christian politician, Michel Aflaq, played a leading role in the foundation of the Arab Nationalist movement. The Ba'ath Party, both in Syria and in Iraq, drew inspiration from his speeches and writings. The cultural associations that were established by Christians played a considerable role in the Arabic renaissance. However, this leading role gradually diminished due to the rise of intolerant political Islamism and totalitarian governments.

Nevertheless, under the secular constitution of 1950, Christians in Syria have enjoyed freedom and equal citizenship. Like others in a plural society, Christians are constitutionally guaranteed freedom to practise their faith, build churches, own properties and benefit from tax exemption. The current Syrian constitution affirms equal rights for all citizens and does not discriminate on grounds of religion or gender. According to the constitution, while Islamic Sharia jurisprudence is the principal source of legislation, Islam is not the religion of the country. Christians are permitted to follow their denominational ecclesial laws in relation to betrothal, marriage, divorce/dissolution, custody and inheritance – matters that fall under the jurisdiction of church courts.

One of the main features of Syria's Christian population is its combination of ethnic and religious identity. The leadership hierarchies of some churches have their patriarchates in Damascus, namely, the Greek Orthodox of Antioch, the Syriac Orthodox of Antioch and the Catholic Melkite of Antioch. Other denominations, such as Armenian Orthodox, Chaldeans and Armenian Catholics, have their hierarchies in neighbouring countries, including Iraq and Lebanon. The continuous existence of church leadership in the capital city and the spread of Christians and their churches and monasteries, both ancient and new, all over the country signify the strong presence and role of Christians.

Like their Muslim fellow citizens, Christians enjoy: free education in public schools and universities; a partially free public health system; government subsidies for food items such as sugar, rice and bread; cheap local transportation; and low income tax. At the same time, some Christians share also the same grievances as their Muslim compatriots in relation to such issues as income inequalities, massive corruption at all levels, unemployment, lack of privileges for those who are not members of the ruling party and migration of rural people into urban areas seeking better employment. Nevertheless, regardless of their political stances, Christians in general manifest loyalty to their country. They do not form an exclusive sect but, while maintaining their faith and religious traditions, embrace the plurality of their society. They contribute to the development of their country, working hard and leading their lives with integrity as guided by their social and religious ethics.

The 2011 Uprising

Across the Middle East, Christians are in the process of being ethnically and religiously cleansed. No one would envy the situation of Christians in Syria after the uprising of 2011, which has led to massive destruction and terrible atrocities across the country, particularly in the city of Aleppo, home to some 40% of Syria's Christians. The unbearable pressures of living in a war zone and being targeted by violent extremists have compelled thousands of Christians to emigrate. Some have been internally displaced while others have sought refuge in neighbouring countries or in the West. The Christian population of Syria has dwindled from around 10% of the national population prior to the crisis to around 4% during it. It is estimated that nearly 700,000 Christians have fled the country.

At least 82 churches have been targeted by Islamist terrorists and destroyed either completely or partially: 28 in Damascus and its suburbs, 15 in Aleppo and its suburbs, 12 in Homs and Hama, 8 in Raqqa and Tabqa, 8 in Hassakeh and Qamishly, 5 in Deir Al-Zor, 6 in Jisr Al-Shugur. Six priests of different denominations were assassinated in cold blood by terrorists during 2013 and 2015. Two bishops of Aleppo were abducted by unknown armed insurgents in April 2013 (see below). Two priests were kidnapped by Al-Nusra Front in October 2012. Furthermore, due to shelling of civilian areas, many people have lost their lives or have been injured and disabled.

The sectarian armed conflict has surprised many Syrian citizens and in particular the Christians, who for decades had been enjoying the safest country in the Arab world, marked by plurality, peaceful coexistence and tolerance between different religious groups. The 'Arab Spring' that began in December 2010 in Tunisia, and then spread to countries such as Egypt and Libya, as well as the turmoil in Iraq since 2003, had been a warning to Syrian Christians that their country might witness a similar development. However, they never imagined the nightmare that would unfold for them from 2011 as their country has been torn apart by the rise of Islamist groups such as ISIS and Al-Nusra, the oppression and corruption of the ruling regime and the interventions of regional and international powers which have fought their proxy wars in Syria.

No wonder Christians in Syria felt threatened and unprotected when the uprising started in March 2011 and even more so when it later took on a militant aspect. Christian communities felt that the rise of militant Islam against the ruling regime, and its initial success, would threaten their very presence and protection as a substantial minority group in the country. This led to a mass exodus of Christians, particularly intellectuals and young people, from Syria. This has come about not because Christians feel unaffiliated or disloyal to their land, nor because they feel they have no stake in its future. The reason for the large-scale emigration is that many Christians feel that their lives and the lives of their children are threatened by a grim and uncertain situation. They fear that a society marked by tolerance, safety, plurality, coexistence and a mosaic type of life will probably be replaced by one that is exclusive, monolithic and fanatically Islamic. Such fears are not exclusive to Christians. Many Muslims have opted to leave the country for similar reasons, particularly those whose political affiliations make them feel vulnerable. Yet, many Christians, despite the atrocities and difficulties of life in a war situation, have opted to remain in the country or have left only as a last resort.

Some minorities among Christians, such as the Assyrians, were persecuted in the north and east of the country, when it was occupied in 2013 by ISIS or Al-Nusra or other militant factions. The Christian population in Raqaa, located in the mid-east part of Syria, on the Euphrates River, had to escape overnight when ISIS occupied the city on 4 March 2013. Christians were given two options, with less than one day to choose between them: either submit to Sharia law and convert to Islam, or leave the area immediately with no possibility of taking any of their belongings. No accurate account can be given as to how many Christians left Raqqa at that time. However, it is estimated that prior to the occupation there were some 5,000 Christians in the city, who were all forced to flee. Some moved west to Aleppo and others south to Damascus.

Life under ISIS rule is harsh. For example, no woman can walk in the streets or be seen by someone else without wearing the *niqab* and completely covering the body, face and hands with a loose-fitting black robe and gloves. No one is permitted to smoke or drink alcohol in public. Men are obliged to go to the mosque on Fridays for prayers, whether they are believers or not. Schools are devoted to religious education and children are obliged to learn the Qur'an by heart. The published curricula for education are based on the extreme Wahhabi type of Islam. Brutal penalties are applied to people who do not abide by the rules and required conduct. These can include beating in public, hanging from a wall, crucifixion and even immediate killing. In late 2015 and early 2016 ISIS invaded villages in Hassake's suburbs – in the north-east, close to the Iraqi and Turkish borders – and Assyrian Christians were kidnapped and tortured. It was reported that some young women were sold in the market (Souq al-Nikhasa) as slaves. Both vendors and customers belonged to ISIS. Some of the kidnapped people were later released but the fate of others is unknown. Many ancient churches in those villages were burned or otherwise completely destroyed.

In Aleppo, two eminent archbishops, Mar Gregorios Yohanna Ibrahim of the Syriac Orthodox Church and Boulos Yaziji of the Greek Orthodox Church, were abducted on 22 April 2013 as they returned from a humanitarian mission at the Turkish border. Their fate remains unknown (the author of this essay was working under the supervision of Archbishop Yohanna Ibrahim). The kidnapping of these two well known church leaders represented a threat to the presence of Christians in Aleppo and elsewhere in the country. In fact, it prompted Christians to recall some dark moments of history when atrocities were perpetrated against them, such as the violent riots of fanatical Muslims in Aleppo in 1850 that led to loss of life of Christians, and the genocide of the Ottoman Empire in 1916 against Armenians, Syriacs, Chaldeans and Greeks.

During the current crisis, Christians have been trapped between two fires, the national Syrian army on one side and the armed 'rebellions', 'moderate opposition' and militant factions on the other. Since the coming of Islam to the country, Christians have not formed any autonomous, ethnic, religious or political groups, or had any specific political ambitions. Rather, they have been involved and engaged in the overall public life of the country. Based on that approach, Christians and churches did not engage in the public demonstrations that took place in early 2011 when the spark of the conflict started, except on an individual and personal basis. They did not take up arms or ally themselves with opposition groups. All young men, however, are conscripted to the national army. On the eve of the conflict, churches voiced some general critique and called for immediate reformation to prevent any escalation of the conflict. For example, Archbishop Yohanna Ibrahim of Aleppo, before his abduction, gave interviews on Syrian television and radio in which he called for peace, prevention of an armed conflict and the sustaining of a unified Syria. Christian communities have never committed any offence or atrocity against any party in conflict. On the contrary, since Christians usually live in urban areas under government control or have moved there for protection, they have been the victims of atrocities perpetrated by militant groups.

Christians of Syria during the current conflict can be classified into four categories. The first is a generally middle-class group of people who used to live on the daily income of small businesses and suddenly lost it because of the war. This category is occupied with sustaining their daily life in a crisis that involves shortages of electricity, water, heating and cooking gas while living with the stress of displacement, poverty, unemployment or even fear of being killed in a bomb attack. This category is not concerned about any engagement in political affairs, but fears that Islamisation of the country will threaten their lives as Christians. Therefore, they do not wish to see any political change and tend rather to sympathise with the current regime.

The second category comprises an elite of wealthy businesspeople and intellectuals. They have lost their prestige during the war and are more concerned about politics than the first category. Although they might criticise the ongoing corruption in the country, they share the same belief that the fall of the current regime would not be in their interest. The alternative that presents itself is an extreme and fanatical type of Islam that will not allow any space for the Christian community. Driven by this anxiety, and because of the absence of any serious unarmed political opposition that could bring peaceful and democratic change to the country, they are inclined to support the political status quo rather than an unpopular opposition.

The third category comprises various educational, intellectual and working people who have suffered greatly in the civil war. They fear that their own lives and the lives of their families are not safe and that the future looks grim. Many people have decided to leave the country, and there is little prospect of their return, especially the young among them.

The fourth category is perhaps the most pivotal, because it comprises the leadership and hierarchy of the various churches, which represent the Christian communities in relation to the government. Many churches also have strong connections and affiliations with churches in the West. The various hierarchies have been able to transcend their divisions through their painful shared experience of the conflict. They have also broken new ground by engaging publicly with the national crisis rather than attempting to remain neutral or taking a passive stance. Church leaders called on the government and the state political leadership to undertake necessary and immediate reforms to achieve greater social justice, advised all parties to avoid armed conflict, advocated for peaceful Syrian dialogue, advised its communities not to take up arms or commit offences against any party, steadfastly resisted any political changes that might lead to the overthrow of the secular regime and its replacement with an extreme religious form of government that would not recognise plurality in society or permit free practice of religion, condemned all atrocities committed against Christians and their premises, and, finally, rejected any offensive international intervention in the country's affairs that might lead to a rule of religious fanaticism. In view of the recent ethnic cleansing of Christians in Iraq at the hands of Islamic militants, the experience of Islamisation in Egypt, fear of takeover by a political-religious radical opposition that will ultimately undermine the presence of Christians as a minority component in the society, and their patriotic loyalty to their country, Christians and their church leaders have been motivated to support the current regime rather than the opposition, which has failed to engage with the Christian community.

What of the Future?

Will Christianity decay in Syria? It is not an easy question to answer. A landmark date for the whole country was 22 December 2016, when the eastern part of Aleppo was finally liberated by opposition forces. This has given some hope to Christians inside and outside the country that they might have a viable future in Syria. Christian churches were pioneers in launching humanitarian relief programmes for displaced and vulnerable people, regardless of affiliation. Eventually, the number of Christians fell drastically due to the unsafe situation and fear of the future, but also because daily life had become unbearable. It is another dark moment in a long history of waves of emigration. However, based on their faith, Christians have not lost hope at any time that this violence and warfare will come to an end, nor have they abandoned their conviction that their fate is bound up with that of other citizens. Their priority is to achieve survival in a safe, peaceful and protected environment that grants them prosperity and participation in the public life of a civil and secular society that respects all citizens equally.

They are looking forward, like other citizens, to rebuilding a new Syria after the war, undertaking the necessary political, social and cultural reforms, and restoring a plural, mosaic, tolerant, coexisting, moderate and peaceful society. This dream is not exclusive to Christians but is shared by many religious and ethnic groups in Syria. Serious joint efforts from both the political authorities and civic society will be required to achieve peace and reconciliation in a country that has suffered greatly from division and violence. Will Christians of Syria be given the opportunity to participate in such efforts or be left in their shadow? This is a question that cannot be answered now. Can Christians be agents of peace and reconciliation in such turmoil? Are they qualified to do so? And would non-Christian communities in Syria consider them credible agents? Christians will need to tackle such questions in an honest discourse sooner rather than later. At the time of writing, little of this work has been done and Christians have remained inactive except for individual efforts.

A significant challenge will be the refitting of Christians as a minority/component in post-war Syrian society. Considering the brain drain of Christians from the country as a result of the displacement caused by the war and the likelihood that most emigrants will not return, the task awaiting the remaining Christians is formidable. Nonetheless, they are looking forward to sustaining their life with freedom to practise religion, as in the past. They will continue to resist the imposition of any fundamentalist, exclusive, discriminatory and aggressive type of government. They will work to sustain a secular government and a secular constitution so that they can enjoy full dignity as citizens and integrate fully in a society that does not undermine them as a religious minority/component. The shape of the post-war Syria will determine how far Christians are able to reintegrate into society. Despite the large-scale destruction, the role of Christians in Syria, with all their diversities and ethnic and linguistic pluralities, will remain active and constructive.

Bibliography

Awad, Najib George, *And Freedom Became a Public-Square* (Berlin: LIT Verlag, 2012).

Badr, Habib, Suad Abou el Rouss Slim and Joseph Abou Nohra, *Christianity: A History in the Middle East* (Beirut: Middle East Council of Churches; Geneva: World Council of Churches, 2005).

Rabo, Annika, '"We are Christians and We Are Equal Citizens": Perspectives on Particularity and Pluralism in Contemporary Syria', *Journal of Islam and Christian–Muslim Relations*, 23:1 (2012), 83–7.

Sahner, Christian, *Among the Ruins* (Oxford: Oxford University Press, 2014).

Tomass, Mark, *The Religious Roots of the Syrian Conflict: The Remaking of the Fertile Crescent* (New York: Palgrave Macmillan, 2016).

Lebanon

Charles Chartouni

To describe Christianity in Lebanon is a complex task, since the different historical, ecclesiological, cultural and political variables are interwoven in an elaborate, minutely calibrated and multilayered way. The situation is further complicated by the protracted conflicts in Lebanon and the ideological and political commitments they have elicited, which have often inhibited the progress of scholarship.

The history of Lebanese Christianity antedates the creation of the Lebanese national entity in 1921, the historical schism between the churches of Rome and Constantinople (1054), the Christological divides before and after the Seventh Ecumenical Council (787) and the Islamisation of the contemporary Near East (622–750), going back to the earliest Christianity – the itinerant ministry of Jesus and the work of the Apostles. Lebanon is mentioned 72 times in the biblical narrative. The modern nation is the product of a multi-textured cultural sedimentation process, and the various expressions of Christianity found in Lebanon today have to be understood within this context. Particular points of reference include the Christological divides (Chalcedonian vs non-Chalcedonian), the historical schism between Rome and Constantinople, the Islamic watershed and the proto-national period extending between the late Middle Ages and the emergence of Greater Lebanon in 1921. Lebanese Christianity is unlikely to be understood without a working knowledge of the historical, archaeological, ecclesiological, theological and cultural factors that have shaped its identity. However, the most decisive demarcation line is the progressive Islamisation in the realms of both geopolitics and civilisation and the pressure this has exerted on Christian communities identified with political and cultural groupings that have lost out in this process.

Another historical landmark relates to the proto-national era of the medieval emirates (1516–1840), which paved the way for the creation of Greater Lebanon in 1921, in contradistinction with the territories of Mount Lebanon, the historical homeland of the Maronite Church. The emergence of the Lebanese national entity marked the origin of a new political model which broke with the dhimmitude paradigm that had organised the life of Christian communities under Islam along a systemic segregated status set by Koranic, hadithic and historically mandated prescriptions regulating the various religious, political, social and institutional aspects of Christian churches and communities.

Lebanese Christianity is distinguished by its ecumenical composition, by its civic and political egalitarianism, which contradicts dhimmitude, and by a legacy of relative political and moral autonomy nurtured through five centuries of proto-national existence. This historical dynamic set in motion a process of overall empowerment that led to the formation of a nation state upon the demise of the Ottoman Empire, based on a constitutional, pluralistic democracy that stipulates a principled civic parity between Muslims and Christians. This institutional structure intertwines with a form of 'civil religion' predicated on a Christian–Muslim profession of civic faith (the National Covenant), which prevents group domination and gears towards a consociational political culture based on elective civil status and inclusive political, economic, social, religious, educational and cultural rights. The external protections provided under the rubric of collective rights do not in principle equate with internal restrictions that cripple individual rights. Nonetheless, there are neither constitutional nor civil religion restrictions which prevent the dynamics of civic integration.

This relatively stable context has proved attractive to historic churches, which have resettled their headquarters in Lebanon or maintained a dual residence while shifting their real governance to Lebanon. This gradual transfer was basically due to their ability to operate for the first time independently, free from any state or ideological control. Their Lebanese repositioning opened up new horizons, allowing them to emerge from a stifling legacy of theological prejudices, intellectual archaism, mental restrictions, minority fears and complexes, and psychological and moral confinement. The very fact of their presence in an open society set in motion a dynamic of intellectual, institutional and mental reform. They were burying a millennium-long legacy of existential sequestration and opening up new horizons.

Christianity in Lebanon, 1970 and 2015

	1970		2015		Average annual growth rate (%), 1970–2015
Tradition	Population	%	Population	%	
Christians	1,436,000	62.5%	2,004,000	34.3%	0.7%
Anglicans	1,800	0.1%	150	0.0%	–5.4%
Independents	13,600	0.6%	30,500	0.5%	1.8%
Orthodox	357,000	15.5%	343,000	5.9%	–0.1%
Protestants	28,100	1.2%	18,900	0.3%	–0.9%
Catholics	989,000	43.0%	1,613,000	27.6%	1.1%
Evangelicals	17,700	0.8%	20,300	0.4%	0.3%
Pentecostals	4,400	0.2%	63,900	1.1%	6.1%
Total population	**2,297,000**	**100.0%**	**5,851,000**	**100.0%**	**2.1%**

Source: Todd M. Johnson and Gina A. Zurlo (eds), *World Christian Database* (Leiden/Boston: Brill), accessed March 2017.

The Maronite Church

The Maronite Church has a unique role in Lebanon and indeed in 1920 played a leading role in the creation of the Lebanese national entity. It emerged as an independent church within the Antiochene branch of Christianity in 742 and can best be understood as a nativist reaction to the expansion of Islam in the region. While recognising its Chalcedonian and Syriac character, one can best understand the Maronite Church under the sociological category of a Messianic movement whose aim is to restore the historical agency of a defeated religious or cultural group. This accounts for its lingering proto-national consciousness and irredentism. The deconstruction of its written sources helps us understand the dynamics that led to the formation of the church and its corollary political expressions. This long historical trajectory witnessed the gradual rise of multidirectional dynamics that led to the restoration of the historical agency of profoundly disenfranchised Oriental Christian communities in the rural areas of northern Syria. Although far from being a unique example of nativist rejection of Islamisation, the Maronite Church was the only one that succeeded in questioning the dhimmitude organisational pattern and its subculture. This occurred only after a long interlude of political quiescence and eschatological spirituality that found organisational expression in the monastic life and ethos, which profoundly impacted social life.

The monastery has always served as a social and moral matrix around which Maronite social dynamics have been organised. This is no coincidence, since the Maronite Church as a religious movement started in 451 as a monastic community organised around the model of ascetic spirituality represented by a monk named Maron. It was through the Crusades that the Maronites began to forge a relationship with the Church of Rome, and in 1189 this was formalised when they asserted their allegiance to the Roman Apostolic See.

Today, the Maronite Church operates an elaborate institutional infrastructure; it has dozens of schools, five universities, vocational training schools run by its religious orders and dioceses, healthcare institutions, five hospitals and dispensaries, and a broad array of social ministries – social housing, micro-lending programmes, medical insurance, retirement homes, shelters for the homeless, palliative care centres, family counselling services and preparation for marriage, hospital ministry, athletic clubs, cultural activities, music schools, artistic training, and job resource and training centres. The Maronite Church is a powerful public and professional actor, mitigating shortfalls in the delivery of public health and educational services on the part of the state. However, the disharmonies between the effective church ministries and the deficient state public services raise questions about the overall public policy configuration and require the creation of an alternative framework. The discrepancies between the civil sector and the public sector necessitate a renegotiation of their boundaries and a redefinition of the notion of public service. There is an urgent need to review the institutional providers of social services – their arbitrating mechanisms, financing modes and regulatory agencies. Its prominence in the public sphere also requires the Maronite Church to play a role in the political life of the country, which often calls for careful calibration between the different interests at play.

The power of its role owes much to its historical contribution to the foundational and civic narratives, almost amounting to a civil religion in the form of a national covenant, which defined Lebanon as a land of Christian–Muslim dialogue. It also played an effective role in federating the different Catholic churches in the Middle East into such bodies as the Council of Catholic patriarchs of the East; the Caritas Foundation, which coordinates the various social ministries of the church; and the General Secretariat of Catholic Schools, which fulfils the same function with regard to educational institutions. However, it has failed so far to create a co-ordinating mechanism between the different Catholic universities, where it plays a predominant role. Since 1990 it has also been a significant player in the Middle East Council of Churches. Another recent development has been the formation of dioceses in Europe, the Americas and Australia to provide for the large Maronite diaspora.

Greek Churches

The Capitulation Treaty of 1536 between Francis I and Suleiman the Magnificent promoted commercial exchanges between France and the Ottoman Empire and paved the way for the creation of a merchant class among Christians. The Greek Catholic Church arose out of the resulting economic and social transformations in such major urban settings as Damascus and Aleppo. The acculturation processes entailed in these transformations favoured the Uniate tendencies within the Greek Orthodox urban merchant class and led to the creation of the Melkite Greek Catholic Church (GCC).

The traditional narrative of the newly created Uniate Church traces its origins to the Fourth Ecumenical Council (the Council of Chalcedon of 451) and the Council of Florence of 1643, which enacted the Union between Rome and the Eastern Churches to transcend the schism of 1054. The nascent church took root in different areas, including the rural areas surrounding Damascus and Aleppo and around Mount Lebanon, where the Salvatorian and Choueirite Basilian orders played major roles. The historical role played by these two orders set the Lebanese moorings of the newly created church and, ever since, Salvatorians have been elected patriarchs. The GCC is a member of the Middle East Council of Churches and an active participant in ecumenical consultations and dialogue. It also runs a network of schools through its various congregations in Beirut, the Metn North and South districts, the Bekaa, the Shuf, and lower and upper South Lebanon.

Known also as the Antiochene Orthodox or the Roman Orthodox Patriarchate of Antioch and all the East, the Greek Orthodox Church of Antioch is headed by the Greek Orthodox Patriarch of Antioch and considers itself the successor of the Christian community founded in Antioch as recorded in the Book of Acts, chapter 11. It is an autocephalous church within the wider communion of Eastern Orthodox Christianity. For practical reasons the patriarchate relocated from Damascus to Beirut, leading to greater ecumenical openness and the development of theological education, particularly through the Orthodox University at Balamand. Notable leadership in these developments was offered by Ignatius IV Hazim, patriarch from 1979 to 2012, who sought to free the church from political manipulation.

The reformist mandate of Ignatius IV Hazim thoroughly restructured the Orthodox Church of Antioch. In this transformational ministry, he worked in active cooperation with Bishop George Khodr, Metropolitan of Mount Lebanon, whose intellectual and ecumenical ministry profoundly influenced the overall posture of his church, and Bishop Elias Aoudeh, Metropolitan of Beirut, whose active public ministry and entrepreneurship revitalised the public role of his church in multiple ways. Energy for this movement of renewal in the church came from the Orthodox youth movement, which exercised great influence from the 1950s to the 1970s. A question today is whether the reform movement will survive the passing of the generation of leaders associated with Ignatius IV Hazim. The church has an extensive diaspora and includes eparchies in western Europe, North America, Australia, Mexico, Argentina and Brazil.

Armenian Churches

The Armenian Churches are represented primarily by the Catholicosate of the Great House of Cilicia, which traces its origins to the missions of the Apostles Bartholomew and Thaddeus in the first century, whereas St Gregory the Illuminator is considered merely as its first catholicos (257–331). The latter is the religious leader credited with the conversion of Armenia to Christianity in 301, when it became the first country to adopt Christianity as its national religion.

As for the Armenian Catholic Church, it claims the same genealogy as the Catholicosate of Cilicia and bears the same title, and is in full communion with the other Catholic Oriental Churches and the Latin Church. This Church is regulated by Eastern canon law. After the Armenian Apostolic

Church broke away from the Chalcedonian communion in the fifth century, various attempts to restore communion with Rome took place, but none achieved lasting success.

The establishment of the Armenian Apostolic Church of Cilicia in Lebanon is due to the Armenian genocide (*Medz Yeghern*), which gradually eradicated the Armenian presence in its historical territories. The formidable task of the past century has been to relocate the Catholicosate of Cilicia, rebuild church institutions, cater to the immediate needs of an uprooted population, and federate the Armenian diaspora, especially after the Catholicosate of all Armenians in Etchmiadzine lost its autonomy following the communist revolution and the rise of the Soviet Union.

The Catholicosate succeeded in a remarkably short time in establishing itself as the federating pole of Armenians throughout the world. It has embodied the Armenian renaissance after the genocide. Catholicos Aram I, the current Armenian primate, has emphasised the need for a contextualised theology that recapitulates from a theological perspective the Armenian tragedy, a theology of the genocide to connect back with the Christian *kerygma* after suffering extermination. This intellectual effort was preceded by decades of moral, psychological, political, economic, social, educational and religious endeavours to rebuild the Armenian presence, give it back visibility and enable it to adjust to the life conditions in a new environment. The Catholicosate has been highly instrumental in protecting Armenian identity, keeping alive the memory, working through the genocidal legacy and federating the international diaspora, in spite of various political pressures and travails. The Armenian Apostolic Church has also been deeply engaged in ecumenical dialogue, at both domestic and international levels. Catholicos Aram I was elected moderator of the central and executive committees of the World Council of Churches for two consecutive mandates between 1991 and 1998.

The Armenian Apostolic Church also played a key role in building up communitarian institutions in various sectors: educational, social, cultural and economic. Particularly significant has been its efforts to develop the training of its seminarians, both at the seminary it created at Bikfayya and at various Catholic universities in Beirut (St Joseph University, Holy Spirit University of Kaslik) and at international Catholic and secular universities, such as the Institut Catholique in Paris, the Pontifical Gregorian University in Rome, Fordham University in New York and the University of Cambridge in England.

The Armenian Catholic Church, however small, has played a major role in communal reconstruction and the protection of Armenian identity and culture. Its Mechitarist monastery of San Lorenzo, near Venice, harbours the intellectual heritage of the Armenian people and its cultural memory.

It has played a highly significant role by federating the Armenian Catholic diasporas throughout the world. As for the small Armenian Evangelical Church, it also played a key role by promoting the Armenian cause in the USA, protecting the Armenian religious and cultural legacy worldwide, and overhauling the educational capabilities of the Armenians, particularly through the unique Armenian higher-learning institution Haigazian College in Beirut. It contributed to a major acculturation process by introducing the Protestant Reformation to Middle Eastern contexts and engaging in a dialogue with those of Armenian Christian heritage.

Protestant Churches

The Protestant churches include those of an ecumenical disposition, such as the Methodists, Presbyterians, Congregationalists, Anglicans and Lutherans, as well as those that take a non-ecumenical stance, such as the Baptists and the Church of God. Protestants depart from the rest of the churches since they derive from the Protestant Reformation and the dynamics of western Christianity. While they have been part of the overall Christian landscape of Lebanon, they have set themselves apart since they had a problem relating to the historical legacy of the native churches. Pastor Wanis Semaan described their predicament as being 'aliens at home'. At one level they are part of the overall Christian communion but theologically and institutionally their dynamics have been very different from those of the Orthodox and Catholic churches.

This picture is less true nowadays, since ecumenism has made huge strides and the conversation between the Protestant churches and the native churches is taking place within the Middle East Council of Churches (MECC) and the Association of Theological Institutions in the Middle East (ATIME). Particularly significant in this regard has been the development of ecumenical theological training, through which students preparing for the ministry draw on the same theological resources, in French, English or German. In this regard Professor George Sabra of the Near East School of Theology (NEST) has initiated an ambitious research programme to investigate the theological legacy of the patristic era and the seven Ecumenical Councils in relation to the Reformed tradition, as a platform for prospective ecumenical dialogues. Meanwhile, the common political and existential challenges facing Christians in the Middle East have added new scope to the ongoing theological and ecumenical debates. Leading pastors in the different Protestant congregations and theological schools like NEST have engaged, at multiple levels, in theological, pastoral and political dialogues between the various Christian churches.

The Protestant churches have made an important contribution to the development of education in Lebanon. They run a network of schools and have their own federation, which works in parallel with the General Secretariat of Catholic Schools. Protestant missionaries from New England in 1835 founded the Syrian Protestant College in Beirut. This institution became the famous American University of Beirut, which is among the leading higher-learning institutions in the Middle East. Their work also resulted in the Evangelical Synod of Syria and Lebanon, a Reformed church with a federated operational structure.

Assyrian and Syriac Churches

This Christian tradition includes four churches, two autocephalous non-Chalcedonian churches – Assyrian and Syriac – and two Catholic churches. The Syriac Catholic and Chaldean churches emerged when parts of the Syriac tradition entered into communion with the Roman Catholic Church in 1781 and parts of the Assyrian tradition did likewise in 1830. They trace their history to apostolic times and the tradition of Saints Thomas (Mar Tuma), Bartholomew (Mar Tulnay), Thaddeus (Addai) and Mari (Assyrian and Chaldean churches), going back to the first Christian communities in Antioch, as recorded in the Book of Acts, chapter 11.

The Assyrian Church is the only one that claims no communion with any other church, be it Roman Catholic, Orthodox, Coptic, Armenian or Protestant. Nonetheless, both the Assyrian and Syriac Orthodox Churches have signed common Christological declarations, stipulating that their doctrinal differences in no way affect the substance of their faith, since these arose because of differences of terminology and culture and the various formulae adopted by the different theological schools to express the same faith. These churches have been very active in the interdenominational and ecumenical dialogue, be it among themselves, with the other Eastern Orthodox Churches or with the Catholic Church, the World Council of Churches, or the Middle East Council of Churches. Patriarch Ignatius I Zakka-Iwass was one of the early presidents of the World Council of Churches.

Two of these churches have their patriarchal residences in Lebanon. At its foundation in 1781–2, the Syriac Catholic Church built its patriarchal residence in Sharfeh. The Syriac Orthodox Church moved its patriarchate from Damascus to Beirut when the civil war started in Syria in 2011. These churches represent small minorities that took shelter in Lebanon after the Turkish massacres between 1914 and 1918 and those in Iraq in 1933. Many of these refugees were transient, on their way to Western destinations. Syriac, Chaldean and Assyrian Christians who remained were a shifting presence, evolving in line with the security barometers in Lebanon and their homelands in Syria, Iraq and Turkey and the solicitations of their new centres of gravity in Scandinavia, Germany, the Netherlands, the USA,

Australia and Canada, where the bulk of their communities ultimately migrated.

In Lebanon they have managed to be part of the intercommunal dynamics, joining the Christian political mainstream set by the Maronite community. Their ecclesial life, social ministries and ecumenical engagement were coordinated in different respects with the Maronite Church. The recent breakdown of the states of Iraq and Syria and the deadly impact on Christians in these lands forced many of them to quit their ancestral homelands overnight and seek shelter in Lebanon before embarking for their final destinations in western Europe, the USA, Canada, Australia or New Zealand. Their plight testifies to the importance of the Christian presence in Lebanon. At the same time, the displacement of Christian communities as a result of the two Iraq Wars, in 1991 and 2003, and then the Syrian civil war from 2011 raises the question of whether we are witnessing the extinction of Christianity in the Middle East.

The Latin Church

The Apostolic Vicariate, created in 1953 by the papal bull *Solent Caeli* of Pope Pius XII, ministers to the small Latin community in Lebanon. It is mostly served by the Latin congregations and a small number of diocesan clergy. Since the late Middle Ages, Roman Catholic congregations, such as the Franciscans, Capuchins, Carmelites, Vincentians, Jesuits, Salesians, Dominicans, Christian Brothers of Jean Baptiste de la Salle and Marist Brothers of Marcellin Champagnat, White Fathers and various female congregations, have contributed greatly to social development in Lebanon. However, while they have had a great impact at the local community level, they have had less success in shaping the political priorities and direction of the nation as a whole. An exception is found with the Jesuits, who played a foundational role in the creation of Greater Lebanon as a nation-state and, through their university, have contributed to the modernisation process at multiple levels, including human rights, democracy, civic and legal cultures, research and development, business and professional ethics, and many different aspects of higher education.

Christians and Society

Consideration of Christian social influence must begin with the role of the Maronite Church in forming the traditions of proto-national and political autonomy. The newly created national entity in 1921 was meant to overcome the asymmetries of an inegalitarian Islamic political culture and create a working partnership based on moral reciprocity and political and civic parity. The new system aimed at 'replacing religious nationalism by a political nationalism' as it was expressed by the Maronite Patriarch Elias el Hoyek, founder of Greater Lebanon. This Rawlsian definition has yielded a consociational democracy that aimed to reconcile the dilemmas of collective and individual rights in a way that prevents group domination and the subversion of individual rights. This dialectical synthesis was burdened by colliding subcultures, the ambiguities of territorial statehood challenged by Arab and Islamic supranational (*ummah*) ideologies and the disruptive interventionism of Arab and Islamic power politics. Nonetheless, Lebanon has been marked by a distinctive political culture in which the notions of Western democracy prevailed, however distorted by the burdens of tribal cultures, endemic political instability and protracted social conflicts. It has been distinguished by the principled distinction between state and civil society, rotation in power, regular elections (though with some exceptions), and intellectual, religious, civil and political liberties. These qualities, despite inconsistency in upholding them, made Lebanon an exception in an Arab region dominated by autocracies and discretionary forms of ideological totalitarianism.

The rise of ISIS (Islamic State or Daesh) poses a grave threat to Lebanon's political order, destabilising its security and raising the spectre of genocide, massive displacement, brutal discrimination and deprivation of basic human rights – as amply demonstrated in Iraq and Syria. After a harrowing 15 years of civil and regional conflicts towards the end of the Cold War era and having lost ground in terms of political and moral autonomy, Christians are apprehensive of the nihilistic drifts of radical Islam. Meanwhile, the small country, already densely populated by a native population of over 4 million Palestinian refugees, has had to accommodate some 1,500,000 refugees from the conflicts in Iraq and Syria. This interlude can be managed temporarily but can be resolved only by a negotiated and sustainable political solution to the Syrian conflict.

Churches and related organisations have been instrumental in evolving elaborate educational, cultural, professional and social strategies and in catalysing the ideas and inputs of sundry societal actors. The Maronite Church is the leading actor in this field, supported by other churches and international Christian organisations. Christians are also prominent in civil society more widely, where their work is informed by their Christian ethics. The politics of subsidiarity have failed so far to negotiate a viable public policy configuration that would allow for effective cooperation between an elaborate civil sector and a profoundly flawed public sector. In this challenging environment, Lebanese Christians continue to operate a dense network of educational institutions and a broad array of social ministries – hospitals; nurseries; retirement homes; rehabilitation centres for the handicapped, young delinquents, former prisoners, drug addicts, homeless persons, prostitutes and victims of domestic violence; social housing; micro-credit programmes; employment resource centres; and relief and social development programmes. They also undertake advocacy work and education in relation to human rights, women's rights and disabled rights.

Christians have played a pioneering role in economic life. They were behind the modernising dynamics in such sectors as finance, industry, agriculture, tourism, media, advertising, financial auditing, entrepreneurship and business consultancy. Though a minority, Lebanese Christians have proved to be a significant resource in the development of the economies of Saudi Arabia, Kuwait and the Gulf. Church universities played a major role in the remodelling and broadening of the professional division of labour, in putting in place the infrastructure for an informational economy and in facilitating the transfer of technology.

The cultural creativity of a regional minority has been expressed by Lebanese Christians in literature, contemporary theatre, journalism, television production, social media, contemporary art, film and publishing. The role of Lebanese Christians was central to the modernising of the Arabic language. Among the leading innovators in the field of Arabic literature were Gibran Khalil Gibran, Mikhael Neaymi, Amine al Rihani, Ramiz Khalil Sarkis (bilingual in Arabic and English), Georges Chehadeh, Venus Khoury-Gatta, Andree Chedid (bilingual in Arabic and French), as well as Said Akl, Youssef al Khal, Ounsi al Hajje and Chawqi Abi Chaqra. Authors such as Amin Maalouf, Wajdi Moawad, Alexandre Najjar, Raymond Khoury and Rawi Hajje are part of the international mainstream. In the field of theatre, Lebanese producers and actors have been able to reach international standards, as seen in the work of Antoine and Latifeh Moultaqa, Mounir Abou Debs, Jalal Khoury, Raymond Gebara and Mounir Maasri. Contemporary Arab journalism was pioneered by Lebanese journalists in Beirut and Cairo who were behind such leading newspapers as *Al Nahar, Lissan al Hal, Al Ahram, Rose al Youssef, L'Orient, Le Jour* and *Le Soir*. The Jesuit press Dar al Machriq was behind the creation of the contemporary publishing industry and a leading force in the production of dictionaries, glossaries, teaching materials and theological writings. The Librairie du Liban became the largest Arabic publisher of academic literature, covering the whole professional spectrum. In music, too, Lebanese Christians have been prominent, as seen in the contribution of such renowned singers and musicians as Sabah, Feyrouz, Wadih el Safi and the Rahbani Family. Lebanese Christian producers, anchors and journalists have been central to the development of the Arab television and advertising industry. In this, as in many other ways, they have been the leading adaptors of Western modernity in the Arab world.

An Uncertain Future

Christianity in Lebanon is at a crossroads and the churches face manifold challenges. First, there is urgent need for internal reform – ecclesiological, theological, ecumenical, ministerial and ethical. Secondly, there is also urgent need to rethink interfaith issues and strengthen dialogue in an imploding Arab world. Thirdly, there is a need to tackle the immediate and long-term fallout of the catastrophe that has overtaken the churches in Syria and Iraq. Fourthly, there is a need to deal with the lingering political stalemates within Lebanon and the unravelling of relationships with neighbouring states, as these have damaged the country's viability and threatened the future of its democracy. Fifthly, there is a need to address problems in the political and business environments, such as corruption, the misappropriation of public funds and resources, and the demise of notions of the common good and social justice. These problems have not spared church institutions and have undermined the credibility of some clergy. Finally, there is also a need to address declining numbers – Christians now represent only just over a third of the total population.

The challenges ahead include the task of reconstruction after a devastating and protracted civil conflict of 15 years, the disarray caused by the Syrian occupation, lasting another 15 years, and the effects of a generalised normlessness, of competing power centres, brittle statehood, a power vacuum and the demise of individual and public morals for the sake of naked power relationships. These are no easy challenges for those who seek to address the issues and keep themselves in line with the evangelical imperatives and their practical mandates. Discernment, moral and practical decision-making have to remain hand in hand in an exercise of continuing calibration.

The imploding geopolitics of the Middle East are having a destructive impact on the already badly bruised, disenfranchised and broken regional churches. The fragile and diminishing Christian community in Lebanon is left with the lofty and challenging task of defending the honour of Christianity, the spirit and imperatives of the Sermon on the Mount, in a world where religion often takes violent forms and politics is morally bankrupt. The intense activity of the churches over the past 25 years, seen for example in the three synods held by the Maronite Church in recent years, has attempted to address the challenges of an uncertain future with a better evangelical and moral compass.

The churches' internal reforms, the issues of interfaith dialogue, the political, social and economic reform agendas, and their contextual theological self-understanding and ministries were extensively dealt with in the documents and declarations of the three synods. What is urgently needed at this stage is an increased coherence to put an end to the chasms between principled statements and ongoing practices. However, the pitfalls of decaying political, social, economic and moral orders have proved highly damaging and hard to repair. Churches are challenged by ugly realities, internal imperfections and inconsistencies, and the evangelical imperatives. They are required to meet these challenges simultaneously, timeously and effectively.

Bibliography

Descy, Serge, *The Melkite Church: An Historical and Ecclesiological Approach* (Boston, MA: Sophia Press, 1993).

Ignatius, Dick, *Melkites: Greek Orthodox and Greek Catholics of the Patriarchate of Antioch, Alexandria and Jerusalem* (Boston, MA: Sophia Press, 2004).

Jenkins, Philip, *The Lost History of Christianity* (New York: HarperCollins, 2008).

Mouawad, Ray Jabre, *Les Maronites: Chrétiens du Liban* (Turnhout: Brepols, 2010).

Salibi, Kamal S., *A House of Many Mansions: The History of Lebanon Reconsidered* (Berkeley, CA: University of California Press, 1990).

Israel

David Neuhaus SJ

The modern state of Israel is one of the countries that constitute the cradle of the Christian faith, known as the Holy Land, the others being Palestine and Jordan. Here Jesus Christ was born, lived, died and rose from the dead, fulfilling the promises of God to the patriarchs, priests, kings, sages and prophets of ancient Israel. Here, too, the first church of believers was established in Jerusalem, and from Jerusalem the Apostles set off to preach the Good News to the ends of the earth. The land and its towns echo in churches throughout the world, in the readings from the Old and New Testaments, in liturgy and song. To this land, Christians have come as pilgrims from near and far to renew and deepen their faith at the holy places that mark the history of salvation. Since the first half of the first century, the Holy Land has been home to Christian communities, whose members have played a central role in the history of this land. Who are the Christians in Israel today? What are the challenges they face? What is their future?

Who Are the Christians in Israel Today?

Christians in Israel belong to a mosaic of communities. First, there is a great diversity of Christian denominations: Byzantine (or Greek) Orthodox and Catholics (who together make up the vast majority of the Christians in Israel), Roman (or Latin) Catholics, Maronites, Armenian Apostolic Orthodox and Catholics, Syrian Orthodox and Catholics, Copts, Ethiopians, Anglicans, Lutherans and a plethora of Evangelical groups. There are also thousands of Messianic Jews, who believe in Christ but do not identify themselves as Christians.

Secondly, in Israel today there is great diversity among Christians with regard to their origins and language. They live in a diversity of socio-political and cultural contexts. The local, rooted Christians are for the most part Arabic speaking, identify themselves as Palestinians and live integrated within Palestinian Arab society in Israel. The majority of this population lives in Galilee; in Haifa and the surrounding villages; and in the towns of Jaffa, Ramla and Lydda (Lod). Long-term resident expatriates mainly serve in church structures and institutions. Most of the Christian hierarchical religious leadership is from this group: Greeks in the Greek Orthodox

Church; Italians and other Europeans, as well as a growing number of Asians and Africans, in the Roman Catholic Church; clerics from Lebanon, Syria, Egypt and Iraq in the Eastern Rite Churches; and English, German, Swedish and American clerics in the Anglican and Lutheran Churches.

An increasing number of Christians of Jewish and other diverse origins live within Jewish Israeli, Hebrew-speaking society. Most of these have immigrated to Israel in recent decades from the countries of the former Soviet Union and eastern Europe as well as from Ethiopia. Finally, a large number of Christians have come to Israel in recent years as migrants – labour migrants, coming predominantly from Asia, and asylum seekers, coming predominantly from Africa.

Christian citizens in Israel today make up about 2.4% of the total population. This constitutes a major decrease in their proportion of the population since 1948, when hundreds of thousands of Palestinian Arabs, Muslim and Christian, left the country as refugees and hundreds of thousands of Jews entered the country as new immigrants. Until 1948, Christians made up about 10% of the population. Currently the Christian population of Israel includes 120,000–130,000 Christian citizens who are Palestinian Arab and Arabic speaking and 30,000–40,000 Christian citizens who are integrated into the Jewish Israeli Hebrew-speaking population, predominantly from the former Soviet Union and eastern Europe. In addition to Christian citizens, the population includes around 135,000 Christian migrants: c. 50,000 Christian migrant workers, legal and illegal (mostly from Asia); c. 35,000 Christian African asylum seekers (mostly from Eritrea); and c. 50,000 Christians who have overstayed their tourist visas to look for employment (mostly from eastern Europe).

The State of Israel was established in 1948, but most Christian communities have maintained older institutional structures that have jurisdiction

Christianity in Israel, 1970 and 2015

	1970		2015		Average annual growth rate (%), 1970–2015
Tradition	Population	%	Population	%	
Christians	79,000	2.8%	189,000	2.3%	2.0%
Anglicans	900	0.0%	1,500	0.0%	1.1%
Independents	3,400	0.1%	37,000	0.5%	5.4%
Orthodox	18,400	0.7%	42,100	0.5%	1.9%
Protestants	8,400	0.3%	13,600	0.2%	1.1%
Catholics	47,100	1.7%	109,000	1.4%	1.9%
Evangelicals	5,800	0.2%	33,500	0.4%	4.0%
Pentecostals	1,800	0.1%	43,600	0.5%	7.4%
Total population	**2,850,000**	**100.0%**	**8,064,000**	**100.0%**	**2.3%**

Source: Todd M. Johnson and Gina A. Zurlo (eds), *World Christian Database* (Leiden/Boston: Brill), accessed March 2017.

beyond the borders of this modern political entity. Many churches maintain their administrative centres in Israeli-occupied East Jerusalem and have jurisdiction over the faithful in Israel and Palestine (West Bank and Gaza Strip), some even stretching further and including Jordan, Cyprus and beyond. Thus, many Christian Palestinian Arab citizens of the State of Israel have ongoing communal relations with their co-religionists in Palestine and Jordan.

A major issue facing Christian Arabs in Israel is emigration from their homeland. This trend, which began in the nineteenth century, is one of the most important threats to the Christian communities in the Middle East today. Israel is experiencing a serious brain drain as the young, the educated and the professionals emigrate, leaving behind a more and more impoverished community. Christians also have smaller families than both Muslims and Jews. The result is that despite an overall slight increase in the number of Christians from year to year, there is a significant decrease in their proportion in the overall population. The concomitant immigration of Christians into Israel has resulted in the creation of vibrant communities who live in fragile circumstances, their members often rootless and without permanent legal status.

Identity in Diversity and Unity

How do Christian Palestinian Arab citizens of Israel define their identity? Many describe them as being in the midst of an identity crisis. Some see themselves trapped between Jewish nationalism, which marginalises them and discriminates against them, and Arab nationalism, increasingly Islamic in its expression, which alienates them.

The fragmentation of the Christian community along denominational lines contributes to an identity crisis. History has divided Christian Arabs into a variety of denominations, whose origins are to be found in the theological debates of the first millennium, the Reformation, and the creation of Eastern Catholic Churches and consequent structural fragmentation. Byzantines, Latins and Oriental Orthodox (Armenians, Syrians, Copts, Ethiopians) compete and coexist in the holy places, and an even greater variety of Christian denominations – Eastern Catholic Churches (Byzantine, Maronite, Syrian, Armenian, Chaldean), Anglicans, various Protestants and Evangelicals – compete and coexist in the daily life of the community. For many, these divisions and the resulting rivalries are a source of scandal. Others insist today that their primary religious identity is Christian rather than Byzantine, Latin or Lutheran. Ecumenical dialogue is not only a formality but a day-to-day reality, in which Christian Palestinian Arabs in Israel, constantly aware of their small numbers, proclaim: 'united we survive, divided we disappear'.

The events of 1948 led to the creation of the State of Israel and the dispossession of hundreds of thousands of Palestinians, both Muslims and Christians. The continuing conflict has produced a series of wars in which the Arab countries have been repeatedly defeated. Fragmentation of the Christian Palestinian Arabs is not only denominational but also geopolitical. After 1948, Christian Palestinian Arabs, like their Muslim compatriots, found themselves in three different socio-political realities. Some became citizens in the newly created State of Israel, some found themselves in territories annexed to the Hashemite Kingdom of Jordan (East Jerusalem and the West Bank) or occupied by Egypt (the Gaza Strip), while many others found themselves in a diaspora, living as refugees. In 1967, Israel occupied East Jerusalem, the West Bank and the Gaza Strip, establishing a military occupation in these territories.

Within the State of Israel, all Arab citizens (Muslim, Christian and Druze) are subject to second-class status, discrimination and marginalisation. For many decades, the fight for equality strengthened the bonds among Christians and between Muslims and Christians. This struggle was led by secular political parties, in which Christians often had leading roles, the most important of which was the Communist Party. Generations of nominally Christian politicians – including communists such as Tawfiq and George Toubi, Emil Habibi and Saliba Khamis, and nationalists like Azmi Bishara and Anglican clerics Shehadeh Shehadeh and Riah Abu El-Assal – worked hand in hand with secular Muslims in the fight against discrimination and marginalisation in Israel. However, a rising Islamic movement in Israel has challenged the secular parties. In recent years, tension based upon the religious divide among Christians, Muslims and Druze has sometimes characterised local conflicts in different Arab locations, the best-known example being the demand by certain Islamic activists to construct a large mosque alongside the Basilica of the Annunciation in Nazareth. The Islamic movement has fomented these conflicts, as have certain elements in the Israeli administration that see advantage in dividing the Arab minority.

Elements within the Israeli administration have consistently followed a policy of 'divide and rule' with regard to the Arab minority. In the 1950s, the Israeli administration worked hard to separate the Druze community from the rest of the Arab population. Young Druze were drafted into the army alongside Jews (Christians and Muslims are not enlisted) and the state promoted a discourse that defined the Druze as a people distinct from the Arabs, with the support of the Druze traditional religious leadership. Similar attempts to separate the Christians from other Arabs failed in that period but have been renewed in recent years and are gaining impetus, supported by some Christian Arabs. The attempt is to foster a 'Christian' identity that no longer defines itself in terms of the Arab world. This current dwells upon the fears of rising Islamic radicalism and promises of material gain for Christians who hope to integrate themselves within the privileged Jewish sector. The most blatant form of this attempt to reformulate identity comes in the attempts to enlist Christian Arab youths into the Israeli army. Led by Greek Orthodox priest Father Gabriel Naddaf and Maronite Israeli army lieutenant Shadi Khalloul, this current promotes the 'Aramaic' rather than Palestinian Arab identity of the Christians in Israel. The Justice and Peace Commission of the Assembly of Catholic Ordinaries in the Holy Land published a letter on this subject in 2013. The Commission said:

> The Church sees her task as one of educating our young people to accept themselves as they are, giving them a balanced human, national and Christian education and an awareness of their history, their rootedness in the land and a sense of identity that integrates the different elements (Palestinian Arab, Christian and citizen of Israel) rather than repressing any one of these elements. The bishops and priests must help the faithful in the midst of this crisis of identity.

The ongoing struggle for Palestinian independence has provided a platform on which Christian Palestinian Arabs can not only surmount their denominational divisions but also unite with Muslims in a joint programme of action. Palestinian Arab church leaders have been outspoken in their condemnation of the Israeli occupation of Palestinian Territories and their demand for Palestinian statehood, among the most prominent being emeritus Latin (Roman Catholic) Patriarch of Jerusalem Michel Sabbah, Greek Orthodox Bishop Atallah Hanna, emeritus Anglican Bishop Riah Abu El-Assal and Lutheran Bishop Munib Younan. Christian Palestinian centres to promote Christian unity and solidarity with the Palestinian cause have sprung up to strengthen this consciousness of being both Christian and Palestinian. Among these can be mentioned the Al-Liqa' Centre in Bethlehem, founded by Greek Catholic Palestinian Arab Israeli citizen Dr Geries Khoury, and the Sabeel Ecumenical Liberation Centre in Jerusalem, founded by Palestinian Arab Israeli citizen Anglican Canon Naim Ateek. Some leaders of the Palestinian Evangelical communities have also integrated into this ecumenical effort to unite Christian Palestinians around the national cause. One example is the collaboration among Palestinian theologians in the composition of the Kairos Document, which formulated a Palestinian 'cry of hope' in the face of the continuing Israeli occupation of Palestine. Within Israel, one particularly Christian face to the struggle for Palestinian rights has been the campaign to rebuild the Christian Palestinian Arab villages of Ikrit and Kufr Bir'am, on the northern Israeli border, which were evacuated in 1948 and subsequently destroyed. This campaign was given prominence by former Greek Catholic Archbishop of Galilee Yusuf Raya, who had arrived in Israel as archbishop in 1968 after participating in the struggle for African American rights in the US South, alongside Martin Luther King. Archbishop Raya was one of the first church leaders to speak out for the rights of the Palestinian Arab citizens in Israel.

The ascendance of radical Islam, which has succeeded in separating the Gaza Strip from the West Bank, has pushed Christians to the margins. The vocal Islamic movement inside Israel has created concerns among Palestinian Arab citizens of Israel, too. The latest series of uprisings in the Arab world, beginning at the end of 2010, has revealed the deep desire of the masses for freedom and dignity but has also opened a Pandora's box of radical Islamic alternatives to secular Arab regimes, constituting a palpable threat to the Christian dream of equality and integration in the Arab world.

At the same time, the growth of new communities in Israel, especially Evangelical and Pentecostal, have also led some Christians to distance themselves from both the traditional churches and their Muslim neighbours. 'Born again' Christians (*mutajadidin*) sometimes justify aspects of Jewish nationalism (Zionism), usually based upon their literal reading of the Old Testament. These communities are often in some kind of relationship with parallel communities of Christians living in the Jewish, Hebrew-speaking milieu.

Christian Palestinian Arab citizens of Israel play an important role within the Arab minority. Christians are often highly educated and serve in the most prominent professions – as doctors, social workers, lawyers, engineers, academics and businesspeople. The best Arab schools in Israel are Christian schools, and some of these are also the best schools in the country overall. Much of the local Arabic-language press, theatre and literature are the fruit of Christian endeavour. One Christian Palestinian Arab writer, Anton Shammas, from the entirely Greek Catholic village of Fassouta, has even been considered one of the leading Hebrew-language authors, after the 1986 publication of his novel *Arabesques*. Christians also have leading roles in organisations that combat discrimination and campaign for human rights. At present, one of the Israeli Supreme Court judges, Salim Joubran, is a Christian. A long series of Christians has served in the Israeli Knesset, most of them members of the communist and other Arab parties, including two who serve in the present Knesset, Basel Ghattas and Aida Touma-Suleiman.

In March 2014, the Justice and Peace Commission of the Assembly of Catholic Ordinaries in the Holy Land published a statement on the continuing attempts of the Israeli authorities to separate Christians from their Palestinian Arab roots, saying,

> We, the heads of the Catholic Church in Israel, would like to clarify that it is not the right or the duty of the Israeli civil authorities to tell us who we are. In fact, most of our faithful in Israel are Palestinian Arabs. They are obviously Christians too. They are also citizens of the State of Israel. We do not see any contradiction in this definition of identity: Christian Palestinian Arabs who are citizens of the State of Israel.... If the Knesset indeed seeks the good of the citizens of Israel, it should invest every effort to legislate laws that remove discrimination, whether it be against Jews or Arabs, Christians, Muslims or Druze. In creating a society that unites all citizens in equality and strives for justice and peace, there will remain no reason to fear for anybody and Israelis and Palestinians, Christians, Muslims and Druze, can live together in mutual respect and dignity, working together to build a better future.

Emigration and Immigration

Alongside emigration of Christian Palestinian Arabs from their homeland has been significant immigration of non-Arab Christians, who have settled within Jewish, Hebrew-speaking society in Israel. These non-Arab Christian populations have created the blossoming of Christian communities and the establishment of makeshift churches in places where churches had not been present, at the very heart of Jewish towns and cities. Today, south Tel Aviv has one of the largest Christian populations in Israel, tens of thousands of Christians, belonging to a plethora of churches, Orthodox, Eastern, Catholic, Protestant, Evangelical, Pentecostal and Messianic, as well a variety of sects. This population, diverse in its origins, introduces new forms of Christianity to Israel.

Christian members of Jewish families and Christians claiming Jewish ancestry have been migrating to Israel since 1948. Granted many of the same privileges as their Jewish co-nationals, they identify mostly as Jews. Among the most well known examples of Christians of Jewish origin who sought to immigrate to Israel are the Roman Catholic Polish Carmelite priest Osvald Daniel Rufeisen, whose demand to be recognised as a Jew in Israel in 1959 made headlines, and the Roman Catholic Dominican priest Bruno Hussar, who founded the Jewish-Arab cooperative village Newe Shalom. The 'Brother Daniel' case raised awareness of this new population of Christians. Structures that were set up to serve their religious needs made Hebrew the language of a Christian population for the first time in the history of the church. The Catholic-founded Work of Saint James, which became a vicariate in 1990, has continually promoted the possibility of being Catholic, Israeli and a Hebrew speaker, integrated within the Jewish population.

Today, after the massive waves of immigration from the countries of the former Soviet Union (about 1 million people between 1990 and 2005), the non-Arab Christians in Israel represent about a quarter of the Christian citizens (between 30,000 and 40,000). This is about 10% of the immigrants from the ex-Soviet Union whom the state defines as being non-Jews. Under pressure to assimilate into the Jewish population, some hide their Christian identities, adopt Jewish customs and even convert to Judaism. The assimilation process is even more successful with the children of these immigrants who are educated in the secular, Jewish Israeli school system, with almost no exposure to the Christian faith and traditions of their parents. The state promotes conversion to Judaism for those perceived as having Jewish heritage, and this is particularly the case within the Israeli army, where young people are encouraged to enter the 'mainstream' by becoming formally Jewish. The Institute for Jewish Studies began its work in 1999 and set its sights on converting thousands of non-Jewish Russians annually, and the Israeli army has its own parallel courses for non-Jewish soldiers.

Tens of thousands of Christian migrant workers and asylum seekers, the majority from Asia and Africa, have boosted the number of Christians in Israel. At the beginning of the 1990s, a stream of African and Asian migrant workers entered Israel, replacing cheap Arab labour as the authorities increasingly impeded Palestinians from the Occupied Territories from entering Israel. An increasingly wealthy Israeli society also began to import tens of thousands of caregivers for the elderly, the handicapped and the sick. Although many migrant workers remained for a limited time in Israel, returning to their countries of origin when their permits expired or when they were deported, some migrants have established families in Israel. The children of migrant families have been integrated into the public school system, becoming Hebrew speakers and largely identifying with their country of adoption. The arrival of the children and their schooling facilitated lengthier stays for their parents, and some migrant families have been granted permanent residence in recent years.

After 2007, when Europe closed its southern borders to Africans fleeing civil war and famine through North Africa, an increasing number of asylum seekers came to Israel by way of Egypt, making their way across the Sinai border. The first stream was mainly from South Sudan and Darfur. They were fast followed by increasing numbers of Eritreans. Israel cannot deport these populations back to their countries of origin because of international conventions but has refused to process the individuals who came into the country as refugees, giving them instead group protection, which can be withdrawn whenever the authorities see fit. Group protection was withdrawn, for example, when South Sudan proclaimed independence and thousands of Sudanese Christians were deported back to a country that was still in the throes of violence and famine. Increasingly, Israel has sought to discourage Eritrean and other African asylum seekers from coming into the country, by setting up prison facilities for those entering and by fortifying the border with Egypt. At the same time, those already in Israel have been pressured to leave, a departure facilitated by the signing of voluntary deportation papers. Nonetheless, the children born to these asylum seekers are integrated in the Israeli Jewish Hebrew-language school system, facilitating a partial integration of their families too.

The new Christian populations constitute a dilemma for a state that defines itself as Jewish. Whereas Christian Arabs are clearly distinguished from the Jewish mainstream because they generally live within an Arabic-speaking milieu, geographically and institutionally separate from the Jewish Hebrew-speaking milieu, many of the new Christians live at the very heart of Jewish society. The new Christian Israeli citizens (mostly from the former Soviet Union and eastern Europe) make no political demands on the state but do seek total social integration. Their children are educated with Jewish children, serve in the army and intermarry with Jews. Small signs of recognition of this Christian presence have appeared. One example is that, since 1996, Christian soldiers in the army can swear their oath of loyalty to the military on a copy of the New Testament. The challenge for these Christians is transmitting their faith to their children in the midst of a strongly secular yet stridently Jewish society. For those Christians who are not citizens, the labour migrants and asylum seekers, the precarious living conditions, exploitation in the labour market, lack of social and medical benefits and growing racism (particularly directed against the Africans) are enormous challenges. Yet here, too, the generation born in Israel to labour migrants and asylum seekers is attracted to the vibrant secular Israeli culture and only rarely continues to frequent the Christian communities and churches in which their parents are at home.

The arrival of new Christian populations has led to the establishment of many Evangelical, Pentecostal and other forms of African, Asian and Latin American faith communities. Many of them are Charismatic and led by individual pastors who rent premises in the neighbourhoods in which the migrants live. Dozens of shop, apartment and bomb-shelter churches are spread throughout south Tel Aviv, the hub of migrant life. Foreign Evangelical and Pentecostal missionaries have also set up local organisations in Israel that not only gather the new Christians but also try to attract Jews and Muslims and Arabic-speaking Christians. Among the Evangelicals and Pentecostals there is also widespread support for Christian Zionism, and organisations like the International Christian Embassy in Jerusalem and Bridges for Peace also engage in pro-Israel lobbying and fundraising. The International Fellowship of Christians and Jews, founded by strongly Zionist Rabbi Yehiel Eckstein, encourages Jewish–Christian dialogue and reconciliation based upon unwavering support for the State of Israel among Evangelicals and Pentecostals.

Suspicion of Christianity and Christians, based on theological arguments ('Christianity is idol worship'), historical hurt ('Christians have treated Jews badly') and ideological animosity ('Christians side with Palestinians in the Israeli–Palestinian conflict'), is common in Jewish Israeli society. This has created a discourse and practice of contempt in some Jewish circles in Israel, leading to manifestations of anti-Christian sentiment in some areas: spitting at traditionally garbed clergy, spraying anti-Christian slogans on churches and institutions, damaging property and making fun of the Christian faith in the media. Particularly at risk in the face of anti-Christian sentiment are the groups of Messianic Jews, many of whom are newcomers to Israel, who believe in Jesus Christ but insist that they are part of the Jewish people. They have been the focus of attacks in word and act by Jewish religious organisations that oppose Christian 'mission' and promote anti-Christian discourse and policy.

Institutions, Service and Inter-community Relations

Christians in Israel live as a mosaic of diverse groups, submerged in worlds that are Muslim (within Arab society in Israel) or Jewish (mainstream Israeli society). Relations with Muslims and Jews are not marginal but are essential for the survival and welfare of these communities. The two majorities, however, are not always sensitive to the Christian presence. In reaction, Christians adopt a variety of strategies:

- *Assimilation.* Some Christians seek to resolve the tension of belonging to a marginal minority by seeking to assimilate within the majority, be it Muslim or Jewish. Although conversion to Islam or Judaism is rare, choices of behaviour that camouflage Christian identity and underline belonging to the dominant majorities are sometimes adopted.
- *Dialogue.* The Christian traditional leadership and some of the laity try to engage the majority, both Muslim and Jewish, in a dialogue that focuses on the need for a discourse of respect, equal rights, shared values and, most importantly, shared citizenship.
- *Withdrawal.* Many Christians, in the face of marginalisation and discrimination, prefer to withdraw from the public sphere and create closed environments where Christians can feel comfortable. Trends in housing and schooling in recent decades have seen the enrolling of most Christian children in Christian private schools rather than in government schools and the creation of housing projects where Christians live isolated from their non-Christian neighbours.
- *Emigration.* Many Christians, in the face of the challenges to being an Arab

and/or a Christian in Israel, choose to seek a better future for themselves and their children in other countries, usually where Christians are the majority.

Despite the small number of Christians in Israel, the Christian institutional presence is very significant in areas where the church traditionally has been present, predominantly in the Arab sector. This institutional presence was built up over centuries, and especially from the nineteenth century onwards included schools, hospitals, orphanages and shelters for the handicapped and the elderly that catered to Christians and an ever-increasing number of non-Christians. Most of these institutions were established by foreign Christians, particularly by Catholic religious orders and congregations. Today, these Christian institutions give prominence to a Christian community, even though small, in areas like Jaffa, Ramla, Nazareth, Haifa and many towns and villages in Galilee. Educational institutions, medical facilities and welfare organisations constitute important arenas in which Christian discourse and values can be promoted in the larger society. The Christian institutional presence in Israel introduces the important reality of a church that serves all, and especially the neediest. As most of the institutions are situated in Arabic-speaking areas, the outreach is predominantly to Muslims.

The continued promotion of Christian institutions at the service of the entire population must go hand in hand with the development of an appropriate Christian discourse about the world in which Christians live. This discourse must also distinguish the Christian contribution as a voice for justice, peace, pardon, reconciliation and selfless love. The Christian presence in Israel is not and will not be measured by its statistical importance but by the significance of its contribution to society, particularly in its service of education, health and relief work and in its language of love.

What Future for Christians in Israel?

Ongoing discrimination against and marginalisation of Christians in Israel weaken already fragile communities that play a very positive role in the life of the country. However, Christians, perhaps more than all other residents of Israel today, are threatened by the ongoing state of war between Israel and the Palestinians. The occupation of Palestinian lands, discrimination against Arab citizens in Israel, violence in the region and socio-political unrest are all elements that threaten the future of Christians as well as everyone else.

Prophets of doom predict that Christians in Israel and throughout the Holy Land are disappearing and that the day will dawn when there are no Christians remaining in the area. Educated Christian Arabs are indeed migrating out of their homeland, and those who stay are having fewer children. Nonetheless, new Christian communities, however fragile, are being formed. Christians have the vocation to contemplate the future with hope, actively engaging the challenges of the present:

1. Christian education needs to deepen a sense of belonging to the land and the particular vocation of being Christian in the land made holy by the history of salvation.
2. Christians need to confront the temptation to emigrate, with a focus on this Christian vocation, and at the same time maintain links with the Christian diaspora in order to garner support for those who stay.
3. Christians need to unite more and more, not only across the divisions of denominational identities but also across the socio-political boundaries that come from the diversity of origins and socio-political contexts.
4. Christian Palestinian Arabs must accommodate the new Christians among them as equal members of the church, and new Christians must get to know their Palestinian brothers and sisters and stand in solidarity with them.
5. Christians need to engage in civil society, bringing to it a discourse that focuses on gospel values like justice, peace, forgiveness and reconciliation as well as demanding the fostering of a civil city in which belonging is based upon citizenship rather than on religious, denominational or ethnic identity.
6. Christians need to identify those Muslims and Jews who are allies in the struggle for a society in both Palestine and Israel in which freedom, equality, dignity and the respect for human rights are foundational.
7. Christians from Israel need to play a greater role in the developing dialogue between Christians and Jews. This dialogue constitutes one of the most astonishing revolutions in the twentieth century, making Christians and Jews partners and allies on many issues, after centuries of suspicion and hostility. Christians in Israel are in the unique position of being the only Christian minority to live in a state in which Jews are the majority.

In January 2015, emeritus Latin Patriarch of Jerusalem Michel Sabbah addressed a congress at the Hebrew University of Jerusalem on the Christian Palestinian Arab citizens of Israel. He was insistent that the Christians in Israel have a vocation:

> The vocation of the Christian is to point the way to peace and to walk in its path. This peace must be built on the dignity of each human being, Palestinian and Jewish. Blessed are the peace makers for they truly serve God and humanity, all humanity, Palestinians and Israelis and the whole region.

Bibliography

Mack, Merav, 'The Status of the Christian Palestinian Communities in Israel: Tensions Between Laity, Clergy, and State', in M. Breger, Y. Reiter and L. Hammer (eds), *Sacred Space in Israel and Palestine: Religion and Politics* (London: Routledge, 2011), 284–310.

Mansour, Attalah, *Narrow Gate Churches: The Christian Presence in the Holy Land Under Muslim and Jewish Rule* (Pasadena, CA: Hope Publishing House, 2004).

Mansour, Johnny, *Arab Christians in Israel: Facts, Figures and Trends* (Bethlehem: Diyar Publisher, 2012).

Munayer, Salim and Lisa Loden, *Through My Enemy's Eyes* (London: Paternoster, 2013).

Neuhaus, David, 'Sixty Years: A Pastoral Letter', 9 August 2015 (http://catholic.co.il/index.php?option=com_content&view=article&id=11368:sixty-years-a-pastoral-letter&catid=28&Itemid=134&lang=en, last accessed 22 November 2016).

Palestine

Bernard Sabella

For Palestinian Christians, Christianity links up to the early church. Some families claim to be descended from the early Christians. The liturgy of both the Maronites and the Syriacs, both Orthodox and Catholic, goes back to Aramaic, the language spoken by Jesus himself. Armenians insist that they have been in contact with the holy places and specifically with the city of Jerusalem since the fourth century, when their nation was converted to Christianity by St Jacob. Copts, whose faith in Christ spread early on in Egypt, associate their presence in Jerusalem and the Holy Land with the arrival of St Helena, mother of the Emperor Constantine, with whom some Coptic Christians made the journey at the beginning of the fourth century. Ethiopian association with Jerusalem dates back to the Middle Ages. Ethiopian pilgrims were known to have visited the holy places from the fourth century.

The Greek Orthodox Church has a long history in the country, stretching back to the Chalcedonian Council of 451, which established a patriarchate in Jerusalem. The Greek Orthodox see themselves as the inheritors of the first church and they speak of how they conserved Jerusalem in the face of all challenges, citing how Patriarch Sofronius met with Caliph Omar to preserve the church's position in Jerusalem when the Muslim armies took it over in 638. With the arrival of the Crusaders in 1099, the Greek Orthodox Patriarchate was removed to Constantinople. It was not until 1845 that the permanent residence of a Greek Orthodox Patriarch was re-established in Jerusalem.

The Latins, as the local Roman Catholics are known, speak of a long history, with the Latin Patriarchate first established during the Crusades. In the long period of absence of the Latin Patriarchate, the Franciscan Order took charge of the holy places and of the spiritual welfare of Roman Catholic adherents in the country. The Franciscan custody of the Holy Land was established in 1217 and covered all the territories around the south-east Mediterranean basin, from Egypt to Greece and beyond, in addition to the Holy Land. In 1847 the Latin Patriarch was allowed to return, and since then the Latin Patriarchate of Jerusalem has had jurisdiction over Israel, Palestine, Jordan and Cyprus.

The Greek-Eastern Orthodox Patriarchate of Jerusalem dates back to the fifth century, when the Council of Chalcedon adopted the Act of Faith, and hence its adherents remained in communion with the Imperial (Royal) See of Constantinople (the term 'Melkite' means royal). In 1752 a Greek Catholic archdiocese was established in Nazareth, and 20 years later the Greek Catholics of Jerusalem were placed under the jurisdiction of the Melkite Patriarchate of Antioch, and have been represented ever since by a patriarchal vicar. Since 1890 the Syriac Catholic Church has had a patriarchal vicar running the affairs of the small community located mostly in Jerusalem and Bethlehem. The Armenian Catholic Church separated from the Armenian Orthodox Church in 1741. In 1842 a patriarchal vicariate was established in Jerusalem. The Maronite Church in Jerusalem and environs is a small one, with a Maronite patriarchal vicariate established in 1895. Most Maronites in the country reside in Galilee, although some families reside in Jerusalem and some in Bethlehem.

Most Protestant churches date back to the nineteenth century, when the various missions made their way to the region in order to evangelise. From 1841 there was a joint Anglican–Lutheran Protestant bishopric in Jerusalem until 1886, when the Church of England took over responsibility for the Anglican part. In 1976 the Anglican Protestant Episcopal Church in Jerusalem and the Middle East was established and an Arab bishop was consecrated at its head. After the Anglican–Lutheran venture failed in 1886, the German Lutheran Church continued to care for the interests of German Lutherans and increasing numbers of local indigenous Lutherans. Since 1979 the Arabic-speaking congregation, the Evangelical Lutheran Church, has had its own Arab bishop. The variety of other Protestant churches in the Holy Land includes the Church of Scotland and Baptist churches. For Christians, in Palestine and worldwide, Jerusalem is clearly the place of roots, ever living and nourishing, as stated in a November 1994 memorandum from the 13 heads of churches in the Holy City.

Christianity in Palestine, 1970 and 2015

	1970		2015		Average annual growth rate (%), 1970–2015
Tradition	Population	%	Population	%	
Christians	53,200	4.7%	69,600	1.5%	0.6%
Anglicans	1,400	0.1%	5,500	0.1%	3.1%
Independents	1,500	0.1%	5,700	0.1%	3.0%
Orthodox	27,700	2.5%	33,100	0.7%	0.4%
Protestants	2,700	0.2%	5,200	0.1%	1.5%
Catholics	19,400	1.7%	16,500	0.4%	−0.4%
Evangelicals	1,700	0.2%	5,700	0.1%	2.7%
Pentecostals	1,300	0.1%	10,200	0.2%	4.6%
Total population	**1,125,000**	**100.0%**	**4,668,000**	**100.0%**	**3.2%**

Source: Todd M. Johnson and Gina A. Zurlo (eds), *World Christian Database* (Leiden/Boston: Brill), accessed March 2017.

The Palestinian Christian Population: Trends

In 2014, Palestinian Christians made up less than 2% of the overall population in both Palestine and Israel. In Israel, indigenous Christians were approximately 1.4% of the total population of Israel (8.3 million) and 7.1% of its Arab population (1.7 million). In Palestine, the local Arabic-speaking Christians made up 1.1% of the entire population of roughly 4.5 million.

To give an understanding of population dynamics, the percentage of indigenous Christians in the overall population stood at its high point, 10.7%, in 1890, with a population of 57,000 Christians out of a total population of 532,000 inhabitants. In 1947, in spite of the Christian population having almost tripled since 1890, the Christian percentage fell to 7.3% of the total population of almost 2 million inhabitants. Between 1947 and 2012, the Palestinian Christian population increased by an estimated 20,000 persons. In contrast, if conditions had been peaceful and normal and if Palestinian Christians had stayed in their homeland, the population would have been expected to increase to 480,000 by 2012.

To give an understanding of the breakdown of the Christian population by denomination, the table below gives estimates of numbers of adherents of different churches in Israel and Palestine in 2014 (more complete totals, including expatriate Christians, are presented in the tables on pages 128 and 141):

Denomination	Israel	Palestine	**Total**	%
Greek Catholics (Melkites)	47,000	1,500	**47,500**	27.9%
Roman Catholics	14,800	18,500	**33,300**	19.6%
Greek Orthodox	42,250	25,000	**67,250**	39.6%
Maronites	7,600	200	**7,800**	4.9%
Syriacs	300	2,300	**2,600**	1.5%
Protestants	700	1,500	**2,200**	1.3%
Armenians	400	700	**1,100**	0.6 %
Copts, Ethiopians, others	6,950	300	**7,250**	4.3%
Total	**120,000**	**50,000**	**170,000**	**100.0%**

The followers of the Catholic Church, in all its variations, represent close to 50% of all Christians in Israel and Palestine combined. Yet numbers are not the primary indicator of the significance of the Christian presence in the Holy Land. That the Christians are an active community in Palestine is illustrated in the following: there are 65 Christian schools (out of 1,800 schools in total), with 25,000 students and 2,500 teachers and supporting staff members. Two out of 13 Palestinian universities have been founded and continue to be run by Christians. Bethlehem University was established by Pope Paul VI upon his visit to the Holy Land in 1964 and is presently run by the De La Salle Brothers community together with local Palestinians. Dar Al Kalima University, College of Arts and Culture, in Bethlehem was established by the Reverend Mitri Raheb, the Palestinian pastor of the Evangelical Lutheran Christmas Church in Bethlehem. Birzeit University, now a secular Palestinian national university, was established by the Palestinian Anglican Nasser family of Birzeit, a town north of Ramallah.

In the health sector, Christians run close to 30% of medical services and hospitals, including Caritas Baby Hospital in Bethlehem and the Anglican hospitals in Gaza and Nablus, besides the Lutheran World Federation Augusta Victoria Specialised Cancer Hospital on the Mount of Olives. There are scores of church-related hospitals and clinics in Jerusalem and throughout the West Bank and Gaza. Of note is the fact that 54% of civil society non-governmental organisations are run and headed by Palestinian Christians, as are 80% of human rights organisations in the Palestinian Territories.

The overall diaspora Palestinian Christian population is estimated at 600,000, taking into consideration waves of emigration prior to 1948, which means that some three-quarters of Palestinian Christians are found outside their homeland. The major Palestinian Christian diaspora communities are found in Chile, where estimates place the numbers of Palestinians at 350,000, and in Honduras, with an estimated Palestinian population of 280,000. In Brazil, Palestinians number close to 60,000. Smaller communities are found in the USA, Australia and dispersed throughout Europe. A majority of these diaspora communities are Christians. The relationships that tie these communities with their towns of origin and with their religious compatriots revolve around political orientations and identity, particularly in times of tension between Palestinians and Israelis. Some financial and professional support is provided but much remains to be desired, as these communities are not organised for the purpose of support of their original towns and villages and for those who stayed. By now, second-, third- and fourth-generation Palestinians have become more rooted in their host societies.

Without delving into the complex and different causes of emigration, politics and economics remain two principal and interdependent reasons for the phenomenon. There are environmental or contextual circumstances that act as push factors on the community. There are also pull factors such as the participation of some Bethlehem craftsmen in the Chicago and Philadelphia exhibitions of the latter part of the nineteenth century, which introduced them and their compatriots to the opportunities then present in America. Stories of the success of early immigrants to Chile in the first decades of the twentieth century also acted as incentive for hundreds of Palestinian Christian families, primarily in the Bethlehem – Beit Jala area, to follow suit. Among the push factors are the vicissitudes of life under foreign rulers, such as the conscription of the eldest sons to the Ottoman army during the First World War; the Arab–Israeli war of 1948, which resulted in 60,000 Palestinian Christian refugees out of a total 725,000 Palestinian refugees; and the continuing conflict since 1967 with its ups and downs that impact population movement in general and that of Palestinian Christians in particular. Recently, the danger posed by the increasing fundamentalist and extremist Islamist groups, such as ISIS in neighbouring Syria and Iraq, along with the predominance of religious identity (as opposed to the broader Arab national identity) and the presence of some in the population who identify with Salafist and extremist religious ideology, add up to a potential push factor for Palestinian Christians to think about emigration.

An Urbanite Educated Community in Search of Stability

The Palestinian Christian community is urbanite middle class, with the attendant socio-economic and cultural characteristics. There do remain Christian communities rooted in the villages and smaller towns in the West Bank, but even these localities are becoming increasingly urbanised. Among the rural communities, Zababdeh in the northern West Bank and Taybeh in the central part of the West Bank, not far from Jerusalem, are examples of significant Christian communities in rural settings. Other towns and villages with significant Christian presence include Birzeit, Jifnah, Aboud, Ein Arik in the Ramallah area and Rafidia in Nablus. On average, Christians are much older than the general population in Palestine or Israel, with a median age above 32 years. This is a reflection of the lower birthrate of the community compared with its Muslim and Jewish counterparts. It is also a reflection of the fact that more Palestinian Christians (10%) are older than 65 years of age than is true of the general population in Palestine (4.4%). The Palestinian Christian community in both Palestine and Israel emphasises the necessity of marriage as ensuring the continuity of the community. The age at marriage is older than that of the Muslim population, which also contributes to a lower number of children.

One of the factors that pushes marriage to later years is the fact that many young women in the Christian community tend to pursue university and higher studies and have successful careers, and they provide a model to emulate. The Christian community is very well educated, with many of its members in the white-collar professions. In surveys undertaken in the Palestinian Territories, Christians were more likely than the general population to seek higher university degrees. The Christian community also looks for long-term advancement of its family members and hence does not necessarily look for immediate satisfaction of needs.

The community considers itself an integral part of wider society and is overwhelmingly willing to serve in the public sphere. Younger members of the community tend to subscribe to centre and left-of-centre politics. An overwhelming majority of Christians believe in non-violent means to achieve an end to occupation and a solution to the long-drawn-out Arab–Israeli conflict. In 2009 a group of Palestinian Christians issued the Kairos Palestine Document 'A Moment of Truth', modelled on the 1985 South Africa Kairos Document ('Challenge to the Church'). This seeks to bring Christian understanding and compassion to efforts at ending Israeli occupation of Palestinian lands and the continuing conflict that is pitting Israelis and Palestinians against each other. The Kairos Palestine Document is an affirmation of the belonging of Palestinian Christians to their society and its aspiration for ending Israeli occupation and establishing a Palestinian state in normal relations within society and with neighbours. The community believes in inter-religious dialogue, especially with Muslim compatriots, but also, to a lesser extent, with Israeli Jews. It is a community concerned with the recent rise of political Islam and the public, emotive and identity-related manifestations that it entails. There is concern about the rise of the Islamist political agenda in neighbouring countries and its implications for the future of Palestinian society and state formation. The community sees political instability as unsafe for its continuity and seeks ways, including emigration, to cope with such instability. The preferred future state in Palestine is one based on the equality of all citizens, not differentiated on the basis of any particular religious or ethnic characteristic. Palestinian Christians view with concern any attempt to make the state a strictly religious domain, while they advocate freedom of religion and worship.

Sunday Mass and Community Continuity

The Christian community in Palestine seems to be more religious in its overall orientation than its sister community in Israel. It expects more of the church than its counterpart in Israel, such as employment opportunities, housing subsidies, educational scholarships and help in issuance of Israeli permits to access places of work, hospitals and other needed services and opportunities. Nevertheless, Sunday mass seems to be a uniting rite and a consensual family obligation for a majority of Christians in both Palestine and Israel. Anyone attending church on Sunday will see whole families participating, with children colourfully dressed. Even families with long-standing disagreements or feuds are seen praying in pews across from each other. Young people usually attend, although those with university and work obligations tend to stay away. Easter and Christmas attract young university students to church, even if normally they do not attend the Sunday mass. Some members of the community who are not particularly religious insist that they attend Sunday mass and the Easter and Christmas celebrations out of respect for tradition and in keeping with the heritage of their fathers and grandfathers, thus contributing to maintaining community continuity. The separation wall constructed by Israel since

2002, with its border-crossing checkpoints and the severing of ties between the traditionally and historically twin cities of Bethlehem and Jerusalem, has sadly prevented Christian Palestinians from moving freely during the yearly celebrations and rituals.

A significant minority of Christians in Palestine view their Christian identity as a defining characteristic, inherited through the family and generations of faithful parents, grandparents and great-grandparents. Yet the religious identity of Christians, unlike that of Muslims, takes second place to that of the Arab Palestinian identity in Palestine. Palestinian Christians generally feel more comfortable with the broader identity of Arab nationalism. They perceive it as an all-inclusive identity that fosters and strengthens ties among all citizens, irrespective of religion or other characteristics. Religious identity as such, even though adhered to as a sign of community continuity and survival, might be perceived as a willingness to separate and to be different from the general population. Much is desired from the church in terms of formation and community leadership. More of the highly educated young people tend to be distant from the church and its spiritual and earthly preoccupations.

Challenging Times

Amin Maalouf, in his book *In The Name of Identity: Violence and the Need to Belong*, speaks of 'patchwork identities', an apt description of the status reality of indigenous Christians in Palestinian and Arab society. The identity is supposed to remain the same under different conditions, as when Christian church leaders, in Palestine and elsewhere in the Arab world, call on Christians to remain rooted in their ancestral and faith identities and hence to be part of their society and its landscape, irrespective of changing environments. Thus Christians are to be loyal to their identities as Palestinians, Arabs, Syriacs, Armenians and so on, rooted in the ancestral traditions of the different churches to which they belong. They are also to be loyal to the language, culture, geography and Palestinian ecosphere, with all its variations and with its flora and fauna. These loyalties pertaining to layered identities are exactly what 'patchwork identities' are all about.

Historically, most Palestinian Christians have opted for the identity of being a Palestinian and an Arab first and then for being a Christian of a particular church. Given the reality of changing religious environments, starting in the late 1970s with the influence of the Iranian revolution, Palestinian Christians, like other Christians in the Middle East, have had to cope with identity issues and challenges. With the increased politicisation of religion in the region and beyond, Christians have tended to react by withdrawing inward, thus heightening their religious identity. The encompassing identity of one Arab nation exemplified by a yearning for one Arab homeland has been replaced by a religious identity that tends to exclude others not of the same religion and hence to increase the feeling of marginalisation among Arab Christians. The sense that the religious sphere is permeating all other spheres contributes to the feeling among some Christians of being excluded and not being members of the 'in-group'.

The invasion of Iraq in 2003, the breakdown of the Iraqi state and the domino effect of that invasion, which culminated in the so-called 'Arab Spring' in 2011, led to the breakdown of a number of Arab states' apparatuses and the relatively recent emergence of more extremist Islamic groups, such as ISIS (Islamic State or Daesh), which have left their impact on the identity, sense of belonging and status of indigenous Christians. The feeling of marginalisation of local Christians, in light of the increased religious identity of the majority Muslim population, was accompanied in both Iraq and Syria with dislocation, dispersal and displacement. This tragic transformation led not only to an accentuation of the religious identity but also to the questioning of the relevance of the national identity and the historical bonds that once united all compatriots. The traumatic experiences of whole Christian communities, among ongoing internecine Muslim and ethnic confrontations that spared no one, led many to the painful conclusion that brute force and power and not the bond of a common identity was the basis of survival.

Although, in Palestine, Christians and Muslims shared the after-effects of both the Arab–Israeli war of 1948 and those of the 1967 June war, and hence a strong feeling of identification with each other took place, the public sphere of recent times has become definitely more religionised. For some, this might have affected the traditionally strong acceptance and mutual accommodation of each other. This is perhaps best exemplified by an exchange during the Second Intifada, designated the Aqsa Intifada, when a Christian involved in its activities was asked by a Muslim youth what, if anything, had he, as a Christian, to do with the Intifada? Aside from this challenging (and ignorant) question, the fact remains that the switch to religion as an identity forces Palestinians to look at their multilayered identities in a critical manner.

The greatest loss from adopting in Palestine an increasingly religious identity, by both Muslims and Christians, is that a process of 'fogging' or 'clouding' of the national–historical narrative has started to take hold. As a result, the ideology of a shared and encompassing political–historical struggle is being replaced not simply by a religious ideology but by a more threatening self and group opportunistic orientation across society. Some, oblivious to the dangers and long-term effects of exclusivist identities, would argue that the religious base underlying the conflict and the struggle is as strong as, if not stronger than, the nationalist base.

Because the adoption of a religious identity, or any other specific identity, transforms the way one looks at oneself and others, individuals need to understand the context(s) that make them think or act in particular ways towards their own group and towards others. One can dismiss the recent intimidation of indigenous Christians in Jerusalem as the work of a fringe group that is unaccepted and condemned by the majority in society. A group of young Muslims, upon hearing the preaching of a religious judge on the 'infidelity' of Christians to the one God, made threats against Christians, and some actually attempted to attack a Christian convent in the Christian quarter of the Old City. But such threats and acts reflect on how the supposedly fringe group members identify themselves and on how indigenous Christians see themselves as a consequence. Palestinian Christians remain adamant that this is their place of roots and that they will not allow any group to intimidate them away from this conviction. Islam, as one of the great religions and civilisations of the world, has always been part of Christians' heritage as Arabs and Palestinians. Nicola Ziyadeh puts it beautifully:

> I and Geries and Tannous and Shnoudah are the inheritors of one Arab Islamic civilization. We worked at one time to build it. We are the children of the land which nourished this civilization. We are Arabs as much as any resident in the Arab land is Arab.... Yes this is my civilization which goes back at least to more than six thousand years. (Nicola Ziyadeh, *Christianity and the Arabs*, 4th edition, Sindbad, 2002, 256–7)

Patriarch Emeritus Gregory III Laham of the Melkite Greek Catholic Church speaks of the indigenous Arab and Palestinian Church as being one with the Mosque and with Islam. This identification with the Islamic heritage is not defensive, nor is it, at this juncture, protective of Arab Christians in light of extremist Islamist identities that seek to exclude them. Nevertheless, we cannot deny that, at present, there is a sense of apprehension and uncertainty among an increasing number of Palestinian Christians. The more there are incidents, incitements or intimidations of a religious nature, in Palestine but also in the wider Middle East, the more likely it is that younger generations will opt to migrate. This sense of apprehension and uncertainty is due not only to the words and acts of extremist Muslim groups but also to those of extremist Jewish groups that desecrate and vandalise holy books, churches and religious symbols, not to speak of the irreverence and aggression shown to Christian monks, priests and nuns on occasion. Religious identities, in their extremes, seem to work towards disharmony, fear and conflict, in contradiction to the purpose of religions.

The political situation also is not helping to resolve the issues emanating from the 'patchwork identities'. The continuing occupation of Palestinian lands, the 'Israelification' of East Jerusalem, the failure of the so-called peace process over the last two decades, with the disastrous impact of the Oslo Accords and the weakening of the Palestinian National Authority by Israeli policies and measures, all contribute towards a 'limbo situation' in which religious identity to a majority becomes an assuring element while to others desiring a more open society, including Palestinian Christians, it adds up to a lack of clarity about future prospects. The internal Palestinian division between the politically secular-leaning Fatah and the 'left'-leaning groups in Palestinian politics and the clearly religiously oriented Hamas does not offer the prospect of consolidating an encompassing Palestinian identity. The support given by a significant number of Palestinians, including some Christians, to the 'confrontationist' position of Hamas, in contrast to the 'accommodationist and pacifist' position of the National Authority, which has not been rewarded by the failed negotiation process with Israel, also points to the problematic nature of the Palestinian identity at this stage.

The 'accommodationist and pacifist' position is coming under attack as having failed to achieve its objectives. The National Authority, nonetheless, keeps insisting that the best prospects for Palestinians lie in opting for non-violent resistance and in pursuing the process of peaceful negotiations. Aside from the right of everyone to adopt political positions and hence to empower the body politic with a variety of views and perspectives, the fact that the division today in Palestinian society is between the 'religious-confrontationist' and the 'secular-accommodationist' leaves no prospects for an invigorating discussion of 'what do we want and where are we going?' Hence, this 'limbo situation', given also the turmoil in the region, encourages many to adopt religious identities that encapsulate their worldview and not to reach out to others and their worldviews. Encapsulated religious identities are narrow and do not allow for understanding others. As such, these identities block attempts to find common ground that would enable Palestinians to overcome the challenges of ending Israeli occupation and establishing their own state with due respect to international conventions and resolutions. The narrow identities do not allow for a vision that would be inclusivist and welcoming of others.

The experience of Palestinian Christians in Gaza since the Hamas takeover in 2007 raises questions about how indigenous Christians would react to a theocratic government in Palestine. While Gaza Christians acknowledge that relations with Hamas are very good, nevertheless some would point out that more than 40% of the Christian population left Gaza between 2008 and 2016. Others expect that within a decade no Christians will be left in Gaza. The reason most often given for departure is that – in addition to the siege and blockade imposed on the Gaza Strip by Israel, which is a major reason – there is a feeling of unease with a government run on religious principles and the all-around permeation of the public sphere with religion, in addition to the wars waged periodically with enormous loss and trauma to the civilian population. It is therefore not surprising that not only Christians want out of Gaza. According to some estimates, more than 50% of the population of the Gaza Strip would leave if given the opportunity to do so.

While Palestinian Christians do not hide their preference for a secular, pluralist and democratic state with equality for all citizens, it is nonetheless reasonable to think of a forthcoming Palestinian state that is run on Islamic religious principles. This probability is borne out by the fact that close to half of the Palestinian population would most likely vote for Hamas in any future elections. While Hamas might not implement an Islamic state right away, its long-term objective is the establishment of a state run on Islamic principles derived from the Holy Qur'an and the Sunnah (example and sayings) of the Prophet. In this eventuality, which is not currently realistic because the chances of holding elections are slim, Palestinian Christians need to assess their status in such a future Palestinian state. Being middle class and accustomed to a lifestyle that prioritises freedom of choice and the pursuit of economic, educational and professional careers in a free and open environment, the likelihood of survival in an environment enveloped by religion will definitely become smaller.

Palestinian Christians remain committed to serve and to identify with their society, irrespective of the challenges and concerns raised by the increasing role of religion in the public sphere. The role of Christian religious institutions and their educational, caritative, healthcare, social and cultural involvement cannot be underestimated. These will continue and, together with other Palestinian civil society organisations, provide hope for the continuity and viability not only of the Christian communities but of a society that is open to all of its citizens and that encourages identification on an inclusivist basis, with due respect to religious and particularistic traits and characteristics of the population and its various constituent groups.

The heritage that our parents, grandparents and great-grandparents left us is that this land of Palestine is ours. Throughout history, the connections and links that crosscut Christian, Muslim, Jewish and other religious and ethnic communities in Palestine were more varied than simply the religious element or the politicised identity of more recent times. As indigenous Palestinian Christians, we cannot ignore the challenges facing our society, be they political, with the objective of ending the Israeli occupation; social, with the shaping of a society that responds to the needs and requirements of all of its citizens in an age of modernity; cultural, with the aim of maintaining the traditions that strengthen our common identity as a people rooted in the land and its history and heritage; or economic, with the strengthening of the opportunities open to young people, irrespective of their religious, political or personal preferences. Without linking up and opening to others, we cannot survive either as Christian believers or as devoted Palestinians. The future is guaranteed by reaffirming the best in our Palestinian past and present, celebrating our humanity and overcoming the prejudices that come with narrow identities, those identities that Amin Maalouf cautioned could lead to violence and the exclusion of others. It is only fitting to end with the optimistic and assertive reflection of Latin Patriarch Emeritus Michel Sabbah, who reaffirmed, in an exchange with young people, that, as Palestinian Christians, we have no option but to stay put on our beloved land, to look fear in the eye and to rely on ourselves and on our fellow Palestinians to overcome the challenges.

Bibliography

Issa, Anton Odeh, *Les minorités chrétiennes de Palestine à travers les siècles: étude historico-juridique et développement moderne international* (Jerusalem: Franciscan Printing Press, 1979).

Kuruvilla, Samuel J., *Radical Christianity in Palestine and Israel: Liberation and Theology in the Middle East* (London: I. B. Tauris, 2013).

Noble, Samuel and Alexander Treiger (eds), *The Orthodox Church in the Arab World 700–1700: An Anthology of Sources* (Dekalb, IL: Northern Illinois University Press, 2014).

Raheb, Mitri, *Palestinian Christians in the West Bank: Facts, Figures and Trends* (Bethlehem: Diyar Publishers, 2012).

Soudah, Romell and Bernard Sabella, *The Sabeel Survey On Palestinian Christians in the West Bank and Israel: Historical Demographic Developments, Current Politics and Attitudes Towards Church, Society and Human Rights* (Jerusalem: Sabeel, 2006).

Jordan

Paulo Maggiolini and Iyad Twal

Jordan's Christians, or the Jordanian Christians, were an essential and original component of the country's socio-political landscape well before the foundation of the Hashemite state. The condition of Christians in contemporary Jordan has frequently been described as 'Jordan, Kingdom of happy Christians'. The relative lack of interest in Jordanian Christianity may be attributed to the fact that the Jordanian Christian communities enjoy a calm and stable existence in the small Hashemite kingdom, at least compared with such unstable countries as Syria, Iraq and Lebanon.

The history of the Christian presence in the contemporary land of Jordan dates back to the first century. Christian Scriptures and traditions attesting to Jesus's visit to this land (Mark 3: 7–8; Matthew 8: 28; John 1: 28–9, 35–9); archaeological evidence, with a considerable number of early churches discovered around the country; as well as church history (recording local martyrs such as Bishop Esterios in Petra and Deodorus and Theophanous in Karak) are all palpable evidence of the original and vivid attachment of Christianity to this territory.

Given its traditional role as a frontier between the Levant and the Arabian Peninsula, during the pre-Islamic centuries the land of today's Jordan served as a sort of 'sanctuary' hosting different Christian communities and favouring encounters and blending between the Roman-Byzantine and Arab traditions. During the third century, Christians persecuted by Diocletian took refuge in its deserts, and later Imperial Byzantine Orthodoxy coexisted alongside the Syrian Miaphysitism of the Ghassan Arab tribes, fully representing the multi-vocal character of early Christianity and attesting to Arab Christians' presence in the country during the pre-Islamic period.

With the arrival of Islam, the local Christian presence entered a long phase of transition. Numerical decline set in and its community and church life began to stagnate. Nonetheless, during the seventh century Christian communities generally continued to represent the majority of the inhabitants. Their vitality is attested by archaeological evidence dating back to the eighth century discovered, for example, in Umm al-Rassas, Madaba and Mount Nebo. With the exception of the two centuries of the Crusades, which partially recovered some of the strategically important areas, after the end of the Umayyad Caliphate in 750 Jordan became increasingly isolated and provincial. During the Mamluk and Ottoman periods it underwent a prolonged crisis in its socio-political and economic life. Christianity stagnated and shrank, and most of its ancient churches were progressively abandoned or ruined. Tribalism became predominant, no matter what the faith professed. Christianity became strongly bound to and inscribed within the local tribal system.

Although Jordan was mainly associated with the Orthodox tradition and part of the diocese of the Greek Orthodox Patriarchate of Jerusalem, the absence of official religious authorities residing within this territory and the poor condition of most of its places of worship favoured the development of a strong sense of popular religiosity and syncretism within both the Christian and the Muslim dimensions. Therefore, before the foundation of the Hashemite Emirate (1921), the prevailing relationship between Muslims and Christians was inspired neither by Islamic scriptural tradition nor by Ottoman legal norms. At the same time, neither was the Byzantine canon decisive.

The nineteenth century saw a slow but steady awakening and revival for both Christians and Muslims. After centuries of de facto autonomy from the dominant centres of imperial power, the land of Transjordan aroused fresh interest. Under the military pressure exerted by Muhammad 'Ali and his son Ibrahim Pasha from Egypt (who between 1831 and 1841 conquered Syria), by Saudi Wahhabism and, finally, by Western colonial ambitions, the Ottoman powers in Istanbul reassessed their attitude toward this land, now perceived to be of strategic importance for controlling and protecting their empire. After 1867 Istanbul employed a variety of instruments to return this territory to its direct authority, such as the imposition of new laws, military repression, the implementation of policies to facilitate the

Christianity in Jordan, 1970 and 2015

	1970		2015		Average annual growth rate (%), 1970–2015
Tradition	Population	%	Population	%	
Christians	83,400	5.0%	127,000	1.7%	0.9%
Anglicans	3,500	0.2%	5,000	0.1%	0.8%
Independents	5,000	0.3%	8,300	0.1%	1.1%
Orthodox	38,600	2.3%	78,100	1.0%	1.6%
Protestants	5,900	0.4%	6,700	0.1%	0.3%
Catholics	30,400	1.8%	29,300	0.4%	−0.1%
Evangelicals	6,000	0.4%	8,400	0.1%	0.7%
Pentecostals	2,100	0.1%	11,300	0.2%	3.9%
Total population	**1,655,000**	**100.0%**	**7,595,000**	**100.0%**	**3.4%**

Source: Todd M. Johnson and Gina A. Zurlo (eds), *World Christian Database* (Leiden/Boston: Brill), accessed March 2017.

settlement of the local nomadic and semi-nomadic tribes (also through the redeployment of foreign ethnic communities, such as Circassians and Chechens from central Europe), reviving old towns and agricultural centres, promoting the arrival of merchants from Syria and Palestine, and initially tolerating Christian missionary activities, especially in the sphere of education and healthcare.

After 1860, Catholic missionaries from France and Italy belonging to the Latin Patriarchate of Jerusalem (revived in 1847) and Protestants, mainly British in origin and affiliated with the Church Missionary Society, increasingly flocked to the land of Jordan. At the same time, the Orthodox Patriarchate of Jerusalem from 1875 dedicated itself to reviving its old activities and presence within this land. Soon afterward, the Melkite Catholic Church re-established its presence and activity. The stratification and differentiation between distinct churches and denominations is a condition that still characterises the Christian presence in Jordan today.

Christian Denominations in Jordan

As in other countries in the Middle East, the Christian presence in today's Jordan is distinguished by the richness and multi-vocality of its ecclesiastical, liturgical and theological traditions. Through conversions, revivals of ancient church institutions, foundations of totally new ones and immigration, the local Christian presence constantly grew and diversified during the twentieth century. In particular, because Jordan remained the realm of tribes and never hosted the high-ranking seats of any of the traditional churches of the Middle East, the consolidation of all the different Jordanian Christian denominations and their institutions proceeded simultaneously with the development of the Hashemite state, entering into its socio-political field without experiencing particular tensions or conflicts. This situation was also favoured by the particularly positive attitude of the Hashemite dynasty towards local Christians.

Christian denominations in Jordan can count on the full recognition of their presence and institutions. Under the terms of the Law on Associations of 2008, the Hashemite Kingdom of Jordan officially recognised 12 denominations: the Greek Orthodox, Roman Catholic, Greek Catholic (Melkite), Armenian Orthodox, Maronite Catholic, Assyrian, Coptic, Anglican, Lutheran, Seventh-day Adventist and Presbyterian Churches. The Baptist Church represents a specific case because, although it is officially registered, it does not enjoy full privileges. With these should be included churches registered as 'societies', such as the Free Evangelical Church, Nazarene Church, Assemblies of God, Christian and Missionary Alliance, and Church of Jesus Christ of Latter-day Saints. Moreover, there are Christian denominations neither registered nor recognised, such as the United Pentecostals and Jehovah's Witnesses. Finally, due to the recent conflicts in Syria and Iraq, Jordan has seen the Chaldean and Syriac presence growing.

Moreover, the constitution grants religious communities the right to create and maintain their own educational institutions (Article 19) and to establish community courts to judge issues relating to the personal status their members (Articles 108 and 109). Nonetheless, recognised non-Islamic religious communities are not eligible for state subsidies and are financially and administratively independent from the state. At the same time, Christian institutions run a network of schools and educational establishments that are widely recognised by both Christians and Muslims for the quality of their teaching. In this framework, the Catholic schools probably represent the most developed network, with 23 establishments directly managed by the Latin Patriarchate of Jerusalem and other institutions administered by other congregations, such as the Franciscans, De La Salle Brothers, Rosary Sisters and Melkite Church. Moreover, fulfilling Pope John Paul II's idea, in 2009 Pope Benedict XVI laid the first stone of the first Catholic university in the country, the American University of Madaba, officially established in 2011. This has strengthened and expanded the educational influence of the Catholic Church in Jordan. Finally, as a further proof of the willingness to contribute to the cultural life and public debate in Jordan and within the so-called Arab world, the experience of abouna.org, promoted by Father Rif'at Bader, represents an interesting initiative of online dissemination in English and Arabic of information, news and analysis on various topics, from the conditions of Christian communities in the Middle East to inter-religious dialogue.

Therefore, since the foundation of the Hashemite state in the 1920s, Christians have enjoyed a peaceful and relatively stable and secure existence. Moreover, the Hashemite Crown has summoned Christian institutions to support and contribute to its initiatives within the fields of inter-religious dialogue and education. This has given them wide visibility in Jordan, as well as regionally and internationally. While official Islam dominates the public sphere, community and ecclesiastical institutions are recognised as leading actors within their constituencies and important factors in improving services in the fields of education and healthcare, to the benefit of all.

The Christian Presence

From the ethno-political perspective, the composite Christian denominational presence in Jordan is relatively homogeneous compared with other Middle Eastern countries. With the exception of the Armenian community, which is not ethnically Arab but which nonetheless has always conformed to Jordanian 'identity', the Jordanian Christians constantly show their attachment to the Arab culture of their Muslim brethren. Moreover, similarly to the rest of Jordanian society, the Jordanian Christian community perfectly mirrors the traditional 'divide' between Transjordanians and Palestinians. Therefore, the Jordanian Church has always perceived its mission and ecclesiastical identity as fully part of the Arab dimension. Similar to Syrian and Palestinian Christianity, Jordanian Christians see themselves as an integral part of an Arab Church, free from nostalgic yearnings for a mythic pre-Islamic, different past. In particular, Christians have constantly related to Muslims on the basis of a common tribal past, sharing the same values and customs. Jordanian Christians, from both the East and the West Bank, have widely identified with the Arabist cause and the Palestinian question.

Therefore, the sense of this shared tribal past and mentality, combined with the positive attitude of the Hashemite governmental system, has given socio-political stability to both Jordanian Christians and Muslims in public life. In Jordan, it is the family, large or small (the tribe), that is the receptacle of values and the guarantor of social and political order. Christians – especially those of Transjordanian origin – and Muslims are receptive to this tribal identification, as they share the same social structures and largely the same social values. Patriarchal values are built on the basis of kinship, such as solidarity between individuals and families.

The Jordanian Christian presence is clearly a demographic minority. Traditionally estimated as between 6% (as officially stated by the monarchy) and 4% of the population, today Christians do not exceed 3%, namely 200,000–220,000 of the 6–7 million Jordanian citizens. Among these Christians, the Greek Orthodox account for almost 50%, whereas the Catholics number approximately 40%, predominantly part of the Latin denomination. The rest is composed primarily of Anglicans and Lutherans, Syriacs and Armenians.

Against this background, Jordanian Christians have always been fully integrated into the economic, cultural and political life of the country, thanks to their dynamism and the guarantees provided by the state. For instance, Marwan al-Muasher can exemplify the range of opportunities open to well positioned and educated Christians in Jordanian politics. Currently vice president for studies at the Carnegie Endowment for International Peace, he earlier served in a number of prestigious political positions in the Hashemite Kingdom. In 1995, following the peace treaty of 1994, he was charged with opening Jordan's embassy in Israel and afterwards was ambassador in Washington, contributing to negotiation of the free-trade agreement with the USA. He served also as foreign minister and in 2004 became deputy prime minister.

Moreover, although the proportion of Christians does not exceed 3% of the Jordanian population, the actual influence and presence of Jordanian

Christians far exceeds this. For instance, 30% of the country's economy has Christians as business leaders – hence the term 'qualitative majority', with which they are pleased to be described. Osama Imseeh, head of the Jordanian Jewellers' Syndicate, well represents the profile of an important Jordanian businessman with strong contacts with the Christian community and active in the intellectual and charitable dimensions.

While the constitution does not recognise the existence of minorities within the kingdom, it grants full equality to all its citizens before the law regardless of their religion, language or race (Article 6). At the same time, the constitution sanctions the right to freedom of worship and religious belief in accordance with the customs and traditions in the country (Article 14). Nonetheless, Islam is the religion of the state and the king (Articles 2 and 28) and, therefore, personal status is to be regulated according to the specific religious affiliation of each citizen.

From the political perspective, the Hashemite Kingdom has always granted Christians full representation through both a quota system and the tradition of appointing one or two Christians as ministers, as palace advisors, to senior ranks in the military and to high positions within the public administration. The nine seats (out of 130) in the House of Representatives reserved for Christians, a quota confirmed in a revision of the electoral law in 2016, is actually overrepresentation compared with their demographic weight. The same electoral law increased the seats reserved for women from 12 to 15. This provision further enlarges possible Christian representation within the House of Representatives.

Since the foundation of the Emirate, the Hashemite regime has developed a very close relationship with Christian institutions on the basis of convergent interests and shared objectives. Recognising the church's institutions and guaranteeing Christians' community life according to a sort of neo-millet approach fostered cooperation and goodwill between Jordanian civil and Christian religious authorities. This condition secured the church's support for the regime and made it possible to integrate community activities within the Hashemite political field. Moreover, the protection of non-Muslim communities fits perfectly into the Hashemite Islamic discourse through which the regime sought to promote its status within the country, the region and globally. Religion has constantly represented an important source of legitimacy for the Hashemite family according to the idea of being kin with the Prophet Muhammad's family and the inherent responsibility to protect non-Muslims living under its authority. Such a discourse further developed during King Hussein's reign. Accordingly, the monarch found in Christian ecclesiastical institutions a valued ally against secularist opposition, both nationalist and leftist, although a number of Christians actively participated in each camp.

In general, Christian educational institutions in Jordan have promoted the legitimacy of the Hashemite monarchy and its distinctive attitude towards Christian Jordanian citizens. At the same time, their social activities have contributed equally to the state, partially making up for its own shortcomings and thus integrating into the specific regime's redistributive strategy. The Jordanian Christian institutions played their role in fostering the stability and durability of the Hashemite regime and state also in terms of services and aid to the refugees who entered the country. In this framework, Christian institutions were able to access the Jordanian public domain, increase their visibility and manage their internal affairs, reinforcing their community boundaries and solidarities. Moreover, the inter-religious dialogue and the promotion of Christian archaeological heritage further reinforced the relationship between the Hashemite regime and Christian institutions. Since the first papal visit to the Holy Land in 1964, the idea of the 'Holy Land' and its archaeological sites entered the Jordanian political domain, becoming an important factor in promoting the historical continuity between contemporary history and past civilisations under the Hashemite emblem. At the same time, the Jordanian Christian institutions were able to inscribe their presence, heritage and traditions within both the Hashemite state project and the World Church dimension, promoting the image of Jordan as an integral part of the Holy Land's geography of salvation.

Jordan's biblical sites have also taken root in the local liturgy and prayers, becoming important focal points for the life of the Christian community. In particular, two places are distinguished for their role and importance. The baptismal site on the River Jordan is where Christians of Jordan organise their annual pilgrimage on 10 January. Thousands of Christians from across the entire country go to the site to pray and celebrate this occasion. The government gave permission to each Christian denomination to build a church there. This site has become for the Christians in Jordan a source of national pride, where they publicly revive their attachment to their faith and homeland. The second place is Mount Nebo, *Syagha* in Arabic, which is a small mountain near the city of Madada , famous for its mosaics portraying the ancient Holy Land, where tradition holds that the prophet Moses saw the Promised Land and where he died and was buried. Every year for the feast of the prophet Moses, thousands of Christians from Madaba and Amman go there to pray and enjoy the environment.

In 1964, when he welcomed the pope at Amman airport, King Hussein stepped into the international spotlight to present himself as national ruler and 'Guardian of the Holy Places', both Muslim and Christian. This historic religious event had political implications, offering the kingdom and its king the opportunity to promote their legitimacy and positive image within the international context. During the 1990s and in connection with the 2000 jubilee, this relationship significantly revived. Needless to say, the political situation was totally different. In 1988 the kingdom officially announced full legal and administrative disengagement from the West Bank, although reaffirming its role as Guardian of the Holy Places, and in 1994 Amman and Tel Aviv signed a peace treaty. Accordingly, the promotion of the Jordanian Christian sites now served to uphold the country as the cradle of the three monotheistic religions, a land of tolerance, religious freedom and peace. International legitimacy and religious tourism became two important factors that reinforced the relationship between the regime and the Christian institutions. With the accession to the throne of Abdullah II in 1999 and after 2001, this discourse became even more preeminent. The Amman Message initiative of 2004 and the commitment to Islamic–Christian dialogue, for example with the initiative of the 'Common Word Between Us and You' of 2007, confirmed King Abdullah II's wish to foster the country's international status, presenting himself as the guarantor of a moderate interpretation of Islam in a world increasingly dominated by the rhetoric of the 'war on terror' as well as the cornerstone of 'Arab diplomacy' in explaining the Arab standpoint.

Syrian Christians in Jordan

The Syrian conflict broke out in 2011 and still continues. Already about 1.5 million Syrians have fled to Jordan, some housed in camps and others in all the cities of the kingdom. The Syrian refugees who arrived in Jordan come from the south of Syria, a part rather poor and predominantly Muslim. Among them, however, were 17,000 Christians who passed through Jordan; after a few months almost all left for Germany, Australia, Canada or the USA – for them, Jordan was a transit nation. At the same time, Jordan also saw the arrival of 35,000 Armenians, who went through Jordan to Armenia. During their stay in Jordan, Caritas Jordan, led by Wael Suleiman, and the local Christian churches offered them rent for housing, school fees for children, medical care and monthly coupons for food. Many local parishes hosted dozens of Christian Syrian families until their departure.

Iraqi Christians in Jordan

Jordan has experienced four different waves of Iraqi immigrants and refugees: the first was in 1991, after the first Gulf War; the second occurred in 1996, after the second Gulf War; the third was in 2003, after the fall of Saddam Hussein; finally, in 2014, with the fall of Mosul and the massacres in Nineveh Plain carried out by ISIS, a fourth wave of Iraqis sought refuge in Jordan. The first two waves of Iraqi refugees (Muslims and Christians) were wealthy, and most of them have already left Jordan, although some have remained and continue to work and develop their own new businesses within the country. Some have even obtained Jordanian passports. The situation of people belonging to the last two waves of Iraqi refugees is different. They are economically poor, especially those who arrived in 2014 after being robbed of everything by radical Islamist militias. The Iraqi Christians who arrived and were registered by the United Nations in 2003 numbered around 10,000. What seems strange, but also understandable, is that none of these Iraqi Christians are considering the option of returning to Iraq in the near future, even if the country becomes more stable. They say that they have been betrayed by their Muslim neighbours, who stole their homes after their departure. Nor do they want to stay in Jordan. Since they are legally refugees they do not have the right to work. They simply want to leave, for such countries as Canada and Australia.

The Jordanian government merely opened its borders to Iraqi Christians; Caritas Jordan ensures all medical care, children's schooling, rent and food. Eighteen Catholic parish centres welcomed their Iraqi brethren for more than a year in parish halls and centres, before they started to rent their own lodgings. In 2014, Caritas Jordan worked with an outlay of nearly US$30 million; 75% of this was in aid of the Syrian refugees (only 1% of whom are Christians) and of Iraqi Christians.

As for religious services and needs, most of the Iraqi Christians who arrived in Jordan belong to the Catholic Syrian or Chaldean Church, with some Assyrians. There is a Syrian Catholic priest, a Chaldean priest and a third Assyrian who are providing the needed services for each community. The Catholic Church of both the Latin and Byzantine rites has opened its premises and churches to Iraqi and Syrian co-religionists. Nevertheless, even in these difficult circumstances, the problems have had a positive impact on faith and religious experience. The strong commitment of the Iraqi Christians and the witness they bore to professing their faith in the face of persecution provided an example to Jordanian Christians. It brought home the fact of persecution elsewhere and the need for a strong personal commitment to their faith. Currently, the Iraqi Christians live on a day-to-day basis in the hope of a better future.

Challenges and Questions for Christians

The combination of the high number of churches and denominations, the demographic minority status of Christians and the role the constitution gives Islam in the country has presented a number of challenges to the Jordanian Christian presence.

First, while ecclesiastical fragmentation is a symbol of the richness and multi-vocality of the Jordanian Christian presence, it also has a negative impact, parcelling and dividing Christian positions towards local state authorities as well as the majority Islamic community. Therefore, fragmented ecclesiology represents an internal challenge to the Arab Christian dimension and it has two different but interconnected effects. On the one hand, the faith of Christians in Jordan is a social faith. Their religious identification is also an expression of their belonging to a specific community or a tribe, and it is inherited. Belonging to and professing the Christian faith is not always viewed as a personal conviction. Divisions between denominations and churches can only increase such a mentality and attitude. A number of serious pastoral initiatives have been taken, and for years the clergy have been exhorting people to adopt a personally active faith. On the other hand, fragmented ecclesiology and divisions between churches put the Christians' future at risk. While this diversity provides a rich ecclesiastical life, and a wealth of cultural, liturgical, spiritual and dogmatic experiences, at the same time the disunity of the churches is an obstacle for missions, and it weakens their message and especially their prophetic role. In this field, the Council of Churches plays an important role in fostering free discussion and expressing a common voice concerning Christianity and its condition. This kind of initiative is also particularly strategic in creating some coordination between the considerable numbers of associations (charitable, youth, cultural or simply religious) that characterise the Christians' presence in the kingdom.

Alongside the interdenominational dialogue, the relationship between Christianity and Islam in the country, the Hashemite Crown has constantly shown its commitment to interfaith dialogue, promoting the development of different initiatives and dedicated institutions such as the Royal Aal al-Bayt Islamic Thought Foundation (established 1980), the Royal Institute for Interfaith Studies in Amman (1987) and the Jordanian Interfaith Coexistence Research Centre (2003). Such interfaith and ecumenical dialogue promotes mutual understanding.

Secondly, Christians have to face a challenge primarily posed by the 'numbers mentality'. Arab Christians in general, and those of Jordan in particular, are well aware that they are a minority. They accept this fact, albeit against what they really wish and hope for in their hearts. Their unease comes from having lived as a minority for centuries, which eventually forged a mentality that might be described as one of 'weak community' or 'Al Dhimma', a psychological condition. This has fostered 'isolated' identities, a tendency that in the past pushed Christians to search for foreign protection or instilled fear to act openly, making them retreat from the public domain. Of course, this attitude has also been fostered by some members of the Islamic majority, hindering the minority's enjoyment of its rights due to the law of rule by the strongest. In a state and society clearly dominated by Islam, the fact of being undoubtedly a demographic minority can foster negative psychological attitudes, persuading Christians to act as a silent minority. This can cause excessive conformism and self-censorship, limiting the Christian presence within the public sphere and favouring a passive acceptance of the positions of whoever intends to impose the logic of majority rule.

Accordingly, the experience of the Muslim Brotherhood in the government at the beginning of the 1990s and the recent development of militant radical movements in the region, although under control within the country, are important factors that can increase such attitudes and behaviours. Certainly, one cannot speak of actual religious persecution in Jordan, but neither can it be denied that religious affiliation has a direct effect on Christians' daily life. In all of today's Arab countries, as in Jordan, there is still the need to develop a 'healthy' mentality and culture in which all can progress and live in total harmony within an inclusive civil society, where the dignity of the individual and the concept of citizenship are valued regardless of religious affiliation. In order to overcome such boundaries and limits, Arab Christian leaders and thinkers prefer to describe the Christians' position as one of 'small numbers' rather than of 'minority'. They emphasise that the presence and role of Christians cannot be evaluated only on the basis of their percentage of the population but should be assessed on the basis of quality and commitment.

Thirdly, although the Jordanian constitution grants the right to freedom of worship and religious belief, the right to freedom of conscience is not contemplated, and this means conversion from Islam to another religion is prohibited. The same principle applies to 'mixed' marriages. A male Muslim can marry a Christian, but a male Christian cannot marry a Muslim unless he converts to Islam. Moreover, there are still unresolved issues related to religious holidays, inheritance and the non-inclusion in public school curricula of Christians' historical role and presence in the country. Accordingly, some textbooks completely ignore the historical presence of Christianity within the country before the arrival of Islam in the seventh century. At the same time, Christianity is frequently explained only through the perceptions and the notions contained in Islam. Furthermore, Christian students enrolled in public schools receive no religious education, which is, in contrast, compulsory for their Muslim classmates. Jordan is one of the few Arab countries to deprive Christian students of this right.

Finally, at the geopolitical and socio-political level, in Jordan, as in other Arab countries, a number of serious challenges and questions must be faced. In fact, the regional instability that surrounds most of the countries where Christians live is a serious threat. Conflicts, violence, occupation, uncertain political futures and forced migration weaken personal and community commitment. All these elements create a perfect 'eject situation' for Arab Christians, who always 'have an eye abroad'. At the same time, the kingdom's difficult economic situation seems to represent the main concern that both Christians and Muslims share. Inequality and unemployment have been the two main drivers for emigration, and recently they were pinpointed as the ever-present issues dominating demonstrations and protests. Therefore, emigration and the brain drain are the first challenges that need to be tackled, because they seriously weaken the Christian presence in the country and within the entire region.

To conclude, although the Hashemite Kingdom has provided its Christian citizens with a level of protection and recognition qualitatively higher than that of most other Middle Eastern countries, there are important issues in their lives where the notions of religious affiliation and tradition tend to supersede those of nationality and citizenship. The recognition of the centrality of Islam in the socio-political system technically reduces the room for manoeuvre for Christians' involvement and contributions. Indeed, although the community and church life are fully respected, the position of individuals appears less protected. This condition is also the result of the specific structure of the Jordanian political field, where the king and the regime (rather than the state system) are the real supreme guarantors of the country's socio-political life. Although this situation is also true for Jordan's Muslim citizens, it has a particular impact on Christians' position within the country. The same controversial situation occurs within the political domain. The quota system is a way of providing Christians with a solid and definite political representation, despite their limited numbers. Nevertheless, the same system paradoxically confines the possibility of representation, both quantitatively and qualitatively, to the sole level of the community and sub-state identities.

Bibliography

Chatelard, Géraldine, 'The Constitution of Christian Communal Boundaries and Spheres in Jordan', *Journal of Church and State*, 52:3 (2010), 476–502.

Kildani, Hanna, *Modern Christianity in the Holy Land: Understanding Christianity and Islam in the Land of Their Origins* (New York: Blessed Hope Publishing, 2014).

Maggiolini, Paulo, 'Christian Churches in the Hashemite Kingdom of Jordan: Citizenship, Ecclesiastical Identity and the Political Role of Christian Communities Within the Jordanian Political Field', *Archives de sciences sociales des religions*, 171:3 (2015), 37–58.

Moucarry, Chawkat, *The Prophet and the Messiah: An Arab Christian's Perspective on Islam and Christianity* (Downers Grove, IL: InterVarsity Press, 2002).

Stetter, Stephan, *World Society and the Middle East: Reconstruction in Regional Politics* (New York: Palgrave Macmillan, 2008).

Iraq

Herman G. B. Teule

The beginnings of Christianity in the lands that constitute present-day Iraq go back to the early second century. It appears that Christianity entered Mesopotamia from Edessa, a Syriac- or Aramaic-speaking town situated west of the Persian border. Though the new faith might have appealed to some members of the local Aramaic Jewish community, the liberal attitude in religious matters of the ruling Arsacid dynasty largely explains the rapid expansion of Christianity.

In 226 a new dynasty rose to power, the Sassanians, who abandoned the liberal religious policy of their predecessors and made Zoroastrianism the Empire's official religion. Initially, the consequences for Christians were not too dramatic. Their numbers increased, and by the beginning of the fourth century we already see the establishment of a first ecclesiastical structure. The subsequent years, however, were characterised by waves of fierce persecution, especially under the long reign of King Shapur II (d. 397), who suspected the Christians of collaborating with the traditional enemy, the East Roman Empire. Many churches and monasteries today still bear the names of the martyrs, such as the monk Pethion in the fifth century, who died at the hands of Shapur and his successors. But the same century also gave the church more freedom, allowing it to organise a number of synods, which decreed that the bishop of the capital, Seleucia-Ctesiphon, would be the first in rank and no longer under the authority of the see of Antioch. It is during this period that the Persian Christians opened themselves up to certain doctrinal developments that had taken place in the Roman world. In 410, at the Council of Seleucia-Ctesiphon, they received the creed of Nicea. Students at the ecclesiastical academies, notably the illustrious School of Nisibis, were introduced to the Antiochian exegetical methods of Nestorius's teacher, Theodore of Mopsuestia, whose Greek writings were translated into Syriac. The School also adopted his Christological preferences, which explains why, throughout the sixth century, the Persian Church professed an outspoken dyophysite or two-nature Christology, emphasising the distinction between the human and divine natures of Jesus Christ.

When, in the middle of the sixth century, so-called Jacobite or Syrian Orthodox Christians from Syria established themselves in central Iraq and began to propagate their miaphysite or one-nature Christology, some theologians felt obliged to react. They developed the idea that each abstract nature (humanity, divinity) was also specific: it was the divinity *of the Word of God* and the humanity *of Jesus of Nazareth* that were united into the one person of Jesus Christ. To denote this specificity, they coined the term *qnomā*. In the course of time, Persian theologians adopted the custom of speaking of two natures and two *qnomē* (plural of *qnomā*), a Christological formula which in the eyes of some looked like the Syriac translation of the Christology of Nestorius, who had held that the acceptance of two natures also required the acceptance of two *hypostaseis*. This latter formula was considered heretical by both the Imperial Church of the Eastern Roman Empire as well as by the miaphysites, because in their eyes it implied a division of Jesus Christ into two persons, and they interpreted the acceptance of two *qnomē* by the Persian Christians basically to be adopting the Christology of Nestorius. This linguistic misunderstanding was the beginning of a process of estrangement between the Church of Persia and the other Christian communities, the latter considering the Persians as heretical Nestorians. It is true that for many centuries the Persian Christians called themselves Nestorians, but this is more to be interpreted as proof of their admiration for Nestorius's intransigent attitude towards the originator of miaphysitism, Cyril of Alexandria, than of the acceptance of the 'Nestorian heresy'. Today, the descendants of the Persian Christians avoid the label 'Nestorian'. A more neutral name used by them was simply 'Easterners'.

In the sixth century, these Easterners, though remaining a minority, developed into the 'national' church of the Persian Empire, with a network of dioceses, monasteries and schools throughout the whole country and the bishop of the capital designating himself as catholicos-patriarch, implying that he was the equal of the incumbents of the great patriarchal sees in the Eastern Roman World. At the same time, the miaphysites succeeded in

Christianity in Iraq, 1970 and 2015

	1970		2015		Average annual growth rate (%), 1970–2015
Tradition	Population	%	Population	%	
Christians	401,000	4.0%	336,000	0.9%	−0.4%
Anglicans	500	0.0%	190	0.0%	−2.1%
Independents	1,600	0.0%	82,000	0.2%	9.1%
Orthodox	98,000	1.0%	124,000	0.3%	0.5%
Protestants	980	0.0%	17,000	0.1%	6.5%
Catholics	300,000	3.0%	186,000	0.5%	−1.1%
Evangelicals	1,200	0.0%	20,600	0.1%	6.4%
Pentecostals	310	0.0%	71,100	0.2%	12.8%
Total population	**9,918,000**	**100.0%**	**36,423,000**	**100.0%**	**2.9%**

Source: Todd M. Johnson and Gina A. Zurlo (eds), *World Christian Database* (Leiden/Boston: Brill), accessed March 2017.

building their own structures, initially around Tagrit (Tikrit), and later additionally to the north. Though dogmatically each other's opponents, both communities used Syriac in their liturgies and literature, the knowledge of Syriac thus being for both an important identity marker.

The Islamic Period

Between 633 and 642, the territory of Iraq came under Muslim rule. Echoes of this situation can already be found in some letters by Patriarch Isho'yahb III (d. 659), who praises the positive attitude of the new rulers towards Christians. In the period of the Damascus-based Ummayads, some bishops allowed themselves to be instrumentalised by the rival Muslim factions who struggled for power in Iraq – with negative consequences for the church, which for many years was not allowed to elect a new leader. When, with the establishment of the Abbasid Empire, Iraq became the centre of the Islamic world, Patriarch Timothy I (780–823) took the decision to move his residence to the newly founded capital, Baghdad, a gesture greatly appreciated by the authorities. It marked the beginning of a fruitful cooperation between Christians and Muslims. Christians occupied important functions in the Abbasid administration; they were also requested to put their knowledge of Greek, and of Greek philosophy and medical science taught in their academies, at the service of Islamic society by making Arabic translations (sometimes through the intermediary of Syriac) of a number of fundamental texts. In this way, they contributed to the development of Islamic science, philosophy and discursive theology (*kalām*).

Despite discriminatory measures that caused some Christians to convert to Islam, the first two centuries of Abbasid rule were characterised by a positive interaction between the two communities, who challenged each other in religious matters, discussing different conceptions of God's unicity, the prophethood of Muhammad or simply religious practice. A famous example is the discussion between Patriarch Timothy I and the Caliph al-Mahdī around 800, during which Timothy refused to call Muhammad a prophet but recognised that because he had brought the message of One God to the people of Arabia and had exhorted his people to do works of justice, he 'walked in the path' of the prophets of Israel. This new interaction with the Islamic world required to Christians adopt Arabic as a second language, though a number of Iraqi Christians, especially those living in the south, were ethnically Arab and proud of their Arab ethnic identity. Whether Arabicised or ethnically Arab, Christians in Iraq were among the pioneers of creating a Christian Arabic theological literature.

The Second Abbasid Period (950–1258) witnessed a process of minorisation: not necessarily in all regions in a numerical sense, but wherein Christians no longer set the standards in the fields of culture and science.

For a short time, the fall of Baghdad in 1258 aroused new hopes in the minds of local Christians, both 'Jacobites' and 'Nestorians', who, because of the initial Mongol sympathy towards them, already dreamed of a Christian empire or were at least eager to cooperate with the new leaders. The Easterners even elected a patriarch of Öngüt origins in order to facilitate contacts with the Mongol court. But by the end of the thirteenth century the Mongols had abandoned their pro-Christian policies and opted for Islam, and a period of decline set in for the Christian communities, leading to their marginalisation. In 1310, a terrible massacre of Christians took place in Erbil, carried out as an act of revenge by one of the Arab generals who served in the army of the Mongol Il-Khan.

Unfortunately, historians have little information about Christianity in Iraq in the fourteenth and fifteenth centuries. The centre of the (Nestorian) church was transferred to Kurdistan. Political unrest, the raids by Timur and waves of persecution by local rulers, though sometimes interrupted by more peaceful periods, destroyed much of the ecclesiastical infrastructure. For several centuries Christians were no longer in a position to develop scholarly activities. The sixteenth century offered a similar picture: raids by Turkic tribes who acted for the Safavid Dynasty which had taken power in Persia, followed by the conquest of Iraq by the Ottomans (1517).

New Churches

By the middle of the fifteenth century, the Easterners had decided that the patriarchal dignity should remain within the same family. It thus became hereditary, passing from uncle to nephew. This decision was counter to the age-old tradition that the patriarch had to be elected and caused resentment among part of the clergy. In 1552, a number of bishops elected Yuḥannān Sullāqā, the abbot of the monastery of Rabban Hormizd (the place of residence of the patriarchs), as their new leader to protest against the fact that the canonical Patriarch Shem`un VII had appointed his 12-year-old nephew as his successor. In the absence of a sufficient number of metropolitans to ordain Sullāqā as the new patriarch, the latter was advised to turn to Rome. After submitting a profession of faith in which he abjured his presumed heretical Nestorian Christology, he was recognised by the pope as patriarch of Mosul, an act not appreciated by Shem`un and his followers. In fact, it was the beginning of a new church that, despite several setbacks and a very complicated history with changing loyalties, in the course of time succeeded in outnumbering the faithful of the 'Nestorian' mother-church. The name given to the new community was the Chaldean Church. Since 1830, it has had a continuous line of patriarchs in union with Rome, who for more than a century would have their residence in Mosul. The most illustrious of these was undoubtedly Joseph VI Audo (1848–97), who opposed Roman interference in the internal management of the Chaldean Church, culminating in his rejection of the dogma of papal infallibility, adopted at the First Vatican Council, which, however, he was forced to accept a few years later. The struggle between Audo and the Vatican is emblematic of the ongoing tension between Latinising tendencies and the struggle to preserve the oriental character of the Chaldean Church.

In this period, the patriarch of the mother-church resided in the village of Qodshanes, in eastern Anatolia, not far from the Iraqi border. His faithful living in Kurdistan were confronted with intense missionary activity on the side of the 'papists', as the Chaldeans were often called. As a result of the archaeological discoveries by the British of some ancient Assyrian sites near Mosul, the 'Nestorians' began to interpret the traditional name Atorāyē, used for their faithful living in the land around Mosul (called in Syriac Ator, merely a geographical designation), as 'Assyrian', as if they were the descendants of the pagan Assyrians mentioned in the Old Testament. It was a label that appealed very much to the missionaries of the Church of England, who started to speak of the Assyrian Church, a name later made official by the Easterners themselves, who today call their church the Assyrian Church of the East.

A similar development took place within the 'Jacobite' community in the eighteenth century and led to the creation of a uniate Syrian Catholic Church. Though the centre of this new church was outside Iraq, a relatively large number of Iraqi Jacobites joined the uniate community and took over some of the originally Jacobite churches and monasteries, comparable to the way the Chaldeans had taken over some of the possessions of the 'Nestorians'.

Next to these four autochthonous churches, which though dogmatically divided are all proud of their Syriac heritage, some new churches established themselves in Iraq. In the seventeenth century, Latin missionaries created a network of small convents. Their activities were highly valued by Rome, which created a (still extant) Latin diocese based in Baghdad. These missionaries worked closely with the members of the newly formed uniate churches. In the same period, Armenians from Iran came to Basra and to Baghdad, which became the see of an Armenian bishop.

After the First World War

During the First World War, tens of thousands of Assyrians and Chaldeans living in Anatolia were brutally massacred. Some Assyrians managed to escape to Iran but were later forced to seek refuge in Iraq, where they were given shelter in a camp near Baquba (30 miles north of Baghdad) in terrifying circumstances. Surviving Chaldeans settled mostly in villages in Kurdistan along the Anatolian border, thus doubling the Chaldean presence in this region (from about 4,000 to 8,000). A number of Armenian refugees established themselves in the same region, mainly in the Kurdish town of Zakho, where they opened a still-extant Armenian church and built a new village, Avzrog. The ethnic profile of these 'Kurdish Armenians' was, however, different: less Armenian than that of their co-religionists in Baghdad and Basra. After the war, when Iraq came under the British mandate, many Assyrians hoped to be compensated for their loyalty to the Entente powers and to Britain in particular. When it turned out that returning to their Anatolian villages was impossible, they pushed for the creation of an independent or semi-independent Assyrian homeland in or near Iraqi Kurdistan, which should enjoy British protection. The British mandatory authorities, though to a certain extent sympathetic towards the Assyrian cause, did not actively support the Assyrians in realising this political objective. They helped, however, the newly ordained patriarch establish his authority and encouraged a number of Assyrian tribesmen to enrol in the Iraqi Levies, a militia created to patrol certain difficult areas, such as Kurdistan. After a few years, the force was entirely Assyrian and came to be known as the Assyrian Levies.

When the mandate came to an end in 1932, the government of the newly formed Kingdom of Iraq suspected the Assyrians of still pursuing their aspirations for autonomy under the leadership of the patriarch. Assyrian armed soldiers, refusing to cooperate with the government, clashed with Iraqi troops and were eventually defeated by the Iraqi army near the village of Simele (Summayl) in Kurdistan on 7 August 1933. This was, however, much more than a military and political conflict. A great many local Christians, including Chaldeans who did not share the nationalist aspirations of the Assyrians, were massacred. Simele thus became the symbol of general anti-Christian violence and is still commemorated each year by the Christians of Iraq on 7 August as Martyrs' Day. In Kurdistan, it is even an official holiday. The patriarch himself was expelled from Iraq and settled eventually in Chicago, which would become the centre of the Assyrian Church for several decades. He was followed by many Iraqi Assyrians, leading to a growing minorisation of the Assyrian element among the Christian population.

The Chaldeans, now by far the largest Christian community in the country, had better understood the signs of the new times and were prepared to limit the role of their patriarch to that of a religious leader and no longer as the head of a nation, as in the Ottoman period. Their adaptation to the new political realities was highly appreciated by the authorities, who welcomed the patriarch as a member of the Senate, a position (although with limited political power) he would hold until the proclamation of the Iraqi Republic in 1958. One of the consequences of successful integration into the Iraqi state was the gradual move of the centre of the Chaldean Church from the north to Baghdad. In 1946, Patriarch Joseph VII Ghanima decided to transfer the patriarchal residence from Mosul to the capital, where his successor, Paul II Cheiko (1958–89), developed an important pastoral and parochial infrastructure serving the faithful, who in the course of time grew to a community of around 250,000. In Baghdad, the Chaldean Church lost a great deal of its ethnic profile and became strongly Arabicised, Arabic replacing Syriac even in the liturgy. Many faithful of the Syrian Orthodox and the Syrian Catholic Churches followed the example of the Chaldeans and settled in the capital. There, in 1954, an Armenian Catholic diocese was also established. In 1956, four American Jesuits founded the al-Hikma University, which developed into an important academic institution, attracting besides Christians also many students with a Muslim background. The same inter-religious openness was also characteristic of the many educational and social institutes established in this period by the Latin-rite Dominican Sisters and by members of the Chaldean religious orders such as the Chaldean-rite Daughters of Mary Immaculate (founded in 1922 in Baghdad) and the Chaldean Sisters of the Sacred Heart (founded in 1915).

The decision in 1964 by the Assyrian patriarch in Chicago to introduce the Gregorian calendar created a schism within the Church of the East. Thomas Darmo, one of the former Assyrian refugees from Anatolia who had found shelter in the camp of Baquba and who after an ecclesiastical career in Iraq and Syria became the incumbent of the metropolitan see of Thrichur (India), led the protests. In 1968, he was consecrated patriarch of a schismatic church, which adopted the name of the Ancient Church of the East and established its centre in Baghdad. Apart from liturgical considerations, traditional tribal rivalries also played a role in the formation of this church, which since 1972 has been under the leadership of Addai II, with his residence in Baghdad. It is clear that in this period the centre of Iraqi Christianity had shifted from the north to Baghdad.

Under Saddam Hussein

In 1968 the Baath Party took power. Its ideology emphasised the Arab character of the Iraqi state. This implied the nationalisation of a number of foreign institutes, including the al-Hikma University, which had to close its doors and was integrated into Baghdad University. Many private Christian schools, hospitals and orphanages suffered the same fate, though the majority of the teachers, being of Iraqi origin, could keep their positions. Despite this development, initially the leadership of the Chaldean Church had no difficulty in cooperating with the new regime, especially since its Arabisation policy was rather mild as far as Christians were concerned. In

1972 the specific cultural and linguistic rights of the Christian communities were officially recognised, offering the possibility of creating a Syriac Academy, which took a number of important cultural and scholarly initiatives. By the end of the 1970s, however, the government had abandoned this policy of overture to the non-Arab populations on Iraqi soil and the Academy had to close its doors.

For some Christians in Kurdistan, less Arabised than those living in the capital, this meant a growing awareness of their ethnic particularity. In 1979 they created the Assyrian Democratic Movement (ADM), although for them the label 'Assyrian' no longer referred exclusively to the Assyrian Church of the East; it was understood as a general identity marker of those Christian communities who used Syriac in their liturgies or literary traditions. It was an attempt to overcome traditional ecclesiastical divisions and rivalries, which in their eyes prevented Christians from playing an effective role in Iraqi society. A number of these new Assyrians joined the Kurdish Peshmerga in their struggle against Saddam Hussein. As a result, an important number of Christian villages (both Chaldean and 'Assyrian') situated within Kurdistan were destroyed during the infamous Anfal campaigns undertaken by the regime in 1986 and 1987.

In central Iraq, the long-lasting Iran–Iraq conflict (1980–8), followed by the First Gulf War (1990–1), took a disproportionately heavy toll on the Christian population. Many youngsters tried to emigrate in order to avoid conscription and the prospect of serving in Iran. The bi-ritual Major Seminary of St John the Evangelist, under the supervision of the Dominicans, in Mosul was left without a sufficient number of students and had to stop its activities. The Seminary, founded at the end of the nineteenth century, had been for many decades one of the major Christian institutions in the country and, known for its high level of theological education, was responsible for the training of both Chaldean and Syrian Catholic clergy. The fact that the liturgy was celebrated according to both the Eastern and Western Syrian (or Assyrian and Syrian Orthodox) rites helped the students look beyond their own communities.

In 1991, after the First Gulf War, Kurdistan was recognised by the international community as an autonomous region; the ADM was rewarded for its participation in the struggle against Saddam Hussein and was integrated into the political system of Kurdistan. ADM politicians, some of whom were given important ministerial positions in successive Kurdish cabinets, were able to take initiatives for the promotion of Syriac culture. This development placed especially the Chaldean hierarchy, which was torn by divided loyalties, in a difficult position: on the one hand, it had responsibility for the traditional Chaldean villages in Kurdistan but, on the other, the majority of its faithful were living in Baghdad. A *modus vivendi* with the government turned out to be possible, and despite the difficult political situation ecclesiastical life continued, partly thanks to the many social initiatives carried out under the supervision of the Chaldean hierarchy. An interesting ecumenical initiative was the creation in 1991 of a school for theology and philosophy, known as Babel College. Though under the supervision of the Chaldean Church, the College attracted students from all communities. The different communities also took initiatives for the preservation of the Christian material heritage: the renovation of some ancient monasteries and churches in and around Mosul and the preservation of hundreds of Syriac and Christian-Arabic manuscripts, often dispersed in different locations and in the hands of private families. An important pastoral initiative was the publication of a cultural-theological magazine *al-Fikr al-Masīḥī* (*Christian Thinking*). The objective of this periodical, started in 1964 in Mosul by a small team of Syrian Catholic priests and taken over by the Dominicans of Baghdad in 1994, is to introduce educated laypeople to new theological developments.

One of the reasons behind the working relationship with the government was that during the period of the international boycott against Iraq, the Chaldean Church was one of very few avenues through which the regime could establish contacts with the international community. A key role was played here by the politician Tariq Aziz, of Chaldean origin, who for many years served as deputy prime minister and foreign minister.

After Saddam Hussein

The overthrow of the Baath regime in 2003 heralded a period of extreme violence and unrest, partly inspired by al-Qaeda and aimed at the Christian population of central Iraq, partly the result of indiscriminate banditry. Thousands of Christians left Baghdad and other cities of the south such as Basra and tried to settle in the north or to go abroad. Local Christian politicians such as the influential Sarkis Aghajan, minister of finance in the Kurdish government, set up an ambitious programme to accommodate these Christian refugees. More than 100 new Christian villages were built around Dohuk and along the Turkish border, whereas many other Christians flocked to Ankawa, an entirely Christian township of 25,000 inhabitants, near the Kurdish capital Erbil. One of the challenges was to integrate these refugees into the economic fabric of Kurdistan, but the urban background of the majority of the refugees, their unfamiliarity with the local Kurdish languages, and the economic situation in Kurdistan made them consider Kurdistan only as a springboard for further migration.

In the meantime, the ADM changed its strategy and, instead of collaborating primarily with the Kurdish authorities, tried to win influence at the federal level. When a new constitution had to be prepared, ADM politicians realised the importance of Christians speaking with one voice and suggested that the constitution recognise a sole Christian Chaldo-Assyrian 'nationality' (*qawmiyya*), an effort at unity that, however, failed. Article 121 of the final constitution adopted in 2005 speaks of the 'administrative, political, cultural and educational rights' of the Chaldeans and the Assyrians as two separate groups. In Kurdistan, too, bringing Christians together under one ethnic label turned out to be impossible. In 2007 Aghajan tried to set up a trans-denominational Chaldo-Syriac-Assyrian (CSA) Council, the objective of which was to coordinate common Christian cultural and political initiatives, but after a few years the Council became a political party itself, competing mainly with the ADM. Despite all internal rivalries, Christian politicians succeeded in securing a minimum Christian representation in both the federal and the Kurdish parliaments. The election law of 2009 determined that from a total of 325 seats in the National Assembly, five seats would be reserved for the 'Christian constituent', whereas the Kurdish parliament of 111 members would include six Christian representatives. Taking into account the dwindling numbers of Iraqi Christians, one could speak of a Christian over-representation, though it should rather be considered as recognition of the fact that, to a large extent, they constitute the autochthonous population of the country.

Since 2003, both ADM and CSA politicians have been working for the political acceptance of the idea of an autonomous Christian homeland. Both parties agree on where it should be located: the so-called Plain of Nineveh, a stretch of land situated in the Governorate of Nineveh, north-east of Mosul. This region still has a number of Christian towns and villages, such as Baghdida (Karakosh) – with a mainly Syrian Catholic and Syrian Orthodox population – and Tell Kepe and Alqosh (both Chaldean), where the inhabitants speak Sureth, a neo-Aramaic language related to classical Syriac. The politicians diverge, however, on the interpretation of autonomy. For the ADM, it should be limited to a form of self-administration, whereas the CSA advocates full self-governance, including legislative and executive powers, comparable to conditions in the Kurdish autonomous region. A second point of divergence is whether this region should cooperate closely with Kurdistan, the CSA preference, or rather with the federal government, as the ADM desires. The underlying question here is whether the future of Iraqi Christianity is with Kurdistan or in central Iraq. The protagonists of the Kurdish option point to the much better safety situation in the Kurdish area, the absence of anti-Christian Islamist parties and the fact that the regional government has received thousands of Christian refugees from the south. The opponents emphasise that, despite centuries of contact, Kurds and Christians in Iraq have never been able to work and live together, and they point to the role of the

Kurds in the Assyrian genocide of 1915 and more recently their failure to protect Christian villages taken by ISIS in 2014. Moreover, they stress that the majority of Christians speak Sureth and Arabic rather than one of the Kurdish languages.

The idea of autonomy, strongly supported by Iraqi Christians living abroad, was, however, opposed by several ecclesiastical leaders. Apart from doubts about the feasibility of the project, they feared that by defining themselves as an ethnic minority, Christians would be marginalised and even ghettoised. The Chaldean Patriarch Louis Raphael I Sako, elected in 2013, repeatedly emphasised how Christians and Muslims in Iraq throughout history have been living together and should now also cooperate in building a new, secular Iraqi society. Other bishops, however, including the Syrian- and Lebanon-based Syrian Orthodox Patriarch Ephrem II, have expressed themselves in favour of an autonomy option, in their eyes the best guarantee of safety for the Christian population and of the preservation of their culture and language.

As to the prospects for autonomy, in 2013 CSA and ADM politicians succeeded in overcoming their differences and submitted a memorandum to both the federal government and the Kurdish authority requesting them to accept the principle of the creation of a separate *mohafaza* (governorate) in the Plain of Nineveh, which would give them the possibility to organise themselves according to the (limited) competences attributed to the governorates. In January 2014, the idea was accepted by the Federal Council of Ministers, but the occupation of the Mosul region by ISIS a few months later and some other political considerations prevented its implementation. After the liberation of the Plain of Nineveh in 2017, Christian politicians brought the issue again to the attention of the authorities. The creation of an autonomous Christian governorate will inevitably rekindle the debate about the relationship of this province with Kurdistan, and federal politicians fear that the region will be drawn into the orbit of the Kurdish region.

Ecclesiastical Developments

The above-mentioned lack of safety in central Iraq greatly affected all churches. Hundreds of the faithful have been abducted or killed, as have members of the hierarchy and the clergy, such as the Chaldean priest Raghid Kanni, together with three deacons (in Mosul in 2007); the Archbishop of Mosul, Paul Faraj Raho (2008); and his Syrian Catholic colleague Basil Cassmoussa (2005). In 2010 a heavy blow was dealt to the Syrian Catholic community of Baghdad when their cathedral was attacked during the weekend liturgy, with more than 50 persons killed. The occupation of Mosul and some major Christian villages in the Plain of Nineveh, such as Karakosh, by ISIS in June 2014 not only triggered a massive Christian exodus to Kurdistan but also destroyed a great deal of the local Christian infrastructure, churches, convents and many private houses. The Christian population of Mosul was given the choice to convert to Islam, to leave the city or to pay the *jizya*, a tax in former periods taken by the Islamic authorities from non-Muslim populations, but already for almost two centuries no longer applied in the Arab world.

This situation of violence required new pastoral strategies. Babel College was transferred to Ankawa-Erbil, which also saw the construction of a new Chaldean clerical seminary and an Assyrian cathedral. To give young people among the Christian refugees the possibility of a future in Kurdistan, the Chaldean Archbishop of Erbil Bashar Warda, in cooperation with the Kurdish authorities, created a Catholic university in 2016, but recent events have undermined the self-confidence of many Christians who dream instead of a better future abroad.

One of the challenges faced by all the autochthonous Christian communities is the increasing presence of evangelical missionaries in Kurdistan and Baghdad. Though traditional Protestant denominations such as the Anglicans have been present in Iraq for more than a century, since the collapse of the Saddam regime new missionaries from the USA have entered the country. These missionaries attract converts not only from the Muslim community but also from the traditional churches, a serious problem to the extent that the Chaldean Church put this issue on the agenda of its synod of 2005.

After the death of Catholicos Mar Dinkha IV in Chicago in March 2015, the Assyrian Church of the East entered a period of vacant see. In the run-up to the elective synod, some intensive ecumenical discussions took place to investigate whether a reunification of the Assyrian Church of the East and the Ancient Church of the East would be possible. In his turn, the Chaldean patriarch, Sako, even proposed to use this vacancy as an opportunity to reunite the three churches. He suggested that Mar Addai II, the patriarch of the Ancient Church of the East, and he himself would submit their resignation to allow the bishops of the three churches to elect a new common leader, who should adopt the principle of communion of faith with the See of Rome. The name of this new church would be a neutral 'Church of the East', without the rival labels 'Chaldean' or 'Assyrian'. However, the traditional antagonisms (liturgical, tribal, ethnic) turned out to be too strong and in September 2015 the synod of the Assyrian Church, taking place in Ankawa-Erbil, elected the metropolitan of Baghdad as the new patriarch. He adopted the name Ghiwarghis III. To show that the future of their Church is intimately related to a strong Assyrian presence in the homeland, the synod decided to move the patriarchal see back to Iraq, a decision much welcomed by Iraqi Christians, who believe in a future for Christianity in their country.

Conclusion

The unstable political situation, uncertainty about the future of the country, massive emigration and the ensuing minorisation of Christians, the influence of Iraqi Christians in the diaspora concerning issues of identity and autonomy, ecclesiastical rivalries and unsuccessful attempts at unity on an ethnic or political level all make the future of a Christian presence in Iraq highly uncertain. Much depends not only on the commitment of Christian leaders, both ecclesiastical and political, to overcome their internal dissensions and to make strategic choices to contribute to building up the country, but also on the willingness of the Iraqi and Kurdish governments to consider Christians as full citizens and even more on the capacity of the Muslim population to accept them as friends and neighbours.

Bibliography

Girling, Kristian, *The Chaldean Catholic Church: Modern History, Ecclesiology and Church–State Relations* (Abingdon: Routledge, 2017).

Rassam, Suha, *Christianity in Iraq* (Leominster: Gracewing, 2016).

Teule, Herman, *Les Assyro-chaldéens* (Turnhout: Brepols, 2008).

Teule, Herman, 'Christians in Iraq. An Analysis of Some Recent Political Developments', *Der Islam* 88 (2012), 179–98.

Wilmshurst, David, *The Martyred Church: A History of the Church of the East* (London: East and West Publishing, 2011).

The Gulf: Bahrain, Kuwait, Oman, Qatar, Saudi Arabia, United Arab Emirates (UAE), Yemen

Hrayr Jebejian

The Arabian/Persian Gulf, located in western Asia between Iran and the Arabian Peninsula, is an extension of the Indian Ocean. Most of the people of the Arabian Peninsula are Arabs whose roots go back generations. Arabic is the official language, though dialects distinguish one region from another. With the expansion of Islam in the seventh century, all of the countries in the area accepted the new religion.

The nomenclature is controversial. Historically it is known sometimes as the Persian Gulf but also as the Arabian Gulf. Iran, the largest country adjacent to these waters and with a population of over 70 million, has throughout its history designated it the Persian Gulf. Modern scholarship and historical records going back at least 2,500 years, to the time of the powerful Pars Empire, agree on the name Persian Gulf. But the nationalism of most of the Arab countries challenges the Iranian position and insists on the name Arabian Gulf. The 1958 coup of Adbulkarim Ghasem in Iraq followed by anti-Iranian feelings in the region after Iran and Egypt ceased all diplomatic relations in 1960 led to a general acceptance of the term Arabian (rather than the Persian) Gulf.

The Gulf region (hereafter 'the Gulf') includes the Kingdom of Bahrain, Kuwait, the Sultanate of Oman, Qatar, the Kingdom of Saudi Arabia, the United Arab Emirates (UAE) and the Republic of Yemen. These first six countries formed the Gulf Cooperation Council (GCC) in Abu Dhabi, UAE, in 1981. The aim of the GCC is to foster peace and security in the region and to develop economic relations among the member countries. The GCC is increasingly becoming an important entity in the Arab world and internationally, assuming the role of an active political power broker in the region.

Christian Presence: Historical Overview

From the fourth century onwards, Christianity flourished in the Gulf, and even when it did not flourish but only survived, it remained a spiritual and cultural force in the Gulf, right up to the present day. The Syriac sources of the Church of the East, also known as the Nestorian Church, document the presence of monasteries from the mid-fourth century onwards. Documentary and archaeological evidence also shows that even after the birth of Islam in 629, the churches remained active until the late ninth century.

Two schools of thought exist on the matter of Christianity's fate after the ninth century. One argues that the persecution of the Church of the East completely removed it from the Gulf. Proponents base this case on the Prophet Muhammad's deathbed words: 'Throughout the peninsula there shall be no second creed'. There is little to substantiate this case, however. In this period, Christians together with Jews acquired *dhimmi* status, a lower status than Muslims in Islamic law, and they had to pay *jizya*, a tax. The second school of thought links the disappearance of the Church of the East to the Greek (Byzantine) theology and philosophy that alienated Arab intellectuals and religious leaders. The economic argument for conversion should, however, not be overlooked: Christians were restricted in their movements, and conversion meant better business and social networks.

Christianity in Bahrain, 1970 and 2015

	1970		2015		Average annual growth rate (%), 1970–2015
Tradition	Population	%	Population	%	
Christians	5,900	2.8%	182,000	13.2%	7.9%
Anglicans	500	0.2%	6,000	0.4%	5.7%
Independents	1,000	0.5%	13,600	1.0%	6.0%
Orthodox	800	0.4%	5,500	0.4%	4.4%
Protestants	1,100	0.5%	6,600	0.5%	4.1%
Catholics	2,500	1.2%	150,000	10.9%	9.5%
Evangelicals	680	0.3%	4,000	0.3%	4.0%
Pentecostals	950	0.4%	44,200	3.2%	8.9%
Total population	**213,000**	**100.0%**	**1,377,000**	**100.0%**	**4.2%**

Source: Todd M. Johnson and Gina A. Zurlo (eds), *World Christian Database* (Leiden/Boston: Brill), accessed March 2017.

Christianity in Kuwait, 1970 and 2015

	1970		2015		Average annual growth rate (%), 1970–2015
Tradition	Population	%	Population	%	
Christians	38,600	5.2%	396,000	10.2%	5.3%
Anglicans	1,500	0.2%	5,000	0.1%	2.7%
Independents	2,400	0.3%	7,000	0.2%	2.4%
Orthodox	13,300	1.8%	80,100	2.1%	4.1%
Protestants	1,700	0.2%	7,400	0.2%	3.4%
Catholics	17,700	2.4%	300,000	7.7%	6.5%
Evangelicals	2,100	0.3%	9,200	0.2%	3.3%
Pentecostals	1,300	0.2%	84,500	2.2%	9.8%
Total population	**750,000**	**100.0%**	**3,892,000**	**100.0%**	**3.7%**

Source: Todd M. Johnson and Gina A. Zurlo (eds), *World Christian Database* (Leiden/Boston: Brill), accessed March 2017.

Christian presence re-entered the Gulf with the first colonial ventures of the Portuguese in 1497, the establishment of the East India Company in 1600 by the British, the Dutch East India Company in 1602 and the American Arabian Mission in 1889. The Reformed Church in America took over the Mission in 1894 and built the first schools for boys in 1905 and the first proper hospital in 1913. These still exist in Kuwait, Bahrain and Oman, although the Mission ceased its activities in 1973.

The preaching of the gospel has yet to bear fruit in the Gulf, since no indigenous Christian community has emerged. Still, a foundation for the future was laid as thousands of travellers, businesspeople and migrants from the Middle East and other places arrived in the Gulf and established churches.

Profiles of Christianity

Two efforts have contributed to the toleration of the Christian community in the UAE. The first was the work of the American Arabian Mission from

Christianity in Oman, 1970 and 2015

	1970		2015		Average annual growth rate (%), 1970–2015
Tradition	Population	%	Population	%	
Christians	2,700	0.4%	197,000	4.4%	10.0%
Anglicans	500	0.1%	7,300	0.2%	6.1%
Independents	380	0.1%	19,100	0.4%	9.1%
Orthodox	650	0.1%	23,400	0.5%	8.3%
Protestants	500	0.1%	3,300	0.1%	4.2%
Catholics	700	0.1%	140,000	3.1%	12.5%
Evangelicals	190	0.0%	5,100	0.1%	7.5%
Pentecostals	330	0.1%	35,200	0.8%	10.9%
Total population	**724,000**	**100.0%**	**4,491,000**	**100.0%**	**4.1%**

Source: Todd M. Johnson and Gina A. Zurlo (eds), *World Christian Database* (Leiden/Boston: Brill), accessed March 2017.

Christianity in Qatar, 1970 and 2015

	1970		2015		Average annual growth rate (%), 1970–2015
Tradition	Population	%	Population	%	
Christians	3,900	3.6%	210,000	9.4%	9.2%
Anglicans	350	0.3%	10,000	0.5%	7.7%
Independents	350	0.3%	10,600	0.5%	7.9%
Orthodox	320	0.3%	5,300	0.2%	6.4%
Protestants	400	0.4%	5,600	0.3%	6.0%
Catholics	2,500	2.3%	170,000	7.6%	9.8%
Evangelicals	280	0.3%	4,400	0.2%	6.3%
Pentecostals	290	0.3%	53,800	2.4%	12.3%
Total population	**109,000**	**100.0%**	**2,235,000**	**100.0%**	**6.9%**

Source: Todd M. Johnson and Gina A. Zurlo (eds), *World Christian Database* (Leiden/Boston: Brill), accessed March 2017.

1889 onwards. In particular, the dedicated ministry of the American doctors and nurses through the Oasis Hospital (established in 1960) in Al Ain won many friends among the Arabs. The second factor lay in the political leadership of Sheikh Zayed Al Nahyan, the founding president of the UAE. Sheikh Zayed welcomed Christians by declaring that he held out his hand to everyone in a spirit of cooperation for the wellbeing of the nation and its people. While the Sheikh's declaration did not grant religious freedom, it signified toleration, respect and collaboration.

The present Evangelical Church, known as the United Christian Church of Dubai, evolved out of the American Arabian Mission in 1962. It expanded into Abu Dhabi in 1966 and today hosts more than 60 different congregations and language groups. Similarly, the present St Andrew's Anglican Church in Abu Dhabi dates back to 1965, and the Chaplaincy of Dubai and Sharjah, known as Holy Trinity, was established in 1970. The Order of Capuchins, who have charge of the Apostolic Vicariate of Southern Arabia (including St Joseph's Cathedral in Abu Dhabi), held the first Catholic worship service

Christianity in Saudi Arabia, 1970 and 2015

	1970		2015		Average annual growth rate (%), 1970–2015
Tradition	Population	%	Population	%	
Christians	18,300	0.3%	1,379,000	4.4%	10.1%
Anglicans	2,000	0.0%	19,000	0.1%	5.1%
Independents	4,800	0.1%	54,800	0.2%	5.6%
Orthodox	2,000	0.0%	50,000	0.2%	7.4%
Protestants	6,900	0.1%	15,500	0.1%	1.8%
Catholics	2,600	0.0%	1,220,000	3.9%	14.6%
Evangelicals	4,300	0.1%	27,500	0.1%	4.2%
Pentecostals	4,600	0.1%	361,000	1.1%	10.2%
Total population	**5,836,000**	**100.0%**	**31,540,000**	**100.0%**	**3.8%**

Source: Todd M. Johnson and Gina A. Zurlo (eds), *World Christian Database* (Leiden/Boston: Brill), accessed March 2017.

Christianity in United Arab Emirates, 1970 and 2015

	1970		2015		Average annual growth rate (%), 1970–2015
Tradition	Population	%	Population	%	
Christians	9,300	4.0%	1,173,000	12.8%	11.4%
Anglicans	1,500	0.6%	14,000	0.2%	5.1%
Independents	100	0.0%	18,100	0.2%	12.2%
Orthodox	2,200	0.9%	74,200	0.8%	8.1%
Protestants	910	0.4%	17,700	0.2%	6.8%
Catholics	4,500	1.9%	1,057,000	11.5%	12.9%
Evangelicals	920	0.4%	12,500	0.1%	6.0%
Pentecostals	230	0.1%	291,000	3.2%	17.2%
Total population	**235,000**	**100.0%**	**9,157,000**	**100.0%**	**8.5%**

Source: Todd M. Johnson and Gina A. Zurlo (eds), *World Christian Database* (Leiden/Boston: Brill), accessed March 2017.

in 1965. To accommodate the growing number of worshippers, two more Catholic churches were built, one in Jebel Ali, Dubai, in 2001, and another in Fujairah, in 2002. Today, the Catholic Church runs five schools in the UAE, at which catechism is taught to all Christian pupils. Diplomatic relations between the Vatican and the UAE were established in 2007.

Indians constitute the largest group of Christians in the UAE. The Syrian Orthodox Church, Mar Thoma Church and Church of South India have large congregations, who worship in English, Kannada, Malayalam, Tamil, Telugu and Urdu. The Indian Pentecostal Church and the New Testament Church also boast very large, active congregations.

Migrant workers from Africa, the Philippines and other Asian countries have formed congregations and worship within the premises of the Anglican and Protestant churches. The Anglican Church in Abu Dhabi hosts 10,000 worshippers and 45 congregations, representing 17 languages. Evangelical expansion in Asia, missions from the West, internal splits among denominations, and the diverse needs of the different ethnic groups have spurred this growth in the UAE's seven emirates: Abu Dhabi, Ajman, Dubai, Fujairah, Sharjah, Ras al-Khaimah and Umm al-Quwain. In fact, of the total population it has been estimated that 13% are Emirati nationals, 23% other Arabs and Iranians, around 50% South Asians and the rest East Asians, Europeans and Americans. The migrant labour force constitutes 40% of the total population.

It is estimated that 160 countries are represented in the UAE, concentrated in Dubai. The latter has stepped forth as a world city and global commercial hub that knows no limits to infrastructure development. It attracts many global professional elites and promotes luxury tourism, entertainment facilities and winter sun resorts. Dubai caters to international tastes and services and ranks as a world cultural centre.

Christianity in Yemen, 1970 and 2015

Tradition	1970 Population	1970 %	2015 Population	2015 %	Average annual growth rate (%), 1970–2015
Christians	1,700	0.0%	36,500	0.1%	7.1%
Anglicans	170	0.0%	1,800	0.0%	5.4%
Independents	1,000	0.0%	4,000	0.0%	3.1%
Orthodox	0	0.0%	8,000	0.0%	16.0%
Protestants	290	0.0%	13,700	0.1%	8.9%
Catholics	120	0.0%	6,000	0.0%	9.1%
Evangelicals	210	0.0%	4,000	0.0%	6.8%
Pentecostals	200	0.0%	6,800	0.0%	8.2%
Total population	**6,156,000**	**100.0%**	**26,832,000**	**100.0%**	**3.3%**

Source: Todd M. Johnson and Gina A. Zurlo (eds), *World Christian Database* (Leiden/Boston: Brill), accessed March 2017.

One of the significant factors of the Christian presence in Kuwait is the local Christian community. Today, the local Kuwaiti Christians number around 300. Historical records indicate that evangelist Yaacoub Shamas came from Mardin, Turkey, in 1919. His extended family also settled in Kuwait, and they still live there. Another noteworthy family is the Gharayebs, who came from Carboran, Turkey. One of its descendants is the Revd Amanuel Gharayeb, the present senior pastor of the National Evangelical Church and spokesperson of the Christian community.

The Catholic Church (established in Kuwait in 1948) is the largest Christian community in Kuwait. Diplomatic relations with the Vatican date back to 1996. The Greek Catholic Church (established 1960) and the Greek Orthodox Church (1961) function to this day, catering to the spiritual needs of their growing congregations. Today, the Evangelical Church, established in 1931 on land given by the authorities, hosts more than 84 congregations of different language, ethnic and denominational groups.

The humanitarian and educational contributions of the Evangelical Church in Kuwait have become well known. Samuel Zwemer and Stanley Millrya, from the American Arabian Mission, opened the first Christian bookshop in Kuwait in 1903. This was followed by the first proper hospital for men in 1913 and another for women in 1919. Lew and Dorothy Scudder played a vital role in the medical ministry, with Dorothy serving for 54 years in Kuwait. Unfortunately, the hospital closed in 1967. Also in 1913, Edwin Calverley opened a school for boys. Students included such notables as Shaykh Fahad bin-Salima Sabah, Kuwait's first minister of health and public works. Although the school is no longer open, its impact on the development of modern Kuwait has been great.

Other churches that boast sizeable congregations are the Armenian Orthodox Church (established locally in 1962), the Anglican Church (1948) and the Egyptian Coptic Church (1961). Indeed, the number of churches and denominations reflect the growing number and diversity of migrant workers and expatriates in Kuwait.

Bahrain has around 500 indigenous Christians who have their own representative in parliament. Expatriate influx from the early 1950s until today, though, has changed the face of the church in Bahrain. Churches and congregations mushroomed while Bahrain's infrastructure and economy prospered. Today, Christians in Bahrain worship in Malayalam (a congregation that started in 1959), Tamil (since 1964), Telugu (1965), Urdu (1969), Amharic, Arabic, Chinese, Korean, Nepali, Sri Lankan and Tagalog. Dozens of other groups meet and worship in their own languages and in their own churches. St Christopher's Anglican Cathedral, founded in 1953, for example, hosts more than 40 different language and ethnic groups. The Catholic Sacred Heart Church was built in 1939.

According to Youssef Haydar, a prominent Bahraini Christian, the American Mission Hospital, founded in 1901, has Bahraini postal box number 1, indicating that it is the country's oldest mission organisation. A significant day in the history of the American Mission Hospital was 17 March 1988, when the minister of labour and social affairs issued ministerial order no. 5, whereby the Hospital was renamed the American Mission Hospital Society of Bahrain. The Hospital remains a viable institution in the country. Similarly, the first 'church school' building was dedicated in Bahrain on 10 June 1906 through the efforts of the American Mission. The Catholic Sacred Heart School (1953) is still run by the Comboni sisters.

The 1950s brought a unique development to the Kingdom: the needs of Christian expatriates living in the various oil camps established by the Saudi Arabian Oil Company (ARAMCO, formerly the Arabian American Oil Company) were recognised. The first personnel to minister openly in the camps were Edwin Lutdens and Harvey Stall, who resided in Bahrain. This ministry still goes on today in the same compound.

Saudi Arabia is the only country in the Gulf that does not allow churches freedom of worship. Even though the Vatican and the Kingdom held several talks about allowing the million or so Catholics working and living in the Kingdom to practise their faith freely, it was all to no avail.

Of the 22 churches that used to operate in Aden during the period of British control of Yemen, only four are still open. These churches, three Catholic and one Anglican, maintain a low profile as much as possible. The latter runs a small clinic, which renders impressive medical services to the local community. In Sana'a, the capital, the Catholic Church meets in a house, while Evangelical groups meet in the hall of a local restaurant. European Lutheran missionaries ran a trade and craft social school in the city of Tai'z.

For years, Mother Teresa's Sisters of Charity took care of the elderly and physically challenged in Sana'a, Tai'z, Aden and Hodeida. However, the decades-long conflict in the ancient country has taken a toll on Christians and Christian missions. Over the years, many missionaries have been killed, churches attacked and hospitals destroyed. In 1998, three Sisters of Charity were assassinated. In 2002, three Southern Baptist missionary doctors were killed at Jibla Hospital. After the incident, the hospital suspended its operation. During the ongoing strife in the country, one of the Catholic churches in Aden was looted and destroyed. For the time being, ministries have been suspended because of the escalating upheaval and chaos in the country.

In 2008, the Catholic Church of Our Lady of the Rosary was the first church to be inaugurated on land granted by the authorities in Qatar. It was followed by the inter-denominational Indian churches, which host an estimated 29 different Indian denominations. The Sts Peter and Paul Coptic Orthodox Church hosts the Ethiopian Church; Greek Orthodox; St James Jacobite Church; and the Anglican Church of the Epiphany, which hosts 67 different congregations and language groups. A steering committee representing all the mainline churches coordinates the various aspects of the Christian community and its relations with the authorities. All these churches are located in one district of the capital city, Doha, which is guarded by police at all times. Worshippers at Church City, as the place is known among Christians in Doha, have to step through x-ray and screening machines to enter the compound.

The church set-up and composition in Oman are similar to those in the other Gulf countries. The Catholic community is the largest and has church buildings in Ruwi, Ghala, Sohar and Salalah, as does the Protestant community in Oman. The latter hosts around 90 different congregations and language groups. The Coptic, Greek Orthodox, Mar Thoma and Syrian Jacobite Churches are also present and have their own facilities for worship. The development of the Christian ministry in Oman, however, was quite different from that in other Gulf countries. The establishment of a maternity hospital in 1913, a school for boys and girls in 1939 and the Muscat Chapel resulted in a purely Omani church. The Omani experience proved that education and medical work that spanned over a period of five decades were effective evangelistic tools to initiate mission among the local community.

In 1987, after the closing of the American School in Muscat, the Reformed Church in America established the Al Amana Centre, an academic interfaith centre. The purpose was to educate a broad cross-section of Christians in the USA and Europe about Islam and Arab culture, in the hope of fostering deeper mutual understanding and peace between East and West. The Centre operates today and provides an important contribution in this field. Presently, its director is the Revd Douglas Leonard.

The change of regime from Sultan Said bin Taimur to his son Qaboos in the summer of 1970 was a watershed. It was no less so for the Omani church. The American Mission gave up the hospital work to the Ministry of Health in 1973, followed by the school. By 1977, the Omani Christian fellowship had begun to quietly fade out of view. A number of their leaders went back to their Muslim faith. The church eventually disappeared in 1984. Presently, the only Arabic-speaking congregations are primarily expatriates from Lebanon, Egypt, Syria, Jordan and other Arab countries.

Scripture Ministry

The Bible Society in the Gulf (BSG), formed in 1999 and a member of the United Bible Societies (UBS) worldwide fellowship, provides all the

Scripture needs of the churches in the Gulf. The BSG runs 18 resource centres in Bahrain, Kuwait, Oman, Qatar and the UAE within church compounds and provides Scriptures in more than 60 different languages. All these centres – including a Bible depot in Aden, Yemen – are officially recognised by the local authorities, and Scriptures are imported legally.

Andrew Thompson, an Anglican priest in Abu Dhabi, sees the importance of resources supplied by the Bible Society shops as opportunities for others to learn about the Christian faith. Catherine Graham, in her extensive independent survey, confirms the latter and adds that the BSG is the only ecumenical organisation with which different church traditions in the region cooperate. She does not find this at all surprising, because the Bible Society has an evangelistic orientation geared to migrant workers in the labour camps, and produces and supplies Scripture materials for them.

Indeed, the Bible Society's programmes are designed to help the migrant community in their daily challenges, to address their spiritual needs and to help them cope with feelings of hopelessness and despair. Hence, Bible Engagement (BE) is the latest strategy the BSG has adopted to engage Christians in the Gulf with the Scripture message of hope. A variety of formats serve this purpose: printed material, audiovisual innovations, storytelling, and training seminars. Research conducted by the BSG in 2014 showed that printed, audio and storytelling are used extensively and almost equally by all churches. This is a significant finding, as it emphasises the importance of continuing to provide Scriptures in different formats to reach all – the literate, semi-literate and illiterate.

Scripture distribution is not a recent phenomenon, though. The American Arabian Mission was the pioneering advocate of Scripture ministry in the Gulf. Its Scripture distribution ministry began as early as 1819. Contemporary records note an officer, Captain Thompson, who even attempted to convert the ruling sheikhs to Christianity. Samuel Zwemer, of Mission to Arabia, who developed educational and medical missions in the region, preached the gospel for the first time to many Muslims, including the ruling sheikh, who allegedly asked for a reading of the gospel and even purchased a large Arabic Bible.

Other pioneers include the Revd James Moerdyk. Facing fierce opposition to his preaching, he immediately realised that the Bible was a book that was forbidden by the local Muslims. His experience reflected that of many missionaries over the years: local people welcomed the medical and educational ministries of the missionaries but not their religious message.

Records show that apart from distributing tracts and selling Bibles, evangelistic work was primarily a matter of personal contact, visits in private homes, and conversations carried on in the environment of the Bible shop or the dispensary. Gatherings were organised in the Arabian Mission's hospital for women, for example, where the Scriptures were read, followed by hymn singing and short talks.

Trends and Status Quo

Present laws in the Gulf do not allow proselytisation of Muslims. However, Christian presence is tolerated, and Christians have the freedom to worship within church buildings that are located inside walled compounds. In this respect, Scriptures are distributed only within the church compounds and need to be stamped with 'For church use only'.

Seventeen Gulf cities provide government land for more than 40 church buildings. Even though churches cannot own land, they have a certain degree of assurance from the local authorities that they will not take these lands back. This privilege of granting land is not extended to all churches and denominations, which means that different church traditions and congregations share the same space. This has and still produces some wonderful examples of cooperation as congregants learn to live together with a shared voice in an effort to foster better relations with government officials and to seek a fruitful ministry among migrant workers. At times, though, this so-called arrangement of forced ecumenism has led and still leads to fierce internal tensions and impedes cooperation among churches because of differences in priorities among those seeking to remedy financial, legal, social or religious needs.

Through numerous consultations with the World Council of Churches and the Middle East Council of Churches, in 2013 church leaders who preside over the Roman Catholic, Eastern Orthodox, Oriental Orthodox, Anglican and Protestant Churches in the Gulf formed an ecumenical body called the Gulf Churches Fellowship. The latter is an association of officially recognised churches in the Gulf, gathered for the purpose of relating to each other, identifying areas of shared concern, and joining together for mutual support in negotiations with Gulf governments when the need arises. The Gulf Churches Fellowship strives to develop a shared voice and common commitment to cooperation among the different churches. Its mission statement highlights that the way forwards requires an effort to build relations of trust and a network of people among all Christian churches of the Gulf that have a shared sense of mission, which is rooted in the churches' common theology.

Hamza Alian explains that most government legislation in the Gulf countries, with the exception of Saudi Arabia, guarantees freedom of worship and the right to exercise religious faith in line with local laws and regulations. The prohibition of the use of church bells in the cities of the Gulf is an example of such regulations. The Revd Thompson does not see such restrictions as persecution. He argues that they need to be seen in context, for often authorities in the Gulf define proselytisation as the indiscriminate distribution of literature, manipulating or coercing others to change their religious faith, and brainwashing.

Some things are considered taboo and cannot be changed. For example, Islamic law restricts interfaith marriages. That is, a Christian man may not marry a Muslim woman unless he converts to Islam. Similarly, a Christian woman cannot marry a Muslim man unless she converts to Islam.

Another issue that is rife in the Gulf is the censorship of websites. Often authorities block those that are deemed to be critical of Islamic values and beliefs. The Revd Thompson mentions the little-known fact that sometimes sites that disrespect other faiths, especially Christianity, are also blocked. Similarly, mosques in the UAE, for example, have to seek prior approval from the Federal Ministry of Justice and Islamic Affairs of topics suitable for preaching. This high degree of political control, some believe, has helped the UAE to become a modern state, secure from Islamic radicalism. Relegation of religion, as Kenneth Christie argues, means that priority is accorded to political leadership, and religious leaders are controlled by the state.

According to World Bank sources, Saudi Arabia comes in at thirteenth place in the world in terms of a business-friendly climate, while Bahrain, the UAE, Qatar, Kuwait and Oman rank twentieth, thirty-third, thirty-ninth, sixty-first and sixty-fifth, respectively. Having said that, recently Washington-based democracy watchdog Freedom House rated these countries as 'not free', except Kuwait, which was deemed 'partly free'. The banning of political parties and lack of freedom of speech, press and assembly are issues often raised by foreign, mostly Western, human rights agencies. Other concerns include migrant workers' living and working conditions, which have often been described as amounting to slavery, especially in the absence of labour laws, labour unions and healthcare, the violation of human rights by confiscating passports and withholding wages, and the physical abuse of domestic workers. In recent years, several countries have introduced some legal protections for maids, for example, but it is too early to judge their effectiveness.

As most Christians in the Gulf are designated as economic migrants, holding on to the language and culture of each and every group becomes crucial. Each language and culture group likes to stick together. As a consequence, the church plays a key role in bringing its flock of the same kind together. For Christian communities in the Gulf, the church is a safe haven where they feel at home and seek refuge during challenging times.

The churches seek to build good relations with the local communities in the Gulf. Rolf Pearson, former General Secretary of the Middle East Council of Churches (MECC) in the Gulf, for example, championed the

Open Doors – Open Minds Foundation, an agency in Dubai that tries to reach out to Muslims, not to convert them but to build bridges between the local community and migrants. The Gulf is a region where dynamic people meet and where millions of migrants come to build themselves a future. These people are often courageous, with open minds, prepared to open closed doors.

Impact of the Christian Presence

The UAE has the highest ratio of expatriates to the local population (84%) in the world, followed by Qatar, Kuwait and Bahrain, the top four countries in the world in terms of multinational societies. A considerable number of these expatriates are Christians. According to the Revd Thompson, with many church buildings being erected, people can see that the Christians are here to stay; hence, the churches' key function is to engage more purposefully with the migrant communities and the locals. To achieve this, there is a need to educate and equip Christians to live their lives with an integrity and authenticity rooted in the Scriptures.

The Gulf provides the opportunity and the platform to many nations and language groups to live together under one roof. The latter is an opportunity for each and every culture to understand the 'other'. According to the Revd Cameron Arenson, Senior Pastor of the Evangelical Church in Abu Dhabi, one important ministry challenge for the Christian church in the Gulf is to create a mission platform for 'Kingdom Impact'; that is, as Christians from all over the world rub shoulders, the Gulf is a dynamic place for the influence of the kingdom of God to spread.

According to the Revd Bill Schwartz, one of the archdeacons of the Anglican Diocese of Cyprus and the Gulf, the church contributes positively to the ongoing efforts of resolving misunderstandings between Christian and Muslim communities. And in this global era of misunderstandings between faiths and cultures, where communities face difficulties living together in one social environment, the Christian presence in the Gulf is contributing to society at large by engaging in interfaith dialogues in education, health services, the workplace, technology and countless media. The aim of the dialogue is to look into the Bible together and interpret its contribution in the various spheres of life, including salvation.

Don Hepburn of the Reformed Church in America describes the mission of Christianity in the region as a very special kind of witness, which is not measured by the number of people converting to Christianity but by the impact it makes on society. Similarly, the Revd John Folmar of the United Christian Centre of Dubai sees the Gulf region as a place where peoples and cultures flow in, with great opportunities for evangelisation. He encourages people to move there and live openly as Christians, among the nations. And living among the nations paves the way for more understanding of the Other, which is the gateway for security and reconciliation. In this sense, today, the impact of the church in the Gulf is immeasurable.

Bibliography

Alian, Hamzeh, *Christians in Kuwait* (Kuwait: Zat Salasel, 2015).

Casper, Jayson, 'Why Christianity Is Surging in the Heart of Islam', *Christianity Today*, 59:7 (11 September 2015), 19.

Graham, Catherine, 'The Gulf Church, Migrant Workers and Muslim Society', unpublished survey, 2009.

Scudder, Lewis III, *The Arabian Mission's Story: In Search of Abraham's Other Son* (Grand Rapids, MI: Eerdmans, 1998).

Thompson, Andrew, *Christianity in the UAE: Culture and Heritage* (Dubai: Motivate Publishing, 2011).

Armenia and Karabakh

Hratch Tchilingirian

In 2001 Armenia celebrated the seventeen-hundredth anniversary of the adoption of Christianity as the state religion. It is believed that two of Christ's Apostles, Thaddeus and Bartholomew, were the first evangelisers of Armenia, in the mid-first century. Tertullian (155 – c. 240) and Eusebius (c. 260–340) record that there were Christians in Armenia as early as the first half of the third century. Armenia was the first nation to adopt Christianity as its state religion, in the early fourth century, when King Tiridates III (ruled 298–330) was baptised by Gregory the Illuminator (c. 240–325), the patron saint of the Armenians. Gregory, a descendant of a noble house in Parthia and brought up as a Christian in Cappadocia, was consecrated a bishop by Leontius, the metropolitan of Caesarea, as the first Bishop of Armenia. He established the Armenian nation's Holy See in Vagharshapat, today known as the Mother See of Holy Ejmiatsin (Etchmiadzin), located 25 km from Armenia's capital, Yerevan. He is called Illuminator for 'enlightening the nation with the light of the gospel' and is considered the first catholicos (patriarch) of the Armenian Apostolic Orthodox Church.

Armenia's formal conversion to Christianity not only meant stronger political and cultural ties with the Roman world, but also determined the future course of Armenian history and culture. As Christianity took roots in the life of the nation, the invention of an Armenian alphabet was necessitated to make the Scriptures and worship services, which were conducted in Syriac and Greek, accessible to the people. In 406, Mesrop Mashtots (c. 355–439) created the Armenian alphabet, under the auspices of Catholicos Sahak (c. 348–438), and soon after, together with a group of associates known as Holy Translators, translated the Bible into Armenian, followed by the biblical, theological and liturgical writings of leading church fathers of the time. This most important era is known as a golden age in Armenian history.

Divided Between Empires

Geographically, Armenia has been at the crossroads of competing empires and regional powers and subject to invasions and destruction. As a result, the size and borders of the country have changed many times. The territory of the Republic of Armenia today is only one-tenth of what it used to be historically. Over the centuries, Armenia was divided between the Persian, Ottoman and Russian empires. It has seen Persian rule (430–634) and Arab domination (c. 654–851), been an independent Bagratids kingdom (885–1079) and was the medieval Armenian Kingdom of Cilicia, or Lesser Armenia (1080–1375). Indeed, the history of Armenian Christianity is intimately woven with the history of the nation and its tribulations. Armenian language, literature, architecture, music and Armenian culture in general have been influenced by the nation's Christian heritage.

Political and social developments of crucial significance in the nineteenth century – for both Eastern Armenians under Persian rule and Western Armenians under Ottoman rule – brought about major legal, organisational and institutional changes in the Armenian Church. Many Armenians looked to tsarist Russian rule for potential relief from Persian rule, which was carried out through virtually autonomous khans in the Caucasus. Indeed, most Armenians of Turkey and Persia viewed the Russians as champions of Christendom against Islam and hoped Romanov Russia would lead them to liberation. Seeking refuge and relief – and as permitted by the Treaty of Turkmanchai (1828) – some 50,000 Armenians from northern Persia emigrated to Russian Armenia. As historian Richard Hovhanissian writes, 'Along the entire route, Armenians welcomed the Russian troops as liberators and rejoiced that the day of deliverance was at hand' (*Armenia on the Road to Independence, 1918,* Berkeley: University of California Press, 1967, 8). But such hopes were to be cut short by the signing of the Treaty of Adrianople in 1829, when Russia agreed to withdraw its troops from Erzerum and Kars. Fearing Muslim retaliation for their support of Russian forces and the undesirability of staying under Ottoman rule, by 1830 some 100,000 Armenians emigrated from the plains of Erzerum and Alashkert to the Transcaucasus, just like their Persian Armenian counterparts.

Christianity in Armenia, 1970 and 2015

	1970		2015		Average annual growth rate (%), 1970–2015
Tradition	Population	%	Population	%	
Christians	859,000	34.1%	2,849,000	94.4%	2.7%
Independents	2,300	0.1%	65,000	2.2%	7.7%
Orthodox	854,000	33.9%	2,534,000	84.0%	2.4%
Protestants	350	0.0%	39,700	1.3%	11.1%
Catholics	0	0.0%	235,000	7.8%	25.1%
Evangelicals	45	0.0%	30,300	1.0%	15.6%
Pentecostals	2,100	0.1%	117,000	3.9%	9.3%
Total population	**2,518,000**	**100.0%**	**3,018,000**	**100.0%**	**0.4%**

Source: Todd M. Johnson and Gina A. Zurlo (eds), *World Christian Database* (Leiden/Boston: Brill), accessed March 2017.

Tsar Nicolas I (ruled 1825–55) had given lavish promises to the Armenians and filled them with hope for political autonomy once liberated from Persian and Ottoman rule. However, all such promises proved to be empty. Soon after the establishment of Russian rule, the tsar attempted to bring the Armenian Church under its control as well. Following negotiations of several years – and in line with its policy on non-Russian religious and ecclesiastical institutions within the empire – in 1836 a church constitution (the *Polozhenie*) came into effect after being ratified by the tsar. The Catholicos of All Armenians accepted the document with reluctance, inasmuch as it curtailed the power of the head of the church, both internally vis-à-vis the bishops and the clergy and externally vis-à-vis the state. This constitution brought the eastern dioceses of the church and the Catholicosate of All Armenians in Ejmiatsin under the tight control of the tsarist government and left the laity virtually out of the administration of the church.

In the western part of the Armenian world, in the Ottoman Empire, more or less the opposite happened. Overwhelming power was given to the laity. A national constitution was established in 1863 for the Armenian *millet* (nation). From as early as 1461 the patriarch was the Sultan's designated head of the Armenian nation in the empire; the absence of clearly defined regulations or a constitution had given titled Armenian dignitaries, the *amiras*, and the wealthy barons of Constantinople great influence over the patriarch and, by extension, the Armenian population. A constitutional commission was set up in 1855 by an imperial edict. A number of drafts were debated over some eight years between conservative- and liberal-minded members of various committees. A final version of the constitution was approved 'by all classes of the Armenian population of Constantinople' and ratified by the sultan on 20 September 1863. As historian Robert Hewsen put it, 'the Armenian millet within the Ottoman Empire thereby entered the modern world' ('Introduction' to *The Armenian National Constitution (1863)*, Cambridge, MA: Society for Armenian Studies, 1987, 2). The constitution drastically reduced the traditional ecclesiastical authority of the Patriarch of Constantinople as well as of the clergy in general. It established the rule of popular general election of all candidates for sacred office in the church. It created organs for the government of the church that were almost completely dominated by laymen, irrespective of the degree of their commitment to the Christian faith. The National Assembly of Deputies, composed mainly of laymen and presided over by the patriarch, was recognised by the state as being the highest representative body and governing authority throughout the Ottoman Empire for the administration of the 'Armenian nation'. The constitution became defunct in the early years of the Turkish Republic.

From the 1890s until 1923, the Armenians were subjected to state-orchestrated and state-executed mass killings, and during the First World War virtual annihilation, in the Ottoman Empire. As a result, an estimated 1.5 million Armenians perished between 1915 and 1923. Today, the large Armenian diaspora, estimated at some 5 million, is made up largely of the descendants of the survivors. More than any other event in history, the Armenian genocide has had a major traumatic effect not only on Armenian identity, but also on Armenia and the Armenian Church.

Under Soviet Rule

Armenian Christianity, as with all other religions in the Union of Soviet Socialist Republics (USSR), suffered enormously under Soviet rule, anti-religious propaganda and state-sponsored atheistic indoctrination. Like its counterparts, the Armenian Church was persecuted, especially in the 1920s and 1930s. A vast number of churches were destroyed, priests were exiled or executed, and assets and treasures of Ejmiatsin were confiscated. The Soviet state, especially in the early decades of the communist regime, spent large amounts of resources and energy in seeking to expunge Christianity from society. By 1940 only nine functioning Armenian churches remained in the entire Soviet Union. It was thanks to the importance of the Catholicosate of All Armenians in Ejmiatsin to the large Armenian diaspora that the centuries-old institution was saved from complete oblivion.

Persecution and pressure eased after the death of Joseph Stalin in 1953, and the election of the Romanian-born Catholicos Vazgen I (Baljian) in 1955 ushered in a new period in the life of the church. Under his leadership, the church gradually came out of its isolation. As the church had a long-established network of dioceses and churches around the world, Vazgen created bridges between Soviet Armenia and the diaspora through Ejmiatsin and strengthened relations with wealthy communities and institutions outside the USSR. This increased the church's prestige in the eyes of the communists, who were ever mindful of projecting a good image abroad, and asserted the catholicos's national position. Moreover, numerous donations from the diaspora enabled Vazgen I to renovate many historic churches and monasteries and to engage in cultural-educational activities inside Soviet Armenia, including the construction of a modern museum and the establishment of a new printing press in Ejmiatsin.

Mikhael Gorbachev's *glasnost* ('openness') and *perestroika* ('restructuring') in the late 1980s was the beginning of a new era for the church under communism and brought changes of attitude in government and society. Matters of church and religion, in general, were openly and publicly discussed. The restoration of the 'national character' of Armenia and Armenian institutions was part of this process, which included, for example, renaming cities, towns, villages and streets. Reclaiming Armenian Christian identity, through baptism, became a common feature of the changes. The return to religion and spirituality, enhanced by *perestroika*, coincided with several major national events and developments that have had a far-reaching impact on Armenia and Armenians: (1) the Karabakh Movement – demanding the reunification of Nagorno-Karabakh (an autonomous region within Azerbaijan) with Armenia – which started in February 1988 and later turned into an independence movement; (2) the devastating earthquake in northern Armenia in December of the same year; (3) the pogroms of Armenians in Azerbaijani towns; (4) the war with Azerbaijan in and for Nagorno-Karabakh; and (5) the subsequent economic and energy blockade of Armenia by Azerbaijan and Turkey, which created harsh conditions for the population, especially in the winters of 1992 and 1993.

The beginning of the Karabakh Movement in early 1988 was a major test of Gorbachev's new policy of openness and a major turning point in Soviet Armenia. The dispute between Armenians and Azerbaijanis over Karabakh – an enclave of only 4,388 km^2 and a population of about 150,000 – is the oldest unresolved conflict in the former Soviet Union, having started in the 1920s. A popular movement for self-determination by Karabakh Armenians turned into a full-scale war between Armenians and Azerbaijanis in 1991. A formal but fragile ceasefire has been in place since May 1994, but dozens of people continue to be killed every year on the line of contact, and the war has not ended.

The role of the Armenian Church, personified in Catholicos Vazgen I (1955–94), in the early stages of the Karabakh Movement was ambiguous. On the one hand, Ejmiatsin was reluctant to publicly oppose the Kremlin's policies; on the other, as an Armenian national institution, the church could not be indifferent to the popular struggle. Catholicos Vazgen argued that Armenia's survival was possible only 'within the great and mighty family of Soviet nationalities' and that popular demands for Karabakh's union with Armenia would not lead to any tangible results. Based on his decades-long experience with Soviet authorities, he feared – as expressed in his appearance on Armenian television – that an anti-Soviet movement would lead to 'offer[ing] Armenia on a platter to our centuries-old enemy'.

The Soviet Armenian government and the Armenian communist leadership in 1989 officially recognised the Armenian National Movement (ANM), which had overwhelming popular support. This was the beginning of the erosion of Soviet power in Armenia. In November of that year, ANM delegates visited Ejmiatsin to meet with the catholicos. Despite Vazgen's earlier cautious stance, the leaders of the Movement still considered him an important national figure and a supporter of pan-Armenian causes, especially in view of the fact that he had influence in the diaspora through the church's dioceses and parishes abroad. In his welcoming address, Vazgen assured the delegates that 'All Armenians, whether believers or not, we consider them true children of the Armenian Church without discrimination'. He explained the role and position of the church throughout the centuries and positioned the church in the centre of national life.

The catholicos, shortly after the overwhelming 'yes' vote for independence, presided over the swearing in of the first democratically elected president of the newly independent Republic of Armenia and gave his blessings. In terms of his standing in Armenia and the diaspora, while the entire communist leadership was discredited, the catholicos was the only national figure who still enjoyed respect and public standing. Less than three weeks before his death in 1994, Vazgen I was the first national figure to be awarded the newly created highest honour of the Armenian state, the Order of National Hero.

Independence of Armenia

The fall of communism and independence of Armenia in 1991 marked the beginning of many unprecedented events in the life of the Armenian nation, in both the Republic of Armenia and the diaspora. Independence has not only radically changed the way the Armenian diaspora — where more Armenians live than in Armenia itself — perceives and understands itself, but has created a 'new' discourse of mobilisation and 'unity', to face the colossal new challenges facing the 'nation'. As a result of post-independence developments, institutional life, both in Armenia and the diaspora, has changed and continues to unfold. While the Armenian Apostolic Church has flourished internally — with the building of new churches, seminaries, charitable institutions and so on — the church has virtually had no functional role in the transitional processes in Armenia and the diaspora concerning how the country and state have been shaped over the last 25 years.

Rampant corruption, social and economic inequalities, a lack of basic legal protection and other state-induced difficulties in post-Soviet Armenia continue to plague society. The 'moral guidance' and 'spiritual anchor' that society expected from the church was not provided. Although the church is respected as a historically significant national institution, its establishment and the clergy remain on the periphery of the country's spiritual life. Decades of state-sponsored atheism in Soviet Armenia and the processes of secularisation and globalisation have had their impact on society.

Since independence, other denominations and religious movements have challenged the primary position of the church and introduced 'competition' in the religious sphere. In addition to Christian denominations, alternative religious movements have appeared in Armenia, including Jehovah's Witnesses, Mormons, the International Society for Krishna Consciousness, Transcendental Meditation and pagans. Nevertheless, the Armenian Church remains the largest national religious institution, with around 500 parishes and churches in over 30 countries around the world and about 700 bishops and priests serving an estimated 8 million Armenians living in Armenia, Karabakh and the diaspora.

A significant event in Armenian Christianity in the twenty-first century was the canonisation of the victims of the genocide in the Ottoman Empire. In November 2014, the Synod of Bishops, headed by the two catholicoi of the Armenian Church, announced that over 1 million 'martyrs' of the atrocities committed during the First World War would be sainted collectively. Previously, the last person who was declared a saint in Armenia was in the fifteenth century. On 23 April 2015, during a solemn ceremony in Holy Ejmiatsin on the centenary of the genocide, the newest saints of the Armenian Church were announced and venerated in the presence of international dignitaries, high-level government officials and thousands of people. This major event provided a symbolic meaning for Armenian society: through sainthood the victims were no longer victims, but victors in the Christian faith, saints who 'live in the glory of God'.

Religion is one of the subjects mandated by the curriculum of state schools in Armenia. To the dismay of non-Apostolic churches, the law grants special privileges to the Apostolic Church, including the right to train teachers of religion for state schools throughout the country. The 1997 Law on Freedom of Conscience and Religious Organisations states that 'within the boundaries of the procedure provided by the Law', the Armenian Church is 'to promote the spiritual education of the Armenian people, including in the educational institutions where the teaching of religion is permitted solely on the basis of the belief professed by the Armenian Apostolic Church and by teachers who have adequate qualification and authorisation from the Armenian Apostolic Church' (Article 17, 2.5). Hundreds of teachers have been trained by the Apostolic Church to teach the 'Armenian brand' of religion in state schools.

The Armenian Brand of Christianity

The overwhelming majority of Armenia's population of 3 million adheres, at least nominally, to the Christian faith. The Armenian Church or the 'National Church', belongs to the Orthodox family of churches, known as the Oriental Orthodox or 'Non-Chalcedonian' Churches. It shares many commonalities with the Byzantine and Slavic Orthodox and Roman Catholic Churches, especially in the liturgy, but differs over certain theological issues.

The Armenian Church has been actively involved in the ecumenical movement since the 1930s and especially through the World Council of Churches since the 1960s. It also has bilateral commissions and dialogues with the Roman Catholic Church, the Byzantine Orthodox Churches, especially the Russian and Greek Churches, the Anglican Church and others. It maintains close working relations with the Oriental Orthodox family of churches with which it is in communion – the Coptic, Syrian Orthodox, Ethiopian and Indian Malabar Churches.

The Catholicosate of All Armenians, also known as the 'Mother See of Holy Ejmiatsin', is the supreme ecclesiastical centre of the church. It is recognised as 'pre-eminent' among the four hierarchical sees of the church, the other three being: the Catholicosate of Cilicia, located in Antelias, Lebanon, founded in 1930, but with roots going back to the thirteenth century; the Patriarchate of Jerusalem, from the early fourteenth century, which is one of the three custodians of Christian holy places in the Holy Land; and the Patriarchate of Constantinople in Istanbul, established in 1461 by the Ottoman Sultan and once the administrator of the entire Armenian 'nation' (*millet*) in the Ottoman Empire.

One of the unique features of the Armenian Church is the involvement of lay people in its administrative, legislative and financial affairs, unlike in the Roman Catholic Church and the Orthodox Churches of the Byzantine tradition. However, decisions concerning faith, dogma and liturgy remain the exclusive domain of the College of Bishops and the catholicos.

Armenian Catholic and Evangelical Churches

There are an estimated 150,000 Armenians around the world who are members of the Armenian Catholic Church and almost 100,000 Armenian Protestants. Both denominations have small communities in Armenia.

Catholicism in Armenia can be traced back to the twelfth century, when Armenians came into contact with the Church of Rome through their ties with the Crusaders in Cilicia. Later in the fourteenth century, through the missionary activities of the Franciscan and Dominican orders, a 'Latinising movement' gained ground among liberal elements in the Apostolic Church. However, it was only in the nineteenth century that the Armenian Catholic Church was formally organised as a separate church. In 1831, the Catholics were legally recognised as a separate *millet* — an autonomous church affiliated with Roman Catholicism — in the Ottoman Empire, with their own hierarchy and catholicos (patriarch). 'Armenian rite' communities are found in Iran, Iraq, Lebanon, Turkey, Jerusalem and the USA.

The roots of Armenian Protestants go back to the nineteenth-century missionary activities of the American Board of Commissioners for Foreign Missions, which expanded an aggressive mission throughout Asia Minor.

After 'painful clashes' with the Armenian Apostolic Church, the Protestants were formally recognised in 1846 by the Ottoman government as a separate community. Subsequently, as a result of their continued affiliation with American missionary organisations, Armenian Evangelicals established many schools and colleges during the second half of the nineteenth century, which benefited thousands of Armenians living in the Ottoman Empire. In 1996, the late Catholicos Karekin I of All Armenians, during a ceremony in Yerevan on the one hundred and fiftieth anniversary of the Armenian Evangelical Church, praised the Evangelicals for their valuable ministry.

Christianity in Karabakh

Soon after Armenia's conversion to Christianity in the fourth century, the Kingdom of Albania in the Caucasus (not to be confused with Albania in the Balkans), which included the provinces of Artsakh (the future Karabakh) and Utik, converted to Christianity through the efforts of St Gregory the Illuminator. Grigoris, the grandson of Gregory, was appointed the head of the Albanian Church around 330. He was martyred in 338 while evangelising in the north-east region of the country, near Derbend (currently Daghestan). His body was brought to Artsakh and buried in a church in Amaras (in the Martuni region). The Albanian Church, having been established by the Armenian missionaries, pledged canonical allegiance to the Armenian Church. An Albanian Catholicosate or holy see was established in 552, when the seat of the head of the church moved from Derbend to Partav. The patriarch of the Albanian Church was given the title 'Catholicos of Aghuank' (Artsakh and Utik) and received his ordination and canonical authority from the Catholicos of Armenia. From the eleventh to the thirteenth century, more than 40 monasteries and religious centres were built in Karabakh through the patronage and efforts of the Armenian princes of Artsakh. Starting in the fifteenth century, the monastery of Gandzasar became the seat of the native catholicos. The existence of a separate catholicosate in Karabakh, with its own autonomous religious institutions, attests to the importance of the region as a religious centre.

In the nineteenth century, the status of the native catholicosate was drastically reduced. When tsarist Russia liberated Karabakh from Persian domination, Catholicos Sarkis of Karabakh, upon his return from exile, was demoted to the rank of metropolitan by the imperial authorities in 1815. After his death in 1828, upon the request of the meliks (princes) of Karabakh, Catholicos Yeprem of All Armenians, in 1830, ordained Baghdassar, a nephew of Sarkis, Primate of the Diocese of Karabakh. He was ordained in the Cathedral of Ejmiatsin in Armenia. Thus, the Catholicosate of Karabakh was reduced first to a metropolitan seat and then to a diocese of the Armenian Church.

Between 1820 and 1930, Karabakh was a hub of vibrant religious and cultural life. The diocese of Karabakh and Swiss missionaries – sent by the Basel Evangelical Association – operated 10 schools in the city of Shushi alone and founded the first printing press in the region in 1828. Church and privately owned printing houses published over 150 titles on biblical, theological, philosophical, scientific and literary subjects, as well as a dozen newspapers and journals. A remnant of this religious-cultural renaissance is the famous Cathedral of Our Saviour (built 1868–87) and an order of women monastics and deaconesses, a rare phenomenon in the Armenian Church, who were involved with social and pastoral work under the aegis of the Karabakh diocese.

The church in the early Soviet period

In 1918, the Bolshevik Revolution gained force in the Transcaucasus. The Russian army disintegrated, and the Ottoman Turkish army marched over the region, threatening the population of the region. Faced with the possibility of a complete Turkish take-over, the representatives of the Georgians, Azeris, and Armenians formed a Transcaucasian Federation, as a preventive measure. But within a few months, by May 1918, the Federation had failed; Georgia, Azerbaijan and Armenia proclaimed independence and became new republics. However, as national administrative boundaries were not clear, the newly established states became embroiled in a series of territorial conflicts. The most protracted and complex of these conflicts concerned mountainous Karabakh.

Having been left to face their own uncertain future, Karabakh Armenians elected a People's Government in August 1918. In February 1919, they dispatched Bishop Vahan of Shushi and Hrant Bagaturian, a member of the Executive Council, to Tiflis to present the case of Karabakh Armenians – the issue of their security and freedom – directly to the representative of Britain, General William Thomson, the military commander in the region during the short-lived period of British control of the region. However, not only were their concerns not addressed, within six months Karabkhis were forced to sign an agreement with Azerbaijan putting Karabakh under the jurisdiction of the latter provisionally until the final outcome of the Paris Peace Conference. This signalled the beginning of the end for the Armenian Church in Karabakh.

In 1923, when under Soviet rule, Mountainous Karabakh became an autonomous *oblast*, the Armenian Church was the first national institution to face the growing Soviet pressure. In 1925, since the city of Shushi was out of bounds for the clergy – the Armenian neighbourhoods had been burnt down and the diocesan headquarters closed – the new prelate sent from Ejmiatsin chose the monastery of Gandzasar as his diocesan centre.

His activities were closely monitored by the Commissar for Internal Affairs of Mountainous Karabakh. In 1929, in a letter to the catholicos in Ejmiatsin, Bishop Vertanes wrote: 'Every day dozens of churches and monasteries are being closed, clergymen are being imprisoned and exiled.... Please help us in this dire situation ... all we are left with is 112 functioning churches, 18 monasteries, and 276 priests'. Soon after, Vertanes was arrested and jailed. He was released in January 1932, as the Soviet court 'did not find [him] guilty of any crime' but was never allowed return to Karabakh. Thus ended the activities and formal existence of the Armenian Church in Karabakh.

The return of the church to Karabakh

In March 1988, in response to the popular uprising and demonstrations in Yerevan and Stepanakert during the previous month, the Central Committee of the Communist Party of the Soviet Union issued a decree on social-economic developments in Karabakh. This created a climate for cultural and religious revival in the region. Prior to the formal reopening of the church, a renewed interest in Christianity and the church was created by visits of preachers from Armenia belonging to the church-loving Brotherhood of the Armenian Church (*Yeghpayragtsutiun*), who, starting in 1987, attracted a group of people who later 'converted' and became 'committed Christians'.

This coincided with the beginning of the 'national liberation movement', when, secretly, protest signatures were being collected in Karabakh. In early 1988, these new converts started to collect signatures secretly for a petition to have churches reopened in Karabakh. The petition was presented to the authorities and a copy was given to the catholicos in Ejmiatsin. This campaign of the 'believers in Karabakh' provided Catholicos Vazken I with additional leverage with the authorities to re-establish the long-defunct diocese. In November 1988, he appointed Barkev Martirossian as Prelate of Karabakh. The newly appointed prelate, together with four priests, came to Karabakh to establish the diocese. The first church was formally reopened on 1 October 1989 at the Monastery of Gandzasar, after six months of preparatory work and reconstruction. On that day, the bishop declared in his sermon: 'Today is the beginning of our victories'. The first task of the church leadership in Karabakh was to renovate churches and provide places of worship.

Between 1989 and 1991, the clergy were involved in active evangelisation throughout Karabakh. Sunday schools were established, and teachers were trained to instruct the children and prepare them for baptism. Weekly lectures on Christianity were presented by the bishop at schools where several hundred students would gather to hear the lectures. A significant project of the diocese of Karabakh was the establishment in Yerevan in

1990 of the Gandzasar Theological Centre, which produced literature and religious publications for both Karabakh and Armenia.

Within a few years of its re-establishment, the Armenian Church had regained its legitimacy not only as a religious institution but also as a national institution to fight alongside the people of Karabakh. Freedom of religion, ushered in by the collapse of the Soviet Union, coincided with the struggle for liberation. The evangelistic efforts of the church were eclipsed by the national aspirations of the people and mass mobilisation for Karabakh's independence. The church was one of the first national institutions to be 'reclaimed' by the people, even those who were unbelievers, as a historically significant source of their religious and national identity. In the early days of the Karabakh Movement until the declaration of independence in 1991, the church played a surrogate role as the advocate of the people and their rights, similar to the role of the churches in Poland and East Germany. In the absence of recognised political leadership, the church became the unofficial representative of the people of Karabakh to the outside world.

The church in Karabakh has assumed responsibility for setting a certain moral and ethical context to the war, on the one hand, and the nation-building process, on the other, by establishing a balance between the national aspirations of the Armenians and their religious values. However, since the declaration of independence, which is not recognised by any country, the role of the church has changed. A priest surmised that between 1989 and 1991, 'the church was much more significant, was much more valuable than perhaps it is today'. Nevertheless, it is still considered by many to be an important moral and spiritual source, as both a national and a religious institution.

Bibliography

Hewsen, Robert H., *Armenia: A Historical Atlas* (Chicago, IL: University of Chicago Press, 2001).

Maksoudian, Krikor, *Frequently Asked Questions about the Armenian Church* (Burbank, CA: Western Diocesan Press, 2010).

Nersoyan, Tiran, *Armenian Church Historical Studies: Matters of Doctrine and Administration* (New York: St Vartan Press, 1996).

Ormanian, Malachia, *The Church of Armenia* (New York: St Vartan Press, 1988).

Papazian, Michael B., *Light from Light: An Introduction to the History and Theology of the Armenian Church* (New York: SIS Publications, 2006).

This essay draws on the author's earlier work: 'The Armenian Apostolic Church', in Lucian Leustean (ed.), *Eastern Christianity and Politics in the Twenty-First Century* (Oxford: Routledge, 2014), 471–97; and 'Religious Discourse and the Church in Mountainous Karabakh', *Revue du monde arménien moderne et contemporain* (Paris) 3 (1997), 67–83.

Georgia and Azerbaijan

Silvia Serrano

Two distinctive features characterise the South Caucasus: it is the cradle of the oldest Christian kingdoms and it is a region with a high level of diversity, including religious diversity. Whereas, up to the current period, Eastern Christianity has played a crucial role in the history of Georgian kingdoms, Islam has gradually expanded in the territory of contemporary Azerbaijan – Shia Islam became the official confession in the sixteenth century. After the break-up of the Soviet Union, religious pluralism was regarded as a challenge to nation- and state-building. The dominant religious groups, Eastern Orthodoxy in Georgia and Shia Islam in Azerbaijan, have strengthened, but religious minorities – including Christian, Muslim and Jewish – still live in both countries. According to the 2014 census, almost 90% of the population of Georgia was Christian, at least nominally, whereas in 2009 Christians were less than 4% of Azerbaijan citizens, mainly among ethnic minorities; 98% of ethnic Azeris identified as Muslims.

The Soviet legacy of official atheism still has an influence on patterns of religiosity and on the public role of religions. The religious landscape also highly depends on the nature of the political regime. Whereas democratisation has been the officially proclaimed goal of successive governments in Georgia, Azerbaijan has remained an authoritarian regime, with strict state control over religious activities.

Historical Background

The Caucasus is an area of early penetration of Christianity. According to legend, in the fourth century St Nino came from Cappadocia and converted Kartli (Greek Iberia, in eastern Georgia). According to tradition, Christianity became the state religion of Kartli in 337. In Egrisi (Greek Colchis, in western Georgia), a Christian Church existed from the first half of the fourth century. The current Georgian Church adopted 483 as the official date when it became autocephalous. In the early seventh century, the split between the Armenian and Georgian Churches over Christological conceptions crystallised religious identities. In the eleventh century, when Kartli and Apkhazeti unified under the Bagratid kings, the authority of the catholicos expanded to all the territory where the language of liturgy was Georgian. After the break-up of the Georgian Kingdom into several independent polities, the catholicos, although deprived of effective power, ensured the permanence of the institution. Despite the weakening of religious life under Persian, Arabic and Turkish domination, and despite feudal fragmentation, the church remained the unifying force of the nation.

Paradoxically, the common faith of the Russians and Georgians exposed the latter to stronger pressures for assimilation than non-Orthodox, peoples: for the tsars, there could not be two Orthodox Churches in the empire. After the incorporation of the Georgian polities into the Russian Empire in 1811, autocephaly was abolished and the Church of Georgia was reorganised as an exarchate under the authority of the Russian Holy Synod. In the nineteenth century, restoration of autocephaly became the claim of the nascent nationalist movement. On 12 March 1917, a church assembly announced the abolition of the exarchate and the restoration of autocephaly, more than a year before the declaration of independence.

Pre-modern culture was intrinsically linked with the early penetration of Christianity. The Georgian word for Georgia, 'Sakartvelo', appeared

Christianity in Georgia, 1970 and 2015

	1970		2015		Average annual growth rate (%), 1970–2015
Tradition	Population	%	Population	%	
Christians	1,650,000	35.1%	3,453,000	86.3%	1.7%
Independents	100	0.0%	86,900	2.2%	16.2%
Orthodox	1,608,000	34.2%	3,323,000	83.1%	1.6%
Protestants	10,000	0.2%	13,000	0.3%	0.6%
Catholics	3,000	0.1%	40,000	1.0%	5.9%
Evangelicals	4,800	0.1%	27,600	0.7%	4.0%
Pentecostals	50	0.0%	54,500	1.4%	16.8%
Total population	**4,707,000**	**100.0%**	**4,000,000**	**100.0%**	**−0.4%**

Source: Todd M. Johnson and Gina A. Zurlo (eds), *World Christian Database* (Leiden/Boston: Brill), accessed March 2017.

Christianity in Azerbaijan, 1970 and 2015

	1970		2015		Average annual growth rate (%), 1970–2015
Tradition	Population	%	Population	%	
Christians	263,000	5.1%	311,000	3.2%	0.4%
Anglicans	0	0.0%	1,900	0.0%	12.4%
Independents	0	0.0%	7,800	0.1%	15.9%
Orthodox	250,000	4.8%	288,000	3.0%	0.3%
Protestants	1,100	0.0%	12,100	0.1%	5.6%
Catholics	12,000	0.2%	560	0.0%	−6.6%
Evangelicals	310	0.0%	4,500	0.1%	6.1%
Pentecostals	0	0.0%	12,100	0.1%	17.1%
Total population	**5,178,000**	**100.0%**	**9,754,000**	**100.0%**	**1.4%**

Source: Todd M. Johnson and Gina A. Zurlo (eds), *World Christian Database* (Leiden/Boston: Brill), accessed March 2017.

in the tenth century to refer to all the Transcaucasian regions that used Kartvelian in the liturgy. The Georgian translation of sacred texts also strengthened Georgian as the dominant language. A secular hagiographic literature began in the fifth century with the *Martyrdom of St Shushanik* (the wife of the governor of a southern province converted by opportunism to Mazdaism, who refused to recant her faith) and continued in the seventh century with the *Martyrdom of Abo Tbileli* (a young Arab converted to the Christian faith). A rich culture developed in monasteries, such as those of the Tao Klarjeti region, in the monastery of Iviron on Mount Athos and in the Academies of Gelati (Imereti) and Iqalto (Kakheti).

The Armenian Apostolic Church has been present in the territory of Georgia and Azerbaijan since the fourth century. The Armenian Diocese in Georgia is one of the oldest and most important dioceses of the Armenian Apostolic Church. The third-oldest church, the Apostolic Church of Caucasian Albania, was founded in 488, on the territory of contemporary Azerbaijan. Originally autocephalous, it soon fell under the jurisdiction of the Armenian Church.

Catholicism also has a long history in the region. In the twelfth and thirteenth centuries, Franciscan and Dominican friars settled in Georgia. Capuchin monks lived in Tiflis (Tbilisi) from 1661 until their expulsion by the Russians in 1845. Many Bagrationi princes and kings, and even patriarchs, got close to Catholicism. The uncle and adviser to Vakhtang VI and author of the first Georgian lexicon, Sulkhan-Saba Orbeliani (1658–1725), converted to Catholicism.

From the end of the eighteenth century, other Christian groups came from Russia. Cossacks and Molokans settled in the territory of southern Azerbaijan, and Dukhobors in southern Georgia. After the Caucasus became part of the Russian Empire, Russians and other Slavs lived in major cities and in rural areas in the governorates of Baku and Elisabethpol. The first Protestant presence also goes back to the nineteenth century, with the establishment of German colonies in several regions of Georgia and Azerbaijan, including in Tiflis, and the building of Lutheran churches. In 1867 the Central Baptist Church was founded in Tiflis.

After the establishment of Soviet rule, all religious communities in Georgia and Azerbaijan were victims of anti-religious policies. Before the Second World War, most churches were closed and the clergy persecuted. For example, only one Armenian church remained active in Georgia. All Baptist churches were closed down and all the male followers were sent to Siberia. Some groups were particularly affected by Stalin's persecutions, on either religious or ethnic grounds: most Lutherans – ethnically Germans – were deported to Siberia and Central Asia, as were non-Christian groups such as Muslims from the Samtskhe-Javakheti region.

In an attempt to involve churches in war mobilisation, Stalin's religious policy shifted in 1943. The major religious groups were then awarded limited rights. A crucial consequence for the Georgian Orthodox Church (GOC) was the recognition of its autocephaly by the Russian Orthodox Church in October 1943. Although other anti-religious campaigns started under Khrushchev, some room for a more active religious life finally opened. In the late Soviet period, and more evidently after the election of a new Catholicos-Patriarch Ilia II (Shiolashvili) in December 1977, the GOC could start recovering. Churches opened to worship, religious publications were authorised and there was a revival of monastic life. In 1983 Ilya II participated in the ceremonies marking the bicentenary of the Treaty of Georgievsk, alongside the head of the Russian Orthodox Church, Pimen, and Armenian Catholicos Vazgen, and he obtained permission to celebrate the fifteen hundredth anniversary of the GOC. In the Soviet period, the church managed to survive as an institution by being perceived as part of the national culture.

Patterns of Growth and Contraction

After the collapse of the Soviet Union, it seemed that major obstacles to religious practice had been lifted, since the constitutions of the newly independent states officially guarantee freedom of religion. Religions started playing a growing public role. In the new political context, the dominant religion (Eastern Orthodoxy in Georgia, Islam in Azerbaijan) became instrumental in consolidating the nation state and legitimising its power. At the same time, the newly independent nations opened to the global religious marketplace.

In Azerbaijan, the political and economic situation led to a dramatic decrease of the two main Christian groups, the Orthodox and the Armenians. Soon after the first demonstrations by Armenians calling for a change in the status of the autonomous district of Nagorno-Karabakh, in February 1988, violence against the Armenian population started. It reached a peak in December 1989–January 1990; as a result, almost the entire Armenian population was forced to leave Azerbaijan, and the Armenian Apostolic Church is now present only in Nagorno-Karabakh, a region not controlled by Baku. Religious heritage has been damaged or destroyed in the Autonomous Republic of Nakhchivan.

The decrease of the Slavic population started in the 1970s and accelerated after 1989 (from 6.2% of the population in 1989 to 1.6% in 2009). The Slavs were not targeted by the assaults against Armenians, but fear of chaos, preference for ethnic Azeri in public service, the lack of knowledge of the language and better opportunities in Russia, among other motives, led them to leave. In addition, higher fertility rates among Azeri women led to the relative decline of the Slavs in the population. At the organisational level, Azerbaijani parishes remain under the jurisdiction of the Russian Orthodox Church. The Orthodox Church has six registered cathedral churches and one chapel in the country.

Protestant and Charismatic–Pentecostal denominations, which came to Azerbaijan during the 1990s, are another important Christian group. They seem less active than during the first decade of independence, possibly because of restrictions imposed by state agencies.

Baku has attempted to exercise strict control over religious activity. Religious organisations are required to register as 'associations' through the State Committee on Work with Religious Associations (SCWRA) and some have faced difficulties functioning. The SCWRA reviews and approves all religious literature for legal importation, sale and distribution. In 2013, out of almost 600 registered groups, 12 were Christian.

The religious 'revival' in Georgia was intrinsically linked with the consolidation of the Georgian Orthodox Church. The GOC has been one of the few national institutions to survive the Soviet era. Its autocephaly was recognised by the Ecumenical Patriarchate of Constantinople in 1990. In independent Georgia, the identification of the nation state with the GOC has led to its institutional reinforcement. The constitution adopted in 1995 asserts the principles of separation of the church and the state and of religious freedom, but it also recognises the special importance of the autocephalous GOC in Georgian history. The relations between the state and the church were further regulated by a 'constitutional agreement' signed by both parties on 14 October 2002. This has provided the church with an official preferential status and with numerous material and symbolic privileges, such as tax exemptions and a say on school programmes.

State funding, though not guaranteed by law, is not prohibited. The GOC has benefited from state support for education and from growing transfers from central and local governments. According to official sources, budget transfers to the church increased from GEL1.29 million (€0.5 million) in 2005 to GEL25 million (€10 million) in 2014. The funds are allocated for religious education, social programmes and media. Additionally, clerics were offered personal gifts. One central issue was the restitution of buildings and goods confiscated during the Soviet regime. The commission in charge of identifying the real estate to be restituted has never been set up, and the transfer of numerous plots and buildings to the GOC has lacked transparency.

The state has also contributed to the symbolic consolidation of the church by intrinsically linking religious and national imagination. The reference to Orthodoxy is present in the symbols and rituals invented by political leaders and instrumental in building a secular state. The presidents of independent Georgia take an oath on the Bible and receive the blessing of the patriarch. One of the first measures adopted by the pro-independence government was to declare official holidays to mark the main Orthodox feasts such as Christmas, Epiphany, Good Friday, Easter Monday, St Andrew, Dormition, Svetitskhovloba (the Life-giving Pillar) and St George. The president and officials, as well as most leaders of the opposition, attend the liturgy at Christmas and Easter and other important Orthodox ceremonies. The first decree signed by President Mikheil Saakashvili, in 2004, was to replace the previous burgundy, black and white flag of the First Republic by a new flag with explicit Christian connotations – five crosses. The arms of the state adopted at the same time feature St George, the patron of Georgia, crowned and surrounded by two lions, and a motto proclaiming that 'unity is strength'.

As a result of these developments, ethnic Georgians tend to identify with Orthodoxy, regardless of their individual religiosity. In addition, the GOC has conducted a very active proselytisation policy, mainly directed towards the ethnic Georgians who converted to Islam during Ottoman rule. Collective baptisms were held in Adjara – a region incorporated into the Ottoman Empire in the sixteenth century – as early as the 1980s.

The dynamics of Christianity have also been affected by demographic trends, although to a lesser extent than in Azerbaijan. Emigration rates have been particularly high among ethnic minorities, including Christian groups such as Armenians, Slavs and Greeks. The result has been a stronger identification between (Georgian) ethnicity and (Orthodox) confession, a changing demographic pattern that is not reflected in official statistical data, since all Orthodox parishes on the territory of Georgia are officially affiliated to the GOC. The above-mentioned factors interact with other factors (rural emigration, dynamic of mixed marriages, etc.) to bring about a decrease of Catholicism in the regions where it was historically present for centuries, such as Samtskhe-Javakheti, where the numbers of *p'rangebi* (Franks), as local Georgian Catholics are called, and of Armenian Catholics are decreasing.

In the first two decades of independence, religious issues were not the priority of the government. No state body was responsible for regulating confessional diversity. Soviet-inherited institutions such as the Council for Religious Affairs were dismantled at the very beginning of the 1990s, and the State Agency for Religious Affairs was created under the prime minister only in March 2014. Apart from the GOC, no religious organisation had a clear legal status; hence such bodies faced hurdles in things like renting premises and importing literature. They could not benefit from state funding or from restitutions. The authorities were late in recognising the problems induced by the rising influence of the GOC in comparison with other bodies. It took another decade after the 'constitutional agreement' was signed to adopt a more balanced legislative framework and to set up tools for its implementation.

The main improvement came with the adoption of an amendment to the Civil Code on 5 July 2011. A religious organisation can now register as an entity in public law or as a private law non-profit organisation, or choose not to register at all. Although representatives of most religious minorities are not fully satisfied with the new rules, the Roman Catholic apostolic administration of the Caucasus and the Diocese of the Armenian Apostolic Church were registered as legal entities in public law. The Jehovah's Witnesses, present in Georgia since the 1950s, registered as a non-profit organisation. Others, such as the Baptists, refused to register for several years. Under a government decree of January 2014, four additional groups (the Armenian Apostolic Ecumenical Church, Muslims, Jews and Catholics) have been entitled to receive state funding as partial compensation for damages during the Soviet regime. New groups will probably be added to the list soon.

Still, property restitution remains a sensitive issue, and a bone of contention between the GOC and other Christian churches. For many years, the Armenian Apostolic Church, the Catholic Church and the Evangelical-Lutheran Church – as well as the Muslim and Jewish communities – have been trying to reclaim property confiscated by the state. The GOC has taken control of some of these churches and claims ownership. As a consequence of these unresolved disputes, some buildings are falling into disrepair. In addition, religious minorities face hurdles in building new churches. Non-governmental organisations (NGOs) have documented numerous cases in which Catholics, Jehovah's Witnesses or Muslims faced pressure from the GOC and obstruction from state authorities when constructing new buildings.

The Evangelical Baptist Church of Georgia (EBCG) is probably the largest Protestant denomination in Georgia (with around 5,000 members) and one of the most influential. The structure is a mixture of congregational and episcopal polity. It is active in the global ecumenical movement and a member of the Conference of European Churches. It emerged in 1991 as a Georgian-speaking branch of the Soviet-era All-Union Council of Evangelical Christian-Baptists, created in 1944. Its development is largely due to the commitment and charisma of Archbishop Malkhaz Songulashvili. He sees the role of the Georgian Baptists as bridging the gap between Georgian Orthodoxy and the European Reformation. Under his leadership, the EBCG has engaged in an unusual method of contextualising the gospel, incorporating Orthodox heritage. It has founded a school for icon painting and uses incense in services. It has a monastic order and holds processions and pilgrimages.

The largest Christian group in territories of Azerbaijan controlled by Baku is the Russian Orthodox Church. The overwhelming majority of its 117,000 members are Russians, of Russian origin, or from mixed Azerbaijani–Slavic families. The Orthodox believers are older than the average population, and have a higher proportion of women. With approximately 4,000 believers, the Apostolic Church of Caucasian Albania is the oldest recognised church in Azerbaijan.

Since independence, many Pentecostal and Evangelical churches have been founded. There is no comprehensive academic study on the denominations newly established in Georgia and Azerbaijan, and quantitative data are unreliable. It appears, though, that the new denominations are more likely to emerge in former industrial centres such as Rustavi. Another assumption is the over-representation of ethnic and Russian-speaking minorities among these groups. In Azerbaijan, they attract mainly former Orthodox or individuals from mixed families. However, even in remote rural regions of Georgia such as Svanetia, the local population remembers that in the 1990s missionary groups came to proselytise.

Such communities have been considered by the government and the population alike to be foreign or non-traditional, and as such they have been particularly vulnerable to discrimination. In Georgia, for example, two Pentecostal Churches, the Assemblies of God and the Word of Life Church, were raided by militant Orthodox groups on several occasions. In Azerbaijan, Jehovah's Witnesses, Baptists and Seventh-day Adventists, among others, were denied registration.

Inter-church Relations

One of the main challenges to balanced and peaceful relations between religious groups in Georgia is the growth of anti-Western and anti-ecumenical feelings inside the GOC. From 1978 to 1983, during the late Soviet period, Catholicos-Patriarch Ilya II was a committed proponent of ecumenism and one of the chairmen of the World Council of Churches (WCC). This position contributed to improving the visibility and the prestige of the GOC on the international stage and was instrumental in promoting a positive image of the USSR among Christians abroad. But criticism of this stance and the lack of consensus among clerics became public after the collapse of the Soviet Union. The activism of anti-ecumenical movements led to strong internal tensions in the 1990s. In April and May 1997, a group of monks from Shioghvim, Betani, David Garedji and Shemokmedi monasteries wrote an open letter to Ilya II describing the ecumenical movement as 'heresy'. They sent an ultimatum asking the Holy Synod and the Catholicos-Patriarch to withdraw from the WCC and to end Eucharistic communion with the churches participating in it. Under the threat of a schism, on 20 May 1997 the Holy Synod decided to withdraw from the European Conference of Churches and from the WCC. Since then, the influence of anti-ecumenism inside the GOC has being growing. The GOC does not recognise the reality of the sacraments celebrated by other Christian churches. A non-Orthodox Christian marrying an Orthodox is required to 'convert', and an Orthodox marrying a non-Orthodox Christian is considered an apostate. Opposition to ecumenism was central to the decision of the GOC to boycott the Holy and Great Council convened in Crete in June 2016.

Dogmatic conceptions and positions on ecumenism have fuelled GOC hostility towards other Christian denominations. In November 1999, strongly hostile reactions to Pope John Paul II during his visit to Georgia revealed the influence of the GOC in shaping negative public attitudes towards other Christian churches and the rise of anti-Catholic feelings within Georgian society. In September 2003, Mgr Tauran, then the Holy See's Secretary for Relations with States, came to Georgia to sign an interstate agreement providing the Catholic Church with a legal status. At the last moment, under pressure from the GOC, Georgian authorities refused to sign the agreement. No further official visit of the Holy See's Foreign Minister could take place until September 2014. The visit of Pope Francis in September 2016 is an indication of the changing balance of power between the patriarchate and the secular authorities.

However, the most negative public attitudes towards non-Orthodox Christians have been against Protestants and 'non-traditional' Christian denominations. They have faced major obstacles to the practice of their faith as well as discrimination in their everyday lives: insults in the public space, obstacles to employment, discrimination in schools and even some cases of forced conversion of children. Up to the 'Rose Revolution' of 2003, Baptists, Pentecostals and Jehovah's Witnesses were the victims of physical aggression from Orthodox radicals – laymen and clergymen – who raided their sanctuaries during services, burnt religious literature and even attacked the flock. According to a United Nations report, there were 150 attacks against Jehovah's Witnesses between 1999 and 2003.

Several radical groups, including Jvari' (Cross) or the Society of John Chrysostom, were responsible for these abuses. One of the most active groups was led by Father Basil Mkalavishvili, a priest who was defrocked in 1995 after criticising the GOC for being too conciliatory towards religious minorities. He created the Eparchy of Gldani – a suburb of Tbilisi – under the jurisdiction of a Greek schismatic church and openly called for a war against non-traditional denominations, which, according to him, had a corrosive impact on Georgia. These groups benefited from the passivity and even the help of the police, from the indifference of larger segments of Georgian society and from implicit support from the patriarchate. Protection from the authorities ended after the Rose Revolution of November 2003. Mkalavishvili was arrested in 2004 and sentenced to six years of detention. The larger and more violent raids ceased, and open aggression towards Protestant and non-traditional communities decreased in Georgia.

Nevertheless, one of the most salient developments in the last decade in Georgian society has been the rising influence of new fundamentalist Orthodox groups who directly challenge the pro-Western orientation of the government and the state-promoted narrative about Georgian identity. On the contrary, they have promoted their vision of the nation based on partly invented traditions and 'Orthodox values'. They share with their counterparts in Russia a common sense of belonging to the 'Orthodox civilisation', as opposed to the decadent West, and the Russian Orthodox Church obviously influences their discourses and agenda. Despite unresolved disputes over parishes in Abkhazia and South Ossetia, links with the Moscow patriarchate remain strong.

In Azerbaijan, the Orthodox Eparchy of Baku also actively watches Protestant and Pentecostal groups, and the main mission is to support historical communities and to counter the influence of non-traditional denominations among them.

Inter-faith Relations

The official display of good relations between the three monotheisms and of state-supported interfaith dialogue can be interpreted as a Soviet legacy. Both Allahshukur Pashazade, the Sheikh ul-Islam and chairman of the Supreme Religious Board of Caucasian Muslims, in Baku, and the Georgian Patriarch Ilya II were already in charge in the late Soviet period. They frequently meet and praise tolerance towards other faiths. At the domestic level, however, the attempt by the GOC to keep its monopoly on religious visibility led to conflicts over issues such as construction of mosques and erection of minarets. In the 1990s and 2000s, the violations of the rights of Muslims remained under-documented. This situation changed with the emergence of active Muslim NGOs such as the Association of Muslims of Georgia, which have attracted the attention of domestic and international watchdog organisations. The defeat of the Saakashvili-backed alliance at the 2012 parliamentary elections was interpreted by radicals as an authorisation of violence against religious minorities. Several clashes occurred and attacks against Muslim communities were carried out before the new government reacted. Other Christian denominations have maintained better relations with Muslim communities. For example, the EBCG carried out charitable activities for Chechen refugees.

In Azerbaijan, there have been tensions over the fate of the historically Georgian Orthodox parishes in the district of Kakh; the flock has complained that their worship is obstructed and the last open church, in Kurmukhi, has been closed down.

Social and Political Influence

Despite obvious trends towards de-secularisation and growing religiosity, the social influence of religion in Georgia and Azerbaijan remains limited in comparison with most countries. Religions – at least dominant religions – have become impressively present in the public sphere. In Georgia, more churches have been built in the last two decades than in previous centuries, most of them financed by well-off businessmen. Participating in public religious events such as processions and attending religious services for the main feasts have become the social norm. High visibility of the dominant religion is an indication that the role it plays in the South Caucasian societies has drastically changed; it is not evidence of growing religiosity. Hence the social and political influence of religions is disconnected from faith. In both countries, the subjective importance of religion is much higher than religious practice. In a 2012 survey, 80% of respondents in Azerbaijan and 92% in Georgia claimed that religion was 'rather' or 'very' important in their daily lives. The figures in 2007 were, respectively, 52% and 72%. But only 16% of the people in Georgia in 2012 said they attended religious services once a week or more. Azerbaijan has an even lower rate of religious attendance, at 5%. Already relatively low, even at the European level, religious practice has being declining. According to a study conducted in 2007, these figures were then 9% in Azerbaijan and 21% in Georgia. Almost twice as many people in 2012 said they attended religious services only on special holidays as in 2010, and frequency of fasting in Azerbaijan has declined from 62% in 2009 to 50% in 2012.

In Georgia, opinion polls show that the catholicos-patriarch is the most popular and trusted figure. However, his recommendations on morals or family matters have limited impact. For example, despite his endorsement of family values and calls for increasing the number of births, Georgia has low fertility rates and some of the highest divorce and abortion rates in the world. The global tendency to invent religion 'made to measure' to fit ambivalent expectations, and of choosing what makes sense while rejecting other aspects, is exacerbated in the case of the Caucasus.

Contemporary Orthodoxy is more about belonging than believing. However, religion is not limited to public demonstrations of patriotism. There are different ways of living one's faith. Some tendencies can be pointed out: a revitalisation of the parishes, the importance of the individual relation between the follower and his or her spiritual father, a revival of monasticism. Various forms of popular religiosity and renewed practices have emerged in the last two decades, such as painting and veneration of icons, participation in processions and pilgrimages or the veneration of Georgian saints. One major event in Georgian Orthodoxy was the canonisation of Monk Gabriel as a Fool for Christ, in 2012. Some Orthodox followers claim a practice more internalised and disconnected from political contingencies. The level and patterns of religiosity are different among minority groups, particularly the non-traditional. They are more focused on spirituality and less motivated by a desire to comply with social norms, and in some cases adherence probably stems from individual choice.

Another limitation to the social influence of religions is that social work remains underdeveloped, for different reasons, such as lack of experience and resources, and a focus on issues related to national identity in the GOC and the Armenian Apostolic Church. Another explanation is that, notwithstanding the collapse of the Soviet-inherited welfare state in the 1990s, and despite the growing role of private actors in this field, people expect that the state, not religious organisations, will provide for the common good in the spheres of education, public health and social protection.

Still, the Orthodox Churches in Georgia and Azerbaijan, as well as the Armenian Diocese in Georgia, are involved in a number of social activities. In many churches, parishioners are engaged in charitable activities such as collecting food or essential goods for the destitute or for internally displaced persons and providing medical support for isolated pensioners, the ill and marginalised households. The GOC is active in the field of education and in the prison system. There are also orphanages in several eparchies. Several social programmes and institutions also work under the Apostolic Administration of the Roman Catholic Church in the Caucasus. The Baptists have created a shelter for the elderly. Social work throughout the country is conducted by the sisters of the Order of St Nino. Newly established Protestant churches have probably been the most active, benefiting from experience and from financial resources from abroad. The social work of all religious groups has been growing.

Religion and Politics

In the context of low attendance, the influence of religions derives from their integration in the political field rather than from their pastoral mission. Indeed, religious issues and confessional belonging have been extremely politicised in the Caucasus. In Georgia, religious attitudes interplay with political attitudes, and disputes over religious issues express political polarisation. Stances on religion often reflect the dividing lines between political factions. Domestic perceptions of confessions are linked with geopolitical change and with official political orientation: those who welcome

Roman Catholicism and Protestant denominations as well as those who fear their influence link their activities with growing Western influence.

Churches are engaged in public debate on various questions, such as relations with neighbouring countries, democratisation, the legitimacy of mass protests, social justice and family policy. The fiercest disagreement has been related to topics that have recently emerged on the agenda, such as gender issues or the rights of sexual minorities. Among major Christian churches, the Evangelical Baptist Church of Georgia is the most committed to promoting gender equality. It recognises the ordination of women; there are women bishops, presbyters and deacons. In 2014, the first Georgian female bishop, Rusudan Gotsiridze, won the US Secretary of State's annual International Women of Courage Award, for advocating gender equality and the protection of minorities, including the LGBT community.

A key event was the assault, led by Orthodox clerics, on a pro-gay-rights rally in Tbilisi on 17 May 2013. The catholicos-patriarch not only refused to condemn the violence against peaceful demonstrators but also called for 17 May to be turned into a 'Family Day', when the strength of the traditional family would be celebrated. Dissension on gender issues and sexual minorities among Georgian Christians reflects polarisation at the global level and is evidence of foreign influence. The GOC holds a similar position to the Russian Orthodox Church, and also that of some American Protestant denominations. It is no coincidence that in 2016, at the initiative of one of the politicians closest to the patriarchate, the annual summit of the World Congress of Families (WCF) was held in Tbilisi.

At the official level, the perception of different religions by the authorities depends on foreign policy. In Azerbaijan, Islam has been securitised, and state policy depends on whether the Muslim community is or is not perceived as a foreign threat. Since 15 October 1996, by governmental decree, foreigners were banned from engaging in religious propaganda. Islamic organisations, not Christian denominations, were the main target, but the latter were also affected. More recently, the maintenance of Christian communities and the lack of persecution of Christians and Jews have become instrumental in creating a positive image of the state in the international arena, in an attempt to silence criticism of human rights violations and the crackdown on opposition. In recent years, and more particularly after the start of the war in Syria and the rise of ISIS, the authorities have been very active in describing Azerbaijan as a tolerant Muslim country, committed to secularity and multi-faith peaceful coexistence. The presence of the Orthodox has become an element of inter-state relations with Russia.

In Georgia, too, religions are instrumental in foreign policy. Whereas a part of the population and the hierarchy of the church have rejected Catholicism as opposed to national values and tradition, liberal politicians have viewed it as a tool for strengthening links with Europe. Secular authorities have done their best to improve bilateral relations with the Holy See, despite the opposition of the patriarchate. In May 2010 President Saakashvili visited the Vatican and met with Pope Benedict XVI. In April 2015 President Margvelashvili met Pope Francis. Despite the relatively small number of their adherents, Protestant Churches influence Georgian politics thanks to their international networks. Sixty foreign guests from 14 countries, including the general secretary of the Baptist World Alliance, attended the wedding of Malkhaz Songulashvili, the Archbishop of the Evangelical Baptist Church of Georgia. The EBCG has also had intensive contacts with international watchdog organisations committed to documenting the violations of religious rights. After the August 2008 war and the severance of diplomatic relations with Russia, Ilya II played a crucial role in maintaining contacts with Moscow, meeting Vladimir Putin on several occasions.

After decades of official atheism and of obstacles to religious practice, religious life has seen a resurgence. One of the main trends has been the diversification of the religious supply, with the arrival of new proselytising groups and the penetration of foreign influences. At the same time, in Georgia – and to lesser extent in Azerbaijan – religion has played a crucial role in nation-building and in the legitimisation of the independent state. In both countries, the representatives of the majority religion have relied on political power to strengthen their institutions and to adapt to the new competitive context. But despite the increased visibility of religions, in both countries practice remains low and religious norms have little influence on lifestyles and on individual and collective behaviour. Whereas Soviet Georgians and Azeris were cut off from religious tradition, the new generation grew up in societies open to religion. What the consequences of religious socialisation will be remains unknown.

Bibliography

Agadjanian, Alexander, Jödicke Ansgar and Evert van der Zweerde (eds), *Religion, Nation and Democracy in the South Caucasus* (London: Routledge, 2015).

Crego, Paul,'The Georgian Orthodox Church', in Lucian N. Leustean (ed.), *Eastern Christianity and Politics in the Twenty-First Century* (London Routledge, 2014), 140–60.

Merlo, Simona, *Russia e Georgia: Ortodossi, dinamiche imperiali e identità nazionale (1801–1991)* (Milan: Guerini e associati, 2010).

Pelkmans, Mathijs, *Defending the Border: Identity, Religion, and Modernity in the Republic of Georgia* (Ithaca, NY: Cornell University Press, 2006).

Peters, C. J., 'The Georgian Orthodox Church', in Pedro Ramet (ed.), *Eastern Christianity and Politics in the Twentieth Century, Christianity Under Pressure* (Durham, NC: Duke University Press, 1988), vol. 1, 286–308.

Major Christian Traditions

Anglicans

Yazid Said

The Medieval Latin phrase *Ecclesia Anglicana* (the English church) reminds us that the title 'Anglican' initially referred to the English nation. The development of various churches across the world which were in communion with the See of Canterbury gave birth to what became known in the second half of the nineteenth century as the Anglican Communion. By the time of the first Lambeth Conference, in 1867, the Anglican presence in the Middle East had already been well established. When it began in the early nineteenth century, the mission was focused mainly on Palestine, Egypt and Iran. While Egypt and Palestine were at first under the same diocesan structuring, the development of Anglican communities in Iran and the Arabian Gulf had separate political and ecclesiastical arrangements. What is now known as the Diocese of Cyprus and the Gulf had its origins in an Act of Parliament of 1877, which also established the Diocese of Lahore, covering parts of India as well as the Arabian Gulf.

One cannot deny that these ecclesiastical developments in the Middle East were part of the history of British imperial interests, a history meticulously documented by a Palestinian civil servant in Mandate Palestine, A. L. Tibawi, under the title *British Interests in the Middle East, 1800–1901* (Oxford University Press, 1961). The balance between mission and imperialism is hard to assess in these contexts, and the chronicles of the history include sharp indictments by locals like Omar Farrukh, who published *Al-Tabshir wa-l-isti'mar* (*Evangelism and Imperialism in Arab Lands;* Beirut: al-Maktabah al-'Asriyyah, 1973). These local commentators were partly right. Indeed, one could see the face of Empire in what became known as All Saints' Cathedral in Cairo and St George's Cathedral in Jerusalem, serving the Mandatory powers of the times. The establishment of a bishopric in Jerusalem was a joint British–Prussian Protestant endeavour that came with the backing of the respective monarchs. The connection to the politics of the time is quite obvious.

However, this was not the full story. The hard work of mission that was behind the later development of Anglican identity in the Middle East is credited mainly to the work of the Church Missionary (now Mission) Society (CMS). They took the lion's share of the work of the Church Ministry among the Jews in Jerusalem (CMJ). CMS, unlike CMJ, engaged in its mission with the wider Christian and Muslim society in the region. With an emphasis on ministry among the Jewish people, CMJ helped establish the first Anglican church in the Middle East, Christ Church inside Jaffa Gate in the Old City of Jerusalem. It was dedicated in 1845 and was designed to look like a Victorian Jewish synagogue. It became the cathedral of the first three bishops. Indeed, the first bishop in Jerusalem, Michael Solomon Alexander, was a converted Jew. In 1881, the Anglo-Prussian union collapsed and the bishopric became solely Anglican under the fourth bishop, George Blyth, who founded St George's Cathedral, dedicated in 1898.

To suggest that these missionary societies were simply concerned with Empire would be a mistake. They were, rather, part of the profound impression made in the Church of England by the pietism of the Evangelical Revival. This movement, which was growing in strength by the end of the eighteenth century, sought to recover the experiential content of the doctrine of justification by faith, by a more overt dependence upon Scripture, together with the preaching of conversion and an emphasis on sanctification. This tradition was one of the major strands in the missionary movement through which the Anglican Communion eventually came into being. One needs to acknowledge, therefore, a religious and theological concern of the missions, which were not simply political. Consequently, and with the support of the second bishop in Jerusalem, Samuel Gobat (who also had oversight of Egypt), CMS established a lasting legacy of missionary institutions – schools, hospitals, pilgrim guest houses, and centres for disabled people and the elderly – some of which continue to exist today, serving societies across the region.

It is clear from some of the writings of the missionaries that they had no intention of creating a local indigenous Anglican Church but, rather, hoped to revive the ancient Eastern Churches with renewed evangelical zeal. Yet, while missionaries had a sincere sense of being sent as disciples of Christ, they had to learn not simply to bring Christ but to discover Christ, so to speak, in the complex religious and political context in which they served. Indeed, whether in Iran, Palestine or Egypt, missionaries learnt a great deal from their friendships with Muslim women and men, often breaking

Anglicans in North Africa and West Asia, 1970

Region	Total population	Christian population	Anglican population	% of region Anglican	% of Christians Anglican
Northern Africa	82,883,000	5,220,000	92,900	0.0%	1.8%
Western Asia	86,037,000	6,330,000	22,700	0.0%	0.4%
North Africa and West Asia	168,920,000	11,550,000	116,000	0.1%	1.0%
Globe	3,682,488,000	1,229,247,000	47,404,000	1.3%	3.9%

Source: Todd M. Johnson and Gina A. Zurlo (eds), *World Christian Database* (Leiden/Boston: Brill), accessed March 2017.

the generalised stereotypes of Islam. In Egypt and North Africa, the most notable women missionaries of the time were Lilias Trotter (1853–1928) and Constance Padwick (1896–1968).

Eventually, the work of these missionaries and institutions resulted in the emergence of a number of local congregations and the formation of native church leadership, such as the Palestinian Church Council in 1905. At the time of the Suez Canal crisis in 1956, the British clergy and bishop had to leave the region. With some pressure from the local leadership, support grew for a native episcopacy. The first Arab bishop, the Rt Revd Najib Qub'in, who was the chairman of the Palestinian Church Council at the time, was consecrated in 1958, with oversight of Jordan, Syria and Lebanon. At this stage, the English bishop in Jerusalem was elevated to the rank of archbishop and was under the direct jurisdiction of the Archbishop of Canterbury.

Archbishop George Appleton, former Archbishop of Perth and the last English-speaking Archbishop in Jerusalem, formed a commission to consider restructuring the Archbishopric in Jerusalem to give the local native churches their own leadership. After an interim period from 1970 to 1976, the current structure was established. Under the new structure, the Anglican Church in the Middle East today forms one province of the Anglican Communion, the Province of the Episcopal Church in Jerusalem and the Middle East, which includes the four dioceses of Jerusalem, Egypt, Iran, and Cyprus and the Gulf. The metropolitical authority was handed from the Archbishop of Canterbury in 1976 to the provincial central synod, which currently has two archbishops: the Primate of the Province (currently the Bishop of Egypt, Munir Anis), elected by rotation, and the Archbishop in Jerusalem (currently Bishop Suheil Dawani).

Apart from the Diocese of Iran, the other three dioceses cover the various countries of the Middle East, stretching from Algeria in the west to Somalia in the south and Iraq in the east. Historically, Syria and Lebanon were not impacted by Anglican missionary activity. But, with the refugee crisis of Palestine in 1948, a number of Palestinian Anglicans went to Beirut and established the first Anglican congregation there. In Damascus, until

Anglicans in North Africa and West Asia, 2015

Region	Total population	Christian population	Anglican population	% of region Anglican	% of Christians Anglican
Northern Africa	223,892,000	9,864,000	534,000	0.2%	5.4%
Western Asia	257,231,000	15,049,000	104,000	0.0%	0.7%
North Africa and West Asia	481,123,000	24,913,000	638,000	0.1%	2.6%
Globe	7,349,472,000	2,414,772,000	90,728,000	1.2%	3.8%

Source: Todd M. Johnson and Gina A. Zurlo (eds), *World Christian Database* (Leiden/Boston: Brill), accessed March 2017.

the eruption of the current civil war, the Anglican presence was limited to chaplaincy work among diplomats and other expatriates.

Across this region today are found an estimated 50,000 baptised Anglican communicants and around 200 congregations. These four dioceses define themselves as Anglican today for two reasons, both concerned with the exercise of authority as established in the Church of England. First, the Church of England never acquired any confessional text comparable to those of the Lutheran and Reformed Churches or to the decrees of the Council of Trent. It did, however, produce a group of documents – the Thirty-Nine Articles of Religion (1571), the Book of Common Prayer (1562) and the Ordering of Bishops, Priests and Deacons (1550) – that contain important teaching and are still referred to collectively as the 'inheritance of faith' in the manuals of the Province of Jerusalem and the Middle East as much as they are in the Church of England. Secondly, the Church of England did not develop an authoritative, contemporary teaching body, comparable to the pope and College of Bishops in the Catholic Church. It did assert that the church has authority in controversies of faith (Article XXI), provided that its decisions do not contradict Scripture, and its bishops are instructed to be vigilant in correction of error.

This exercise of authority suggests that the Anglican Church tends to be both broad in scope and diverse in method, a matter that allowed the Church in the Middle East to cope with the challenges it has faced in the region across its history. The mission had to face the complexities of both colourful and varied ecclesiastical traditions and a constantly and rapidly changing political context. To begin with, admitting a new Protestant bishopric in Jerusalem in 1841 required a *firman*, or authority, from the Ottoman caliph; in other words, it required diplomatic measures and political persuasion. The Anglican Church also had to learn how to engage the ancient Christian churches from the start. The Archbishop in Jerusalem is given the title 'in' Jerusalem and not 'of' Jerusalem, on the assumption that he does not take the place or compete with the Archbishop *of* Jerusalem, the Greek Orthodox patriarch who is the successor to St James, the first bishop of Jerusalem. This assured the Orthodox Church of Anglican support for its historic patrimony on behalf of all Christians. Similarly, the

Changes in Anglicans in North Africa and West Asia, 1970–2015, growth rate, % per year

Region	Total population	Christian population	Anglican population
Northern Africa	2.2%	1.4%	4.0%
Western Asia	2.5%	1.9%	3.4%
North Africa and West Asia	2.4%	1.7%	3.9%
Globe	1.5%	1.5%	1.5%

Source: Todd M. Johnson and Gina A. Zurlo (eds), *World Christian Database* (Leiden/Boston: Brill), accessed March 2017.

Archbishop of Canterbury signed an agreement with the Coptic patriarch of Alexandria in which he committed the Anglican Church to serve the Orthodox Churches. Indeed, the newly established Anglican presence started a theological college for the Coptic Orthodox Church in the patriarchate in Cairo that produced one of the future popes of Alexandria, known as Kyrilos the Reformer.

The title Archbishop in Jerusalem was only recently re-established to affirm the Anglican bishop in Jerusalem as representative of the Anglican Communion in Jerusalem and successor to the Church of England archbishops in Jerusalem. The title also emphasises the significance of Jerusalem in the history of the faith, Jerusalem being the only city that does not have a mother church, so to speak, as it is the city of Jesus's resurrection, where he first established the community of witnesses to his resurrection and poured upon them the promise of the Father, the Holy Spirit.

As with other Christian traditions, there exist among Anglicans both church theologies and theologians' theologies. The former are contained in teaching documents, statements, catechisms and liturgies issued or authorised by bishops and synods. The latter comprise a vast range of theological scholarship and spiritual writing. Generalisations are necessarily uncertain and controversial, but certain features can be observed among Anglican Middle Eastern missionaries and native thinkers, with differences across the two centuries of their existence.

First, the inevitable engagement with other faiths and the production of some of the most important works and guides to interfaith dialogue and mission were notable features of the nineteenth century and continue to be of vital importance today among Middle Eastern Anglicans. Notable scholars among the early missionaries were Temple Gairdner (1873–1928), a prolific Arabist and a scholar of the medieval Muslim luminary Abu Hamid al-Ghazali (d. 1111). Gairdner's pupil, Constance Padwick, was heavily engaged with Egyptian Sufi communities and deepened her own Christian devotion by engaging in the study of Muslim prayers. She called for the establishment of contemplative religious orders in the Muslim world. This work continued with the prolific output of the Assistant Bishop in Jerusalem and major scholar of Islam, Kenneth Cragg (1913–2012). Bishop Cragg combined a grateful acknowledgement of Islam's witness to God and a celebration of all that Christians and Muslims have in common with a persistent and sensitive Christian critique of Islam. The present author is a native Palestinian child of the Diocese of Jerusalem whose scholarship on Ghazali and Islam has been heavily informed by these luminaries of Middle Eastern Anglicanism.

Secondly, a number of the schools and hospitals that were established in the nineteenth century continue to function under the auspices of the four dioceses today, many being of vital importance to the region. They continue to be the focus of pride in the writings and statements of current church leadership in the region. However, the vocation to Christian mission of these institutions has undergone radical change with the recession of Empire and the emergence of nation states in the Middle East. Most of these schools and hospitals have been absorbed into state medicine and state education systems, not least to maintain state financial support. Their sense of mission has had to change accordingly.

There are two notable exceptions to this rule. The first is the Anglican hospital in Gaza City, which is totally dependent on donations and support from friends of the Diocese of Jerusalem. It continues to offer free services to needy individuals and families in one of the world's most deprived communities.

The second exception is St George's College in Jerusalem, a centre in Jerusalem for interfaith and Christian scholarship serving the worldwide Christian community. An Anglican Communion foundation supports the College's work. St George's College provides vital services not only to the worldwide Christian church but also to the local pastoral scene; it is limited by the current political map from reaching out to the whole Middle East. The pastoral and sacramental ministries across the region today are restricted to non-proselytism or circumscribed in their relevance to local culture and faith patterns. This means that ministry tends to be limited to well established Anglican families in the region. Reaching out to non-Anglican Christians and non-Christians generally is often viewed with suspicion and in some places is met with political opposition. Therefore, parochial life tends to focus on maintaining the small flock, not just through Sunday worship, but also through various parish activities during the week that aim to give parishioners a sense of belonging and purpose, while the clergy do their best to maintain good ecumenical and interfaith relations in their respective communities. In this context, St George's College has become one of the main resources for continued education of the clergy and their own pastoral needs.

Thirdly, with the establishment of local leadership in the province, and in face of political turmoil, especially after 1948, the Anglican Church became a force to reckon with nationally. However, this came with both positive and negative effects. It was positive to the extent that it raised important theological questions relating to the pastoral needs of the Palestinian Christian communities in the light of the establishment of the State of Israel. The Palestinian Christian political climate was one of increasing awareness of the need to relate to the biblical narrative of Israel afresh. This was in the light of Western support for controversial policies of Israeli governments that often justified their claims on biblical grounds.

It was important to relate to this particular pastoral concern of the local Christians, especially regarding how to remain faithful to the biblical tradition. The successive Palestinian Anglican Bishops in Jerusalem have all been in the forefront of political debates. It was, however, Canon Naim Ateek who led the movement that became known as Palestinian Liberation Theology, which created and maintained a distinctive local theological voice for the confused and hurt Palestinian communities in the region. As with other Liberation Theology movements, Palestinian Liberation Theology proposed a Christian presence that is politically engaged and culturally decentralised.

On the other hand, negative developments arose from the political context of the region. First, the constant political struggles meant that the small Christian communities in the region as a whole and Anglicans in particular were dwindling in number, with many opting to find more sustainable lives elsewhere in the world. The consequence of this is that the smaller the communities become, the more likely it is that churches generally are defined solely by what the hierarchs say and do; and even when that is well said and done, it increasingly lacks a credible connection to what the mission of the Body of Christ is meant to be. While this has been the current trend across the different churches, the onus of the work in church institutions is often thrown on to Christians present in lay capacities. Two distinctive laywomen in the region who stand out are Suhayla Tarazi, herself a Greek Orthodox Christian, who has led the Anglican hospital in Gaza with distinction and profound devotion; and Betty Majaj, the Anglican former director of the Princess Basma Centre for disabled children in Jerusalem. Both have offered tireless service to their communities under the umbrella of the Anglican Church. The church is also defined by the example of such outstanding lay leaders.

In addition, the nationalisation, so to speak, of the leadership in the region has also frozen the concept of church leadership in a defensive post-colonial stance as the definitive structure of the church, thus allowing non-theological power struggles rooted in nationalism and ethnocentrism to flourish, with damaging effect. Local theologies have not been engaging such questions. In many ways, the Anglican mission in the Middle East is still learning how to live with local contexts, which is not a bad sign in itself. But this also means that its mission is fraught with difficulties. The church in the Middle East needs to think afresh about the meaning of leadership in relation to the church's practice and mission so that it becomes good news for all the peoples of the region, beyond ethnocentric definitions: a challenge to both the official establishment and the Liberation Theologians.

Bibliography

Badr, Habib (ed.), *Christianity: A History in the Middle East* (Beirut: Middle East Council of Churches, 2005).

Jacob, W. M., *The Making of the Anglican Church Worldwide* (London: SPCK, 1997).

Markham, Ian, Barney J. Hawkins, Justyn Terry and Leslie Steffensen Nunez (eds), *The Wiley-Blackwell Companion to the Anglican Communion* (Oxford: Wiley-Blackwell, 2013).

Sachs, William L., *The Transformation of Anglicanism: From State Church to Global Communion* (Cambridge: Cambridge University Press, 1993).

Ward, Kevin and Brian Stanley (eds), *The Church Mission Society and World Christianity, 1799–1999* (Grand Rapids, MI: Eerdmans; Curzon, 2000).

Independents

Duane Alexander Miller

The plight of the ancient Christian communities in the Middle East is well known. What is less well known is that there is also a young community of Christians that is experiencing rapid growth, from Algeria to Iran and from Saudi Arabia to Syria. These are believers in Christ from a Muslim background.

For the purposes of this chapter, the term 'Independent Christian' is used as shorthand for these believers from a Muslim background (BMBs). The majority of these BMBs self-identify as Christians when there is sufficient freedom and security to do so. In terms of doctrine and practice, most of these BMBs would be broadly considered Evangelical, with a small minority belonging to the Latin, Eastern or Oriental churches. This focus on BMBs is not to deny the existence of other kinds of Independent Christians. As with any part of the world, there are always organic, people-led formations that emerge independent of any church, and these sometimes take the form of movements or informal Christian groups.

It is estimated that there are hundreds of thousands of BMBs throughout the region, with the greatest concentrations being in Algeria (380,000) and Iran (100,000). Estimating these numbers is notoriously difficult. Various religious and social groups have motives either to exaggerate or to minimise the number of BMBs in their countries.

Legal Challenges

While theologically there is much overlap, treating BMBs separately from Evangelical Christians in the region is appropriate for a number of reasons. One is that BMBs are limited in terms of their leadership roles in local churches. Most of the countries in this region will not legally permit or recognise conversion from Islam to Christianity. Therefore, while BMBs may teach or preach in a local church, they can never function as legal representatives of that church in terms of business transactions or issuing official documents like baptismal certificates. In other words, the 'independence' is legally enforced.

There are exceptions, but the default position throughout the region is that conversion out of Islam is not possible. A Muslim can legally convert to Christianity in Israel and Turkey. Lebanon has blasphemy laws but no apostasy law, which leaves it somewhat indeterminate. In some other countries, like Jordan and Egypt, converts have tried to have their religious conversion acknowledged by the courts, but without success. The consensus of the Islamic Sharia is that conversion out of Islam, or apostasy, is a capital crime. One authentic *hadith* of the Prophet Muhammad reads, 'Whosoever changes his religion, slay him' (Al Bukhari 52: 260).

While most states will not legally recognise religious conversion out of Islam, it is also true that public execution of an apostate by the state is rare. Field research and autobiographical conversion narratives outline a few broad tendencies regarding the fate of BMBs. Some converts remain quiet about their new faith and are marginally involved in a church, likely a home church. Other converts are outspoken about their new faith, which generally leads to persecution and sometimes incarceration. Converts who do not renounce their new faith and who do not die while in jail might be released and compelled to leave the country. If a convert's change of faith is made known and a non-state actor carries out the punishment prescribed by Sharia, the death of the convert typically is concealed or the police do not actively pursue the executioner.

For some BMBs this situation is intolerable. They regard it as unjust and an affront to the inherent human dignity. That Christians are free to convert to Islam while Muslims may not leave Islam is seen as hypocritical. That families, neighbours and nation states sometimes use coercion is interpreted as a sign of the weakness of Islam in winning the hearts and minds of its adherents. One can identify a strong tendency in many of the autobiographical conversion narratives of BMBs to advocate for greater respect for human rights and more social change. This advocacy is born precisely from the converts' new vision of God and humanity. The artefact of the theology-making is then an intense desire to transform unjust social structures, which can be interpreted as a type of liberation theology.

Motives for Conversion

Given the very real difficulties experienced by these BMBs, it is reasonable to ask about the motives for their conversion. Synthesising the findings

Independents in North Africa and West Asia, 1970

Region	Total population	Christian population	Independent population	% of region Independent	% of Christians Independent
Northern Africa	82,883,000	5,220,000	67,400	0.1%	1.3%
Western Asia	86,037,000	6,330,000	44,500	0.1%	0.7%
North Africa and West Asia	168,920,000	11,550,000	112,000	0.1%	1.0%
Globe	3,682,488,000	1,229,247,000	96,342,000	2.6%	7.8%

Source: Todd M. Johnson and Gina A. Zurlo (eds), *World Christian Database* (Leiden/Boston: Brill), accessed March 2017.

of various studies, the following is a fairly comprehensive list of reasons given regarding conversion:

1. the character of Jesus, for example in his interactions with women;
2. truth – Christianity answers questions that Islam could not, and the Bible is a source of truth;
3. finding a new community in God's family;
4. the need for forgiveness and the conviction that forgiveness need not be earned;
5. the desire for a personal relationship with God;
6. dreams, vision, miracles;
7. disappointment with Islam or disappointment with Muhammad;
8. a religion characterised by love – God is loving, Jesus is kind and loving, Christians are loving people.

Religious conversion almost always embrace several factors from this list. Conversion is usually a gradual process, even if it culminates in one moment of decision or surrender, perhaps represented by saying a prayer of dedication or receiving the sacrament of baptism.

Challenges Related to Families and Gender

Another key locus of complexity and challenge for BMBs relates to family. Not only is it illegal to convert from Islam to Christianity or any other religion, but this legal reality also has broad repercussions in family life. For instance, Sharia does not allow a Christian man to marry a Muslim woman. So even if a woman BMB has been a practising Christian for many years, she cannot marry a local Christian man. If a male BMB marries a Christian woman, then according to Sharia their children must be Muslims and will be so designated legally. This means that if they attend a public school they will likely have to take classes on Islam and they will be treated as Muslims by teachers, despite their parents trying to raise them as Christians. Juggling multiple social identities is something that adults are used to, but it can be very confusing for children.

Independents in North Africa and West Asia, 2015

Region	Total population	Christian population	Independent population	% of region Independent	% of Christians Independent
Northern Africa	223,892,000	9,864,000	195,000	0.1%	2.0%
Western Asia	257,231,000	15,049,000	483,000	0.2%	3.2%
North Africa and West Asia	481,123,000	24,913,000	678,000	0.1%	2.7%
Globe	7,349,472,000	2,414,772,000	420,149,000	5.7%	17.4%

Source: Todd M. Johnson and Gina A. Zurlo (eds), *World Christian Database* (Leiden/Boston: Brill), accessed March 2017.

Some churches have addressed this difficulty by encouraging BMBs to marry other BMBs. According to Sharia, this is simply a Muslim marrying another Muslim, but it also means that any children born to the union will be Muslims legally. As a result, the above difficulties would still be present. Furthermore, because they would be considered a Muslim couple, any legal family matters would be regulated by Sharia, including matters related to divorce or inheritance. Finally, BMBs might be given an Islamic burial in a Muslim graveyard by their extended family, even if that is contrary to their wishes. Legally recognised members of the church would have their conscience respected, receiving Christian burials with readings from the Bible and not the Qur'an, and be buried in a Christian cemetery with the faith family they chose. Again, these are examples of what BMBs must deal with as 'unofficial Christians'. They might attend a given church for much of their lives, but in an important sense they remain, albeit involuntarily, 'independent'.

While the experiences of women and men converts are not fundamentally different, it is possible to identify some tendencies. For instance, when women are asked about their motive for conversion they are more likely to identify a personal friendship with a Christian or Jesus's way of interacting with women as of particular importance. Conversely, they are less likely than male converts to identify disappointment with Islam as a key factor leading to conversion. Throughout the entire region there is also a tendency to allow greater freedom to men than to women. As such, it can be particularly difficult for a young woman who is a seeker or convert to regularly attend a Christian meeting.

The legal difficulties were summarised above, but often the main source of persecution for BMBs comes from their immediate or extended family. The most extreme form of persecution is extra-legal execution, purportedly carried out in order to uphold the Sharia and protect the honour of the family. What is more common is not to allow girls or young women to leave the home until they 'come to their senses' and return to Islam. A young man is often treated as if he were dead, with no one in the family being allowed to interact with him. As such, BMBs tend to place a great deal of emphasis on their new family – the church.

Changes in Independents in North Africa and West Asia, 1970–2015, growth rate, % per year

Region	Total population	Christian population	Independent population
Northern Africa	2.2%	1.4%	2.4%
Western Asia	2.5%	1.9%	5.4%
North Africa and West Asia	2.4%	1.7%	4.1%
Globe	1.5%	1.5%	3.3%

Source: Todd M. Johnson and Gina A. Zurlo (eds), *World Christian Database* (Leiden/Boston: Brill), accessed March 2017.

Ethnicity and Identity

The intersection between ethnicity and Christianity is complex and varied. Some ethnic groups traditionally have been strongly identified with Islam, such as Turkish or, in many places, Arab ethnicity. For BMBs in such contexts – Turkey, the Arabian Peninsula, the Maghreb – a key challenge is to identify and formulate ways to prove that they are still loyal members of their nation state and ethnic group even though they have departed from Islam as a religion. People commonly belong to multiple communities or groups, and such BMBs are trying to prove that they can still be, say, Saudis and Arabs, even while no longer subscribing to the teachings of Islam.

A further complication is discerning what exactly Islam is. If it is interpreted as an opposing religion, then it makes sense to vigorously reject it and its practices, and many BMBs do precisely that. But if Islam is interpreted as a civilisation or culture, then perhaps one can retain aspects of Islam that do not contradict the teachings of Jesus Christ and his apostolic community. While the dominant trend is to interpret Islam as a competing religion and thus to reject it, the question is still an open one for some BMBs.

In other ethnic contexts, however, becoming a Christian is a way to preserve and assert one's cultural identity. Two of the countries with the largest numbers of ex-Muslim Christians are Algeria and Iran. In each we find a large non-Arab ethnic group: Kabyle Berbers and Persians, respectively. For both groups, Christianity is not only a way of relating to God but also a way of relating to God that affirms their distinct heritages, languages and local customs in the face of Islamo-Arabic hegemony. Seen as being different to Islam, Islamo-Arabic hegemony has insisted on Arabic names and prayer in Arabic and dismissed the history of the peoples prior to the advent of Islam as *jahiliyya,* or the age of ignorance. Iranians, for instance, found much in the Bible that affirms their heritage, with entire books like Esther and Tobit taking place in their land. Kabyle Berbers of Algeria were affirmed in their ancestral language when Christians started broadcasting a radio programme in it. This was reinforced by the translation of the New Testament and then the Old Testament into their language. Worship, singing, teaching, Bible reading – all of these are carried out in the vernacular among the Kabyle and Persians. For them, Christianity in its translatability created a space to know God and be known by God in their own linguistic and cultural identity.

Before moving on, it is appropriate here to mention one other, quite small, group of believers in Christ – those from a Jewish background. These believers are commonly called Messianic Jews, though many Jews in Israel do not regard them as authentic Jews. There is a great deal of diversity among them, with some devoutly keeping Torah and questioning doctrines like the Trinity, while others in their theology and religious practices resemble American Evangelicals. Messianic Jews find themselves in a similar situation to the Christian Turks, trying to argue that they are indeed Jewish even while holding to the conviction that Jesus of Nazareth was God's promised messiah.

In sum, the interaction of a new Christian faith with existing membership in an ethnic and perhaps national community compels local Christians to engage creatively in the formulation of new identities, though the journey to a new and stable identity can go in different directions.

BMBs and the Existing Churches

In some countries BMBs will find no existing church to join or be influenced by. This would usually be the case in most of Saudi Arabia, Yemen, Libya and Tunisia. In other places there are ancient, indigenous churches like the Copts of Egypt or the Syriacs of the Levant as well as more recent Catholic and Protestant arrivals. How established churches interact with BMBs exhibits a great deal of variety. Three main tendencies can be identified.

1. *Rejection*. Many of the indigenous churches of the Middle East managed to survive by becoming introverted and quietist. This was an understandable strategy for self-preservation in the context of *dhimmitude* (the conditions of non-Muslims under Islamic rule). The clergy are aware that welcoming a BMB would be interpreted as a gross offence against Islam and Muhammad, endangering the properties and safety of local Christians. A common instinct thus is to turn away Muslim enquirers, or at best to direct them to Evangelical churches where they might be welcomed.
2. *Secret inclusion*. Sometimes a priest or pastor will secretly baptise an individual convert or convert family, providing pastoral care to them, but without visibly and publicly incorporating them into the congregation. The strategy is to respect the spiritual hunger of the seeker while also safeguarding the security of the local Christians. This makes the formation of a new convert identity difficult, however.
3. *Open inclusion*. The church baptises seekers and incorporates them into the normal life of the church. The most obvious danger is that the church or local Christians might become subject to violence at the hands of Muslims who are offended by this action. Aside from violence, though, many Christians from the Middle East are instinctively suspicious of converts. They might wonder whether the convert is insincere or acting as a spy for a local extremist group or the government, or whether perhaps a male convert wants to marry one of the Christian girls and then, once that happens, go back to Islam. This might seem like paranoia, but both

have in fact happened. What is needed is sensitive but keen pastoral care, both for the new believer and for the existing congregation.

Zakaria Boutros, a Coptic Orthodox priest, is a good example of the third avenue. He openly evangelised Muslims in Egypt but was later forced to flee. For years he has utilised new technologies like the Internet and satellite television to share the Christian message with millions of Muslims throughout the Arab world. His gracious personality and profound knowledge of Islamic history, the Qur'an and the life of the Prophet have combined into a fruitful ministry that has claimed thousands of converts over the years. He once described his approach to evangelism as 'short, sharp and shocking'.

Key Challenges for the Future

One of the critical challenges for the future of BMBs in the region, and indeed throughout the world, is the development and refinement of pastoral care for BMBs. This will need to avoid lionising converts, which often happens when these believers visit the West, while at the same time not treating converts with suspicion or holding them to a higher standard than existing church members.

A second challenge is related to raising children. As mentioned above, adults are used to acting in different ways among different people – juggling identities is something we have learned to do. But what to do with children? Two families in Egypt, all converts, sent their children to the same school. One set of parents told their child to be bold and acknowledge that while his identity card said he was Muslim, he was in fact a Christian. The other family told their son that while the family is really Christian, people at school think he is Muslim, so just go along with it.

A third challenge is related to work. Once their faith becomes known, many BMBs lose their jobs. Churches and ministries with access to foreign money are loath to hire such persons, concerned that this might lead to false conversions or create an unhealthy sense of dependence. On the other hand, leaving people to starve after they have adopted your faith is unethical. BMBs and those working with them can find ways to train new believers so they can run their own businesses, thus providing for their own needs while avoiding unhealthy dependence.

A fourth challenge is related to leadership formation. Traditional seminary education is usually unavailable or unaffordable, while informal apprenticeship can lead to gaps in knowledge or ministerial competence. Will BMBs be able to find a way to harness the Internet along with structured mentorship programmes in order to provide a new generation of educated and mature ministers?

A final challenge is related to Islam itself. As noted above, disappointment with Islam is a key factor leading to people leaving Islam for Christianity. With continued upheaval in the region and the proliferation of violence carried out in the name of Allah and his Prophet, all indications point to a continuing, regular stream of enquirers, seekers and new converts.

Bibliography

Andrew, Brother and Al Janssen, *Secret Believers: What Happens When Muslims Believe in Christ* (Grand Rapids, MI: Revell, 2008).

Bultema, James, 'Muslims Coming to Christ in Turkey', *International Journal of Frontier Missiology*, 27:1 (2010), 27–31.

Greenham, Ant, *Muslim Conversions to Christ: An Investigation of Palestinian Converts Living in the Holy Land* (Pasadena, CA: William Carey International University Press, 2011).

Kraft, Kathryn, *Searching for Heaven in the Real World: A Sociological Discussion of Conversion in the Arab World* (Oxford: Regnum, 2013).

Miller, Duane Alexander, *Living Among the Breakage: Contextual Theology-Making and Ex-Muslim Christians* (Eugene, OR: Pickwick Publications, 2016).

Eastern Orthodox

Georges Tamer

The particular part of the Orthodox world that is the subject of this essay (the following essay deals with the Oriental Orthodox world) encompasses the four patriarchates of Constantinople, Alexandria, Antioch and Jerusalem, which together with Rome constitute the oldest Churches of Christendom. After the birth of the Church on Pentecost Sunday, which was in consequence of the redemptive works of Christ – his death on the cross and his resurrection – the disciples began to proclaim the Good News (gospel), beginning from Jerusalem. The Book of Acts reports missionary deeds along the coast of Phoenicia, northwards to Antioch, a city of significance at that time, where the followers of Jesus Christ were called Christians for the first time (Acts 11: 26). Here, the first congregation was founded, consisting of not only converted Jews but also evangelised pagans. This previously non-existent situation posed to the young church the fundamental question of whether the pagans who had joined it should be subject to the Mosaic laws in order to enter into Christianity. The disciples decided this matter at the Council of Jerusalem around AD 48 (Acts 15: 1–29). With this development, the process of crystallising an autonomous Christian identity, which gradually set itself apart from Judaism, commenced. With the successful reception of gentiles in Antioch, Christianity took its first universal forms. It is from here that Paul undertook his first missionary journey. The pastoral experience he gained in this first multi-ethnic and multicultural Christian community shaped his theology decisively.

Orthodox Self-understanding

The Orthodox Churches of the East (Eastern Orthodox) understand themselves as a continuation of the first church – encompassing all Christians of true faith across all ethnic and cultural boundaries – of the Roman Empire, of which Constantinople, the capital under the Emperor Constantine, became the new Rome. According to the self-conception of the 'Eastern Romans', they, too, were Romans (Greek Ῥωμαῖοι), whose Arabic demonym, 'ar-Rūm', is also testified to by the Qur'an in the eponymous Surah 30 (Surah 30, verse 2), whereas the term 'Byzantine' is perceived as foreign and inauthentic. Unified in the Orthodox faith of the early church, these churches maintain ethnic and linguistic diversity.

The Orthodox Churches have defined and formulated their faith over the course of their long history of contentions over heresies and deviant theological teachings. Though the Ecumenical Councils have played important roles in this, so have local developments, because the local church represents the entire church in its fullness. The Orthodox creed is the Nicene–Constantinopolitan Creed, in which Orthodox Christians confess, *inter alia,* the oneness of God, the essential equality of the Son with the Father, his two natures – divine and human – his redemptive works and return, as well as the proceeding of the Holy Spirit solely from the Father, one baptism, and the resurrection of the living and the dead in the age to come. The Orthodox faith was passed on uninterrupted over generations, in writing as well as orally; it consists not only of theoretical teachings ('orthodoxy' means 'true faith') but equally right action, truthful practice corresponding to the faith (orthopraxy). In the Orthodox Churches, great value is ascribed to the passing on of traditions, because through them the authenticity of the teaching and the connection to the early church of the Apostles can be ensured. The passing on of Orthodox beliefs and practices, however, concerns an unfinished, continually living tradition that comprises upcoming generations next to those past and in its vitality takes into account modified historical circumstances. This corresponds to the church's self-conception as the living body of Christ in the world.

The spiritual heritage of the Eastern Orthodox Churches is grounded in Christ, the incarnate God, who for the redemption of humanity died on the cross and rose again. At the centre of Orthodox theology stands therefore not an abstract entity or body of writing, but a living person who unites

Overall Orthodox in North Africa and West Asia, 1970

Region	Total population	Christian population	Orthodox population	% of region Orthodox	% of Christians Orthodox
Northern Africa	82,883,000	5,220,000	4,410,000	5.0%	84.5%
Western Asia	86,037,000	6,330,000	4,411,000	5.1%	69.7%
North Africa and West Asia	168,920,000	11,550,000	8,821,000	5.2%	76.4%
Globe	3,682,488,000	1,229,247,000	142,550,000	3.9%	11.6%

Source: Todd M. Johnson and Gina A. Zurlo (eds), *World Christian Database* (Leiden/Boston: Brill), accessed March 2016.

Eastern Orthodox in North Africa and West Asia, 1970

Region	Total population	Christian population	Eastern Orthodox population	% of region Eastern Orthodox	% of Christians Eastern Orthodox
Northern Africa	82,883,000	5,220,000	39,500	0.0%	0.8%
Western Asia	86,037,000	6,330,000	2,885,000	3.4%	45.6%
North Africa and West Asia	168,920,000	11,550,000	2,924,000	1.7%	25.3%
Globe	3,682,488,000	1,229,021,000	118,275,000	3.2%	9.6%

Source: Todd M. Johnson and Gina A. Zurlo (eds), *World Christian Database* (Leiden/Boston: Brill), accessed March 2017.

the divine and human in himself, without either one limiting his freedom. The conduct of Jesus Christ is determined by love that leads to life, by overcoming death through his voluntary death. Therein lies the heart of the Christian message: through the voluntarily acting love that knows no bounds, Christ accepts the others, the sinful humans, just as they are and sacrifices himself for them, in order to change them into a new creation and give them eternal life. Such love is associated with suffering, which is marked by joy and bears its opposite in itself, inasmuch as this constitutes a transition into the overcoming of suffering. The cross – whose sole deep meaning is love – and the resurrection are two sides of the same coin. Being a Christian in the world means following Christ, above all freely mediating to people this limitless love with word and deed.

Saints and Icons

People who have endeavoured until death to live according to the above ideal of life are venerated as saints in the Orthodox Church and regarded as guides and role models for people who labour for the same goal as long as they live. Among the saints are counted the Apostles, the church fathers, the martyrs and the great ascetics. Honoured above all others is Mary, who made the incarnation of Christ possible by his receiving a human body through her. In keeping with the belief in Christ's two natures, she is held to be not only the mother of the man Jesus but also simultaneously the mother of God (*Theotokos*), whom she, in the state of virginity, conceived and to whom she gave birth. The saints are venerated in Orthodoxy because they have dedicated their lives to God, be it in asceticism, charity or the

Overall Orthodox in North Africa and West Asia, 2015

Region	Total population	Christian population	Orthodox population	% of region Orthodox	% of Christians Orthodox
Northern Africa	223,892,000	9,864,000	7,437,000	3.3%	75.4%
Western Asia	257,231,000	15,049,000	8,569,000	3.3%	56.9%
North Africa and West Asia	481,123,000	24,913,000	16,006,000	3.3%	64.3%
Globe	7,349,472,000	2,414,772,000	282,167,000	3.8%	11.7%

Source: Todd M. Johnson and Gina A. Zurlo (eds), *World Christian Database* (Leiden/Boston: Brill), accessed March 2016.

Eastern Orthodox in North Africa and West Asia, 2015

Region	Total population	Christian population	Eastern Orthodox population	% of region Eastern Orthodox	% of Christians Eastern Orthodox
Northern Africa	223,892,000	9,864,000	15,400	0.0%	0.2%
Western Asia	257,231,000	15,030,000	4,933,000	1.9%	32.8%
North Africa and West Asia	481,123,000	24,894,000	4,949,000	1.0%	19.9%
Globe	7,349,472,000	2,411,984,000	218,529,000	3.0%	9.1%

Source: Todd M. Johnson and Gina A. Zurlo (eds), *World Christian Database* (Leiden/Boston: Brill), accessed March 2017.

martyr's death. They continue to live with God after their physical death and consequently constitute living members of the body of Christ. As they have completed the 'good fight' (2 Timothy 4: 7), they can, through their intercessions, support those members of the church who still remain in the world in their efforts to obtain sanctity. They are not mediators between God and the believers, because Jesus Christ alone plays this role. They attend to the struggling believers in their lifelong pursuit to lead a life in Christ. Essentially, holiness requires all-encompassing effort and takes up an entire lifetime. According to Orthodox understanding, sanctification is a life's work that concludes only with death. As long as people live, they are threatened by failure. Hence the canonisation of saints can take place only after their deaths.

Portrayed on icons, the saints are constantly present in the community. The veneration of the icons is not directed at the lifeless matter (such as wood and paint) but to the people portrayed iconographically; they represent the human nature in the state of sanctification. In Orthodoxy, icons are perceived as theological expressions; they are visible messages of the reality of a new life immersed in the glory of God. They represent the history of salvation in the presence of the praying community and thus function as open windows to a new world. In this context it is noteworthy that the depiction of people in Orthodox iconography does not faithfully follow the human physiognomy and the exact measurements of body parts. The bodies presented iconographically, especially the faces, reflect a transcendent reality beyond this world. Theological content is conveyed

Changes in overall Orthodox in North Africa and West Asia, 1970–2015, growth rate, % per year

Annual growth rate, 1970–2015	Total population	Christian population	Orthodox population
Northern Africa	2.2%	1.4%	1.2%
Western Asia	2.5%	1.9%	1.5%
North Africa and West Asia	2.4%	1.7%	1.3%
Globe	1.5%	1.5%	1.5%

Source: Todd M. Johnson and Gina A. Zurlo (eds), *World Christian Database* (Leiden/Boston: Brill), accessed March 2016.

Changes in Eastern Orthodox in North Africa and West Asia, 1970–2015, growth rate, % per year

Annual growth rate, 1970–2015	Total population	Christian population	Eastern Orthodox population
Northern Africa	2.23%	1.42%	−2.07%
Western Asia	2.46%	1.94%	1.20%
North Africa and West Asia	2.35%	1.72%	1.18%
Globe	1.55%	1.51%	1.37%

Source: Todd M. Johnson and Gina A. Zurlo (eds), *World Christian Database* (Leiden/Boston: Brill), accessed March 2017.

symbolically by means of painting. As an example, I would like to explain briefly the icon of Christ's resurrection.

The resurrection of Christ, known as 'the feast of all feasts', stands at the centre of Orthodox faith. Despite all the differences in detail, the icon always contains the same symbols. In the middle of the resurrection icon stands the pre-eminent figure of the victorious Jesus, with the marks of the crucifixion visible on at least one of his hands and clothed in powerfully radiating white, surrounded by a bright pointed oval framed with stars, representing the divine glory. This oval actually looks similar to a burial cave, which, through the resurrection, has been transformed into a space of divine victory and eternal life. Standing on pieces of his cross, he stretches out his arms to Adam and Eve and pulls them both out of Hades. Death, which through the sin of the first humans became part of human nature, has been destroyed with the resurrection of Christ. In one variation of the icon, Christ can be seen holding his rather long cross with his left hand like a victory sceptre and piercing deep into the heart of death (or of Satan), which is represented by the corpse of an old man. The cross here acts as a spear with which death, the consequence of satanic temptation, is stabbed down and also as a plough, with which the resurrection harrows Hades. The scattered keys and broken locks indicate the destruction of the gates of Hades. Jesus, with his resurrection, has freed humans from the shackles of death. The prophets of the Old Testament appear on the icon to the right side of the resurrected Jesus and testify to the freeing event. Among them are, most notably visible, John the Baptist, David and Abel, the first man killed after the Fall. On some resurrection icons the Apostles stand on the left side of Jesus as witnesses of the event. The Old and New Testaments are gathered around the resurrected Jesus. In the background of the icon are angels who proclaim the good news to the world.

The icons form a crucial component of the Orthodox liturgy. In this way we arrive at the heart of Orthodoxy. 'Liturgy' means 'public service' – the Greek compound *λειτουργία*, from the verb *λειτουργώ*, is compiled from the words λαός/λεώς/λειτός (people) and *ἔργον* (service). Liturgy consists of the work that changes the offerings of the faithful (bread and wine) into the body and blood of Christ. The liturgy is performed not by the clergy only but by the whole community. In the liturgy, the community gives expression to its unity. The liturgy is in Orthodoxy the treasure chamber of theology, formulated in poetic language and sung in beautiful melodies.

Centrality of the Liturgy

The Eastern Orthodox Church is a liturgical church par excellence, not only in the uninterruptedness of its ancient tradition of worship, but also because of the place that worship occupies in the life of the faithful and in the constitution of church dogma. The Orthodox Church is known for the wealth of its liturgy, a wealth that reflects a theological position. Orthodox Christians experience their membership in the church through liturgy. The liturgy is considered both a source and an expression of Orthodox theology. The liturgy maintained the church's identity and continuity in an ever-changing world. Thus, in the Orthodox Church the *lex credenda* and the *lex orandi* cannot be separated from each other. The rule of worship is nothing other than the rule of belief.

Worship in the Orthodox Church takes place in connection with three cycles of time: daily, weekly and yearly. These cycles together constitute what may be called 'the liturgy of time'.

The daily cycle is the basis of the liturgy of time. It consists of the services: Vespers, Compline, Nocturne, Matins and the Hours (the First, the Third, the Sixth and the Ninth Hour, together with the so-called Inter-Hours). As is the case in the Jewish liturgy, the liturgical day of worship in the Orthodox Church begins at the evening, and so Vespers is the first service in the liturgical day. The structure of the services and their relation to one another can be understood only in connection to the theology of time that they contain and express. This theology of time is clearly expressed in Vespers and Matins, in which four themes follow one another in sequence.

The beginning of the liturgical day is brought into connection with the creation of the world. The theme of sin and the Fall follows, as expressed in Psalms 140/141, 141/142, 129/130 and 116/117, which are chanted in the Vespers. After the theme of salvation and the coming into the world of the Son of God, expressed through procession with a candle and the hymn 'O joyful light', comes the theme of the End, the *Eskhaton*, expressed through the prayer of Simeon in Luke 2: 29–32.

The Compline, the service after supper and before going to bed, signifies the end of an active period of time and the beginning of the period of rest. It contains a contemplation of personal sins and faults committed in the day passed. Salvation is fulfilled through Jesus Christ, who is 'at all times and at every hour, both in heaven and on earth, worshipped and glorified', as a concluding prayer says.

The Nocturne emphasises the coming of Jesus Christ at the end of ages and indicates that people must always be prepared to meet the Lord.

Matins, the morning service, contains the same themes in the opposite order. Matins represents an ascension to the meeting of light and contains a cosmic thanksgiving based on the perception of God's glory in the world. At sunrise the exclamation 'Glory to You, who has shown us the light' and the doxology reflect Christian joy and the assurance of God-given salvation.

The Hours refer to biblical motifs and events. The main topic of the First Hour (Prime) is the new day that may be in the light of God. The Third

Hour (Terce) mentions the coming of the Holy Spirit to the disciples, which is reported to have happened at the third hour on the Jewish Pentecost Day (Acts 2: 15). Following the narratives of the gospels (Matthew 27: 45–6), the Sixth Hour (Sext) focuses on the crucifixion of Jesus and the Ninth Hour (None) on his death.

The weekly cycle is based on Sunday, the so-called 'eighth day', 'the day of the Lord', the day of His resurrection and His presence in the Eucharist. In the liturgical weekly cycle, Sunday does not simply replace the Sabbath, which is considered the day of awaiting. This is, in the Eastern Orthodox Churches, the day of commemoration of the dead, who expect resurrection, and also the day when Christ, in the tomb, descended into Hell to assure the dead of liberation. Thus, Saturday is considered, together with Sunday, as a Eucharistic day.

The weekly cycle does not have its own separate services. Its material, entirely hymnographical and non-biblical, is inserted into certain parts of the daily services, depending on the day of the week. Each day of the week has its own liturgical theme, which is expressed in a series of canticles. Monday is dedicated to the angels, as the first creatures of God. Tuesday is dedicated to the prophets and the righteous of the Old Testament, who awaited the Messiah. They are all represented through John the Baptist, the Forerunner of Jesus. Wednesday is dedicated to the betrayal of Christ through Judas. Thursday is dedicated to the Apostles and the saints of the New Testament, represented through St Nicholas (Bishop of Myra, third to fourth century). Friday is dedicated to the crucifixion and death of Jesus and it is, like Wednesday, a day of fasting, because both days present the peak of human refusal of God, which is the original sin.

The yearly cycle is the most complex of the three cycles. It includes three parts. The first is the liturgy of the *Menaion* (month), which consists mainly of hymns dedicated to the fixed feasts, fasts and commemorations of the saints. The material is divided according to dates, beginning with 1 September. The second part is the liturgy of the period of the Great Lent, including three preparatory pre-Lenten weeks, six weeks of Lent and the Passion Week. The liturgical book is the *Triodion*. The third is the liturgy of the Paschal period, consisting of the services of Easter, Easter Week and the time between Easter and Pentecost. The liturgical book is the *Pentecostarion*. The liturgy of the yearly cycle includes both biblical and hymnographical material, which is inserted into the structure of the daily cycle.

A basic character of the liturgy is the commemoration of past events, which are presented in the liturgy as if they were happening now. This kind of presenting the past, of recapturing past events, is not a simple reminder of what occurred once and does not exist anymore; it aims, rather, at occupying the present time with events from the life of Christ and the saints. In the liturgy, these events are made living, are animated through the Holy Spirit, who remains living in the church. They exist in the present time of the church, constituting a new living reality of sanctification. This is not identical with the recalling of a past 'golden age', such as the time of *awā'il* in Islam, that has to be imitated in the present. The Orthodox Church believes that, through the real presence of the Holy Spirit, the past and the present are unified into one living spiritual reality and that persons who lived in Christ or died for the sake of their faith in him are still alive as parts of his living Body, which is the church. There is no past situation that has to be repeated, but rather an uninterrupted life in Christ, who is 'the same, today, yesterday and for ever' (Hebrews 13: 8) and who constitutes the everlasting midpoint of the church, whose life is continuously renewed through the Holy Spirit.

The Eucharist

The Eucharist, the ceremony of the Holy Communion, based on Christ's last supper, is not essentially connected with any definite time. However, the celebration of the Eucharist is placed within the framework of the liturgy of time, so that being neither bound essentially to time nor determined by it, it is a 'correlative' of time (Alexander Schmemann, *Introduction to Liturgical Theology*, New York: SVS Press, 1986, 44). This is seen even more clearly in the weekly cycle, where the Eucharist has a special day, the Lord's Day or Sunday. Its connection with this day is based on the special meaning of Sunday as the day of Christ's resurrection, as the so-called 'eighth day', which is in a sense different from the usual week; it indicates a different time, the time of the new life in Christ. It can hardly be doubted that the Eucharist has a basic character as the Feast of the Church, as the expression and actualisation of its eschatological fullness. The time of the Eucharist is something special; what it expresses in time fulfils time and gives it another standard of measurement.

The entire life of the Christian and the entire life of the church on earth receive their significance and their secret fullness from the *Eskhaton*, from the end and fulfilment of time, since everything is connected with this end and everything is judged and illuminated in relation to it. But this end can become a force, which transforms life and transmutes the state of expectation into joy and triumph only because it is not something in the future only, but rather something that has already come, already begun, and is being eternally actualised and fulfilled in the Eucharist. The everlasting life of the resurrected Jesus will appear at the End, which is already in existence. That New Aeon (age, era) will begin in which the faithful are already participating; that same Lord will appear who is present in the Eucharist. Thus the church is experienced as new life in new time, existing within this old world and its time for the express purpose of its salvation and renewal.

The Eucharist is *the* mystery of the church, its eternal actualisation as the Body of Christ, united in Christ by the Holy Spirit. Therefore the Eucharist is not only the most important of all liturgical services, it is also the source and goal of the entire liturgical life of the church. The Eucharist does not reproduce or symbolise past events of Christ's life; it manifests their efficacy and the church's actual participation at the salvation of Christ established by these events.

The idea that the Eucharist is the mystery uniting the whole church prevents in the Orthodox Church the multiplication of masses. No more than one Eucharist may be celebrated each day; similarly, a priest, or bishop, is not allowed to celebrate twice on the same day. However, when priests are lacking, exceptions are allowed out of pastoral needs.

The *Anaphora*, the central prayer before offering the gifts in the Liturgy of John Chrysostom (which is the most-used Eucharistic service in the Orthodox Church), expresses nothing else but giving thanks to God for his gracious deeds towards mankind throughout history. In full awareness of God's effective presence, the faithful give thanks happily for everything he has done to humanity, 'seen and unseen'. Thus, the church becomes the medium in which God and humanity meet. In Orthodox theology, thanking God is, further, a distinct means to know him. Since humanity cannot know God by reason, it is thanking that creates an existential state through which humanity becomes able to know God through acknowledging his gracious deeds to humankind since the beginning of the world. It is not at all a theoretical knowledge, but knowledge gained through participation at the joyous situation created by thanking. Being in such a state does not mean to neglect 'natural' time and usual life conditions, including passions and temptations. Instead, all conditions of human life are to be taken seriously and transmitted into the Eucharistic state of gratitude.

The Eucharist is therefore the manifestation of the church as the new age. By participating in Christ's Last Supper, Christians receive into themselves his new life and his Kingdom. The eschatology of the Eucharist is not turning away from the world, but it is above all the affirmation of the reality, the certainty and the presence of the Kingdom of Christ that is 'within' this world, but which will be manifest in its all glory only at the end of this world.

In the Orthodox Church, liturgy does not mean simply a rite or a means of contemplation. It has at its centre an access to the mystery of salvation through receiving the Holy Communion. This spiritual act is a lived experience with practical dimensions in personal life, family life and community life. God's salvation of humanity happened through a divine action: the Incarnation of Christ. The Orthodox Church believes that Jesus Christ was as real a human being as each one of us, with only one exception: he did not sin. His divine nature is revealed through his deeds of salvation and in a special way through his voluntary crucifixion, death and resurrection. These deeds are also the manifestation of his infinite love. In the same manner as Christ's divinity and love were revealed through deeds, so it is possible for Christians to partake in Christ's love and be a real image of him, if they live in a Christian way. Real worship is not only in the church during liturgy, but also in 'the liturgy after liturgy' that is to be fulfilled in society outside the church, in full responsibility towards God and the entire creation. From this standpoint, the *ora* and the *labora*, the *via contemplativa* and the *via activa*, are perfectly combined. The purpose of the liturgy is to sanctify time and place, to change the world into 'the kingdom of the Father, and of the Son, and of the Holy Spirit, now and forever, and throughout all ages' (the opening words of the Liturgy of John Chrysostom).

Islamic Context

The Eastern Orthodox Churches have been in close contact with Islam since its rise in Arabia in the seventh century. Christians obviously lived in this context. The Qur'an contains many Christian elements. Mary and her virgin birth of the wondrous Jesus (*ᶜĪsā*) are described; he is a prophet and holds an exceptional position among the prophets. In the Qur'an the central doctrine of Islam – the absolute oneness of God (*tauḥīd*) – is developed particularly in contention with the Christian doctrines of the trinity and Jesus's divine nature. Muhammad's first wife, Khadīja, was most likely a Christian. The majority of the population in the Islamic empire remained in the first three centuries Christian. Christian theological writings in Arabic, the language of the Qur'an, have existed at least since the time of Theodor Abu Qurra (died between 825 and 830). Testimonies from the end of the ninth century indicate that the liturgy of John Chrysostom was celebrated partly in Arabic, along with Greek and Syriac, in certain places in the empire. Arabic gradually established itself among the Orthodox Christians of the Levant. During the second half of the nineteenth century their intellectuals and writers made considerable contributions to the modernisation of Arabic literature and the development of new strands of thought in Egypt and Lebanon. It was also Orthodox Christians who in the first half of the last century founded secular parties and campaigned for the separation of state and religion.

The Eastern Orthodox Churches, along with all other churches, are presently located, from Egypt through the Arabic countries to Turkey, in countries with predominantly Muslim populations. The Arabisation of the church, however, took place in the Orthodox Church of Antioch, while Greek still dominates the patriarchates of Alexandria and Jerusalem. The fact that Arabic has for centuries been the common language of Christians and Muslims has led to the development of common thought structures that are anchored by the tangible coexistence and joint encounter of political and economic challenges. According to its self-conception, the Orthodox Church of Antioch is an Arabic Church; this is also how it is perceived by Arab Muslims. Because of its long history in the land of Islam and the common Arabic language, some of its great figures, such as Metropolitan George Khodr (born 1923) of Mount Lebanon, have played a leading role in the development of Christian–Islamic understanding. This Church, which does not have a national character, is firmly committed to the peaceful coexistence of religious communities, cultural diversity and mutual openness towards others.

Renewal Movements

A distinctive occurrence in the modern history of this Church is the founding of the Orthodox Youth Movement (known as MJO: Mouvement de la Jeunesse Orthodoxe) in 1942 by the previously mentioned George Khodr and a group of students. Thereafter, the Antiochian Orthodox Church experienced a renaissance that manifested itself in the formation of Bible circles and study groups, revitalisation of the spiritual lives of the members, improvement of education for the clergy, strengthening the roles of the lay people in the communities and dioceses, founding of monastic communities and strengthening the ministry to the needy and socially weak. Particularly the renewal of monastic life offers to the faithful more opportunities to worship in monasteries and ask for spiritual guidance. The accomplishments of the Orthodox Youth Movement also include the founding of the An-Nour (The Light) Publishing House and the magazine of the same name. The founding of the University of Balamand in 1988 on the compound of the eponymous monastery in northern Lebanon is among the fruits of the extensive educational work undertaken in this context.

Similarly, a movement of renewal of monastic and spiritual life started in the 1960s in the Coptic Orthodox Church around the famous monk and priest Mattā al-Miskīn, Matthew the Poor (1919–2006). A prolific theologian and author of highly spiritual writings, he left 181 books and numerous articles. Under his spiritual leadership St Macarius Monastery in Wādī an-Natrūn became the centre of spiritual and theological renaissance, which reached out beyond the borders of Egypt.

Eastern Orthodox Churches have been committed members of the ecumenical movement since its inception. They are members of the Middle East Council of Churches, headquartered in Beirut. Through the organisation of regular theological meetings, common prayer services, consultations on urgent political and social issues, and cooperation in charity projects, particularly during wartime, these Churches demonstrate their awareness of the importance of ecumenism for the future of Christianity.

As right faith and right praxis are inseparably related to each other in the Orthodox Churches, the life of the individual and the life of the community are considered as real expressions of faith. In this sense, the faithful participate regularly in the Eucharist and other church mysteries. Many of them enjoy the guidance of a spiritual father or at least maintain strong ties to monastic communities, where they can get spiritual support. This is particularly appreciated in countries torn by civil war and disturbances. However, it can also be observed that, under economic pressure, people who need to have more than one job to survive with their families find less time to attend church services.

Among the major developments in the modern history of the Eastern Orthodox Churches is the large-scale emigration of its members since the beginning of the nineteenth century from their home countries to Europe, and especially to North and South America and Australia, in search of better political and economic conditions. As a consequence, large communities and dioceses that now comprise the majority of the members of these churches emerged in the diaspora. While longer-established dioceses and parishes like those existing in North America are better prepared to incorporate Orthodox new immigrants, the younger dioceses in Europe struggle with the humanitarian challenge of helping newcomers to settle. The recent political developments in Syria and Iraq have immensely contributed to the emigration of Orthodox Christians from the Middle East. Should peace remain absent in the region, the Eastern Orthodox Churches will have to fear for their existence in the foreseeable future in parts of these regions. At best, the shrinking of these Churches would signify the decline of their role in their countries of origin. Churches seem to be unable to stop this trend. Long-term planning to create new jobs and thus offer young people incentives to stay in their countries is not clearly recognisable.

Bibliography

Coniaris, Anthony, *Introducing the Orthodox Church: Its Faith and Life* (Minneapolis, MN: Light and Life, 1982).

Hopko, Thomas, *The Orthodox Faith. Vol. 1, Doctrine and Scripture; Vol. 2, Worship; Vol. 3, Church History; Vol. 4, Spirituality* (New York: SVS Press, 2016).

Schmemann, Alexander, *Introduction to Liturgical Theology* (New York: SVS Press, 1986).

Schmemann, Alexander, *The Historical Road of Eastern Orthodoxy* (New York: SVS Press, 1997).

Ware, Timothy, *The Orthodox Church: An Introduction to Eastern Christianity*, 3rd edn (London: Penguin Books, 2015).

Oriental Orthodox

Aho Shemunkasho

The Oriental Orthodox family comprises: the Syriac Orthodox Church of Antioch, with the Malankara Orthodox Christians in Kerala, southern India; the Coptic Orthodox Church of Alexandria in Egypt, with the Ethiopian Orthodox Tewahedo Church and the Eritrean Tewahedo Orthodox Church; and the Armenian Apostolic Church with the Holy See of Etchmiadzin near Yerevan, the capital of Armenia, along with the Catholicosate of Cilicia in Lebanon, the Patriarchate of Istanbul and All Turkey, and the Patriarchate of the Holy Land and Jordan, with residence in Jerusalem. All these churches are of apostolic origin and have their roots in the Middle East and India. The Armenian tradition refers to Jesus's disciples Bartholomew and Thaddeus. For Syriac Christianity, the Apostle Peter missioned in Antioch, the disciple Addai (Thaddeus) in Edessa and the Apostle Thomas in India. Coptic Christianity goes back to St Mark's mission in Alexandria and the Ethiopic Orthodox Church is related to Philip, Bartholomew and Matthew.

In the East Roman territory, Alexandria and Antioch played prominent roles in spreading Christianity. Up until the fifteenth century, Syriac-Antiochian Christianity, along with the East Syriac Christian Church of Persia, missioned beyond their territorial boundaries in Asia Minor and Mesopotamia, and their activity reached the Caucasus in the north; Ethiopia, Eritrea and the Gulf region in the south; and along the silk roads in India, Central Asia and China in the east. The Coptic Alexandrian missionaries spread Christianity also beyond their borders in Egypt and North Africa and reached as far as Ethiopia and Eritrea. While both Antiochian and Alexandrian Christianity identify themselves as universal churches, the Armenian Apostolic Church understands itself as a national church and holds to the historical fact of being the first nation adopting Christianity, with the conversion of King Tiridates the Great through St Gregory the Illuminator in 301. The Eritrean Orthodox Church, Ethiopian Orthodox Tewahedo Church and Malankara Orthodox Syrian Church, which all proclaimed independence in the last century, are considered to be national churches too.

The Oriental Orthodox churches are in full communion with each other, as they share the theological definition of the first three universal councils – Nicaea in 325, Constantinople in 381 and Ephesus in 431 – but, in particular, rejected the Council of Chalcedon in 451. Each church is independent and has its own pope, patriarch or catholicos, and there is no hierarchy between the churches. As a consequence of the Council of Chalcedon, the Oriental Orthodox churches were isolated from the imperial Christianity of the Roman and Byzantine Empire, and some of their leaders were persecuted, particularly in the sixth century. With western Christianity having spread beyond European borders since the sixteenth century, western missionaries converted some Oriental Orthodox Christians to Latin Christianity, and with the emergence of the eastern Catholic churches, and partly also the eastern Evangelical churches, Oriental Orthodox churches weakened in their traditional homelands.

Due to historical developments in the last millennium, the Oriental Orthodox churches lost a large part of their homeland in the Middle East and demographically their presence has changed dramatically, particularly in the last century, since the end of the Ottoman Empire. Because of political instability in their homelands, members of all churches emigrated to Europe, the USA, Canada and Australia, where they established and are still in the process of establishing new parishes, dioceses, churches and monasteries, due not to missionary work and conversion but rather to looking after the dispersed communities. Each church is facing different challenges in the different states in the Middle East and similar challenges in the diaspora.

Over the centuries there have been various attempts to clarify and unify the different Christological points of view, such as by Severus of Antioch (d. 538), or during the time of the Crusades. Meeting each other always offers a golden opportunity for understanding each other. Through migration to the west and because of the recent ecumenical process, Oriental Orthodoxy has come into contact with Latin Christianity as never before. In particular, the unofficial ecumenical dialogues of the foundation Pro Oriente in Vienna since its establishment in 1964 have led to mutual ecumenical agreements between each Oriental Orthodox church and the Roman Catholic Church, in which the Christological dilemma of the

Oriental Orthodox in North Africa and West Asia, 1970

Region	Total population	Christian population	Oriental Orthodox population	% of region Oriental Orthodox	% of Christians Oriental Orthodox
Northern Africa	82,883,000	5,220,000	4,370,000	5.3%	83.7%
Western Asia	86,037,000	6,330,000	1,525,000	1.8%	24.1%
North Africa and West Asia	168,920,000	11,550,000	5,895,000	3.5%	51.0%
Globe	3,682,488,000	1,229,021,000	20,926,000	0.6%	1.7%

Source: Todd M. Johnson and Gina A. Zurlo (eds), *World Christian Database* (Leiden/Boston: Brill), accessed March 2017.

Council of Chalcedon has been put to one side. There have also been very promising ecumenical discussions with the churches of Byzantine Orthodoxy and with the Evangelical and Anglican Churches.

At the beginning of the modern ecumenical process, the heads of the Oriental Orthodox churches met for the first time in Addis Ababa, Ethiopia, from 15 to 21 January 1965. They acknowledged their common faith and communion and emphasised the need for stronger work together. In 1998 the heads signed a mutual agreement to meet annually and to continue all official ecumenical dialogue with the other churches as a family together and no longer individually, and accordingly they take part in the global ecumenical movements as a family.

The Coptic Orthodox Church of Alexandria

Today there are about 12 million Coptic Orthodox Christians in Egypt, and there are also about 2.5 million in other parts of Africa, the Middle East and the western diaspora. Particular strong communities are found in Sudan with about 0.5 million, in Canada and the USA, each with about 200,000, in Australia with 75,000, in Libya with 60,000 and in Italy with 30,000.

The indigenous Coptic Christians in Egypt see themselves as the heirs of the ancient Egyptians, with a rich history from Egypt's pharaonic period and hieroglyphic literature that goes back as far as the fourth millennium BC. The Coptic Christians describe themselves as the ethno-religious people of ancient Egypt, as philologically the term 'Copt' derives from the old Bohairic (*kubti*) and Sahidic (*quptaion*) used for the indigenous people of Egypt.

In the Christian era, in reference to the Bible, the evangelist Mark is the founder of the Alexandrian Church (Acts 18: 24); according to tradition, he died as a martyr in AD 68 in Alexandria. The current pope, Tewadros II, was elected in 2012 as the one hundred and eighteenth pope of Alexandria. Christianity spread very fast in Egypt. Historically it can be traced back to Bishop Demetrius in the second century. Already in early Christianity the Alexandrian school, along with the Antiochian school, was very influential

Oriental Orthodox in North Africa and West Asia, 2015

Region	Total population	Christian population	Oriental Orthodox population	% of region Oriental Orthodox	% of Christians Oriental Orthodox
Northern Africa	223,892,000	9,864,000	7,421,000	3.3%	75.2%
Western Asia	257,231,000	15,030,000	3,611,000	1.4%	24.0%
North Africa and West Asia	481,123,000	24,894,000	11,033,000	2.3%	44.3%
Globe	7,349,472,000	2,411,984,000	61,368,000	0.8%	2.5%

Source: Todd M. Johnson and Gina A. Zurlo (eds), *World Christian Database* (Leiden/Boston: Brill), accessed March 2017.

in theological controversies and contributed to the dogmas of the whole church through the work of such theologians as Clement and Origen, Athanasius and Cyril. Resulting in the Nicene–Constantinopolitan Creed, the first three ecclesiastical councils were shaped by Alexandrian teaching. The Alexandrians searched for a true understanding of Christianity that offers salvation for the whole universe. This can be seen in the surviving patristic literature and also through the discovery of the rich Nag Hammadi Library in Upper Egypt in 1945. The 13 codices provide a number of gnostic texts witnessing to the struggle of defining 'orthodox' faith.

In the second and third centuries, the Copts used Greek, but, using the Greek alphabet, they developed the Coptic alphabet for the Coptic language and literature. The Coptic language has been lost as a native language through Arabisation, but is still partly used in the liturgy. There is some effort to revive it, but the current challenge with political instability in Egypt does not offer any real opportunity.

Next to the language and culture, for Coptic Christians two significant spiritual factors play an important role in shaping their identity. The first is the apostolic biblical foundation, which has an immense impact on the daily life of Coptic Christians. The second is the monastic tradition, which influenced the whole of Christianity. The account of the biblical foundation goes back before the time of the Apostle Mark. The Copts see their land blessed through the Patriarch Joseph as a starting point of the Jewish exile into Egypt (Genesis 37: 28ff.) and Jesus's flight to Egypt with Mary and Joseph (Matthew 2: 12–23). Both Joseph and Jesus fled from Judea and took refuge in Egypt. Joseph and Mary fled with Jesus to Egypt to escape King Herod's massacre of the innocent children, and after Herod's death they returned home. Through the visit of the Holy Family, blessing was bestowed upon the country, just as Isaiah had prophesied: 'Blessed be Egypt' (Isaiah 19: 25). Jesus's return to Judea is also seen in reference to the prophecy of Hosea: 'and out of Egypt I called my son' (Hosea 11: 1). The spread of Christianity and the building of churches, in the view of Coptic

Changes in Oriental Orthodox in North Africa and West Asia, 1970–2015, growth rate, % per year

Annual growth rate, 1970–2015	Total population	Christian population	Oriental Orthodox population
Northern Africa	2.23%	1.42%	1.18%
Western Asia	2.46%	1.94%	1.93%
North Africa and West Asia	2.35%	1.72%	1.40%
Globe	1.55%	1.51%	2.42%

Source: Todd M. Johnson and Gina A. Zurlo (eds), *World Christian Database* (Leiden/Boston: Brill), accessed March 2017.

Christians, represents the fulfilment of Isaiah's prophecy: 'Then the Lord will be known to Egypt, and the Egyptians will know the Lord in that day and will make sacrifice and offering' (Isaiah 19: 21). This tradition is alive in Egypt, and Coptic Christians commemorate the visit of the Holy Family in a number of pilgrim churches. It is believed that they left certain traces behind at these sites, such as Christ's footprint on a stone in St Mary's Church in Sakha, a stone that was used for kneading dough by Mary in Samannound, or trees (called after the Virgin Mary) in Belbeis and in Ain Shams in whose shade the Holy Family rested. There are hundreds of such places, churches and monasteries in Cairo related to the visit of the Holy Family and shaping Coptic Christian spirituality. Thus, with such a tradition grounded upon biblical references, Egypt became special for Christians and gave them a unique role in keeping the Christian faith alive.

Monasticism is the second feature through which Coptic Christianity strongly influenced the ascetic and spiritual movement in the whole church. St Anthony the Great (d. 356) became the father of all monks when he went into the desert of Egypt and lived as a hermit. Many other hermits followed him. Pachomius (d. 348) started his life as a hermit too, but he realised the difficulties involved for beginners and weak monks and nuns. Therefore he founded a first monastery around 320 at Tabennissi, where more than 100 people joined him and lived nearby. Thus, Pachomius organised a community life for the monks that is called cenobitic. The idea is to escape from all sorts of worldly temptations and follow Christ totally, to be united with him, to realise and fulfil his will and to worship God day and night, like the angels in heaven. The biography of Anthony, written by Athanasius of Alexandria, and the other hagiographies are full of ascetic exercises, struggles against the demonic powers and miraculous victories over them. *The Life of Anthony*, written in Greek, was soon translated into Syriac, Latin and other languages and became a 'best seller' in the whole Christian world.

Today, the Coptic Orthodox Church is experiencing a revival of monasticism and spirituality all over the country and in the diaspora. Since the middle of the twentieth century, many ordinary and professional people from all walks of life have left their jobs and become monks and nuns. This is seen as a modern renaissance of monasticism. Spirituality and vivid faith are very much present also in the local churches. Two renowned figures contributed to this development: one is the previous pope, Shenouda III (d. 2013), and the other is Matta al-Maskin (d. 2006). Both followed in the steps of St Anthony in the desert. Pope Shenouda III chose the solitude of the Egyptian desert in 1954 and lived as a hermit for six years in a cave he carved for himself. From 1950 the monk Matta al-Maskin lived as recluse for 12 years, and other monks followed him. For a while Matta al-Maskin was also the spiritual father of Shenouda III. After he was appointed to St Macarius monastery in the Wadi al Natrun in 1969, he built up the monastery, and by 1981 more than 80 monks had joined him. With the other monks, his monastery focused on the service of the poor, both Muslims and Christians, and offered to build up teaching of catechumens through the Sunday schools. Although controversial at the beginning, this became the principal structure for religious education for the whole church. Because of various theological disagreements, such as over the issue of theosis, his relation to Shenouda III was marked by controversy. In 1971, Matta was a candidate for the patriarchal throne. In the 40 years of his episcopate, Pope Shenouda III was very influential and a well respected authority among both Christians and Muslims. In 1962 he was ordained as Bishop for Christian Education and became the President of the Coptic Orthodox Theological Seminary. He focused on pastoral work and religious education. He was gifted in preaching, and as patriarch from 1971, he conducted a weekly meeting where thousands of people came to St Mark's Cathedral. He encouraged the faithful to hold to the faith of their forebears. Thus, both of them inspired the whole church spiritually with their literary creativity and catechetical teaching, filled the monasteries with monks and nuns, and filled the Sunday schools all over the world with people studying the Bible and learning the liturgy.

The political instability in the country is of great concern to Christians. The state speaks of freedom of religion but declares Islam to be the state's official religion. Conversion to Christianity is prohibited and there is harsh punishment for any blasphemy. Copts have been targeted over the centuries, but the recent political upheaval has brought more violence, persecution and discrimination. The Copts are not well represented in the government and blame it for not protecting them. Churches as well as homes have been set on fire. There have been physical attacks and property has been taken. Since the beheading of 21 Copts on a beach in Libya in 2015, there have been a number of brutal attacks on churches, such as during Advent 2016 in St Mark's Cathedral in Cairo and during Holy Week 2017 in Alexandria and Tanta. The Christians killed for their faith are venerated as martyrs. Martyrdom is not confined to the past; it is still present among all the Oriental Orthodox churches and has become part of their identity. The Ethiopian and Eritrean Orthodox Churches belong to the Coptic tradition (see Vol. 1 of the Edinburgh Companions to Global Christianity, 264–76).

The Armenian Apostolic Church

Tablets written in golden letters and decorated with gold crosses are famous all over Armenia and can be found in various places, such as in the residence of the Catholicos of all the Armenians in Etchmiadzin. The gold-inscribed tablets have become a symbol for Christians and for the ethnic identity of Armenians. They are important for them in the same way the Ark of the Covenant was for the people of Israel, housing the tabernacle with the two stone tablets of the Ten Commandments. Traditionally, the beginning of Christianity in Armenia is attributed to the missionary work of Thaddeus and Bartholomew. According to legend, Thaddeus first converted Abgar the Ukomo in Edessa and then went to Armenia. Both Thaddeus and Bartholomew died as martyrs in Armenia. There is evidence of some Armenians being Christian as early as the second century, but Gregory the Illuminator played an important role for the Christian identity of the Armenians. Gregory converted Tiridates III and baptised him with other members of the royal family in 301. In the same year Tiridates III adopted Christianity as the state religion. Therefore, the Armenians are considered to be the first nation to have adopted Christianity. Gregory was sent back to Caesarea, his homeland, and was ordained as the first catholicos of the Armenians. Gregory was married and had children before he chose the ascetic life. His son Aristaces became the second catholicos of the Armenian Church. Today, in the Armenian tradition there are two catholicoi and two patriarchs, who are all of equal status according to Armenian tradition.

The creation of the Armenian alphabet in 406 by Mesrop Mashtots, who was commissioned by Catholicos Sahak, is the second most important historical event for the flourishing of Armenian Christianity and Armenian literature in general. Up until this time the Armenians depended on Greek and Syriac literature, but with the translation of the Bible and liturgy into Armenian, along with some other theological and philosophical works, the nation could develop its own literature, and this led to the renaissance of Armenian culture in general.

The Armenians were present at the first two ecumenical councils with their catholicoi and in the third council with a delegate of the catholicos. Although not present at Chalcedon in 451, they officially rejected Chalcedon's Christological definition of the two natures in Christ in a local council in 506, and were separated from the Byzantine and Roman Churches.

Since 1411 the Armenian Church has had four independent hierarchical leaders, two catholicoi and two patriarchs. Today, the supreme head of the Armenian Apostolic Orthodox Church is Catholicos Karekin II, with his seat in Armenia, but he has jurisdiction only over his territory in Armenia and not over the other three heads. Because of the Armenian genocide and the deportation of the survivors in 1914 and 1915, the seat of the Catholicosate of the Great House of Cilicia moved to Antelias in Lebanon in 1930.

Today it is occupied by Aram I, whose jurisdiction, with that of his bishops, covers the whole of the Middle East, Europe and the Americas.

The Holy Land and Jordan have their own patriarchate, with its seat in Jerusalem. The current patriarch is Archbishop Nourham Manougian. The second patriarch is Archbishop Mesrob Mutafyan, who is on the seat of the Patriarchate of Constantinople and All of Turkey.

The laity play a significant role in the Armenian Apostolic Orthodox Church – more so than in other churches. They also participate in the Holy Synod. With the arrival of Western missionaries, a relatively small number of Armenians became Catholics or Evangelicals. The Catholic Mekhitrist Order, founded by Mekhitar of Sebastia (d. 1749), played an important role in collecting old manuscripts, building up libraries in Venice and Vienna and contributing to the revival of arts and literature. Particularly in the last two centuries, a number of outstanding figures contributed to the renewal of faith and culture, national aspiration and emancipation of the Armenians, such as Catholicos Nerses Ashtaraketzi (in office 1843–51), Catholicos Mkrtich Khrimian (1892–1907), clergyman Komitas Vartabet (1896–1935) and Patriarch of Constantinople Maghakia Ormanian (1896–1908).

The Armenian Apostolic Orthodox Church suffered harsh political conditions, persecution and genocide at the end of the Ottoman Empire. However, towards the end of the period of Soviet rule the Armenians started to recover and look after their ethno-religious and cultural identity. In particular, the tremendous work of Catholicos Vazken I (1955–94) and the restoration of the Cathedral of Etchmiadzin with other churches motivated the Armenians and paved the way for the independence of Armenia in 1991. The re-evangelization and the renewal of the religious community along with the renewal of the monasteries are high on the agenda of the Armenian Apostolic Orthodox Church.

Although it is a small country and has only about 15% of the territory that the Armenians occupied before the genocide, the modern Republic of Armenia is a great strength to Armenian culture and religion. It is a place where the Christian tradition in all its aspects can survive and be further developed.

Altogether there are about 11 million Armenians worldwide, but only around 3 million live in the Republic of Armenia and in Karabakh. In their ancestral land in modern Turkey only about 60,000 are left, mainly in Istanbul. In contrast, before the genocide, there were over 2 million there. It has been estimated that the biggest community, of up to 2.5 million, are in Russia, 1.5 million in the USA, 750,000 in France, 250,000 in Ukraine and 100,000 in Lebanon. With the focus on the Christian ethno-national identity, the Armenians are in a strong position to keep their tradition and language alive in the diaspora.

The Syriac Orthodox Church of Antioch and all the East

Among the Oriental Orthodox Churches, the Syriac tradition, with its rich history, contributed most to the development of Christianity in the past. With its Syriac-Aramaic literature and the symbolic, poetic and Semitic theology that it shares with the East Syriac Church, it is seen as the third pillar of Christianity, along with the Greek Byzantine and Latin Western traditions. The patriarchal seat was in Antioch, where Peter and Paul were before they went to Rome. And Antioch, as the capital city of Syria in the East Roman Empire, became the centre of Syriac Christianity. Traditionally, Addai (Thaddeus) converted King Abgar Ukomo, who invited Jesus to Edessa to cure him of illness. Instead, Addai went and healed and converted the king, along with all the members of the royal family.

There is historical evidence that Christianity was already in Edessa at the beginning of the second century. Edessa played a significant role in the translation of the Bible and liturgy, and its Aramaic dialect, called Syriac, became the canonical language of the whole of Syriac Christianity. Particularly in the first Christian millennium, many famous schools and monasteries, such as those of Edessa, Nisibis and Qeneshrin, were established, producing distinguished scholars who wrote influential works. With their geographical position on the borders between East and West, and along the silk roads, they served as a bridge and dealt with different cultures and empires. Rich Syriac literature has survived, comparable to the Greek and Latin, and remains witness to special features of the Oriental Semitic and poetic genre. But since the massacres of Tamerlane in the fourteenth century, throughout the years of the Ottoman Empire and during the genocide of 1914–15, Syriac Christians lost their visible presence in society and became a tiny minority, even in the heart of their homeland.

Despite being geographically widespread in the past and highly productive, the monasteries and schools are disappearing as they fight for survival in their Middle Eastern homeland and in different ways also in the Western diaspora. The official patriarchate is in Bab Touma, Damascus, Syria, where it has been located only since 1959. Prior to that it was in Homs (1933–59), Mardin (1293–1933), Malatya (1034–1293) and Antioch (until 1034). Because of the present Syrian war, some of the administration is carried out in Atchaneh, near Beirut, Lebanon. The effect of the political instability is also reflected in the moving of the Patriarchal Theological Seminary after it left Mardin in 1933: Zahleh, Lebanon (1939–46); Mosul, Iraq (1946–62); Zahleh again (1962–8); Atchaneh, Lebanon (1968–78); Damascus, Syria (1984–96); Ma'arat Saydnaya, Syria (since 1996). For the first time, in 2015 Patriarch Mor Ignatius Ephrem II opened a patriarchal seminary in Salzburg, Austria; at present, it is still in the process of establishing itself.

In the whole of the Middle East, the number of Syrian Orthodox Christians is declining, but in the West it is increasing. This is the case because of the dramatic change in the south-east of Turkey, Iraq and Syria. The regions where Syriac Christianity survived naturally in its original places, with its ancient monasteries and churches, are becoming devoid of indigenous Syriac Orthodox Christians, called Arameans or Assyrians, such as in Turabdin in Turkey, the region of Nineveh in Iraq and Gozarto (Jazirah) in northern Syria. With this change, the main question concerns the survival of Syriac Orthodox identity, with the Syro-Aramaic language and its Oriental-Semitic theological and cultural features.

Since there are no empirical data on the Syriac Orthodox Christians, all the numbers cited in various sources are approximate. Equally, due to emigration it is clear that the numbers of the faithful have changed dramatically in Turkey, Syria and Iraq. It is almost impossible to guess how many are going to remain when the war is over and Christians can settle again. In Syria there are four dioceses, with their seats in Damascus, Homs, Aleppo and Hazakeh, with altogether about 33 priests and parishes, seven monks, two monasteries, two schools and less than 100,000 faithful.

There are also four dioceses in Turkey. The biggest is the patriarchal vicarate of Istanbul, with about 20,000 faithful, most of them originally from Turabdin, Mardin, Diyarbekir and Adiyaman, now served by seven priests in seven parishes. The archdiocese of Turabdin was the largest until the 1970s, but its numbers declined from about 80,000 to less than 2,000 people, 13 priests, 11 monks, 13 nuns and six monasteries. Most of the churches are still maintained but are empty and in the process of being confiscated by the state. The Archdiocese of Mardin is reduced to less than 1,000 people, mainly in Mardin, two monks, one monastery, one priest, three nuns and six churches. The patriarchal vicariate of Adiyaman was re-established in 2006, with one bishop, one priest and around 1,000 faithful.

In Lebanon there were about 25,000 Syrian Orthodox Christians before the war, but the number increased immensely through immigration from Syria and Lebanon. The seats of the three archdioceses are in Beirut, Bouchrieh and Zahleh, with one bishop in Atshane, Bikfaya. There are two monasteries, 10 priests, 5 monks, 12 nuns, one school and one orphanage.

In Iraq there are still three historical archdioceses, with their seats in Baghdad, Mar Matay Monastery and Mosul, with 25 priests, five monks, three nuns and about 30,000 faithful. In the Holy Land there are two parishes, with the seat of the patriarchal vicarate in Jerusalem, in St Markus Monastery, two priests, three monks, two parishes in Jerusalem and Bethlehem, with about 2,000 faithful, and one parish with one priest in Amman in Jordan, with about 2,000 Christians.

A new diocese has been established in the Gulf region, in Dubai, with one parish for the faithful originally from the Middle East (around 500 people) and one large parish for workers from India. With the emigration of the faithful to the West, seven dioceses have been established in Europe, two in the USA, one in Canada, one in Argentina, one in Brazil and one in Australia. The largest community in Europe is settled in Germany, with over 100,000 faithful, two bishops, one monastery, one monk and over 65 parishes, each with its own priest. The second biggest is in Sweden, with about the same numbers. The third biggest is the patriarchal vicariate in the Netherlands, with 14 parishes, one monastery, three monks, three nuns and around 30,000 faithful. Switzerland and Austria form a single diocese, with the bishop's seat in the monastery in Arth, Switzerland, and comprising nine priests, two monks, one nun and about 15,000 members. The Bishop of Belgium is also in charge of the small community in France, and in the UK there is a bishop in London with a small community.

The Patriarchal Vicariates in the USA are relatively small. The Diocese of New Jersey has one monastery and 20 priests serve in Florida, Georgia, Illinois, Indiana, Massachusetts, Michigan, New Jersey, New York, Rhode Island, Texas, Virginia and Washington, DC. Smaller is the Patriarchal Vicariate for the Western United States, with the bishop's seat in Los Angeles, five priests serving in Burbank, Orange, Los Banos (all in California) and Portland, Oregon. In Canada the bishop has five priests, serving in Quebec and Toronto, Ontario. With the bishop, four priests serve in the Patriarchal Vicarate of Argentina in La Plata, Cordoba, Frias, Santiago del Estero, and Buenos Aires; and two priests serve in the patriarchal vicarate of Brazil in São Paulo and Campo Granda. Some local people converted, but their number is unknown. In Central America, the Caribbean Islands and Venezuela, a new community of Syrian Orthodox Christians has been emerging since 2013. In particular, over 0.5 million indigenous people of Guatemala converted to the Syrian-Orthodox Church under the leadership of Eduardo Aguirre-Oestmann. The diaspora community in Australia and New Zealand remains small. The seat of the patriarchal vicarate is in Sydney, with seven parishes in Australia and one in New Zealand.

These numbers show how indigenous Aramaic-speaking Christians have spread worldwide but have lost most of their historical land. Despite being heirs to a rich tradition, as a minority everywhere and without proper political support they find it impossible to keep alive their Christian tradition with the Aramaic language. It is in danger of dying out both in the Middle East and in the Western diaspora. The largest population of the Syrian Orthodox Church is in Kerala, India (see Vol. 3 of the Edinburgh Companions to Global Christianity).

Bibliography

Brock, Sebastian P., et al., *The Hidden Pearl: The Syrian Orthodox Church and Its Ancient Aramaic Heritage*, 3 vols (Rome: Trans World Film, 2001).

Chaillot, Christine, *The Coptic Orthodox Church: A Brief Introduction to Its Life and Spirituality* (Geneva: Inter-Orthodox Dialogue, 2005).

Krikorian, Mesrob K., *Christology of the Oriental Orthodox Churches: Christology in the Tradition of the Armenian Apostolic Church* (Vienna: Peter Lang, 2010).

Meinardus, Otto F. A., *Two Thousand Years of Coptic Christianity* (Cairo: American University in Cairo Press, 2013).

Papazian, Michael B., *Light from Light: An Introduction to the History and Theology of the Armenian Church* (New York: SIS Publications, 2006).

Protestants

Mitri Raheb

The Protestant presence in the Middle East goes back to first half of the nineteenth century. While the Presbyterians were successful in their mission in Egypt as well as in Lebanon, Syria and Iraq, Lutherans started their work in Palestine and remained mainly there.

Protestants in Syria and Lebanon

The American Board of Commissioners for Foreign Missions, a joint body of Presbyterians and New England Congregationalists, decided in 1818 to start a mission in the Middle East. In 1827, a nucleus for the first Protestant congregation in the Middle East was formed in Beirut and Middle Eastern Protestantism was born. It took, however, 20 years for the first national Evangelical church to be established, that of Beirut, on 31 March 1848. In the second half of the nineteenth century more Protestant churches were established throughout Lebanon and Syria, forming in 1920 a single synod called the National Evangelical Synod of Syria and Lebanon. In the wake of Arab nationalism, the National Evangelical Synod of Syria and Lebanon became fully independent from the Board of Foreign Missions of the Presbyterian Church, USA, in 1959. The synod, which follows Reformed theology and the Presbyterian form of government, is a member of the Fellowship of Middle East Evangelical Churches (FMEEC), the Middle East Council of Churches (MECC), the World Council of Churches (WCC), as well as the World Communion of Reformed Churches (WCRC).

The National Evangelical Church of Beirut did not join this synod but constituted in the early 1960s together with nine other Presbyterian churches the National Evangelical Union of Lebanon. The highest governing body within the Union is its General Assembly, which is formed of both clergy and laity. Its polity is Congregational. The presiding senior pastor of the Beirut Church is traditionally the president of the Union. Since 2002 the Beirut Church has hosted the International Community Church, which caters for refugees and migrant workers. The National Evangelical Union of Lebanon is a member in the FMEEC, the MECC and the WCRC.

The ministry of both Presbyterian church bodies, the National Evangelical Union of Lebanon and the National Evangelical Synod of Syria and Lebanon, was negatively affected by the civil war in Lebanon (1975–90).

Most of the churches of the National Evangelical Union of Lebanon were destroyed or deserted, including the main church building and congregation of the National Evangelical Church of Beirut. A new church building was built and rededicated in 1998. Four (out of 23) of the churches of the National Evangelical Synod of Syria and Lebanon in south Lebanon were deserted, as their members were displaced as a result of the civil war and the Israeli invasion of south Lebanon. More painful for the synod was the war in Syria that started in the wake of the so-called Arab Spring. Five of the 20 Presbyterian churches in Syria were destroyed. As a result of the wars in Lebanon and Syria, a majority of Protestants were internally displaced or emigrated to other countries. Although a few Protestant theologians at the outbreak of the Arab Spring were in favour of the demonstrations and opposition calling for democracy and larger political participation, the overwhelming majority of the Protestants of Syria were supportive of the Assad government and preferred the stability of the familiar to the unknown. With the emergence of ISIS in north-eastern Syria in 2014, Protestants became more and more frightened and unsure about the future. The National Evangelical Synod of Syria and Lebanon became very much involved in humanitarian aid: through the support of partner churches in the USA and Europe, the synod developed a relief programme to assist Christian as well as Muslim refugees, helped in providing housing for displaced members, opened new elementary schools in the Beqa' Valley for the children of Syrian refugee families and started renovating and rebuilding churches where possible.

Presbyterian churches in both Syria and Lebanon continue their educational ministry, which was started by the missionaries in the first half of the nineteenth century. After the civil war in Lebanon, several schools were deserted and closed. Today, the National Evangelical Union of Lebanon runs several elementary schools and one high school, in addition to the Schneller Vocational/Technical School at Khirbet Qanafar. The National Evangelical Synod of Syria and Lebanon runs over 20 schools and kindergartens in Syria and Lebanon, in addition to two conference centres.

Of importance is the Near East School of Theology (NEST), which dates back to 1932. Today, NEST is jointly sponsored and managed by the National

Protestants in North Africa and West Asia, 1970

Region	Total population	Christian population	Protestant population	% of region Protestant	% of Christians Protestant
Northern Africa	82,883,000	5,220,000	204,000	0.0%	3.9%
Western Asia	86,037,000	6,330,000	117,000	0.1%	1.9%
North Africa and West Asia	168,920,000	11,550,000	322,000	0.2%	2.8%
Globe	3,682,488,000	1,229,247,000	204,584,000	5.6%	16.6%

Source: Todd M. Johnson and Gina A. Zurlo (eds), *World Christian Database* (Leiden/Boston: Brill), accessed March 2017.

Evangelical Synod of Syria and Lebanon, the Union of the Armenian Evangelical Churches in the Near East, the Episcopal Diocese of Jerusalem and the Evangelical Lutheran Church in Jordan and the Holy Land. A new campus of NEST was inaugurated in 1971. The civil war in Lebanon took its toll on NEST. It lost teachers through emigration and its student body was reduced to one-third of its pre-war size. After the end of the civil war in 1990, NEST tried to attract students from Sudan, and later from Germany, through the Studies in the Middle East (SIME) programme, which is still fluctuating according to the volatile political situation in Lebanon. In 2010 NEST launched its Centre for Middle Eastern Christian Heritage. The Centre preserves, catalogues and publishes important documents, most of which have been stored in the School library's rare-books section.

The Protestant Church in Lebanon played an important role in shaping the music of the Protestant churches in the Middle East. In 1878 the first Evangelical hymnal was printed. The Fellowship of Middle East Evangelical Churches sponsored its latest revision in 1990. This hymnal is used by all mainline Protestant churches in the Middle East, thus shaping Protestant worship identity and providing an important intra-Protestant platform that glues these churches together.

The Union of the Armenian Evangelical Churches

The Union of the Armenian Evangelical Churches in the Near East celebrated in 2011 its one hundred and sixth-fifth anniversary, dating its beginning to the year 1846, in Istanbul. Following the Armenian genocide during the First World War, tens of thousands of Armenians, many of whom were Protestants, had to escape from Turkey and were scattered throughout the Middle East. A majority of the Armenian Evangelicals fled to Syria and Lebanon. In 1924 several Armenian Protestant churches formed the Union of the Evangelical Churches in the Near East. The location of the Armenian Protestant churches that form the Union is an expression of this history of displacement. Eleven churches are in Syria (mainly in Aleppo and Kassab, with one in Damascus); six are in Lebanon; three are in Teheran, Iran; two in Greece; two in Istanbul, Turkey; one in Alexandria, Egypt; one in Baghdad, Iraq; and one in Sydney, Australia. In the wake of the Arab

Protestants in North Africa and West Asia, 2015

Region	Total population	Christian population	Protestant population	% of region Protestant	% of Christians Protestant
Northern Africa	223,892,000	9,864,000	764,000	0.3%	7.8%
Western Asia	257,231,000	15,049,000	250,000	0.1%	1.7%
North Africa and West Asia	481,123,000	24,913,000	1,015,000	0.2%	4.1%
Globe	7,349,472,000	2,414,772,000	451,054,000	6.1%	18.7%

Source: Todd M. Johnson and Gina A. Zurlo (eds), *World Christian Database* (Leiden/Boston: Brill), accessed March 2017.

Spring and especially from summer 2012 onwards, when Aleppo became a major conflict zone with fierce military activity and the town of Kasab was isolated from the outside world, a new wave of Armenian emigration took place. It is estimated that in 2013, about one-third (10,000) of the Armenian Protestant community fled from Syria to Lebanon, and another third to Armenia. This second displacement while Armenians were commemorating the one hundredth anniversary of the genocide made many Protestants wonder whether there is a future for them in the region. They see Lebanon as a station on the way to the ultimate diaspora in the USA, Canada or Australia. This war and its implications for the churches led the Union to launch relief work providing food, financial support, tuition fees, medical support, housing and schooling for displaced members.

The Union of the Armenian Evangelical Churches in the Near East is organised according to the Congregational governing system and doctrinally subscribes to Reformed theology based on the Heidelberg catechism. The official language of the Union is Armenian, and the denomination's headquarters are in Beirut. The Union is a member of FMEEC, MECC, WCRC and the WCC. Strong ties exist between the Union and other Armenian Protestant bodies in the Armenian motherland as well as the diaspora. Together with the Armenian Orthodox and Armenian Catholic Churches, the Union operates two homes for the elderly in Beirut and Aleppo, as well as a sanatorium in Lebanon. The Union has an expanded educational network consisting of 23 schools, four high schools and the Haigazian University in Beirut, in addition to four conference centres, in Syria, Lebanon, Turkey and Iran.

The Evangelical Lutheran Church in Jordan and the Holy Land

The roots of the Lutheran presence in Palestine go back to the German Protestant involvement with the region. On 7 December 1841, Frederick Wilhelm IV, who had become King of Prussia in 1840, signed an agreement with Queen Victoria of England aiming to establish in Jerusalem a 'Bishopric of the United Church of England and Ireland'. By 1879 there were 12 Protestant congregations in the Holy Land. These churches, the fruits of English as well as German mission work, adopted the Anglican

Changes in Protestants in North Africa and West Asia, 1970–2015, growth rate, % per year

Region	Total population	Christian population	Protestant population
Northern Africa	2.2%	1.4%	3.0%
Western Asia	2.5%	1.9%	1.7%
North Africa and West Asia	2.4%	1.7%	2.6%
Globe	1.5%	1.5%	1.8%

Source: Todd M. Johnson and Gina A. Zurlo (eds), *World Christian Database* (Leiden/Boston: Brill), accessed March 2017.

form of church structure, with a bishop at the top. Among the German missions, three were important for the development of the Lutheran Church: Kaiserswerther Deaconesses, who started, among other things, the first Protestant female school, Talitha Kumi; Johann Ludwig Schneller, who started the first Protestant orphanage, combined with the vocational school in Palestine; and the Jerusalem Society, which took over the congregations and school in Bethlehem in 1860, to found four new congregations. In 1886, after the establishment of a united Germany under Bismarck, the German Protestants separated from the Anglican Church, creating their own structure under a German Propst. The Lutheran identity of the Protestant congregations coming out of the German mission work was crystallised only after the direct involvement of the Lutheran World Federation (LWF) in Palestine in 1947. With the help of the LWF, a Lutheran church was established and officially recognised by the Jordanian government in May 1959. It was called the Evangelical Lutheran Church in Jordan (ELCJ). In 1979 the first Arab bishop was elected to succeed the German Propst as the head of the church. To adjust to the changing political realities, the Lutheran synod adopted in 2005 a new name for the church, the Evangelical Lutheran Church in Jordan and the Holy Land (ELCJHL).

Though a small church, the ELCJHL plays a significant role in five main areas. The first is education. Today, the ELCJHL operates three co-ed schools (K1–twelfth grade) with more than 1,200 pupils in three cities in the Occupied Territories (Bethlehem, Beit Sahour and Ramallah), in addition to a kindergarten in Jerusalem. The percentage of Muslim students varies according to region from as low as 20% to as high as 80%. In that sense, the Lutheran schools provide an important platform for a Christian–Muslim 'dialogue of life'. In 1996, a new Lutheran college was opened in Bethlehem. With Dar al-Kalima University College of Arts and Culture, a first-of-its-kind Lutheran higher institution was established, with a focus on the arts and tourism.

The second area for Lutheran involvement is that of contextual theology. Lutheran Palestinian theologians were among the first to work on developing a Christian theology for the Palestinian context. They became involved in drafting the 'Theology and the Local Church' document in 1988 and the Kairos Palestine Document in 2009. The works of Palestinian Lutheran authors are widely read and circulated, locally, regionally and internationally.

The third area is ecumenism. In 1974 the ELCJ became an official member of the LWF and in 2013 a member of the WCC. On the regional level, the ELCJHL was a founding member of the Near East Council of Churches in 1964; in 1974, of the Fellowship of the Middle East Evangelical Churches; as well as of the MECC. On 26 January 2006 an agreement of full mutual recognition was signed in Amman, Jordan, by the representatives of the ELCJHL, the National Evangelical Union of Lebanon, the Evangelical Presbyterian Church in Egypt, the Union of Armenian Evangelical Churches in the Near East, the National Evangelical Synod of Syria and Lebanon, the National Evangelical Church in Kuwait and the synod of the Evangelical Church in Iran. In this declaration the different churches recognised each other as 'authentic expressions of the one church in Christ, declaring a full communion with each other and mutual recognition of ministry and ordination of Pastors and ministers'.

The fourth area in which the ELCJHL became involved is the gender question. The ELCJHL was the first church in the Middle East to allow for the ordination of women. In 2015 the synod of the ELCJHL voted to adopt a constitution for their new court. The constitution that was adopted accepted full gender equality and justice in family life, including inheritance.

The fifth area of Lutheran involvement is interfaith dialogue. Lutherans were among the first to become engaged in Christian–Muslim dialogue in the early 1980s. In 2008 Diyar, one of the leading Lutheran organisations in Palestine, launched a new initiative on 'Religion and State'. This initiative culminated in launching the document 'From the Nile to the Euphrates: The Call of Faith and Citizenship'. Another important contribution of the Lutheran Church was in the field of Christian–Jewish dialogue. This started in the late 1980s, parallel to the political dialogue between the Israeli left and the Palestinian intelligentsia. The ELCJHL was instrumental in creating the Council of Religious Institutions in the Holy Land (CRIHL), bringing the hierarchies of the three monotheistic religions in Jerusalem together. The ELCJHL continues to play a prophetic role within the Israel–Palestinian context, demanding the end of the Israeli occupation, a democratic Palestinian state and peaceful coexistence between the two peoples (Israelis and Palestinians) and followers of the three religions (Judaism, Christianity and Islam).

The Evangelical Presbyterian Church of Egypt

The first Presbyterian missionary arrived with his wife in Egypt in November 1850. They started their work in Lower Egypt, in Cairo, Alexandria and the Nile Delta. On 13 April 1860 the first Egyptian Presbyterian Synod was organised. It was expanded in 1899 to include the Sudan, thus forming the Synod of the Nile. The church experienced continuing maturity and growth, with the establishment of schools, hospitals, development programmes for self-governance and social service projects.

The Nasser revolution of 1952 that overthrew the monarchy and, soon after, ended British occupation brought major transformation to Egyptian society through land reform laws and the nationalisation of most private companies and institutions, including the Suez Canal. Those events were an important turning point in the life of the church as well. Celebrating its centennial in 1958, the Evangelical Church of Egypt gained its independence, with full self-governance and fully self-supporting. Following the Suez crisis of 1956, most missionaries had to leave and the church exercised full autonomy. Acknowledging its Coptic (i.e. Egyptian) heritage, the church became known as the Coptic Evangelical Church. Under the leadership of its General Secretary, the late Revd Dr Samuel Habib, the church joined the WCC and WARC (World Alliance of Reformed Churches), participated in forming what is now the MECC and started new outreach programmes, to combat poverty and to foster self-development. The entity that undertook those programmes was registered with the Ministry of Social Affairs in 1960 under the name of the Coptic Evangelical Organisation for Social Services (CEOSS). In the course of its 55 years of experience, CEOSS became a leading national agency, spawning and training numerous local organisations that focus on sustainable development. According to its statistics, CEOSS reaches 2 million people at any one point. It has spearheaded inter-cultural and inter-religious dialogue programmes, tackling issues of citizenship, democracy and civil society. Dar al-Thaqafa, CEOSS's publishing arm, has become a major contributor to the advance of Arabic Christian writings as well as social educational literature.

With the proliferation of other Evangelical denominations, in 2004 the official name of the Church became the Evangelical Presbyterian Church of Egypt. It is now the largest Protestant church in the Middle East, consisting of eight regional presbyteries, about 270 congregations, 300 pastors and 25 schools, while local congregations operate 55 others. The synod also manages a number of conference centres and two major medical centres. Several clinics are affiliated with local congregations.

In 2013, the Evangelical Theological Seminary in Cairo (ETSC) celebrated its one hundred and fiftieth anniversary. Besides studies equipping students to become pastors, the Seminary offers evening courses for its Lay Academy and special short-term courses in women's studies. On the occasion of its sesquicentennial, the ETSC inaugurated a new Centre for the Study of Middle Eastern Christianity. Behind this centre is a shift towards a more contextualised approach to theology and biblical interpretation. The ETSC is paying urgent attention to the challenge and the opportunity presented by approximately 120 Evangelical worshipping fellowships and communities that are without pastors. Some of these are located in remote villages and cannot afford a pastor; others are Evangelical members who have followed urban migration to cities that were constructed in desert areas in the late 1980s and 1990s.

The Evangelical Presbyterian Church of Egypt has been involved in several dialogue initiatives. It started a dialogue in 1988 with the Coptic Orthodox Church. Under the guidance of the late Pope Shenouda III and the Revd Samuel Habib the two churches discussed issues related to baptism and salvation. However, the dialogue stopped in 1991. Another important approach to dialogue has been the Bayt al-'ayla al-misriya (the House of the Egyptian Family). During a visit of the Imam of al-Azhar to Pope Shenouda on 7 January 2011 and following the attack on the Church of Sayidat al-Najah in Baghdad in late December 2010, the Imam suggested to the Pope the creation of Bayt al-'ayla al-misriya, with the aim of 'preserving the Egyptian personality and identity' and restoring Christian and Muslim values, respecting differences and strengthening the values of citizenship in both religions. The idea of this inter-religious dialogue was in place prior to the 25 January 2011 revolution and was able to address Egyptian society and to call for unity when things seemed to be getting out of control after the revolution. The new situation in Egypt after the election of the Muslim Brotherhood's Mohamed Morsi forced the churches in Egypt to come closer together and to develop a shared position regarding dialogue and peaceful coexistence with non-Christians, and to seek opportunities for shared social and cultural initiatives. On 18 February 2013 the National Council of Christian Churches in Egypt was founded, with five member churches: the Coptic Orthodox, the Coptic Catholic, the Greek Orthodox, the Anglican and the Evangelical Presbyterian.

The 2011 revolution presented an important challenge for Egyptians in general and Christians in particular. Different from the position taken by the late Coptic pope Shenouda III in backing President Mubarak to the end, the leadership of the Protestant community remained neutral. On 1 February 2011, the Protestant community issued a statement supporting President Mubarak's intended peaceful transfer of power. Eight days later and two days before the ousting of Mubarak, the Protestant community issued another statement praising the youth of the revolution as well as the role of the Egyptian military and calling for a democratic and civic state based on equal citizenship. The Protestant churches also expressed their willingness to engage in a national dialogue not based on their religious identity but rather on their national responsibility. The statement praised the role of the Protestant youth and their positive involvement at Tahrir Square. Christian youth had participated actively at Tahrir Square, thus demonstrated a visible Christian presence in the public realm. The Evangelical Presbyterian Church did not issue a separate statement in connection with the revolution; however, one week before the ousting of Mubarak, on 5 February, seven of the leading pastors and figures published a first-of-its-kind statement supporting the youth revolution and the call for democracy, a peaceful transfer of power and a new constitution based on a secular, civil society and equality of all citizens. The statement demanded the application of the Universal Declaration of Human Rights. On 3 December 2011 the Muslim Brotherhood's Freedom and Justice Party and the Salafist Nour Party had a sweeping victory in the elections to both houses of parliament. That victory brought some doubts and fears among secular Muslims as well as the Christians of Egypt. Yet, the Evangelical Presbyterian Church of Egypt opened a dialogue channel with the leadership of the Muslim Brotherhood. On 28 February 2012, 17 leaders of the Evangelical Presbyterian Church met with five leaders from the Muslim Brotherhood at their headquarters and issued a joint statement on issues related to citizenship, freedom of religious practice and Egyptian unity and identity. However, the election of Mohamed Morsi as President of Egypt on 17 June 2012 and his policies of Islamisation aroused serious anxieties among secular Muslims, Christians and the military. For this reason, the Evangelical Presbyterian Church welcomed the 30 June 2013 counter-revolution and did not see it as a coup d'état, as it was regarded by the West, but a genuine dissatisfaction of the Egyptian people with the ambitious rule of the Muslim Brotherhood.

New hymns were popular during the revolution. While the older pieces dating to the 1940s had a focus on individual spirituality, several of the twenty-first-century pop hymns are more communal prayers for the blessing of Egypt and its people. Besides political matters, the question of the ordination of women is currently being debated, despite synod approval in 2010.

Protestant churches in Sudan

The first Protestant missionaries arrived in Sudan in the 1890s following the defeat of the Mahdist movement and the beginning of Anglo-Egyptian rule. While American missionaries started the Presbyterian mission in south Sudan, Coptic evangelical missionaries were sent to the north of Sudan to pastor the many Arab Christians who were hired by the new government in public administration, commerce and education. The division between north and south Sudan is not only geographical, but also religious and racial. While the population in the south is exclusively Black African and they are generally followers of African traditional religions, the majority of those in the north are Arabs and mainly Muslims. While several tribal languages dominated the south, Arabic was the official language spoken in the north. It was during this era that the Synod of the Nile in Egypt sent the first Coptic Presbyterian pastor, Jabra Hanna, to Sudan. He established the first Presbyterian church in Khartoum, in 1903. Within the first decade of the twentieth century, several churches were established, leading to the formation of the Synod of Sudan Presbytery in 1912. This synod remained part and parcel of the Synod of the Nile throughout the era of independence, from 1955 until 1965. Today, there are 14 congregations in Sudan Presbyterian Evangelical Church and they run several Protestant schools as well.

The history of Sudan since its independence has been marked by division and war. The conflict between the north and the south resulted in two painful civil wars (1955–72; 1983–2005) and others wars in neighbouring countries resulted in large-scale migration from south Sudan to the north, especially to the Khartoum area. Many of migrants were Christians, including Protestants. Within these eras of civil wars, three coups d'état took place (in 1958, led by Ibrahim Abboud; in 1969, led by Gaafar Nimeiry; and in 1989, led by Omar al-Bashir). Under the rule of Omar al-Bashir, the National Islamic Front, led by Hassan al-Turabi, introduced a top-down Islamisation policy based on Sharia law, which was geared mainly towards the Africans in the south, but led many Christians in the north to emigrate and escape the sanctions and the deteriorating economic situation. Nevertheless, this Islamisation policy and persecution resulted in resentment of Sharia and a growing Christian movement. In order to cope with this church growth, many young Protestant Sudanese were sent in the 1980s and 1990s for theological training to the Near East School of Theology in Beirut and/or to the Evangelical Theological Seminary in Cairo.

Most of the Protestant churches in Sudan were established in the middle of the twentieth century and belong to the Reformed tradition: the Sudan Interior Church, which stands in the Baptist tradition; the Sudanese Reformed Presbyterian Church; the Sudanese Church of Christ; and the Pentecostal Church of Sudan. The last is considered the fastest-growing church in Sudan. All of these churches are members of the Sudan Council of Churches and they have congregations in Khartoum and in the Republic of Sudan. However, most of their congregations and members are found today in the independent Republic of South Sudan.

Protestant Churches in Iraq and the Gulf Region

The first Protestant communities were established in Iraq as early as the first half of the nineteenth century. Armenian Presbyterians established churches in Baghdad, Mosul, Kirkuk and Basra. The Protestant church in Iraq, however, was not able to grow to the same extent as in other regions. The Iran–Iraq War (1980–8), followed by the Iraqi invasion of Kuwait in 1991, and the war to liberate Kuwait, the sanctions that were imposed on Iraq after that, then the invasion of Iraq by the USA in 2003 took a major toll on Christians in that country. It is estimated that following the invasion of Iraq in 2003 over 1 million Christians fled Iraq to neighbouring countries like Jordan, with many ultimately migrating to the USA, Canada or Australia. Out of the six Presbyterian churches, only three survived this turmoil while the other three lost many of their members.

In addition to the Presbyterian churches in Iraq, other Protestant churches of the Reformed tradition exist today in the Gulf region. The National Evangelical Church in Bahrain dates back to 1889; and the National Evangelical Church in Kuwait was founded in 1931. From the 1950s these churches experienced immense growth due to the discovery of oil in that region and the consequent influx of migrant workers from Syria, Lebanon, Egypt and Palestine. In the late twentieth century, with the mega construction projects that took place in the United Arab Emirates, Qatar and Oman, hundreds of thousands of Asian migrant workers came to work in the Gulf, many of whom were Christians. The Gulf is today the only place of the Middle East where the number and percentage of Christians is on the increase. Almost all churches in the Gulf developed into multi-lingual, multi-national and multi-ethnic churches where services are held by the hour in diverse languages to cater for the different communities. In all these countries, with the exception of Saudi Arabia, the governments provided land to build churches and allowed people to enjoy freedom of worship as long as they respect the laws of the country. None of the migrant workers are naturalised and so they remain tolerated as foreigners, with some in very difficult conditions, despite living in affluent countries. The Bible Society in the Gulf ministers to many of these migrant workers.

Other Protestant Churches

Several other Protestant churches exist in the Middle East. The Baptists came to the region in late nineteenth century, followed by the Church of God, the Church of the Nazarene, the Christian Missionary Alliance and others. Starting in the late 1970s, an influx of Evangelical theological seminaries was visible. The fact that most of these churches are not organised on a regional level makes it difficult to cover them in any detail within the scope of this essay.

Conclusion

The Protestants of the Middle East are a double minority. As Christians, they are a numerical minority within a Muslim majority. As Protestants, they are a minority within the Christian minority. However, the Protestants in the Middle East reject any minority complex that would isolate them from their neighbours. They see themselves, with the exceptions of the Armenians and Sudanese Africans, as Arabs who have to contribute to their societies. As founders of the ecumenical movement in the Middle East, they were eager to work together with the other churches in the region and beyond. Although their influence today is much weaker than it was in the nineteenth century, they continue to play a role much bigger than their numbers imply. They face today, together with Christians of other denominations, several challenges. The first has to do with the prevailing political realities in the aftermath of the Arab Spring, the rise of political Islam, and the ongoing Israeli occupation of Palestinian land. Their response to these challenges takes different forms, ranging from developing diverse forms of contextual theologies to becoming more engaged in ecumenical and interfaith dialogue. A major focus in the early twenty-first century has been on exploring new ways of looking at faith and citizenship. The second challenge has to do with their demographic decline due to displacement, emigration and lower birth rates. It is foreseeable that several Protestant churches may not survive in certain areas of the Middle East. Nevertheless, the Protestants continue to introduce new thinking in the region, as the question of the ordination of women shows. In January 2010 the sixth general assembly of the FMEEC adopted a proposal that 'supports the ordination of the women in our churches in the position of ordained pastor and her partnership with men as an equal partner in decision making'. Their calling is to continue to push the envelope towards more inclusive societies, based on equality, freedom and grace.

Bibliography

Badr, Habib, et al. (eds), *Christianity: A History in the Middle East* (Beirut: Middle East Council of Churches Studies and Research Program, 2005).

Raheb, Mitri, *Das Reformatorische Erbe unter den Palaestinensern* (Guetersloh: Guetersloher Verlag, 1990).

Raheb, Mitri, *Sailing Through Troubled Waters: Christianity in the Middle East* (Bethlehem: Diyar, 2013).

Sharkey, Heather J., *American Evangelicals in Egypt: Missionary Encounters in an Age of Empire* (Princeton, MA: Princeton University Press, 2008).

Trexler, Melanie E., *Evangelizing Lebanon: Baptists, Mission, and the Question of Cultures* (Waco, TX: Baylor University Press, 2016).

Catholics

Anthony O'Mahony

The Eastern Catholic families of churches in North Africa and West Asia are a complex religious, political, ecclesial and cultural reality. There are one Latin and six Eastern Catholic patriarchal churches, as follows, with global membership statistics from *Annuario Pontifico* 2017: the Latin patriarchate of Jerusalem (in Israel 27,500, including up to 2,000 Hebrew-speaking Catholics – plus 50,000 migrant workers; in the Palestinian Territories c. 20,000 Latin-rite Catholics; in Jordan 50,000, plus 35,000 foreign workers and a number of Iraqi Catholic refugees); Maronite Catholic Church (3,498,707); Melkite (Greek Catholic) (1,568,239); Armenian Catholic Church (757,726); Chaldean Catholic Church (628,405); Syrian Catholic Church (195,765); and the Coptic Catholic Church (187,320). In the region, Eastern Catholics are far from negligible, with approximately 3 million across the Middle East, or approximately a fifth of all Christians in the Middle East. They also have a large diaspora associated with movements of peoples during the twentieth century and further expanding as a result of recent conflicts in Iraq and Syria.

Each of these churches is smaller, in terms of numbers, than its Orthodox counterpart, with the exception of the Chaldean Catholics in relation to the Assyrian Church of the East. On a country basis, however, Eastern Catholics are sometimes in the majority. This is the case in Lebanon, where the proportion is two-thirds Catholic to one-third other Eastern Christian; in Israel, with Melkites being the largest denomination (c. 70,000–90,000, or two-thirds of Christians); and in Iraq, where the Chaldean Catholic Church is the largest denomination (70,000 in 2017, or around half of all Christians). Among the Eastern Catholic churches, the Maronites are the majority in Lebanon, the Greek Catholics in Israel and in Syria, the Latins/Melkites in Jordan, and the Chaldeans in Iraq; almost every community has its strongholds. Only the Catholic Syrians and Armenians are minorities everywhere. However, this excludes the many millions of Catholics, especially large numbers of Syro-Malabar and Malankara Eastern Catholics, who live and work in the Arabian Gulf states, as well as migrant workers across the region, who often work in challenging and, for the Church, pastorally difficult circumstances. These migrants present a pastoral challenge to all the Eastern Catholic churches, which frequently find it difficult to respond, as their resources are often directed to maintaining contact with their own diaspora.

The Latin Church

The origins of the Latin Church, especially the important Latin patriarchate of Jerusalem (re-established in 1847), can largely be traced back to the Western settlements during the Crusades, or linked, especially in the modern and contemporary era, to diplomatic relations between Europe and the East, especially the transformation of the Holy Land during the nineteenth century. Today, the Latin patriarchate of Jerusalem comprises an increasingly complex ecclesial cultural and spirituality milieu, including profoundly different realities between the states of Jordan, Palestine, Israel and Cyprus.

The Holy Land is also home to large numbers of Catholic religious orders that represent global congregations of monks and nuns (e.g. Cistercians, Benedictines and Carmelites). The holy places for the Catholic Church are under the guardianship of the Franciscan Order, who also work across the Christian communities, not just in the Holy Land but in the wider Middle East, especially Egypt and Syria.

The Latin patriarchate of Jerusalem represents Palestinian Christians in a particular way, especially with the appointment of the first Arab patriarch, Michel Sabbah, in 1989. Patriarch Sabbah made a significant contribution to Christian theological thought in the context of relations between Palestinians and Israelis, in support of a vital Christian presence in Palestine, which has experienced a growth in Islamist currents in political society and culture, and on relations between Jews and Christians. Sabbah's pastoral letter 'Reading the Bible Today in the Land of the Bible' (1993) was an important Christian response to interpretations of Scripture that provided support for political theologies that made an exclusive claim to the land.

The Latin patriarchate and the Franciscan Order educate large numbers of Palestinian Christians and Muslims – they increasingly have had to respond to a growing migrant Christian population in Israel that numbers close to 150,000. This includes, for example, large numbers of

Catholics in North Africa and West Asia, 1970

Region	Total population	Christian population	Catholic population	% of region Catholic	% of Christians Catholic
Northern Africa	82,883,000	5,220,000	437,000	1.0%	8.4%
Western Asia	86,037,000	6,330,000	1,643,000	1.9%	26.0%
North Africa and West Asia	168,920,000	11,550,000	2,081,000	1.2%	18.0%
Globe	3,682,488,000	1,229,247,000	658,552,000	17.9%	53.6%

Source: Todd M. Johnson and Gina A. Zurlo (eds), *World Christian Database* (Leiden/Boston: Brill), accessed March 2017.

Filipinos whose family and children are growing up in an Israeli and Hebrew-speaking society, which requires a distinct pastoral response. In ecclesiological terms, the Latin patriarchate of Jerusalem is a unique institution for the global Latin Church and represents an increasingly diverse and transnational community in the heart of the Holy Land, face to face with both a dominant Muslim society among the Palestinians and an overwhelmingly Jewish population in Israel.

It is within this ecclesial–cultural context that the emergence of Hebrew Catholicism in the modern state of Israel might be seen as the most recent expression of Eastern Christianity in the Middle East. Hebrew Catholic churches, or *kehilla* (Hebrew meaning 'community'), known also as Oeuvre de Saint Jacques l'Apôtre (the Association of St James), were established in 1955 within the jurisdiction of the Latin patriarchate. The decision to found the Oeuvre was prompted principally by the patriarchate's pastoral solicitude for the Catholics, some several thousand of them, who arrived in Israel as refugees or immigrants in the years following the Second World War and the creation of the State of Israel (1948) and who continued to arrive throughout the 1950s. They came almost invariably from the countries of Eastern Europe and were either converted Jews (or descendants of such converts) or Catholic spouses in mixed marriages and their (often) baptised children – though in a few cases they had no connection at all with Jews and Judaism and were simply anxious to emigrate from their countries, now communist or in the process of becoming so. The patriarchate was conscious of its duty to those immigrants and – fearing that because of differences of mentality and language, as well as because of the complexity of the socio-political situation, the immigrants might not easily find their place within the normal parochial organisation – favoured the creation of a distinct framework within its jurisdiction specially designed to meet their needs. It was accepted that the pastoral centres envisaged would adopt Hebrew, it being the lingua franca for immigrants originating from a number of different countries. The statutes of the Oeuvre, approved on 11 February 1956, exhorts its members to:

Catholics in North Africa and West Asia, 2015

Region	Total population	Christian population	Catholic population	% of region Catholic	% of Christians Catholic
Northern Africa	223,892,000	9,864,000	1,419,000	0.6%	14.4%
Western Asia	257,231,000	15,049,000	5,713,000	2.2%	38.0%
North Africa and West Asia	481,123,000	24,913,000	7,132,000	1.5%	28.6%
Globe	7,349,472,000	2,414,772,000	1,204,386,000	16.4%	49.9%

Source: Todd M. Johnson and Gina A. Zurlo (eds), *World Christian Database* (Leiden/Boston: Brill), accessed March 2017.

> Acquire an understanding of the mystery of Israel. We insist upon a Biblical formation; we try to promote a Jewish Christian culture and a spirituality in conformity with that culture.... [We aim] to combat all forms of anti-semitism, attempting to develop mutual understanding, sympathy and friendly relations between the Catholic world and Israel.

The majority of those who supported the creation of the Oeuvre seemed to have felt that, even though an open missionary drive among Israeli Jews would, under the circumstances, be unthinkable, their task was to make the Christian faith accessible to those Hebrew-speaking Israelis whom God might prompt to seek membership in the Church. A smaller number of the 'founding fathers' were (and still are) motivated by a much larger vision, which could be summed up as a desire to implant the Church within the Jewish people in such a way that Jews who become Christians should be able to preserve their national character in much the same way that members of any other people or nation are able or invited to do.

In fact, the *kehilla* were granted permission by the patriarchate and the Vatican to have the liturgy in Hebrew as early as 1957. The community has always been under the Sacred Congregation for the Oriental Churches. In November 2003, Pope John Paul II appointed a French monk and abbot of the Benedictine monastery at Abu Gosh, Jean-Baptiste Gourion, as Titular Bishop of Lydda of the Latin patriarchate of Jerusalem, and charged him with pastoral care of Hebrew-speaking Catholics in the Holy Land. Gourion was born in 1934 in Oran, Algeria, to a Jewish family, but converted to Christianity in 1958. He died on 23 June 2005 but no bishop has been appointed to replace him. The *kehilla* have several *foyers* in Tel Aviv, Haifa, Jerusalem and Beersheva, which together constitute several thousand members. However, today large numbers of migrant Christians are now part of this community via their association with Hebrew and Israeli society.

Diaspora Communities

All Eastern Catholic churches have significant diaspora communities, with displacement due to recent conflict, especially in Iraq and Syria. This reality will almost certainly grow into permanent settlement. The Middle Eastern

Changes in Catholics in North Africa and West Asia, 1970–2015, growth rate, % per year

Region	Total population	Christian population	Catholic population
Northern Africa	2.2%	1.4%	2.7%
Western Asia	2.5%	1.9%	2.8%
North Africa and West Asia	2.4%	1.7%	2.8%
Globe	1.5%	1.5%	1.4%

Source: Todd M. Johnson and Gina A. Zurlo (eds), *World Christian Database* (Leiden/Boston: Brill), accessed March 2017.

Christian diaspora in North and South America, Australia and Europe is an important and dynamic reality for all the churches. South America has, since the late nineteenth century, attracted large numbers of Eastern Christians from the former Ottoman territories. Today, these communities have grown into a significant reality. For example, there is a large Maronite presence in South America, including three Maronite dioceses: Buenos Aires, Argentina, with an estimated 700,000 faithful; São Paulo, Brazil, with 468,000 members; and Mexico City, with 157,000 faithful. In addition, there has been large-scale Melkite emigration to Latin America, with dioceses based in São Paulo (443,000) and Mexico City (4,700), as well as apostolic exarchates in Argentina (Cordoba) (310,700), Caracas (26,600) and Mexico (4,700). Armenian Catholics have dioceses based in Buenos Aires (16,000) and Mexico (12,000), and Syriac Catholics the Apostolic Exarchate for Venezuela (20,800). There has been no historic migration of Chaldean or Coptic Catholics to South America. Today, Eastern Catholics from the Middle East have moved to other Western destinations – Australia, the USA, Canada and to a lesser degree Europe. For example, in the wake of the Iraqi catastrophe large numbers of Chaldean Catholics have left the region. In North America they constitute the Eparchy of St Peter the Apostle (San Diego), with 65,000 faithful; the Eparchy of St Thomas the Apostle (Detroit),with 180,000; and the Eparchy of Mar Addai (Toronto), with 35,000. In Australia the Eparchy of St Thomas the Apostle (Sydney) has 32,000 faithful. Within a decade the Chaldean Catholic Church has gone from being a predominantly Iraqi and Middle Eastern ecclesial community to a global reality, with all the attendant pastoral and identity challenges to which a single church must respond effectively.

This diaspora contributes to making Christian identity in the Middle East often a contested one, caught between an 'Arab' Christian identity and an 'Eastern' Christian identity. The jurisdiction of each church normally corresponds to a definite territory, but emigration of numerous faithful has also given it a personal character. This is a significant issue for the churches. For example, three-quarters of Maronites reside outside Lebanon. The churches have responded by creating numerous ecclesial structures in the West to help retain the link between the land of origin and these new Middle Eastern Christian spaces. Despite these continued contacts, the diaspora often has less of a focus upon Middle Eastern identities – Arab, Egyptian, Lebanese, Palestinian, Syrian – when articulating Christian identity. Spirituality, monasticism and distinct theological accounts associated with early Christianity are increasingly coming to the fore. Over time, outside the region Middle East Christians experience an inevitable distancing from the reality of the day-to-day life of Muslim culture and society of the Near East; the faithful of the diaspora feel themselves, by contrast, members of a global Christianity. For young people who have grown up abroad, it becomes difficult to associate the country and original language of their parents with religious faith, to necessarily connect individual religious sentiment and attachment to the community. Due to a lack of pastoral resources and because of their affiliation with the wider Catholic Church, Eastern Catholics from the West Asia region, particularly the Middle East, often become Latins within one or two generations.

Eastern Catholic Churches

The Eastern Catholic churches represent several distinct cultures and histories, making their collective the most cosmopolitan and diverse tradition in the Middle East today.

The Melkite (Greek Catholic) patriarchate of Antioch emerged in the eighteenth century following a schism in the Antiochian patriarchate of the Orthodox Church. Distributed between Lebanon, Syria, Israel, Jordan and Palestine, but with a large diaspora in the nations of the two Americas and small communities dispersed from Egypt to Gulf region, the faithful of the Melkite patriarchate constituted the only Catholic Church of the Middle East to follow the Byzantine liturgical tradition. The Melkite Church jealously protects its particular ecclesial character and vocation in relations between the Catholic Church and the Christian East. The Melkite Catholic hierarchy was presided over from 1947 by a notable figure, Patriarch Maximos IV Sayegh (1878–1967), a native of Aleppo. His successor, elected by synod on 22 November 1967 and choosing the name Maximos V, was the Bishop of Galilee, Georges Hakim. He was born in Egypt in 1908, was a student of the Jesuits in Cairo and at the important seminary for the training of Melkite Greek Catholic clergy of Saint-Anne in Jerusalem, and was consecrated in 1943 for the Palestinian Eparchy, where he carried out intense work on behalf of the Arab families of Nazareth and the surrounding areas. The new patriarch, who immediately found himself having to tackle problems linked to the nationalisation of the schools in Syria, was enthroned in the Cathedral of Saint Elias in Beirut, confirming right from the start of his patriarchate the major outlines of the programme pursued by his predecessor. Therefore it fell to him to apply in the Melkite Church the conciliar norms that emerged from Vatican II, tackling the delicate problem of an *aggiornamento* in harmony with the Eastern traditions in the areas of priestly formation and life, pastoral and ecumenical activity, and social commitment. Under the leadership of Maximos V, too, the patriarchal synod continued to carry out its traditional role, but the Melkite Church also experienced other ecclesial episodes of importance, such as the first general assembly of the clergy, held near Beirut in May 1969 and chaired by the patriarch himself. Patriarch Gregory III Laham (born 1933, elected 2000) led the Melkite

Church – committed to the ecumenical identity and dialogue in the context of strengthening the presence of Christianity in the Middle East – until he was succeeded by Patriarch Joseph Absi in June 2017. Since March 2011 the Melkite Church has suffered greatly due to the conflict in Syria, which put great pastoral and financial burdens upon the church as it sought to care for displaced members of its community. Patriarch Gregory III had a particularly delicate task negotiating with the Syrian government in a period of acute civil and religious strife while maintaining the idea of a diverse society with a significant Christian element as a defining character of the plurality that made Syrian religious and political culture a distinct mosaic. The conflict brought the church closer to the community; however, since 2011 many Melkites have left the country.

The patriarchate of Antioch for Syriac Catholics is dispersed in Syria, Lebanon and Iraq, with various settlements also in the Holy Land, Jordan, Egypt and the two Americas. Syriac Catholics, despite the modesty of their numbers, have exercised considerable influence within the wider Catholic Church. Patriarch Ignatius Gabriel I Tappuni (1879–1968; patriarch from 1929, cardinal from 1935), elected immediately after the transfer of the patriarchal see from Mardin to Beirut in 1929, ruled the Syriac Catholic Church for almost 40 years and was an extremely influential figure both in the region and in Europe. The Syriac Catholic community has been devastated by the conflict in Iraq, especially its uprooting by radical Islamists and the ongoing Sunni–Shiite conflict from its three main centres, Baghdad, Mosul and Qaraqosh in the Nineveh Plain, which has the largest concentration of Syriac Catholics in the region (60,000). Today, the Syrian Catholic Church is led by Patriarch Ignatius Joseph III Younan (born 1944, elected 2009).

The Maronite Church, which has its origins in the fourth or fifth century, is a unique ecclesial and religious culture. It emerged gradually over many centuries in the province of the patriarchate of Antioch, from a small rural Syrian community quite distinct from the rest of the Chalcedonian Church, which was then in real decline. Maronite identity is complex: accepting the Council of Chalcedon, Syriac in rite, Catholic in faith and discipline, and in union with the See of Rome. The Maronite Church and Lebanon's destiny are intimately connected; if, on the one hand, in the years following the Second World War it experienced a period of exceptional economic prosperity, on the other hand it experienced the destabilising effects of political and social crises linked to the Israeli–Arab conflicts and the persistent political demands from the Muslim and Druze communities. The role of the patriarch as a representative of the Christian church in the public sphere in the Middle East has grown in significance, especially in the context of religious leadership in the Middle East. The patriarch often has acted as an intermediary between the Christian community and the state; however, this role has not been universally welcomed among Christians.

Today, the Maronite Church is led by Patriarch Bechara Boutros Cardinal Raï (born 1940, elected 2011, cardinal 2012), who has proved to be a very active diplomat in relation to the Syrian civil war, which impacts upon Lebanon and in wider ecumenical and political circles; uniquely he visited the Russian patriarch in 2012. The most recent phase of the conflict, the hoped-for transformation of political governance in state and society associated with the so-called 'Arab Spring', has encouraged Christian leaders such as Cardinal Raï to call for a 'Christian Spring' that would pave the way for an 'Arab Spring for the Arab peoples' to benefit from a climate of peace, justice and brotherhood. Raï further expressed the hope that the Arab regimes might be transformed into democratic regimes, separating religion from the state, strengthening civil liberties and human rights, observing the right to respect difference and embracing diversity in unity. Cardinal Raï uniquely visited the large Maronite community in Israel (20,000 in 2016), making this one of the first pastoral visits by any Middle East patriarch to the Holy Land. In November 2017 Patriarch Rai held a state visit to Saudi Arabia to discuss Christian presence in the region including the important question of the possibility of Christian worship in the Kingdom and wider Gulf region. In the Maronite Church the eremitical instinct has always been a spiritual current closely associated with its origins. Today, in the Qadesh Valley, this ancient vocation is continuing to attract persons who wish to live their lives in solitude but with full integration with the life of the church through prayer and spiritual guidance.

The Armenian Catholic patriarchate of Cilicia emerged in the eighteenth century. The destruction of the Armenian people during the genocide in the early twentieth century also impacted upon the Armenian Catholics, which led to the transfer of the patriarchal see from Constantinople to Beirut in 1928, preserving in the ancient Ottoman capital an archbishopric with jurisdiction over the 2,500 faithful (in 2017) resident within the confines of Turkey. Of the dioceses existing before the Great War there remained only Alexandria, Aleppo and Ispahan, to which would be added Beirut (1928), Baghdad and Kamichlié (1954), and the two patriarchal vicariates of Damascus and Jerusalem. The first Armenian patriarch elected in the Lebanon after 1928 was Monsignor Arpiarian (1931–7), who was succeeded by Gregory Petros Agagianian (born in 1895 in Akhaltzikke, in the Caucasus; in post from 1937 until 1962; cardinal in 1946; pro-prefect and then prefect of the Congregation Propaganda Fide 1958–70; died in Rome in 1971). After Agagianian stepped down from the patriarchate (1962), the Synod of Armenian Bishops, held once again in Rome, called as his successor his auxiliary Louis Batanian, born in Mardin (Turkey) in 1899, who took the name Ignatius Petros XV. A man viewed as strongly conservative and formed in the Roman model, Patriarch Batanian remained at the head of the Armenian Catholic community until 1976, when he offered his resignation to Pope Paul VI, having reached the age limit in accordance with the norms of the decree *Christus Dominus*. In the years of his pastoral leadership, Batanian showed himself to be very sensitive to the conditions of the poorest among the Armenian faithful, and he founded an orphanage for boys in Anjar (Lebanon). Perhaps less open at the ecumenical level, the patriarch nevertheless agreed to go to Soviet Armenia, at the invitation of the Gregorian Catholicos of Ečmiadzin, Vazghen I, to assist at the celebrations in his honour and to inaugurate a monument in memory of the victims of the 1915 genocide. In such circumstances the Catholic prelate was able to carry out discreet soundings about the conditions of Armenian Catholics in the Caucasus regions. Batanian's successor, Hermaiag (born Vart) Ghedighian, elected on 3 July 1976, belonged to the Venice Mekhitarist order, in which he had spent all of his ecclesiastical career and of which became Abbot General in 1964. Appointed Patriarchal Vicar of the Diocese of Beirut and consecrated on 30 May 1971, at the age of 65 years, Ghedighian had also collaborated, during his long stay in Italy, in the work of the codification of the Eastern Canon Law. Considered by some to be a 'transition' patriarch, Ghedighian nevertheless proved his ability and prudence in guiding the Armenian Catholic community of the Middle East in a particularly difficult period. After he stepped down in 1982, the patriarchal see of Cilicia of the Armenians was occupied by John Petros XVIII Kasparian. The Syrian civil war since 2011 has devastated the Armenian Catholic Church, with numbers leaving Aleppo and Damascus for the Armenian Republic. The Armenian Church is gradually moving its centre of gravity from the Middle East to the Caucasus, with some 600,000 registered in that region, many emerging after the end of the Soviet Union in the states of Armenia and Georgia. Patriarch Gregory Peter Ghabroyan (born 1934, elected 2015) leads the church today.

The Chaldean Catholic patriarchate of Babylon is unique among the Eastern Catholic churches in the Middle Eastern area, in that it surpasses, in terms of numbers of faithful, the ancient and glorious Assyrian Church of the East, from which it separated in the sixteenth century. The Chaldean community was dispersed largely in Iraq and Iran. In the middle of the twentieth century the church was led for 11 years by Patriarch Yousef VII Ghanima, who in 1947 had succeeded Yousef Emmanuel II Thomas, who himself had been leader of his church for almost half a century. Yousef VII, who transferred his residence from Mosul to Baghdad, where the greatest number of Chaldean faithful were now to be found, was succeeded in 1958 by Paul II Cheikho, Bishop of Aleppo, born in 1906 in Alqoch, student of the patriarchal seminary in Mosul and of the Pontifical Oriental Institute in Rome, Bishop of Aqra in north Iraq from 1947 to 1957, then transferred to the Syrian Eparchy of Aleppo, which he ruled for just 14 months, until his election as head of the Chaldean Church. Having taken possession of his own see on 20 March 1959, Patriarch Cheikho personally carried out a pastoral visit to his faithful, out of which arose the urgency of creating new pastoral and social structures. This primary objective was made even more indispensable by the concentration of the Chaldeans in the Iraqi capital. The patriarchate moved from Mosul to Baghdad, thus following the majority of Chaldeans who had moved from the north of the country due to ongoing Kurdish civil conflict. The Iran–Iraq War during the 1980s further undermined the community, with large numbers of young men being killed during the conflict. The Iraq–Kuwait War in 1991, followed by a decade of sanctions leading to the 2003 invasion by the US-led coalition, brought further trauma to the community. Since 2003 nearly 70% of Chaldean Catholics have left Iraq, making the church global due to migration and thus transforming its relationship with the Middle East. This is particularly noted in the transitional Chaldean population in Turkey, which, associated with the Archeparchy of Diarbekir, had 2,900 members in 1990 but 48,594 in 2016, with many of these waiting to leave the region for the lands of exile and diaspora. Emmanuel Delly III was elected in 2003, succeeding Patriarch Bidawid. The Chaldean Catholic Church in Iran has shrunk by half since 1990. For example, the Metropolitan Archeparchy of Tehran numbered 5,500 in 1990 and 2,000 in 2017; the Metropolitan Archeparchy of Urmya and Eparchy of Salmas shrank from 2,250 in 1990 to 1,350 in 2017 and the Archeparchy of Ahwaz from 340 in 1990 to just 25 in 2017. Patriarch Louis Raphael I Sako (born 1948, elected 2013) leads today in a much changed and challenging context. Ecumenical endeavour has been, to date, a central part of Patriarch Sako's leadership, seeking Christian unity in the context of the crisis in Iraq.

The small Church of the Catholic Copts lost its first patriarch on 2 February 1958 with the death of Markos II Khouzam, whom Pope Pius XII had appointed 11 years previously, thus re-establishing the post, which had remained vacant since 1908, following the resignation, in rather turbulent circumstances, of its first titular, Kyrillos Makarios. In 1958, too, the pope wanted to reserve to himself the choice of the new patriarch and called to succeed the late Markos II his auxiliary Stephanos Sidarouss (Stephanos I). Born in Cairo in 1904, the new patriarch was the son of pasha Sesostris Sidarouss, former ambassador of Egypt in the USA. Ordained a priest in 1939, having studied law and political sciences in Paris and worked as a lawyer at that time, Sidarouss belonged to the Congregation of the Mission, in which he had held teaching roles until 1946, when he returned to Egypt to run the Coptic seminary in Tahta. A year later he received his episcopal consecration and became auxiliary to Patriarch Markos. Under the pastoral leadership of Stephanos I (who was created cardinal in 1965 and who retired in 1986), the Coptic Catholic Church consolidated its modest presence in Egypt. Patriarch Stephanos I, who took part in the work of the Second Vatican Council, equally tried to promote ecumenical dialogue with the Orthodox Coptic Church and the Greek patriarchate of Alexandria, thus contributing to the prospect of reconciliation and collaboration after years of indifference and aggressive proselytism. Today, Patriarch Ibrahim Isaac Sidrak (born 1955, elected 2013) leads the Coptic Catholics of Egypt.

Contemporary Challenges

A significant challenge for Christianity in the Middle East has been ecclesial division in a context that urgently needs an ecclesiology that proclaims unity in diversity, an ecumenical theology concerned to change attitudes. The challenges of diversity call for creativity with regard to ecclesiology. Jean Corbon, the well known Catholic ecumenist, wrote: 'The Christian Middle East appears as the microcosm of the universal ecumenism: there where the greatest diversity had abounded in division, the grace of Communion in unity has over-abounded' ('Ecumenism in the Middle East', in *Christianity: A History in the Middle East*, ed. Habib Badr, Beirut: Middle East Council of Churches, 2005, 871–83, at 882).

The following examples demonstrate that difference is now to be seen as enriching rather than dividing. The Balamand Declaration, issued after a meeting held in Lebanon in 1993, was an important stage in the official dialogue between the Catholic Church and Eastern Orthodox Church, expressing a clear rejection of 'uniatism', which was considered a major obstacle in relations between Eastern Catholics and Eastern Orthodox. The ecclesiological notion of a 'return to the Catholic Church' was declared obsolete. Catholic proselytism at the expense of the Orthodox is replaced by a desire for collaboration in evangelisation. Vittorio Peri, leading Italian scholar of ecumenism who had been involved in the dialogue from its early stages, has reminded us that the ecclesiological teaching and canonical praxis of both Catholic and Orthodox Churches expressed this conviction. They now realised that their relation of communion was better described by the theology of sister churches rather than by the theology of 'returning' to one mother church, which each identified exclusively with themselves. Despite the importance of this document in the history of relations between the Catholic and Orthodox Churches, the Balamand process has met with a mixed reception across Eastern Catholic and Eastern Orthodox theological and ecclesial communities in the Middle East and also among the Eastern Catholic and Eastern Orthodox Churches in Eastern Europe.

A further example is the Melkite project for union with the Eastern Orthodox Church of Antioch, which reflects deeply the scale of the change of attitude. Unique in the region, it nevertheless demonstrates an increasing awareness by the churches of the Middle East of sharing in the destiny of the Arab Muslim world. Jean Corbon famously referred to the ecclesial and cultural context of Antioch as 'L'Eglise des Arabes' ('the Church of the Arabs') in his work of that name in 1977. Since the Second Vatican Council, relations between the two Melkite Churches of Antioch have become more and more fraternal, giving rise to a deeper reflection about the reunification of the Antiochian patriarchate. The project of ecclesial communion, presented in a statement following the meeting of the Melkite Catholic Synod of July 1996, is the fruit of a series of efforts undertaken to bring these two Melkite branches of the Antiochian patriarchate closer. It was also a very bold undertaking that was called into question by Rome and Constantinople, both uncertain about how a local agreement based in Antioch might impact upon their relations in a wider setting.

The Christological agreements between the Catholic Church and the Oriental Orthodox churches have met with much success. The origins of this are not just with the meeting of Pope Paul VI with heads of the Oriental Orthodox churches after the Second Vatican Council; the way had been prepared by the encyclical 'Sempiternus Rex' of Pope Pius XII, which declared that the so-called, but wrongly described, 'monophysitism' of the non-Chalcedonian Christians was purely verbal. The patriarchs of the Armenian, Coptic and Syriac churches all have signed significant Common Declarations of Faith with the heads of the Catholic Church – Paul VI, John Paul II and Benedict XVI. This Christological consensus is undoubtedly one of the most significant fruits of the ecumenical engagement of our time.

A third example is the remarkable agreement for Eucharistic hospitality between the Chaldean Church and the Assyrian Church, with the acceptance of the anaphora of Mar and Addai. This agreement allows for the faithful of the two sister-churches of the East Syrian tradition of ancient Mesopotamia the Chaldean Catholic Church and the Assyrian Church of the East to worship and receive communion where the respective faithful have no church of their own – as is often the case in the growing diaspora in the West as a consequence of the Iraqi war and continuing conflict across the region. The Agreement recognizes the validity of the Eucharistic celebration according to the East Syrian Anaphora of Addai and Mari, which is considered one of the most ancient formula in uninterrupted use since the third century. Of great significance is the recognition of the Anaphora as an authentic tradition for the wider Church for it never contained the Institution Narrative – 'This is my Body…", "This is my Blood…' in the first person and direct discourse, as in later Eastern and Western liturgies.

Ecumenism is not just a formality between the churches but a strategic idea key to survival and for charting a plural identity – as witness – in opposition to rigid ideological religious nationalism which has become such a powerful current in the region.

The complex history and ecclesial culture of Middle Eastern Christianity generally have not been appreciated in the modern encounter between Western and Eastern theology. In many accounts the Christian East is fixed in historical terms, clearly oriented towards divisions on Christology in early Christianity. In its engagement with Western Christianity, Middle Eastern Christianity has struggled to retain its specificity. That said, the Christian tradition has been encouraged, especially since the Second Vatican Council, to 'breathe fully with two lungs, the Western and the Eastern', an expression used by John Paul II. Sebastian Brock, however, building upon this idea, emphasises that the Syriac Christian tradition extends and develops our understanding of this scheme. He argues that the church is endowed not just with two lungs but that there is also a third lung from which it needs to breathe: the tradition that can be termed 'the Syriac Orient' ('The Syriac Orient: a third "lung" for the church?', *Orientalia Christiana Periodica*, 71:1 (2005), 5–20, at 5). The diverse and cosmopolitan character of the Eastern Catholic churches continues to demonstrate the significance of culture for the expression of Christianity in a Middle East marked by a crisis in Islam with regard to the questions of history, modernity and the continuing temptation towards the totalising characterisation of the religious other.

The Catholic Church in its various forms continues to make a significant contribution to education at all levels across the region as part of its distinctive commitment to the social and cultural needs of all local Christians – though this often includes educating large numbers of Muslims. Catholic charities often work through the Eastern Catholic communities to give material and medical aid to members of society who are at the margins due the growing levels of social-economic distress brought about by conflict and environmental changes. Dialogue between the Catholic Church and Judaism and Islam has a priority place in the life of the churches, supported by pontifical institutes based in Rome. The question of Jerusalem has never been far from the modern papacy since the first pilgrim visit of Paul VI, in January 1964, to Jerusalem and the Holy Land. Since then, all popes have followed this itinerary of returning to the sources of Christianity in the lands of its birth, to reflect and speak about the challenges of our times. All popes have insisted upon the importance of a strong Christian presence in Jerusalem so that its vocation as a meeting place between all three monotheistic religions – Judaism, Christianity and Islam – remains a reality.

To sum up, Christianity originated in the Middle East. 'Eastern Christians' still speak of pluralism and a personal liberty, with their 'vocation' (to use a term often used in connection with them) of denying by their very existence the deadly confrontations that today are putting North Africa and West Asia to fire and sword. The meaning of the presence of Eastern Christians in this region and the question of their remaining or not raises that of a real citizenship (*muwatana*), based in a state under the rule of law with governance that seeks the 'common good', which must include a cultural capacity to assimilate the idea of religious freedom as part of the human quest. Christianity in this region has a witness beyond itself: it is to be hoped that the churches of East and West rise rapidly to this challenge, for the key to the future of this important region might lie with the few.

Bibliography

'Christianity and Jerusalem', special issue, *International Journal for the Study of the Christian Church*, 5 (2005).

'Eastern Catholics in the Modern Middle East', special issue, *Heythrop Journal* (2004).

O'Mahony, Anthony and Emma Loosely (eds), *Christian Response to Islam: Muslim–Christian Encounters in the Modern World* (Manchester: Manchester University Press, 2010).

O'Mahony, Anthony and Emma Loosely (eds), *Eastern Christianity in the Modern Middle East* (London: Routledge, 2010).

O'Mahony, Anthony and John Flannery (eds), *The Catholic Church in the Contemporary Middle East* (London: Melisende, 2010).

Evangelicals

Wafik Wahba

The word 'Evangelical' derives from the Greek εὐαγγέλιον (*euangelion*), which was used by the early church to refer to the 'good news' it proclaimed to the world. For most of Christian history the word was used as an adjective, indicating the Christian proclamation of the gospel. Most churches throughout history referred to their proclamation of the gospel as an evangelical endeavour. All Orthodox and Catholic churches in West Asia and North Africa usually refer to their tradition as evangelical, meaning proclaiming the good news of the gospel. During the Reformation in the sixteenth century, references were made to those who followed the Reformation movement as evangelicals. The German word *Evangelische* was widely used to refer to those who followed the Protestant movement, and the term became synonymous with Protestantism in Europe until now.

By the mid-nineteenth century, however, the word 'evangelical' was widely used as a noun – referring to particular groups of Christians as 'Evangelicals' – denoting their belonging to the Evangelical tradition. The shift in reference, from evangelical concepts and ideologies to a distinctive movement of identifiable people, became evident in Europe and North America by the end of the nineteenth century due to several revival and evangelistic events. These common features marked the beginning of a new movement, known as Evangelicalism. This essay focuses on the life and ministry of North African and West Asian Christians who belong to the Evangelical movement or tradition. They belong to numerous ethnic groups and they reflect various cultures and languages that extend from Armenia and the Gulf states in West Asia to Morocco in North Africa.

The Evangelicals of North Africa and West Asia

The number of Christians in the region where Christianity began has declined drastically, from a thriving community in the fourth century to a small minority by the twenty-first century. The advance of Islam from the seventh century resulted in the Christians being reduced from a majority population to a minority by the fourteenth century across the region. Today, the majority of the population in North Africa and West Asia are Muslims, with Christians comprising 5% of the total population. The majority of those Christians adhere to various Orthodox traditions.

Between the eleventh and fourteenth centuries, Catholic missions resulted in the establishment of various Catholic churches in the region. By the mid-nineteenth century various Evangelical communities were also present across North Africa and West Asia.

The Evangelical tradition was introduced to the region by Anglican, Lutheran and Presbyterian missions from the late eighteenth century. By the mid-nineteenth century the Presbyterian presence was the most dominant, and this continued until the mid-twentieth century, when other Evangelical communities, such as Baptists and Pentecostals, started to flourish in the region. The early Anglican and Presbyterian missionaries initially sought to reach out to the larger Muslim population. They faced significant challenges and so turned to the Christian communities, which were largely Orthodox. By the mid-twentieth century the presence of various Evangelical communities alongside the dominant Orthodox churches was very much in place. At first, many Evangelical churches adopted the worship style, theology and organisational structures of the Western churches from which the missionaries came. However, the shift to indigenised forms of worship, theology and administrative systems was quickly realised. After all, North African and West Asian Christians have a long history of Christian tradition, and they are very much aware of it. Today, there are more contemporary Christian songs and lyrics in Arabic than in any other language.

The spirit of antagonism between the traditional Orthodox churches in the region and the newly arrived Evangelical communities has started to give way to a spirit of cooperation and better understanding over the last 50 years or so. Many Orthodox churches were inspired by the worship style of the Evangelicals as well as their emphasis on the role of Scripture. In fact, the former Orthodox pope of Alexandria, Shenouda III, started a weekly Bible study in the main cathedral in Cairo, which was attended by thousands of people. Bible study groups are now a prominent feature of many Coptic and Armenian churches in the region.

The formation of the Middle East Council of Churches in the 1960s, in which Presbyterian, Anglican and Lutheran churches played leading roles, brought a new spirit of understanding and cooperation between the

Evangelicals in North Africa and West Asia, 1970

Region	Total population	Christian population	Evangelical population	% of region Evangelical	% of Christians Evangelical
Northern Africa	82,883,000	5,220,000	186,000	0.0%	3.6%
Western Asia	86,037,000	6,330,000	62,700	0.1%	1.0%
North Africa and West Asia	168,920,000	11,550,000	248,000	0.2%	2.2%
Globe	3,682,488,000	1,229,247,000	105,953,000	2.9%	8.6%

Source: Todd M. Johnson and Gina A. Zurlo (eds), *World Christian Database* (Leiden/Boston: Brill), accessed March 2017.

Orthodox, Evangelical and Catholic churches in the region. Several joint ministries initiated by the Council attended to the needs of victims of wars and dislocation that characterised the region for decades. The Middle East Council of Churches is the only ecumenical council that includes the Catholic Church as a full member.

Evangelical leaders from the region played significant roles in the formation and leadership of global Evangelical bodies such as the Lausanne Movement and the World Evangelical Alliance. Their contribution to the global church is significant as they link the Church of Christ to its historical roots in the region where Christianity began. Meanwhile, Evangelicals in North Africa and West Asia take noteworthy leadership roles in parachurch organisations such as Youth with a Mission, Youth for Christ, the InterVarsity Christian Fellowship and Agape Ministries (Power to Change), which reach thousands of people with the gospel message.

Evangelicals in North Africa and West Asia, as well as Christians of the region in general, represent diverse ethnic groups, whose identification with Christianity goes back to apostolic times. The Assyrians, the Christians of today's Iraq and Syria, still speak the very language used by Christ, Syriac, which is a variation of Aramaic. Armenians have their own distinct language and culture. Egyptian Christianity is rooted in its Coptic language and tradition. Most North African Christians speak Amaziric and belong to the Amaziric culture. Greek is the official language used in Cyprus and in other Orthodox contexts across the region.

Unfortunately, many Christians in countries like Iraq and Syria have been massacred or forced to emigrate in recent years due to continuous conflict in their countries. This trend of massacring and persecuting Christians has a long history in the region. In recent history, 2 million Armenians were massacred between 1915 and 1922. Over the last 60 years or so, large numbers of Christians across the region were forced to leave their countries due to persecution. Countries like Jordan, Syria and Palestine boasted large numbers of Christians, reaching over 30% of the population, at the beginning of the twentieth century. But today Christians in those countries represent less than 5% of the total population. Lebanon was a majority Christian nation until its civil war (1975–90). Today, some

Evangelicals in North Africa and West Asia, 2015

Region	Total population	Christian population	Evangelical population	% of region Evangelical	% of Christians Evangelical
Northern Africa	223,892,000	9,864,000	834,000	0.4%	8.5%
Western Asia	257,231,000	15,049,000	242,000	0.1%	1.6%
North Africa and West Asia	481,123,000	24,913,000	1,076,000	0.2%	4.3%
Globe	7,349,472,000	2,414,772,000	331,190,000	4.5%	13.7%

Source: Todd M. Johnson and Gina A. Zurlo (eds), *World Christian Database* (Leiden/Boston: Brill), accessed March 2017.

estimates suggest that Lebanon is less than 30% Christian. An estimated 3 million Egyptian Christians have left Egypt since the 1960s due to persecution and harassment. For the most part, North Africa and West Asia have been drained of their native Christians, with dire consequences for the life and ministry of the church in the region. Meanwhile, in the last 20 years or so, a large number of non-Christians (some estimate over 3 million) have accepted the Christian faith. This trend of non-Christians coming to Christ is increasing for several reasons, including the availability of the Christian message through social media as well as dissatisfaction with their own religious beliefs and traditions. It is not an exaggeration to say that more than half of contemporary Evangelicals in North Africa and West Asia come from a non-Christian background and have accepted the Christian faith very recently – during the last 10 years or so.

Evangelicals' Prevailing Trends and Witness

Many remarkable trends characterise the life and witness of Evangelicals in North Africa and West Asia. In the midst of much turmoil and persecution, the Evangelical community, along with other Christian communities in the region, has continued to bear witness to the love of God manifested in the good news of the gospel through many contributions to the larger community. The Evangelicals' presence in North Africa and West Asia has created new opportunities for ministry and witness in the region. Evangelicals have been instrumental in transforming their communities through preaching the gospel, education and social services, among other ministries. It is worth highlighting some of the prevailing trends and contributions made by Evangelicals in the region.

Communicating God's word

Evangelicals' form of worship, centred on the teaching and preaching of the gospel, necessitated the translation of the Bible into several modern languages, such as Arabic, Armenian and Syriac. Evangelicals across the region are known for their contribution to the translation of Scripture from the mid-nineteenth century onwards. The Bible societies of Egypt and Lebanon took the initiative in completing the translation of the Bible

Changes in Evangelicals in North Africa and West Asia, 1970–2015, growth rate, % per year

Region	Total population	Christian population	Evangelical population
Northern Africa	2.2%	1.4%	3.4%
Western Asia	2.5%	1.9%	3.1%
North Africa and West Asia	2.4%	1.7%	3.3%
Globe	1.5%	1.5%	2.6%

Source: Todd M. Johnson and Gina A. Zurlo (eds), *World Christian Database* (Leiden/Boston: Brill), accessed March 2017.

into modern Arabic. Modern translations of the Bible in the Armenian and Syriac languages were completed in the early twentieth century. The Algerian Bible Society has been very active in completing the translation of the Bible into Amaziric.

The very first translations of the Bible from its original Greek and Hebrew took place in the region during the second and third centuries. Several Coptic and Syriac translations of the Scriptures were used for more than 1,000 years before the Bible was translated into any modern European language. Such emphasis on the centrality of Scripture contributed to forming a new generation of discipled Christians who are committed to their Christian faith and witness. Despite the socio-religious reality of the region, where open evangelism is restricted or even prohibited, Evangelicals have been able to carry their active witness to the gospel through education, social services and more recently through social media.

Education

The emergence of Evangelical churches was usually accompanied by the establishment of educational institutions. Evangelicals established hundreds of primary and secondary schools along with institutions of higher education across the region for the purpose of educating Christians and non-Christians alike. The American universities in Beirut (1866) and Cairo (1919) were founded by Evangelicals to provide quality higher education in order to influence change in the wider society. As thousands of influential leaders graduated from such prestigious institutions over the last 150 years, they were able to promote significant change in society by introducing freedom of thought and democratic principles in governmental and institutional sectors across the region.

Evangelicals in the region also pioneered women's education as early as the beginning of the twentieth century. They established numerous schools and universities that welcomed women and men for the purpose of building a modern society. Women in countries like Egypt, Syria, Lebanon, Iraq and Iran assumed several governmental positions and gained the right to vote in the early twentieth century. Quality education, pioneered by Evangelicals, prepared and empowered women for such leadership roles. Evangelicals have been extremely active in promoting gender equality, which has resulted in social change across the region during the twentieth century before the current widespread social collapse.

Social services

One of the most remarkable trends characterising Evangelicals in the region is their active participation in providing social services to the wider society. Several hospitals and health facilities were established by

Evangelicals. Many Evangelical social organisations minister to their constituencies through healthcare programmes, support for small businesses and provision of new agricultural techniques. For example, the Lebanese Society for Educational and Social Development (LSESD) serves thousands of people through social programmes. It is currently supporting hundreds of refugees from Syria. The Coptic Evangelical Organisation for Social Services (CEOSS) reaches 2 million people through educational, health and social programmes, enabling them to break the cycle of poverty and oppression. The House of Hope in Algeria is providing much-needed social and educational programmes in several cities. Social services have resulted in significant transformation of the conditions of several communities across the region. In general, the administrative structures introduced by Evangelicals, whether in church ministry, education or social services, have provided a participatory model where people are given the chance to choose their leadership and be active participants in decision-making. Such a model has become a catalyst for democratic and participatory structures in the wider society.

Social media

Social media present an unprecedented opportunity for Evangelicals in the region to share the Christian faith with the wider society as well as strengthening the life and witness of the Christian community. In the 1990s, satellite television became available and several Christian channels used the opportunity to present the Christian faith in areas where millions of people had never heard the gospel message before. Today, there are more than 15 Christian satellite television channels broadcasting in various languages, including Arabic, Amaziric, Armenian, Persian and Turkish. More recently other forms of social media, such as Facebook and Twitter, have become instrumental in sharing the Christian faith with the wider society and supporting Christians across the region. Social media became instrumental in clarifying Christian beliefs and practices in a society that was often confused and hostile in relation to the Christian faith, while, at the same time, enhancing the life and witness of the already marginalised Christian communities. In West Asia and North Africa, where open evangelism is often prohibited, social media became one of the most effective forms of sharing the Christian faith. Today, millions of non-Christians across the region are interested in exploring Christianity, something that almost never happened during the last 13 centuries of Islamic domination.

The Power of Prayer in the Face of Persecution

One of the most significant characteristics of Evangelicals in the region is an emphasis on prayer. While prayer has always been a mark of

Evangelicalism, a renewed emphasis on prayer has flourished in the last 20 years. In the face of continuous persecution, and even torture and massacre, prayer became instrumental in giving Christians the power to cope with distressing realities. Through the power of prayer, Christians were able to extend forgiveness to those who committed atrocities against them. One of the most interesting outcomes of the prayer movement is the exposure of the lies that dominated the region for centuries. Although one cannot say that countries across the region today are more democratic or less corrupt than before the uprisings of the early twenty-first century, a remarkable change is taking place in exposing the sources of corruption, injustices and confusion that have dominated the region for many centuries. The prayer movement also resulted in unity among Christians. Different denominations were able to unite in prayer and common witness rather than stressing their differences.

As Christians in North Africa and West Asia are currently facing new cycles of persecution, trusting in God's provision and protection through prayer is proving instrumental for endurance and living witness. The conflicts in Syria and Iraq have resulted in the uprooting and scattering of millions of inhabitants, many of them Christians. Thousands of Christians have been killed and kidnapped. Across the region, Christian homes have been destroyed and properties have been confiscated. Churches have been bombed in Egypt, Syria and Iraq.

Christianity in North Africa and West Asia is associated with a history of spirituality that goes back to the early centuries of the Christian faith. It was in the deserts of Egypt and Syria that the spiritual movement known as monasticism started and flourished, and by the fourth century it had become a global movement that was credited with a key role in spreading Christianity. Today, Christians in North Africa and West Asia are clinging to this great Christian heritage of spirituality. They very much comprehend the reality that being a faithful Christian carries with it a willingness to live a sacrificial life, including the ability to extend forgiveness and even reconciliation to those who persecute us. Paul's words to the Corinthians provide an apt description of the Christians in North Africa and West Asia today: 'hard pressed on every side, but not crushed; perplexed, but not in despair; persecuted, but not abandoned; struck down, but not destroyed' (2 Corinthians 4: 8–9, NIV).

Bibliography

Hutchinson, Mark and John Wolffe (eds), *A Short History of Global Evangelicalism* (New York: Cambridge University Press, 2012).

Lewis, Donald M. and Richard V. Pierard (eds), *Global Evangelicalism: Theology, History and Culture in Regional Perspective* (Downers Grove, IL: IVP Academic, 2014).

Naguib, Makram *Al-Waqi' Al-Injili fi Al-Sharq Al-Awsat* [*Contemporary Evangelicalism in the Middle East*], (Cairo: Dar Al-Thaqafa Publishing House, 1997).
Stiller, Brian C., Todd M. Johnson, Karen Stiller and Mark Hutchinson (eds), *Evangelicals Around The World: A Global Handbook for the 21st Century* (Nashville, TN: Thomas Nelson, 2015).
Zaki, Emil and Venus Nicola, *Al-Kanisa Al-Injiliah Al-Mashikhiah fi Misr* [*The Evangelical Presbyterian Church in Egypt*], (Cairo: Dar Al-Thaqafa Publishing House, 2015).

Pentecostals/Charismatics

Eric N. Newberg

The presence of Pentecostalism in North Africa and West Asia is significant, among other reasons because this region includes the lands of the Bible. The beneficiary nations listed in Acts 2 include residents of two countries in Northern Africa – Egypt and Libya – as well as Arabs (Acts 2: 9, 11). Although the earliest Christians might not have used the term 'Pentecostal', they perpetuated the dynamic of the Christian Pentecost as the source of the growth and empowerment of the church. The primary stimulus of the growth of Pentecostalism today is to be found in its recipients' experiences of the Holy Spirit.

We can distinguish at least two categories of Pentecostalism in this region: indigenous Pentecostal groups that operate under a veil of secrecy due to constraints imposed by Islam, and those founded as branches of Pentecostal groups from abroad. The indigenous Pentecostal groups are largely constituted as house churches and do not hold publicly announced meetings. Those planted by missionaries and expatriates include the Assemblies of God, the Church of God (Cleveland), the Foursquare Gospel Church, the Full Gospel Businessmen's Fellowship International, YWAM (Youth with a Mission) and Christ for all Nations. Churches in the former group are typically independent and hardly ever rely on external assistance, while many groups in the latter category rely on outside funds, literature and sometimes personnel from mission headquarters in the West. The indigenous Pentecostal groups have embarked on their own mission activities, planting branches in host countries and in other parts of the world by means of a reverse mission process.

Albeit in relatively small numbers, people in North Africa and West Asia are attracted to become Pentecostals by two common features, namely, emphasis on a personal religious experience of spiritual rebirth, and manifestations of charismatic gifts such as speaking in tongues, prophecy, healing and miracles. Most Pentecostal groups emphasise 'holiness' (moral purity). Across the board, they are intensely interested in religious experience rather than in ritual or formal liturgy. Pentecostals in this region as elsewhere are noted for preaching a 'prosperity gospel'. Some have assimilated prosperity ideas from North American Pentecostalism. Yet, the commitment to the gospel of prosperity fits in well with values of indigenous cultures, where talismans such as the evil eye are displayed in plain sight to ensure prosperity, health and protection from malevolent spiritual forces. Expatriate African Initiated Christian groups, such as the prophetic churches, have expanded in the Middle East as part of the new African diaspora. These Pentecostal groups attract people because they are seen to be helping people in their everyday lives.

Modern Pentecostalism was introduced to North Africa and West Asia by missionaries associated with classical Pentecostalism. As with other Western missionaries, Pentecostals in North Africa and West Asia largely failed to gain adherents among non-Christian peoples and gained most of their converts by proselytising Orthodox and Catholic Christian communities rather than by evangelising non-Christians. Even today, leaders of the historic indigenous churches of the Middle East express resentment of Pentecostals and Evangelicals for weakening their communities against Islam. At present there is no formal cooperation between the Middle East Council of Churches and any Pentecostal body in this region.

Pentecostalism came to the Arabian Peninsula later than to the Maghreb and the Levant. Currently, the presence of Pentecostalism in the region has increased due to economic migration related to globalisation. Many countries in this region, especially the Gulf countries, have great wealth from oil but acute labour shortages, which they have met by means of immigration. Transient migrant workers make up two-thirds of the labour force in these countries. South Asians constitute the largest non-Arab expatriate community in the Gulf states. Temporary migrants are accorded no political representation. Their wages are less than those of their Western or Arab counterparts. Compelled by the pressures of globalisation, these migrants find better economic prospects as contract workers than they would as free labourers in their home countries. In the 1960s and 1970s multiple Christian congregations were established in several Gulf states, primarily in urban centres. The rulers of the Gulf states have been very tolerant, even donating land for the construction of churches. Every Friday thousands of Christians gather to worship the God of the Bible, often

Pentecostals/Charismatics in North Africa and West Asia, 1970

Region	Total population	Christian population	Pentecostal/ Charismatic population	% of region Pentecostal/ Charismatic	% of Christians Pentecostal/ Charismatic
Northern Africa	82,883,000	5,220,000	48,400	0.0%	0.9%
Western Asia	86,037,000	6,330,000	21,300	0.0%	0.3%
North Africa and West Asia	168,920,000	11,550,000	69,700	0.0%	0.6%
Globe	3,682,488,000	1,229,247,000	62,683,000	1.7%	5.1%

Source: Todd M. Johnson and Gina A. Zurlo (eds), *World Christian Database* (Leiden/Boston: Brill), accessed March 2017.

at the same time as Muslims meet for Friday prayers in their mosques. Pentecostal churches are among the several expatriate groups of Christians in the Arabian Peninsula.

How Pentecostals relate to the Islamic states and societies of North Africa and West Asia can be surmised from a survey of the Pentecostal presence in selected countries. Like all branches of Christianity in this part of the world, Pentecostalism has had to contend with the obstacles imposed by Islamic hegemony.

North Africa

In terms of visible appearance, Pentecostals are few and far between in Algeria, with only one officially recognised Pentecostal congregation affiliated with the Assemblies of God. However, the Pentecostal presence in Algeria might be more robust, judging from a 2006 law establishing 'conditions and regulations for the practice of non-Muslim services'. This law was aimed specifically at Evangelical and Pentecostal preachers who had gained conversions among indigenous Berbers. Many of these converts remain 'secret believers'.

Before the outbreak of war in Libya in 2011, more Christians lived in Tripoli and Benghazi than in any other country in North Africa, aside from Egypt. Since Muammar Qaddafi's fall in 2011, Islamist groups have harassed Christians and forced them to convert. At present most of the Christians in Libya are foreign workers, along with a small indigenous Christian community. A sizeable number of the Pentecostals in Libya are migrant workers in the oilfields from sub-Saharan African countries.

The Assemblies of God has a substantial presence in Egypt. These churches continue to support the orphanage established by the pioneer Pentecostal missionary Lillian Trasher in Asyut and a small prenatal clinic in a poor section of Cairo. In the past 50 years a charismatic renewal movement has emerged among Egypt's Copts. Coptic clergy and laity have turned to charismatic Christianity – mostly couched in familiar Orthodox terminology – in order to strengthen belief, spirituality and communality.

Pentecostals/Charismatics in North Africa and West Asia, 2015

Region	Total population	Christian population	Pentecostal/ Charismatic population	% of region Pentecostal/ Charismatic	% of Christians Pentecostal/ Charismatic
Northern Africa	223,892,000	9,864,000	742,000	0.3%	7.5%
Western Asia	257,231,000	15,049,000	1,315,000	0.5%	8.7%
North Africa and West Asia	481,123,000	24,913,000	2,057,000	0.4%	8.3%
Globe	7,349,472,000	2,414,772,000	644,267,000	8.8%	26.7%

Source: Todd M. Johnson and Gina A. Zurlo (eds), *World Christian Database* (Leiden/Boston: Brill), accessed March 2017.

Middle East

Pentecostals occupy a small yet vital and growing sector of the Christian space in Israel. Pentecostal churches include local branches of international denominations (the Assemblies of God, the Church of God, the Church of God of Prophecy), independent charismatic ministries (Cornerstone, Voice of Healing, Congregation of the Lamb on Mount Zion, House of Bread Church, Christ to the Nations), African Initiated Churches (Church of Pentecost, Resurrection Power, Living Bread Ministries International, Beth-El Prayer Ministry), independent local churches in the West Bank (Immanuel Church) and Messianic churches in Israel (King of Kings Assembly). Of these churches, the two most vital indigenous congregations are King of Kings Assembly in Jerusalem and Immanuel Church in Bethlehem.

Large numbers of non-indigenous Christians, attracted by its economy, have migrated to Israel. Many of these workers from Eastern Europe, Asia and Africa are Pentecostals. Much to the dismay of the Israeli government, a large number of African migrant Pentecostals were able to ensconce themselves in Israel. They found their way to Israel between the late 1980s and early 2000s, coming mostly from Ghana, Kenya and Nigeria. The opportunity for migrant labour emerged as a result of the first Palestinian Intifada (Uprising), in 1987–91. In response, the Israeli government erected checkpoints in order to control the movement of Palestinian workers into Israel. This resulted in a wholesale exclusion of non-citizen Palestinians in the West Bank and Gaza from working in Israel, and dramatic changes ensued in the Israeli labour market. Whereas Palestinians constituted 4.5% of the Israeli labour force in 1993 and migrant workers accounted for 1.6%, by 2000 the proportion of Palestinians had dropped to 3.3% and that of migrant workers had risen to 8.7%. By 2003 the proportion of migrant workers had increased to 10–12% of the labour force. About half of the migrant workers came to Israel as documented labourers, the other half as undocumented. The number of government permits issued to employ overseas workers increased from 4,200 in 1990 to 9,600 in 1993 and then

Changes in Pentecostals/Charismatics in North Africa and West Asia, 1970–2015, growth rate, % per year

Region	Total population	Christian population	Pentecostal/Charismatic population
Northern Africa	2.2%	1.4%	6.3%
Western Asia	2.5%	1.9%	9.6%
North Africa and West Asia	2.4%	1.7%	7.8%
Globe	1.5%	1.5%	5.3%

Source: Todd M. Johnson and Gina A. Zurlo (eds), *World Christian Database* (Leiden/Boston: Brill), accessed March 2017.

10-fold, to 103,000, in 1996. By 2000 the Israeli economy had become heavily dependent on transnational workers.

In the same period, other pathways were available for African migration to Israel, some legal and others illegal. Large numbers of Ethiopians came to Israel seeking asylum from political and military conflict and others came under the right of *aliyah*. In addition, growing streams of undocumented migrants made their way to Israel by means of what has been termed the 'tourist loophole'. Given Israel's profound archaeological, biblical and religious significance for several world religions, the Holy Land attracted pilgrims, some of whom extended the period of stay allowed by their tourist visas and slipped unnoticed into the Israeli economy as undocumented workers. This loophole facilitated the entry of tens of thousands of migrants from West African and other countries. The African migrant workers replaced the newly excluded low-paid, low-skilled Palestinian workers from the West Bank and Gaza, cleaning houses and offices, serving in restaurants and hotels, caring for children and the elderly, and performing other low-wage, physically demanding jobs. The majority of the African migrant workers settled in the poor neighbourhoods of Tel Aviv, especially around the old Central Bus Station, where they found relatively cheap housing, discount shops and food markets, good bus transportation to all parts of the city and country, and the company of other migrant workers, including Africans.

Most African migrants to Israel joined a church made up of fellow Africans. These churches tended to be Pentecostal and/or affiliated with the African Initiated Christianity (AIC) movement. The Africans in Israel derive spiritual, social, economic and political benefits from their churches. In fact, the African churches have become the centre of the lively African community in Israel. At their peak, more than 40 such congregations were meeting in the southern part of Tel Aviv. Theologically, the African churches in Israel can be identified with all three types of AIC churches: African-Ethiopian churches, Prophet Healing churches (also called Spiritual or Zionist churches) and neo-charismatic churches. Most of the Africans interviewed by Galia Sabar in her ethnological research described their churches as 'Pentecostal'. The African migrant churches emphasise the power and gifts of the Holy Spirit; the experience of the Holy Spirit in trances, healing and deliverance; the existence of witches and spirits; narrative theology; and the prosperity gospel. As with Pentecostal churches worldwide, the services in these churches provide release and a feeling of community and togetherness. The churches function as an extended family in providing support for members by means of rites of passage for marriage and death. Most African churches maintain their connection with Africa by offering lectures and seminars on political issues in home countries. Church leaders assume a political role in lobbying for improved living conditions and legal status. The churches provide not only a sense of belonging but also practical assistance. Church members help new arrivals find housing and work, explain the bus routes, teach housecleaning skills, and share tips about wages, hours, work conditions and how to get along with Israelis. The vitality of the African churches in a Jewish state with a small Christian minority augments their importance.

In Lebanon there are three Assemblies of God congregations and a Muslim Background Believers church with 50 congregations. Many of the Pentecostals in Lebanon are migrant workers from Africa and the Philippines, some of whom are undocumented. In her research on Ethiopian Pentecostal churches in Lebanon, Bina Fernandez found that these churches afforded migrant female domestic workers a sense of support, community and agency that functioned as a means of resisting domination by oppressive Muslim employers. More than 5,000 people of many nationalities attend an annual festival of Pentecostal churches in Lebanon for a weekend in March. According to Fernandez, the Pentecostal churches have created a safe space for migrant workers, in which forms of mutual support create a counterculture, empowering their members to navigate the underground world of undocumented workers.

In Jordan there are 16 Assemblies of God congregations. Emphasising conversion and baptism of the Spirit, these congregations are concentrated in the Amman area and are foreign-led. They operate a healthcare clinic in Amman. One Pentecostal congregation with 100 adult members is affiliated with the Church of God (Cleveland). This congregation is Holiness-Pentecostal, emphasising conversion, sanctification and baptism of the Spirit. It is also expatriate-led.

In Syria, the only known Pentecostals are a network of house churches that meet secretly. Prior to the American invasion of Iraq in 2003 there was a substantial Pentecostal community in the country. However, the unintended consequences of the invasion have been devastating for all the Christian communities and many Pentecostals are among those who have fled from the country.

The Gulf

Many who come to Saudi Arabia as domestic workers are Pentecostals. They act as a conduit in connecting other domestic workers with Pentecostal fellowships. Pentecostals have excelled at attracting expatriate workers of Chinese, Ethiopian, Korean, Filipino and South Asian extraction. In many instances Saudi employers confiscate the passports and identity papers of their domestic workers and allow them to leave the home only once a week to go to church. In these cases, Pentecostal churches function as sanctuaries for undocumented workers who have turned to freelance work to escape oppressive conditions.

More than half of Kuwait's population does not hold citizenship. Of these, most are foreign workers from the Levant, South Asia, the Philippines and Ethiopia. Foreign workers comprise a large part of the membership of the churches in Kuwait. Two Arab Pentecostal churches in Kuwait are known for effective evangelism.

The government of Bahrain allows expatriate Christians to worship freely as long as they do not evangelise Muslims, which is illegal. No Bahrainis admit to being Christians, but there are a considerable number of secret believers. Most of the Christians are expatriate workers from India, the Philippines, the UK and the USA. House churches are active, particularly among Filipino expatriate workers.

Although no outreach to the indigenous population is officially permitted in the United Arab Emirates (UAE), religious freedom is enjoyed by Christian groups. The ruling families have loaned land and allowed the construction of compounds for Christian communities. Immigrant workers constitute the strength of Christianity in the UAE.

Oman tolerates (and is mildly supportive of) the religions of its foreign workforce. Christian proselytism of Muslims is forbidden; therefore, virtually all of Oman's Christian population is foreign. Since 1973, expatriates have been freely allowed to worship according to their religious affiliations, build religious compounds and proselytise among other expatriates.

In Qatar the government recently adopted a policy of allowing expatriate Christians to worship in public and to construct church buildings. Qataris who accept Christian faith outside of Qatar have faced ostracism by their families when they publicly acknowledge their conversion. There are practically no indigenous professing Christians in Qatar. Almost all of the Christians in Qatar are expatriate workers.

The Yemeni constitution stipulates that proselytising Muslims is strictly prohibited. If a Muslim seeks information from another religion, this is considered apostasy, punishable by death. Nonetheless, it is thought that there are some secret believers in Yemen. Any national Christians are crypto-Christians. Most Christians in Yemen are migrant workers of Middle Eastern, Ethiopian, Indian and European extraction. There are no known Pentecostal churches in Yemen.

Conclusion

Pentecostalism in North Africa and West Asia does not share the bright prospects for growth projected for the movement worldwide. The demographic status of Pentecostalism in this region corresponds to that of other segments of Christianity. According to the Pew Research Center, the

Middle East – North Africa region is home to less than 1% of the world's Christians. Only about 4% of the region's residents are Christian. Although Christianity began in this area, it now has the lowest overall number of Christians and the smallest share of its population that is Christian. Christians are a minority in every country. Almost half of the Christians in the region live in either Egypt or Lebanon. Pentecostals represent a relatively small segment of the Christian population and are faced with formidable obstacles to the growth of their movement due to the spread of Islamism. Yet we can conclude, based on our findings, that at the margins of the societies of this region a growing number of people continue to encounter the Spirit of God and experience profound transformation, evidencing the markers of Pentecostal spirituality.

Bibliography

Bailey, Betty Jane and J. Martin Bailey, *Who Are the Christians in the Middle East?* (Grand Rapids, MI: Eerdmans, 2003).

Fernandez, Bina and Marina de Regt (eds), *Migrant Domestic Workers in the Middle East* (New York: Palgrave Macmillan, 2014).

Im, H. Chandler and Amos Yong (eds), *Global Diasporas and Mission* (Eugene, OR: Wipf and Stock, 2014).

Johnson, Todd M. and Gina A. Zurlo, 'Ongoing exodus: tracking the emigration of Christians from the Middle East', *Harvard Journal of Middle Eastern Politics and Policy*, 3 (2013–14), 39–49.

Willen, Sarah S. (ed), *Transnational Migration to Israel in Global Comparative Context* (Lanham, MD: Lexington, 2007).

Key Themes

Faith and Culture

Elizabeth Monier

This essay focuses on the interaction between Christian faith and culture in the modern North Africa and West Asia region. Christianity was born here, but today this region is largely made up of Muslim-majority nations, adding to the complexity of unravelling the relationship between Christian faith and culture. Moreover, 'culture' is itself a term that is difficult to define neatly. Although a strong case exists for culture as 'semiotic practices', or the practices of meaning-making, culture can be problematic as an analytic category. While acknowledging this difficulty and the complex nature of both the concept and the regional context, the purpose of this essay is not to solve these dilemmas. Rather, the focus is to summarise and explain some of the dominant perspectives through which Christians in this region relate their faith to their culture (and vice versa), culture being understood here as the semiotic practices that express the meanings that a particular community attaches to its collective existence.

Since most of the region forms part of the Arab and Islamic world, the discussion concentrates on examining how the different denominational and national Christian communities relate to Arab and Muslim culture when Christianity is the minority religion. As well as considering how Eastern Christians relate to the transformation of their homelands to majority Muslim lands and the ways in which this informs their cultural interactions, this essay highlights points of interaction between Christians and the prevailing cultures of the region. These patterns of cultural activities highlighted among Eastern Christians where they are minoritised groups are then briefly compared with the patterns in states where Christianity has a more dominant status. The chapter examines Armenia as an example of a non-Arab Christian-majority state but also highlights the case of Lebanon, which can be considered an exception among the Arab nations in terms of the strength of Christian influence.

Transition from Christianity to Islam

The Middle East is the site from which the major monotheistic religions emerged and evolved. This imbues the region with theological import and symbolic meaning so that the land and its link to faith remain a powerful element in narratives of local Christian cultures and expressions of faith.

Eastern Christians often place themselves in a line of succession from the earliest Christians, asserting their longstanding territorial links and the authenticity of their faith and culture as both ancient and Eastern. In a region that gradually came under the rule of Islam from the seventh century and subsequently underwent a process of Islamisation and Arabisation, this sense of original belonging remains a vibrant pillar in Christian culture. There is attachment to pre-Islamic local cultures, histories and languages that have become part of modern Christian identity because they offer an alternative to Arab or Islamic heritage that is nonetheless deeply rooted in the local. Christian faith thereby continues to be used by Christians as an anchor for their shared communal life within a Muslim-majority region and as an expression of the uniqueness of their religious identity and related cultural practices.

Palestinian Christians employ two such narratives. The first is that of 'living stones' (*al-Hijara al-Haya*) and the second is the Church of Jerusalem as the mother church (*Umm al-Kana'is*). The expression 'living stones' is drawn from the Bible (1 Peter 2: 5) and underscores the idea that Palestinian Christians' culture is rooted in the Holy Land, inherited from the very first Christians. This biblical heritage and historical rootedness shape a unique communal identity that is supplemented by the second narrative, which is the Church of Jerusalem as the first church or mother church. The Orthodox Church of Antioch also defines its faith and community with a similar narrative of historical rootedness and biblical heritage, by referring to the New Testament verse 'The disciples were first called Christians in Antioch' (Acts 11: 26).

The importance of establishing an early origin for the church and with national territory as linked to biblical heritage can also be seen in the case of the Coptic Orthodox Church in Egypt. The Coptic Church traces its foundation to St Mark, making it an apostolic church. Copts also refer to a Bible verse to link themselves with a biblical heritage: 'Blessed be Egypt my people' (Isaiah 19: 25). Egypt features in the New Testament when the Holy Family go into exile there and the Coptic Church has a cherished tradition concerning the places where Mary, Joseph and Jesus stayed during this time. This includes the Virgin Mary Tree located in el-Matariya in Cairo, which stands as a tangible witness to this tradition and its importance to Coptic faith and culture. For many Copts, then, history and culture merge with religious practice and rootedness in the land of Egypt. This underpins the narratives used to express and interpret Coptic traditions and status in a majority-Muslim society and in a region most often associated today only with Islamic civilisation.

The centrality of the Holy Land in the emergence of Christianity clearly forms a strong narrative, but this heritage has also been shaped by the transformation of the region after the emergence and then domination of the Islamic faith and culture. How the various Christian denominations interacted with this process has influenced modern expressions of identity and cultural practices. In the early days of the expansion of the Islamic empire, local Christian communities were in the majority and often played a significant role in the development of Islamic civilisation through the transmission of knowledge, such as the major contribution that Christian philosophers made to intellectual culture during the Abbasid Caliphate. As the Islamisation and Arabisation processes continued and Muslims gradually became the majority, this influence waned, though it has never disappeared entirely.

The impact also swung the other way, as some of the Christian communities living under the protection of Islamic rulers found themselves cut off from other Christian denominations, and these therefore evolved partially disconnected from each other. Many of the denominations were not in communion with each other until the present day, and the later wave of Western missionaries who came to the Middle East led to the creation of new denominations, some in communion with the Catholic Church and others linked to one or another of the Protestant denominations. With such barriers erected between Eastern Christians and the steady increase in Muslim power and spread of Arab culture, the Islamic milieu inevitably became a factor in the way Christian cultural practices were developed and enacted. This was especially the case for those Christian denominations that were not concentrated in a specific territory where Christian culture could develop in relative isolation.

Christians and Arab Culture

The impact of Islamisation and Arabisation on Eastern Christian culture was uneven, with pre-existing religious practices, customs and heritage fusing with the new layer of Islamic civilisation. It was stronger where the Arabic language was adopted. While religious differences set Christians apart from Muslims, Arab culture – notably language and history – has acted as a shared discourse, and engagement with Arab identity is one of the factors that can be identified as continuing to influence the different faith/culture dynamics of present-day Eastern Christians.

One of the most significant intellectual movements of the nineteenth and twentieth centuries in this region was that of Arabism. As the Ottoman Empire declined and Western influence became stronger, shifts in the Arab lands led to the *Nahda* or Arab Renaissance as the various peoples of the region began to look for new ways to organise their social and political lives and to determine their relationships with modernity and the state. There were so many different strands and approaches that space is not sufficient here to detail them. Nevertheless, it is important to note that Eastern Christians across the region, particularly in Syria, Lebanon and Palestine, were contributors to and often leaders of these debates. The movement had its origins in a concern for Arabic culture and the modernisation of the Arabic language in the writings of Christian thinkers such as Nasif al-Yazigi and Butrus al-Bustani. They saw in the revival of Arab culture a way to produce a more inclusive culture, where shared Arabness bound people together, in contrast to the Ottoman millet system where religious identity put people into different categories. As Arab nationalism developed from Arabism it took on political overtones, and in this way Christians contributed to the development of national political cultures.

For these Christians, belonging in terms of Arab culture and/or national culture is influential in how they understand their religious culture as well. For example, the Antiochian Church spent decades attempting to raise up Arab clergy to lead them in Jordan, Palestine and Syria, rather than the Greek priests who had dominated clerical authority. This campaign to Arabise the church illustrates the importance of Arab belonging for Jordanian Christians. Similarly, the power struggle over patriarchal elections in Jerusalem in the 1930s unpacked a long-running controversy between the Greek hierarchy and the Arab congregation over the question of the national character of the institution and how emphasising the Arab culture of the community was a form of resistance against Greek cultural imperialism within their churches.

The rise of Arabism and nationalism bore fruit in terms of offering Christians more access and more visibility in society, and they became more involved in the arts and media during the same period. Christians were behind the flourishing of the press, first in Lebanon and then in Egypt. In 1876 Egypt's iconic newspaper *al-Ahram* was established by Syrian Greek Catholics Salim and Bishara Takla, and a year later the first national newspaper owned by a Copt, *Al-Watan*, was published by Mikhail Abd al-Sayid. Education was also a huge area of influence, mainly due to Western missionary work in the region that focused on establishing schools. These schools continue to be regarded as prestigious and they educate both Muslim and Christian students. Because these interfaces, particularly in the arts and education, were less overtly political, Christian presence continued for longer, albeit to a lesser extent, after political and intellectual roles generally declined in the latter half of the twentieth century. This visibility should not be equated with influence, however.

In terms of the public visibility of Christianity, the arts have perhaps been the most successful point of interaction. Some of the icons of Arab music and cinema such as Fairouz, Yousef Chahine and Naguib al-Rihani are Christians. Lebanese singers like Fairouz and Majda al-Roumy are best known for their secular music but have also recorded popular versions of religious music, and the famous Egyptian singer Abdul Halim Hafez (1929–77) referred to the Messiah and to the gospels in one of his songs. The song *'Ala Ardaha* (1967) was written by a Muslim for a Muslim singer and is about Jerusalem rather than the Messiah per se, but is framed in the telling of Jesus's story. It did provoke controversy, and al-Azhar, the highly respected Islamic University in Cairo, requested that the lyrics be altered to be in line with Islamic beliefs concerning Jesus. It was also made a condition that the song was sung only outside of Egypt, but in the end it became known in Egypt and especially appreciated by Copts.

In literature, among some of the best-known writers in Arabic are Khalil Gibran, a Lebanese Christian, and Edwar al-Kharrat, an Egyptian Christian. Christian writers commonly include Christian themes and characters in their work, and Christians as characters are not absent in Arabic literature in general. Christian characters also appear in film and television, especially in Lebanon, where the larger Christian population continues to be reflected in its media, music and arts scenes. The centre of Arab film and television is Egypt, and in the mid-twentieth century it was common to see many Christian names in Egyptian film credits and even as major characters in films such as *Hassan wa Morcos wa Cohen* (1954) and *Shafiqa Al-Qibtiya* (1964). However, in the late twentieth century this presence waned under the influence of Islamism, which permeated national life.

Egypt later witnessed a new increase in Christian characters and themes on screen, particularly since the early 2000s, most notably *Beheb al-Cima* in 2004 and *Hassan wa Morcos* in 2008. While the title of the latter referenced the 1954 film *Hassan wa Morcos wa Cohen*, the 2008 film was without the Jewish character (Cohen) and was a heavy-handed attempt to promote the message of national unity between Muslims and Christians. The increased treatment of Coptic issues in the media often provokes controversy, however. There was an outcry against the portrayal of Christians in *Beheb al-Cima*, and the film *Wahed-Sefr* (2009) incited sharp criticism for its focus on the theme of divorce in the Coptic Church. This demonstrates that increased visibility of Christians and Christianity in national culture is not automatically welcomed by Christians themselves.

Not all Eastern Christians see themselves as Arabs, regardless of how integrated they are into Arab cultural heritage, and part of preserving their cultural heritage is undertaken by emphasising the non-Arab aspects of their cultural identity. The use of the various neo-Aramaic dialects today is an important distinguishing factor in maintaining cultural heritage and maintaining links with the biblical past of the community because of the idea that the Aramaic language and culture are close to what Jesus would have known. Emphasising the non-Arabness of the culture then becomes a quick and common way to frame the Christian community and its practices as different.

In reaction to the rise of the Arab nation state and disintegration of the Ottoman order, movements rose up among some Eastern Christian communities against Arabism and nationalism. Assyrian nationalism sought to create a broad non-Arab identity incorporating those descended from ancient Assyrian and Aramaic peoples from across the Syriac churches. Some of the Maronites of Lebanon constructed a similar frame to promote a non-Arab Aramaic and Phoenician heritage for both Lebanese Christians and Lebanon itself. But this trend went much further in Iraq than in Lebanon. The massacres Iraqi Christians experienced during the First World War and after the end of the British Mandate led to unease with the idea of being incorporated into an Arab nation. They feared that pan-Arabism would lead to the loss of their culture and unsuccessfully petitioned the League of Nations to set up an autonomous area for Assyrians or their removal to a region remaining under British Mandate. Later, under Saddam Hussein's Arabisation campaign, they underwent forced removal from their traditional territories and forced integration into a society defined as Iraqi and Arab by eliminating their distinctive culture with its ethno-religious basis.

Spaces for Christian Culture

Despite such different perspectives on belonging to Arab culture and contributions to Muslim civilisation, individual Christians continue to play roles in the social, cultural and political life of the modern Middle East. Yet these contributions and activities in the public sphere have not usually facilitated any significant impact for Christian faith itself on national cultures or regional consciousness. Additionally, the ability to contribute and participate in national culture is not stable but is influenced by fluctuations in broader social and political trends. This section looks at the alternative spaces Christians have formed to express the aspects of their cultural life that are forged by their faith and reveals the significant concerns they have with preserving and transmitting their religious culture and the strategies they employ to do so.

In many of the states of the Middle East, where Christians are a numerical minority, the de facto involvement of Christians and Christian culture in public life is limited by often unspoken rules. Since the everyday marginalisation occurs on the basis of religion, it is logical that faith forms part of the alternative. In Egypt, for example, the church acts as a separate space where Christians can exercise their specific faith and culture. This space is symbolically protected by the walls around the churches and monasteries and guarded by Coptic Church leaders through the maintenance of good relations with the state. Consequently, the church plays a pivotal role in structuring and preserving Coptic cultural life, especially since the Sunday School Movement of the 1950s saw efforts to revive the teaching of Coptic heritage, including Coptic history, hagiographies and the Coptic language. The church also runs a programme of social and cultural activities such as youth retreats to monasteries, the provision of IT services and broadcast of television programmes. In 2008 a large Coptic Orthodox Cultural Centre was established by the church to provide a library, museum, media studios and a conference hall, with the aim of preserving Coptic heritage.

The Coptic Church also oversees a massive media production arm running satellite channels and websites and producing films, books and newspapers, but these cultural artefacts are largely unseen in the national public sphere. An exception is the weekly newspaper *Watani* ('My Homeland'), which can be purchased alongside other Egyptian newspapers from public stores and not only from within the church. In fact, the editor, Yusef Sidhom, believes that up to 10% of the readership are Muslims. Yet the reality is that while some products of Coptic faith and culture are seen in the public sphere, the open performance of others or the perception that Copts have too much influence in the public sphere often leads to tensions.

In Iraq, too, the church is a key space in which Christian cultural life is performed, preserved and transmitted. Each denomination runs its own programme of social and educational services for its community. While the primary activity has been religious education, there are increasing numbers of publications, websites, radio stations and even satellite channels, such as Ishtar TV. Youth groups are another major focus. Again, churches are not simply places of worship but also act as social and cultural meeting places, with resources such as libraries and function rooms. Cultural centres were also established in Iraq, especially in the Kurdish region, where there has been more freedom to express Syriac culture since the 1990s – and these produce publications in Arabic and Syriac about the faith and history of the community. They also promote writers, music and theatre so that faith and the community spaces provided act as a cultural medium for the whole community and not only the practising members. This is supplemented by a vibrant music and literary scene in the Syriac language and specialised media such as the Assyrian International News Agency (AINA), established in the diaspora.

Christianity as a Majority Faith

The preceding discussion has focused on the context that applies to most of North Africa and West Asia, where Islam has become the religion of the majority and various forms of Arab culture prevail nationally. However, it must be noted that Lebanon is a major exception to that rule. Unlike the rest of the region, where Christians became a minority relative to Muslims centuries ago, Lebanese Christians were a numerical majority until recently. While it is unofficially acknowledged that they no longer retain this numerical strength, Christians maintain their strong influence and remain highly visible. Lebanese culture reflects this, with Christians prominent in all aspects of national life and Christianity forming a significant and public aspect of Lebanese culture, media, politics and society.

In Lebanon the churches ring their bells openly and Sunday is a day of rest. All the Christian festivals are national holidays, and icons and religious statues are commonly seen on roadsides and not just inside churches. One of Lebanon's most famous landmarks is the prominent statue of St Mary known as Our Lady of Lebanon at Jounieh, which looks down from an elevated vantage point and marks a shrine and an important site of pilgrimage. This high visibility of Christian faith and culture marks Lebanon out among the Arab nations. In fact, some Lebanese Christians, notably the Maronites, continue to distinguish themselves from Arab culture by reiterating the idea that Lebanese Christians are Phoenician or Aramaic and not Arab. They also emphasise Lebanon's connections with Western culture to distinguish themselves from Arab culture, and this is particularly important to Maronites who are in communion with the Catholic Church. This can partly explain the widespread use of the French language. The 1943 constitution included a compromise made by those who wanted to define Lebanon as an Arab state and those who objected, and that was to describe Lebanon as having an 'Arab face' – that is, not necessarily Arab, but having an Arab character. This was amended in later constitutions after the civil war, however, to describe Lebanon as being Arab in identity and belonging, thereby conceding that Lebanon is culturally and linguistically part of the Arab world. Nevertheless, the debates over Lebanese identity continue.

This tension between faith, culture and Arab/Islamic identity also applies to the Armenian communities that exist within a number of modern Arab states. The Armenians were historically spread across an area that is now Turkey, Iran, Georgia and Azerbaijan. Under the Ottoman Empire they were a separate millet with authority over their personal status affairs and, like other Eastern Christians, Armenians have a language and biblical heritage that distinguishes their denomination from that of their neighbours, both Muslim and Christian. Armenians do share a number of characteristics with the Eastern Christians living in Arab states, such as a narrative concerning the ancientness of the church and its apostolic foundation and the central role of the church in preserving and transmitting Armenian culture. Ninety-five per cent of Armenians are thought to belong to the Armenian Apostolic Church, which traces its origins to Saints Thaddeus and Bartholomew and represents one of five ancient Oriental Orthodox denominations. Another central narrative is that Armenia was the first nation to adopt Christianity as its state religion. These aspects merge faith and culture by tracing the history of Armenia to biblical heritage and emphasising the importance of place and rootedness in the region.

The experiences of Armenians in Arab lands are vast and varied, so I will focus here on the question of faith and culture in the modern Armenian state. The Armenians established a state after the First World War, but after just two years it was incorporated into the Soviet Union, and regained its independence only in 1991. This means that Armenian faith and culture have also been influenced by the regional context until modern times, despite the existence of the Armenian nation today. Perhaps because of the struggle to remain different from the Islamic culture of the Ottoman period and then Soviet culture, the Armenian Church remains central. Certainly the history of Armenian interactions with the nations and peoples surrounding Armenia plays a significant role in modern expressions of faith and culture. One of the central themes is the collective memory of the Armenian genocide under the Ottoman Empire, when Armenians were killed or forcibly displaced from their traditional territories in Turkey. Collective memory of the Armenian genocide and the religious infrastructure of the Armenian diaspora together provide a strong basis for mobilisation and Armenian identity. It is also a question that permeates the narratives of the Armenian state, which seeks recognition of the genocide and raises awareness about the process of cultural genocide it claims Turkey has continued to undertake.

The church is considered vital for counteracting cultural genocide and preserving Armenian culture and identity, both in the Armenian diaspora and in the national life of the Armenian state. Article 8.1 of the Armenian constitution states that 'The Republic of Armenia recognises the exclusive historical mission of the Armenian Apostolic Holy Church as a national church, in the spiritual life, development of the national culture and preservation of the national identity of the people of Armenia'. Despite this attachment to the church, Armenia's legacy as a former Soviet state has affected the relationship between faith and culture, so that strong identification with the church does not necessarily translate into widespread religious observance. This phenomenon is also present in other post-communist areas, such as Georgia, and demonstrates the vital cultural role of the church and faith even where religious observance has declined.

Conclusion

Despite the transition of much of this region from a Christian to a Muslim majority, land remains intertwined with the faith and culture of Eastern Christians, both for those remaining in the region and for those in the diasporas. Territory is a link to the history and heritage of Eastern Christians that connects faith and culture. Therefore, while Christian religious culture is distinct from the prevailing culture, it is also authentic and indigenous and not 'other', because land and faith are linked and together permeate cultural meaning-making. Eastern Christians have played prominent roles in Islamic civilisation at various periods, and as individual citizens Christians contribute strongly to the social, political, intellectual and cultural life of their nations.

Yet while Eastern Christians are a part of the local, national and regional cultures of North Africa and West Asia, their faith is not normally fully expressed through the public sphere. Instead, parallel but separate spaces are formed, often through the church, or at least using the faith-based community structures, in place to establish cultural centres, which act as community platforms. These separate spaces are vital for preserving the different social and cultural practices of Eastern Christians, so regardless of levels of religious observance, the church continues to act as cultural space, and faith as a significant cultural medium.

Exceptions can be found where Christians are numerically stronger. Lebanon is an exception in the Arab world and Armenia is a case where Christians are the national majority. In these cases the numerical strength of Christians is reflected in all aspects of national culture, as evidenced by the greater visibility of their faith traditions and the prominence of the church's role in national life. This has not isolated these Christians from the processes and dynamics that have impacted Christians in the rest of this region, however. Culture remains closely linked to the church and is often expressed and defined in relation to the faiths and cultures of neighbouring communities and states, which in this region tend to be Arab and Muslim-majority societies.

Bibliography

Donabed, Sargon, *Reforging a Forgotten History: Iraq and the Assyrians in the Twentieth Century* (Edinburgh: Edinburgh University Press, 2015).

Griffith, Sidney H., *The Church in the Shadow of the Mosque: Christians and Muslims in the World of Islam* (Princeton, NJ: Princeton University Press, 2008).

Iskander, Elizabeth, *Sectarian Conflict in Egypt: Coptic Media, Identity and Representation* (London: Routledge, 2012).

Kartveit, Bard, *Dilemmas of Attachment: Identity and Belonging Among Palestinian Christians* (Leiden: Brill, 2014).

Tadros, Mariz, *Copts at the Crossroads: The Challenges of Building Inclusive Democracy in Egypt* (Cairo: American University in Cairo Press, 2013).

Worship and Spirituality

Rima Nasrallah

Christianity in this part of the world has historically expressed itself in multifarious ways, languages and traditions, such that it is hard to compile them together. However, despite the great variety, the many traditions have developed within comparable contexts; have interacted, borrowed and reacted to each other; and express themselves today under similar circumstances. We shall therefore tackle this issue by looking at certain themes that have shaped and defined the worship and the spirituality of Christianity as it is lived today in North Africa and West Asia.

Worship, Language and Identity

Despite the fact that the great majority of Christians in the region live in Arabic-speaking countries and environments, most of the church traditions use a different specific and ancient language in worship. The Christians can be divided in a variety of ways and along many different lines, such as doctrine, language, geography or ecclesiology. However, today the language divide has come, in many instances, to override the doctrinal as well as the geographical groupings. It has recently acquired a weight in identity demarcation and is uniting communities that until recently were, to a certain extent, enemies. The five major language groups have for centuries lived alongside each other and experimented with the incorporation of each other's languages when circumstances demanded it. Yet, original 'pure' language (or as much of it as one can retrieve) and its use in liturgy has become a core element to preserve and re-appropriate.

The five different groups of languages we refer to are: the Syriac–Aramaic family, with the use of one form of Syriac in the liturgy; the Coptic family, with its roots mainly in Egypt; the Armenian family; the Byzantine-Greek family; and finally the languages of a variety of communities, both Catholic and Protestant, with their roots in Western countries. For the last group, language has been a more functional matter and therefore the appropriation of the Arabic language in the liturgical context has been easier.

All these languages have been in use since the dawn of Christianity. Centuries of doctrinal controversies and mutual excommunications re-grouped Christians along doctrinal lines, such as the Chalcedonians, the non-Chalcedonians and the pre-Chalcedonians. Even if, at the grass-roots level and in rural areas, the borders have always been more fluid, foreign interference from both outside the Christian communities as well as outside the East demarcated these borders more clearly. The Ottoman millet system – under which the various religious communities were allowed to rule themselves as far as their internal affairs were concerned – sharpened the divide and sometimes forced certain groups to exist one under the other artificially, as was the case with the Syriac Orthodox and the Armenians. In addition, Catholic missionaries as early as the sixteenth century were concerned about clear demarcations and purity of the faith. As they focused on their 'foster children' and prospective Uniate churches, it was their mission to eliminate liturgical and ritual elements that were not in accordance with the practices and beliefs of the Roman Catholic Church. In the case of the Maronite Church, a clear distinction from what was pejoratively referred to as the Jacobite Church (Syriac Orthodox) was of paramount importance.

However, a combination of events and movements promoted a different regrouping, where language acquired other dimensions. The horrific genocides and massacres of the beginning of the twentieth century against Armenians, Syriacs and Assyrians resulted in the uprooting and displacement of small communities into new areas in the Middle East, with different cultural and linguistic styles. The now small communities had to deal with the double challenge of dealing with their past and finding ways to survive in the present. While in their daily lives many of them had to gradually adopt the Arabic language in its local dialects, it is in their liturgy that they found space to express their identity and the continuation of the culture that otherwise had been lost.

Soon after, promises of possible homelands made by the Mandate nations in the Middle East for the various ethnic minorities fed lingering desires for self-governance and reawakened ethnic and nationalistic feelings. The church in its rituals and continuity was the perfect ally for fostering these frustrated identities, and language was one of the first identity markers that needed to be reinforced. A return to a heavier usage of old forms of the language became the trend in liturgy.

An element that contributed even more to this attention to ethnicity and specificity was Vatican II and its constitution on the Sacred Liturgy. A call to a rediscovery of roots and appreciation for the particular forms of worship encouraged many Uniate churches and in turn their Orthodox counterparts to dig deeper into their heritage and to reincorporate a language that had sometimes been replaced by Latin in the Catholic segment.

Today's tumultuous events in the Middle East have brought more pressure on questions pertaining to the existence and continuity of these shrinking and threatened communities. Dealing with the issue of the large diaspora and pondering how to keep the link with the mother church led to the issue of language again. Yet, at this point, communities that can no longer claim a majority or seniority status have to ally together under the banner of language, creating a feel of internal cohesion for the sake of survival. It is in this context that, for example, the Syriac-speaking family – which for centuries have been divided along doctrinal lines – could come together today and create Syriac centres of study and seminaries that can host and train Chalcedonians (Maronite), non-Chalcedonians (Syriac Orthodox) and pre-Chalcedonians (Assyrian) together.

Time, Space and the Material World

The liturgical heritage in North Africa and West Asia is a product of influences that overlapped and mixed at different times and moulded a plethora of liturgical practices. Jewish-Semitic, Persian-Babylonian, Constantinopolitan-Byzantine, Jerusalem-Byzantine, Syriac, Alexandrian, Latin and even a flavour of global Evangelical strands constitute the layers of the worship experience. While these various combinations produced liturgies that share a family feel, they are not the same. Eastern and Oriental Churches are known for their rich collections of anaphoras, some – like the Syriac Orthodox – counting more than 80 versions. Nevertheless, from the sumptuous and majestic Byzantine tradition to the extremely bare Assyrian liturgy, certain understandings of time, space and the material world clearly mark these communities at worship.

All these, with the exception of the more recent family of Protestant and Evangelical churches, reflect in their liturgies a certain understanding of time that stretches from creation till the end of time. Church structure as well as the annual liturgical rhythm present the faithful with 'all' of history. Churches that are particularly marked by a Byzantine tradition confront the worshippers, via their iconography and frescoes, with a time that precedes our presence and continues beyond it. Not only are biblical events visually and prominently portrayed, but so also are prophets, saints, bishops and future hopes. Most churches are built to reflect the cosmos, with a dome painted with clouds and stars as well as heavenly creatures evoking cosmic dimensions and events. Time in general is sanctified and the liturgical year offers a continuous succession of seasons centred around Easter and punctuated by fasts and feasts with readings that give a reminder for each tradition of its place in salvation history. One can think here of the fast or Rogation of the Ninevites observed by the Church of the East, through which a link is drawn to Jonah's activity in Nineveh.

Not only does the year have a rhythm, but so too does the week, and the hours of the day are structured around prayer times as well as dietary observance. The liturgical year, the week as well as the hours all follow the rhythm of the life of Christ and the remembrance of the Virgin Mary. A week commemorates the Annunciation on Wednesday. The cross, the dead and the martyrs are remembered on Friday, and Sunday re-enacts the resurrection with liturgical prayers and acclamations. The day follows a similar pattern: matins commemorate the resurrection, while vespers commemorate the cross. Churches and the faithful today pick and choose what they participate in and design their own liturgical time, sometimes borrowing from several traditions at once.

This approach to time as being eternal is depicted in the Eucharistic liturgies and their movements. All Eastern and Oriental liturgies have highly developed rites of preparation that take place behind closed curtains or screens. Even more, Eucharistic liturgies are preceded by matins or morning prayers performed by priest and deacons. Churches that follow their tradition in a strict manner observe the rites of the preparation of the clergy the preceding evening. Therefore, when the worshippers join a Eucharistic liturgy on a Sunday morning they are joining something that has already been set in motion. They join a worship that started before them and will continue after they leave, carrying home the blessed bread (*antidoron*) . This perception is intensified by the renowned length of Eastern and Oriental liturgies (even if today attempts are made to shorten them) as well as the movement of prayers and litanies that carry many repetitions and cycles. Furthermore, one cannot help but be reminded of how ancient that faith is when hearing chants that carry tunes of Byzantium or Pharaonic Egypt, or when listening to liturgical languages such as the Krabar classical Armenian dialect, today incomprehensible to the laity, and in obsolete elements of the liturgies such as the dismissal of the catechumens and the closing of non-existent doors. One of the purposes of these liturgies is to take up the worshipper into their long history and witness.

This understanding of time and history, and the role each of these traditions plays within it, makes of today's threats of discontinuity, assimilation and loss of identity due to emigration and the shrinking of the communities an even more existential struggle. 'History' itself and the concept of time are threatened. The understandings of both space and the material world are also specific in this context. The liturgy and worship in these churches find their epitome in physical sanctuaries that parallel the universe in their architecture, giving the entire created world a sacramental dimension and spilling over to impinge on the daily lives of people in their private homes, in their communities and in their pilgrimage places.

All liturgical celebrations, no matter how poor the community is or how simple the rite is, are rich with vestments, liturgical objects, icons, images, candles, oil, water, food and relics. The material world, due to a general (even if diverse) Semitic influence, is embraced. Mainly within the churches of the Syriac tradition, the world is seen as creation transformed (as Ephrem the Syrian proposed). Despite a very important and ever-present monastic heritage that might suggest a rejection of the world, it is not the materiality of the world that is despised. On the contrary, the doctrine of the incarnation – appropriated in various ways in the different traditions – offers a new place for the material that can assist the symbolic expressions in worship and liturgy. This is expressed both in the presence of material objects and in their use in a highly stylised and theatrical manner, such as during the complex rites around the preparation of the bread and wine, the small and large processions of gospel and elements, or in the funerary procession on Good Friday that involves a shroud and flowers.

Not only are the created world and material objects liturgically important, but the human body in its movement and participation is also vital to all liturgical expressions. Eucharistic liturgies, feasts, private devotions in homes (most often around an altar) as well as pilgrimages all rely on the involvement of the body. The liturgies of the East are highly participatory and multisensory. The first step taken in church is a threefold total immersion in baptismal waters. Most traditions practise total-immersion baptisms, followed by generous chrismation with myron on all extremities and sense organs, as well as processions and communion. In liturgical celebrations, the faithful participate with chants and responses, in processions and prostrations, in kissing Scripture and icons, in lighting candles and inhaling incense, in eating and drinking as well as fasting and kneeling.

Moreover, Christians in the East today intensify this bodily involvement and participation with new or rediscovered practices. In Egypt, for example, it is a tradition among Copts to tattoo their wrists with a Coptic cross, particularly on Mount Mokattam. In Lebanon and Syria, one can frequently spot people dressed in the blue outfit of Mary or the green and red gown of St Elijah or the black tunic of St Charbel as they dedicate themselves to saints in prayer or as a result of pledges. Crosses and icons are worn as jewellery by both males and females. Rosaries are carried around necks and wrists. A fabric belt brought from shrines and worn under one's clothing is also common, as are a number of pins, bags containing blessed objects or other small relics. The sacred remains close to one's body at all times and blessings and protection are confirmed.

Besides being moving bodies and decorated bodies, these bodies are also eating bodies. Food is crucial in much of the spiritual context of the region. Orthodox theologians see a tight relationship between regular eating and Eucharistic eating, one giving meaning to the other. Religiosity is expressed in the acts of fasting and then feasting, where bodies are controlled and subdued and then richly enchanted by lavish and communal eating. Fasting and feasting, though targeting the body, have traditionally been communal as well. When Jesuit missionaries arrived in North Africa and West Asia in the seventeenth century they attempted to transform this communal behaviour into a more personal, individual act, yet people continue to approach fasting and feasting as participation in the community of believers and solidarity with fellow practitioners. Many feasts – such as the Assumption/Dormition of the Virgin Mary, the Feast of the Finding of the Cross, or the Feast of Mar Zaia – are celebrated around a large pot of food that community members take turns in stirring. Women and men of all ages are included in preparing a multitude of dishes, sweets and drinks to be consumed communally over an extended period of time, all night long or all weekend.

Pilgrimages, Saints and Apparitions

One cannot but acknowledge the importance of the Holy Land historically for the three Abrahamic religions. Jerusalem has been the object of various conflicts because of its holy position in the eyes of many and it is still in its environment seen as the pilgrimage place par excellence. However, for local Christians, pilgrimage is not only related to one place but is a mode of living. Local Christians, most of whom for political reasons cannot visit the Holy Land, have their own plethora of pilgrimage destinations. Visiting what is considered a holy place, be it a monastery, a birthplace of a saint or a scene of a miracle, is very natural. The borders between pilgrimage and tourism or recreation are very thin, and local Christians do not feel uncomfortable joining a sacred visit to a shrine with a day out with friends and family. Yet pilgrimages and visits to holy places are also connected and related to a deep quest and desire for healing. As is the case with all pilgrimage, it is the sick who are brought to holy sites with a request for healing or after being healed as an act of thanksgiving. Ex-votos representing the request are offered in the shrines. The Syrian Saydnaya monastery's inner chapel, for example, is wallpapered with metal sheets in the shape of hands, feet and other body parts. St Charbel's shrine in Lebanon is covered by heaps of crutches and wheelchairs testifying to miracles.

Marriage and childbearing are particularly popular reasons for pilgrims to flock to certain destinations and seek the intervention of saints or places known for such requests. Unmarried daughters in Cairo are pledged and parents and family members pray for their marriage by visiting certain places. Women seeking to bear children are brought to shrines where they spend the night in prayer, light candles or even, in extreme cases, eat the wicks of the candles. From Egypt to Iraq, the land is speckled with monasteries and shrines hosting not only Christians but also their Muslim and Druze neighbours, all seeking similar interventions.

It is not only an abundance of holy sites that is apparent in this region, but also a visible presence of saints. Each country and each tradition has its own traditional as well as contemporary saints. However, saints cross boundaries very easily and tend to become common to many, regardless of denominational divisions. Their pictures and images can be seen along the streets, on electricity poles and church walls, as well as on car widows, inside home altars and shared via Facebook posts. During the past 30 years, a number of new saints were canonised by Rome as well as declared by local patriarchal sees. Interestingly, many of the new saints are either persons who have known a long history of suffering, such as the Lebanese St Rafqa, or groups of recent martyrs, such as the victims of the Armenian genocide.

Nevertheless, the Virgin Mary remains the most prominent of all saints. The majority of pilgrimage sites are related to her and a number of days and weeks are dedicated to her. As early as the third century, traces of Marian devotion are found in Eastern churches. The Council of Ephesus in 431 and the pronouncement of the title Theotokos accentuated this devotion and formalised it. Eastern Orthodox churches are both visually and liturgically tangled with the Theotokos. St Ephrem's poetry, in the Syriac tradition, venerates Mary as the symbol of the complex and extraordinary relation between the church and Christ; even in the Church of the East the consistent rejection of the title Theotokos never prevented its theologians from elevating Mary. The elaborate Feast of the Dormition of Our Lady (15 August for the Greek Orthodox, Syriacs and Maronites; 22 August for the Copts), preceded by 15 days of fasting, is still the spiritual and social highlight of the summer. Shrines and pilgrimage sites dedicated to Mary are visited by the faithful from every tradition and religion. Yet George Khodr, eminent Orthodox theologian, underlines that in the Eastern Orthodox tradition, 'Mary is never separated from her Son, either in the hymnological domain or in the pictorial' ('The mother of God the Theotokos and her role in God's plan for our salvation', *Ecumenical Review* 60:1–2 (January–April 2008), 29). Popular icons such as the Hodigitria (Guide), Eleusa (Tender Mercy) and Oranta (Praying) often found today in homes and churches testify to this.

Nonetheless, this rich, ancient and diverse Mariology of the East runs parallel to and in fusion with other images of Mary. With the arrival of the Jesuit missionaries in the seventeenth century, the iconography of the East was derogated and immediately supplanted by a different kind of art, of Italian and French provenance. Jesuit missionaries introduced a very different image of Mary through both the arts and new forms of piety. The Mary they introduced was more feminine and realistic than the one depicted in Eastern icons and appears mostly alone, without her son. With the missionaries, new themes were introduced, such as Mary's Ascension (in place of her Dormition), the Immaculate Conception, the Lady of the Rosary and the crowning of the Virgin. May became the Marian month and new practices of pilgrimage, harsh bodily exercises of devotion and flowery processions with the statue of the Virgin Mary were introduced.

Eastern Christians appropriated this new piety and blended what they knew of Mary with this new emphasis on meekness and purity. In popular piety these different images run both in parallel and in merged forms. New dogmas and apparitions in the nineteenth and twentieth centuries increased Marian devotion and practices. Some of the apparitions experienced in Jerusalem and in Cairo had major impacts both sociologically and spiritually. These fuelled national feelings and reinforced political positions, particularly during times of war, such as the apparitions of the Virgin at Zeitoun in Egypt between 1968 and 1970. In Jordan and Palestine a form of mysticism has developed, and visions are experienced in connection with the Virgin Mary. At the beginning of the twentieth century, a statue of the Virgin Mary was erected on a mountain overlooking the Lebanese coast to commemorate 50 years of the doctrine of the Immaculate Conception, its size too formidable to be shaken by Vatican II's modernising enterprise and its more biblical position on Mary and her liturgical retrenching. Today's piety extends beyond the borders of the region, and many believers visit places such as Lourdes and Medjugorje or adorn their homes with objects and images imported from the international scene.

The Context of Islam

Despite the doctrinal and liturgical differences among the Christians of this region, all these communities have lived for hundreds of years under similar circumstances and experienced comparable events in a rather dominant and general Islamic environment. An outsider might be struck by the similarities between certain worship practices and piety among Eastern Christians and Muslims. Coptic worship practices of total prostration, certain Syriac tunes, or the separation of men and women in the worship space and the covering of the head with a veil are some of the obvious similarities. As mentioned above, many Muslims visit Christian pilgrimage sites, share in the veneration of Mary, appropriate certain Old Testament prophets, and parallel prayer and fasting practices known in Christian monastic circles. Christians and Muslims in the East have lived and developed very close to each other and their spiritual and cultural practices have pollinated each other.

Nevertheless, the content of Christian spirituality developed in contrast with many elements of Islam. An emphasis on the incarnation, on the coming of God into our world, is a major theme, in contrast to the Muslim understanding of God. The late Orthodox Patriarch Ignatius IV emphasised the incarnation as the great contrast with Islamic spirituality, when God not only came closer to humans but became one of us at a certain time in a certain place, in the Middle East itself, changing the understanding and the approach to the value of the human and the created world and the way humans relate to God. The greatness of God emphasised in the regular Islamic call to prayer is carried by Eastern Christians and plays as a refrain in their ears but is balanced by a closeness expressed sacramentally in public and private worship.

Living and developing with Islam means that practices as well as doctrines react and are ever challenged by this reality. Throughout the ages, the development and the visibility of Christian worship were affected by the Islamic environment's fluctuating level of tolerance and acceptance. This has impacted the way the different communities across the region understand themselves and practise their faith. It has meant that in many cases Christian communities became introverted and careful about spiritual expression. Liturgical development went hand in hand with the level of religious freedom in the country, and innovation in liturgical matters came most of the time through the door of coping rather than creativity.

Restrictions on some worship practices, coupled with a history of massacres and displacement, are reflected in liturgical practices through a general undertone of sadness. Most Eastern liturgies dedicate a considerable segment to the commemoration of martyrs and remembrance of the dead. This is highlighted in the Armenian and the Syriac traditions and heard clearly in the Assyrian pre-Eucharistic hymn for the dead.

Besides living under or alongside Islam, and maybe also because of it, the Christians of the region are characterised by a religious ontology. The arrival of modernity and the Arab Renaissance did not dramatically alter the general sense of omnipresence of mystery that reigns in this part of the world. The worldview of the Eastern Christian is essentially religious, and separation of the secular and the religious realms is rarely possible.

The Christian East in a Global World

The twentieth and twenty-first centuries have witnessed great changes in a region emerging from a long imperial and colonial or Mandated period. The twentieth century started with massacres and starvation affecting many Christian communities and redistributing them inside the region and throughout the world. This reshuffling of Christian communities continues in different forms in the twenty-first century and the repercussions on the worship and spirituality of these communities are still to be fully analysed. One of the obvious results, though, is the diaspora of Eastern Christians throughout the world and its interaction with mostly Western spiritualities and ontologies. Eastern and Oriental Christians have either formed diaspora communities in Europe, the Americas and Australia or merged with existing Christianity or secular society. This fact plays a great role in the self-understanding and spirituality of the churches. The Maronite Church in its patriarchal synod of 2006 addressed this issue extensively and re-evaluated its liturgical theology in its light. The Greek Orthodox patriarchal see, in less formal ways, ponders similar questions. Assyrians, Armenians and Syriac Orthodox all have to redefine their understanding of ecclesiology and liturgy in this new context.

Another major event affecting the Christians of the East has been the creation of the State of Israel in 1948. Not only did this event shake the area as a result of consequent wars and waves of Palestinian refugees, but it also created a conundrum regarding the Christian position towards the Holy Land and the use and understanding of the Old Testament. The Holy Land, now inaccessible to most Christians, became for some a deep and frustrated desire and for others a more spiritualised and abstract concept. Scriptural readings and hymnody were both affected as selective readings, term substitutions and, sometimes, total omissions were practised in order to avoid mixing theological terms with political connotations. This remains a wound and a predicament for all Christians.

The twentieth century brought not only massacres and displacements but also spiritual revivals. The Greek Orthodox Church witnessed the establishment of its massive Orthodox Youth Movement at the beginning of last century. This Movement led to a spiritual revival, monastic renewal, evangelical engagement and liturgical awakening. The Coptic Church experienced a similar impulse through its Sunday School Movement, which started earlier in the nineteenth century and intensified in the twentieth, bearing fruits both in monastic renewal and in diaconal and pastoral life. As for the Maronite Church, its trajectory has been more complex, with its intensive contact with Rome, yet in its own way it has experienced a self-reinvention in its liturgical practices, with a distinctive move to a more Syriac flavour adapted to Lebanese culture.

All these movements translated into new hymnology, choirs and prayers as well as a revival of old tunes and poetry. New worship books, hymnals and lectionaries have been published in recent years and made available in the pews. More participation in liturgical moments is promoted and these are more visible and transparent. Many churches have adopted new technology, such as video projectors, electronic keyboards, microphones and pre-recorded music, to enhance participation and visibility.

This has been accompanied by a reinvention of monasticism, in which old monastic and even ascetic forms can coexist with new open monasteries that can host retreats, meetings and youth events. Monasteries have become more and more central in the lives of worshippers in ways that fit each liturgical family.

Coupled with this is a focus on the youth. Within Uniate churches the focus on the youth started early on and inspired the other Eastern churches. Today, a multitude of youth organisations and spiritual associations host young people and keep them close to their tradition in the new spirit of renewal. In many cases this spirit of renewal comes with Charismatic undertones, where massive assemblies of young people gather to worship with body and spirit in a manner reminiscent of large Evangelical youth events elsewhere in the world.

The last centuries have also witnessed the arrival of new types of spiritualities in this region. Though small in relative numbers, Protestant and Evangelical groups have been forming in the East since the mid-nineteenth century through contact with American, British and German missionaries. The Protestant groups in their wide variety – Anglican, Presbyterian, Baptist and Pentecostal – created a new spiritual reality to be dealt with and to be challenged by. Despite their small numbers, they had a great impact, via their schools and social involvement, on the spirituality of the East. They introduced forms of worship and ecclesiology different from those common in the area. Evangelicals emphasised from the start the centrality of the Bible. They encouraged the involvement of the laity, individual spiritual relation with God, introspection, the desire for spiritual growth and religious education. They introduced new musical styles, architectural layouts and understandings of materiality and sacramentality. Though the relationships between Protestants in general and the older churches have not always been smooth, their spiritual impact cannot be overestimated. It is their presence that inspired the Sunday School Movement in Egypt and drove many churches to seek greater biblical knowledge and to appropriate newer forms of Christian education. Today, Protestants are known for their simplicity in worship styles and their focus on the cognitive aspect of faith, expressed through elaborate didactic sermons and prayers.

Conclusion

Nowhere can the long and tumultuous history of the Christian presence in North Africa and West Asia be more clearly witnessed than in the complexity and diversity of its worship practices. With the increased pressure, migration and emigration, its richness is in danger of either being lost or becoming obsolete. In order to avoid dissolving into host communities, the diaspora response is in most cases a closing in on oneself and clinging to old customs. The Christians of the region are facing critical times in which they have to discover how to carry their heritage into new contexts without turning their vibrant spirituality into museology.

Bibliography

Badr, Habib (ed.), *Christianity: A History in the Middle East* (Beirut: Middle East Council of Churches, 2005).

Heyberger, Bernard, *Chrétiens du Monde Arabe: Un Archipel en Terre d'Islam* (Paris: Editions Autrement, 2003).

O'Mahony, Anthony and Emma Loosley (eds), *Eastern Christianity in the Modern Middle East* (London: Routledge, 2010).

Parry, Ken (ed.), *The Blackwell Companion to Eastern Christianity* (Chichester: Wiley-Blackwell, 2010).

Valognes, Jean-Pierre, *Vie et Mort des Chrétiens d'Orient: Des origines á nos jours* (Paris: Librairie Aethème Fayard, 1994).

Theology

George F. Sabra

Two preliminary remarks need to be made before a discussion of theology in North Africa and West Asia (NAWA) is attempted. The first remark is geographical and terminological: geographically, this essay is supposed to cover the region of NAWA but, since theological output and reflection have been most intense and most prevalent in the part of the region that includes Syria, Lebanon, Jordan, Palestine/Israel and Egypt, the designation 'Middle East' is used below. The second remark is about the use of the term 'theology'. Theology could mean different things to different people and traditions. Theology could mean 'religious thought or speech in general'; it could also mean, more restrictively, as in traditional Eastern Orthodox discourse, 'the doctrine of God in himself', as distinct from the doctrine of God in relation to the creation ('economy'); or it could mean the intellectual discipline of the Christian faith reflecting on and expressing the truth of God and all that relates to God. It is under the umbrella of this last sense that 'theology' is used here.

Hence, theology here means reflection on the Christian faith and its relation to various aspects of intellectual, social and political life in the Middle East in the contemporary period. The discussion is thus limited to what would fall under 'systematic theology' and so does not cover theological productions in the areas of biblical studies, church history, liturgy, Christian ethics, or hagiographic, devotional, homiletical and spiritual writings. A survey of Middle Eastern Christian publications in Arabic from 1950 to 1990, conducted and published by the Middle East Council of Churches, showed that the majority of writings were of a devotional or homiletical nature and that very little had been produced in the area of systematic reflection on contemporary issues of thought and life. This is still more or less the case in the second decade of the third millennium, but with an increase in historical and liturgical theological writings. There are today writings, of both devotional and apologetic character, emerging as a response to the current experiences of suffering and persecution of Christians. Contemporary confessional writings stress the distinctive historical, spiritual and doctrinal identities of the different traditions. None of these, however, falls within the purview of this essay. They are 'theology' in the widest sense of the word, and not in the specific sense of the scholarly undertaking of the Christian faith reflecting on its object (God) and its situation in the contemporary world – namely the task of systematic theology.

Covering theology in the Middle East is not an easy task, not only due to the paucity of theological writings proper but also because the variety of Christian traditions in the Middle East is so large that one cannot simply trace and describe the development and characteristics of a single movement of thought. The various Christian traditions have different conceptions of what it means to 'do theology' or what counts as theology, due to the vast cultural differences among them concerning the approach and method of the theological enterprise. Moreover, the various traditions and churches live in different social, political and cultural contexts that shape their theological outlooks, despite the fact that they all live in one area called the Middle East. Thus, it seems best to approach the topic thematically. In what follows, major themes that dominate theological reflection will be briefly introduced and their most important directions will be pointed out.

Following David Tracy's identification of the social location of theology as church, academy or society, it can clearly be seen that theology in the Middle East is inspired mainly, but not exclusively, by issues arising from society. Theological reflection in the Middle East is not so much inspired or challenged by Christian faith's conversation with philosophy and the sciences, nor primarily by the need to clarify and interpret the gospel to the church. It is, rather, prompted by political, social and inter-religious questions and issues that arise from the context of the life of the churches in that region of the world. Two main contexts form the world of Middle Eastern theology and provide it with issues, questions and challenges: Middle Eastern Christianity lives in the larger world of Islam, and it lives in the world of the Arab–Israeli conflict. These two worlds or contexts are obviously inter-related, and many issues and themes overlap from one to the other, but for the sake of clarity it is helpful to view and treat them as two distinct areas of theological interest and reflection. Needless to say, each one is actually a very general theme that includes many subthemes.

Christianity in the World of Islam

Christians in the Middle East have been living in the world of Islam for the last 14 centuries. Muslims have been the rulers and shapers of society throughout those centuries. Although Islamic rule has taken various forms, Christians have been viewed and treated as religious minorities in the abode of Islam. Christian thinkers and theologians have tried to deal with this situation of being a minority in lands dominated by another religion, and this has given rise to many themes for theological reflection, including (1) making theological sense of Islam and the role of Christianity in the world of Islam; (2) Christian–Muslim dialogue; and (3) questions of cultural and religious identity and the political order of society.

Christian theologies of Islam

Trying to make theological sense of Islam is an old undertaking among Christians in the Middle East; it is the natural result of the historical encounter between the two religions. Many of the positions developed early on in the history of that encounter have been re-presented today in somewhat different forms, but new ones have been articulated as well. One of the earliest theological responses to Islam was the view, first articulated by John of Damascus in the eighth century, that Islam is a kind of Christian heresy. This view continues to be maintained today, not only in the popular Christian mind but also by some writers and theologians. The work of Abu Musa al-Hariri (an alias for a twentieth-century Lebanese Maronite scholar), which purports to show that Islam is basically a revival of the Ebionite heresy, is a prime example of this school of thought. Al-Hariri nowhere employs the word 'heresy', but the implication of the identification of Islam with Ebionite teachings is clear enough. The writer's intent is not to denigrate Islam but to show that, since the 'Christians' (*nasara*) of the Qur'an have nothing to do with the orthodox Christians of the seventh century or the Christians of today, all attempts to create a rapprochement between Christianity and Islam today on the basis of the Qur'an are misleading and erroneous. Christianity is not what Muhammad thought it to be, and Islam after the Qur'an is not what Muhammad intended. Such a conclusion, if acknowledged by both sides, would have vast implications for Christian–Muslim dialogue.

Islam as a legitimate form of Jewish Christianity is another Christian theological reading of the Arabian religion. The works of Al-Ustadh al-Haddad (an alias for a twentieth-century Syrian Melkite priest who lived and wrote mostly in Lebanon) claim to show that Islam is nothing but the Arabic version of Jewish Christianity which dates back to the times of the Apostle Paul; the *nasara* of the Qur'an are those Jews who believed in Christ but who had separated from the apostles after the Council of Jerusalem (Acts 15). Al-Haddad concludes that Muslims and Christians are actually of one religion, in the sense that they derive from one origin. What unites them is the Naziritism (*nusraniyyah*) of the Qur'an, but that is not Christianity. Yet this common ground between them, the Nazirite origin, could and should foster mutual understanding and dialogue between Christianity and Islam today. Islam is not a Christian heresy; it is a legitimate continuation of the Jewish response and adherence to Jesus and his message.

Another theological position, Islam as part of salvation history, has been propounded by two Lebanese Maronite priests and scholars of Islam,

Michel Hayek (1928–2005) and Youakim Moubarac (1924–2005). Both relate Muhammad and Islam to figures and events in the Old Testament. Hayek considers Islam to be an 'Ishmaelism'. Just as Isaac is father of the Jews (then Christians), Ishmael is father of the Arabs and Muslims, and both are part of God's plan of salvation. Hayek reinterprets Romans 9–11 to include Ishmael and his descendants in the Abrahamic blessings to all nations. Islam thus informs Christianity about something that escapes it – the fulfilment of the promise to Ishmael. Islam is neither a Christian heresy nor a Jewish sect; it is of Abrahamic origin. It is God's dispensation to the Arabs, the descendants of Ishmael, who also prefigures Christ. Moubarac is within the same sphere when he argues for Islam as an 'Abrahamism', namely, an authentic monotheism – an Abrahamic religion like Judaism and Christianity. The origin of Islam is thus in Abraham, not his descendants. Islam is the Arabic version of Abraham's faith, and so it is an authentic and autonomous religion. Muhammad is not an innovator, but a reformer; he simply repeats the monotheistic message of Abraham but Arabises it.

Islam as a religion that affirms Christian truths is yet another direction for theological thinking about the Arabian religion. This is sometimes called the Christian reading of the Qur'an. While it does not theologise Islam as a whole, and so refrains from offering a theological theory of Islam, this approach studies the Qur'anic references to Christ and tries to show that many of its teachings and statements confirm Christian belief about him, provided that the Islamic text is examined critically. Titles given to Christ in the Qur'an, such as 'word from God' and 'spirit from Him', are, it is claimed, indicative of a high Christology that traditional interpreters of the Islamic holy text have failed or refused to see. This theological direction is usually associated with the Orthodox theologian George Khodr, among others. The theological starting point is the patristic teaching (by Irenaeus of Lyons and Justin Martyr) about the *logos spermatikos*. The *logos* was incarnated in Jesus the Christ, but its presence in the cosmos predates the historical event of Christ. Thus there is truth outside the Bible and the church, but it is not independent of the truth of Christ, and it is not final.

Finally, Islam as an independent and legitimate religious approach to God is a theological direction that is just beginning to see the dawn in the Middle East, specifically in Lebanon. The Lebanese philosopher and former Greek Catholic priest Mouchir Aoun has adopted this position of religious pluralism in his theology of religions. Influenced by the works of John Hick and Paul Knitter, Aoun argues that God uses religions as a means of revelation to different peoples in different times and contexts. Only God is absolute, and our religions are always relative. Islam, thus, like Christianity and Judaism and other religions, is a legitimate religious approach to the absolute mystery that is God. This pluralist approach to the theology of religions is well known in the West, but it has not yet become a school of thought in the Middle East, for it does not seem to have many intellectual adherents. Nevertheless, it is there, and it might eventually become more widespread and find more vocal support.

These are the major theological directions that express the Middle Eastern Christian theological concern with Islam. This is an area of thought and reflection that has occupied thinkers and theologians and continues to do so. It has given rise to many creative attempts to think theologically about Islam.

Christian–Muslim dialogue

Very closely related to the foregoing, and in many ways inspired by and based on it, the theme of dialogue between Christianity and Islam occupies an important place in the theological production of Middle Eastern Christians. The activity of dialogue itself is a wide undertaking that was originally (from the mid-twentieth century in Lebanon) and for quite some time initiated and sustained mainly by Christians, although today many initiatives are coming from the Islamic side as well. It covers the writings of theologians and scholars of religious studies but also the work of centres of dialogue at the main institutions of higher learning. Lebanon is home to the largest number of centres and organisations that are involved in dialogue, with academic institutions such as the University of St Joseph (Roman Catholic), the University of Balamand (Orthodox), the Harissa Seminary of St Paul (Melkite) and the Near East School of Theology (Protestant), among others, housing centres and forums of dialogue that regularly organise activities and issue publications. Other regional organisations, such as the Middle East Council of Churches and the Arab Group for Muslim-Christian Dialogue, as well as local ones, such as ADYAN (Lebanon), also organise activities and encounters of dialogue and produce writings. Following the end of the Lebanese civil war (1975–90), and most likely because of it, significant events and encounters of inter-religious dialogue have produced numerous publications. The themes of dialogue are wide and varied; they range from classical theological topics – such as the Trinity, Christology, revelation, prophecy and prophethood, the historicity and redemptive significance of the death of Jesus, the holy texts, and the essence of religion – to more ethical topics (justice, mercy, violence, bioethical issues), as well as political, social and cultural issues such as common living, co-citizenship, human rights, secularism, relation to the West, peace, response to modernity and education. To be sure, 'dialogue' itself – its nature, value, goals – is also a topic of reflection and discussion. Theologians and scholars on the Christian side, such as Adel Theodore Khoury, George Khodr, Paul Khoury, Mouchir Aoun, Kirillus Bustros and Tarek Mitri, are some of the prominent names in this dialogical undertaking, publishing mainly in the Arabic language. Present-day Christian–Muslim intellectual interaction is no longer predominantly polemical and apologetic as it was in the past. It is now dialogical – but dialogue is understood differently by those engaged in it. The dominant underlying assumption is that dialogue is a means of clarifying and understanding each other's positions and beliefs, an exercise for eliminating misunderstandings and misconceptions through comparing and contrasting the two religions, with the aim of enhancing peaceful coexistence and better relations between their adherents.

If, however, dialogue is to be understood in the profound Platonic sense of a common journey on the way to seeking truth or, following Jürgen Moltmann's affirmation that 'truth for us human beings is dialogical' and 'only in dialogue with each other can we discover truth', then the undertaking of Christian–Muslim dialogue in the Middle East, especially in its theological dimension, is not yet there. To engage in a theological dialogue between Christianity and Islam on this level requires much more self-criticism and self-questioning than are available or possible in the present day. Dialogue partners are rarely on the same level of willingness and ability to apply objective, historical-critical and rational methods in self-understanding and self-questioning, which is a prerequisite for any fruitful profound and genuine dialogue. There are small but significant attempts, however. A recent joint publication entitled *Divine Hospitality: The Theology of the Other in Christianity and Islam* (by Fadi Daou and Nayla Tabbara, Lebanon: Saint Paul Publications/Adyan, 2011) is a promising beginning, despite the fact that the overall atmosphere of Islamic religious resurgence in the region is not at all conductive to the dialogical endeavours.

Cultural/religious identity and political order

Living among Muslims and under Islamic rule for 14 centuries, Christians of the Middle East have had to face questions relating to their cultural identity and heritage, as well as to the order of society. Being a religious minority in the larger political world of Islam, and though often tolerated and well treated – at least by the standards of the day – Christians were, nevertheless, always considered as not fully equal to Muslims in the political and social orders. This status, sometimes called 'second-class citizenship', has occupied the minds of Christian thinkers, especially since the late nineteenth century and up until the present day. What does it mean to be a Christian in the larger Islamic world? What is the cultural identity of Christians in the Middle East and Arab world? What is the best political order for such a common living?

There have been two tendencies in the attempt to face such questions. One direction has been to seek common cultural and social ground with the larger Islamic majority, thus to adopt the position that the cultural heritage of Arab Christians is Arab and Islamic civilisation. Identifying with the majority in this way enabled Christians to say that their causes and outlooks are no different from those of their Muslim co-citizens and that the best political order for the common living of Muslims and Christians is that of secularism. If Christians in the Arab and Islamic countries espoused the causes and aspirations of their co-citizens and did not identify themselves as socially, politically and culturally distinctive, then they would be treated as equal citizens and they could build, together with their Muslim partners, a secular, just and equal society (and state). The political versions of this option have been Arab nationalism and pan-Syrian nationalism, and many Christian thinkers have allied themselves with those ideologies, while theologians such as George Khodr, Gregoire Haddad and Andrea Zaki supplied the theological basis for such an outlook.

The other tendency is much more cautious and conservative in relation to identifying totally with Arab and Islamic culture. While Christians in the Middle East participate genuinely in Arab and Islamic culture and civilisation, that is not the sole constituent of their cultural or social identity. Being part of the Mediterranean culture, which is not purely Arab, or having roots in their own pre-Islamic cultural identity (such as Phoenician and Canaanite in Lebanon or Coptic and Pharaonic in Egypt), is also a constituent of a distinctive identity for Christians in the region. Taking very seriously Islam's rejection of a separation of religion and state (and society), this tendency is sceptical of a secular solution for the age-old problems of minorities in Islamic societies. Secularism might be an ideal solution, but it is not realistic; a confessional (sectarian) system (as exists today in Lebanon) might not be the ideal solution, but it is certainly the least evil. This latter position has been voiced by Christian thinkers (Michel Chiha, Charles Malik), but it has not been given a theological expression similar to the first one. With the rise of Islamic fundamentalism in the countries of the Middle East since the early 1980s and the Islamist revival that engulfed the outcome of the Arab Spring, the secular option seems to be fading, but it is still too early to tell what the outcome of the political and social upheaval in the Arab and Islamic world of the Middle East will bring and how Christian theology will deal with it.

The Arab–Israeli Conflict

The establishment of the State of Israel in 1948 was a major earthquake in the region and its tremors continue today. Some of those tremors, such the Arab–Israeli wars, Israeli–Palestinian armed conflicts and the internal effects on Arab countries and societies, have been stronger and more damaging than the earthquake itself. The effects of this major event and its ramifications for Christian theological thinking in the Middle East were not immediately felt and taken up. Arab Christian thinkers and theologians dealt with it as a political and humane cause of justice and suffering, especially for refugees.

In the mid-1970s, when the Israeli political discourse became more and more biblical, and religious discourse about the land and the divine right of the Jewish people to the land came to the fore, Christians in the Arab countries found themselves on the defensive, intellectually and theologically speaking. The Old Testament, to which the new Israeli religio-political discourse was appealing, is the book of the Christian church in its Orthodox, Catholic and Protestant/Evangelical forms. That first part of the Bible now became a target of attack for many in the region as being the book of the 'enemy'. Christian theologians have been dealing with the question of the status, meaning and relevance of the Old Testament in the church ever since. It is a major topic of theological writing and reflection. Despite some neo-Marcionite positions, even among Christian writers, the overwhelming tendency has been to defend and preserve the Old Testament. This defence takes many forms, including (1) the patristic shadow/reality scheme (Orthodox positions); (2) the supercessionist scheme (most Catholic and some Protestant positions); (3) the more Lutheran law/gospel interpretation; (4) the Reformed 'alongsidedness' of the two Testaments; or (5) a more Liberationist approach that sees that first book of the Bible as the book of the poor and oppressed (Mitri Raheb). Whatever the position taken, it is clear that the issue of the Old Testament continues to be a major topic of theological reflection for Middle Eastern Christian theology. Related to this, of course, are the topics of the land, the status of the covenant with the Jewish people today (Romans 9–11) and the significance of the Jewishness of Jesus for Christology. All these have been topics of discussion and debate in publications, ecumenical dialogues and conferences in the Middle East for at least the last five decades.

The sustained theological effort to deal with the Arab–Israeli conflict began seriously after the 1967 war; a first and major document here is one produced by a group of Lebanese and Syrian theologians and thinkers, entitled 'A theological perspective on the Arab–Israeli conflict' (Jean Corbon, George Khodr, Albert Lahham, Samir Kafity and Gabriel Habib). Many other statements and conferences and studies followed, especially within the context of the Middle East Council of Churches and its various activities of dialogue with Western churches. But it was in the latter half of the 1980s that the Christian Palestinian engagement with the questions of justice and occupation produced what has been called a 'Palestinian theology of liberation'. The main representatives of this theology were the Palestinian Anglican Canon Naim Ateek and the Lutheran pastor Mitri

Raheb. The former was the first to write a monograph, *Justice and Only Justice* (London: Orbis Books, 1989), with a subtitle describing his effort explicitly as a Palestinian theology of liberation. Statements of the Roman Catholic Patriarch of Jerusalem at the time, Michel Sabbah, as well other writings and declarations by pastors, priests and bishops, may also be considered part of this Palestinian theological movement. Besides dealing with the themes mentioned above about the status of the Old Testament, the theology of the land, election and the covenant, the Palestinian theology of liberation concentrated also on hermeneutical questions of the interpretation of Scripture, contextuality in theology, the meaning of 'Israel' and the meaning and implications of Zionism, not just as a Jewish movement, but also in its 'Christian' form. Critique of Christian Zionism – the theological position that the current state of Israel can (and should be) justified on theological basis within an apocalyptic and dispensationalist theological scenario – became a major focus not only of Palestinian Christian theology, but also of Arab Christian theological output in Lebanon, Syria and Egypt. Palestinian liberation theology was very much a response to the Western Christian 'Israel theology', and it was mainly an ecumenical Christian effort aiming at dialogue, especially with Western Christian theological circles. Today, one does not hear much about a 'theology of liberation' anymore, but rather a call for contextual theology, as well as a call for a 'theology of resistance'. The 2009 'Kairos Palestine' statement, entitled 'A Moment of Truth', written by a group of Palestinian Christian lay and religious leaders and theologians, represents the largest recent effort to challenge Western churches 'to revisit theologies that justify crimes perpetrated against our [Palestinian] people and the dispossession of the land' and declares 'that the military occupation of our land is a sin against God and humanity, and that any theology that legitimizes the occupation is far from Christian teachings'.

Conclusion

These are the two large spheres within which theology in the Middle East orbits – the world of Islam and the world of the Arab–Israeli conflict. This is not to deny that Middle Eastern Christian theologians have also dealt with other topics and themes, more doctrinally or ecumenically oriented, but those others have not been the dominant trend or concern of Christian thinkers in that region. Christians' presence among Muslims and their entanglement in a political conflict with tremendous social, economic, cultural and religious ramifications and effects have largely shaped their sphere of theological discourse in the Middle East. If one were to ask today whether one of those two large spheres is more influential and more absorbing than the other, one would, I believe, have to say that the 'world of Islam' is obviously the dominant one. To be sure, the two 'worlds' in which the Christians of the region live are very inter-related and overlapping, but they are not the same thing. The issues, questions, challenges and even existential threats that are emerging from recent developments in the world of Islam, especially after the events of what has been called the Arab Spring, clearly show that Middle Eastern Islam, in its varied manifestations and in the directions it is taking, is the main concern for Middle Eastern Christians. Some theologians are just beginning to reflect on and study the recent events in the Arab Middle East, especially the rise to power and prominence of Islamist groups in many countries, and the effects on Christians and what a Christian theological response ought to be (Najib Awad on Syria; Andrea Zaki on Egypt; Mitri Raheb on Palestine and elsewhere). The presence, role and fate of Middle Eastern Christians again form a topic of reflection and discussion in many Christian and inter-religious circles in the Middle East. These attempts are still in their beginning stages, but they clearly indicate that Christians in the Middle East are again confronted by the 'world of Islam' – a world that seems to be moving not only towards more internal political and religious divisions but also towards political versions of Islam that are increasingly exclusivist and inaccessible to dialogue.

Bibliography

Fleyfel, Antoine, *La théologie contextuelle Arabe. Modèle Libanais* (Paris: L'Harmattan, 2011).

Sabra, George, *Fi sabeel al-hiwar al-maskouni: maqalat lahoutiayah injiliyyah* [*Towards Ecumenical Dialogue: Evangelical Theological Essays*] (Beirut: Dar el Nafir, 2001).

Sabra, George, 'Two ways of being a Christian in the Muslim context of the Middle East', *Islam and Christian–Muslim Relations* 17:1 (January 2006), 43–53.

Sabra, George, 'Middle Eastern Christian theologies of Islam and the prospects of dialogue', in Sidney H. Griffith and Sven Grebenstein (eds), *Christsein in der islamischen Welt. Festschrift für Martin Tamcke zum 60. Geburtstag* (Wiesbaden: Harrassowitz Verlag, 2015), 613–33.

Zaki, Andrea (ed.), *Nahwa lahout 'arabi mou'aser* [*Towards a Contemporary Arabic Theology*] (Cairo: Dar el-Thaqafa, 2007).

Social and Political Context

Mark Farha

It would be easy to pen a swan song to the impending extinction of the presence of Christians in the Middle East, the very cradle of Christianity. In fact, given the ongoing escalation of conflict and spectre of state collapse, along with the spreading contagion of sectarianism and terrorism, it might be even more difficult to compose anything other than an obituary of a community withering away in its own birthplace and cradle.

Amidst the unfolding scene of gloom and doom, it bears repeating that not just Christians but also their Muslim compatriots have fled the Middle East conflict zones in droves. For Christians as a minority community, this exodus has disproportionately compounded a longstanding demographic diminishment. The upshot is that in many instances, including Palestine itself, Christians are on the path to extinction. While the emergence and proliferation of a host of violent terrorist groups raising the banner of jihad have contributed to this sorry state of affairs, it is important to underscore that many prominent Muslim leaders across the spectrum have time and again emphasised the need to protect and preserve the Christian presence in the Middle East. In some cases, such as Lebanon, quotas of political representation were built into the constitution itself, although such safeguards could not arrest the long-term spiral of downward demographic trends.

Ironically, one of the chief causes of Christian emigration lies in decisions to intervene taken in the Western capitals with which Middle Eastern Christians are habitually associated, both positively, as cultural emissaries of education and science, and negatively and polemically, as putative 'fifth columns'. As in the present, Christian presence in the region has always been adversely affected by conflicts, including wars instigated and exacerbated from outside the region. Thus, a major Christian exodus followed both the First World War and the Iraq War of 2003. The latter misadventure arguably set the precedent for no less calamitous subsequent regime change operations in Libya and Syria. Lofty dreams of democracy – whether pursued under Wilsonian, neoconservative or liberal agendas – have resulted in the nightmares of disintegrating states and societies.

In light of these broad regional constellations, Christians have been and continue to be faced with three options:

- withdrawal, surrender and, ultimately, martyrdom or exile;
- (armed) resistance and the establishment of sub-state cantons;
- proactive, peaceful participation in the political process, society and economy.

Historically, all three options have been pursued, with mixed results.

The first, isolation and martyrdom, is arguably etched into both the early theology and history of Christianity and the life of Jesus. The Coptic calendar, for instance, commences in AD 284, the 'year of martyrdom', commemorating Diocletian's persecution. Likewise, in Lebanon and Iraq, Maronite and Chaldean historiography, respectively, are full of sectarian references and memories of massacres and martyrdom at the hands of Byzantine, Persian and Muslim overlords. The monastic ideal of withdrawal remains, to this day, alive in the mountains and monasteries of south-eastern Turkey, Lebanon and the anchorites in the Egyptian desert. This model of abject self-surrender and passive contemplation may have (inadvertently) contributed to the survival of Christianity in the region, although it always was embraced only by a small, select minority.

The second option, of taking up arms, has been attempted in isolated incidences such as the Lebanese civil war or, more recently, vigilante militias seeking to protect besieged neighbourhoods and enclaves in Syria and Iraq. It is a negative, defensive, stopgap measure aimed at mere survival, not a long-term strategy for a flourishing community. More often than not, Christian communities were unable to marshal enough military might themselves, thus making alliances and patrons attractive. In the Iraqi case, for example, almost 90% of Christians have sought refuge in Kurdish areas centred around Erbil.

Lastly, the third option, of integration and participation, has arguably been the most popular and the most promising strategy. Historically, Arab Christians have been a mainstay of the Arab Enlightenment and continue to exert a vital influence in intellectual discourse and across the audio-visual media sphere, advertising, construction, contracting, banking and finance. Many of the region's landmark newspapers and political parties, such as the daily *Al-Ahram* and *al-Nahar* newspapers, the Wafd party in Egypt, the Popular Front for the Liberation of Palestine, the Syrian Social Nationalist Party in Lebanon and Syria, and the Baath in Syria and Iraq, were founded or co-founded by Christian Arabs. Yet the unabated political polarisation and sectarianisation has rendered this third, pragmatic option of participation increasingly difficult to realise. In some cases, the commercial success of Christian entrepreneurs could rebound negatively as they became objects of envy and extortion during times of revolutionary agitation, as was the case after the overthrow of King Farouk in Egypt in

1953 and of King Faisal in Iraq in 1958, or indeed in wake of the toppling of Saddam Hussein in Iraq after 2003 and, more recently, the campaign against Syria after 2011. All of these cataclysms set in motion a steadily escalating series of expropriations, expulsions and terrorist attacks that targeted and displaced Christians. The fate of Middle Eastern Christianity in particular, and moderation in general, continues to be tied to sound, stable and secular governance. Yet neither local, regional nor international players exhibit sufficient interest in prioritising stability or secularism. Instead, we find the witting and unwitting fomenting of sectarianism for the purpose of wars (mis)perceived to be in the national interest.

The Political Predicament

A review of the historical record might suggest that Christian and other minorities in the region have, as a rule of thumb, tended to fare better under magnanimous monarchs and autocrats than during periods of populist agitation. The obvious exception to this paradoxical pattern has been Lebanon, perhaps the most democratic state in the region. Moreover, representing a possible paradigm for the intractable conflicts in Syria and Iran, Lebanon's consensus Republic is explicitly based on an integrative and pluralist, rather than a majoritarian and exclusivist, system. Unlike its southern neighbour Israel, the Lebanese state does not identify itself with a distinct religion, nor does it discriminate on the basis of ethnic identity. The debate remains whether in fact winner-take-all democracies or states privileging a particular sectarian group (such as Iran, Israel and Saudi Arabia) are well suited to protect diversity or the rights of minorities. This question is as relevant to Christian communities in majority Muslim or Jewish states in the Middle East as it is to Muslim and Jewish minorities pressing for their civil rights in India, Europe or the USA. The Arab Spring brought into stark relief the peril of democracy serving as a catalyst for vicious communalisms. Matters came to a head in Iraq and Libya after the ousting and execution of the dictators Saddam Hussein and Muammar Gaddafi, and in Egypt after the end of the Mubarak regime, when the democratically elected Muslim Brotherhood leadership slighted and excluded Egyptian Copts along with secular-minded Muslims. Yet even before the Brotherhood's reign, several studies documented the rise of attacks against Copts and the silencing – and assassination – of liberal Muslims.

If and when fundamentalism did erupt in the region, it was attributed in facile fashion to prior repression. In what has become an orthodox, dominant narrative, the unfolding violence that swept over Algeria in 1991 and Egypt in 2012 has often been explained as an all-but-karmic 'natural reaction' to the toppling of duly elected Islamists, just as the gruesome acts perpetrated by the Syrian opposition have either been ignored entirely, or, if covered, related to the brutal crackdown by the Assad regime. Yet whether it be the carnage of the civil war in Algeria; the expulsion of over 1 million Christians across Iraq and Syria; the desecration of ancient churches and monasteries in Iraq, Syria and Egypt; the (re)institution of polygamy and slavery in Libya post-revolution; the ritualistic, celebratory and sadistic slaughter of captives by ISIS; or even the gory cannibalism by one of the members of the 'moderate' Free Syrian Army aired on the BBC, pointing to a given regime's injustice or iron fist falls short of providing a comprehensive explanation, let alone a justification for pathological atrocities perpetrated on the defenceless.

Geopolitical Cynicism and Complacency

If the plight of the Middle East's Christians is so dire, why, one may wonder, has the 'Christian' West not rushed to their aid, or at least heeded their opinion? Generally speaking, Christians do not figure as key considerations in the corridors of power in Paris, London, Washington or Berlin. When it comes to the Middle East, the formulation of the 'core national interest' in US or European foreign policy is dictated by lobbies serving the interests of arms manufacturers, Israel and the oil industry. While historically France has served as the patron of the region's Catholics, and Russia has acted as a guardian of the region's Orthodox communities, the USA, ever since its entry as the new superpower after the Second World War, has rarely, if ever, put the fate of Christians high on its list of priorities. The sorry state of Christians might receive mention in the annual report on the state of religious freedoms published by the State Department, but amidst the greater tectonic forces pitting Saudi Arabia and Israel against Iran, and Sunni versus Shia, Christians usually find themselves as collateral damage caught in the cross-hairs at worst and suffer benign neglect at best. This became even more abundantly clear during the Arab Spring, when US foreign policy did not put the fate of minorities high on the agenda. While the USA would periodically petition for the inclusion of minorities in the successive iterations of the opposition coalitions in Syria, ultimately it was militias with an Islamist orientation that were leveraged and supplied with arms on the battlefield against Gaddafi and Assad by the USA, France and the UK.

For Western states, meeting Israel's demands and ensuring the inflow of Gulf oil and capital remain paramount concerns, both in official declarations and in covert action. Israel made no secret of aiding and abetting jihadist rebels in Syria to put pressure on Bashar al-Assad and Iran. Of the dozens of Israeli bombing campaigns in Syria, none targeted the al-Qaeda-affiliated opposition, let alone ISIS. The former head of Mossad, Efraim Halevy, confided openly on Al Jazeera that Israel would readily treat al-Qaeda fighters in its hospitals but never extend the same favour to Hizbollah. In the blunt words of Israel's former ambassador to the USA, Michael Oren, Israel 'preferred the bad guys who weren't backed by Iran to the bad guys backed by Iran'. Sowing discord and playing with the sectarian fire is always a risk-laden strategy, yet it has certainly paid off for Israel thus far, as the campaigns against Saddam, Assad and Gaddafi drove a wedge between Sunnis and Shia, as had been recommended in strategy papers by pro-Israeli think-tanks such as Brookings, Rand and the Project for a New American Century from 1999 onwards.

By the same token, US foreign policy has shown a consistent habit of siding with jihadists to hasten regime changes, with devastating consequences for moderate Muslims as well as Christians. During the Arab Spring, Secretary of State Hillary Clinton, Chair of the Senate Foreign Relations Committee John McCain and Senator Lindsey Graham openly met with and honoured notorious Islamists such as Abdel Hakim Belhadj and Mahdi al-Harati in Libya. With the blessing of the administration, the CIA endorsed and armed jihadists in Libya and Syria in collaboration with Turkey and Gulf states. The integral links between 'moderate' and militant branches of the Syrian and Libyan opposition became evident when fighters from the Free Syrian Army and freelancers from Libya readily defected to ISIS. Both the USA and the European Union made fateful decisions to lift restrictions on weapons shipments to Libya and Syria, in the process fuelling the raging fire.

While the preservation of civil rights and democracy might be pledged as a slogan, a bevy of intolerant Islamist movements – whether they be Shia in Iraq or Sunni in Syria – have directly and indirectly been supported by Western powers in order to tap into the 'Arab street' or to advance regime change. Even after what should have been a bitter lesson, Thomas Friedman of the *New York Times* has gone so far as to counsel sparing ISIS so as to leverage their terrorism against the Assad regime. Prior to Friedman, former CIA director David Petraeus openly advocated arming an al-Qaeda offshoot, the al-Nusra Front, in order to combat ISIS. The fact that al-Nusra had engaged in transgressions against Syrian Christian communities clearly was and is not of concern to strategists such as Petraeus or pundits like Friedman. On the chessboard of global geopolitics, the region's ancient Christian communities are but dispensable pawns.

This has been particularly so since a 'new cold war' between Russia and the USA has been stoked to such a degree as to obstruct vital cooperation in the fight against ISIS and other terrorist organisations. Few would contest Moscow's consistent fight against terrorism, making it the natural ally of Washington, as President Putin does not cease to emphasise. There have been a few encouraging signs. President Trump has come under heavy assault by the war-prone establishment and intelligence apparatus for as much as suggesting amicable relations with Russia, leaving the field open for jihadism to fester.

Political Polarisation

Geopolitically, Christians then are increasingly caught in the crossfire of the escalating showdown between the USA and Russia on the one hand, and the conflict between Sunni Saudi Arabia and Shia Iran on the other hand. Toxic tribalisms and set 'us versus them' binaries emanate from these conflicts to dominate the media and hold mentalities captive. Nowhere did the stark choice imposed by this fault-line become more apparent than in Lebanon, where approximately half the Christian forces sided with the 'March 8' Shia axis, represented locally by Hizbollah, while the other major Christian political factions of 'March 14' supported a US–Gulf state alliance. The dilemma was clear: should Christians support the status quo of a Syrian regime that, its repression notwithstanding, had historically protected Christians, or should they back a regime-change campaign which, democratic slogans notwithstanding, was dominated by jihadist militia hailing from all corners of the world? The predicament was only heightened by the tragic precedent of the Iraq War, which had led to about 1 million Christians being displaced from their homes.

Indeed, the 2003 Iraq War is often identified as the point of origin and fulcrum for a spreading cancer of sectarian strife and state disintegration. At that point, the USA decided to wage a war – without UN approval – making good on the Iraq Liberation Act of 1998, which declared 'that it should be the policy of the United States to seek to remove the Saddam Hussein regime from power in Iraq and to replace it with a democratic government'. Instead of birthing democracy, however, the war unleashed the genie of sectarianism and a series of horrific suicide bombings, which have continued until the present day.

Since the Iraq War, a clear dichotomy has crystallised in the region, pitting two camps against each other: a Sunni axis led by Saudi Arabia, and a Shia antagonist led by Iran. Compounding the peril, each of these poles is sponsored by a nuclear patron power, the USA and Russia, respectively. In this cynical geopolitical game of proxy wars playing off Iran against Saudi Arabia and Shia again Sunni, Christians and other minorities such as the Yazidis have time and again ended up as casualties. The clarion calls of almost all major Oriental churches entreating the USA to abstain from reckless regime change operations have time and again fallen on deaf ears in Western capitals and the echo chambers of think-tanks often funded by arms manufacturers and regional states intent on settling scores. What is more, there is no Middle Eastern Christian lobby of comparable influence and cohesion to match the influence of the Israel lobby in Washington, DC. When the Lebanese Maronite Patriarch Rai and President Michel Aoun warned of a bloody repetition of the Iraqi state collapse on Syrian soil in 2012, they instantly found themselves charged with being apologists for dictators, even though both had a long record of opposing Syria. Indeed, the spectre of sectarian strife and Islamic fundamentalism was often raised by the likes of Assad, Gaddafi, Ben Ali and Mubarak themselves, ostensibly as a pretext in order to ward off critiques of their regimes. While these warnings at the time were glibly dismissed as blatant exercises in self-serving opportunism, the subsequent proliferation of militant movements bore out the worst of these fears and substantiated the concerns of besieged Christians as well.

The Psychological Predicament

Perhaps one of the greatest problems facing Christians and other minorities in the region is the pervasive denial and abiding amnesia of the very existence of a sectarian malady and terrorist thought. Such oblivion is not just a chronic symptom of the sectarian protagonists in the Middle East themselves, but also afflicts Western media and scholarship covering the region. Partly out of fear of being branded bigots, a number of scholars have also done their utmost to avoid attributing ideological origins to the crisis in Islamic political discourse in general, and to the discrimination and terrorist acts perpetrated by jihadists against Christian and other communities in particular. Yet in point of fact it must be understood that the Arab media sphere and the Internet are brim full not just with anti-Christian rhetoric but also with accusations of treason levied by popular sheikhs and their acolytes at anyone deemed unorthodox or beyond the pale, even within the house of Islam. Akin to the populist waves sweeping across the globe, which may take on xenophobic contours, fear of the 'other' and rampant jingoism are jeopardising pluralism and civil peace across the Middle East. The hysteria is such that both Sunni and Shia apocalyptic literature has spread rapidly over the last decade. Moreover, as is the case with all sectarian animosity, eventually even members of the same sect find themselves riling each other. A case in point is the bitter divide between Sunni states supporting and opposing the Muslim Brotherhood.

In part due to this broad underestimation of the region's societal infrastructure of sectarianism, decision makers in the US administrations post-9/11 have been led to believe that the greater Middle East agenda, the enfranchisement of a hitherto politically alienated populace, would usher in democracies that, ultimately, would recognise and secure Israel. Yet even as promises were made of an impending 'spring' of democracy, to many observers it was clear that any wholesale destruction of prior state structures in the wake of a bombing campaign was bound to spawn a communalist backlash. Ironically, some of the most ardent neoconservative champions of wars against Middle Eastern states have tried to portray themselves as righteous combatants of Islamophobia, while at the same time creating the toxic grounds of devastation and despair in Iraq, Syria and Libya on which fundamentalism would thrive and spread like a fungus.

In sum, while sectarianism is habitually dismissed as a Western plot or conspiracy in the Middle East, it has been equally dissembled as a false pretext in the West used by despots to legitimise their iron grip. Ironically, popular regimes are more likely to foment sectarianism than authoritarian ones. There is in fact, contrary to widespread and oft-recycled charges, no indication that Bashar al-Assad ever overtly incited against Sunni Muslims, nor would it have been in his interest to do so given the Alawites' status as a demographic minority in Syria.

Likewise, Sunni autocrats and monarchs could and can afford to institute protective measures for Christian communities while warding off charges of heresy. The King of Bahrain and the Emirs of Kuwait, the United Arab Emirates (UAE) and Qatar have granted permissions for the building of churches, thereby overruling demagogic religious leaders who have issued calls for the expulsion of Christians from the entire Arabian Peninsula as allegedly mandated according to religious texts. As a consequence, one of the bright spots for Christians in the Middle East is their thriving success under the rule of reformist-minded monarchs, as opposed to revolutionary populists, let alone communal militia. This holds true even today, as Christians inhabiting the Gulf states have actually seen a marked improvement not just in their material livelihood but also in the civic freedoms of religion as well. Gigantic development projects have spurred a demand for qualified Arabic-speakers, many of whom happened to be Christian Arabs from the Levant and Egypt. In turn, the Gulf states have allowed religious freedom to flourish, overseeing the construction of churches and temples for their large expatriate communities. Christians have never enjoyed as many freedoms as they have in the past two decades in Kuwait, Bahrain, Qatar, Oman and the UAE.

Levantine Christians, by contrast, once a pillar of Christianity in the Middle East, have been buffeted by civil wars and confessional conflict, whether it be the successive wars with Israel (1948, 1967, 1973, 2006, 2008), the protracted Lebanese civil war (1975–90) or, indeed, the more recent conflicts in Iraq (2003) and Syria (2011–), which all have taken a devastating toll on Christian communities in these countries. Whereas the Gulf states have seen an influx of Christians in the years and decades succeeding the 1973 oil boom, the Mashriq or Fertile Crescent (Syria, Lebanon, Palestine, Iraq) has seen a steady emigration and evisceration of

Christian communities. The tragic fate of the Christian communities in Iraq after the US invasion of 2003 would be replicated in Syria after the 2011 uprising. Yet the wave of uprisings and toppling of regimes since 2011 has been deleterious to the fabric of all Arab states, sects and societies.

Conclusion

In the grander scheme, the violence that marred the Arab uprisings has led to the erosion of the state and the entrenchment of a security state confronted with terrorism and bent on repression of opinion and a curtailment of civil rights, not to mention the mind-boggling increase of expenditure on arms. Perhaps most concerning, there has been a gradually escalating ideological polarisation on the global, regional and local levels alike. Christians have been caught in the crossfire of the regional Sunni–Shia showdown, which in turn is partly fuelled by the new cold war stoked between the USA and Russia, which are each supporting Sunni and Shia proxy powers in the region. Realpolitik currently has a tough stance, with communal passions running high and cold war hysteria reaching fever pitch in the USA.

The NATO interventions to achieve regime change in Libya and Syria have brought to power radical jihadists of all stripes. Even the most moderate factions in the Syrian opposition have been reluctant to unequivocally endorse full equality before the law. The USA is compromised insofar as it is supporting states such as Israel and Saudi Arabia, which discriminate on the basis of ethnic and religious identity. Jewish, Sunni and Shia expressions have been embodied in states. The near exclusive focus on ISIS, Hizbollah and Hamas as terror groups leaves out a far larger swathe of militant movements and ideologies that have practised ethnic cleansing.

In all this, it is important to underscore that, according to credible polls by Pew, a majority of American, European and even Arab public opinion was opposed to these interventions planned and executed by an unaccountable elite bent on war. While there is significant and disturbing support for anti-Christian, jihadist groups, including ISIS, there are also hopeful signs of momentum towards a more civil society. War-ravaged societies such as Iraq and Lebanon demonstrate strong opposition to sectarianism. Recent polls in both countries show a significant majority of respondents calling for a separation of religion and state.

While the sources of the maelstrom of sectarian violence haunting Christian communities in the Middle East are manifold, the intensification of an artificially concocted new cold war between the USA and Russia, as well as the rivalry between Saudi Arabia and Iran, has further aggravated conflicts in Syria, Iraq, Libya, Yemen and elsewhere. Conversely, it can be asked to what degree the Syrian civil war itself has invited US–Russian competition over regional spheres of influence, if not hegemony. And how might a revised US–Russian relationship positively contribute to a de-escalation of the (proxy) conflict in Syria and narrow the fault-lines riddling the region?

Meanwhile, the spreading contagion of sectarian strife has thus far not led the superpowers to bury the hatchet and fully coordinate actions against militant movements. Regional peace in the Middle East, and indeed global peace, hinges on a fundamental redefining of foreign policy strategies according to joint long-term security interests. While there have been intermittent encouraging signs of incipient diplomatic activity between the USA and Russia as regards Syria, given the magnitude of the crisis of sectarianism, much more is required, particularly in light of the unabated tensions between Saudi Arabia and Iran. Indeed, the latter two regional players and their allies must be forced by the USA and Russia to the same negotiating table. Allowing these two powers to rattle sabres is bound to lead to further escalation, culminating in a regional and possible global war, given the critical geostrategic interests at stake.

In a supremely uncanny irony, precisely 100 years after President Wilson went to Congress to petition a declaration of war against Germany to make 'the world safe for democracy', President Trump ordered the launch of a barrage of Tomahawk cruise missiles on Syria. Perhaps in part due to the remaining influence of neoconservative hawks in his administration, Trump is in danger of betraying his campaign promises of desisting from regime-change delusions his predecessor had championed in Iraq, Libya and Syria. President Obama might have subsequently expressed his pride in not having bombed Syria, but in 2016 the USA dropped 12,192 bombs on Syria and 12,095 on Iraq, ostensibly to fight ISIS.

Politically, Christians in the region have at best been footnotes and statistics, and at worst dispensable pawns on the broader chessboard of regional geopolitics. Henry Kissinger at one point is said to have suggested that the besieged Christians of Lebanon might seek refuge in Canada. Yet the 'Arab Christian', to cite the late Kenneth Cragg, was rooted in the region even before Islam. The Middle East's Christians remain critical bridge-builders between East and West, the umbilical cord connecting Orient and Occident, in both past and present. While periodically their besieged state did lead to foreign intervention, more often than not they clarified misunderstandings and reduced tension between Islam and Christianity. Should they disappear entirely, crusading and jihadist demagogues will find it that much easier to revive and realise their diabolic dream of a clash of civilisations.

Perhaps the most fundamental challenge facing Christians in the Middle East is the pervasive tendency to ignore or discount their fate. The US and European mainstream media have, in part due to their ties to the political establishment and a hysterical animus towards Russia, refused to adequately cover their predicament. In their concerted effort to promote regime changes, the media were prone to underplay or censor the extent of the sectarian agenda and acts perpetrated by most of the rebels sponsored by NATO and intelligence agencies. The excessive lionisation – and whitewashing – of a largely Islamist and often brutal opposition in all states of the Arab Spring, and the excessive vilification of autocratic regimes, has exacerbated the crisis.

Moreover, the most influential state, Israel, itself has lent moral, logistic, medical and even military support to interventions in Iraq and al-Qaeda-affiliated militia in Syria. Today, Israel has officially joined forces with major Sunni Gulf states against Shia Iran and its proxies, above all Hizbollah in Lebanon. Through its own diplomatic cables, the USA has pursued a strategy of playing on Sunni fears of Iranian expansionism. But while such strategies might succeed in splitting Islamic opposition along sectarian lines, and galvanise Sunnis against Shia and state against state, the region's Christians and moderate Muslims are likely to bear the brunt of the repercussions.

The Middle East is currently passing through a tempest. Caught in its throes, Christians face stark choices, ranging from resignation to emigration. Perhaps the most sensible strategy for Middle Eastern Christians to pursue is to ally with moderate Muslims across the region who are equally aghast and harassed by the spectre of budding terrorism and jihadist Islam. It bears repeating that the sympathy expressed for the victims of terrorist attacks carried out in the name of Islam is manifold and sincere, even as prejudice might afflict all cultures and religions, and the pandemic of suicidal cults across the region has continued unabated. For Christian communities to survive in the Middle East, a broader diplomatic détente would be necessary. Otherwise, far from being a 'card' in the hands of Western powers, as is often alleged, Christian communities will continue to be human debris in devastating wars of civilisation and oil, of fervid ideologies and cold interests.

Ironically, historically many Oriental Christians acted as a vital link between East and West, serving as traders and translators between Islam and Christendom. Their absence would only foster deeper misunderstandings. For, contrary to the polemicists' defamations, most Arab Christians are not Trojan horses in the region. Historically, they are more akin to a leaven of civilisation who contributed to the achievements of the Middle East. The divestment of the region of its ancient Christian communities will thus spell an impoverishment of culture and dialogue.

The region is now at a critical crossroads, in which security and sectarianism, reason and passion are pitted against one another. Regimes are weighing the costs of rallying believers around the sectarian flag, on the one hand, against the opportunity cost of a spreading cancer of terror in the name of faith, on the other. The Middle East's vulnerable Christian communities should stand as a warning against such communal passions. As the great powers plot and plan, civilians of all faiths are suffering. The region's Christians are treading once again on a *via dolorosa*.

Bibliography

Awad, Najib George, *And Freedom Became a Public-Square: Political, Sociological and Religious Overviews on the Arab Christians and the Arabic Spring* (Berlin: LIT Verlag, 2012).

Cragg, Kenneth, *The Arab Christian: A History in the Middle East* (Louisville, KY: Westminster John Knox Press, 1991).

Farha, Mark, 'Searching for sectarianism in the Arab Spring: colonial conspiracy or indigenous instinct?', *Muslim World*, 106:1 (2016), 8–61.

Farha, Mark and Salma Mousa, 'Secular autocracy vs. sectarian democracy? Weighing reasons for Christian support for regime transition in Syria and Egypt', *Mediterranean Politics*, 20:2 (2015), 178–97.

Lukasik, Candace, 'Conquest of paradise: secular binds and Coptic political mobilization', *Middle East Critique*, 25:2 (2016), 107–25.

Mission and Evangelism

Heather J. Sharkey

Beginning in the seventh century, when conquests forged the early Islamic empire in West Asia and North Africa, Muslim rulers allowed Christian subjects to practise their religion but forbade them from making converts. Combined with incentives encouraging conversion to Islam and with laws that effected Islamisation (e.g. by identifying children born to Muslim fathers and non-Muslim mothers as de jure Muslims), Islamic state policies eroded Christian communities over the next millennium. In the eighteenth century, but even more in the early nineteenth, circumstances changed somewhat as the mounting influence of 'Western' or European powers – above all, France and the UK – emboldened Catholic and Protestant missionaries to head to the region. There, missionaries imparted ideas, some recognisably 'religious' (e.g. about how to pray), others broadly cultural (e.g. about how to dress). These missionaries attracted relatively few converts, yet set wide-reaching social changes in motion. In the mid-twentieth century, faced with technological opportunities and postcolonial political constraints, Middle Eastern Christian missionaries, along with European, American and other partners, embraced broadcast media such as radio and television to convey their messages. By the early twenty-first century, the Internet was enabling evangelists to build 'digital cathedrals' among scattered and often anonymous followers.

This essay explains the constraints and opportunities that shaped Christian life in Islamic West Asia and North Africa, while illustrating the relevance of historical legacies for mission and evangelism today. A grasp of this history will enable observers to appreciate long-running challenges that local Christians have faced; enduring traditions of Islamic law and statehood; and cultural sensitivities surrounding Christian evangelism in the region, especially among Muslims.

The Cusp of the Islamic Era

By the seventh century, when Islam and an Islamic state emerged in Arabia, Christianity was the official religion of the Eastern Roman or Byzantine Empire, while small Christian communities also flourished in Persia. Middle Eastern Christianity was diverse – even fissiparous – as a result of theological controversies that had caused churches to splinter. For example, in Egypt, those who insisted on Christ's indivisible human and divine natures broke off in the fifth century to form the Coptic Orthodox Church. Many historians have argued that the fractured state of Middle Eastern Christianity translated into a lack of Christian unity that eased the Muslim path in conquest.

Islam emerged in western Arabia in the early seventh century, when a merchant named Muhammad (c. 570–632) imparted messages, which he called transmissions, from God. His followers later compiled these messages into a text called the Qur'an (literally, 'recitations'). Calling themselves Muslims, meaning those who submit (to God), these followers attested to the defining credo of Islam: 'there is no god but God and Muhammad is His prophet'.

By his death in 632, Muhammad was a political leader, too. He guided the fledgling Muslim community in organising devotional and social life and waged wars to consolidate Muslim control over Arabia. Those who succeeded Muhammad as political leaders or caliphs (from the Arabic word *khalifa,* meaning 'successor') of the Muslim community created an Islamic empire beyond Arabia. Within a decade, greater Syria and Egypt fell under Muslim control; by the century's end, so had North Africa as far west as Morocco. Muslim armies secured the Tigris–Euphrates region (Iraq) and overthrew the Persian empire (Iran) by killing its shah, or king, in 651. Moving north-west, Muslim armies pushed the Byzantine Empire towards what is now western Turkey. Constantinople (Istanbul) persisted as the last enclave of the Byzantine Empire before falling to the Ottoman Empire in 1453. The Ottomans, whose rulers, or sultans, upheld Sunni Islam as the religion of state, expanded into south-eastern Europe before conquering greater Syria and Egypt in 1517 and moving farther still, eventually, to what is now Algeria in the west and Iraq in the east. The Ottoman Empire collapsed after the First World War, when Allied victors dismantled it and contrived borders for several countries.

The Legacies of Islamic Statehood

In the early seventh century, as Muslim imperialists devised policies for ruling non-Muslims, they looked first to the Qur'an, which referred to Christians and Jews as 'people of the book' – fellow believers in God and heirs to the Scriptures. Indeed, the Qur'an recognised an affinity to the Christian and Judaic traditions by identifying Muhammad as the last among many prophets, including Jesus and Moses. This affirmation of familiarity – even familiality – modulated Muslim rulers' treatment of conquered Christian and Jewish peoples while easing their transitions to Muslim rule and, through conversion, to Islam itself. The early Islamic empire's treatment of Christians also reflected deals that Muslim leaders made with Christian communities amidst the first conquests. If Christians submitted to Muslim rule, paid a tax called the *jizya* to support the Muslim state and its military, and accepted subordination, then Muslims guaranteed Christians things in return: protection, freedom of worship and the ability to pursue livelihoods unmolested. In short, Muslims recognised Christians as *ahl al-dhimma* ('people of the pact') or simply *dhimmis*. In time, Muslims remembered the various ad hoc conquest agreements as 'the Pact of Umar', after a man named Umar who ruled as caliph of the early Islamic state. Associated initially with Christians of Syria, the Pact of Umar became generalised to Jews, too. According to the Pact, Christians could not, for example, build or repair churches without permission from Muslim rulers. Restrictions on church-building in countries like Egypt today harken back to this early arrangement. Another persistent restriction was the ban on non-Muslims functioning as armed soldiers within Islamic state domains. (The Ottoman state, for example, did not draft Christians and Jews until 1909, and even then, during the First World War, placed them on 'labour battalions', where they were non-combatants, doing things like building roads.)

Across the centuries, the Pact of Umar inspired clothing rules, which Muslim rulers periodically declared and enforced. These rules determined what colours or types of clothing Muslims, Christians and Jews could wear in public and enabled people passing in the street to 'read' each other's religions at a glance. In Aleppo, Syria, in 1814, for example, Muslim authorities ordered Christian men to 'return' to wearing blue turbans. Yet as clothing fashions changed, the Pact of Umar's points about dress lapsed as well. For example, within a few centuries, no one could remember what it meant for Christian men to wear the *zunnar* belt, which the Pact insisted they do. Through a combination of mid-nineteenth-century Ottoman state reforms on the one hand, and influence from foreign Catholic and Protestant missionaries and other 'Western' people on the other, religious dress codes fell away. Thus, when missionaries required children in their schools to wear 'Western' styles – getting all boys to wear, say, white shirts and dark trousers whether they were Christian or not, or all girls to wear tailored dresses with hair uncovered and coiffed – their efforts had both religious and political implications.

Islamic laws that jurists codified reinforced the subordination of Christians while offering further incentives to becoming Muslim. Islamic inheritance laws, for example, which persist in most Middle Eastern countries today, barred non-Muslims from inheriting from Muslims. Thus Christian relatives of recent converts to Islam lost inheritance rights unless they joined the Muslim community. Islamic laws stipulated that anyone could join Islam, but no one could leave once converted or born to the faith. Leaving Islam (through conversion, or more egregiously in the view of Muslim jurists, through denial of God or atheism) was apostasy, a crime theoretically punishable by death. While Christians and Jews could join Islam, *dhimmis* could not convert to other religions; thus Jews could not become Christians, just as Christians could not become Jews. At the same time, again, Islamic law deemed children of Muslim fathers to be Muslim. As specified in the Qur'an, Muslim men could marry Christian or Jewish women on the grounds that such women were believers in God. Implied was the expectation that Christian and Jewish men could not marry Muslim females. These laws about marriage also persist today in Middle Eastern countries. Islamic law, meanwhile, recognised slavery, regarded it as licit for Muslim men to have sexual relations with their female slaves, and considered children of female slaves and free Muslim fathers to be Muslims and free. During the early Islamic era of imperial expansion through conquest, when 'intermarriage' with Christian females was common (to use the euphemism favoured by scholars to describe Muslim men's relationships with females who may have been technically wives, slaves or war captives), paternity offered important routes to Islamisation.

The attrition of Christian communities during the Islamic era varied in pace and extent. In some places, such as what are now Tunisia and the Republic of the Sudan (northern Sudan), Christianity disappeared before the modern period. Elsewhere, Christians persisted in small numbers – accounting for perhaps 7% of the Egyptian population, for example, by the sixteenth century. This dwindling led to what some have called the 'introversion' of Christian communities, which tried to avoid further attrition through individual cases of conversion or intermarriage by turning inward. Preservation of the already Christian – not evangelisation of the non-Christian – became the priority of indigenous churches.

How could Christian communities grow under Islamic rule? Historically, there were two ways: either through natural increase or at each other's expense. Missionary-sponsored Catholic and Protestant churches eventually did the latter, by seeking members from small Christian communities that persisted in Islamic domains.

Modern Missions: When and What

Many historians start the 'modern' era around 1500 – 46 years after the publication of the Gutenberg Bible, and eight years after the Spanish kingdom of Ferdinand and Isabella expelled its Muslim and Jewish subjects and deployed Columbus to seek a western route to the Indies. Modern Christian missions to the Middle East started around this same time, when Roman Catholics appealed to Orthodox Christian church leaders in Egypt and West Asia. Early-sixteenth-century Catholic missions entailed a kind of ecclesiastical diplomacy: they tried to persuade church leaders to recognise Vatican authority and lead congregations with them.

Missions penetrated more deeply during the eighteenth century, when various Catholic missionaries – especially Jesuits, Franciscans, Carmelites and Lazarists – started work in towns and villages in West Asia and North Africa. It helped that, by the eighteenth century, the Ottoman Muslim ruling classes were becoming, on the one hand, more open to foreign European (and especially French) fashions, customs and ideas and, on the other hand, more eager to initiate reforms amid territorial threats from France, the Russian Empire and other 'Western' competitors. During the eighteenth century, Catholic missionaries arrived with military advisors, merchants and diplomats (the last offering missionaries some consular protection). These connections had the long-term disadvantage of associating missionaries in the mind of many Ottoman peoples with the variegated if vague forces of Western imperialism. Indeed, in the mid-twentieth century, an awareness of this history prompted some Muslim critics of modern Christian missions to argue that Christian missionaries had been Western imperialism's most culturally insidious agents.

The first Protestant missions in the Middle East might have been the Moravian Brethren, a small number of whom settled in Cairo during the mid-eighteenth century. Alas, the Moravians, who worked in Egypt for eighty years, left no archive, so historians know little of their doings. Protestant missions expanded dramatically – and left more of a paper trail – in the early nineteenth century. In 1819 the American Board of Commissioners for Foreign Missions (ABCFM), a joint Congregationalist and Presbyterian enterprise, sent missionaries from Massachusetts to the Holy Land. Finding Jerusalem crowded with Christians already, these 'pioneers' (as many American supporters of missions later remembered them) headed towards what they saw as emptier regions or 'frontiers' in West Asia. Many others along the Protestant spectrum subsequently reached the Middle East and North Africa: assorted Presbyterians, Episcopalians or Anglicans, and Lutherans; later, Methodists, Baptists, Quakers, Latter-day Saints (Mormons) and Pentecostals; and more. Some represented small, independent faith missions. Others evangelised widely but were adamantly non-denominational, to the extent of not fussing about which, if any, church a believer attended. During the nineteenth century, new Catholic and Protestant missions emerged that focused explicitly on the West Asia and North Africa. The non-denominational Protestant North Africa Mission, and the Catholic Comboni Brothers (in the Nile Valley) and White Fathers (initially in Algeria), stand out.

Muslim rulers across history rarely cared about which sects Christians followed or how they practised religion at home or in church. Christians were generally able to move from one church to another without incurring disapproval from Muslim authorities – a point that helps to explain the Catholic strategy of cultivating Middle Eastern Christians and establishing breakaway Catholic churches from Orthodox traditions. These included, for example, the Coptic Catholic Church in Egypt, the Armenian Catholic Church in Anatolia (now Turkey) and the Melkite Greek Catholic Church in what are now Syria and Lebanon.

Propelled by universalist evangelical ideals, Protestant missionaries generally hoped to share the gospel with everyone. Yet realities of life in Islamic societies tempered their aspirations. Thus, while Protestant mission might have seemed very different from Catholic mission in theory, Protestant missionaries in practice tended to do as Catholics did by focusing on people who were Christian already and then founding new Protestant churches – among Egyptian Copts, Armenians and so on. Meanwhile, some Catholics, like Protestants, evinced broadly evangelical sensibilities by welcoming Muslims, Jews and other non-Christians who approached them. In certain places – such as the Kabylie region of north-eastern Algeria – Catholics also pursued energetic missions to Muslims – although in this Algerian case, missionaries benefited from the heavy-handed, even brutal, French colonial regime that favoured Christian settlers.

The Heyday of Foreign Missions

Historians often call the late nineteenth century and early twentieth century a 'golden age' of foreign missions. This effervescence among Protestants owed much to the popularity of evangelical and social reform movements, though global political and logistical factors were also involved. For a start, colonial powers protected Christian missions: Catholic and Protestant missionaries alike gained latitude, for example, in French-controlled Algeria. Global migration was relatively free: few states monitored passports. Technological advances made long-distance travel cheaper, faster and easier, while medical advances (in everything from vaccinations to understandings of hygiene) averted diseases and deaths from childbirth. During this period, Christian missionaries could arrive in places like Tunis or Tanta (in Lower Egypt) and settle down expecting to enjoy reasonably good health and comfort, staying as long as funding from abroad continued.

Missionaries came from so many different countries, social strata and churches that they variously collided and colluded. National rivalries surfaced – among Catholics, for example, a sense of French versus Italian competition – and prompted many missions to stake out turf (or, to use the delicate wording of early-twentieth-century Britons, to 'establish spheres of influence') in what they did or where they did it. Consider, for example, the British and Foreign Bible Society (BFBS) and the American Bible Society (ABS), two non-denominational Protestant publishing missions that sold versions of the same book. In 1937, after years of bickering behind the scenes, executives in London and New York signed a treaty (or, as they called it, a 'scheme of cooperation'), such that the BFBS 'claimed' Lower Egypt and the ABS 'claimed' Upper Egypt, while they both agreed to 'occupy' Cairo.

Social contacts across national and organisational lines led to productive friendships and alliances, too. Two important figures behind the Edinburgh 1910 World Missionary Conference – W. H. T. Gairdner on the British (Anglican) side and Charles R. Watson on the American (Presbyterian) side – had become comrades in Egypt. Within the Middle East, this spirit of camaraderie and ecumenism eventually extended to Orthodox and Catholic Christians, so that by 1984 the Middle East Council of Churches, based in Beirut, counted Protestant, Orthodox and Catholic churches as full and active members.

Women played critical roles in Middle Eastern missions. In societies where gender divisions were sharp, the ability of 'Western' females to mingle with women and children – and to transcend gender divisions by also interacting with men – enabled them to have a deep and broad social impact. By promoting female literacy (especially in Bible reading) and participation in churches (e.g. by encouraging women to join men in congregational worship), and by modelling female scholarship and professionalism (as teachers, translators and more), Catholic and Protestant women missionaries helped to transform gender relations in the Middle East. Their work abroad also reverberated into societies that sent them. During the mid-nineteenth century, for example, British and American women missionaries who wanted to do medical evangelism among women and children in places like Syria and Egypt helped to open to women the doors of UK and US medical schools, which had hitherto been for men only.

Missionary Natives

Catholic and Protestant foreigners boosted the modern revival of Christian mission in the Middle East, but local Christians did, too. Nineteenth- and early-twentieth-century European-language sources make frequent but passing references to locals, whom they call 'native' evangelists or catechists, 'colporteurs' (meaning Bible and Christian tract distributors) and 'Bible women'. Since few of these locals left records, historians know relatively little about them. Nevertheless, by considering a few cases of 'missionary natives' (a term that aims to recognise their significant roles while acknowledging their marginalisation relative to 'Western' missionaries) one can better appreciate local contributions to evangelism in West Asia and North Africa.

Consider the colourful career of Said Jureidini, Greek Orthodox Christian by birth and atheist by inclination, who in 1893 sailed from his native Mount Lebanon to New York. After a stint performing the sword dance before camels at the 'Wild East' exhibit of the Chicago World's Fair, Jureidini had a 'born-again' experience during a visit to Missouri, which inspired him to start a Baptist mission back home. Thus began a long-running exchange between Arab Christians from Maronite Catholic, Greek Orthodox and other churches who became Baptists in what is now Lebanon and Americans of the Southern Baptist Convention.

Stories of the first Protestant missions to the Sudan – what became the Anglo-Egyptian Sudan in 1898, the Republic of the Sudan in 1956 and the two republics of Sudan and South Sudan in 2011 – typically begin with a British and American duo who arrived in Khartoum in 1901 after the colonial conquest. In fact, the first evangelist to arrive was an Egyptian man named Gabra Hanna, who reached Khartoum around 1899. Educated and ordained by American Presbyterian missionaries as a pastor of the Egyptian Evangelical Church, and employed as a colporteur of the BFBS, Gabra Hanna pioneered Protestant missions in the Sudan by spreading biblical tidings.

Both the ABS and the BFBS depended on local evangelists for their West Asian and North African missions. They sent colporteurs into markets and cafés; on to trains and trams; even into bars and brothels, where they felt people most needed solace or counsel. They chose colporteurs who could talk easily to people around them, selling Bibles and preaching informally. In Mediterranean ports, through which soldiers, sailors and migrants passed, both Societies employed some 'Hebrew Christians': men of Jewish origin who had embraced Christianity without relinquishing their Jewish customs and who often spoke multiple languages – Arabic, Yiddish, Turkish, Italian and more. In the long run, after dislocations that followed the emergence of Israel in 1948 and the rise of the Arab–Israeli conflict, some Hebrew Christians blended into Protestant churches, such as Anglicans in the UK; others joined Messianic Jewish communities in places like the USA (where they combined a sense of Jewishness with belief in Jesus as Messiah); still others settled as Jews in Israel.

The Bible societies also funded programmes to train Bible women, hire them and pay them salaries. Unlike colporteurs, who were generally itinerant, Bible women usually stayed in one place. They made home visits to women whom they taught to read and understand the Bible, informally preached, mediated in family disputes and visited female patients in mission hospitals. Historians know little about individual Bible women.

Sometimes one can glean a name here and there from church and mission obituary notices, which mention, for example, Mahiba Mishriq Haddad (d. 1912), who worked in fin-de-siècle Damascus, and Umm Nahariyya (d. 1949), who evangelised in Cairo.

Among men, a few prominent missionary natives converted from Islam. For example, Johannes Awetarian (born Muhammad Shukri Effendi, 1861–1919) preached throughout what is now Turkey, Bulgaria, the Caucasus, Central Asia and Xinjiang (western China). Awetarian, who converted to Christianity after reading a Turkish Bible, interacted with American, Swedish and especially German missionaries, and also with the BFBS, which sponsored his translation of the gospels into Kashgar, the Turkic Uighur language spoken around Xinjiang. The Egyptian evangelist Kamel Mansour (born Ahmad Mansur, c. 1880 – c. 1960), memorised the Qur'an as a child and studied at al-Azhar (the distinguished Sunni Muslim university in Cairo) before scandalising his family by converting to Christianity. Strikingly, Kamel Mansour followed the path of his elder brother, Mikhail Mansur (born Muhammad Mansur), an imam in a mosque who sought baptism from Catholic missionaries in Cairo before joining the Evangelical (Presbyterian) Church. Kamel Mansour married a Syrian Catholic woman and taught Arabic at an American mission school before dedicating himself to work as a 'lay evangelist' among Muslims, preaching throughout Egypt and running a hostel in Cairo for Muslim men who professed Christian belief. Arrested in 1930 on charges of defaming Islam, but acquitted possibly as a result of British intervention, Kamel Mansour illustrated the possibilities and risks of pursuing Christian mission to Muslims.

Missions to Muslims

Two trends converged in the late nineteenth and early twentieth century to make the careers of former Muslims like Johannes Awetarian and Kamel Mansour possible. First, the Ottoman reforms of the mid-nineteenth century – the Tanzimat – set a mood of change and reform. Most important was Sultan Abdulmajid's edict of 1856, which included lofty if vague assurances about religious liberty. Second, 'Western' powers stood ready to intervene on behalf of foreign missionaries and occasionally protégés. Even US President Abraham Lincoln intervened in 1861, as civil war was exploding in the USA, by writing to Said Pasha, Ottoman governor and de facto ruler of Egypt. Lincoln sought clemency for a former Syrian Catholic priest turned Protestant preacher who had incurred the wrath of Muslim authorities in Egypt by helping a woman who wanted to revert to Christianity after divorcing her Muslim husband. Lincoln's intervention proved effective at a time when some Middle Eastern potentates, like Said Pasha of Egypt, were eager to secure goodwill from outside powers during this period of high Western imperialism.

In the mid-nineteenth century, the Ottoman state stopped punishing apostates from Islam. Yet popular Muslim hostility to Christian evangelisation, together with the refusal of Muslim authorities to register converts from Islam to Christianity (with implications for marriage, inheritance and the like), meant that social barriers to evangelising Muslims remained. At the same time, Muslims who dared profess Christian belief faced grave threats from their families. In practice, therefore, nineteenth-century reforms never had the liberalising impact for which missionaries had hoped – a point still apparent in the early twenty-first century.

Opportunities for Christian mission to Muslims contracted after 1930 as modern Islamist movements emerged, such as the Muslim Brotherhood (founded in Egypt in 1927), which called for the assertion of Islamic laws in modern states. Forms of nationalism emerged, too, among Muslim activists who were 'secular' insofar as they did not support explicitly religious forms of statehood but who nevertheless accepted historic principles of Muslim hegemony. During the early to mid-twentieth century, both Islamist and secular Muslim nationalist movements evinced strong anti-imperial and anti-colonial dimensions – and these derived partly from suspicions surrounding Christian missionaries.

During the twentieth century, as West Asian and North African countries gained independence from colonial control or (as in Turkey and Iran) informal Western imperial pressures, Muslim policy-setters cancelled policies that had favoured Christian missionaries. New laws banned the teaching of Christianity to Muslim students, placed religious education under state control and intervened in the appointment of teachers and the setting of curricula. In the postcolonial period, visa requirements tightened, so that missionaries from abroad became more likely to make only short visits to support local Christians, who assumed control over churches and social services. At the same time, West Asian and North African Christians (who were minorities in being both small in number and politically vulnerable) focused on service among Christians – with a notable exception being the Coptic Orthodox Church of Egypt, which began in the early 1950s to send missionaries to followers of traditional religions in what is now South Sudan.

New media technologies offered creative, flexible and cost-effective opportunities for evangelising across distances, making face-to-face contact less imperative. Radio came first, with programming that had the potential to reach – as an Assemblies of God minister noted in 1958 – 'the atheists, the non-Christians, the man [sic] on the street, as well as the man [sic] at church'. In the late twentieth century, Lutherans in Lebanon devised talk-show radio programmes that they broadcast throughout the Middle East from bases in Beirut, Monrovia (Liberia), Monte Carlo and Cyprus. By 1983, the Lebanese affiliate of a US televangelical enterprise – which also had a base in Cyprus – broadcast 10 hours of daily programming, seven days a week, consisting of everything from sermons and songfests to Christian-themed soap operas and children's cartoons. From the late 1990s, the Internet offered opportunities for evangelism via personal computers, while in the early twenty-first century, mobile telephones allowed people to watch and hear Christian content. Christian radio, television and Internet evangelism provided greater privacy and anonymity for those who wanted to see or listen to Christian programming, whether they were in Beirut, Baghdad, Riyadh or elsewhere, even as it made assessing the impact of this evangelism next to impossible. Muslims found these Christian media approaches so compelling that some charismatic Muslim preachers copied them. In the late 1990s, for example, the Egyptian 'Amr Khaled adopted the friendly, cheerful styles of Christian evangelists to devise a kind of 'Islamic televangelism', which appealed to fellow Muslims.

As the twenty-first century opened, some Muslims were showing interest in Christianity or professing faith in Christ without openly converting. To avoid the social stigma associated with apostasy, and the chronic harassment that usually came with it from officials and families, some ardent believers stayed Muslim on the books (with implications for laws affecting their family life) while becoming what some called 'Muslim believers in Christ'. By some accounts, Muslims turning to Christianity reflected alienation from oppressive regimes or harsh ruling factions that politicised Islam. In other cases, turns to Christianity occurred as people found solace in hard times through radio, television or Internet outreach. Conversions also occurred among Muslims in the diaspora – especially among immigrants, their children and their grandchildren – who had more freedom to profess Christianity in, say, France, Argentina or Australia than in Turkey, Egypt or Kuwait.

Conclusion

In 1820, when the pioneer American missionaries Levi Parsons and Pliny Fisk reached Jerusalem, they already knew about the forbidding reputation that the region held for Christian evangelism. And yet, both men aspired to the universal mission that their sponsor, the ABCFM, supported. Just a few years before their dispatch, the ABCFM had declared that 'the great pillars of the Papal and Mahommedan impostures', referring to Catholicism and Islam, respectively, were 'tottering to their fall', making the time ripe for reaching all the peoples of the region. The ABCFM's discursive juxtaposition, and assumed near equivalence, of Catholicism and Islam was possible at a time when the European history of Catholic–Protestant discord and competition still loomed large in Western Christian imaginations. Sentiments like these persisted. In 1870, 50 years after the departures of Parsons and Fisk, delegates of the United Presbyterian Church of North America (UPCNA) – sponsor of missions to Egypt and what is now Pakistan – met in Pittsburgh and deliberated whether Catholic baptism was 'legitimate'. The answer, they concluded, was no. 'The church of Rome is not a church of Christ, because she rests on a false foundation.' Elaborating, they declared that 'the Church of Rome was once a Christian [sic] Church, yet, by a gradual departure from the truth as in Jesus, and corruption of the faith once delivered to the saints, she has lost all claim to that character'.

Such comments would be hard to imagine today. We are living in the post-Edinburgh-1910 era of greater Christian ecumenism, inclusiveness and lower-case 'c' catholicity – and in the post-Vatican II era, too. We are a half-century beyond Pope Paul VI's *Nostra Aetate* of 1965, the 'Declaration on the Relation of the Church with Non-Christian Religions', which affirmed common values with Hindus, Buddhists, Muslims and others while seeking to improve – and, after the Holocaust, atone for – Christians' relations with Jews. *Nostra Aetate*'s recognition of fellowship with non-Christians underlined its implicit acceptance of Christian diversity.

While relations among Christians have greatly improved in West Asia and North Africa during the past century (as one can see today from the composition of the Middle East Council of Churches), and while Protestant–Catholic conflicts in Europe and North America have receded, mistrust and rancour still run high in Christian–Muslim relations, beyond circles of those who connect as friends, colleagues and neighbours or through interfaith dialogue. Some of this Christian–Muslim tension relates to immigration. Just as American Protestant anti-Catholic sentiment (as reflected in the UPCNA's 1870 rejection of Catholic baptism) responded in the late nineteenth century to anxieties over working-class Irish and Italian immigration, so European and American anti-Muslim sentiment or Islamophobia today owes something to recent flows of immigration. Against this context, the history of Christian ecumenism and Protestant–Catholic relations might offer ground for optimism about possibilities for ameliorating Christian–Muslim relations. Just as relations among historically embattled Christian groups improved dramatically in the twentieth century, so Christian–Muslim relations might improve in the future.

Anyone interested in Christian mission in the contemporary Middle East must understand the steep historical barriers to Christian evangelism and in some respects to Christian living in the Islamic states of the Middle East. Many Muslims are proud that Islamic states across history proved broadly tolerant of Christians when they engaged in private, individual worship. Nevertheless, almost all Islamic states have restricted the *public* profession or performance of Christian identity. Some of these legacies remain visible today in West Asian and North African countries where laws limit or prohibit conversion from Islam while restricting marriage, inheritance and child custody in ways that favour Muslims – and above all, Muslim men. Assumptions among Muslims about what Christians can do, or how they can or should behave, also linger, and these legacies in the realm of mentalities may prove especially hard to change.

Bibliography

Badr, Habib (ed.), *Christianity: A History in the Middle East* (Beirut: Middle East Council of Churches, 2005).

Bailey, Betty Jane and J. Martin Bailey, *Who Are the Christians in the Middle East?*, 2nd edn (Grand Rapids, MI: Eerdmans, 2010).

Murre-van den Berg, Heleen (ed.), *New Faith in Ancient Lands: Western Missions in the Middle East in the Nineteenth and Early Twentieth Centuries* (Leiden: Brill, 2006).

Pacini, Andrea (ed.), *Christian Communities in the Arab Middle East: The Challenge of the Future* (Oxford: Oxford University Press, 1998).

Sharkey, Heather J., *A History of Muslims, Christians, and Jews in the Middle East* (Cambridge: Cambridge University Press, 2017).

Gender

Donna Rizk

In our modern twenty-first-century world, challenges of gender discrimination and inequality are still prevalent among a number of Christian communities across the globe. Concentrated patriarchal societies still induce such discrimination, which is rooted deeply within political, societal and cultural dimensions. Countries facing such challenges exist in the region of North Africa and West Asia, which has a history of religious persecution and marginalisation against women in particular and even more so towards women of faith. The history of this region has seen a variety of religious and political impetuses that have influenced and dominated the socio-theological atmosphere with regard to gender. From ancient empires, the Arab conquest, European invasions and occupations, the Crusades, civil wars, the reigns of dictators and religious oppressions and persecutions, North Africa and West Asia have experienced a plethora of changes that have shaped how gender is addressed inside and outside the church communities. This essay focuses on the roles and views of women in the Orthodox church, since the majority of Christians in the region belong to that tradition.

Women and their functionality within Orthodox church communities have been marginally addressed, primarily among the Orthodox in the eastern hemisphere. If gender issues are discussed inside or outside the church, the discourse is often characterised by fear, being subject to the perception that the topic is taboo and should not be accorded unconstrained discussion without the supervision of the hierarchy. Alternatively, women who do express feelings of oppression might be led to accept (whether directly or indirectly) that such feelings are to be seen as a vital aspect of their spiritual journey, where the Christian woman should bear her 'cross' – an analogy to the sufferings of Christ, in which her cross involves exposure to the church's gender-based discrimination.

A large number of Orthodox communities found in North Africa and West Asia are preoccupied with issues of survival and feel that they do not have the luxury of attending to 'trivial' matters like gender. Those countries which have had Orthodox communities since the early centuries of Christianity are found to be more progressive in acknowledging the position of women in the church at large. However, their progression is still minimal and relatively lacking. In ancient Orthodox communities such as those found in Egypt, Sudan, Israel and Cyprus, women's leadership roles are not integrated into a system within the life of the church. Their role is neither identifiable nor unified across the board. For example, the roles of women chanters or readers within the liturgical setting in these churches are almost non-existent. When it is suggested that there could be more integration of women into leadership roles, the general response implies that this would automatically lead to the ordination of women to the priesthood and thus to compromising the Orthodox tradition. Such negative responses cripple the progression of the church in clearly identifying and addressing gender discrimination against women and diminish their value, status and importance within the life of the church.

A different approach can be found in other Orthodox communities, such as those in Armenia, Georgia and in some Syriac churches, where it is common practice for women to have minor roles in the services. Women in both the Syriac and Armenian communities are more often than not the leading choir or chanters during liturgical services. Women readers are common in the practice of the Armenian Apostolic churches. The ethos of these churches does not betray underlying discriminatory views, practices or marginalisation with regard to women and gender. This might be due, in part, to Western cultural influences in these countries and previous colonial occupations by Western powers. Particularly for the Armenians, women have been highly regarded since early Christian history and, in modern times, women had leading political roles during the period of Soviet rule. Their holding positions of authority acknowledged the importance and perspective of women within the socio-cultural atmosphere, which in turn inevitably affected how women are integrated and viewed in their church communities.

The modern feminist movement from the 1960s and 1970s undoubtedly contributed to the shift in how women are viewed and their functionality within society and, consequently, in the church. Questions about women's status among the various church traditions (Orthodox, Catholic and Protestant) have become ubiquitous, although more prevalent in the West. Patriarchal societies along with the hierarchy in church communities have to face these questions. Typically, when speaking about the role of women in the church, the topic of the ordination of women arises. The Orthodox church universally has a general consensus that women have never been ordained as priests. Maintaining a male-only clergy is believed to be strongly grounded in Scripture and tradition. Such answers are often received with despair by feminist groups, who consider that the church hierarchy is motivated by a sense of threat, a determination to secure its own position and a discriminatory attitude with regard to gender.

Other ecclesial communities, such as Anglicans and Protestants, in the countries of the Middle East have recently endorsed the ordination of women. In June 2011, the first female priest was ordained in the Anglican Church. Egyptian Protestant communities soon followed, though with much opposition. These discussions in turn have challenged the Orthodox communities to address women's roles in the church, but they remain steadfastly opposed even to the ordination of women to the diaconate, except in the Armenian Apostolic Church. The Catholic Church has not permitted ordination of women, though much discussion has taken place about the need for more women to be integrated into higher ecclesiastical roles. For the Orthodox church, there needs to be a clear understanding of the distinct role of women in parallel with the ordained clergy, a distinction that does not imply inequality. These roles are often juxtaposed in such a way as to imply male superiority, which is contrary to the church's doctrine on the equality of women and men.

Role of Laity and Clergy

In the church today, the role of the laity is often perceived (and at times treated) as subservient to the ordained orders. Laypeople often are viewed in contrast to the clergy – and consequently are spoken of in negative terms: they are *not* ordained, are *not* consecrated, do *not* have authoritative and leadership roles in the church and are *not* endowed with spiritual gifts like the clergy.

It can be argued, however, that the exact opposite is true. Lay members of the church have received initiation into the church by the Holy Spirit, through the rites of baptism and chrismation. Thus, each person has been *ordained*, is *consecrated* and receives specific charisma(s) from the Holy Spirit *for* and *in* the church. Members thus become the *laos*, the people of God. This is affirmed by the Apostle Peter when he writes 'you are a chosen generation, a royal priesthood, a holy nation, his own special people' (1 Peter 2: 9). Thus, the *laos* of God are accepted into the church in an affirmative manner and all members – laity and clergy, female and male – are received equally and given the indwelling and charisma of the Holy Spirit. But because a disconnect exists between what is true and what is practised, this causes tension and divisions in the church. In some Orthodox churches, the difference between a member of the clergy and a layperson is regarded as highly significant.

This disparity between laity and clergy is, in part, a result of the understanding of ministerial ordination in Western traditions, which has inevitably influenced the Orthodox church and particularly its members who are living in the diaspora and the Western world. The influence of the pronouncements of the magisterium in the Catholic Church, for example, have affected how the Orthodox church views spiritual gifts, authority and ministerial involvement as a result of Catholic missionaries entering Egypt in the eighteenth and nineteenth centuries. The working of the Spirit of God, which ushers the *laos* into the church and gives each a gift for the 'profit of all' (1 Corinthians 12: 7) has been reduced to these two levels of witness. In this way, the diversity of gifts, differences of ministries and diversity of activities that the Spirit administers to the *laos* of God (1 Corinthians 12: 4–7) has been abridged and marginalised. As a result, laypeople, no longer viewed in light of being part of this royal priesthood, become mere numbers among the masses in the church. They might feel like bystanders, passive attendees, not in full participation in the life of the church, particularly during the liturgical services. Since they are *not ordained* into the ministerial priesthood and thus do not participate in the aesthetics of the divine services, there is not much to 'do'. These feelings of isolation and passivity unfortunately are often expressed in laypeople's participation (or lack thereof) in the church at large. The gifts they received by right of their baptismal ordination and anointing in chrismation are suppressed and silenced and they find no authentic purpose for their presence in the church.

Further to this, women are even more likely to feel marginalised within the life of the church. Gender inequality is experienced on a socio-cultural level outside and sometimes inside the church. The tension is increased because women have to struggle with patriarchy in society at large, and this tension is exacerbated when another layer is added with the division between clergy and laity. Elisabeth Behr-Siegel, an influential contemporary lay Orthodox theologian, has argued that, when properly understood, Orthodox theology teaches that the Spirit does not abolish differences of sex and culture but rather transcends them. The gifts of all are needed if the common spiritual house is to be built.

Some voices in different Christian communities, including the various Orthodox churches in North Africa and West Asia, have been calling for reform so that women can have a more participatory role, particularly in liturgical services. Feminist members even argue for the ordination of women, in light of the church's belief in the equality of women and men. However, the Orthodox church, being a hierarchal church and being well integrated in the patriarchal system of the socio-cultural world of North African and West Asian communities, is extremely slow in moving forward with the issue of gender equality, let alone women's ordination. The fear of women having a more 'authoritative' role in the church is often the underlying issue, and usually theological arguments are used as a scapegoat to justify the discrimination women face. In the climate today in Egypt, for example, the issue of women's purity has become a point of debate and the hierarchy are divided on whether women should approach the Eucharist during the menstrual cycle (a practice that dates back to the third century, though it is unknown when or how long this practice was enforced for sanitary reasons not relating to theological doctrines). Such minute prohibitions on women reflect the scale of the challenge women are facing in the Orthodox church.

Nevertheless, whether or not the Orthodox church officially makes provision for the active participation of women in its practices, it cannot prohibit the living reality that women play an integral role and are vital to the survival and growth of the church. So, then, what are women's current roles in the life of the church and how can their functions lessen gender inequality?

Women Deacons

As Orthodoxy has met the Western world due to the diaspora and Western missionaries, the traditional forms of Eastern Christianity have interfaced and intermingled with Western practices and social influences. This intermingling caused a number of pastoral and theological questions to arise regarding the role of women, and such questions have undoubtedly escalated in modern times as a result of the rise of feminism in both the Western and the Eastern worlds.

In modern times, women are seen as the primary keepers of the Orthodox faith. It was they who upheld churches and prevented them from being destroyed during communist rule. Under the Soviet Union, many women – mostly elderly women – were secretly baptising children. They also assisted in parish duties, mediated among public officials to keep church legislation intact as much as possible, and taught the faith in secret. After this deathly regime, the people of the Orthodox churches have these women to thank for their survival.

The living tradition of the church historically also had a specific order for women's ministry. This order, officially known as the diaconate, was mainly *for* women *by* women. The female diaconate was ordained by the laying on of hands, a *charismatic* gift from the Spirit. The role of female deacons was to minister to laypeople (mostly women and children) and to assist the local bishop in specific ecclesiastical tasks, usually aiding with the liturgical order during the services and adult female baptisms. However, this role is almost extinct in the majority of Orthodox churches today. One way forward might be for the church, as the *laos* of God, to revive such an order so that women may be more included in the church at large. In light of current discussions on women's role in the church and their ministerial involvement, this order is greatly needed – both for women who are called to the diaconate and for the laypeople who are being served as a result. The rest of the community, in turn, would benefit from the exercise of such a charisma in the church.

The existence of women deacons (or deaconesses) throughout history is a reality that cannot be denied. Such accounts can be found in Scriptural, patristic, canonical, hagiographical and historical texts. The modern Orthodox debate about women deacons is not whether they existed historically but whether they were ordained with the laying on of hands by the bishop. Kyriaki Fitzgerald has convincingly argued that women deacons were indeed ordained. On the basis of close study of Byzantine liturgical texts, she concludes that the ordination of women deacons took place in the same way as any other ordination to major orders. It occurred during the celebration of the Eucharist and at the same point in the service when a male deacon would be ordained. The woman deacon would be ordained at the altar by the bishop and would later receive Holy Communion together with the other clergy.

It is important to understand that when one speaks about female deacons, it is not a rank or a step towards the priesthood; the order was a very practical and needful ministry in the life of the church. In Scripture, we know of St Phoebe, who worked with St Paul (Romans 16: 1–2) and is called a *diakonos*. She is known as being 'the Equal of the Apostles' and is the prototype for female deacons in the Orthodox church. Junia (who is named as an Apostle by St Paul in Romans 16: 7), St Tryphena and St Tryphosa (Romans 16: 12), Priscilla (Romans 16: 3), St Tabitha (Acts 9: 36) and St Lydia (Acts 16: 14) are recognised as female deacons as well. Among early patristic writers, Clement of Alexandria, Origen, John Chrysostom and other historical witnesses mention the rank of female deacons. In the *Apostolic Constitutions* and the *Didascalia* female deacons are mentioned as an active ministry in the church, and their role was in many ways similar to that of the ordained male deacon in the early church. The role of female deacons was essential to the life of the church. According to the *Didascalia,* the church was in 'need of the ministry of a deaconess for many things'. She educated the people (not only women), assisted the priests and deacons in female baptism, visited widows and the sick, and helped administer order during the liturgical services.

There have been a number of attempts to revive the order of the female diaconate in the past 30 years. It was agreed at an Inter-Orthodox Theologian Consultation in 1988 that the female order would be restored and it would represent a positive response to many of the needs and demands of the contemporary world. Some people (both lay and clergy), however, have a lurking fear that restoration of this order will pave the way for women to ask for ordination to the priesthood. This fear betrays misunderstanding of and unfamiliarity with this order, as well as a failure to understand the difference between the order of the priesthood and that of the diaconate. These observations have contributed to the entrenchment of hierarchy in the church and, as a result, provoked questions about women's roles in the church, clericism and the whole issue of equality within the life of the church. Historically, neither the female nor male deacon's orders were regarded as a preliminary stage to the priesthood. These orders were sacred and specific in their own right, without being directly linked to the ordination of a presbyter or bishop. Both the female and the male deacon were ordained to be the representatives of the bishop in his pastoral concern for the community, and thus the diaconate ought to be regarded as a fully fledged order of the ordained ministry, with its own unique integrity.

Among the Orthodox churches today (both Eastern and Oriental), the Armenian Apostolic Church seems to be the only one that has fully ordained deaconesses. It has had ordained female deacons throughout its history – since about the fifth century. However, this practice is rare and mostly performed for consecrated nuns. Nevertheless, if a woman is ordained for work in a parish, her ordination and dress are now often seen as a foreign rite in many of the churches. In February 2017, however, there was a significant development when the Eastern Orthodox Patriarch of Alexandria ordained five African women in Congo to the order of the diaconate – an unprecedented and historical event for the Church of the East, particularly in West Africa.

Other Orthodox churches have deaconesses, but nominally, with certain tasks. The Syriac Church has consecrated women or girls to participate in the church choir and liturgical hymns. The Coptic Church has a large number of deaconesses, who perform a variety of ministerial activities throughout Egypt and in the diaspora. However, the Holy Synod decided in 1998 that the ordinational prayer is not to be said for the deaconess, but a 'rite of blessing' instead. The other Orthodox churches do not officially have any ministerial order for deaconess besides occasional cases of women participating in the choir (although they are usually called 'choir' girls and not deaconesses) and in the specific cases where nuns are consecrated and assist in specific services within the walls of their monastery.

The female diaconate's role today is as needed as it was in the early church, if not more so. The role of women is crucial to the church, and if their significance is not recognised, all members of the church – both men and women – will be the poorer. The church, according to its living tradition, must facilitate such roles, especially those that were administered and essential throughout history. Such roles for women assist in restoring their dignity and acceptance as valuable and active members among the *laos* of God. This affirmation is vital for the dynamism of the community and the progression of the life it gives to its members.

Bodily Purity in the Church

Another recent so-called 'controversial' topic with regard to gender inequality in the churches of North Africa and West Asia concerns bodily purity in the church. The concept of 'purity', particularly in relation to the body and its normal functions, has been a topic of high interest and heated contestation in recent years among Orthodox Christian communities. The Orthodox Christian doctrinal understanding of purity is linked to belief in sanctification, that is, God making the human person holy in collaboration with the person's will to be sanctified. However, this doctrine has not always been expressed consistently in practice. Purity (and impurity) has been misconstrued and confused with Judaic and other cultural notions relating to the body. Thus, for example, communities in this region, primarily among the Orthodox churches, continue to support the belief that women should be prohibited from participating in the sacramental life of the church (namely the Eucharist) during the time of their cycle and post-partum. It is taught in some circles that the woman during this time is effectively bleeding and should not approach the holy mysteries; she is 'unworthy' and 'unclean'. Such negative affirmations of her bodily 'un'-cleanliness (whatever one may perceive as 'un'-cleanliness here) are linked to her spiritual ability to be accepted and found worthy by God to participate in the sacrament of the Eucharist.

Many ardent debates among the various Orthodox communities have taken place within the past 30 years. Challenges to the misconception of bodily purity linked with the notion that a woman is unworthy before God and the church have been presented by various theologians from Greek, Coptic and Russian Orthodox churches. Yet these different traditions still uphold a practice that was initially put forth by the third-century Patriarch Dionysius of Alexandria in what was later established as a church canon. Some parishes in these traditions have effaced this practice in recent years, stating that such ideologies are unorthodox and irrelevant to Christian purity. However, the approaches depend on the belief of the local bishop or priest.

Discussions came to head during 2015–16 in Egypt when a book entitled *Women and the Eucharist* was published in both Arabic and English by the Coptic Orthodox Monastery of St Macarius in the desert of Skete. The book's intention was to present to the Orthodox community how the idea that women are unclean and not fit to partake of the Eucharist is an unorthodox practice and must be removed from the life of the church at large. The book was received with mixed reviews among members of the clergy and laity across the globe, but it was primarily discussed and circulated in Egypt. From each group, some welcomed the book with eagerness and enthusiasm for change; others among clergy and laity alike strongly rejected its content, stating it was unorthodox to go against the doctrines of the church. The book gained much attention, to the extent that it was discussed at the annual synod meeting of the Coptic Orthodox Church in May 2015. A committee was delegated by Patriarch Tawadros II to investigate further how the church should respond to the research contents of the book and the heavily divided opinions concerning the subject among both clergy and laity throughout the Western and Eastern hemispheres.

A few months after the synodal meeting, an unofficial post was released by the allocated synodal committee regarding the topic of women and purity. The statement affirmed that the church does not teach that women are unclean during their cycle or post-partum, nor does the Holy Spirit leave them during these times. It further stated, however, that every woman must follow the practice of the church by abstaining from communion during these specific times as well as abstaining from marital relations before partaking of the Eucharist, the latter prohibition applying equally to men. Additionally, it proposed that a child can be baptised at any time. However, the statement did not elucidate whether the mother can be present (if the child is baptised before the 40 days for boys or 80 days for girls, set by the canon of the church, the mother cannot be present during the sacrament as she is still considered to be under the time of unpreparedness).

In November 2015, another book was released, by a diocesan bishop by the name of Baphnotius, located in a small village in Upper Egypt. His book, *Women and Christianity*, covered several topics in support of the book published by St Macarius Monastery earlier that year, including the theology of the sacraments in the Orthodox church, the rule of 40/80 days for the baptism of boys and girls, marital relations and menstruation. This book also proved to be controversial among the clergy and laity in the Coptic community and it caused further commotion among church communities within and beyond Egypt. The book was soon refuted in a 14-page response by a fellow Coptic bishop by the name of Agathon, who presides over the province of Maghagha in Egypt. The division on this topic rapidly escalated across the Coptic community particularly, and there seemed to be no immediate solution in addressing the deeply rooted gender-based issues on the concept of bodily purity, which can be traced back to the time of Dionysius of Alexandria. Shortly after such escalations and irresolvable heated debates alongside the various publications from clergy, Egypt immediately faced a turning point when it was hit by a terrorist attack – mainly aimed at women and children (ironically yet tragically) – on 12 December 2016 at St Peter's Church at the Coptic Cathedral in Cairo. After such an appalling event (devastatingly, it took a bomb to bring back the mind of the church to unity and prayer) the debate on women and the church quickly dissipated, yet remains unresolved.

Thus, the issue remains unaddressed on an official ecclesiastical level and the church in the twenty-first century awaits thorough and reputable research on the topic, not only from a theological perspective but also from a pastoral, social and cultural stance, where underlying notions of gender discrimination and treatment are key factors. The official hierarchs of the church among the various communities, not only in Egypt but throughout North Africa and West Asia, need to congregate and discuss this vital topic. An active approach is needed in order to take account of the needs of the people of the church and to prevent misconceptions about gender from debilitating the vitality of each church's community.

Future Prospects

The church, as the living icon of God and dwelling place of the Spirit, is always moving. If the members, including the hierarchy of the church, acknowledge and actualise this reality, the gap between gender discrimination and women's roles in light of the 'other' will be lessened. The people of God should not be afraid to raise and discuss pastoral and theological issues even if the topics of enquiry may be found outside of the Orthodox tradition. Today, as throughout history, the theologians of the church must be equipped on every occasion to undertake this task in addressing such questions for the sake of the people. The church must be relevant and alive – it cannot keep old ways of thinking due to fear of deviating from tradition (e.g. the belief that allowing female deacons will lead to female priesthood), but it must stand firm in its beliefs and its practices.

The church, as it aims to be modern, dynamic and relevant without wavering in its adherence to theological truths, must adjust to the pastoral needs of the people. This will involve countering gender discrimination before it cripples the church at large. Movements driven by the need for women to be more included in liturgical settings and as equal members must be on the agenda of the churches today. Women must be described and treated as clean, and ordained ministers, as Christian lay members. This can be actualised only if such arbitrary and archaic practices as women's purity laws in the church are done away with, while maintaining the official doctrines of the church. The language of purity must be incorporated into the teachings of the clergy and hierarchy as second nature and should be taught from each church's lectern regularly. Such basic shifts will, over time, address the underlying issues of discrimination against women and the undertones of gender inequality so that the gap between teaching and reality will be closed.

Furthermore, the people of God – both male and female – must recognise their common nature. Mistreatment of one member by another should be regarded as heresy. To treat males and females differently, despite their fundamental equality as humans created in the image of God, is as grave as saying the Spirit is not equal with the Son or the Father (Arianism). For humanity, being made in the image of the Trinity reflects this equality, as the Trinity, being Divine Persons, are equal among themselves in divine nature.

In a true Orthodox understanding, there can be no final separation between male and female. Mystically, they both are bearers of the image of God. As a result, they find fulfilment in each other, since they were made part of each other from the beginning. And this fundamental equality has to be applied to the issue of clergy and laity. Both in theology and in practice, it is of great importance today that the Orthodox churches recover their calling to ensure that all of their members, lay and clergy, male and female, find unity in the oneness of the church.

Bibliography

Behr-Sigel, Elisabeth, *The Ministry of Women in the Church* (Pasadena, CA: Oakwood Publications, 2011).

Fitzgerald, Kyriaki, *Women Deacons in the Orthodox Church* (Boston, MA: Holy Cross Press, 1999).

Larin, Vassa, 'What is ritual im/purity and why', *Saint Vladimir's Theological Quarterly* 52:3–4 (2008), 275–92.

Meinardus, Otto, *Christians in Egypt: Orthodox, Catholic and Protestant Communities Past and Present* (Cairo: American University in Cairo Press, 2006).

Zakarian, David, 'The representation of women in early Christian literature: Armenian texts of the fifth century' (DPhil Thesis, University of Oxford, 2015).

Religious Freedom

Ewelina Ochab

Since the rise of Daesh and the establishment of the so-called caliphate of Daesh in Syria and Iraq in 2014, religious diversity in North Africa and West Asia has come under serious threat. It has been argued by several authorities – including the Council of Europe, European Parliament, US Department of State, UK House of Commons, Canadian government and parliament, Australian parliament and French parliament – that the atrocities committed by Daesh against religious minorities are genocidal in nature. Such recognition and, importantly, a call to action are crucial to preserving religious diversity in the region. However, it is often forgotten that the persecution of or discrimination against religious minorities did not start with the rise of Daesh. This trend has been evident in North Africa and West Asia for many years and has led to a crisis of religious pluralism in the region, especially since the Arab Spring. Also often overlooked is the link between state limitation of religious freedom and religiously targeted attacks (including terrorism).

The pre-Daesh religious discrimination and persecution are continually ignored in the debates on Daesh genocide in Syria and Iraq. However, freedom of religion for minority groups has been restricted in both countries, either through government policies or by social discrimination and persecution that was not adequately investigated and prosecuted. This atmosphere of impunity effectively authorised further discrimination and persecution. The Daesh genocide did not happen overnight. Under certain circumstances, genocide can develop from war crimes and crimes against humanity. However, this progression takes time and often happens with an attendant ignorance by the state or international community, which gives the perpetrators licence to continue. Any failure on the part of the state or the international community to act, and to act promptly, can lead to an escalation of atrocities until they reach the threshold of genocide. Iraq is the best example of such a progression. Christian minorities were leading reasonably good and safe lives in Iraq under Saddam Hussein. However, after the fall of Saddam in 2003, this changed. Christian minorities began to be targeted. Discrimination and persecution increased significantly. The atmosphere of impunity for religiously targeted attacks gave terrorist groups like Daesh the best conditions in which to flourish. The Daesh genocide was not the beginning of the crisis of religious pluralism in the region but the consequence of limiting freedom of religion.

The kernel of the crisis of religious pluralism in North Africa and West Asia is at the level of freedom of religion in the region. What does freedom of religion mean in North Africa and West Asia? How is it protected? Who benefits from it? How does it accommodate religiously targeted attacks and/or terrorism? What is the link between government control of religion and religiously targeted attacks? These questions are often wrongly dismissed. However, answering them might help to address the issue of persecution of religious minorities in the region. The central aim of this essay is to scrutinise the level of freedom of religion in North Africa and West Asia, its limitations and the consequences of those limitations. It is argued that freedom of religion in North Africa and West Asia does not comply with international standards and the international obligations of individual states. The stance on freedom of religion in the region for Christian minorities is explained and presented by dividing the analysis into two key areas: governmental and non-governmental limitations, including discrimination and persecution. Furthermore, the essay explains that governmental controls on freedom of religion are clearly linked to religious violence and persecution by non-governmental actors, either individuals or groups. This demonstrates why targeting only the religious discrimination, persecution or violence perpetrated by non-governmental actors is not able to address the issue adequately, or indeed at all. Both elements have to be addressed in order to ensure that religious minorities can live out their faith and so that religious plurality is preserved. Lastly, the essay indicates some changes that, if introduced, would help to ensure that the right to freedom of religion or belief is the right of all, in accordance with international law.

The Level of Freedom of Religion

Islam is the majority religion in North Africa and West Asia. In many countries where Islam is the majority religion, it is also the state religion. This is an important consideration, chiefly because Islam, as a religion prescribing 'correct' actions among individuals, has a close relationship with the law in those countries where it is the state religion. Indeed, Sharia law plays a crucial part in those countries' legal systems. However, concepts within Sharia law might not be consistent with international standards of freedom of religion, and this has an impact on the lives of religious minorities. When discussing the situation of Christians and followers of other religions in the region, one must consider the impact of living as a member of a minority faith in a country where the legal system is designed for members of a faith they do not share.

Are Christian minorities free to live out their faith in North Africa and West Asia? The World Watch List 2017 report *Open Doors* indicates that this is not the case. It reveals that the persecution of Christians is 'extreme' in Syria, Iraq, Yemen and Sudan. There is a 'very high' level of persecution in Libya, Saudi Arabia, Qatar, Egypt, the Palestinian Territories, Jordan and Tunisia, and a 'high' level of persecution in Algeria, the United Arab Emirates, Bahrain and Oman. The challenges faced by Christians might differ from state to state. However, it is possible to identify certain trends that are characteristic of the region. As the World Watch List 2017 shows, North Africa and West Asia have high levels of discrimination against and persecution of Christians. In reality, this means that in these countries being Christian is perceived as highly risky or, at a minimum, the ability of Christians to express their faith in everyday life is severely limited.

In Yemen, Islam is the state religion and all legislation is based on Sharia. The Yemeni constitution does not guarantee freedom of religion – only 'freedom of thought and expression of opinion'. Conversion from Islam is prohibited and punished with the death sentence. However, converts are given three opportunities to repent to be acquitted. Proselytising is prohibited. Religious minorities constitute less than 1% of the Yemeni population. The number of Christians in Yemen is assessed at a few thousand. The ongoing conflict in Yemen is being used by Daesh to gain new territories. Christians are often targeted in the process.

The Sudanese constitution recognises the right to freedom of religion. However, as the Sudanese legal system is based on Sharia law, Islam is widely given preference and Christians' opportunities to live out their faith are severely limited as a result. Apostasy from Islam and encouraging apostasy against Islam are criminal offences. It has been reported that the government refused permits for the building of new churches, censored religious materials, limited missionary work and detained church members.

The Libyan constitution assures 'non-Muslims the freedom to practise their religious rituals'. Furthermore, religious discrimination is prohibited constitutionally. Nonetheless, the constitution pronounces Islam to be the state religion, the result of which is a limit on the freedom of religious minorities. Some estimates suggest that the number of Christians in Libya could be as low as 20,000, out of a population of more than 6 million. Only just over 100 Christians living in Libya are actually Libyan. Libyan Christians are forced to keep their faith secret. The Christian migrants enjoy more freedom to live out their faith. However, because of terrorism and the growing presence of Daesh in Libya, Christians living in Libya are under threat.

Morocco is a predominantly Muslim country. Christians and other religious groups constitute less than 1% of the population. Christians and other religious minorities in Morocco face discrimination and persecution. There are reports of limitations to the right to freedom of religion in areas where this freedom involves freedom of expression or freedom of association. It was reported that the Moroccan government has the right to criminalise debates or presentations questioning the legitimacy of Islam.

In the Palestinian Territories, Christians constitute a small minority of approximately 70,000 people (out of a population of less than 5 million). The persecution of Christians is most severe in Gaza, where there are only about 1,300 Christians left. While Christians are generally discriminated against, Muslim converts to Christianity are specifically targeted by Islamic extremists and harassed to convert back to Islam. The discrimination and persecution of Christians in the region has contributed to an exodus of Christians that continues to this day, threatening the existence of Christianity in the region.

The above-mentioned examples are arguably those countries in North Africa and West Asia where Christians are most persecuted because of their religion and hence cannot enjoy their freedom of religion fully or at all. Although the situation in other countries across the region is not as extreme, this does not mean that Christians can live out their faith freely. One of the best examples would be the situation in Jordan. Christians constitute a small minority, of approximately 170,000 people (out of a population of 7.9 million). Christians are, reportedly, reasonably free to live out their faith. Nonetheless, even in Jordan Christians face a number of challenges. Christians, as other non-Muslims, are effectively (but not legally) prohibited from proselytising Muslims, and Muslims are effectively prohibited from converting from Islam. Converts to Christianity experience some social ostracism and abuse. Turkey is another country with a better situation for religious freedom; however, it still fails in some respects to adhere to the international obligation to guarantee and protect the right to freedom of religion. Christians and other religious minorities face a threat of violence and vandalism. Considering the above-mentioned examples of discrimination and persecution of Christians and other religious minorities observed throughout North Africa and West Asia, one can question whether 'freedom of religion' in North Africa and West Asia can be called freedom at all.

What Is 'Freedom of Religion'?

It may be argued that freedom of religion or belief exists in North Africa and West Asia only as far as it concerns Islam. Religious minorities, including Christians, do not enjoy the same right to freely practise their faith as the Muslim majority. Christianity constitutes a minority religion in most countries across this region. Hence, the right to freedom of religion or belief among Christian minorities should be protected through the general provisions on freedom of religion and the special provisions for minority groups. However, the empirical data, as explained above, indicate that such protection is not yet a reality. In many parts of North Africa and West Asia, not only are Christians severely restricted from living out their faith, but their identity as Christian itself increases their chances of experiencing persecution. This is clear from research undertaken by Open Doors and other organisations, including Aid to the Church in Need and In Defence of Christians.

The majority of North African and West Asian countries considered in this volume are parties to the International Covenant on Civil and Political Rights (ICCPR), with the exception of Saudi Arabia and Oman. Freedom of religion, within the right to freedom of thought, conscience and religion, is affirmed in and protected under Article 18 of the ICCPR. The right to freedom of religion is further protected under Article 18 of the Universal Declaration of Human Rights (UDHR) and the 1981 UN Declaration on the Elimination of All Forms of Intolerance and of Discrimination Based on Religion or Belief. Also, freedom of religion is incorporated in the Universal Islamic Declaration of Human Rights (UIDHR) and in the Cairo Declaration on Human Rights in Islam (CDHRI). However, both documents contain a number of provisions that, despite referring to freedom of religion, are not consistent with the above international standards of freedom of religion.

Despite the fact that Article 18 of the ICCPR provides for the uniform definition of freedom of religion, the exact particulars of this right can differ from state to state. This is because of differences in constitutional traditions and values between individual states. However, the Article 18 right to freedom of religion provides a core that must be incorporated within domestic provisions on freedom of religion, in order for them to comply with international law. As confirmed by the UN Human Rights Committee in its General Comment No. 22:

> The right to freedom of thought, conscience and religion (which includes the freedom to hold beliefs) in article 18.1 is far-reaching and profound; it encompasses freedom of thought on all matters, personal conviction and the commitment to religion or belief, whether manifested individually or in community with others.

When speaking of religious freedom it is not enough to grant religious minorities the right to practise their faith in the private sphere, within families or behind closed doors. Religious minorities must enjoy the same rights to express their faith in the public sphere. This includes being able to build churches and establish places of worship, follow rites and traditions, speak about their faith to others within their faith or those of other beliefs, pray in public, wear appropriate religious signs and symbols, and choose their own religion and critique or interpret it freely. As is clear from the examples provided earlier in this essay, this is not the situation in North Africa and West Asia. Indeed, being able to live out their faith at home is often the only possibility for Christians in North Africa and West Asia. However, with the rise of Daesh and terrorist atrocities in the region, even the private practice of a minority faith can bring people under the threat of persecution and abuse. Despite the voluntary acceptance of obligations under international law as signatories of the ICCPR, the right to freedom of religion under Article 18 has not been adequately implemented in most of the countries discussed. And even if adequately incorporated into domestic legal systems, the empirical reality suggests that freedom of religion remains a promise yet to be fulfilled.

An aspect of religious freedom not often discussed when considering this right under the law is whether the Muslim majority can enjoy freedom of religion. Contrary to the general misconception, it has also to be emphasised that the restrictions on the right to freedom of religion are not an issue exclusively faced by religious minorities in North Africa and West Asia. In countries where the right to freedom of religion of minorities is restricted, even members of the majority faith cannot always fully enjoy the right to freedom of religion. In Algeria, Islamic service may be performed only in mosques sanctioned by the state. The law prescribes how the services must be performed. All religious associations must be registered with the government and approved by the Ministry of Religious Affairs. Only government-authorised, -hired and -trained imams can conduct prayers in mosques. Criminal law prescribes high fines for disobeying this rule. This suggests that, even for Muslim people living in predominately Muslim states, 'freedom of religion' is far from consistent with the international legal standard. Hence, protecting the right to freedom of religion and ensuring adherence to the international standard on freedom of religion would benefit all, not just members of religious minorities.

Governmental Restrictions on Freedom of Religion

The main challenges to freedom of religion in North Africa and West Asia can be presented as governmental and non-governmental restrictions, with governmental restrictions being any legislation or policy that might adversely affect minority groups, and non-governmental restrictions being the wide range of acts conducted by individuals and groups (including terrorist groups) within society discriminating and persecuting people based on religious beliefs or practices.

The main governmental restriction on freedom of religion, as presented above, consists of a failure to incorporate adequately, or at all, the international standards on freedom of religion into domestic law (or in not amending existing legislation to meet international standards). Government-imposed limitations on freedom of religion vary and can include the prohibition of particular religions or beliefs; penalties for conversion or attempted conversion; restrictions on preaching, distribution of religious literature or broadcasting; giving preferential treatment to particular religious groups; and stigmatisation of, or the use of force against, members of particular religious groups.

In Bahrain, Christians and other religious groups (including the Shia Muslim community) are subject to government-imposed limitations on the right to freedom of religion. Any religious meeting must be authorised in advance. Muslim religious groups are required to obtain a licence to meet from the Ministry of Justice and Islamic Affairs, while non-Muslim religious groups are required to register with the Ministry of Social Development. Further registrations might be needed with the Ministry of Education, the Ministry of Culture, the Information Authority or the Ministry of the Interior. Many Christian churches are already registered; however, some Christian groups have been refused registration. It is illegal to hold a religious meeting without a prior official permit. Proselytising of Muslims is illegal.

In Morocco, the constitution incorporates several provisions that may be read as restricting the right to freedom of religion. The constitution places Islam above other religions, increasing the likelihood of other faiths experiencing persecution. Despite a reference to the free exercise of beliefs, the constitution is otherwise predominately focused on Islam. Therefore, it may be argued that the provisions allow the free exercise of belief only so long as it is Islamic belief. This is observed clearly in Article 3, which states, 'Islam is the religion of the State, which guarantees to all the free exercise of beliefs'; this gives the impression that religion freedom within Islam and its forms is allowed, but not freedom to hold non-Islamic beliefs. The constitution includes many provisions prohibiting activities or expressing opinions that would 'challenge' Islam.

Other examples of how governments can limit freedom of religion include criminal laws that directly or indirectly target religious minorities – for example, blasphemy laws. Although such blasphemy laws might not have any direct wording aimed at non-Muslim religious groups, they are easily used to target the public practice of minority faiths. As a result, speech perceived as offensive towards those of the religious majority can be prosecuted. This is the case, for example, in Tunisia. In Tunisia, any speech deemed 'to cause harm to the public order or public morals' can be prosecuted under the Penal Code. This also applies to acts that 'intentionally disturb other persons in a way that offends the sense of public decency'.

A similar situation is to be observed in Bahrain. Religious minorities are allowed to publish and distribute religious materials, so long as such material is not anti-Islam and does not criticise Islam. The media law prohibits anti-Islamic publications and broadcasts. Any such media content is subject to criminal prosecution with a possible sanction of imprisonment for 'exposing the state's official religion for offence and criticism'. In February 2014, four people were arrested and charged with defaming Islam. The charges were based on information and images published on social media.

In a number of North African and West Asian states there exist strict punishments for incitement to convert. The incitement to conversion can often be very broadly interpreted, posing danger to individuals of different faiths. In 2010, 150 Christian foreign residents of Morocco were expelled or declared persona non grata by the government without any due process, under the accusation of proselytisation. Subsequently, meetings of Christians were raided by police. Reports of government harassment became more frequent. In February 2014, US citizens were arrested on allegations of proselytising. Muslim converts to Christianity are often pressured to denounce their faith. It was reported that the government places various restrictions on non-Islamic religions, including monitoring of meetings and monitoring of individuals and organisations suspected of religious and political activism. The government further restricts the distribution of non-Islamic religious materials.

These are only a few examples of how the state may limit the right to freedom of religion while giving an impression of upholding it, through the preferential treatment of a majority religious group. The right to freedom of religion means nothing if there is no choice between faiths. North Africa and West Asia are notorious for such religious restrictions. It was reported by the Pew Research Center that, in 2011, Egypt had the most restrictions on freedom of religion in the region; restrictions on religious freedom have largely increased since the Arab Spring in 2011. Other countries where restrictions on religious freedom were and remain severe are Algeria, Bahrain, Iraq, Kuwait, Libya, Oman, the Palestinian Territories, Qatar, Sudan, Syria and the United Arab Emirates.

It must be emphasised that government-imposed restrictions on freedom of religion have an effect on society. By refusing to guarantee or protect the right to freedom of religion, including for minorities, governments reinforce and uphold the discrimination against religious minorities by both governmental and non-governmental actors. If a government excludes certain groups from human rights protections, it sends a message to the population that such excluded groups can be freely subjected to discrimination. Furthermore, government-imposed limitations on religious freedom do not have to be expressed in law; for example, they could include a failure to intervene, investigate or prosecute when religious groups are subjected to discrimination and persecution. Such omissions create impunity for religiously motivated crimes in their societies.

Non-governmental Limitations

As mentioned above, government-imposed limitations have an effect on society as a whole as they can reinforce discrimination against and persecution of religious minorities by non-governmental actors, be they individuals or groups. This is because government restrictions add legitimacy and impunity to the discrimination and persecution committed by non-governmental actors. Such discrimination or persecution may range from intimidation and harassment to religiously targeted attacks, armed conflicts and acts of terrorism. Impunity for such acts created by government inaction can beget further crimes and contribute to generalised instability in such countries.

Non-governmental discrimination and persecution are deeply rooted in many North African and West Asian states – so deeply, in fact, that it is not only governments in the region who oppose the right to freedom of religion as guaranteed under international law. A study conducted by the Arab Institute for Human Rights in 2015 suggested that two out of three people in Tunisia opposed the right to freedom of religion. It follows that, even if a government introduces law and policy consistent with the international standards for freedom of religion, this is not enough to change societal attitudes. In a number of states, despite changing governmental attitudes to freedom of religion, it is often the discrimination, persecution and threats of violence from members of society and even from the families of the victims that limit their enjoyment of the right to freedom of religion. For example, in Tunisia, despite religious conversion being legal, religious converts face discrimination and persecution. In 2012, there were reports of beheadings of Muslim converts to Christianity. This is not an unfamiliar situation in other parts of the region.

While freedom of religion is limited throughout North Africa and West Asia, in some areas minorities are facing annihilation. The situation faced by religious minorities in Syria and Iraq represents an extreme example of how restrictions on the freedom of religion have given legitimacy to widespread social discrimination and violence. The Christian population of Syria was estimated at 700,000 in 2016, a massive decrease from more than 2 million in 2011. In Iraq, there were approximately 200,000 Christians left, from some 1.4 million in 2003. In 2014, after Daesh proclaimed the so-called caliphate in many regions of Iraq, the situation for Christian minorities there deteriorated and continues to be critical. In June 2014,

Daesh invaded Mosul. The Christian population, more than 30,000 people, were given an ultimatum: convert to Islam, pay a 'protection' tax, leave Mosul or face death. Christian homes were marked with the Arabic letter N, for Nazarene. Thousands of Christians fled to the Nineveh Plains, their indigenous region. In August of that year, Daesh took control of the Ninevah Plains and committed further atrocities.

In Syria and Iraq, Daesh has unleashed a genocidal campaign against religious minorities, significantly affecting these countries' demographics. Daesh aimed to establish a purely Islamic state through the targeting of non-Muslims. They would likely have succeeded but for the efforts of the Coalition against Daesh, a coalition of 68 states that combined their military efforts to stop their advance. Nonetheless, the Daesh atrocities have destroyed much of the Christianity and religious pluralism in Syria and Iraq. There is still a risk that Christianity may disappear from its region of origin, in the Levant, and the presence of Daesh across other countries within the region, including Tunisia, Algeria, Egypt, Yemen and Saudi Arabia, is also a cause for concern. Towards the end of 2016, Daesh had been losing its territories in Syria and Iraq, but reports of Daesh taking over new regions in North Africa and West Asia continue to circulate. As Daesh is making its way through North Africa and West Asia, Christian communities in the region continue to face grave risks.

As demonstrated above, governmental limitations on freedom of religion and the consequent discrimination against religious minorities cannot be separated. There is a clear link between governmental limitations on freedom of religion and religiously motivated violence. North Africa and West Asia, especially the Middle East, have the highest level of government restrictions on religious expression. A 2013 study conducted by the Pew Research Center on the Arab Spring indicated that before 2011, the level of state-imposed limitations on freedom of religion was very high, much higher than in any other part of the world. Religiously targeted attacks were common, perpetrated within society and by terrorist groups. The study further indicated that the aftermath of the Arab Spring has seen increased restrictions to freedom of religion, both in the region and globally.

Conclusion

Freedom of religion in North Africa and West Asia does not mean the same thing as in the Western world. Freedom of religion in the predominately Muslim region means freedom to practise Islam. However, religious minorities, including Christians, are often prevented from practising their religion freely, especially in public. Religious minorities experience different degrees of restriction, depending on the state in which they live; however, it is clear that freedom of religion for minorities across the region is far from consistent with international standards. States in the region have ignored the rights of religious minorities to benefit from protections derived from their status as minorities.

The future of religious freedom in the region is contingent upon the protections afforded to religious minorities and the accommodation of an interfaith dialogue aimed at promoting tolerance and guaranteeing religious pluralism. In order to address these challenges, it will be necessary for states to take steps to recognise and follow international obligations to protect the right to freedom of religion. This will involve ensuring that domestic protections of the right to freedom of religion meet international law standards in accordance with Article 18 of the ICCPR. This will include ensuring that all cases of alleged criminal behaviour are investigated and prosecuted in accordance with due process and the rule of law.

It must be emphasised that the needs and actions to be taken would differ from state to state, depending on the degree of discrimination and persecution. For example, considering the level of atrocities perpetrated by Daesh in Iraq, which will have a long-lasting effect on the religious minorities, the actions undertaken by the Iraqi government would have to address the vulnerability of the religious minorities. To ensure any future for religious minorities in Iraq, the government may have to establish safe zones where religious minorities can exercise their faith freely, without any fear of repetition of the persecution. After years of discrimination and persecution in the region, this might be the only chance to preserve religious pluralism in Iraq.

Protections of freedom of religion and the protection of religious minorities are not exclusive. Religious minorities should be able to rely on and benefit from both. Perceiving religious groups as minorities does not weaken the status of the groups. It is the empirical reality derived from laws and policies not recognising their right to freedom of religion fully (or at all) and from polices favouring one religious group above another that makes the minorities vulnerable. Religious minorities require additional protections because their right to freedom of religion is not implemented adequately (or at all). This translates into non-governmental discrimination and persecution reaffirming the weak status of religious minorities.

However, above all, it is essential to continue monitoring and assessing the situation of religious minorities in North Africa and West Asia. Only by doing so will it be possible to recognise at an early stage practices that threaten the existence of religious minorities and the religious pluralism in the region. Such monitoring is especially crucial when states fail to do so. It is also plausible to conclude that governmental institutions would not be able to fulfil this role, since some of the discriminatory practices are reinforced by state actors.

Despite the fact that the freedom of religion or belief of religious minorities is at a serious risk, the role of the West in administering the monitoring of religious freedom in the region remains a sensitive issue. However, considering the deteriorating situation of religious minorities and the inadequate state response to the issue, the involvement of the West in this process may be unavoidable. Nonetheless, in order to be effective, any involvement of the West will need to put the religious minorities first. The solutions to the problems encountered by religious minorities must be established in close cooperation with the persecuted religious minorities themselves. The appropriate role of the West will be to offer support rather than to impose solutions.

Bibliography

Addicott, Jeffery F., Md Jahid Hossain Bhuiyan and Tareq M. R. Chowdhury, *Globalization, International Law, and Human Rights* (Leiden: Martinus Nijhoff, 2007).

Kalanges, Kristine, *Religious Liberty in Western and Islamic Law* (Oxford: Oxford University Press, 2012).

Marshall, Paul, Lela Gilbert and Nina Shea, *Persecuted: The Global Assault on Christians* (London: Thomas Nelson, 2013).

Ochab, Ewelina U., *Never Again: Legal Responses to a Broken Promise in the Middle East* (Vienna: Kairos, 2016).

van de Beek, Abraham, Eduardus A. J. G. Van der Borght and Ben P. Vermeulen, *Freedom of Religion* (Leiden: Brill, 2010).

Inter-religious Relations

Najib George Awad

The area that spreads along the northern Mediterranean coasts of Africa and over the western end of Asia is a homeland for communities that are rich in their multi-cultural, multi-ethnic and multi-religious backgrounds. This is especially the case at the western end of Asia and Egypt (also known as the Middle East), where diversity and plurality are socially and anthropologically conspicuous and influential. The people of the Middle Eastern region are predominantly Arab in culture (the Jews of Israel and the small ethnic communities of Kurds, Armenians, Sūrianies, Assyrians and Cherkessians partially excepted) and Muslim in belief (including in Turkey and Iran). Be that as it may, any study of the inter-religious relations in the region must focus on how the non-Muslim communities relate to the Muslim majority and how they establish a living space for themselves within that *Sitz im Leben*. Within this particular context, any understanding of inter-religious relations in this mainly Arab-Muslim setting must circle substantially around the 'dialogue' phenomenon and its inter-religious nature.

In observing the inter-religious dialogue practised in the Middle East today, one soon realises that it is characterised by the two central aspects. First, it is strictly, even narrowly, a Christian–Muslim dialogue. That is, it is relationally an incomplete dialogical process, since the third major historical Abrahamic religion, Judaism, which was born in, and certainly still belongs to, that region, is not part of it. One can observe a single Arab-Muslim interest in developing an inter-relation with Judaism in the academic context of Morocco, where Moroccan Muslim scholars and religious figures do study Judaism and try to create a sustainable religious inter-relation with the Moroccan Jewish community. One can also observe some Muslim interest in dialogue with Christianity and Judaism alike in the Turkish intellectual arena. This dialogical interest is practised in particular by the organisations of the politically persecuted Islamist scholar Fethullah Golen, whose institutes and centres are now forced to pursue this inter-religious activity outside Turkey, as Recep Tayyip Erdoğan's ruling regime has pursued a systematic campaign of oppression against Golen and his movement inside the country since at least summer 2016. Despite these two potentially promising examples, one cannot but realise that the almost century-long Arab–Israeli conflict became the main reason behind the absence of any serious dialogue between the three Abrahamic monotheistic religions in the region. This conflict does not have any foreseeable solution. So, any dialogue between the Christians and the Muslims of the region with the Jews does not seem likely to feature in inter-religious relations in the foreseeable future.

Second, the Christian–Muslim inter-religious relations in the region have a long history. They represent the oldest inter-religious encounter between Christianity and Islam in human history. Since the early seventh century, the Peninsular Muslims embarked on establishing their own empire and civilisation after the death of their prophet, Muhammad. They expanded outside their desert homeland into the fertile crescent of the northern and western borders of Greater Syria, Mesopotamia, Persia, Egypt and up to the Atlantic edge of northern Africa. There, the Muslims encountered the local inhabitants, who were predominantly Christians, Jews and Zoroastrians. Syrian, Arab, Greek and Coptic historical manuscripts and records from that early Islamic era (seventh to ninth centuries) tell stories of inter-religious dialogical encounters between Muslim leaders and caliphs and Christian prelates and theologians, such as the meeting of Caliph Omar (b. al-Khaṭṯāb) and Sophronius, the Patriarch of Jerusalem; the meeting of Patriarch John I and 'Amr b. al-'Āṣ; the dialogue of the caliph al-Mahdī with Patriarch Timothy I; and the dialogue of the Melkite Chalcedonian theologian Theodore Abū Qurrah with Muslims in the court of the caliph al-Mā'mūn. Christian–Muslim relations in the Middle East are, thus, not just the oldest in history: they are probably the most important source of knowledge for understanding and acquiring necessary and useful lessons on how to conduct fruitful, effective and meaningful inter-religious communication and interaction between these two religions in particular, and other religions in general.

Inter-religious Dialogue, Yesterday and Today

There is, however, a considerable difference between Christian–Muslim relations in late antiquity and the Christian–Muslim relations that one can observe today in the region. That difference can be perceived coherently only when we examine the fundamental nature of any dialogue or inter-religious relations. Christian–Muslim dialogue tried to achieve two ultimate purposes at its beginning in the early Islamic era. The first was creating a peaceful and tolerant coexistence between Christian locals and the newly arriving Muslims. The second purpose was founding this inter-relation on reliable and trustworthy mutual understanding, perception of particularities and exertion of mutual influence. On the level of practically living or coexisting together, attention has centred predominantly on commonality and similarities. The Christians consistently wanted to assure the new

Muslim rulers that they really could share the same space and the same living situation because they (the locals) and the newly arriving Muslims probably had enough common understanding. One can frequently detect such orientation in the extant *Kalam* (apologetic theology) texts that were written by Christian theologians and authors from all church backgrounds throughout the centuries. On the level of coexistence, similarities and parallels were emphasised and highlighted more than anything else.

The above conceded, emphasising similarity was not always sufficient, let alone rationally convincing, to create the needed inter-religious relationality at the level of mutual understanding, perception of particularities and enjoying reciprocal influence. Muslims and Christians alike did not shy away from the substantial religious, cultural and intellectual discrepancies between their traditions. Both religious sides opted willingly for dialogue on these discrepancies and assessing them based upon pure reason and logic. This was the birth of *Kalam*: the science of developing a logical and rational explanation for theological and religious convictions. What we learn from this with regard to inter-religious relations in the history of this region is the following: to make the other understand who you are and to understand who the other is, you and the other need to understand each other's 'otherness' and discern your distinctions sufficiently. To achieve this, one needs to shed light not just on similarities but also on differences and distinctions, because part of who the Christian is and who the Muslim is lies particularly in what makes her a 'Muslim' and not someone else and what makes him a 'Christian' and not another 'Muslim'. The mutual understanding and influence require sincere, transparent manifestation of differences and this, in turn, is a passage towards inter-relationality.

This is a lesson one can glean from ancient inter-religious relations in the region. It is a lesson that is required to correct a detectable one-sidedness in today's Christian–Muslim interactions in the Middle East (if not in the world overall), namely the singular emphasis on achieving mere coexistence. This one-sidedness occupies the Middle Eastern inter-religious scene today because people are primarily concerned about living and surviving together in the midst of a boiling and deeply disturbed *Sitz im Leben.* Christians and Muslims alike are preoccupied with the question of 'how can I live with the other?' By contrast, little attention is devoted to understanding one another's specific identity and exploring what this means for a religious and intellectual relationship. Such one-sidedness has started to become counterproductive. How can people live with the different others in the same space and effectively inter-relate to each other if they do not fully perceive how the others understand and interpret that life and the idea of 'inter-relation' from their religious and cultural mind-set? Perceiving this is not possible without exploring differences (rather than merely accentuating commonalities) and without recognising the mind-set of the other (and not just finding a peaceful and diplomatic way to exist side by side). Coexistence without mutual understanding and reciprocal impact is mere survival, just as reciprocal understanding without coexistence is just theory. Either way alone empties inter-religious dialogue of its core nature and impoverishes its meaning.

Inter-religiosity in Contemporary Context

In the predominantly Arab-Muslim context of the region, attention to the inter-religious relations between Christianity and Islam occupies centre stage. From the last two decades of the twentieth century up until today, this attention generated numerous local and international conferences, panels, workshops and meetings on the ramifications and orientations of inter-religious relations in the region. These activities were more frequent and regular before the beginning of the Arab Spring and the wars in Syria and Iraq. The presence of ISIS since 2013–14 in Syria and Iraq has prevented the religious communities in that region from engaging in any dialogue, since they have been preoccupied with the ISIS onslaught that aimed to eliminate all those who do not conform to its own religiosity and dogma, whether Christians, Shi'ites or Sunnis.

Some examples one can mention of the activities and outcomes that were generated for reflecting on and fostering inter-religious relations in the region include the Colloquium on Mutual Views and Changing Relations between Christians and Muslims (University of Balamand, Lebanon, 27–29 August 1997); the Consultation on Cooperation in Christian–Muslim Studies (Middle East Council of Churches, Beirut, 29–31 August 1997); 'Christians and Muslims Together: A Charter for a Dialogue of Life and Common Action' that was produced by the Arab Working Group on Muslim–Christian Dialogue (Cairo, Egypt, 20 December 2001); Marqab al-'aych al-Mushtarak fī Lubnān (the Observatory of Christian–Muslim Relations in Lebanon); an international conference on Muslim–Christian dialogue entitled 'Sustainability of Peace and Consolidation of National Unity' (Khartoum, Sudan, 4–6 July 2007); an international conference entitled 'Religion and the Rule of Law in the Near East', by the Royal Scientific Society (RSS) (Amman, Jordan, 27–28 February 2008); and the colloquium 'Religion and Civil Society' organised by the Royal Institute for Inter-Faith Studies (RIIFS) (Amman, Jordan, 18–20 May 2009).

The documents generated by these conferences reveal that the main enquiry in relation to this subject was as follows: notwithstanding their religious claims of owning *alone* 'the truth', do Christians and Muslims believe that a societal and political plurality is tenable on the basis of each religion's acknowledgement of the other religious community's equal rights and a common willingness to cooperate in achieving ultimate good for all people? Probing the core content of this enquiry reveals that the principal and notional perspective on this question centres exclusively on finding filial and peaceful coexistence in such a complex multi-religious context, wherein the historical roots of ethnic, cultural and religious minorities dig many centuries deep in their human and cultural existence in the pre-Islamic soil of that geographical location. Such a deep concern clearly makes the ultimate driving force behind the inter-relation between religions primarily existential, societal and coexistential in nature, much more than being intellectual, methodological, epistemological or logically analytical-critical in orientation. Rather than meeting around a theologically, epistemologically or intellectually driven inter-relation, the inter-religious inhabitants of this context often busy themselves with making the Christian–Muslim dialogue an instrument in the service of creating a state of coexistence that is capable of allowing people to live together in dignity, justice, responsibility and openness towards all the members' aspirations and challenges alike. To fulfil this happy aspiration, the tendency is to over-stress agreement and commonality at the expense of critical and analytical correspondence over theological, intellectual and cultural distinctions. The outcome of such a dialogical orientation is to attend to ethical, political and sociological pragmatic necessities and survival strategies and nothing else. Religion per se and religious dialogue become just tools in the service of educating the public on peace-making and on human rights and common rules of conduct, rather than also an opportunity for discerning differences and similarities with regard to the Muslims' and Christians' understandings of human nature and existence in the light, for instance, of their beliefs in God and their interpretations of God's relation to the world.

This predominant orientation in contemporary Christian–Muslim relations in the Middle East is one-sided. It focuses on 'praxicology' at the expense of 'theology' and on 'how to exist with the other' at the expense of 'what "existence with another" as such means for me and the other'. Such one-sided concentration may enable Muslims and Christians to coexist side by side. However, it does not per se guarantee that these two religious communities truly understand each other's core identities and mind-sets, which make each one of them who it is and not the other. Such an epistemic dimension is capable of transforming the existence of these two religious communities from a state of 'islands coexisting in one ocean' into a state of 'communities existing in symbiosis': communities in mutual interaction and a reciprocally influential inter-relationality.

No inter-religious relation can reach that symbiotic inter-existence unless it is founded on a theological and epistemological understanding of the other religion's thought-form and content. This understanding is not to be shaped according to the pragmatic and relativist needs, necessities and preferences of those religious people who relate to each other on the sole level of the concern about peace-making, security, acceptance and survival. It should be constructed, instead, on a critical and open interaction with each religion's faith discourse and worldview. Theology is by nature far from merely the outcome of a slavish reflection or mirroring of life's practical daily needs and conditions, and it should not be patronised or dictated by the pragmatist preconditions and expectations of the inter-relating and dialoguing partners. Eastern Christianity in the Arab-Muslim world would not be truly relevant, let alone adherent, to its own religious faith if it founded its belief in inter-religious relation and dialogue on the sheer urgency of particular, circumstantial political and sociological challenges and needs, which forces these Christians to improvise a religious formula that can be used in guaranteeing a peaceful and secure coexistence with Muslims. The belief in inter-religious relationality and dialogue per se must be founded, first and foremost, on these Christians' theological understanding of God's stance on other religions.

Dialogical inter-relationality derives its constituents and purposes from the theological understanding upon which religious persons rely to construct their views and interpretations of inter-relation as '*inter-religious* relation' and of dialogue as '*inter-religious* dialogue'. For example, the religious person who departs from an exclusivist/discriminatory approach that denies any trace of divinity or truth in other religions will then get involved in a controversial debate and confrontational relation with the religious other. The focus will be solely on casting suspicion on the other's cultural, ethical and societal worth, not to mention proving the falsehood of the other's belief system and endeavouring eventually to win this other into the challenger's own belief circle in a proselytising strategy. Such an inter-religious relation will not be dialogical and it will fail to create symbiotic coexistence, potentially even threatening any already existing peaceful, tolerant state of presence used by these religious communities to survive together. Even if the terminology, the manners of communication, the conversation strategies and rules of such interaction are peaceful, reconciliatory, embracive, filial and charitable, they will fail to validate the presumptive rationale that underpins these communication means and skills. In this case, what avails symbiosis will be both relating sides' willingness to reassess and scrutinise critically together the theological understandings that bring them into the inter-religious relation's or dialogue's meeting circle with exclusivist and conflictive mentalities.

The methodologically organic relation between inter-religious relation and dialogue and its epistemic constituents and preconceptions, and the necessary maintaining of this constructive/systematic relation, is what needs to be profoundly pondered and performed in inter-religious relations, not just in Christian–Muslim relations and dialogues in the Arab-Muslim Middle Eastern region, but equally in every inter-religious venue all over the global village in which we live today. There is a need to cure the intellectual dialogical 'schizophrenia' that manifests itself in the fact that those who are involved in Christian–Muslim dialogues are starkly divided into either experts in theological issues alone or specialists in the non-religious, secular matters only: they are either narrowly 'theologians', who hardly pay attention to matters of legislation, economy, politics and sociology, or they are one-sidedly politicians and public figures, who rarely, if ever, know anything about faith and religious thought-forms. Such schizophrenia reflects a mutated inter-relationality that can easily get infected by conclusions extracted from hermetically sealed and static perspectives of knowledge.

Any balanced inter-religious dialogue conducted for the purpose of creating a healthy inter-religious relation needs to be proportionately developed after a dual attention to life and thought, to practices and convictions, to coexistence and to webs of meaning, to practical commonalities and to epistemic distinctions alike. The Christian–Muslim inter-relations and dialogues in the region are invited to travel conceptually beyond the dialogical inter-relationality per se, deeper beyond its mere practising and strategising frontiers. They are invited to pause at and carefully decipher the relation between any dialogue and its foundational conceptual and theological premises in the first place. This involves a progression from thinking merely about the best means and facilities of conducting a dialogue into pondering the *pre*-dialogue, the *pre*-inter-relation principal religious world-view and epistemological driving-thought that motivate the Christians and Muslims to inter-relate and dialogue with the other; the one, that is, that implicitly or explicitly colours these inter-relating sides' understandings and interpretations of what they contribute to the inter-relation and the dialogical encounter, as well as their understandings and interpretations of what the others offer to the same encounter.

Lessons for Today's Inter-religious Dialogue

Reading the extant historical records of the inter-relation and dialogue between Christians and Muslims in the history of inter-religious coexistence in the North African and West Asian region since the seventh century demonstrates that the theological understanding and the attention to it has never escaped the mind of the inter-relating and dialoguing members of these two religious communities. The concern about coexistence has always been accompanied by, if not also influenced deeply by, an equal concentration on understanding and conceiving the theological and epistemological differences between the two faiths' discourses. This section of the essay will present some basic lessons one can glean from the history of Christian–Muslim inter-relation and dialogue in the context of the Arab-Muslim world. These lessons are necessary to guarantee that any dialogue between religions will be conducted in a proper and balanced manner that will turn that dialogue eventually into an entrance for developing an inter-religious relation that does not abort any potential symbiotic coexistence.

In my participation in inter-religious dialogues in the region, I learned from first-hand experience that these interactions were always more constructive and productive when the dialoguing partners avoided the 'pro' and 'anti' stances in their communication with their interlocutors. By 'pro', I mean presuming that a certain faith, teaching, viewpoint, interpretation, presumption or identity is always right, accurate, flawless or unblemished. On the other hand, 'anti' in my experience designates an assumption that the aforementioned things are always wrong, negative and suspiciously hostile and untrustworthy. In Christian–Muslim dialogue, I learnt that abiding with my identity as 'Christian' need not be fulfilled by opting for a 'pro-Christian' or 'anti-Muslim' stance. Similarly, I also realised that my avoidance of this orientation has correspondingly encouraged the Muslims to abide with their own faith without needing to defensively manifest this in terms of 'pro-Islam' or 'anti-Christianity'. That experience enabled me to perceive the valuable success the Christians and Muslims achieved in their inter-religious relations when they managed to relate to each other in a symbiotic manner and whenever they avoided that 'pro–anti' mentality and embraced each other as different, yet not necessarily antagonistic and contradictory in a 'black-vs-white' or 'truth-vs-falsehood' mentality.

One of the problematic consequences of inter-religious dialogues has stemmed on some historical occasions from the fact that one dialoguing partner would relate mistaken explanations of his or her own faith, leading the other to develop judgemental depreciation of a religious explanation that is, actually, based on a wrong presentation of that religion's content. An example of this is the Gospel of Barnabas. This text is problematic for Christians and they consistently point out its inaccuracy when in discussion with non-Christians. The reason is that the content of this fourteenth-century text shows that its Jewish-Italian author is knowledgeable about Islam, but he ignores Christianity and fills his book with crudely inaccurate geographical, historical and religious data on Jesus's life and ministry.

Inter-religious relation is by nature, and inter-religious dialogue is by purpose, a pre-emptive pre-conflict state of being and acting against conflict. This inter-relationality and its dialogue must be conducted so that no management or resolution of any conflict would be needed at all within the context of an inter-religious coexistence. When Christians and Muslims dialogue in the Middle East, they do not usually do so because the Christian and Muslim groups in this region were involved in religious wars or massacres, as one could find in the history of some African countries (e.g. Sudan and Nigeria). Even when the civil war broke out in Lebanon, it was more political than religious in nature. In this context, religious dialogue is not necessarily conducted to fulfil a conflict-resolution purpose, but rather to make sure that the religious factions in one society maintain a peaceful coexistence that will pre-empt any need for conflict resolution in the future. If conflict resolution is required, it should precede the interfaith relation and dialogue: without peace and a situation of positive coexistence, dialogue and inter-relationality are not possible. In other words, conflict resolution and management require diplomacy, but diplomacy is not actually a guarantor or a definite source of inter-relation and dialogue. In the context of the Middle East, inter-religious relations and dialogues are needed to guarantee the success of any conflict resolution, should a religious conflict take place.

In inter-religious relations and dialogues, one should apply the same critical scrutinising method of interpreting and applying rules of understanding evenly to the other's faith and to one's own alike, and in an equally courageous openness. For example, a dialoguing side that follows the historical-critical method of investigation will be communicating in parallel and never in correspondence with a dialoguing counterpart who follows a literalist, proof-texting method of investigation. On the other hand, a similar communication failure and 'conversation of the deaf' will occur when one dialoguing side is searching for the meaning of religious texts, whereas the other side is busy seeking the origin(s) of the same religious texts. The inter-relating sides need to clarify their webs of interpretation and methods of investigation and understanding in order to create one inter-related dialogue and interaction and not end up pursuing two parallel, if not contradictory, relating states that eventually broaden the cultural, existential and societal gap between them instead of narrowing it.

To offer examples of this, before the Christians and Muslims in the region start to make a fruitful dialogue on the subject of 'the sources of legislation' in the state (one of the main controversial subjects in that context), they need to articulate lucidly how each of them understands the ideas of 'legislation' and 'law'. For Muslims, 'law' means 'Sharīʻa', which is derived directly from the religious teaching and textual heritage of Islam. For Christians, it does not mean anything derived directly from religious texts. This is not mere distinction in semantics; it is a substantial difference in cognition. The same applies to the notion of 'civil society' (another crucial subject in that context). Today, both Arab Muslims and Christians speak about this notion and call for it in the Arab world. But, a careful perception of what each group speaks about demonstrates that each group actually has connotations and interpretations of that concept that are historically, conceptually, textually and politically starkly different from each other. Each side derives its understanding of this concept from different sorts of intellectual tradition: Muslims from the history of the Prophet and *Fiqh*, Christians from the history of Hellenic-Christian thought in the West. The participant in dialogues on such subjects in the region would feel that the two interlocuting sides are actually talking in parallel rather than to each other and that they need to discern the distinct webs of meaning they follow to start dialoguing with each other on the sort of civil society the Arab world can have in the future.

Whither Inter-religious Relations?

The history of inter-religious relations in North Africa and West Asia teaches us that the inter-religious dialogical experience between Christians and Muslims in that region has never been created after a static, absolutely correct, 'recipe', with fixed and easily arranged ingredients. Inter-religious relations in the history of the Christian–Muslim coexistence in the region has always been a journey, a frankly adventurous and sometimes inevitably risky sojourning through the deep water of coexistence with those who are other than you, who are different in a far from figurative or superficial manner. For Eastern Christians in the Arab-Muslim region, inter-religious relations and dialogues were not, and never will be, mere choices they opted for at certain stages of their life with the Muslims. Ever since they started, inter-relation and dialogue have been the Eastern Christians' primary method for guaranteeing peaceful life with Muslims. They are the core identity-forming constituents that are inherent in their presence (not just existence) as 'Christians' in a Muslim world.

In light of the drastic situation in that part of the world and the multi-faceted confessionalist and geopolitical conflicts that have affected it since 2011, the Christians find themselves facing, side by side with their Muslim compatriots, the very same existential crisis and are challenged by the following question: 'How should these Christians aid their Muslim compatriots in facing the tsunami of fanaticism and religious-confessionalist hatred that threaten the existence of both equally?'

Nevertheless, the post-Arab Spring (or the late Arab Spring) *Sitz im Leben* and its ramifications in the region today strongly imply that another 'to-be-or-not-to-be' inter-relation and dialogue needs to be urgently attended to and conducted in the heart of the Muslim world itself, namely between the Sunnis and the Shi'ites of the region. The urgent need for such an inter-relation and dialogue in the midst of the carnage between these two Muslim factions has recently overshadowed all other inter-religious relations. The survival of Islam in the region seems today to be also depending on such a Muslim–Muslim inter-relation and dialogue. In the midst of this context, inter-religious relations and dialogues assume great importance as the factor most likely to salvage the situation and create viable coexistence. There is a desperate need to move from mere Christian–Muslim inter-relation and dialogue to a Muslim–Muslim one, wherein the Christians can play a mediatorial, bridging role between the two antagonists. It is to be hoped that the success of this mediatorial role will enable the people of the region in the future to extend the boundaries of inter-religious relations and dialogues beyond Christianity and Islam, paving the way for a possible Abrahamic inter-relation and dialogue between Christianity, Islam and Judaism, in the midst of the land that gave the three of them birth and mothered them all equally.

Bibliography

Awad, Najib George, *And Freedom Became a Public-Square: Political, Sociological and Religious Overviews on the Arab Christians and the Arabic Spring* (Berlin: LIT Verlag, 2012).

Awad, Najib George, 'Is "Post-Christendom" a Relevant Hermeneutical Framework to the Situation of the Christians in Greater Syria? Towards a Critical Appraisal', *Post-Christendom Studies Journal*, 1 (2016), 31–76.

Cheetham, David, Douglas Pratt and David Thomas (eds), *Understanding Interreligious Relations* (Oxford: Oxford University Press, 2013).

Goddard, Hugh, *A History of Christian–Muslim Relations* (Edinburgh: Edinburgh University Press, 2000).

Sabra, George F. (ed.), *Hiwār al-Haqīqa min Ajl al-Hayāt Ma'ān* [*Dialogue of Truth for Life Together*], 3 vols (Beirut: Near East School of Theology Publications, 2004, 2008, 2013).

Monastic Movements and Spirituality

Anna Poujeau

From the second half of the twentieth century, the Middle East witnessed a major renewal of Christian monasticism, marking the social, political and religious landscape of this predominantly Muslim region. Unmatched for several centuries, the revival of these movements with their monastic spirituality is reflected in the re-founding of ancient monasteries, often centuries old, or the foundation of new monasteries wherever the political context makes this possible, as in Lebanon, Jordan or Syria. Three processes of re-founding and founding monasteries can be identified: the rediscovery and renovation of ruins of an ancient place of worship; the enhancement of a place associated with a saint through the construction of a monastery; and the construction of a new monastery specially designed for a community of monks or nuns aiming to renew the monastic tradition among young people. All three types of monastery, capable of sheltering numerous communities and welcoming thousands of visitors, participate in an important re-Christianisation of the national territories of this region. The renewed monasticism, the re-founding of monastic movements and the revival of monastic spirituality have become strong political and religious symbols that place the region's various Christian communities fully in their political and social contexts, even in cases where governments show little sympathy for members of religious minorities, as in Egypt, Iraq and Turkey.

In Egypt, from the end of the 1940s, the numerous Coptic monasteries – often in poor condition – were newly occupied by important communities and were being renovated. During the same decade in Lebanon, pilgrims who had come to the monastery of Saint Maron of Annaya to pray at the tomb of Father Charbel, a hermit monk of the Lebanese Maronite Order who died in 1898, experienced blessings and miracles. In 1950, his tomb was opened and witnesses observed the good state of conservation of his remains. The hermit monk Charbel was finally canonised by the Vatican in 1975. These events, which brought tens of thousands of devotees to the monasteries of Lebanon, undoubtedly gave a new impetus to the monastic movements throughout the country.

Without looking to the past, these movements fit fully into their context and modernity. Indeed, inherited from the past but turned towards the future, monasticism inscribes the Christian community into modernity. Vocations became more numerous, and many monasteries of all denominations were restored, such as the Greek Orthodox monastery of Nouriyye near the town of Batroun (Lebanon). In the mid-1960s, two nuns from the Syrian monastery of Saydnaya were commissioned by the Greek Orthodox ecclesiastical authorities to rebuild a female community in the ruined monastery then occupied by Palestinian refugee families. In Syria in the late 1970s, the Greek Orthodox patriarchate of Antioch and All the East – the largest church numerically in Syria – gave new impetus to a monastic revival in the country. Thus, although in the 1950s only three Greek Orthodox monasteries were still active in the country, at the end of the year 2000 there were several dozen, as well as some Greek Catholic, Syriac Orthodox and Syriac Catholic monasteries.

Similarly, on the borders of Syria, Turkey and Iraq, in the region of Tur Abdin – in Syriac 'the mountain of the servants of God', so called because of the numerous monastic communities that settled there during the first centuries of Christianity – there was a revival of Syriac Orthodox monasticism from the mid-1990s onward. Vocations are increasing and the monasteries are renovated thanks to donations from the Syriac diaspora spread mainly throughout northern Europe and the USA. Although this sometimes poses significant political and land issues with the Turkish authorities and the local Kurdish communities, the monasteries of the region, particularly the Mor Gabriel monastery, founded in the fifth century, have again become important centres for the learning and the dissemination of the Syriac language and culture. We should also mention the case of the monasteries of northern Iraq, which, despite the disastrous national political situation, underwent conservation and renovation work in the late 1980s, notably due to the efforts of the Syriac Orthodox Church – whose patriarch of Iraqi origin, Ignace Zakka II (1932–2014), resided in Damascus – and of the Dominican Friars present in the plain of Nineveh since the end of the nineteenth century. The oldest monastery in Iraq, Mar Elia (Saint Elijah), near Mosul, was partially restored in 1986. Unfortunately, it was razed to the ground in 2014 by Daesh following the invasion of the region by the extremist Islamist group.

Monasticism, Holiness and Worship

In many cases, these efforts to renovate the monasteries are accompanied by a revival of monastic vocations. Men and women do not hesitate to give up the culture of consumerism and, despite the difficulties of daily life in a monastery, monastic vocations are more and more numerous among both men and women. In Egypt and in other countries of the region, the cult of saints and miracles lies at the heart of these vocations. Saints are indeed an important focus of worship throughout the whole region, and the monastery – always dedicated to a saint – is a privileged place of worship, for both the present monastic community and the faithful, Muslims as well as Christians, who make pilgrimages there in order to obtain graces. The renewal of monastic movements and spirituality, witnessed progressively from the second half of the twentieth century, is accompanied by a real passion (among both religious and lay worshippers) for the saints and miracles. On the holy day of the saint to which the monastery is dedicated, thousands of visitors flock to the place of worship to celebrate and implore him or her. In Egypt, as in Syria, Palestine, Lebanon and elsewhere in the region, major celebrations take place in the monastery for several days, during which individual and collective prayers alternate with dances, music and festive gatherings with family and friends around lavish meals composed of sheep sacrificed in honour of the saint. For instance, in Palestine every year in March, thousands of people join the Greek Orthodox monastery of Saint Gerasimus in Deir Hajla in the Judean desert. Monks and nuns as well as ecclesiastical authorities encourage these celebrations, which testify to the importance and strength of monasticism for the population and bring to the monastery devotees willing to make large gifts in thanks for the miracles that the saint grants to all, be they Christians or Muslims. More generally, these practices are part of the increased religiosity of the lay Christian population at large in the region.

The lay faithful who come on pilgrimages to celebrate and implore the saints to whom the places of worship are dedicated, however, are not the only ones to establish relations with the saints. On a daily basis, the members of the monastic communities who dedicate their lives to the patron saints of their monasteries – from whom they often derive their personal vocation through an apparition or a dreamlike vision – establish close links with them. Thus, in the accounts that the nuns of the monastery of Saint Thecle in Syria give of their existence at the monastery, their relationship with the patron saint of the place of worship is the focal point around which they grow spiritually. The role of the saint in the various monastic movements of the region is absolutely fundamental. There may even be a superposition of the saint and the monk. Therefore, some monks and nuns – such as Father Charbel and the nun Rafqa in Lebanon – were canonised by the Vatican in the second half of the twentieth century. Even some ecclesiastical authorities – such as Cyril VI in Egypt, who was a monk before being Patriarch of the Copts under President Nasser – are considered saints by their communities. While the processes leading to the recognition of holiness vary considerably between those advocated by the Vatican's strict rules (with processes of beatification and canonisation) and the much more informal ones of the Eastern churches (based on popular support), the effects are the same among those who recognise the authority of the Vatican (Uniates) and among the Orthodox, both on the monastic movements themselves and on the spirituality of the religious and the laity.

Holiness is one of the founding pillars of monasticism in the region. Therefore, in order to understand all the stakes involved in the renewal of monastic movements, it is essential to understand that these are intimately linked to the processes and logics underlying the construction of holiness, which, far from being new, have a historical depth that is not to be neglected. Holiness is at the heart of both the processes of construction of monastic movements as well as the modes of daily organisation of monastic communities. This is largely because, from the time of their founding in the first centuries of Christianity (to which we shall return later) until now, Oriental monastic movements have ignored the notions of order and rule, strictly speaking, at least as they have been perceived in Latin monasticism since its foundation. In Egypt, Syria, Mesopotamia and even more widely in the East, monastic movements are not unified within various orders, nor are they organised by precise rules that would dictate activities, missions and the spirituality of the monks and nuns. The monastic communities form distinct groups of men and women, and even if they may be related through their common adherence to a church (such as Greek Orthodox, Coptic, Syriac Orthodox) and their common submission to the patriarch of their church, their direct links are in fact very weak. The monastic movements of this region indeed claim that they belong to the rule of Saint Basil, which is generally distinguished by its extreme flexibility and its deeply reflective character.

A Spirituality of Renunciation

Beyond the great political, religious and social diversity of the various national contexts in which today's monastic movements take place, their renewal marks the formidable historical continuity of Eastern Christianity since the age of primitive Christianity. Indeed, although taking place extremely late, this renewal is part of the regional history of holiness, monasticism and ascetic spirituality that, far from being linear, has been marked by numerous ruptures and transformations. To study the monastic movements and the spirituality inspiring them today, a historical approach is unavoidable, not only for the theoretical necessity of placing this phenomenon in its historical context but also for the methodological concern of taking into account the word of the men and women currently engaged in monasticism. Indeed, through their highly reflective stories about themselves and their religious, social and political conditions, they place their own existence and that of the communities to which they belong in diachronic depth. This aims to rebuild a continuity between themselves and the first ascetics and monks of the region as well as the famous saints who constitute important points of reference for them.

In this context, questions of vocation and monastic spirituality are absolutely central. In fact, the spirituality that inspired the first monks continues to inspire the monks of today: renounce the world, renounce oneself and build a relationship with God that is as direct as possible. The construction of the relationship with God is, however, based on ascetic practices that often differ significantly according to the practitioner's age and community. Nonetheless, in the various monastic movements it is possible to identify very old structuring logics based on the principles of autonomy and emancipation, especially of political and ecclesiastical power. From the first centuries of Christianity, monastic movements have sprung from the will of men and women to free themselves as much as possible from their existential condition and worldly needs. They have sought to organise communities less constrained by social order in general and by political and economic contingencies in particular. For these men and women the issue has been to get out of the world and to create a society of consecrated individuals entirely devoted to the search for God. To pursue this objective the question of asceticism is essential. As defined by Max Weber in 1958, asceticism is a way to free people from their nature and their impulses through extreme self-control.

If asceticism is therefore not an objective but a means of reaching God, Weber adds, it is invariably hostile to authority. Here we find the essentially emancipatory objective of asceticism and monasticism. The aim is to be freed from the logics of power. Outside the world, men and women engaged in monastic movements seek to create a different society. In this sense, it is possible to agree with Jean Séguy that these men and women are guided by a utopia. This he defines as 'Criticism of the present by a past or normative principle, in the perspective of another future' ('Pour une sociologie de l'ordre religieux', *Archives de sciences sociales des religions*, 57:1 (1984), 62). This utopia aims at the transformation of society and seeks to free women and men from their condition and worldliness. The pursuit of this utopia responds to the essential need of monks and nuns to free themselves from carnal life in order to attain the good life. But if this utopia is profoundly transcendent in the sense that it is always open and is intended to be surpassed, it is nonetheless a variable historical and social phenomenon: how radical it is varies according to the period in which it is pursued.

Since late antiquity, the men and women who, generation after generation, have chosen to give their lives an exemplary religious direction have done so in ways that have varied according to the times, regions, theological quarrels, and ascetic and spiritual currents. Monasticism has a fundamentally protean character that, over time, allows it to persist while renewing itself despite political, social and religious contexts, which are at times frankly hostile to the extreme way of life it advocates. Indeed, at first glance, monastic asceticism marks a radical break with one of the essential elements of life in society, namely its family structure and thereby the reproduction of society. Even though marriage, family and reproduction were a matter of survival for the population in the Roman Empire, women and men 'renounced the flesh' for the resurrection of the dead and to prepare for the end of time announced by the Christian doctrine as it had been widely taught and transmitted by Saint Paul. Indeed, the formation of women's communities dates back to the first century. Thus, choosing to break with the family, the first members of the monastic communities inaugurated an extreme and extra-worldly way of life.

Historically, Syria–Mesopotamia is, with Egypt, one of the cradles of Christian monastic movements. In the fourth century, in Upper and Lower Egypt, the hermits of Saint Anthony (250–356) and Saint Pachomius (292–346) went into the desert, firstly to practise prayer and meditation in almost absolute eremitism and secondly to found a community there in a closed place under the authority of a superior. After them, in less than a century, hundreds and thousands of monks chose to live in this hostile environment, in total destitution. This movement spread in Syria–Mesopotamia with, however, some specificities. Several works on the conditions of the emergence and the peculiarities of monasticism in Syria in relation to Egyptian monasticism show that until the seventh century, a considerable number of monks engaged in extreme ascetic practices, such as Stylitism, Saint Simeon Stylites being one of the most celebrated representatives. But then there are other, more extreme ascetic practices, which have now fallen into oblivion. The monks of the time thus exercised in their asceticism a certain violence that, moreover, was directed both towards themselves and towards other. For Peter Brown, if Egypt is indeed the cradle of monasticism, at the time of the Roman Empire of the East 'Syria was the great province for ascetic stars.... [T]he holy men who minted the ideal of the saint in society came from Syria, and, later, from Asia Minor and Palestine – not from Egypt' (Peter Brown, *Society and the Holy in Late Antiquity*, London: Faber and Faber (1982), 109–11).

Movements Beyond the Mundane Order

Nevertheless, in spite of the radical particularities of these 'virtuosos of the religious' (Weber) – in comparison with other clerics, from a more formal and institutional point of view – in the age of primitive Christianity there was not yet a real separation between the secular clergy and the regular clergy; the population of the monks is then ill-defined and is neither secular nor clerical. There is, however, another fundamental difference between men of religion in general – who were all ascetics, from the simple cleric to the bishop – and the lay Christian population. Therefore, until the fourth century, one cannot really speak of monasticism in Syrian–Aramaic Mesopotamia, and it is more accurate to speak of 'protomonachism' or 'first asceticism'. Later, the ecclesiastical structures adopted the more classical model of Christianity in the late Roman Empire, in which members of the secular clergy and ascetics were radically different in their religious practices and ways of life. This split also led to many heresies. Political and religious tensions between clerical institutions and monastic movements, which constitute a real *topos* of the history of Christianity, are therefore very old. Varying in strength according to the epochs, they participated in the construction and the specificities of the different monastic movements through the ages. Hence, classically, the monastic society of that period, which was not unified, was already established as a counter-society in relation to ecclesiastical institutions, which were extremely hierarchical and structured around the figures of the bishop and the episcopal college. As it was, the rapid collapse of the official church in Syria in the fifth century and the great Councils of Ephesus and Chalcedon gave considerable freedom back to the monks.

Despite the fundamental change in the structure of the church from this time on, the relationship between the monks and the faithful remained very close. The monks chose their disciples among them and formed more or less stable monastic communities. In this particularly competitive monastic world, many monks also wished to exercise a certain magisterium in society and did not hesitate to instigate major ecclesiastical conflicts such as the one concerning the unity of the natures of Jesus Christ. Moreover, monasticism did not develop in a truly hostile environment. Indeed, the first monks appeared in the region where Christianity had practically become the official religion of the Roman Empire. And, unlike the martyrs of the first centuries, who had no choice but to go into the desert or to the mountains to escape religious persecution, the monks themselves had a real social visibility.

The integration of the monk – who, according to Brown's expression, is a holy man – in society made him a real 'hinge-man' and 'man of power' (Brown, *Society and the Holy in Late Antiquity*, 118) who was able to resist the power of the great lords. The 'holy men' were very popular and crowds of people visited them. In analysing the context of the emergence of the 'holy man' as well as his role in his era, Brown clearly shows that the latter certainly did not entirely devote himself to a contemplative life. On the contrary, he had an important role in society and was even considered, at the time, to be an individual capable of managing the internal problems of a village or a region and defending the interests of the peasants against the landowners. The category of the sacred to which the holy man was attached then had a real function: it enabled him to exercise a role in society.

In the Christian tradition, monks have never been figures of stability. On the contrary, they always evolved on the margins of the church and were agitators. Far from ignoring this fact, however, for centuries the prelates and monks have referred to them as eminent representatives of Christianity, who have always been able to defend their society against the powers of one side or another and who, to a certain extent, continue to do so. In a way, the function the members of the monastic movements have today has been inherited from the monks of the first centuries. Of course, it is difficult today to speak of them as 'holy men or women', but the saints to which the monasteries are dedicated and to which the monastic communities devote themselves entirely, allow them to continue to exercise this function. It is for this reason that the relations established by the monastic communities with the saints are so important.

This essential detour via the category of the sacred developed by the works of Brown, which specifically examine the role and the place of the one he calls 'holy man' at the time of the emergence of the first monastic movements, makes it possible to restore a texture and a social and political density to the members of the monastic movements and to the spirituality that inspires them. By restoring their social depth to the monks and the communities they form, the historical and anthropological approaches of monasticism come together to characterise this religious phenomenon. Thus, even more firmly than utopia – although this is not contradictory – it is indeed the protest against worldliness that the monastic movements seem to embody and which guides the monastic spirituality in this region. In any case, this is what the first Syrian ascetics, then considered to be the holders of great supernatural powers, did by cursing their enemies in the name of God, practising exorcisms or even generously distributing graces to the devout coming to ask for cures, as well as resolving their economic disputes with the great lords of the cities. They appeased the evils of humanity, while at the same time contesting a social and political order that governed by force. Monastic movements have an original and structuring aspect, more or less acute depending on the period and, if not revolutionary, at least contentious, undoubtedly contributing to their dynamism and permanence in the region.

Furthermore, we must note how subversive it is for educated, middle-class men and women to forgo the conventional lifestyle of getting married and having children, to go against tradition and choose to devote themselves to a monastic life. For women, in former times and also today, running away from marriage and joining an order despite their family's opposition is even more subversive. This aspect is certainly an indication of what today continues to animate monastic spirituality. The choice made by monks and nuns to lead an ascetic existence in order to bear witness to their belief in Jesus Christ is quite different from that of members of the secular clergy who enter the service of the church. The latter inscribe their religious vocation in parishes, bishoprics and patriarchies. And in Egypt, Palestine, Lebanon and Syria, according to their hierarchical status, they are linked to the political figures of the country and take their place in a worldly order, at the heart of which political and economic relations and often patriarchy and cronyism prevail.

Mainstays of the Christian Community

As we have seen, monasticism is a singular way of life and expression of the Christian faith. The Arabic term for 'monasticism', *rahbana,* is built on the root *RHB*, which means 'fear'. The monk is indeed 'he who fears God'. The monks and nuns are outside a worldly hierarchy to which the members of the secular clergy belong, and for this reason monks and nuns may be said to be outside the world. Moreover, the verb *tarahaba,* which is used in Arabic to designate the action of these men and women, precisely means 'to isolate oneself from society by entering the monastery in order to worship God'. It also designates the one who takes the monastic vows (poverty, chastity and obedience) and who sacrifices himself or herself to God. The members of the secular clergy, for their part, take no vows, but engage in their priesthood through a ceremony based on the notion of 'promises', *nuzur* in Arabic. Moreover, men who are already married can become priests in the Eastern rites, including those who belong to churches recognising the authority of the Vatican. Nowadays, according to monks and nuns, people visit the monasteries and give them gifts because they remain strong points of identification for the Christian population of this region, and they certainly have become even more important since the end of the 1960s and the official closure of borders between several countries in the region and Israel, as well as the banning of Christians from the region (except Jordanians and Egyptians) from Israel and consequently from carrying out the Great Pilgrimage to Jerusalem. According to monks and nuns, the saints of the monasteries then gained importance in order to become again the 'symbolic resourcing of a community and to attract the Christian community towards a deeper religious and spiritual experience' (excerpt from an interview with a Greek Orthodox monk, 2003, Syria).

Monks and nuns thus receive many visitors, and it is much more common for a Christian from the region to visit the members of the monastic movements than to visit the prelates of the churches, with whom relations are extremely distant. Their ties with the population provided the members of the monastic movements with a certain power over the latter, which in many respects was more important than that of the prelates. Nevertheless, this separation and sometimes opposition between monasteries and their communities on one side and the churches and their prelates on the other, which monks and nuns tend to emphasise, must be qualified. First, the superiors of the monastic movements are ambivalent: they are the links with the prelates and represent, in some ways, the authority of the latter in the monastery. Then, on the side of men, we must remember that bishops are often monks and that the patriarchs are chosen from among the bishops, and therefore potentially from among the monks. Therefore, for men, the only holders of religious authority in the Eastern churches, there is a possible circulation between secular clergy and regular clergy. This essential nuance certainly allowed the monastic movements to maintain themselves despite their profound rejection of the power of clerics.

Indeed, it is legitimate to wonder how, without this fundamental nuance, monastic movements and ascetic spirituality could to this day occupy a place of such great importance in the Christianity of this region for both the religious and the laity. This is certainly the reason why the patriarchs of the Eastern churches, who are the supreme repositories of religious and political authority over church members, have not ceased since the second half of the twentieth century to encourage the creation and renewal of monastic movements and the spread of ascetic spirituality. Hence, in 1977, the Greek Orthodox Patriarch of Antioch and All the East, Elias IV Moawad, made the following declaration in one of his official speeches:

> The creation of monastic communities is an indication of the spiritual maturity of the faithful.... The Church needs both clergy in the parishes and religious in the monasteries. A Church that does not have these two complementary aspects is not complete.... Without monasteries we are guided solely by the bishops, and a bad bishop can lead his community towards evil. Herein lies the importance of the monasteries. Monasteries have always been the history and protection of Orthodoxy.

Seven years later, in August 1984, the new patriarch of the church, Ignatius IV Hazim, reaffirmed the idea in an interview with the Lebanese daily *al-Nahar*: 'Monastic communities are one of the most important elements to pursue our goal of renewal. Monasticism is one of the purest elements of the Church.'

Conclusion

Excerpts from the speeches of these two heads of the Greek Orthodox patriarchate of Antioch and All the East from 1970 to 2012 show that they pursued the same objective: establishing monastic movements as one of the essential dimensions of their church. According to them, the members of the monastic movements thus have two important functions: the protection of the church and the whole community – secular and religious – and the perpetuation of tradition. Monastic movements and ascetic spirituality are therefore conceived as structuring elements of the church and of the community. Thus, despite the tumultuous changes in the region that have affected the monastic communities as well as the rest of the population, monasticism is not in decline. On the contrary, faithful to their subversive tradition, monks and nuns do not hesitate to oppose the political power that attempts to manipulate the Christian communities, as we can observe in Syria. The monk and priest Paolo Dall'Oglio, as well as his monastic community of the Syriac Catholic monastery of Mar Moussa, located in the region of Homs (Syria), openly called for support for the Syrian revolution as early as 2011. In 2014, the Greek Orthodox nuns of the monastery of Saint Thecle in Syria refused to accuse the rebellion of persecuting them because of their religion. They even declared to the official media that rebels had saved them from death when the fights between the Syrian army and the rebels took place around the monastery. Hence, we can see how monastic communities offer a political and religious voice freed from the clientelist constraints in which patriarchal institutions are often caught up and that prevent Christians from having a real non-communitarian political commitment.

Bibliography

Brown, Peter, *Society and the Holy in Late Antiquity* (London: Faber and Faber, 1982).

Brown, Peter, *The Body and Society: Men, Women and Sexual Renunciation in Early Christianity* (New York: Columbia University Press, 2008 [1988]).

Poujeau, Anna, *Des monastères en partage. Sainteté et pouvoir chez les chrétiens de Syrie* (Nanterre: Société d'ethnologie, 2014).

Séguy, Jean, 'Pour une sociologie de l'ordre religieux', *Archives de sciences sociales des religions*, 57:1 (1984), 55–68.

Weber, Max, *The Protestant Ethic And The Spirit Of Capitalism* (New York: Charles Scribner's Sons, 1958).

Ecclesiology

Gabriel Hachem

Since the war in Iraq and Syria, the Christians of the Middle East have been subject to much international concern, as their presence is more than ever threatened by major challenges. They represent a source of the most ancient Christianity and are the last witnesses to the gospel in this region. Their role has often marked the life of people and contributed to the constitution of the country in which they are 'embedded'. Their diversity reflects both a wealth of theological, spiritual and cultural traditions as well as a series of divisions that still separate their different churches as a result of theological controversies and cultural and political conflicts.

The current situation of Christians in the Middle East, in its political, social and ecclesial complexity, can be confusing at first sight. They differ from one another in their theologies, liturgies, spiritualities, histories, cultures and languages. How should one distinguish between what is held in common and what marks the ecclesial and confessional identity of each of them? What is their current mission and what role can they play as religious and ethnic minorities in the midst of current crises? This essay seeks to shed light on the situation by offering an analysis of ecclesiology – how the churches of the region understand themselves.

The Mystery of the Church

Ecclesiology is the mystery of the church as an approach, discourse, and historical realisation. Clearly, these three elements are inseparable, especially in the East, where the life of the church is understood to be the response of the people of God to the convocation (Hebrew *qahal*) of the Spirit. This response becomes 'liturgy', meaning a reflection of the Trinitarian Mystery in worship for the glory of the Father, Son and Holy Spirit. The church is liturgy and liturgy is where the Father's plan is realised through the incarnation of the Son and the power of the Spirit. In the Eastern churches, everything is liturgical: theology, poetry, iconography, hymnography, rites, sacraments, *diakonia* (service) and fraternal charity. This practice of the mysteries allows no separation between 'being a Christian' and living as church. This witness, to the point of martyrdom if necessary, is the manifestation of this being.

This ecclesiological foundation has accompanied the Eastern churches and marked their history, to the extent that this mystical approach has become synonymous with their being. This is why Western Christians sometimes speak of Eastern Christianity as a world of 'magic' or 'marvels'.

The Christian Middle East is a complex reality; it is one and diverse at the same time. The Church of God is no exception to this rule. Although she is one and uniform in Jerusalem, she permits diversity in Antioch, where 'the Church was born under the sign of plurality', as stated by Jean Corbon in his book *L'Eglise des Arabes* [*The Church of the Arabs*] (Paris: Cerf, 1st edn, 1977, 21). The Judeo-Christian community opens to the nations and embraces the pagan-Christian element (Acts 15). Later, this diversity extends to all the Eastern regions, and the mixing of different elements builds the catholicity of the church, which from that point on incorporates Jews, Greeks, Romans and Syrians.

The history of the Middle East has often been shaken by political turmoil, marking the life of Christian communities with suffering. This suffering is due to multiple factors *ad intra* and *ad extra*. Theological debates of the fourth and fifth centuries led to painful separations that last to this day. The advent of Islam in the seventh century and the rapid invasion of the patriarchal territories of Jerusalem, Antioch and Alexandria separated these churches from their sisters. But Islam also became, like Judaism, an essential element in the constitution of Eastern Christianity.

Between the seventh and twentieth centuries, many different dynasties and Muslim regimes ruled in the East. Christians were first considered citizens entirely set apart, before they became *dhimmis*, that is to say second-class citizens, and treated as 'foreigners' to the Muslim *ummah* (nation). Political events and their ramifications have marked the life of the Eastern churches, which have adapted consecutively to Caesaropapism under the Byzantine Empire, cooperative citizenship under the Umayyad and Abbasid caliphates, and finally to the status of *dhimmis* or minorities with special status in return for paying the capital tax. Persecutions are often their lot; their witness to Christ even unto martyrdom became their major challenge. The Syro-Chaldean and Armenian genocides perpetrated a century ago are just a flagrant illustration.

Ecclesiological Characteristics of Patriarchal Churches

The Eastern churches, regardless of denomination, call themselves 'apostolic' in the dual sense of founded by an Apostle and continuing to live according to apostolic tradition. Their structure is intimately related to the apostolic ministry that is perpetuated through apostolic succession, especially in the episcopate, one male bishop for each church, who is the guarantee of apostolicity (fidelity to apostolic teaching). As a successor of the Apostles, the bishop is the icon of Christ present in his church on its way to the Kingdom of God. He presides over the community as the *protos* (first) and at the Eucharistic celebration as the *proestos* (one who holds the place of Christ). This apostolic succession is seen in the East as the guarantee of unity, catholicity and holiness of the Church of God realised in a particular place.

The ecclesiology of the East is a Eucharistic ecclesiology. The communion of the church manifests itself and lives in the synaxis (the Eucharistic gathering). In Eastern thinking, the church is the Eucharist and the Eucharist manifests the church as the sacrament of Christ. This synaxis is always the celebration of a memorial, the actualisation of the economy of salvation, and the anticipation of the end times. The liturgy therefore has an important place in the life of Eastern Christians; it is where they excel in the aesthetics of architecture and art for the glorification of the Holy Trinity.

The communion among the churches is also assured by apostolicity, whose sign is the historical episcopate. To offer the same worship to God, proclaim the same gospel, celebrate the same mystery of faith, transform time (*chronos*) into favourable moments (*kairos*) as well as the material world into the Kingdom of God, all of this is what it means to be in communion with the Trinity, with each other and with the world. They claim in their theological discourse that the universal church is the communion of the local or particular churches with the episcopate as its apostolic structure.

The recognised structures for ecclesial communion are the proclamation of the Word, sacramental communion and fraternal life in a diocese headed by a bishop. These structures, developed in the East, form the theological and ecclesial foundation of patriarchal and synodal practices. From the fifth century on, this synodal practice granted to the Eastern churches a patriarchal structure confirmed in the Codex of Justinian. The patriarch is somehow the 'first among equals', the one who calls, chairs and speaks for the synod. The patriarch and the synod together constitute the patriarchal structure of the Eastern churches: no synod without a patriarch and no patriarch without a synod. According to Canon 34 of the Apostolic Canons, the patriarch is the first who must not decide anything without the other. In this sense, the patriarchate is the cornerstone of Eastern ecclesiology and pentarchy; that is to say, the agreement of the five apostolic patriarchates in the order established at the Council of Chalcedon (451) constitutes its ultimate expression, especially during the celebration of an ecumenical council.

The ecumenical council appeared in the fourth century. This was a new synodal structure established to express the communion of the whole church spread throughout the world (*oikoumeni*). However, the criteria for ecumenicity and for reception remain undetermined and are not accepted by all the churches. The ecumenical councils of the fourth and fifth centuries were crucial for the formulation of Christian dogma concerning the incarnation, the hypostatic union of two natures in the person of Christ, and in the divinity of the Holy Spirit. This conciliar way (*via concilii*) maintained communion between the Roman Catholic Church and the Greek or Byzantine Eastern Church until the fifteenth century. The Council of Florence, 1438–9, was the last council held between the two churches and was not fully received.

Orthodox patriarchal churches still maintain the patriarchal structure of the first millennium. Besides the apostolic patriarchates of Constantinople, Alexandria, Antioch and Jerusalem, minor patriarchates have formed that are characterised by their national identity (such as the Russian, Serbian and Romanian patriarchates). The celebration of communion between these churches and its ultimate expression are realised in the convocation of a Holy and Great Synod or a pan-Orthodox synod. However, at times the autocephaly that ensures their independence makes this convocation difficult and compromises it.

Monasticism was born in the East – Syria, Egypt and Palestine. It developed there, as witness to anticipation of the resurrection and as a royal road to *sequela Jesu*, an imitation of Christ by a total detachment (*kenosis*), to the point of martyrdom. Monastic centres are havens of Eastern Orthodoxy, oases of faith for spiritual renewal. The communion with the local bishop is the sign of the incorporation of their monasteries in the church. Their mission consists in that. In the Coptic Orthodox Church in Egypt, the monastic life is a reflection of the vitality and spiritual dynamism of the whole church. The monasteries are often seen as places of pilgrimage. They are visited by the faithful who wish to rediscover the purity of faith in living strong spiritual moments by engaging in prayer and meditation. Through the centuries, some monasteries played a prominent role in the conservation of manuscripts and transmission of the Bible. The monastery of St Catherine in the Sinai is an example, known among other monasteries for its precious manuscripts.

Western Missions and their Impact

From the sixteenth century, the ecclesiological structure of the Eastern churches faced a double Western model, presented and supported by the Catholic and Protestant missions alike. This confrontation has had a significant impact on ecclesiology in the East.

First, from the fifth century the Roman Catholic Church has opted for a centralised or pyramidal ecclesiology. As Yves Congar has argued, the 1054 schism between the Roman Catholic Church and the Greek/Byzantine

Church was brought about by a progressive state of estrangement between the two. Therefore, Catholics developed an exclusivist ecclesiology stating that 'outside the Catholic Church there is no salvation'. This unilateral development has reinforced the belief that the Roman Catholic Church is the Church of Christ. Concerned with the salvation of non-Catholics, Rome established the Congregation for the Propagation of the Faith (Propaganda Fide) in 1622, with mission and conversion as its goal. Roman missions, established in the East in the second half of the sixteenth century, organised themselves under the care of the new Congregation and introduced new concepts in ecclesiology and soteriology. The dedication of the Latin missionaries for the salvation of the 'condemned' Easterners became the foundation and theological justification for these missions. Their method was to open schools and to send top students to Roman universities to train and to be ordained. Once these students were back in their country, they would assist the missions. Sinking into poverty, social injustice and ignorance that prevailed under the Ottoman Empire, groups of Orthodox faithful considered the Latin missionaries to be 'saviours'. The vacant patriarchal see was their opportunity to declare their union with the Roman See. The Eastern Catholic churches emerged (Greek Melkite, Chaldean, Armenian, Syriac and Coptic). This movement, called by the orthodox 'Uniatism', far from contributing to the unity of the church, has multiplied divisions in the East.

The Eastern Catholic churches have largely abandoned the theology of their fathers and adopted the post-Tridentine Latin theology. They thus introduced the Roman concept of papacy, with its universal jurisdiction, and an exclusivist principle of salvation. They added the Filioque to the Nicene–Constantinopolitan creed and preached the doctrine of transubstantiation as defined by the Council of Trent.

As far as liturgy was concerned, the Melkites, envious of the Roman rites and liturgy, introduced Corpus Christi in their calendar and removed the feast of Gregory Palamas, considered by the Romans to be a heretic. Religious practices of Latin origins have spread in all the Eastern Catholic churches. Processions, novenas and worship of the Blessed Sacrament have multiplied in parishes and shrines. In the sacrament of initiation, baptism and confirmation are celebrated separately, contrary to tradition, and first communion has become a common practice.

The Catholic ecclesiology, at the time, had a tendency towards standardisation. The Eastern churches translated and taught the Tridentine catechism to comply with Roman instructions. Some among them were Latinised more than others because they believed they could play the role of bridge between East and West on the principle of 'dual communion'. However, in doing so they fell into the ecclesiological ambiguity they always suffer: Eastern but attached to the Roman Church, Orthodox but having become Catholic, and patriarchal but subject to the authority of the pope. The Eastern Catholic churches live thus in an ecclesiological tension: they are not recognised by the Orthodox, nor is their ecclesial being deeply respected by the Catholics. The question remains: what is their place and role within the communion of churches?

Protestant and Evangelical missions arrived in the East in the late eighteenth century. They had the same foundations and the same theological justification as their Latin counterparts. From America or Europe, they applied the same methods, creating schools and selecting the brightest students to train in the West and to become pastors. In return, these pastors were devoted to the mission and became the right hand of Western missionaries. However, unlike the Latin missions that led to the birth of the Eastern Catholic churches, Protestant and Evangelical missions have contributed to the establishment of Reformed and Evangelical churches or communities in the Levant. These new Christian communities suffer from the same ambiguity of identity and ecclesiology as Eastern Catholics because they are regarded as corollaries of colonialism. In fact, up until the ecumenical era in the 1960s, they used European languages in worship, teaching and administration. Some pastors were Europeanised to the point that they distinguished themselves from the indigenous people in the countries where they lived and ministered.

Inspired by Martin Luther, the Reformers rose against a poor concept of individual salvation. The massive practice of indulgences at the expense of education in the faith was the starting point of this revolution. However, strongly held ecclesiological principles have caused some resistance to the ideas of the Reformation among Easterners attached to their discipline, their sacraments and their liturgical rites. The Protestant Reformation remains, nevertheless, a major event in the modern history of global Christianity. It reiterated and defended the first foundations of the Christian faith, including justification by faith alone, the primacy of the Word of God, the importance of the common priesthood of the people of God and the apostolic ministry as a 'service'. The reception of the Counter-Reformation prevented the Catholic churches of the Middle East from opening up to the Reformation and achieving a critical analysis. Similarly, the Orthodox churches showed greater resistance to innovations that seemed inadequate for their ecclesial traditions and for their ecclesiology. How, then, did Protestant churches and Evangelical communities come to exist in the region? Schools and educational institutions, colleges and universities were the privileged place of encounter with the Reformation, through the study of biblical texts and openness to post-Renaissance European civilisation. Competition between Catholic and Protestant missionaries had beneficial effects in this area. The social work of missionaries was also a way to implement the principles of the Reformers. But the decisive factor, in my view, lies in the dedication and witness of missionaries themselves, who presented life and spiritual role models.

In the specific historical context of the eighteenth, nineteenth and early twentieth centuries, while the Ottoman Empire increasingly became a 'sick man', the contribution of Western missions was of considerable benefit to the people of the region. In theology, the scholastic method (mainly Thomistic) was introduced and Easterners were introduced to Western theological method. In matters of worship, a personal relationship with God, expressed in individual prayer as well as some liturgical rites, allowed the faithful to experience new horizons of spiritual life. Personal Bible reading has been promoted by vernacular translations, as well as the new tradition of Bible study. Sunday schools also contributed, in turn, to the listening, discernment and meditation of the Word of God. In teaching, education and training, the impact of the missionaries is undeniable. In this area, the Catholic and Orthodox churches are indebted to the Reformation!

One 'Church of the Arab'

The concept 'Church of the Arabs', coined by Jean Corbon, initially applied to the Church of Antioch in the land of the Arabs. This is strictly an ecumenical concept that sprang from a historical fact. The churches that exist today in the ancient territory of this patriarchate have the same roots, the same patristic and theological heritage and the same culture. They form the Church of Christ in this determined 'place' and were given the same mission. Going back to the Antiochian sources can only bring unity to this church and heal its secular wounds. Similarly, working for its unity leads its components to their common identity.

It seems entirely justifiable to apply today this concept in the Middle Eastern territory since the ecclesiological analysis, presented in the preceding paragraphs, shows how various factors and events have shaped the identity of the Church of Christ in this region. Four families of churches are present: (1) the Oriental Orthodox churches, the Assyrian Apostolic Church, the Eastern Orthodox churches; (2) the Eastern Catholic churches; (3) Protestant and Reformed churches; and (4) the family of free Evangelical communities, the international Pentecostal movement, the Assemblies of God, the Baptist Church, the Seventh-day Adventist Church.

The Coptic, Armenian and Syriac Churches form the family of Oriental Orthodox churches. They are in full communion in faith, sacraments and service. They affirm their fidelity to the apostolic tradition and preserve traditional ecclesiology as far as the discourse on the mystery of the church and the liturgy are concerned. The same applies to monastic life and moral instruction. The ecclesiastical hierarchy enjoys great authority and full respect from all members. The bone of contention with other churches is primarily theological and specifically Christological. The separation dates back to the Council of Chalcedon and focuses on the concept of nature (*physis*) and the union of the divine and the human in the one person of Christ. Since the 1960s, these are open to ecumenical dialogue, especially at the regional and international levels.

The family of Eastern Orthodox Churches relates to the three apostolic patriarchates of Antioch, Alexandria and Jerusalem. These communities are descendants of the Byzantine Empire. They are in full communion despite the canonical and disciplinary independence of each. Until the mid-nineteenth century, they were still 'Hellenised'. The patriarchate of Antioch has taken a different path and Arabised itself, while the other two patriarchates are still dominated by the Greek hierarchy. In Jerusalem, the hierarchy is Greek while the people are Arab; in Alexandria it is the same story, while the effective expansion of the patriarchate happens on the side of the African continent beyond Egypt and North Africa.

The Apostolic Assyrian Church of the East is an ecclesiological entity on its own. Withdrawn from the Council of Ephesus (431), accused of Nestorianism and martyred by successive persecutions, this notable church of a tradition dating back to the Apostles Addai and Mari is now weakened by the dispersion of the faithful around the world. The majority of the Assyrians found refuge in the Chicago area in the USA. Recently, the Assyrian Church opened to international ecumenical dialogue, while the dispute with the Orthodox Copts does not seem yet resolved. This church is part of the family of the Syriac churches, even if its language, called 'Eastern' in relation to the Euphrates, contains some changes compared with the 'Western Syriac' used by the Syriac and the Maronite Churches.

The Eastern Catholic family consists of Armenian, Chaldean, Coptic, Maronite, Melkite Greek Catholic and Syriac Churches, whose emergence is linked to Catholic missions. They are a minority compared with the mother churches, with the exception of the Chaldean Church, where the number of faithful is greater than that of the Assyrians. The identity of Eastern Catholics established itself especially in the early twentieth century, after the publication in 1895 of the apostolic letter of Pope Leo XIII entitled *Orientalium Dignitas*. This papal document reclaimed the value of the Eastern Catholic churches and reminded the missionaries that they are at the service of the Eastern churches. This measure, combined with financial subsidies, endowed these churches with an internal organisation as well as educational and social institutions that are the cause of great pride. Since Vatican II, they seek to define their place and role in the communion of churches. They equally promote a synodal approach through the national assemblies of patriarchs and bishops as well as the Council of the Catholic Patriarchs of the East, formed in 1991.

Protestant and Reformed churches established in the East invested increasingly in integrating in the ecclesial soil of the Middle East while keeping their own identity. Reformed and Presbyterian communities have been growing in Lebanon and Syria. The Lutheran and Episcopalian (Anglican) Churches are present in Egypt, Palestine and Jordan. Engaged in the ecumenical movement since its birth, they came together first in the Near East Christian Council. In fact, Protestants in the Middle East are the developers and pioneers of ecumenism. In 1964, the Syriac Orthodox Church of Antioch joined this Council, which became therefore the Near East Council of Churches. Later, Greek Orthodox (1974) and Catholics (1990) became board members of the Council, now called the Middle East Council of Churches (MECC). Presbyterian and Reformed communities prefer a synodal structure that goes beyond 'congregations'. We can cite as examples the National Evangelical Synod of Syria and Lebanon and the Evangelical Synod of the Nile (Egypt and Sudan). Reformed, Lutherans and Episcopalians together form the Fellowship of the Middle East Evangelical Churches.

The new Evangelical communities are a small minority in the region. Their ecclesial nature, their understanding of mission and salvation, give them a suspect proselytising character. In their biblical teaching and charismatic style, they are related more to their churches and communities of origin rather than to Eastern Christianity. Their ecclesiological model seems totally foreign to the churches of the region because it insists on the primacy of Scripture and neglects the tradition of the Fathers and sacramental practice. Some of these communities are not recognised by the civil authorities and face difficulties in confessional regimes related to the status of persons.

Ecumenical Vocation of Christian Presence

'Ecumenism in the East is a matter of life or death', stated Melkite Patriarch Maximos IV. The creation of the MECC marks par excellence the ecumenical moment and the most appropriate place for the expression and promotion of communion among the different churches in the region. It is an ecumenical body, a forum where Christians meet to learn about each other as the Church of Christ in Arab lands. This ecclesiology of communion inevitably results in the synodal way, the soul of the Eastern churches. But synodality requires recognition of the other, in its own identity and openness to the diversity of Christians in the Middle East. Together, they can promote a common theological reflection and adequate models of unity appropriate to their context.

Before being a movement or way of thinking, ecumenism is first a common life in the service of a common mission. The particular Eastern context is one of mixed marriages and common pastoral concerns. In 1991, a declaration of recovery of communion was signed by patriarchal Syriac and Greek Churches of Antioch decreeing the *communicatio in sacris* (worship in common). In 1996 the Melkite Greek Catholic Church undertook an initiative with the Greek Orthodox Church. It is based on the fruits of the dialogue since 1982 within the Joint International Commission for Dialogue between the Catholic Church and the Orthodox Church: the ecclesiology of communion, the concept of sister churches and the common heritage. Archbishop Elias Zoghby (former Archbishop of Baalbek, Lebanon) tried to base this initiative on the principle of 'dual communion'. But circumstances did not seem ripe for either side – the opinions of the Roman Curia and the patriarchate of Constantinople were not favourable – and the project has not been implemented. On the other hand, in the Council of Catholic Patriarchs of the Orient (CCPO) and with the synodal work with the Greek and Oriental Orthodox Churches, a protocol of pastoral understanding was signed aimed at addressing such issues as mixed marriage, first communion and the development of a common catechetical curriculum. This is an expression and a suitable preparation for the resumption of full communion in three sensitive areas. The reception of this protocol is quite satisfactory; the need for new protocols is increasingly felt and there is always the need for a common pastoral work.

Since its inception, the Church of Antioch has been open to all currents of Christianity. It has become a model of diversity despite the vicissitudes of history; its ecclesiology is an ecclesiology of communion. It is unfortunate that so far the Apostolic Assyrian Church of the East and the new Evangelical communities are not integrated in the MECC. The causes are different but the Council is aware that it should remain open to all, in order to be the mouthpiece of all Christians in the region.

The Global Christian Forum, born of the Council a little before 2000, focuses on the meeting of all the churches and Christian communities in a new ecumenical configuration that drives away institutionalisation. Since 2007, the Forum has taken, in collaboration with the MECC and with the blessing of church leaders, the initiative to visit the churches in the region and to organise consultations between them. The aim is a common reflection for the sake of promoting cooperation and common witness to the gospel in the current situation.

The Christian presence in the Middle East constantly encourages churches to take the context into account in their ecclesiology because the mystery of the church is always embodied in a 'place' and a specific culture. But the context shows that, despite the different cultural identities of the churches in the East, the highest common value appears to be Arabism. It also shows a model of common life between Jews, Christians and Muslims that is almost unique in the world, even if coexistence has not always been easy for over 13 centuries. As for human and social cohesion, it has proved rather authentic. With their knowledge, expertise, art and ingenuity, Christians have contributed to the development of society in the countries in which they live. As much as they have profited from this experience, they feel called to act as guardians of this convivial tradition to promote a model of inter-religious relations that should enrich the dialogue between different religions.

Since the 'Arab Spring', a new wave of violence invaded the entire region. The political instability that has lasted since the *Nakba* (the Palestinian defeat), social injustice and the deteriorating economic conditions have revived the haemorrhage of emigration and fuelled the return of violence. The events that have emptied the Mosul area of its Syriac and Chaldean people dispersed them on the road of suffering and destruction. This human tragedy is currently wasting the living forces of churches and driving them once again to face martyrdom. The courage of these Christians and their commitment to their faith never ceases to amaze the world.

Despite the relentless rise of Islamic extremism and the ravages of ISIS, Christians are invited to distinguish Islam from Islamic extremism. With all citizens, they want to fight terrorism, to reject the use of violence and to promote a culture of justice, peace and harmony. Such a project cannot be achieved without surpassing the minority complex and the deployment of rooting efforts in their countries. The road seems long, from the temptation of isolation to the confirmation of identity and citizenship in a state of law. To promote a civil society with the 'other' of a different religion appears today as a manifestation of communion and an updated form of ecclesiology.

Towards an Ecclesiological Pluralism

This essay on ecclesiology in the Middle East attests to the existence of several ecclesiological models. The first ecclesiological challenge is to receive and recognise this ecclesiological pluralism: to accept diversity of ecclesiological models in a synodal structure that safeguards the unity; to welcome new Evangelical communities and launch a dialogue on soteriology, eschatology and missiology; and to develop the practice of synodality in the service of 'being together' and of 'Church of the Arabs'. The second challenge is a theological one: how to promote together a contextual theology and an appropriate ecumenical model. To what extent is traditional theology prepared to include in its considerations new questions about forms of the apostolic ministry in a secularised society, the role and ministry of women in the church, the diverse sacramental structures, the exercise of authority, moral discernment in fundamental morality or bioethics, and collaboration in the protection of creation? The third challenge has to do with the relationship with other religions and specifically with Islam in its many manifestations. Can we truly speak of Islamic–Christian dialogue? Is it not more about a spiritual solidarity and cooperation to maintain peace and harmony in the context of a common life?

In a few words, the major challenges of ecclesiology in the East are: (1) to face together, beyond denominational affiliations and institutional compromises, the demands of the Christian presence in the East as the realisation of the Church of Christ in Arab lands; (2) to stay faithful to the gospel and the common tradition, without neglecting the new reality of the context; (3) to walk together, live in Church together, celebrate the mystery of God together, and witness to Christ together. In this way, hope can be rekindled and the Church of God can be manifested.

Bibliography

Badr, Habib, Suad abou el Rouss Slim and Joseph Abou Nohra (eds), *Christianity: A History in the Middle East* (Beirut: Middle East Council of Churches, 2005).

Corbon, Jean, *The Wellspring of Worship*, 2nd edn (San Francisco, CA: Ignatius Press, 2005).

Corbon, Jean, *L'Eglise des Arabes*, 2nd edn (Paris: Cerf, 2007).

O'Mahony, Anthony and John Flannery (eds), *The Catholic Church in the Contemporary Middle East* (London: Melisende, 2010).

Valognes, Jean-Pierre, *Vie et mort des chrétiens d'Orient: Des origines à nos jours* (Paris: Fayard, 1994).

Christian Media

Sara Afshari

Churches in North Africa and West Asia have adopted modern media in order to modernise their presentation of Christianity, to reach the unreached, to make their presence and the truth of their faith visible, and to connect to the wider world. The aim of this essay is to give an analytical overview of Christian media in the North Africa and West Asia region. Therefore, after stating the context, it will give a brief introduction to the function of media technologies in the region. Then it will introduce Christian media, using satellite channels as an example of their function. Finally, it will explain the importance of Christian media as well as point to current challenges.

Although Christians began using modern media technologies from their inception, the Christian churches in North Africa and West Asia had, at first, a slow start in this field as these technologies were regarded with suspicion. The two main concerns were: whether media had the ability to present the doctrine and the sacraments of the church and whether the safety of Christian communities would be at risk. The Catholics in Lebanon were the first to start television broadcasting in Arabic. Télé Lumière (Noursat) started in 1991 from Beirut, Lebanon. The new millennium brought rapid growth to Christian media in the region. One can detect several reasons for the fast adoption of media, the first being the fact that the churches saw opportunities to modernise their presentation of Christianity to reach the younger generations of Christians as well to as to spread their message more widely. Another reason was that, with the threat to their existence through persecution and discrimination, especially with the accelerated growth of Islamic extremism and its broadcast hate speeches against Christians, the churches felt a need to protect themselves, their identity and their right to exist. They did this by making their presence visible and the truth of their faith known to the region, as well as by connecting to the wider world and global Christianity in order to strengthen their position. The massive migration of Christians from and within the region was another reason to employ media, that is, to spiritually nourish and connect the diaspora communities to their home church communities.

Therefore, in this context Christians in North Africa and West Asia integrated media into the life of the church by employing all types of media technologies: old media (print, radio, including sound recording and television), the new/digital media (such as websites, weblogs, webTV, GooglePlus, online broadcasting) and social media (such as YouTube, Twitter, Facebook, Instagram, WhatsApp, Snapchat). However, the churches have focused their resources largely on old media, mainly on television programming, print and sound recording, with other types of media being given a secondary place, mainly as an accompaniment to their television programmes and video preaching.

Their approach to digital and social media has been influenced by the hierarchical systems of the churches, the lack of understanding of the functions and implications of social media, as well as limited media literacy and economic struggles among their focus audiences. For example, television has become a necessity for the majority of households in North Africa and West Asia as not everyone has a computer at home or even knows how to operate one. In addition, owning a satellite dish is a one-time cost but accessing the Internet is an ongoing cost. However, the Christian media in this region are very much situated within the modern world and globalisation. On the one hand, they belong to the religious media marketplace, while, on the other hand, they are part of the regional media, although professionally, socially and politically they have been slow to find their place in the larger media world in North Africa and West Asia. To analyse the work of Christian media it might be helpful to first give an overview of the function of media technologies in this region.

Media in North Africa and West Asia

The arrival of satellite channels, and later the Internet, in North Africa and West Asia was celebrated for their potential to bring political reforms and democracy into the region, to overthrow dictatorial regimes. They were also welcomed by the Arab regimes for publicising their political and ideological views locally and internationally. For that reason, most analyses and discussions on this subject outside the region have focused on democratisation and political reform. Within the region, by contrast, they have focused on pan-Arabism and Islamic ideologies – mainly strengthening the regimes. Therefore, from the beginning, the use of media and the task assigned to them were narrowly defined and heavily linked to political reform.

The 2009 Iranian uprising, the Green Movement and the 2011 Arab Uprising have been boldly called 'Twitter revolutions' and 'Facebook revolutions'. Yet, after nearly three decades of media revolution, not only did democracy not develop but the region has been more in turmoil than ever. In addition, satellite and Internet media have deepened the political, cultural, social and religious struggles of both the Middle Eastern regimes and their societies, while at the same time creating new opportunities, alternatives and creative empowerment for their users and participants. For this reason, it has become difficult, if not impossible, for governments to diminish or control the spread of the Internet and satellite channels. Nonetheless, heavy restrictions and domination have been practised by the majority of Middle Eastern regimes, through the frequent closing down of media organisations, persecution and imprisonment of journalists and individuals, and restrictions on online materials and access to new technological equipment. Each government has taken its own distinct approach. For example, Egypt and Saudi Arabia have provided satellite space (NileSat and ArabSat, respectively) for three purposes: first, to control the flow of information; secondly, for their national security; and thirdly, for the preservation of Arab identity and Islamic values. At the same time, however, many of the Arab regimes under controlling and restrictive guidelines have allowed the semi-privatisation of media. Iran, by contrast, has kept heavy control over all media platforms. It banned satellite channels, nationalised the Internet provision and has kept aggressive control over the print industry. Nevertheless, despite Iran's uncompromising stance, one can argue that among all the Middle East regimes Iran is the least successful in controlling the spread of media among its population, especially among the youth.

Satellite and Internet media have also created opportunities for minority groups to make their presence more visible and their voices heard, including promoting their religious ideologies. For instance, Christians have taken advantage of the media to reach out to their communities, to make their faith known to Muslims, as well as to offer to the wider society educational, inspirational and developmental programmes. However, in general their work, in comparison with Islamic media, has not been widespread. For example, the Islamic media (and other Islamic propaganda) – influenced by Christian televangelism and a business model of media, and with professional use of satellite channels and especially the Internet – have contributed significantly to the rise of Islamic extremism and increased the persecution of minorities, including Christians in the Middle East. Their founders are more experienced entrepreneurs and media players, with multimillion-dollar budgets. In contrast, Christian channels have to operate with minimal resources, limited budgets, limited media experience and very tight security, and in some places under severe persecution.

Despite all these factors, the region is home to various Christian satellite television channels, numerous Internet-based ministries and social media activities. The majority of churches and Christian communities have also taken advantage of the technology for their spiritual and social growth, for they too recognise the power of media to strengthen the bonds between believers and the churches and reinforce Christian practice among their members, as well as to spread their message more widely. Therefore, most of the leaders of the churches are in one way or another involved in Christian media activities. For example, if one enters a well established church somewhere in the Middle East, especially in churches in Egypt, Lebanon and Jordan, one can see media communication tools everywhere, such as digital projectors, television sets, good sound systems and even high-definition video-cameras. Notices invite visitors and members to look at their websites and watch or listen to the latest sermon or use other resources, as well as encouraging them to join their social media platforms such as Facebook or WhatsApp, or to watch their video clips on YouTube. Furthermore, if one travels to Tunisia, Algeria, Iraq or Palestine, and visits small churches or house churches and speaks to ordinary Christians, one is likely to hear stories of either their involvement with Christian media production or the impact of Christian media in their faith and lives, such as their experience in coming to faith.

Nonetheless, one can argue that the significance of Christian media in the Middle East is not in the technology or media platforms but in the power of active and participative human elements, both the leadership and the laity (producers and users), who connect Christians with one another, with their Muslim neighbours and with the wider world. Although Christian media have not yet found their place or established strong relationships within the larger Arab media world, their messages of hope, peace and forgiveness have contributed to sustaining hope for peace and tolerance within the Arab world in such a way that some Arab media have broadcast their messages or produced similar programmes themselves. For example, in two heart-breaking incidents, the beheading of 21 Copts in Libya on 12 February 2015 and the bombing of two Coptic churches on 9 April 2017 (Palm Sunday), which left 43 Christians dead, both committed by Daesh, the majority of Christian media broadcast messages of peace and forgiveness to the Arab societies and their Muslim neighbours, especially through the testimonies of some of the families of the martyrs, who offered their forgiveness to the murderers of their loved ones.

The Case of Satellite Television Channels

The complexity of functions of media, especially digital and social media, makes it difficult to analyse their work briefly. For that reason, I will use the case of satellite television channels as an example of the role of Christian media. The reason for choosing satellite television channels is that they are still the main players, especially since the development of digital broadcasting, which has provided them with the opportunity to adopt multi-layered media platforms for their content, which has increased their visibility online and on social media platforms as well. As a result, their audience can choose when and how to view and participate in their preferred programmes. Secondly, although Christian social media and Internet activities are a significant part of the history of Christian media in North Africa and West Asia, many people, depending on the country and their government's policies on bandwidth and censorship, as well as age groups, have only limited or controlled access to the Internet.

Around 25 Christian channels broadcast their programmes in Arabic and/or North African languages. Catholics in Lebanon were the first group to start Christian television broadcasting, in 1991, calling their station Télé Lumière (Noursat). Télé Lumière now runs 10 other channels, five on different satellite frequencies and the other five as Internet-based channels. After that came SAT-7, founded by Terence Ascott, which with ecumenical vision went on air in May 1996. Now it has four television channels in the Arabic language. The Coptic Christians at first joined SAT-7 but later started their own broadcasting, with a different approach: the channels are not run directly by any church but by individual groups within the Christian community for the purpose of supporting the churches. Their international television channel is called CTV. Besides CTV there are four other channels that serve Coptic Christians in North Africa and West Asia. Other than the above three main groups, channels that are available locally belong to Evangelical Protestant denominations and operate primarily from outside the region, mainly from the USA and Europe.

One can categorise Christian media into three types. The first category is those whose focus is on their own congregations and churches, such as Catholic Télé Lumière and the Coptic channels. The second type focus on the needs of the churches as well as Arab communities, Muslims and Christians alike, with their educational, developmental and teaching programmes. SAT-7, Miracle TV and Al-Karama TV are prominent in this category. The third category are channels whose main aim is to undertake evangelism; therefore their focus is mainly outside the church constituency. Those in the first category produce most of their programmes locally and with a denominational focus. Those in the second category produce a significant percentage of their programmes within the region, with an ecumenical and inter-denominational approach. Those in the third category produce almost all their programmes outside of the region, mainly in Europe and North America.

Based on the above categories, one can summarise the significance of Christian media in their three functions. The first is to serve Christian communities and churches, to take the churches and their teachings into people's homes, especially to Christians in remote areas who might not be able to attend a church otherwise and to those who for security reasons do not go to church. The second function is to carry out evangelism on behalf of the churches. The third function, which has not yet been utilised and explored fully, is to offer educational and inspirational programmes to all and to be a voice of freedom, justice, equality and peace for Christians and non-Christians alike. SAT-7 Arabic is one of the few channels that has a vision to do so, but it is still at an early stage.

The Importance of Christian Media

Christian media have many great opportunities, including broadcasting the message of hope, faith and love, as well as promoting forgiveness, peace and reconciliation in a devastated West Asia and North Africa, bringing Christian history to life, strengthening the Christian presence and promoting the contributions of Christians to their societies, making Christian faith available to all.

In 1954 a comedy film was produced in Egypt called *Hassan wa Morcus wa Cohen*. Hassan was a Muslim, Morcus was a Christian and Cohen was a Jew. All were able to work and live together despite their religious differences. In 2008 a new film was produced, called *Hassan wa Morcus* – because the Jewish community had almost disappeared from Egyptian society, Cohen was deleted. Recently even some Muslims, both in Egypt and elsewhere in the region, have raised their concerns over the shrinking of the Christian community. There might soon be a film called simply *Hassan*. There is also a growing fear worldwide that Christianity might soon disappear from its birthplace. The intensification of sectarian conflicts, the persecution and discrimination against Christians, civil wars, unrest and uncertainty in the region, migration and displacement have all contributed to the decline of Christianity in the Middle East. Many have left and those who have stayed, as George Makeen, programming director of SAT-7 Arabic channels, said in an interview with the author in May 2016, 'remain physically but not emotionally; the young people are full of passion, dreams and visions, but not for their community and society in the Middle East, for their dreamland is somewhere in the West'.

Christian media can strengthen the place of Christians within Middle Eastern societies through, firstly, providing a platform for individual Christians to speak about their dreams and to reflect their diversity. (At the moment, politically and religiously, whenever governments or other authorities and groups want to talk to Christians they go to the church leaders. Almost all the Christian television channels are in the hands of pastors and church leaders; the voices of individuals are not heard.) Secondly, as George Makeen said in the interview, 'if you want to protect them you need to present their history'. Christian media have great opportunities and platforms to reconstruct Christian history, their collective memories, warm traditions and silent customs, critically and objectively, in connection with their Middle Eastern culture and heritage. This strengthens the roots of Christians in the region. At present, many Christians have disconnected themselves from their non-Christian societies and communities. As Makeen said, 'We think we have nothing to do with Arabs or we are victims. We see ourselves closer to the West than to our Arab neighbours.' The retelling of Christian history in connection to Middle Eastern cultures will also strengthen the relationship between Christians and their Muslim neighbours. It allows Muslims to hear the forgotten chapters of their history and heritage. In almost all North African and West Asian countries, the history of Christianity in the school textbooks has been neglected, reduced to only a few pages or forgotten altogether. In the light of history and faith journeys in the Middle East, Christian media have the ability to speak on human rights, religious freedom, women's rights and people movements, which can pave the path towards peace, healing, forgiveness, reconciliation, respect and tolerance.

Voices for Peace and Hope

One of the most noteworthy clips on SAT-7 Kids is Maryam's interview in January 2015. Maryam was then a nine-year-old Iraqi Christian schoolgirl. Her house and school were destroyed by Daesh and her family had to flee and live in a refugee camp. Essam, the SAT-7 Kids reporter, asked her, 'What are your feelings towards those who drove you out and destroyed your home and school?' Her response – speaking of hope, faith and love – was overwhelming. The clip went viral in the Middle East and beyond. Even Al Arabiya, a Saudi-owned news agency, featured it on its website, and MTV, a Lebanese channel, broadcast it. Al Arabiya wrote, 'The Iraqi girl faces Daesh with love … and teaches the world a lesson of love, forgiveness and faith in God.'

The reason that Maryam's short interview went viral was her whisper of hope, love and courage. Hers is a voice that conceives a new path, a new way of thinking and new behaviour. Maryam's story also challenges the mentality of the Middle East, and offers alternatives: forgiveness, love and inclusivism: 'God loves everybody [even Daesh] … I will ask God to forgive them … they are in the hands of Satan.' Through this simple yet profound response Maryam offered a new way of thinking which shows the ability of Christian media to empower and project the voices of hope and courage that are already there, and voices that challenge people's pre-set mentalities.

Globalisation and modernity have not weakened the place of religion in North Africa and West Asia. However, both the increase of religious violence and wars being covered by global media have caused some to question their religious views and/or created the desire to experiment with different spiritual ideologies or non-religious ideologies. Among them are those who dare to call themselves 'atheists' and others who are in search of something different. For example, there are numerous websites, weblogs and social media sites (e.g. Facebook pages) on atheism in Arabic that speak of doubts and struggles with religion, which might seem odd in a region that has witnessed the growth of religiosity over the last few decades. Although this new movement is partly a reaction to what has been happening in the region, in this situation Christian media have the ability to offer hope, reconciliation with God and a new definition of 'self', 'truth' and 'God', as well as an alternative viewpoint.

Challenges Facing Christian Media Today

There are a number of challenges that Christian media face. The first relates to their strategy of doing mission. Many Christian media have not been able to form a more inclusive vision and strategy that includes and involves all North African and West Asian communities. In other words, it has been challenging for many media ministries to develop a triangular relationship strategy with audiences as agents of change on one side, the local societies with their religious and cultural worldviews, including their contemporary struggles, on another side, with the third side of the triangle being their messages.

The next challenge is related to their understanding, or lack of understanding, of social and digital media functions and implications. Traditionally, audiences/users utilised media simply to read, watch or obtain products and aids. Increasingly, however, audiences/users utilise media platforms to create, modify, share and discuss topics. One of the implications of this has been that power over the content (theology) has been taken from church leadership (pastors) by individual users. This represents a social and digital media phenomenon that has impacted the work of Christian media, especially in the area of monitoring, understanding and responding to different media activities. Adding to this problem is the fact that the majority of people who run churches' social and digital media platforms are volunteers, whose focus is primarily on their content rather than their audience.

This brings us to the next challenge that Christian media face, which is understanding participation, in other words, what audiences do to the received messages. How do they negotiate and interpret media messages into their context and on their social media platforms? Many teachers and preachers on Christian media still think that their audiences are the same as, or similar to, their listeners in the church pulpits – passive yet positive recipients. This might be because Christian media focus mainly on their content (programming), with the majority of audience response being from their regular and loyal hearers, who tend to give positive feedback. Lack of funds and expertise have made it difficult for them to conduct any scientific qualitative research in order to gain an elevated understanding of their audiences' participation with the message.

Both challenges – limited understanding of functions and implications of social and digital media and audiences' participation – have caused many Christian media ministries and churches to be unable to develop an up-to-date strategy and engage effectively with both the media and their users. This in turn has challenged the hierarchical system of the churches and Christian organisations by giving more power to the audiences and laity. That means ordinary members of the churches as well as users of media can produce and distribute Christian teachings and messages without seeking the approval of their church.

Adding to the above challenges, the high cost of media productions, limited funds and donors' demands have impacted Christian media performance and strategies. The issues of security and persecution – especially for those who are operating within the region, particularly in areas such as human talent, content and sharing information on who should be on-screen, what to share and how much to share – have been other concerns. The lack of a Christian media hub or summit where Christian media organisations and others involved in media can trust, participate, share and learn from each other has caused major duplication, with limited diversity in productions, content, presentation and audience follow-up.

All the above challenges have left many Christian media organisations unable to develop a brand identity effectively in the media market through which their audiences and users can verify their aims and objectives and point to their uniqueness. With the issue of identity comes the topic of language and contextualisation of the text. This has been another challenge for many media ministries. For language is more than just an agreed, practical arrangement of grammar and vocabulary by which we talk to each other: 'it is a crucial arena in which struggles for power take place over such things as whose reality is represented in language and whose isn't' (Peter Horsfield, *From Jesus to the Internet: A History of Christianity and Media*, Oxford: Wiley-Blackwell, 2015, 6–7). To what extent has the reality of the region and Christian communities been presented on Christian media?

Conclusion

This essay has given an analytical overview of the work and place of Christian media in North Africa and West Asia. It points out the significance of Christian media in the region as well as the challenges they face. Besides supporting Christian communities, serving the churches and offering an alternative spiritual perspective, they are also voices of Christians in the region with an ability to restore hope and promote peace and tolerance.

The region is in turmoil. Religious minorities as well as majority groups have been suffering at the hands of sectarian groups and caught in intractable conflicts. Christian churches have been bombed, burned and destroyed. Christians, like other minorities, have been kidnapped and killed and many have been pushed into refugee camps. Many have left, and while those who have stayed have remained physically they have not necessarily stayed spiritually and emotionally. Therefore, both the communities of the region and its Christian churches need the assistance of Christian media to broadcast and promote voices of hope and peace and to promote forgiveness and healing. Moreover, the perpetration of violence in the name of religion has persuaded some to question their own belief system. Christian media have been playing a crucial role in reaching the dispersed Christian communities, providing their audiences with an alternative faith perspective as well as reintroducing the forgotten and silenced heritage and culture of Christianity into contemporary discourse.

However, Christian media in a highly fragile region are faced with a number of challenges: the issues of security, trust and persecution have prevented them from developing more inclusive strategies, strengthening their relationship with their audience or conducting qualitative and quantitative audience research. The problem of funds and the competitive fundraising market have resulted in low-quality, monotonous productions with limited diversity, and limited capacity to hire professionals in the field, as well as compromised their vision and strategies. Therefore, the challenges they face have affected their working strategy, negatively impacted their performance and limited their responses to the needs of Christian communities and the wider societies in the region.

Bibliography

Campbell, Heidi A. (ed.), *Digital Religion: Understanding Religious Practice in New Media Worlds* (New York: Taylor and Francis, 2012).

Cohen-Chen, Smadar, Richard J. Crisp and Eran Halperin, 'Perceptions of a Changing World Induce Hope and Promote Peace in Intractable Conflicts', *Personality and Social Psychology Bulletin*, 41:4 (2015), 498–512.

Feldt, Jakob and Peter Seeberg (eds), *New Media in the Middle East* (Odense: University Press of Southern Denmark, 2006).

Horsfield, Peter, *From Jesus to the Internet: A History of Christianity and Media* (Oxford: Wiley-Blackwell, 2015).

Moll, Yasmin, *Islamic Televangelism: Religion, Media and Visuality in Contemporary Egypt* (2010). Available at http://www.arabmediasociety.com/articles/downloads/20100407165913_Mollpdf.pdf (accessed 12 June 2016).

Displaced Populations

Kristian Girling

This essay explores the causes of Christian displacement in West Asia in the late twentieth and early twenty-first centuries and considers some of the most prominent examples of local communities forced into changed circumstances. Christian decline has arisen largely due to four factors: (1) interventions of external state actors to alter local governments, as has happened in Iraq, Libya and Syria; (2) disinclination by the numerically largest religious tradition in the region – Sunni Islam – to help sustain societies capable of plurality; (3) a lack of overarching vision and willingness to cooperate among churches to secure their presence; and (4) migration in search of a better life and employment. These issues, taken together, substantially set back the maintenance of the Christian populations, even to a subsistence level.

The crisis for Christianity is situated in a wider context of socio-political uncertainty in many states in North Africa and West Asia, which acts as a catalyst for Christian displacement. Such uncertainty has been ongoing since the re-emergence of Islam as a qualifying factor in identity for Muslims beginning in the mid-twentieth century and as most forcefully expressed through the work of figures such as Hassan al-Banna and Ruhollah Khomeini. The reality of an Islamic revival might previously have been restricted to one or two states, such as the Islamic Republic of Iran, but an attachment to Islamist or revolutionary Shia ideologies has increased, and sympathy for the increased utilisation of Islam as a means of societal regulation in public life – if not its actual establishment – is ubiquitous across West Asia (outside of Armenia, Georgia and Israel).

The prevalence of such attitudes increased among Muslim communities following the Arab states' defeat by Israel in the 1967 Six-Day War and was consolidated in the aftermath of the 2003 Iraq War. The coalition invasion permitted dissenting voices and a new status quo to emerge. Although Islamic revivalist movements and a general economic decline from the late 1960s impacted strongly upon Christians, the invasion of Iraq and overthrow of Saddam Hussein fundamentally altered the norms of behaviour and weakened stability as a prevailing societal factor in the Middle East. Where previously external interventions such as the 1990–1 Gulf War might have been only half-measures in societal change, the transformative nature of the 2003 Iraq War removed any illusion that the established order, and hence Christian security, in the Middle East was set in perpetuity.

'Being' a Christian in North Africa and West Asia to 2003

To clarify the situation, four scenarios for Christians can be suggested for the period 1945–2003 in North Africa and West Asia. The first is states with relatively stable Christian populations who nonetheless lacked opportunities to take a full part in socio-political life due to cultural or religious stipulations. This included Egypt, Iran, Palestine, Iraq and Jordan, in each of which Christians were able to maintain a position, though in circumstances that inhibited the popular and active representation of Christianity. The second is states in which Christianity had a secured position, either via statutes, as in Israel and Lebanon, or through a longstanding model of strong inter-communal relations, as in Syria. The third scenario is states in which Christianity was (and is) effectively prohibited on a de facto basis or else actually illegal, as in Saudi Arabia. The fourth scenario is states in which Christianity was present but numerically so minor as to inhibit a large-scale presence in society, as in Turkey, Algeria, Morocco, Libya and Tunisia. In all these contexts few Christians would consider themselves minorities, outside of the numerical sense of the term. The consistent Christian contributions to societies in the region and to civilisational development more widely prohibit them from being considered a minor influence. Furthermore, utilising 'minority' tends towards accepting the Islamic paradigm of *dhimmi* status and an atmosphere of 'dhimmitude', which furthers the notion of Christians as outside the apparent norms of Middle Eastern life and as reliant upon Muslim communities to legitimise their presence.

Islamisation of Culture and the Loss of Lay-state Paradigms

A central issue that has forced Christians to reconsider their position since 2003 is the increase in confessionalisation, with one's religious identity becoming the primary paradigm by which to relate to others and express one's metaphysical sense of self. In line with confessionalisation, Islam as a force in society tends towards the regulation of not only its own communities (via customs and laws) but also other communities' affairs. Not every state in the Middle East implements such policies, but the rejuvenation of Islam as something that impacts on all areas of life has, since the 1970s and the popularisation of Islamism, inhibited Christianity's public presence.

For example, both Syria and Iraq have sought strongly to inhibit Islamism's spread. From the 1960s (and until 2003 in Iraq) both held to rule by Arab nationalist political parties that followed Baathist ideology (although slightly differing versions) and maintained *laïcité* as a central aspect of their governance. Religious identity in public life was acceptable insofar as it was not political (which was suppressed). The state as directed by the party was the only arena in which political development of national policies and identity was permitted. External to this arena, activity could occur as long as ideology derived from alternative religious, political or cultural sources did not attempt to effect change on a national level or weaken the Baathist hold on the means of coercion in the state. Such a separation of the overall direction of Iraqi and Syrian societies goes deeper than the English term 'secularism', which emphasises more attempts to suppress overt displays of religion in public life. The desire to advance such a paradigm of *laïcité* is linked not just to fulfilling Baathist ideological imperatives but also to the need to sustain a societal mentality that could unite the plural Iraqi and Syrian populations and to oppose the rise of Islamist or revolutionary Shia groups.

After the invasion of Iraq and the start of the Syrian conflict in 2011, however, the emphasis on identity as defined by religious background has emerged and transformed inter-communal relations and the perceived status of non-Muslims in society. To be outside the *ummah* has become the qualifying factor for Christians in their engagements with Muslims. Where once Christians' vertically integrated presence sustained them and their identity, they are now present in societies that are unwilling to deal with religious 'difference'.

As a result of the ubiquitous nature of Islam and its influence on social regulation, to be a minority in the Middle East is beyond just a neatly defined religious, sociological or anthropological category. It is something that defines your ability to represent yourself and your identity in public life. Christian identity springs not only from your own culture but also from another and determines the extent to which faith and deference to the divine regulate society as a whole. To be a Christian in the contemporary Middle East is, then, to be dispossessed of the ability to orient society in an explicitly Christian direction and, on a political level, to have limited ability to direct or alter the status quo outside of cooperation with other communities.

The Christian situation today is similar in some respects to that of Middle Eastern Jews in the mid-twentieth century. There is a widespread ambivalence about their presence, due to their religion, and persecution has undermined their resilience to remain in states across the region. Furthermore, cultural, political and legal stipulations regarding their status offer limited opportunities to retain their long-established position in the Middle East. Nevertheless, the situation is distinctive because Christians have no relatively secure state – except perhaps Lebanon – in which to seek self-imposed exile. Also distinctive is the lack of awareness of the scale of anti-Christian attitudes in the Middle East, which has been exacerbated since the American-led 'interventions' in the region from the late twentieth century. Longstanding antipathy can be expressed through such stereotypes as Christian association with Crusaders and neo-conservative political Christian movements, which fail to represent how highly distinct Middle Eastern Christians are from Western Christian identity and Western political institutions.

A wider difficulty is that no external power (with the possible exception of the Russian Federation) is undertaking 'rescue' efforts to secure the Christian presence through political and military means, whereas Israel can rely on the support of the USA. Furthermore, the Jewish communities were and are able to focus on the State of Israel and share in the Zionist movement. Christians, in contrast, do not have a unifying political identity or national ambitions and largely have not emphasised their Christianity in a political manner, choosing instead to remaining fully integrated into Middle Eastern societies and in no way set apart from them.

Direct Persecution

The level of physical persecution that Christians currently experience is seemingly inversely proportional to how previously well integrated and prominent they were in the Middle East, especially in those cases of extreme violence in Iraq, Syria and Egypt. The scale of and commitment to violence by those perpetrating it varies, but violence as a means to deny Christians a place in Middle Eastern societies has become a sustained and normal occurrence. Destruction affects cultural heritage sites, church property, individuals and groups, as does large-scale ethnic cleansing. As of 2016, the latter was reserved to those Christians in the reach of ISIL/Da'esh and its allies. Da'esh/ISIL aimed at the systematic removal of Iraqi and Syrian Christians with a 'scorched earth' policy applied to churches, monasteries and shrines and the repossession of Christian businesses and homes for its own purposes. This was done in order that the communities are denied a link with their origins and to deny their place in history, indeed to make Christian life as something ahistorical and outside of what is perceived as an Islamic account of history. Da'esh/ISIL's efforts also focused on creating some type of sacred territory and emphasising the purity of that land as free from non-Muslims.

Destruction of Christian cultural heritage has been conducted in such a manner as to obscure the historical events that most prominently impacted upon Christians. Armenian Christians have been part of Syrian society for centuries; however, this population expanded as a result of the Armenian genocide. Refugees either were sent to Syria or subsequently settled there, having been driven out of Asia Minor. A major centre of Turkish ethnic cleansing was the city of Deir ez-Zor in eastern Syria, where at least 150,000 Armenians were murdered. Subsequently it became an Armenian pilgrimage site, with a memorial church opened in 1991. The church's destruction by ISIL and its allies in September 2014 struck at the heart of Armenian communal memory and in effect was akin to destroying a major Jewish memorial dedicated to those killed in the mass executions of the Second World War. The meaning and symbolism of this type of destruction would be known and understood well in Middle Eastern Christian contexts, underlining ISIL/Da'esh's commitment to managing not just the future of the territories under its control but also the past of the peoples whom it has conquered.

The other pattern of attacks expediting displacement of communities in Syria from 2011 but also earlier undertaken in Iraq from 2003 are targeted campaigns against leading bishops and priests in which they were kidnapped, tortured and/or murdered. The most high-profile incidents have included the martyrdom of the Chaldean Archbishop of Mosul, Polos Faraj Raho, in 2008 and the abduction of the Syriac Orthodox and Antiochian Orthodox archbishops of Aleppo, John Ibrahim and Paul Yazigi (whose fates remain unknown), in 2013. Aleppo and Mosul are strongholds of Syriac Christian culture, and the targeting of the bishops was a deliberate attempt to undermine figures who were highly articulate on behalf of their communities and widely respected beyond the local Christian constituencies.

One of the most difficult aspects of Iraqi Christian life has been the change in societal attitudes and the weakening of relationships once regarded as strong. Where previously Christians and Muslims largely would have mixed freely socially, from 2003 Christians have been isolated by former friends, with at best their presence popularly regarded as anachronistic in a supposedly 'Muslim' Iraq and at worst seeing their neighbours involved in anti-Christian activities. Such events might be regarded as more challenging to deal with than Da'esh/ISIL-led physical persecution, given that many of the terrorists are of non-Iraqi background and hence in no way tied by bonds of shared national or ethnic identity.

With the advance of Da'esh/ISIL across northern Iraq from 2014 and the ethnic cleansing of 100,000 Christians from the Nineveh Plain region, we see the destruction of a centre of ecclesial life that had existed continuously for more than 1,700 years. For churches whose preceding generations have contended with persecution under a variety of rulers, from Sasanian to Baathist, and survived, the intervention of Da'esh and its ability to alter the social make-up of Iraq has an air of complete finality. These circumstances are comparable to the loss of Kosovo for the Serbs in terms of the spiritual, religious and cultural heritage that the two regions have respectively for Iraqi and Serbian Christians.

These are some of the most egregious examples of persecution and are not representative of every state. However, challenges exist even in countries that maintain greater commitment to permitting the religious life of members of the non-dominant religious tradition. In Israel, for example, local Christians face unofficial discrimination and attacks on their property from Orthodox Jews. It should be noted that such attacks are not undertaken through the prism of anti-Palestinian feeling but rather via vandalism of Christian buildings with the use of explicitly anti-Christian slogans. Nonetheless, Israel offers a level of security to the Christians resident there and is the only state in the Middle East where some type of freedom of religion as might be understood in the West is permitted by law. Israeli authorities also cannot avoid engaging with the Christian population, as it has increased through the migration of expatriate workers, particularly from the Philippines. However, Christians are greatly challenged by Israeli encroachments on their churches and cultural heritage sites, particularly in Jerusalem.

For Christians in Palestine the situation is extremely difficult, as they are in circumstances that on a daily basis lead to the loss of natural dignity. They are also spiritually challenged by cognisance of their geographical proximity to the foundational sites of the events of Christ's earthly life while at the same time being unable to fully express their faith as a result of the retrenchment of Islamist narratives among Palestinian elites. Palestine was once more capable of plurality, and Christians were often the leading voices and actors in Palestinian affairs – similar to circumstances in Syria and Iraq. As Arab nationalism is no longer perceived as a means to advance states' socio-economic development, so Islamism has become a preferred option to engage in resistance to Israel and serves as a means to unite the Palestinian national cause with the advance of Sunni Islam internationally. The decline of Palestinian Christianity is such that we can note an ongoing real struggle to sustain it in a manner that reflects the heritage of the area and its significance to Christians internationally.

This denial of the Christian presence as an effective 'actor' in that environment follows in part from a lack of popular international discourse on Jerusalem's status as a centre of Christian activity. The city remains under-acknowledged for its integral importance to Christianity, and limited consideration is given to the effects of conflict on the Christians resident in the city. This has been an ongoing problem since the occupation of East Jerusalem in 1967 and the overarching implementation of several political and religious narratives competing for dominance that exclude the Christian voice.

The status of Egyptian Christians is high, insofar as they could not really be described as a dispossessed minority. However, despite the Coptic community's size it is increasingly displaced from Egyptian society. From the second half of the twentieth century it has not been well represented politically, in the security services or in state bureaucracy, which has substantially weakened the Copts' position following President Mubarak's overthrow in 2011. In general, the Copts' have been characterised by regular difficulties in retaining a status within public life that is more than just at a level of acceptance. Nevertheless, Egyptian Christianity is advantaged through its geographical spread throughout the country, which ensures it is not perceived as entirely outside mainstream society and sustains its presence within Egyptian Islamic culture more thoroughly.

Egyptian society since the mid-twentieth century can be characterised by two trends that broadly split the population in half – support of either Islamism (via the auspices of the Muslim Brotherhood) or a lay-state paradigm. Crucially, the latter has the backing of the armed forces, which have served as the greatest brake on the Brotherhood's influence in Egypt. The Arab Spring exposed this divide, with elections followed by military intervention in turn overthrowing the Muslim Brotherhood-led government of Mohamed Morsi in 2013.

Emerging Islamist paradigms at the government level have also been seen under the regime of President Recep Erdoğan in Turkey, where a once staunchly lay paradigm in official life has been dislodged and replaced by a revivification of Sunni Turkish nationalism. This is of concern not only to Christians in Asia Minor but also to Christians more widely, with Armenian and Syriac Christians strongly aware of the role that Sunni-led anti-Christian narratives played in the genocide during the First World War. Erdoğan has also overseen the occupation of parts of northern Syria and Iraq in a purported bid to secure Turkish borders from ISIL/Da'esh while simultaneously making the case for Aleppo and Mosul to be returned to Turkish rule as per the Ottoman Empire. Both cities are longstanding centres of Christian life and culture, indicative of the geopolitical interests that can override Christian interests.

The Christians of Libya, Algeria, Tunisia and Morocco have been greatly challenged following the start of the Arab Spring in 2011. In the former three states this has precipitated change in political structures, with Libya the most radically altered. Christianity in North Africa has not formed a prominent part of society since the eighth century, with the Islamic invasions and occupation seeing its rapid diminution. Under French, Spanish and Italian rule from the nineteenth century there was a relative Christian resurgence, insofar as public Christianity became a feature of North African life among European residents. Those who remained following the end of European rule continue to form some of the largest proportions of the Christian communities. Nonetheless, in Libya the Coptic population is the largest (around 60,000), and throughout North Africa covert Muslim converts to Christianity are found in growing numbers. Overall, however, Christians form less than 1-2% of the total population in these states. Large-scale displacements of the Christian populations have not taken place on a physical level in Morocco and Tunisia in the late twentieth and early twenty-first centuries. However, societal attitudes and cultural stipulations against Christian activities see the communities pushed to the margins of public life. In Algeria, Islamist activity has been a prominent factor affecting Christians, most notably resulting in the murder of Pierre Claverie, Roman Catholic Bishop of Oran, in 1996, while the overthrow of Muammar Gaddafi in 2011 has seen the expansion of anti-Christian violence in Libya by Da'esh/ISIL. The most prominent incident was the abduction and murder of 21 Coptic men in January 2015.

Christianity in the Caucasus

Christians in the Caucasus have, like communities in the Middle East, been marked by the long-term effects of Islamic rule, but unlike in the Middle East they have also felt the full force of Soviet communist ideology. These two factors have expedited Christianity's re-emergence as a chief marker of national identity in Armenia and Georgia since 1991 and have seen the status and popular appreciation of ecclesial institutions often rising far higher than for other national bodies.

Armenia and Georgia are distinctive in the wider context of this essay as overwhelmingly Christian states by population, and since the end of the USSR they have not seen displacement as a result of anti-Christian persecution. However, Armenia continues to be affected by the genocide's legacy – we recall this caused the deaths of at least 40% of the contemporary Armenian population but is still denied as a historical reality by the Turkish state – and fears of twenty-first-century neo-Ottoman ambitions of Turkey that colour relations between the countries and present a potential threat to the Armenian Christian tradition.

Georgia has been greatly impacted as a result of being a focus of wider geopolitical interests that have affected inter-Christian relations, especially between the Georgian and Russian Orthodox Churches. Competing visions for the national political orientation of Georgia – more favourable either to the Russian Federation or to NATO – have undermined the ability of local communities to determine their own affairs and have directly affected many. The ethnic Georgian populations in the autonomous regions of South Ossetia and Abkhazia in north-western Georgia, for example, were strongly impacted by the 2008 Russo-Georgian War, with up to 200,000 people migrating to Georgia proper as a result. For Georgians, the conflict with Russia can be seen through a religious lens: the Georgian Orthodox community regained ecclesial independence from the Russian Church only in 1917, after 200 years of Russian jurisdiction. The heightened tension between the states since 2008 is perceived as an ongoing attempt to reassert Russian cultural, religious as well as strategic influence over the Georgian state and society.

Azerbaijan is a majority Sunni Muslim state in which Christians form less than 5% of the population (fewer than 500,000 people); the majority are of the Russian or Georgian Orthodox tradition. Christian displacement in Azerbaijan is a sensitive issue for the contemporary government as the large Armenian community that once resided in Azerbaijan proper has, since the fall of the USSR, relocated to the autonomous Nagorno-Karabakh Republic in the south-west of the country, on the border with the Republic of Armenia. The movement of population was expedited from 1990 following a pogrom against the Armenian population of Baku. Conflict between Armenia and Nagorno-Karabakh on the one hand and Azerbaijan on the other has been a feature of post-Soviet life, with a major war from 1992–4 and outbreaks of fighting continuing to 2016. If not acknowledged officially, Christian and Muslim identity continues to underpin conflicts in the region alongside ethnic and national rivalries.

Internationalisation of West Asian Communities

The loss of Christian presence relates not only to push factors such as persecution but also to pull factors and the attraction of higher socio-economic status and opportunities in the Americas, Australasia and Europe. The rate and scale of change during the twentieth and twenty-first centuries has been such that the diaspora communities can form larger proportions of the total populations of particular churches than those resident in West Asia. This is particularly the case for the churches that predominate in Armenia, Iraq, Lebanon, Palestine and Syria. As of 2014, the Melkite Catholic Church, for example, whose patriarchate is in Damascus, had as many community members resident in Australasia and South America as living throughout the Middle East (about 700,000). This imbalance in the distribution of the populations is an organisational challenge for church leaders seeking to ensure that the entire community's varied needs can be met. The status of women and questions of vocation or education can differ markedly between Baghdad and Buenos Aires.

Migration from the region is such that West Asian Christianity is typified by its international nature and dispersal to states far removed from its geographical and cultural points of origin. The growth of communities in the Americas and Australasia is especially large, with Europe (particularly

Sweden) also becoming a hub for migrants and refugees. What has been termed 'diaspora' can also be regarded as an opportunity for missionary work. For example, the Antiochian Orthodox Church in the USA has been one of the most prominent in attracting American converts. Such efforts challenge both sides, presenting differing visions of the Christian life and drawing in those concerned by changes in churches in the West with an interest to engage with a Christian culture distinctive from their own.

The integration of Middle Eastern Christians into life in the countries of the diaspora and an array of political jurisdictions is an ongoing process, yet for many it is not in any way out of the ordinary. Ecclesial identity may end on Sunday, with the rest of the week focused on the same life lived as any other citizen. Questions of national allegiance are generally settled for second-, third- or fourth-generation immigrants. Visions of the past or of the 'mother country' are seen through the lens of parents' memories or extended family still resident in the region. The difficulties that contemporary native (mother country) communities experience are still of great concern, and such events frequently inspire charitable activities to alleviate the situation of those in the 'homeland'.

The scale of Middle Eastern Christian migration internationally is dealt with by states with varying degrees of success. The effort to 'integrate' communities is confounded by ongoing assumptions that the Middle East is solely a place of Muslim–Jewish dichotomies and that to be Arab, Turk or Persian necessitates being Muslim. The assumption of Western and Middle Eastern political interests as necessarily antagonistic also ensures that the reception of non-Muslims from the Middle East is very poorly understood as to its practical manifestations. A principal disadvantage is that migrants for the most part are being settled in post-Christian societies that lack sufficient religious literacy to comprehend fully the challenges that Christians of the Middle East have faced and the causes of their migration.

Conclusion

Christians in Syria and Iraq have often been noted as being most severely dispossessed through the effects of statewide conflicts and their experience of direct persecution by Da'esh/ISIL. In contrast, those in Egypt, Palestine and Turkey still face violence (albeit on a smaller scale) but are often more restricted by other factors – in the Palestinian case most apparently by the effects of the occupation by Israel, and in Egypt and Turkey by the movement away from a lay-state paradigm in government life to one that encompasses a greater position for traditional Islamic stipulations and which inhibits the presence of the Christians in these societies. Such a status quo situates the Christians as permanent outsiders and diminished in terms of the contributions that they would normally make to wider society.

If Christian demographic decline continues, the effects on Middle Eastern culture are likely to be striking; region-wide actions would be needed in to prevent such decline. Those most badly affected other than the Christians themselves are likely to be Western states when they come to seek interlocutors in the region most open to popular contemporary ideologies of human rights and religious freedom. Few other constituencies in the Middle East would be willing to fully support such concepts. Such concerns have been strongly reflected in the thought of Antoine Audo SJ, the contemporary Chaldean Bishop of Aleppo. He has consistently articulated the 'difference' that Christians make in the Middle East, a difference that goes beyond just a distinctive religious commitment. The Christian difference offers a voice between competing dichotomous conflicts and seeks plurality and a hope for an accommodating, as opposed to an exclusionary, ethos for the future of Middle Eastern society – one open to meeting and dealing with problems on an inter-communal basis as opposed to a unipolar paradigm dominated by a single religious tradition.

The future of Christianity in the Middle East, especially in Syria and Iraq, is very uncertain, and will continue to be so without some form of distinctive and comprehensive engagement between local stakeholders and major external powers. One key actor that could make a significant difference to the overall direction of external Christian efforts to alleviate the crisis is the Holy See. However, the pontificate of Pope Francis has been marked by a lack of concerted effort (and indeed real policy development) to meet the challenges of the situation. Under John Paul II and Benedict XVI, Vatican foreign policy and interest in Eastern Christianity were more sharply focused, based on the former's interest in ending Soviet rule and raising awareness of Christianity in Eastern Europe and Russia and the latter's strong concern with sustaining the Christian presence in the Holy Land and determining realistic means for Christians to survive in predominantly Islamic societies and cultures. That said, given Pope Francis's February 2016 meeting with the head of the Russian Orthodox Church, Patriarch Kirill, in Cuba, it might be thought that closer coordination to support the Christians of the Middle East could be forthcoming – a practical ecumenism that sees the joint efforts of the principal figures in Eastern and Western Christianity directed towards highlighting the Christians' plight, seeking action from those states now committed to interventions in the region, and raising awareness of the particular difficulties of the Christian communities. Nonetheless, action is required now and on a wide scale if the Christians are not to be reduced to a token minority, further forgotten in the West, or to be known only through museum exhibits.

Bibliography

Griffith, Sidney H., *The Church in the Shadow of the Mosque: Christians and Muslims in the World of Islam* (Princeton, NJ: Princeton University Press, 2008).

Leustean, Lucian (ed.), *Eastern Christianity and Politics in the Twenty-First Century* (London: Routledge, 2014).

O'Mahony, Anthony and Emma Loosley (eds), *Eastern Christianity in the Modern Middle East* (London: Routledge, 2010).

Rowe, Paul S., John H. A. Dyck and Jens Zimmerman (eds), *Christians and the Middle East Conflict* (London: Routledge, 2014).

Ye'or, Bat, *The Decline of Eastern Christianity Under Islam. From Jihad to Dhimmitude: Seventh-Twentieth Century*, translated by Miriam Kochan and David Littman (Madison, NJ: Fairleigh Dickinson University Press, 1996).

Conclusion

The Future of Christianity in North Africa and West Asia

Mariz Tadros

The introduction to this volume began by noting the twenty-first century genocide in Iraq and the centennial commemoration of the Armenian genocide. Up to August 2017, the United Nations (UN) recognised the Yazidis as victims of ISIS genocide, but it did not extend such recognition to the Christians. Such politics of denial are déjà vu. One hundred years after its occurrence, the Armenian genocide is still being denied global recognition: only 28 countries worldwide acknowledge it. While all definitions of what constitutes a genocide are debatable, the UN standard definition of a genocide reads:

> any of the following acts committed with intent to destroy, in whole or in part, a national, ethnical, racial or religious group, as such: killing members of the group; causing serious bodily or mental harm to members of the group; deliberately inflicting on the group conditions of life calculated to bring about its physical destruction in whole or in part; imposing measures intended to prevent births within the group; forcibly transferring children of the group to another group. (http://www.un.org/en/genocideprevention/genocide.html, accessed 23 August 2017)

The definition entails two processes – the intention to omit and the systematic targeting of a group on account of their particular identity.

A *longue durée* reading of history is illuminating, showing how a politics of denial and/or omission repeatedly undergirds mainstream narratives' handling of religious targeting of Christians. Several myths have been perpetuated across the decades to obscure the scale and intensity of assault and justify the targeting. Such myths include that Christians have provoked local Muslim sentiment by flexing their muscles; that they collude with the West or are its corollaries; that they are not 'real' Christians; that it is really a class war cloaked in sectarian terms; that they prefer autocracy over democracy; and that they have come under assault because of the disenfranchisement of the Muslim world by Western powers. Certainly there is a need to avoid romanticising the trajectories of the Christians in North Africa and West Asia (NAWA), and there is a need to acknowledge incidents of abuses of power for which they are responsible. However, this volume has sought to challenge some of these myths and misconceptions and to expose their origins and ideological roots. The struggle for recognition is not intended to promote victimology but to acknowledge injustice and prevent future recurrences. Indeed, the stories of Christians, as this volume shows, are about active agency, resistance, adaptation and innovation. However, the politics of non-recognition need to be challenged because, other than its distortion of complex realities, its outcome is the absence of concerted action to address the scale of the existential threat. The disappearance of Christians from the Middle East will not only represent a loss in terms of world heritage but will also pose a threat to the praxis of religious, cultural and social pluralism in the region more widely.

In view of the highly volatile nature of the ever-changing geopolitical power configurations influencing the region, in particular the Middle East, it would be of little value to present a number of future scenarios as is common in foresight approaches. There are simply too many unpredictable political twists and turns, too many opaque and behind-the-scenes regional and global players, and too many ripple effects of changes in one setting that might impact upon others.

To a very large extent, the future of Christians in the NAWA region is tied to the political, social and economic stability of countries at large. The predicament of Christians, as with Muslims and others, is tied to systems of governance, the future of conflict and ideology (e.g. whether democratic or authoritarian, secular or theocratic). However, what will be argued below is that although certain overarching determinants of survival affect all the populations of the region, the affiliation of individuals and groups with Christianity means that some factors will affect them differently. In the twenty-first century, the hardship and suffering experienced by most of the populations, especially in the Middle East – against the backdrop of wars and civil conflict, security instability and economic inequalities – is acute. However, in addition to all of the above, Christianity faces an existential threat because of the diminishing numbers of adherents in the countries, in particular those of the Middle East. Below, reflection on three themes is offered. The first is the necessity of advancing a holistic approach to attaining substantive security; the second is the various levels of collaborations and solidarities critical for an enabling environment; and the third theme is the repertoires of capturing and preserving the dynamic spiritual and cultural heritage of the Christian populations of the NAWA region.

Substantive Security

In the twentieth century, in many countries of the Arab world, there was a prolific body of scholarship highlighting how the acquisition by Christians in the region of their full citizenship rights would be the natural outcome of the removal of authoritarian rulers who had wrongly convinced their populations that they were the buffers against Islamism. In the twenty-first century, with many countries in the region in disarray, there is recognition that the single most influential factor for survival is the extent to which any setting is able to shield religious minorities.

While all populations have suffered from insecurity – with factors such as age, gender, class, disability, geographical origin and political orientation making certain individuals and groups especially vulnerable – we argue that the targeting of Christians and other politically non-empowered religious and ethnic minorities will lead not merely to encroachment upon civilians but to the extinction of ancient communities altogether. The withdrawal of physical security often happens when the police retreat from upholding the basic rule of law, a characteristic of fragile states irrespective of regime type. With the exception of the wealthy, who can afford their own private security systems, whole populations suffer. However, religious minorities such as the Christians in Iraq, Syria, Egypt, Sudan, Palestine, Libya and other settings collectively become targeted for looting, physical assault, confiscation/occupation of property or kidnapping by groups that know that their numerical status as a minority will mean they cannot fend for themselves. Such groups might be inspired by ideology (subjugation of the non-Muslims), economics (exploitation) or both (e.g. war booty). Hence, to secure the most basic level of survival, the (re)instatement of the rule of law is critical. This requires first a recognition that a security system that is blind to religiously driven sources of vulnerability will ultimately fail. Feminist scholarship has shown how a gender-blind security system can overlook the power relations that increase women's vulnerability to particular kinds of insecurities and which are exacerbated by class and geographical location (e.g. for poor women in remote settings). It has also exposed the prejudice with which security systems undermine women's security needs, whether deliberately or inadvertently.

Similarly, a religiously sensitive lens needs to be brought to bear on the provision of security services. This will need to explore ways in which security provision has increased Christian communities' vulnerability – for example, by not responding to complaints of hate speech or mobilisation of mobs. It will also need to address the institutionalised prejudice against protecting religious minorities, including Christians. In the twenty-first century, in particular following the Arab revolts, we have witnessed the increasing porousness of national borders, which has allowed the free movement of militants, weapons and ideology. Christian minorities in Libya, Syria, Egypt, Iraq, Palestine and elsewhere have been the targets of assaults, often involving the collusion of internal and external actors.

However, while this most basic level of the rule of law is a prerequisite, it is not sufficient to ensure survival. The provision of political and economic security is critical. If political settlements in Iraq and Syria turn out to be exclusionary (as they were in Egypt), Christians are highly likely to feel that they contain too few guarantees of power sharing and will not prevent more exclusionary political projects from being rolled out in the future. Moreover, economic security is integral. In the occupied Palestinian Territories and Iraq, for example, there are concerns that in the absence of opportunities for young people to compete for jobs on a level playing field and for families to meet basic survival needs, the incentive to stay in the home country is very slim. This conundrum, however, applies to most of the countries of the NAWA region. The challenge across the region is that the departure of those who are often most capable of migrating, the middle classes, deprives the community left behind of social and human capital as well as the material support they offer to the less privileged.

Here there is a clear tension between the aspirations of the clergy and the people. The clergy recognise that places of worship with ancient roots risk becoming museums if no people are left to worship in them. They recognise that heritage is best protected when it is a living one. However, calls upon populations to stay rather than migrate are problematic when people feel they are being required to sacrifice their children's future opportunities – a sacrifice not required of unmarried church leaders.

The other level of security critical for the continued presence of Christians in the region is that associated with the ability to build the necessary trust in the community. Vernacular understandings of security relate to what is needed to make local communities safe. If neighbours and friends cannot be trusted, how can social cohesion be forged? The difficulty lies in communities that have witnessed a high level of violence and where Christians feel betrayed by those who reported on them in return for a bounty, took advantage of their vulnerable position for economic gain or joined the chorus of hate speech against them. While, undoubtedly, many undocumented stories of Muslims who heroically risked their lives in order to rescue Christians can be found in all settings, nonetheless where ruptures in relations have occurred, many Christians question the conditions under which trust will ever be possible again. Such security needs transitional justice, community healing and reconciliation processes built from the bottom up over time, enabled by a supporting national climate.

The future of Islamism

As many of the essays have shown, Christians and Muslims have lived in peaceful coexistence and collectively mobilised against internal and external oppressors during several historical phases. However, also emerging as a pattern from the contributions to this volume is the direct correlation between the introduction (or deepening) of a Sharia-inspired system of governance and the institutionalisation, formally or informally, of a hierarchy of rights premised on religious affiliation. In other words, citizenship as an identity and a set of rights and duties becomes tied to the interpretation of Sharia being applied. This is in no way to suggest that no violations of the rights of non-Muslim citizens occur under secular regimes in the NAWA region. To the contrary, and undoubtedly, many factors account for the varied experiences of citizenship in different parts of the region. Moreover, Islamist groups – political forces and movements that seek to create a state that is governed in accordance with their interpretation of Sharia – do not have a singular ideological standpoint on religious minorities. Different religious leaders, groups, movements and centres of learning and issuance of fatwas (religious opinions) have different and changing doctrinal positions on the rights of minority groups. However, in all of the cases under study here, the greater the leadership's pronouncement of a commitment to Islamising a system of governance, the more likely it is that the terms of engagement for members who belong to a religious minority become exclusionary.

This is irrespective of the political order enforced, be it a democratically elected leadership such as the Muslim Brotherhood in Egypt or the AKP in Turkey, a totalitarian monarchy such as Saudi Arabia, or a so-called Islamic state such as ISIS in Syria and Iraq. Under the authoritarian regimes of Mubarak in Egypt and Gadaffi in Libya, and prior to the assumption of power by Hamas in Gaza, some Western think-tanks argued that if only Islamist movements were given a chance to govern, they might prove to be more pluralistic and acquiescent to the rights of religious minorities than their critics assumed. Against the backdrop of severe encroachments on the rights of Christians under the Muslim Brotherhood in Egypt and Hamas in Gaza, and under the rule of Islamist militias in different parts of Libya, the compatibility between Islamist political forces' assumption of power and tolerance for religious pluralism has transpired to be non-existent. This is partly because of the conservatism of the interpretations of Sharia that have informed their praxis of citizenship, and partly on account of deep, historical and systemic social systems of prejudice. Hence, the removal of authoritarian regimes and the instatement of electoral democracy is no guarantee of the advancement of religious pluralism and inclusivity. Certainly, the greater the authoritarian nature of theocratic rule, the less space there will be for resistance or opposition from religious minorities. A religious minority such as Christians can be excluded under the rubric of majoritarian democracy. In effect, the ideology of a regime, and not only how democratic and free it is, will be critical for the survival and flourishing of twenty-first-century Christian communities in the NAWA region.

One of the most critical features of the increasing Islamisation of social and political orders is the tendency to homogenisation. Such homogenisation can take subtle forms, such as encouraging the majority not to mix with or befriend those who do not conform to a particular interpretation of religion or those who belong to another religion. Homogenisation can also take more overt forms by, for example, institutionalising Islamic education for all, irrespective of their religious affiliation. Homogenisation is harmful to religious pluralism, not only across religions but also within religions, making tolerance of diverse interpretations or different expressions of the same faith very limited.

The second inference, building on the first, is that while economic and social grievances sometimes become the main drivers of exclusion in the lives of Christians and non-Christians alike in the region, the ideological appeal of jihadism will continue to represent a threat to Christians independently of the political predicament of ISIS. At the time of writing, military battles to liberate parts of Iraq and Syria from ISIS rule were underway. While Christians, like many others living in the ISIS-occupied region, will be relieved that the occupation of their settings has ended, this by no means suggests that the existential threats facing Christians in Syria and Iraq or the region more broadly have abated. While ISIS has represented a highly performative, ruthless movement that systematically targeted non-Muslim minorities, including Christians (as well as non-compliant Muslims), other jihadi movements continue to thrive and to have global outreach. Their work is enabled and facilitated through collaborators from within communities, who might or might not have links to militant movements. What fighting ISIS brought to the fore was the difficulty of combating a movement whose recruitment appeal is universal and whose operation knows no territorial boundaries. Despite the geographical disparity in the distribution of Christians across the NAWA region, alarm over what the political ascendency of an Islamist regime might mean for Christians is widely shared. The extent to which future political settlements in the region will recognise that Islamist citizenship is now considered a contradiction for Christians remains to be seen.

Cross-cutting Solidarities

In a multi-ethnic, multi-religious setting like the NAWA region, where strong international and regional actors influence local power configurations, Christian leaders and communities have historically had to make strategic choices regarding ententes, coalitions and alliances. The level of solidarity varies: it might be a temporary collaboration, take the form of an entente that is premised on friendly relations but is non-binding, or take the stronger form of an alliance revolving around engagement that binds together actors in recognition of mutual interests. The country essays as well as the thematic essays in this volume cumulatively suggest that the survival of the Christians in the NAWA region might be contingent upon different levels and kinds of solidarities: coordinated global action that is informed by 'religious literacy' (see below); engagement across religious divides in religiously heterogeneous populations; and strengthening inter-denominational ecumenism.

While this volume has focused on Christians in the NAWA region, with many of the country chapters highlighting varying levels of persecution and encroachment, it is acknowledged that this is happening against the backdrop of the greatest crisis in population displacement witnessed in contemporary history, on a scale that surpasses what was witnessed in the aftermath of the Second World War. A report from the United Nations High Commissioner for Refugees found that, worldwide, 65.6 million people were displaced at the end of 2016 (http://www.unhcr.org/uk/news/stories/2017/6/5941561f4/forced-displacement-worldwide-its-highest-decades.html, accessed 14 August 2017). Although displacement is a global phenomenon, it is also acknowledged that the occurrence of five simultaneous conflicts in the NAWA region (in Libya, Yemen, Iraq and Syria, and the Arab–Israeli conflict) has accentuated the impact on the peoples of this region. Very little disaggregated data are available on the proportion of Christian populations displaced in relation to the broader communities and the extent to which their experiences of relocation (whether temporary or more permanent) have been influenced by their religious identity. Undeniably, however, the global response to the displacement of large populations has been the subject of many scathing critiques. What has been less adequately explored and understood is the extent to which international humanitarian policy has been sensitive to the ways in which belonging to a religious minority might influence both people's experiences and their coping strategies. For countries in the NAWA region whose populations have experienced genocides, such as Israel and Armenia, what would citizen solidarity look like?

Moreover, only recently has the role of international powers in arming actors whose policies have contributed to the ascendency and activity of terrorist networks come under scrutiny. Studies using process tracing to uncover the impact of arming governments and non-state actors who endorse jihadism on the vulnerability of religious minorities, including Christians, in the region are still few and far between. In some cases, a number of seemingly inconsistent policies are being rolled out. For example, while Qatar allows its migrant and professional workers to practise their Christian faith with relative freedom, the country has also been accused of funding jihadi organisations regionally whose 'portfolio' would also include the religious targeting of Christians (http://www.huffingtonpost.com/entry/qatarism-and-fund-of-terrorism_us_5956479de4b0326c0a8d0f78, accessed 15 August 2017).

Secondly, solidarity between Christians and non-Christians in the NAWA region will become particularly pertinent against the backdrop of a broader movement against religious homogenisation. While potential collaborations across religious divides are many, depending on the power configurations on the ground, three are of particular significance. The most common form of entente is that between religious leaders and heads of state; however, as highlighted earlier, this is becoming increasingly complex, with many more stakeholders involved. State leaders who profess a commitment to inclusiveness and pluralism that goes beyond rhetoric tend to have a major impact on the threshold of tolerance for religious-inspired inequality prevalent in governmental practices. This is perhaps because many of the contexts of the NAWA region feature authoritarian regimes in which centralisation of the top-down exercise of power is high. Conversely, state leaders who play the 'sectarian card' to divide and rule (as in colonial times) as a means of maintaining the monopolisation of power tend to increase the Christian vulnerability to vilification and prejudice. As systems of governance become increasingly sophisticated and complex, however, it is the 'collective' involved in multi-tiered levels of leadership that is influential. For example, beyond the role of the head of state, the role of the security apparatus in most of these countries is critical for the positioning of Christians, since religious difference is considered a matter of national security. Leadership is also influential at the level of church hierarchy. The success of church leaders in shielding their communities from persecution lies not only in their ability to create positive rapport with the rulers of the country but also in preventing a compromising of their rights through their cooption. Here again, beyond the central role of the head of the Christian community, other tiers of leadership in the church, comprising bishops or even highly influential local clergy, can determine the positioning of Christians in a particular context.

Throughout most of the past centuries, the religious community's loyalty to the local or national ruler often was used as a proxy for their patriotism and rejection of foreign intervention. However, entering the twenty-first century, the terms of engagement in some parts of NAWA are shifting. Should the international community be mindful of the importance of inclusive political settlements? Undoubtedly, safeguards for inclusive political settlements in some regional contexts need to be instated in order to ensure state accountability with regard to the preservation of religious and cultural diversity in religiously heterogeneous communities. However, there can be no alternative to fostering local solidarities between people. People-led movements that cross religious divides and mobilise around social justice issues are few and far between in the NAWA region, but they have almost always had a strong youth constituency. In the twenty-first century, more youth-led movements might emerge to mobilise around agendas that bring people from different religious backgrounds together for progressive social and political change, in particular in view of the evident 'youth bulge' characterising the demographics of the region. One of the challenges will certainly be how people can overcome religious differences without having to forgo their identity in the process.

The third kind of collaboration might be dialogues between religions, which until now have been predominantly Christian–Muslim, often involving multiple leaderships on both sides. The Catholic Church has been particularly active in several dialogues with Muslim and Jewish groups and leaders in the NAWA region. The Orthodox churches have also been involved in a number of dialogues, often of a bilateral nature with Muslim leaders, although perhaps for political reasons Christian–Jewish dialogues have been more on the fringes. Beyond the creation of goodwill on a religious leadership level, the extent to which they have trickled down in their impact is an area needing further research.

Finally, the challenges of building solidarities within and across Christian denominations are discussed at length in this volume. Surprisingly, despite the very different traditions, standpoints and denominational affiliations from which the authors of this volume speak, two points of congruence emerge: first, what appear on the surface to be theological contentions and disputes are sometimes underpinned by political struggles; and second, semantics has a role in creating misunderstandings and forging rifts. While much progress has been made to identify where the obstacles lie and seize opportunities to arrive at a common ground, a number of challenges to inter-denominational and cross-denominational solidarities remain. The heterogeneity of positions within the church hierarchies (reflecting different standpoints in relation to ecumenical unity) is a major challenge within all churches. The disconnect between ecumenism at the highest levels of church leadership and the churches at the local level can be dramatic. Perhaps one of the reasons why the role of lay movements at the local level in forging bridges across and within denominations has been almost invisible in the NAWA region is the very limited scope for people's mobilisation through civil action in most of these contexts. Highly centralised systems of governance have severely inhibited the emergence of lay-led movements across NAWA, in sharp contrast, for example, to

Latin America, where such mobilisation from within the Christian communities is much more perceptible.

The Power of Internal Repertoires

The religiously inspired targeting of Christians in many parts of the NAWA region have meant that most interventions in support of Christian communities have focused on their physical safety. This is an understandable response, in particular when it corresponds to the priorities of vulnerable Christians themselves in terms of addressing the material need for physical protection, and the education and health needs of their families. Certainly, as we saw from Palestine/Israel, where Christianity began, without addressing the material needs of the oldest Christian communities in the area, their presence will diminish, making holy sites restricted to seasonal worship. Large-scale displacement and migration might disrupt continuity in the preservation of the distinctive identity and heritage of scattered communities. Recognising the social, cultural and religious repertoires of identity is critical for the individual's cognitive sense of wellbeing as well as for the preservation of the Christian community. One most obvious measure is the restoration of churches, shrines, manuscripts, archives and other tangible religio-cultural heritage places of worship and artefacts. Other than the importance of preserving the ancient roots of Christianity as a matter of world heritage, many of these sites represent a dynamic link between the history and the present for these Christian communities. The narrative of continuity and rootedness is often built around the memories that were formed around individual and collective experiences in these places – in other words, the stories that people share and tell about these places.

However, there is another form of heritage that is at risk – the intangible cultural heritage – that is critical for the survival of Christian communities. According to UNESCO, intangible cultural heritage includes the 'oral traditions, performing arts, social practices, rituals, festive events, knowledge and practices concerning nature and the universe or the knowledge and skills to produce traditional crafts' (https://ich.unesco.org/en/what-is-intangible-heritage-00003; accessed 10 August 2017). Preserving the cultural heritage of Christian communities, whether thriving (as in Armenia and Georgia) or under threat (as in many other countries of the NAWA region), can be seen by some as potentially detrimental if it encourages the ghettoisation of Christians or if it encourages exclusionary rejection of others who do not share the faith. On the other hand, it might encourage Christians to be integrated without being assimilated (maintaining a cognitive sense of their identity), and engaging with heritage may also bring to the fore stories of communal coexistence and solidarity. The preservation of the spiritual, cultural and social living heritage of Christians draws on the repertoire of stories, practices and historical narratives of what it is to be a Christian. It can evoke sentiments and insights on turbulent change as well as continuity and resilience. The ability of people to capture their own stories and heritage is important for self-representation. The production of one's own knowledge can be a source of community pride and restoration of a sense of agency (especially for those coming from conflict-torn and fragile contexts). It can also challenge narratives that objectify, essentialise or are written from very different standpoints. It can be cathartic if people are empowered to be in charge of the process of capturing and sharing their history and experience, establishing the link between the past and present and their future aspirations and visions. Historically, the emphasis in Christian communities in the NAWA region (with a few exceptions) has been on documenting the more tangible dimensions of heritage in addition to the languages and histories of the churches. While these efforts have been central to preserving important elements of heritage, there continue to be many undocumented dimensions. The history of the church has sometimes tended to mean the history of the patriarchs, priests and clerics. The heritage of the people in terms of everyday practices has been under-researched. The capture of intangible culture has tended to focus on music, rites and rituals. The folklore, the interface between the religious and non-religious, has also tended to be missing from heritage captured and preserved. The voices of women and youth in particular tend not to be represented.

The opportunities afforded by the technological advances made in the twenty-first century can facilitate the widespread sharing of living heritage among Christians and others in geographically dispersed parts of the world. The use of cutting-edge technologies in preservation and dissemination may represent new ways to reach the youth. While the primary purpose of using new technology may be the empowerment of Christian communities themselves in capturing, valuing and celebrating their own repertoires of heritage, technology can perhaps also challenge narratives of negation surrounding the status and role of Christians in the NAWA region. Sceptics may consider heritage capture and preservation a luxury, a measure that should be deprioritised until the region's conflicts are resolved and the predicament of the Christians in highly unstable contexts is settled. However, there is an urgency to the challenging of dichotomous thinking between material and immaterial priorities that does not take into account the multiplicity of policies and interventions needed in a context where the stakes are very high. Much of the predicament of the Christians of the NAWA region is contingent upon the unintended outcomes of geo-strategic policy choices by global, regional, national and even local actors. In the immediate term, much is dependent on whether they are able to secure substantive security and engage in building solidarities across different divides that enhance their negotiating position. In the long term, there are the unintended outcomes at the local level of changing contexts. For example, if the oil economy of the Gulf changes, this would undoubtedly impact the social contract between the residents of these states and the migrant workers. The ways in which this will affect the Christian guest-worker population in the NAWA region whose original homelands are often fraught with religious targeting remain to be seen.

However, as they have done before, Christian communities will also draw on the spiritual, social and cultural repertoires of strength, inspiration, resistance, subversion and resilience in order to adapt to changing realities. Solidarity on the part of local and national stakeholders favouring an inclusive society and politics will be key to countering those in favour of a more religiously, politically, socially and culturally homogenous polity. Solidarity from international civil society organisations (including but not to restricted churches) that favour justice, inclusion and human rights will be key to disrupting and challenging the patterns of omission and negation that characterise many mainstream international narratives about Christians in the NAWA region.

Bibliography

Malik, Habib C., *Islamism and the Future of the Christians of the Middle East*, 1st edn (Stanford, CA: Hoover Institution Press, 2010).

Philpott, Daniel and Timothy Shah (eds), *Under Caesar's Sword* (Cambridge: Cambridge University Press, 2018).

Rowe, Paul S. (ed.), *Routledge Handbook of Middle East Minorities* (London: Taylor and Francis, 2018).

Tadros, Mariz, 'Christians Coping with Insecurities in the Aftermath of the Arab Revolts: Converging and Diverging Strategies', *Review of Faith and International Affairs*, 15:1 (2017), 21–30.

Tadros, Mariz, *Decrypting Copts' Perspectives on Communal Relations in Contemporary Egypt Through Vernacular Politics (2013–2014)*, IDS Working Paper 456. Available at http://www.ids.ac.uk/publication/decrypting-copts-perspectives-on-communal-relations-in-contemporary-egypt-through-vernacular-politics-2013-2014 (accessed 24 August 2017).

Appendices

Christianity by Country

The table that begins overleaf provides a quick-reference, country-by-country listing for Christianity and its major traditions for all the countries that appear in this volume. These statistics are found in the *World Christian Database* (see Methodology and Sources) and all figures relate to 1970 and 2015. Small numbers are left unrounded to distinguish known small populations from zero but do not represent precise estimates.

The columns are as follows:

- Country (name of country in English)
- Region in which country is located
- Total population of country (United Nations estimate, 1970, 2015) and total numbers and percentage of population in each tradition
- Percentage mean annual growth rate, 1970–2015.

The last page of the table presents regional totals.

Country	Region	Tradition	1970 Population	1970 %	2015 Population	2015 %	Growth rate (%), 1970–2015
Algeria	North Africa	Total population	14,550,000	100.0%	39,667,000	100.0%	2.3%
		Christians	100,000	0.7%	69,100	0.2%	−0.8%
		Anglicans	800	0.0%	90	0.0%	−4.7%
		Independents	16,100	0.1%	48,400	0.1%	2.5%
		Orthodox	2,700	0.0%	1,400	0.0%	−1.5%
		Protestants	4,400	0.0%	13,500	0.0%	2.5%
		Roman Catholics	76,500	0.5%	5,700	0.0%	−5.6%
		Evangelicals	3,600	0.0%	27,000	0.1%	4.6%
		Pentecostals	3,500	0.0%	21,400	0.1%	4.1%
Armenia	West Asia	Total population	2,518,000	100.0%	3,018,000	100.0%	0.4%
		Christians	859,000	34.1%	2,849,000	94.4%	2.7%
		Independents	2,300	0.1%	65,000	2.2%	7.7%
		Orthodox	854,000	33.9%	2,534,000	84.0%	2.4%
		Protestants	350	0.0%	39,700	1.3%	11.1%
		Roman Catholics	0	0.0%	235,000	7.8%	25.1%
		Evangelicals	45	0.0%	30,300	1.0%	15.6%
		Pentecostals	2,100	0.1%	117,000	3.9%	9.3%
Azerbaijan	West Asia	Total population	5,178,000	100.0%	9,754,000	100.0%	1.4%
		Christians	263,000	5.1%	311,000	3.2%	0.4%
		Anglicans	0	0.0%	1,900	0.0%	12.4%
		Independents	0	0.0%	7,800	0.1%	15.9%
		Orthodox	250,000	4.8%	288,000	3.0%	0.3%
		Protestants	1,100	0.0%	12,100	0.1%	5.6%
		Roman Catholics	12,000	0.2%	560	0.0%	−6.6%
		Evangelicals	310	0.0%	4,500	0.1%	6.1%
		Pentecostals	0	0.0%	12,100	0.1%	17.1%
Bahrain	West Asia	Total population	213,000	100.0%	1,377,000	100.0%	4.2%
		Christians	5,900	2.8%	182,000	13.2%	7.9%
		Anglicans	500	0.2%	6,000	0.4%	5.7%
		Independents	1,000	0.5%	13,600	1.0%	6.0%
		Orthodox	800	0.4%	5,500	0.4%	4.4%
		Protestants	1,100	0.5%	6,600	0.5%	4.1%
		Roman Catholics	2,500	1.2%	150,000	10.9%	9.5%
		Evangelicals	680	0.3%	4,000	0.3%	4.0%
		Pentecostals	950	0.4%	44,200	3.2%	8.9%
Cyprus	West Asia	Total population	614,000	100.0%	1,165,000	100.0%	1.4%
		Christians	469,000	76.5%	822,000	70.5%	1.3%
		Anglicans	6,000	1.0%	10,000	0.9%	1.1%
		Independents	2,200	0.4%	8,500	0.7%	3.0%
		Orthodox	450,000	73.4%	765,000	65.7%	1.2%
		Protestants	3,100	0.5%	5,900	0.5%	1.4%
		Roman Catholics	6,400	1.0%	11,300	1.0%	1.3%
		Evangelicals	2,800	0.5%	6,300	0.5%	1.9%
		Pentecostals	540	0.1%	13,900	1.2%	7.5%

Country	Region	Tradition	1970 Population	1970 %	2015 Population	2015 %	Growth rate (%), 1970–2015
Egypt	North Africa	Total population	34,809,000	100.0%	91,508,000	100.0%	2.2%
		Christians	4,574,000	13.1%	7,673,000	8.4%	1.2%
		Anglicans	1,000	0.0%	2,000	0.0%	1.6%
		Independents	45,600	0.1%	118,000	0.1%	2.1%
		Orthodox	4,252,000	12.2%	7,305,000	8.0%	1.2%
		Protestants	137,000	0.4%	487,000	0.5%	2.9%
		Roman Catholics	139,000	0.4%	260,000	0.3%	1.4%
		Evangelicals	102,000	0.3%	394,000	0.4%	3.1%
		Pentecostals	43,000	0.1%	571,000	0.6%	5.9%
Georgia	West Asia	Total population	4,707,000	100.0%	4,000,000	100.0%	−0.4%
		Christians	1,650,000	35.1%	3,453,000	86.3%	1.7%
		Independents	100	0.0%	86,900	2.2%	16.2%
		Orthodox	1,608,000	34.2%	3,323,000	83.1%	1.6%
		Protestants	10,000	0.2%	13,000	0.3%	0.6%
		Roman Catholics	3,000	0.1%	40,000	1.0%	5.9%
		Evangelicals	4,800	0.1%	27,600	0.7%	4.0%
		Pentecostals	50	0.0%	54,500	1.4%	16.8%
Iraq	West Asia	Total population	9,918,000	100.0%	36,423,000	100.0%	2.9%
		Christians	401,000	4.0%	336,000	0.9%	−0.4%
		Anglicans	500	0.0%	190	0.0%	−2.1%
		Independents	1,600	0.0%	82,000	0.2%	9.1%
		Orthodox	98,000	1.0%	124,000	0.3%	0.5%
		Protestants	980	0.0%	17,000	0.1%	6.5%
		Roman Catholics	300,000	3.0%	186,000	0.5%	−1.1%
		Evangelicals	1,200	0.0%	20,600	0.1%	6.4%
		Pentecostals	310	0.0%	71,100	0.2%	12.8%
Israel	West Asia	Total population	2,850,000	100.0%	8,064,000	100.0%	2.3%
		Christians	79,000	2.8%	189,000	2.3%	2.0%
		Anglicans	900	0.0%	1,500	0.0%	1.1%
		Independents	3,400	0.1%	37,000	0.5%	5.4%
		Orthodox	18,400	0.7%	42,100	0.5%	1.9%
		Protestants	8,400	0.3%	13,600	0.2%	1.1%
		Roman Catholics	47,100	1.7%	109,000	1.4%	1.9%
		Evangelicals	5,800	0.2%	33,500	0.4%	4.0%
		Pentecostals	1,800	0.1%	43,600	0.5%	7.4%
Jordan	West Asia	Total population	1,655,000	100.0%	7,595,000	100.0%	3.4%
		Christians	83,400	5.0%	127,000	1.7%	0.9%
		Anglicans	3,500	0.2%	5,000	0.1%	0.8%
		Independents	5,000	0.3%	8,300	0.1%	1.1%
		Orthodox	38,600	2.3%	78,100	1.0%	1.6%
		Protestants	5,900	0.4%	6,700	0.1%	0.3%
		Roman Catholics	30,400	1.8%	29,300	0.4%	−0.1%
		Evangelicals	6,000	0.4%	8,400	0.1%	0.7%
		Pentecostals	2,100	0.1%	11,300	0.2%	3.9%

Country	Region	Tradition	1970 Population	1970 %	2015 Population	2015 %	Growth rate (%), 1970–2015
Kuwait	West Asia	Total population	750,000	100.0%	3,892,000	100.0%	3.7%
		Christians	38,600	5.2%	396,000	10.2%	5.3%
		Anglicans	1,500	0.2%	5,000	0.1%	2.7%
		Independents	2,400	0.3%	7,000	0.2%	2.4%
		Orthodox	13,300	1.8%	80,100	2.1%	4.1%
		Protestants	1,700	0.2%	7,400	0.2%	3.4%
		Roman Catholics	17,700	2.4%	300,000	7.7%	6.5%
		Evangelicals	2,100	0.3%	9,200	0.2%	3.3%
		Pentecostals	1,300	0.2%	84,500	2.2%	9.8%
Lebanon	West Asia	Total population	2,297,000	100.0%	5,851,000	100.0%	2.1%
		Christians	1,436,000	62.5%	2,004,000	34.3%	0.7%
		Anglicans	1,800	0.1%	150	0.0%	−5.4%
		Independents	13,600	0.6%	30,500	0.5%	1.8%
		Orthodox	357,000	15.5%	343,000	5.9%	−0.1%
		Protestants	28,100	1.2%	18,900	0.3%	−0.9%
		Roman Catholics	989,000	43.0%	1,613,000	27.6%	1.1%
		Evangelicals	17,700	0.8%	20,300	0.4%	0.3%
		Pentecostals	4,400	0.2%	63,900	1.1%	6.1%
Libya	North Africa	Total population	2,114,000	100.0%	6,278,000	100.0%	2.4%
		Christians	58,800	2.8%	46,600	0.7%	−0.5%
		Anglicans	380	0.0%	60	0.0%	−4.0%
		Independents	2,700	0.1%	1,700	0.0%	−1.1%
		Orthodox	47,000	2.2%	27,800	0.4%	−1.2%
		Protestants	3,900	0.2%	3,500	0.1%	−0.2%
		Roman Catholics	3,700	0.2%	11,200	0.2%	2.5%
		Evangelicals	1,800	0.1%	1,500	0.0%	−0.4%
		Pentecostals	390	0.0%	2,600	0.0%	4.3%
Morocco	North Africa	Total population	16,040,000	100.0%	34,378,000	100.0%	1.7%
		Christians	109,000	0.7%	34,800	0.1%	−2.5%
		Anglicans	600	0.0%	1,600	0.0%	2.2%
		Independents	1,400	0.0%	4,700	0.0%	2.8%
		Orthodox	900	0.0%	570	0.0%	−1.0%
		Protestants	5,000	0.0%	3,800	0.0%	−0.6%
		Roman Catholics	100,000	0.6%	22,500	0.1%	−3.3%
		Evangelicals	1,300	0.0%	4,100	0.0%	2.6%
		Pentecostals	800	0.0%	4,200	0.0%	3.7%
Oman	West Asia	Total population	724,000	100.0%	4,491,000	100.0%	4.1%
		Christians	2,700	0.4%	197,000	4.4%	10.0%
		Anglicans	500	0.1%	7,300	0.2%	6.1%
		Independents	380	0.1%	19,100	0.4%	9.1%
		Orthodox	650	0.1%	23,400	0.5%	8.3%
		Protestants	500	0.1%	3,300	0.1%	4.2%
		Roman Catholics	700	0.1%	140,000	3.1%	12.5%
		Evangelicals	190	0.0%	5,100	0.1%	7.5%
		Pentecostals	330	0.1%	35,200	0.8%	10.9%

Country	Region	Tradition	1970 Population	1970 %	2015 Population	2015 %	Growth rate (%), 1970–2015
Palestine	West Asia	Total population	1,125,000	100.0%	4,668,000	100.0%	3.2%
		Christians	53,200	4.7%	69,600	1.5%	0.6%
		Anglicans	1,400	0.1%	5,500	0.1%	3.1%
		Independents	1,500	0.1%	5,700	0.1%	3.0%
		Orthodox	27,700	2.5%	33,100	0.7%	0.4%
		Protestants	2,700	0.2%	5,200	0.1%	1.5%
		Roman Catholics	19,400	1.7%	16,500	0.4%	−0.4%
		Evangelicals	1,700	0.2%	5,700	0.1%	2.7%
		Pentecostals	1,300	0.1%	10,200	0.2%	4.6%
Qatar	West Asia	Total population	109,000	100.0%	2,235,000	100.0%	6.9%
		Christians	3,900	3.6%	210,000	9.4%	9.2%
		Anglicans	350	0.3%	10,000	0.5%	7.7%
		Independents	350	0.3%	10,600	0.5%	7.9%
		Orthodox	320	0.3%	5,300	0.2%	6.4%
		Protestants	400	0.4%	5,600	0.3%	6.0%
		Roman Catholics	2,500	2.3%	170,000	7.6%	9.8%
		Evangelicals	280	0.3%	4,400	0.2%	6.3%
		Pentecostals	290	0.3%	53,800	2.4%	12.3%
Saudi Arabia	West Asia	Total population	5,836,000	100.0%	31,540,000	100.0%	3.8%
		Christians	18,300	0.3%	1,379,000	4.4%	10.1%
		Anglicans	2,000	0.0%	19,000	0.1%	5.1%
		Independents	4,800	0.1%	54,800	0.2%	5.6%
		Orthodox	2,000	0.0%	50,000	0.2%	7.4%
		Protestants	6,900	0.1%	15,500	0.1%	1.8%
		Roman Catholics	2,600	0.0%	1,220,000	3.9%	14.6%
		Evangelicals	4,300	0.1%	27,500	0.1%	4.2%
		Pentecostals	4,600	0.1%	361,000	1.1%	10.2%
Sudan	North Africa	Total population	10,233,000	100.0%	40,235,000	100.0%	3.1%
		Christians	318,000	3.1%	2,016,000	5.0%	4.2%
		Anglicans	90,000	0.9%	530,000	1.3%	4.0%
		Independents	500	0.0%	19,900	0.1%	8.5%
		Orthodox	107,000	1.1%	102,000	0.3%	−0.1%
		Protestants	53,200	0.5%	256,000	0.6%	3.5%
		Roman Catholics	62,900	0.6%	1,099,000	2.7%	6.6%
		Evangelicals	76,900	0.8%	407,000	1.0%	3.8%
		Pentecostals	100	0.0%	141,000	0.4%	17.5%
Syria	West Asia	Total population	6,379,000	100.0%	18,502,000	100.0%	2.4%
		Christians	667,000	10.5%	1,136,000	6.1%	1.2%
		Anglicans	50	0.0%	4,600	0.0%	10.6%
		Independents	2,600	0.0%	4,600	0.0%	1.3%
		Orthodox	464,000	7.3%	714,000	3.9%	1.0%
		Protestants	20,900	0.3%	33,500	0.2%	1.1%
		Roman Catholics	179,000	2.8%	386,000	2.1%	1.7%
		Evangelicals	8,500	0.1%	11,400	0.1%	0.6%
		Pentecostals	390	0.0%	22,800	0.1%	9.5%

Country	Region	Tradition	1970 Population	1970 %	2015 Population	2015 %	Growth rate (%), 1970–2015
Tunisia	North Africa	Total population	5,060,000	100.0%	11,254,000	100.0%	1.8%
		Christians	27,300	0.5%	24,000	0.2%	−0.3%
		Anglicans	150	0.0%	80	0.0%	−1.4%
		Independents	1,200	0.0%	2,400	0.0%	1.5%
		Orthodox	250	0.0%	230	0.0%	−0.2%
		Protestants	630	0.0%	890	0.0%	0.8%
		Roman Catholics	25,000	0.5%	20,000	0.2%	−0.5%
		Evangelicals	480	0.0%	660	0.0%	0.7%
		Pentecostals	570	0.0%	2,400	0.0%	3.3%
Turkey	West Asia	Total population	34,772,000	100.0%	78,666,000	100.0%	1.8%
		Christians	290,000	0.8%	181,000	0.2%	−1.0%
		Anglicans	2,000	0.0%	12,000	0.0%	4.1%
		Independents	2,100	0.0%	19,700	0.0%	5.1%
		Orthodox	226,000	0.7%	78,800	0.1%	−2.3%
		Protestants	24,300	0.1%	15,000	0.0%	−1.1%
		Roman Catholics	26,500	0.1%	42,700	0.1%	1.1%
		Evangelicals	5,100	0.0%	7,000	0.0%	0.7%
		Pentecostals	490	0.0%	18,300	0.0%	8.4%
United Arab Emirates	West Asia	Total population	235,000	100.0%	9,157,000	100.0%	8.5%
		Christians	9,300	4.0%	1,173,000	12.8%	11.4%
		Anglicans	1,500	0.6%	14,000	0.2%	5.1%
		Independents	100	0.0%	18,100	0.2%	12.2%
		Orthodox	2,200	0.9%	74,200	0.8%	8.1%
		Protestants	910	0.4%	17,700	0.2%	6.8%
		Roman Catholics	4,500	1.9%	1,057,000	11.5%	12.9%
		Evangelicals	920	0.4%	12,500	0.1%	6.0%
		Pentecostals	230	0.1%	291,000	3.2%	17.2%
Western Sahara	North Africa	Total population	76,900	100.0%	573,000	100.0%	4.6%
		Christians	31,600	41.1%	880	0.2%	−7.6%
		Independents	0	0.0%	100	0.0%	5.3%
		Roman Catholics	30,000	39.0%	780	0.1%	−7.8%
		Evangelicals	0	0.0%	30	0.0%	7.9%
		Pentecostals	0	0.0%	73	0.0%	4.5%
Yemen	West Asia	Total population	6,156,000	100.0%	26,832,000	100.0%	3.3%
		Christians	1,700	0.0%	36,500	0.1%	7.1%
		Anglicans	170	0.0%	1,800	0.0%	5.4%
		Independents	1,000	0.0%	4,000	0.0%	3.1%
		Orthodox	0	0.0%	8,000	0.0%	16.0%
		Protestants	290	0.0%	13,700	0.1%	8.9%
		Roman Catholics	120	0.0%	6,000	0.0%	9.1%
		Evangelicals	210	0.0%	4,000	0.0%	6.8%
		Pentecostals	200	0.0%	6,800	0.0%	8.2%

Region	Tradition	1970		2015		Growth rate (%), 1970–2015
		Population	%	Population	%	
North Africa	Total population	82,883,000	100.0%	223,892,000	100.0%	2.2%
	Christians	5,220,000	6.3%	9,864,000	4.4%	1.4%
	Anglicans	92,900	0.1%	534,000	0.2%	4.0%
	Independents	67,400	0.1%	195,000	0.1%	2.4%
	Orthodox	4,410,000	5.3%	7,437,000	3.3%	1.2%
	Protestants	204,000	0.3%	764,000	0.3%	3.0%
	Roman Catholics	437,000	0.5%	1,419,000	0.6%	2.7%
	Evangelicals	186,000	0.2%	834,000	0.4%	3.4%
	Pentecostals	48,400	0.1%	742,000	0.3%	6.3%
West Asia	Total population	86,037,000	100.0%	257,231,000	100.0%	2.5%
	Christians	6,330,000	7.4%	15,049,000	5.9%	1.9%
	Anglicans	22,700	0.0%	104,000	0.0%	3.4%
	Independents	44,500	0.1%	483,000	0.2%	5.4%
	Orthodox	4,411,000	5.1%	8,569,000	3.3%	1.5%
	Protestants	117,000	0.1%	250,000	0.1%	1.7%
	Roman Catholics	1,643,000	1.9%	5,713,000	2.2%	2.8%
	Evangelicals	62,700	0.1%	242,000	0.1%	3.1%
	Pentecostals	21,300	0.0%	1,315,000	0.5%	9.6%
North Africa and West Asia	Total population	168,920,000	100.0%	481,123,000	100.0%	2.4%
	Christians	11,550,000	6.8%	24,913,000	5.2%	1.7%
	Anglicans	116,000	0.1%	638,000	0.1%	3.9%
	Independents	112,000	0.1%	678,000	0.1%	4.1%
	Orthodox	8,821,000	5.2%	16,006,000	3.3%	1.3%
	Protestants	322,000	0.2%	1,015,000	0.2%	2.6%
	Roman Catholics	2,081,000	1.2%	7,132,000	1.5%	2.8%
	Evangelicals	248,000	0.2%	1,076,000	0.2%	3.3%
	Pentecostals	69,700	0.0%	2,057,000	0.4%	7.8%

Methodology and Sources of Christian and Religious Affiliation

Todd M. Johnson and Gina A. Zurlo

Unless otherwise designated, the demographic figures in this book, both in the full-colour section and in the tables throughout, are from the *World Christian Database* (Boston, MA: Brill). This essay offers a concise explanation of methods and sources related to the database. It is adapted from longer treatments in Todd M. Johnson and Brian J. Grim, *The World's Religions in Figures: An Introduction to International Religious Demography* (Oxford: Wiley-Blackwell, 2013) and David B. Barrett and Todd M. Johnson, *World Christian Trends* (Pasadena, CA: William Carey Library, 2001). The *World Christian Database* (*WCD*) includes detailed information on 45,000 Christian denominations and on religions in every country of the world. Extensive data are available on 234 countries and 13,000 ethno-linguistic peoples, as well as on 5,000 cities and 3,000 provinces. Information is readily available on religious activities, growth rates, religious literature, worker activity and demographics. Sources are evaluated and reviewed on a weekly basis by a professional staff dedicated to expanding and updating the *WCD*, and the database is updated quarterly.

The Right to Profess One's Choice

The starting point of this methodology is the United Nations 1948 Universal Declaration of Human Rights, Article 18:

> Everyone has the right to freedom of thought, conscience and religion; this right includes freedom to change his religion or belief, and freedom, either alone or in community with others and in public or private, to manifest his religion or belief in teaching, practice, worship and observance.

Since its promulgation, this group of phrases has been incorporated into the state constitutions of a large number of countries across the world. This fundamental right also includes the right to claim the religion of one's choice, and the right to be called a follower of that religion and to be enumerated as such. The section on religious freedom in the constitutions of very many nations uses the exact words of the Universal Declaration, and many countries instruct their census personnel to observe this principle. Public declaration must therefore be taken seriously when endeavouring to survey the extent of religious and non-religious affiliation around the world.

Religious Demography

The origins of the field of religious demography lie in the church censuses conducted in most European societies. For many years and in many countries, churches produced the most complete censuses of the population. They achieved this largely by recording baptisms and funerals. These data, however, were seen not as referring to specific religious communities, but rather to the larger homogeneous societies. With the decline of national churches in Europe beginning in the nineteenth and continuing into the twentieth century, governments began tracking births and deaths, eventually replacing churches as the main bodies collecting detailed information on human populations. Although thousands of sources for international religious demography are available, ranging from censuses and demographic surveys to statistics collected and reported by religious groups themselves, little has been done by scholars in religion, sociology, or other disciplines to collect, collate and analyse these data.

Sources

Data for religious demography fall broadly under five major headings:

1. Censuses in which a religious question is asked

In the twentieth century, approximately half the world's countries asked a question related to religion in their official national population censuses. Since 1990, however, this number has been declining as developing countries have dropped the question, deeming it too expensive (in many countries each question in a census costs well over US$1 million), uninteresting or controversial. As a result, some countries that historically included a religion question have not done so in their censuses since 1990. National censuses are the best starting point for the identification of religious adherents, because they generally cover the entire population.

2. Censuses in which an ethnicity or language question is asked

In the absence of a question on religion, another helpful piece of information from a census is ethnicity or language. This is especially true when a particular ethnic group can be equated with a particular religion. For example, over 99% of Somalis are Muslim, so the number of Somalis in, say, Sweden is an indication of a part of the Muslim community there. Similarly, a question that asks for country of birth can be useful. If the answer is 'Nepal' there is a significant chance that the individual or community is Hindu. In each of these cases the assumption is made (if there is no further information) that the religion of the transplanted ethnic or linguistic community is the same as that in the home country.

3. Surveys and polls

In the absence of census data on religion, large-scale demographic surveys such as MEASURE (Monitoring and Evaluation to Assess and Use Results) and Demographic and Health Surveys (DHS) often include a question about the respondent's religious affiliation. In some instances, demographic surveys by groups such as UNICEF (the United Nations Children's Fund) include a religious affiliation question. Demographic surveys, although less comprehensive than a national census, have several advantages over other types of general population surveys and polls. Demographic and Health Surveys (DHS) are highly regarded by demographers and social scientists, and provide valuable nationally representative data on religion. Surveys can also be commissioned in light of a dearth of data on a particular subject and results can be used to search for correlations between different variables.

4. Scholarly monographs

Every year, scholars publish hundreds of monographs on particular religions or religions in particular countries or regions. Such monographs differ from other sources in that they attempt to provide an overall profile of religion in an area or country, bringing to light local sources of quantitative data as well as qualitative information that provides layers of context and background.

5. Religion statistics in yearbooks and handbooks

Religious communities keep track of their members, using everything from simple lists to elaborate membership reports. The most detailed data collection and analysis is undertaken each year by some 45,000 Christian denominations and their 4.7 million constituent churches and congregations of believers. The latter invest over US$1.1 billion annually for a massive, decentralised and largely uncoordinated global census of Christians. In sum, they send out around 10 million printed questionnaires in 3,000 different languages, covering 180 major religious subjects reporting on 2,000 socio-religious variables. This collection of data provides a year-by-year snapshot of the progress or decline of Christianity's diverse movements, offering an enormous body of data from which researchers can track trends and make projections. Statistics collected by religious communities often enable researchers to distinguish between two categories of religionists – practising and non-practising – based on whether or not they take part in the ongoing organised life of the religion.

In addition to the above categories, there are governmental statistical reports, questionnaires and reports from collaborators, field surveys and interviews, correspondence with national informants, unpublished documentation, encyclopaedias, dictionaries and directories of religions, print and web-based contemporary descriptions of religions, and dissertations and theses on religion. The best practices in determining the religious affiliation of any population utilise as many sources as possible.

Affiliation

There are at least two different perspectives on what it means to be a Christian: professing Christians and affiliated Christians. Utilising the United Nations Universal Declaration of Human Rights as a foundation, 'professing Christians' means all those who profess to be Christians in government censuses or public-opinion polls, that is, who declare or identify themselves as Christians, who say 'I am a Christian' or 'We are Christians' when asked the question 'What is your religion?'

However, not all those who profess to be Christians are affiliated to organised churches and denominations. Therefore, 'affiliated Christians' are those known to the churches or known to the clergy (usually by names and addresses) and claimed in their statistics, that is, those enrolled on the churches' books or records, with totals that can be substantiated. This usually means all known baptised Christians and their children, and other adherents; it is sometimes termed the 'total Christian community' (because affiliated Christians are those who are not primarily individual Christians but who primarily belong to the corporate community of Christ), or 'inclusive membership' (because affiliated Christians are church members). This definition of 'Christians' is what the churches usually mean by the term (and thus the *WCD*), and statistics on such affiliated Christians are what the churches themselves collect and publish. In all countries, it may be assumed with confidence that the churches know better than the state how many Christians are affiliated to them. This therefore indicates a second measure of the total Christians that is quite independent of the first (government census figures of professing Christians).

Children

The family is by far the most important instrumentality through which individuals acquire personal, cultural and social self-identification. In consequence, children of church members are more likely to remain members than those whose parents are not church members. Children of ardent and practising Christians usually are, to the extent that their years permit, ardent and practising Christians. However, many churches do not enumerate children under 15 years. One reason is that it has been widely noted that most conversion crises occur in the 13–20-year age group in Christian families or in majority Christian contexts. On this view, therefore, children who have not yet reached 15 cannot reasonably be expected to be practising and believing Christians. The *WCD* takes the opposite view: children and infants also can properly be called Christians, and can actively and regularly (to the extent of their ability) practise the Christian faith. Consequently, where Christian denominations do not count children in their membership rolls, their membership is reported in our adult category. A total community figure is calculated (in the absence of any additional information from the denomination) by adding in the average number of children reported in United Nations statistics for the given country. Thus, the total community figures are comparable from one denomination to the next whether or not they count children in their membership.

Choice of Best Data Available

Religious demography must attempt to be comprehensive. In certain countries where no hard statistical data or reliable surveys are available, researchers have to rely on the informed estimates of experts in the area and subject. Researchers make no detailed attempt at a critique of each nation's censuses and polls or each church's statistical operations. After examining what is available, researchers then select the best data available until such time as better data come into existence. In addition, there are a number of areas of religious life where it is impossible to obtain accurate statistics, usually because of state opposition to particular tradition(s). Thus it will probably never be possible to get exact numbers of, for example, atheists in Indonesia or Baha'i in Iran. Where such information is necessary, reasonable and somewhat conservative estimates are made.

Reconciling Discrepancies in Survey Data

There are post-survey strategies that help general population surveys better reflect the actual composition of a particular country. For instance, if in a survey of 1,000 people, 60% were women and 40% were men, but we know that women and men are each 50% of the country's total population based on a recent census, then each woman's response on the general population survey would be weighted down by a factor of 500/600 and each man's response would be weighted up by a factor of 500/400. Such adjustments are called weighting.

Other adjustments made to general population surveys may require taking into account that they are meant to be representative of only adult populations. Therefore their results require adjustments, particularly if some religious groups have more children than others in the same country. This requires either a complete roster of members of each household or some other way to estimate of the number of children living in the household with the adults. When a complete roster is unavailable, most estimates of religious affiliation of children assume that they have the same religion as their one of their parents (usually assumed by demographers to be the religion of the mother). Differences in fertility rates between religious groups are particularly useful in estimating religious differentials among children. This is because demographic projections carry forward children born to women. It may introduce some bias to the degree that the father's religion is more likely to be the religion of the children than the mother.

Example: Coptic Church in Egypt

At times, the results from government censuses and information from religious communities can be strikingly different. For example, in Egypt, where the vast majority of the population is Muslim, government censuses taken every 10 years have shown consistently for the past 100 years that a declining share of the population declare themselves as or profess to be Christians. In the most recent census, some 5% identified as Christian. However, church estimates point to a percentage figure three times larger (15%). This discrepancy may be due to overestimates by the churches or attributed, at least in part, to social pressure on some Christians to record themselves as Muslims. Further, according to news reports, some Egyptian Christians have complained that they are listed on official identity cards as Muslims. It also might be that church reports include Egyptian Christians working as expatriates outside Egypt, while the census does not, or that the churches simply overestimate their numbers.

Such a lack of clarity is compounded by media reports and even Egyptian government announcements repeatedly claiming that Christians make up 10% or more of the country's approximately 80 million people, despite the fact that the census repeatedly reports only 5%. The highest share of Christians found in an Egyptian census was in 1927 (8.3%). Figures for Egyptian Christians declined in each subsequent census, with Christians seemingly making up 5.7% of the Egyptian population in 1996. The report from the most recent census, conducted in 2006, does not, however, provide data on religious affiliation, but a sample of the 2006 census data is available through the Integrated Public Use Microdata Series, International (IPUMS). They sample the same Christian share (about 5%) as the latest Egyptian Demographic and Health Survey, with a sample size of 16,527 women aged 15–49 years.

According to the Pew Forum's analysis of Global Restrictions on Religion (see www.pewforum.org), Egypt has very high scores for government restrictions on religion as well as high scores for social hostilities involving religion. These factors might lead some Christians to be cautious about revealing their identity. Regardless of the actual number, it is very likely that Christians are declining as a proportion of Egypt's population, even if their absolute numbers are not falling. On the one hand, Christian fertility in Egypt has been lower than Muslim fertility. On the other, is possible that large numbers of Christians have left the country, although a 2012 study by the Pew Forum on the religious affiliation of migrants around the world has not found evidence of an especially large Egyptian Christian diaspora.

Dates of Statistics

It is important, in changing situations, to know the exact date (year, perhaps also month and sometimes even day) to which particular statistics apply. This methodology compares government statistics of religion with statistics from religious communities themselves; but in doing so, it must be remembered that a government census (or a public-opinion poll) is almost always taken on a single, known day; whereas, by contrast, religious statistics are compiled over a lengthy period – perhaps three, four or even five years from the local grassroots counting of heads to final compilation of totals by a large denomination or church. Denominational totals published in 2015 therefore probably refer to the situation in 2012, 2011 or even 2010.

Counting Pentecostals

Three types of Pentecostals

For the purpose of understanding the diverse global phenomenon of Pentecostalism, it is useful to divide the movement into three kinds, or types. First are denominational Pentecostals, organised into denominations in the early part of the twentieth century. Second are Charismatics, individuals in the mainline denominations (primarily after the mid-twentieth century). Third are Independent Charismatics, those who broke free of denominational Pentecostalism or mainline denominations to form their own networks.

Pentecostals (Type 1)

Pentecostals are defined as Christians who are members of the explicitly Pentecostal denominations whose major characteristic is a new experience of the energising ministry of the Holy Spirit that most other Christians have considered to be highly unusual. This is interpreted as a rediscovery of the spiritual gifts of New Testament times and their restoration to ordinary Christian life and ministry. Classical Pentecostalism usually is held to have begun in the United States in 1901, although most scholars have moved to a 'multiple origins' theory of the birth of modern Pentecostalism, emphasising early activity outside of the Western World. For a brief period, Pentecostalism expected to remain an interdenominational movement within the existing churches, but from 1909 onwards its members increasingly were ejected from mainline bodies and so forced to begin new organised denominations.

Pentecostal denominations hold the distinctive teachings that all Christians should seek a post-conversion religious experience called baptism in the Holy Spirit and that a Spirit-baptised believer may receive one or more of the supernatural gifts known in the early church: the ability to prophesy; to practise divine healing through prayer; to speak (glossolalia), interpret or sing in tongues; to sing in the Spirit, dance in the Spirit, pray with upraised hands; to receive dreams, visions, words of wisdom, words of knowledge; to discern spirits; and to perform miracles, power encounters, exorcisms (casting out demons), resuscitations, deliverances, or other signs and wonders.

From 1906 onwards, the hallmark of explicitly Pentecostal denominations, by comparison with Holiness/Perfectionist denominations, has been the single addition of speaking in other tongues as the 'initial evidence' of one's having received the baptism of the Holy Spirit, whether or not one subsequently experiences regularly the gift of tongues. Most Pentecostal denominations teach that tongues-speaking is mandatory for all members, but in reality today not all members have practised this gift, either initially or as an ongoing experience. Pentecostals are defined here as all associated with explicitly Pentecostal denominations that identify themselves in explicitly Pentecostal terms, or with other denominations that as a whole are phenomenologically Pentecostal in teaching and practice.

Among Protestants (coded as 'P-') are Pentecostal denominations such as the Assemblies of God. Sub-categories of Oneness, Baptistic, Holiness, Perfectionist and Apostolic were retained from earlier research. Each minor tradition within Pentecostalism is considered to be 100% Pentecostal (all members of Pentecostal denominations are counted as Pentecostals).

Charismatics (Type 2)

Charismatics are defined as Christians affiliated to non-Pentecostal denominations (Anglican, Protestant, Catholic, Orthodox) who receive the experiences above in what has been termed the Charismatic movement. The Charismatic movement's roots go back to early Pentecostalism, but its rapid expansion has been mainly since 1960 (later called the Charismatic renewal). Charismatics usually describe themselves as having been 'renewed in the Spirit' and as experiencing the Spirit's supernatural and miraculous and energising power. They remain within, and form organised renewal groups within, their older mainline non-Pentecostal denominations (instead of leaving to join Pentecostal denominations). They demonstrate any or all of the *charismata pneumatika* (gifts of the Spirit), including signs and wonders (but with glossolalia regarded as optional).

Type 2 recognises the existence of Pentecostal individuals within the Anglican, Roman Catholic, Orthodox and Protestant traditions. These are designated 'Charismatic' and evaluated by country as Catholic Charismatics, Anglican Charismatics and so on, designating renewal within an existing tradition. For example, the beginning of the Charismatic movement in Anglican churches is described by Episcopal priest Dennis Bennett in *Nine O'Clock in the Morning* (Alachua, FL: Bridge-Logos, 1970). Traditions are assessed to determine what percentage of adherents identify themselves as Charismatics, ranging from 0% to 100%. Self-identification percentages for Charismatics were calculated by contacting renewal agencies working within denominations.

Independent Charismatics (Type 3)

While the classification and chronology of the first two types is straightforward, there are thousands of churches and movements that 'resemble' the first two types but do not fit their definitions. These constitute a third type and often pre-date the first two types. For lack of a better term, these are called 'Independent Charismatics'. Part of the rationale for this term is the fact that they are largely found in the Independent category of the overall taxonomy of Christians. Thus, Type 3 includes Pentecostal or semi-Pentecostal members of the 250-year-old Independent movement of Christians, primarily in the global South, of churches begun without reference to Western Christianity. These indigenous movements, although not all explicitly Pentecostal, nevertheless have the main features of Pentecostalism. In addition, since Azusa Street, thousands of schismatic or other Independent Charismatic churches have come out of Type 1 Pentecostals and Type 2 Charismatic movements. They consist of Christians who, unrelated to or no longer related to the Pentecostal or Charismatic denominations, have become filled with the Spirit, or empowered by the Spirit and have experienced the Spirit's ministry (although usually without recognising a baptism in the Spirit separate from conversion); who exercise gifts of the Spirit (with much less emphasis on tongues, as optional or even absent or unnecessary) and emphasise signs and wonders, supernatural miracles and power encounters; but also do not identify themselves as either Pentecostals (Type 1) or Charismatics (Type 2). In a number of countries they exhibit Pentecostal and Charismatic phenomena but combine this with rejection of Pentecostal terminology. These believers frequently are identified by their leadership as Independent, Postdenominationalist, Restorationist, Radical, Neo-Apostolic or 'Third Wave.'

Thus, the third type is Independent Charismatics (also known in the literature as neo-Charismatics or neo-Pentecostals) who are not in Protestant Pentecostal denominations (Type 1) nor are they individual Charismatics in the traditional churches (Type 2). Type 3 is the most diverse of the three types and ranges from house churches in China to African Initiated Churches to white-led Charismatic networks in the Western world. It includes Pentecostals who had split off from established Protestant denominations (Type 1) and who were then labelled as Independent. Independent churches formed by Charismatic leaders (Type 2) who founded new congregations and networks are also included. Some Independent Charismatics speak in tongues, but healing and power evangelism are more prominent in this type than in the other two.

Three types together

One difficulty that has plagued all researchers and historians of Pentecostalism is what to call the overarching movement. Some have used 'Pentecostalism' or 'Global Pentecostalism', while others have used 'Charismatic'. Still others have used 'Pentecostal and Charismatic'. David Barrett originally used the lengthy phrase 'the Pentecostal and Charismatic Renewal of the Holy Spirit', which he later shortened to 'Renewal'. He then coined the term 'Renewalist' to refer to all three waves or types. For the purposes of this series, we use the term 'Pentecostals/Charismatics' to refer to all three types.

A demographic overview of Pentecostals/Charismatics (all types) illustrates the complexities of both the spread of the movement across the countries of the world and the striking diversity of the churches themselves. While current ways of understanding Pentecostals, Charismatics and Independent Charismatics reveal a global movement of immense proportions, perspectives on classification, counting and assessment of the movement are likely to continue to evolve. In the meantime, hundreds of millions of Christians across all traditions will continue to participate in the movement – bringing vitality in some denominations and schism in others. They will also promote social transformation in some communities and show little participation in others. What is certain is that, for the foreseeable future, Christianity as a whole will continue to experience the growth pains of this global phenomenon.

Counting Evangelicals

Any effective and comprehensive method for counting Evangelicals must take into consideration denominational affiliation, self-identification and theology. The results of counting Evangelicals are directly related to denominational membership figures. Strictly speaking, denominational affiliation means official membership on a church roll.

Method 1: Individuals in denominations that are 100% Evangelical

The first category of Evangelicals includes individuals who are found in denominations that are coded 100% Evangelical. That is, membership of an Evangelical council (national, regional or global) is assessed for every denomination and those denominations that have Evangelical affiliations are classed as 100% Evangelical. Consequently, 100% of the members of these denominations are considered Evangelical. Using this method alone, the *WCD* estimates there are 150 million Evangelicals in the world. As of 2010, the nine largest 100% Evangelical denominations in the world were all Protestant, and the five largest 100% Evangelical denominations were found in Brazil, Ethiopia, Nigeria and Indonesia, reflecting the global scope of the movement.

Method 2: Individuals who self-identify as Evangelical in non-100% Evangelical denominations

For those denominations not identified as 100% Evangelical, an estimate is made of the percentage (0–99%) of members who self-identify as Evangelical. Self-identification percentages for Evangelicals in non-100% Evangelical denominations are verified by contacting key figures within each denomination, and each estimate is sourced in documentation housed at the Center for the Study of Global Christianity. Adding together figures from both 100% and partially Evangelical denominations gives a total of 285 million Evangelicals worldwide. Looking at both 100% and non-100% Evangelical denominations reveals that the movement has a significant presence beyond Western Protestantism. Some of the denominations with the most Evangelicals are within Anglicanism in the global South, such as the Anglican Church of Nigeria and the Church of Uganda. Chinese house churches (classified as Independents) taken together constitute the denomination with the third most Evangelicals globally. The United Kingdom (the Church of England) and the United States (the Southern Baptist Convention), however, are still important locations of the movement.

Method 3: Evangelicals not affiliated with any denomination (Unaffiliated Evangelicals)

To date, no studies have addressed directly how many Evangelicals are denominationally unaffiliated. However, two well known realities (in Western Christianity, in particular) appear to provide indirect evidence for this undocumented trend. The first is reflected in recent research indicating the unaffiliated are not uniformly non-religious. The Pew Research Center reported that 68% of America's unaffiliated believe in God. It is reasonable to assume that a notable proportion of Christians is among the ranks of the unaffiliated by virtue of Christianity being the largest religion in many of the countries studied. The second reality is the acknowledged fact that unaffiliated Christians often attend and are active in churches, including Evangelical churches, without becoming official members. These unaffiliated Christians profess allegiance and commitment to Christ but do not maintain church affiliation.

Dynamics of Change in Religious Populations

The question of how and why the number of religious adherents changes over time is critical to the study of international religious demography. It is more complex than simply 'counting heads' via births and deaths – a well established area in quantitative sociological studies – but in addition involves the multifaceted areas of religious conversion and migration. The migration of religious people has only in the past few years become a more researched area of demographic study, and issues surrounding religious conversion continue to be under-represented in the field. Data on religion from a wide range of sources – including from the religious communities themselves, as well as governments and scholars – must be employed to understand the total scope of religious affiliation. Given data on a particular religion from two separate points in time, the question can be raised, 'What are the dynamics by which the number of adherents changes over time?' The dynamics of change in religious affiliation can be reduced to three sets of empirical population data that together enable enumeration of the increase or decrease in adherents over time. To measure overall change, these three sets can be defined as follows: (1) births minus deaths; (2) converts to minus converts from; and (3) immigrants minus emigrants. The first variable in each of these three sets (births, converts to, immigrants) measures increase, whereas the second (deaths, converts from, emigrants) measures decrease. All future (and current) projections of religious affiliation, within any subset of the global population (normally a country or region), will account for these dynamics, and the changes themselves are dependent on these dynamics.

Births

The primary mechanism of global religious demographic change is (live) births. Children are almost always counted as having the religion of their parents (as is the law in Norway, for example). In simple terms, if populations that are predominantly Muslim, for example, have more children on average than those that are predominantly Christian or Hindu, then over time (all other things being equal) Muslims will become an increasingly larger percentage of that population. This means that the relative size of a religious population has a close statistical relationship to birthrates.

Deaths

Even as births increase their memberships, religious communities experience constant loss through the deaths of members. Although this often includes tragic, unanticipated deaths of younger members, it most frequently affects the elderly members. Thus, changes in health care and technology can positively impact religious communities if members live longer.

Births minus deaths/total fertility rate

The change over time in any given population is most simply expressed as the number of births into the community minus the number of deaths out of it. Many religious communities around the world experience little else in the dynamics of their growth or decline. Detailed projections rely on a number of estimated measures, including life expectancy, population age structures and the total fertility rate. This means that any attempt to understand the dynamics of religious affiliation must be based firmly on demographic projections of births and deaths.

Converts to

It is a common observation that individuals (or even whole villages or communities) change allegiance from one religion to another (or to no religion at all). Unfortunately, one of the problems in studying conversion is the paucity of information on it. Reliable data on conversions are hard to obtain, for a number of reasons. Although some national censuses ask people about their religion, they do not directly ask whether people have converted to their present faith. A few cross-national surveys do contain questions about religious switching, but even in those surveys it is difficult to assess whether more people leave a religion than enter it. In some countries, legal and social consequences make conversion difficult, and survey respondents might be reluctant to speak honestly about the topic. In particular, Hinduism is for many Hindus (as is Islam for many Muslims) not just a religion but also an ethnic or cultural identity that does not depend on whether a person actively practises the faith. Thus even non-practising or secular Hindus may still consider themselves, and be viewed by their neighbours, as Hindus.

Converts from

Conversion to a new religion, as mentioned above, also involves conversion from a previous one. Thus, a convert to Islam is, at the same time, a convert from another religion. In the twentieth and twenty-first centuries, the most converts from Christianity were and continue to be found largely among those in the Western world who have decided to be agnostics or atheists.

Converts to minus converts from

The net conversion rate in a population is calculated by subtracting the number of 'converts from' from the number of 'converts to'. Conversion to and conversion from will likely continue to play a role in changing religious demographics in the future.

Immigrants

Equally important at the international level is how the movement of people across national borders impacts religious affiliation. Once religious communities are established through immigration they often grow vigorously (for a time) via high birth rates.

Emigrants

In a reversal of nineteenth-century European colonisation of Africa, Asia and parts of the Americas, the late twentieth century witnessed waves of emigration of people from these regions to the Western world. The impact on religious affiliation is significant.

Immigrants minus emigrants

In the twenty-first century, international migration continues to have a significant impact on the religious composition of individual countries. One can try to anticipate the way in which expected immigration and emigration trends will affect a country's population over time. One profound change to be expected is the increase of religious pluralism in almost every country of the world. Increasing religious pluralism is not always welcomed and can be seen as a political, cultural, national or religious threat.

The six dynamics discussed above determine changes in religious demographics. Gains are the result of three positive dynamics: births, conversions to, and immigration. Losses are the result of three negative dynamics: deaths, conversions from, and emigration. The net change in religious demographics is the result of gains minus losses. The balance of dynamics can be reflected in any proportions (for example, mainly births for gains, mainly conversions from for losses) but can also be represented by pairing the gains and losses by type: births versus deaths, converts to versus converts from, and immigrants versus emigrants. In each case, the net change (either positive or negative) will be the difference between the two. This means that any attempt to understand religious affiliation in the past, present or future must be firmly based on demographic dynamics. A proper awareness of these dynamics and their significance is thus vital both for undertaking and for interpreting studies of the future of religion.

Measuring Growth Rates

The rates of growth, increase, decrease or decline of membership in many congregations can readily be measured from their annually reported statistics. This has been done by obtaining the statistics for two different years, where possible five years apart (to minimise the effects of roll-cleaning and other annual irregularities), usually 2000–5 and 2005–10, and working out the average annual growth rate as a percentage. Great care must be taken in such computations to ensure that the statistics used are measuring exactly the same entity (especially geographically) for each of the two years concerned. Growth, as a percentage increase or decrease per year, must be measured by dividing any annual increase by the identical category of total. Thus a church, for example, in a particular country with 500,000 total adherents (including children) in 2005 which grows to 600,000 total adherents (including children) in 2010 shows an increase of 600,000 minus 500,000 = 100,000, which divided by 5 = 20,000 a year, which divided by the mean membership of 550,000 gives an increase rate of 3.64% per year. In practice, the methodology follows a more accurate method by using the 1970 to 2015 figures for each denomination to arrive at average annual growth rates.

There are different ways of measuring the growth of a religious body. First, one can measure either adults only, or total community including children. Secondly, the growth rate of a church or religious grouping can be measured over a single day, or a month, a year, a decade, or 50 years – and all will yield differing results. This survey is concerned primarily to measure long-term rates. A growth rate measured for a specific religious body over a two- or three-year period may not be sustained over a decade.

Projecting Religious Populations

The starting point of future studies is natural growth of the total population of the country or region of interest, using demographic projections as a baseline. Three major areas beyond natural growth are utilised to improve the projections. First, birth and death rates vary among religious communities within a particular country. Secondly, increasing numbers of people are likely to change their religious affiliations in the future. Thirdly, immigration and emigration trends will impact a country's population over time. The highest-quality projections for religious communities are built on cohort-component projections – ones that use differential rates for each religion: age-specific fertility rates by religion, age structure in five-year age-and-sex cohorts by religion, migration rates by religion, and mortality by religion.

Unfortunately, this kind of detail is not yet available for many countries (half of censuses do not ask a question about religion). Fortunately, the process of filling in missing data using demographic and smaller-scale general population surveys is underway, and as these data become available through the Pew–Templeton Global Religious Futures Project, researchers will have access to these data through the *World Religion Database*, where they will be archived in full, with summary results available at the Pew Forum's website. In the meantime, projections cannot solely rely on the cohort-component method. Instead, they use a hybrid projection method. First, the 2015 religious composition of each country is established as the baseline. Then, utilising the United Nations medium variant cohort-component projections of populations for five-year periods up to 2050, future religious shares are modestly adjusted from the 2015 baseline. Adjustments are based on analysis of past differential growth rates of religious groups, factoring in historical patterns of religious switching and possible future attenuation of past trends. Finally, these projections take into account how immigrants might alter the future religious composition of country populations.

Ethno-linguistic People Groups

A problem for social science research is the lack of available survey and polling data in non-Western countries. While the United States and many European countries have a long history of engaging in this kind of research, many – often more underdeveloped – countries can be difficult to access and/or speak languages difficult for Western researchers. The *WCD*'s method directly addresses this methodological challenge through its additional taxonomy of the world's ethnic groups, which are paired with religious statistics.

A 'peoples' taxonomy must take into account both ethnicity and language. The approach taken in 'Ethnosphere' in Part 8 of the *World Christian Encyclopedia* was to match ethnic codes with language codes, which produced over 13,700 distinct ethno-linguistic peoples. Not all combinations of ethnicity and language are possible, but nevertheless every person in the world can be categorised as belonging to an ethno-linguistic people (mutually exclusive). For example, there are ethnic Kazaks who speak Kazak as their mother tongue and ethnic Kazaks who speak Russian as their mother tongue. These, then, are two separate ethno-linguistic peoples.

The work of determining the religious breakdown of ethno-linguistic peoples was begun in the 1970s in Africa, where many Christian churches reported the ethnic breakdown of their congregations. Utilising data gathered by religious bodies and in government censuses, estimates of religious affiliation for all peoples was completed in the mid-1990s and published in the second edition of the *World Christian Encyclopedia*. These data continue to be updated and published in the *World Christian Database* and *World Religion Database*.

Each distinct ethno-linguistic group in a country is assigned varying shares of the 18 categories of religion. For example, the Japanese in Japan are reported as 56% Mahayana Buddhist, 23% various New religionist, 10% agnostic, 3% atheist, 2% Shinto and 1% Christian. Each group is traced throughout the world with the assumption that whatever their religious breakdown is in their home country will be the same abroad. This allows researchers to locate Christian people in predominantly non-Christian countries. For example, the *WCD* reports that Pakistan – a majority-Muslim country – is also home to over 2 million Christians. While Christians are found among Muslim-majority people groups (for example, Punjabi at 4% Christian), they are also present in the country as ex-pats, such as French (65% Christian) and British (70% Christian).

Conclusion

There are a variety of issues related to finding and choosing the best data sources of religious affiliation. Censuses are generally accepted as the most reliable, but there are times when they fail to present the full picture, for example because they omit certain regions of a country or because they do not ask clear or detailed questions about religion. General population surveys can often fill the gap, but, depending on their quality, they may also have some bias. At times, religious groups may have very different estimates of their sizes than are found by censuses and surveys, but for some types of data, such as denominations of Protestantism, estimates by the groups may be the best information available. Finally, for religions such as Islam, Hinduism, Buddhism and Judaism, subgroup information is routinely missing from censuses and surveys. Estimates for the subgroups of these religions often rely on indirect measures, such as ethnic groups likely to adhere to a particular subgroup or expert analysis of multiple ethnological and anthropological sources. Thus, it is important to take into consideration many different kinds of data in order to arrive at the best estimate of a particular religious population in a country.

Index